CONTENTS

PREFACE

The continued popularity and widespread use of this text has prompted this revision which is designed to update the contents of the book while retaining both its basic organization and the conceptual framework that underlies its treatment of ethical issues. Revisions and additions of new material are incorporated into every chapter and new cases have been included while old ones have been updated. I have been particularly anxious to ensure that the revision recognizes the importance of international business and the diversity that demographics have brought into the workplace. For the teacher or reader who would like to know what substantive changes have been made to the text, I have appended a paragraph describing these changes at the end of this preface.

The primary aims of the text remain pretty much the same. They are: (1) to introduce the reader to the ethical concepts that are relevant to resolving moral issues in business; (2) to impart the reasoning and analytical skills needed to apply ethical concepts to business decisions; (3) to identify the moral issues involved in the management of specific problem areas in business; (4) to provide an understanding of the social and natural environments within which moral issues in business arise; and (5) to supply case studies of actual moral dilemmas faced by businesses.

Although the author of a text on business ethics need not apologize for writing on this subject, he or she does owe readers at least some indication of the normative assumptions that underlie what he or she has written. In the hopes of partially discharging this debt and in order to outline the structure of this book, I will describe its major parts and the main assumptions underlying each part.

The text is divided into four parts, each containing two chapters. Part One provides an introduction to basic ethical theory. My central assumption here is that in the absence of any moral standards we humans would be in the kind of situation that the seventeenth century philosopher Thomas Hobbes called a "state of nature"; that is, a situation in which there is nothing to moderate the self-interested competition that Hobbes aptly called "a war of every man against every man." In order to advance one's aims in such normless situations each individual must strive to overcome every other individual. Yet the havoc this striving creates is itself destructive of those aims. Thus, by striving to protect their private interests in the absence of any moral standards, people are led to act collectively in ways that actually harm those interests. Moral standards allow us to break out of these kinds of dilemmas, because they alone provide the basis for the trust and cooperation on which social institutions can be erected.

The central idea in Part One, therefore, is that moral standards serve the function of lifting us out of the dilemmas posed by normlessness and thereby leave us all better off than we would be without them. I elaborate this idea in Chapter 1, where I also indicate how we come to accept these moral standards and how such standards govern our moral reasoning. Chapter 2 critically discusses three kinds of moral principles: utilitarian principles, principles based on moral rights, and principles of justice. These three kinds of moral principles each provide a partial solution to the dilemmas created by normlessness and they lie at the basis of most of our own moral reasoning. They can therefore legitimately serve as the criteria for resolving the ethical dilemmas raised in our business world.

Having defined the social functions of moral standards and having identified three basic criteria for resolving moral issues in business, I then bring the resulting theory to bear on specific moral issues. Thus, Part Two examines the ethics of markets and prices; Part Three discusses environmental and consumer issues; and Part Four looks at employee issues. I assume in each part that in order to apply a moral theory to the real world we must have some information (and theory) about what that world is really like. Consequently, each chapter in these last three parts devotes several pages to laying out the empirical information that the decision-maker must have if he or she is to apply morality to reality. The chapter on market ethics, for example, provides a neoclassical analysis of market structure; the chapter on discrimination presents several statistical and institutional indicators of discrimination; the chapter on the individual in the organization relies on two models of organizational structure.

Each chapter of the text contains two kinds of materials. The main body of the chapter sets out the conceptual materials needed to understand some particular moral issue. This is followed by discussion cases that describe real business situations in which these moral issues are raised. I have provided these discussion cases on the assumption that a person's ability to reason about moral matters will improve if the person attempts to think through some concrete moral problems and allows himself or herself to be challenged by others who resolve the issue on the basis of different moral standards. These kinds of challenges force us to confront the adequacy of our moral norms and motivate us to search for more adequate principles when our own are shown to be inadequate. I hope that I have provided sufficient materials to allow the reader to develop a set of ethical norms that he or she can finally accept as adequate.

I owe a very large debt to the numerous colleagues from whom I have shamelessly borrowed ideas and materials. They all, I hope, have been duly recognized in the notes. I owe a different kind of debt to Arthur Andersen & Co. who generously underwrote a five-year series of workshops on the teaching of business ethics in business school courses, especially to Don Baker and Bob Baechle, the Arthur Andersen partners who oversaw the project. I was fortunate enough to be able to help design and teach in these workshops in which over a thousand business school faculty from around the country participated. My conversations and dealings with these faculty gave me a deepened understanding of the special needs that business school instructors have for pedagogical materials in business ethics. I hope that this new understanding has influenced this revision.

Although revisions have been made to virtually every section, the following substantive additions to the last edition are noteworthy: In Chapter 1 new sections have been added discussing the multinational corporation and ethics, virtue ethics, sex-based differences in moral development, and ethical relativism; in Chapter 2 a discussion of moral principles in international contexts has been inserted; Chapter 3 incorporates new materials on international competition; Chapter 4 now includes a discussion of the causes of price-fixing; in Chapter 5 the statistics on pollution and natural resources have been updated and new discussions of the troubling problems of ozone depletion and global warming, as well as an expanded discussion of ecological ethics have been added; Chapter 6 has a new discussion of markets and consumer protection; in Chapter 7 the tables and statistics on racial and sexual discrimination have been updated, and new discussions have been added of recent Supreme Court decisions on affirmative action, emerging demographic trends, sexual harassment, and accommodating diversity in the workplace; Chapter 8 now includes new discussions of insider trading, whistleblowing, and participative management.

ACKNOWLEDGMENTS

I would like to acknowledge my gratitude to these publications for permission to reprint the following materials:

Excerpt on page 174 is from *The New York Times,* June 9, 1979. Copyright © 1979 by the New York Times Company. Reprinted by permission.

Excerpt on page 117 is from Timothy Smith, "South Africa: The Churches vs. the Corporations." Reprinted by permission from *Business and Society Review,* Fall, 1975. Copyright © 1975 by Warren, Gorham and Lamont, Inc., 210 South Street, Boston, Mass. All rights reserved.

Excerpt on page 117 is from Timothy Smith, "Whitewash for Apartheid from Twelve U.S. Firms," *Business and Society Review,* Summer, 1977, pp. 59–60. Reprinted by permission from *Business and Society Review,* Fall 1975, Number 150. Copyright © 1975 by Warren, Gorham and Lamont, Inc., 210 South Street, Boston, Mass. All rights reserved.

Part One

BASIC PRINCIPLES

Business ethics is applied ethics. It is the application of our understanding of what is good and right to that assortment of institutions, technologies, transactions, activities, and pursuits which we call "business." A discussion of business ethics must begin by providing a framework of basic principles for understanding what is meant by the terms "good" and "right"; only then can one proceed to profitably discuss the implications these have for our business world. The first two chapters provide such a framework. Chapter One outlines some of the major moral issues that arise in business and describes what business ethics is in general. Chapter Two describes three approaches to ethical issues which together furnish a basis for analyzing ethical issues in business.

1

ETHICS AND MORAL REASONING

INTRODUCTION

Large-scale business organizations staffed by professional managers dominate modern economies.[1] They are the basic source of income and wealth for virtually every citizen. They are the engines of production for every nation and the ultimate source of every government's tax revenues. Yet for all the marvelous abundance they make possible, these contemporary organizations have also created some of the major ethical crises of our century, crises that their professional managers are forced to face and resolve.[2]

On April 24, 1985, for example, Warren M. Anderson, the sixty-three-year-old chairman of Union Carbide Corporation, had to make a disappointing announcement to angry stockholders at their annual meeting in Danbury, Connecticut. Ander-

[1] The dominant role of the large-scale corporation is described in Edward S. Herman, *Corporate Control, Corporate Power* (New York: Cambridge University Press, 1981). For a history of the rise of the large-scale American corporation and of the role managers have played in that history, see Alfred D. Chandler, Jr., *The Visible Hand: The Managerial Revolution in American Business* (Cambridge, MA.: Harvard University Press, 1977); for a comparable treatment of European corporations, see Alfred D. Chandler, Jr., and Herman Daems, eds., *Managerial Hierarchies: Comparative Perspectives on the Rise of the Modern Industrial Enterprise*, (Cambridge, MA.: Harvard University Press, 1980).

[2] For monthly coverage of ethical crises faced by managers see *Corporate Responsibility Monitor* (Corporate Information Services, 464 Nineteenth St., Oakland, CA 94612).

son, who had been jailed briefly by the government of India on charges of "negligence and criminal corporate liability," had been devoting all his attention to the company's mushrooming problems.[3] His announcement concerned the complete breakdown of negotiations with officials of the Indian government: They had rejected as inadequate an estimated $200 million compensation for the deaths of 2,000 people and the injuries of 200,000 others which had been caused in December 1984 by a poisonous leak of methyl isocyanate gas from a Union Carbide pesticide plant located in Bhopal, India. In the wake of more than $35 billion in suits filed against the company on behalf of the victims, several insurance agencies had canceled the company's liability coverage reported to total only about $200 million. The company's stock tumbled. Angry stockholders filed suit charging that they had suffered losses of more than $1 billion because the company's managers had failed to warn them of the risks at the Indian plant. Analysts predicted the company would be forced into bankruptcy. Ironically, the Union Carbide plant in Bhopal had been losing money for several years and Warren had considered closing it.

The deadly methyl isocyanate gas that leaked from the Union Carbide plant was a volatile and highly toxic chemical (500 times more poisonous than cyanide) used to make pesticides; it reacts explosively with almost any substance, including water. Late at night on December 2, 1984, the methyl isocyanate stored in a tank at the Bhopal factory started boiling violently when water or some other agent accidently entered the tank. A cooling unit that should have switched on automatically had been disabled for at least a year. Shakil Qureshi, a manager on duty at the time, and Suman Dey, the senior operator on duty, both distrusted the initial readings on their gauges in the control room. "Instruments often didn't work," Qureshi said later. "They got corroded, and crystals would form on them."

By 11:30 P.M. the eyes of workers at the plant were burning. But they remained unconcerned since, as they later reported, minor leaks were common at the plant and were often first detected in this way. Many of the illiterate workers were unaware of the deadly properties of the chemical. Not until 12:40 A.M., as workers began choking on the fumes, did they realize something was drastically wrong. Five minutes later emergency valves on the storage tank exploded and white toxic gas began shooting out of a pipestack and drifting toward the shantytowns downwind from the plant. An alarm sounded as manager Dey shouted into the factory loudspeaker that a massive leak had erupted and workers should flee the area. Meanwhile, Qureshi ordered company firetrucks to spray the escaping gas with water to neutralize the chemical. But water pressure was too low to reach the top of the 120-foot-high pipestack. Dey then rushed to turn on a vent scrubber that should have neutralized the escaping gas with caustic soda. Unfortunately, the scrubber had been shut down for maintenance fifteen days earlier. As white clouds continued to pour out of the pipestack, Qureshi shouted to workers to turn on a nearby flare tower to burn off the gas. The flare, however, would not go on since its pipes had corroded and were still being repaired.

Panicked workers poured out of the plant and the lethal cloud settled noise-

[3] All material concerning Union Carbide and the Bhopal plant, including all quotations and all allegations, is drawn directly from the following sources: The *New York Times*: 25 April 1985, p. 34; 9 December 1984, p. 1E; 16 December 1984, pp. 1, 8; 28 January 1985, pp. 6, 7; 30 January 1985, pp. 1, 6, 7; 31 January 1985, p. 6; *San Jose Mercury News*: 6 December 1984, p. 16A; 12 December 1984, pp. 1, 1H; 13 December 1984, p. 1; *Time*: 17 December 1985, pp. 22–31.

lessly over the neighboring shantytowns of Jaipraksh and Chola, drifting down narrow dirt streets into temples, shops, and tiny slum shacks. Hundreds died in their beds, choking helplessly in violent spasms as their burning lungs filled with fluid. Thousands were blinded by the caustic gas, and thousands of others suffered burns and lesions in their nasal and bronchial passages. When it was over, at least 2,000 lay dead and 200,000 were injured. The majority of the dead were squatters who illegally had built huts next to the factory. Surviving residents of the slums, most of them illiterate, declared afterward that they had built their shacks there because they did not understand the danger and thought the factory made healthy "medicine for plants."

Union Carbide managers from the United States built the Bhopal plant in 1969 with the blessing of the Indian government, which was anxious to increase production of the pesticides it desperately needed to raise food for India's huge population. Over the next fifteen years pesticides enabled India to cut its annual grain losses from 25 percent to 15 percent, a saving of 15 million tons of grain or enough to feed 70 million people for a full year. Indian officials willingly accepted the technology, skills, and equipment that Union Carbide provided, and Indian workers were thankful for the company jobs without which they would have had to beg or starve since India has no welfare system. In return, India offered the company cheap labor, low taxes, and few laws requiring expensive environmental equipment or costly workplace protections. In comparison to other factories in India, the Union Carbide plant was considered a model law-abiding citizen with a good safety record. Said a government official: "They never refused to install what we asked."

At the time of the disaster, the pesticide plant in Bhopal was operated by Union Carbide India Ltd., a subsidiary of the American Union Carbide Corporation in Danbury, Connecticut, which had a controlling interest of 50.9 percent in the Indian company. The board of directors of Union Carbide India Ltd. included one top manager from the parent Union Carbide Corporation in the U.S. and four managers from another Union Carbide subsidiary based in Hong Kong. Reports from the Indian company were regularly reviewed by the managers in Danbury who had the authority to exercise financial and technical control over Union Carbide India Ltd. Although day-to-day details were left to the Indian managers, the American managers controlled annual budgets, set major policies, and issued technical directives for operating and maintaining the plant. But before the tragedy, the Indian subsidiary had been doing poorly. In an effort to contain annual losses of $4 million from the unprofitable plant, local company managers had initiated several cost-cutting programs. Only a year before, the number of equipment operators on each shift had been reduced from twelve to five; morale dropped and many of the best operators quit and were replaced with workers whose education was below that required by company manuals. Although Warren Anderson and other American Union Carbide Corporation managers insisted that responsibility for the plant's operations rested with the local Indian managers, they hastened to say that all cost-cutting measures had been justified.

Critics of Union Carbide in America charged that Union Carbide managers in the United States had an ethical obligation never to have introduced such a dangerous and complex modern pesticide technology into a country with a highly unskilled workforce and a largely illiterate population. Moreover, they said, even if Indian environmental and safety laws set lower standards, managers should have insisted on the same standards prevalent in the United States and should have audited the plant frequently to ensure compliance. In their defense the American managers pointed out that only two years before they had sent three engineers from the United States to survey the plant and had told the Indian managers to remedy ten major flaws in safety equipment and procedures the engineers found. The Indian managers had written back that the problems were corrected. "We have no reason to believe that what was represented to us by Union Carbide India Ltd. did not in fact occur," said the U.S. managers. The U.S. managers had considered closing the failing plant a year earlier, but Indian city and state officials had asked that the company remain open to preserve the jobs of thousands of workers in the plant and in dependent local industries.

The Bhopal disaster was the worst industrial accident in history.[4] Its sheer size forced Union Carbide's managers to confront in public the kinds of difficult ethical dilemmas that managers often must face alone and that we will examine in this book.[5] One issue Union Carbide managers were forced to address concerned the relationship between business and the society in which it operates. Although the Union Carbide plant in India adhered to India's environmental and safety laws, these laws set fairly low standards. Did the managers of Union Carbide have any obligation to do more than what the law required? Is it enough for a business simply to follow the law?

Another issue dealt with the obligations a manager has to people inside and outside the company. What obligations, for example, did company managers have toward the illiterate squatters who built their shacks next to the Bhopal factory although it was illegal to do so? What obligations did they have toward plant workers who were illiterate and untrained, who had to work with equipment that often broke down, who were alleged to have served as human "leak detectors," but who all willingly accepted the jobs the company provided? What obligations did they have toward stockholders who invested their money in a company they knew involved financial risks?

A third issue Union Carbide managers had to face was the issue of moral responsibility. Who was morally responsible for what happened: American managers? The Indian managers? The workers at the Bhopal plant? The parent corporation in the United States? Its Indian subsidiary? The Indian government? The squatters? The issue of responsibility was crucial because it involved determining who should pay for what happened and what they should pay. What compensation, for example, should a company provide for parties it harms? And how is an agent's responsibility determined?

[4] For fuller accounts of the Union Carbide disaster, see S. Prakash Sethi and Paul Steidlmeier, *Up Against the Corporate Wall*, 5th ed. (Englewood Cliffs, NJ: Prentice Hall, 1991), pp. 374–94, and Paul Shrivastava, *Bhopal: Anatomy of a Crisis* (Cambridge, MA: Ballinger Publishing Company, 1987).

[5] Complete annotated bibliographies on ethical issues in business may be found in Donald J. Jones and Helen Troy, *A Bibliography of Business Ethics, 1976–1980*, (Charlottesville, VA: University Press of Virginia, 1982); Donald J. Jones, *A Bibliography of Business Ethics, 1981–1985* (Lewiston, NJ: The Edwin Mellon Press, 1986). An extremely useful bibliography that is regularly updated and that also contains lists of audiovisual materials, of periodicals that publish business ethics articles, and of centers that deal with business ethics issues is *Bibliography of Business Ethics and Business Moral Values*, by Kenneth M. Bond. Copies of the bibliography may be obtained by writing to Professor Kenneth Bond, College of Business, Humboldt State University, Arcata, CA 95521.

Finally, the Bhopal tragedy also raised larger issues about the role of American business in the world. How should the needs of Third World nations be balanced against the dangers that modern technologies involve? Should U.S. managers exercise tighter control over the managers of foreign subsidiaries even when they—and their government—insist on independence? These dilemmas in turn raised other questions about profits, private enterprise, and capitalism itself. In the end, was the Bhopal tragedy caused by a drive for profits inherent in capitalism? Did profit considerations pressure Indian managers to disregard plant safety? Was capitalism itself the culprit?

The moral dilemmas raised by the Bhopal disaster were magnified by the size of the tragedy and the international setting. But they were the kinds of dilemmas that domestic managers must also face, even if on a smaller scale. Domestic managers also face, for example, the moral issues raised by the "external" effects businesses have on society. Consumer groups accuse business of inflicting dangerous products on an unsuspecting public, of unethical sales practices, and of using advertising to manipulate vulnerable groups such as children.[6] And environmentalists claim that business growth policies have consumed our wild lands, forests, and natural resources while creating major and potentially catastrophic pollution crises.[7]

A second kind of ethical dilemma that domestic managers often face concerns the "internal" conflicts that business organizations create among their own members and constituencies, including managers, employees, and stockholders. Employees accuse managers of being negligent in their moral duty to care for the safety of their employees and of recklessly exposing them to hazardous chemical substances.[8] Civil rights groups declare that the hiring and promotion policies of many businesses still discriminate against minorities, women, and the aged, thereby violating their moral rights to equality.[9] Stockholders file resolutions charging

[6] "Corporations Can't Ignore Consumer Movements," *San Francisco Examiner*, 20 February 1991; "Two Major Banks Charged With Use of Deceptive Ads," *Wall Street Journal*, 18 December 1990; "Makers of Juice Box Accused by New York of Deceptive Claims," *Wall Street Journal*, 11 December 1990; "Toy Retailers, Importers Sued Over Product Safety," *Washington Post*, 21 August 1990; "War-Toy Makers Mobilize as Sales Rise," *Wall Street Journal*, 31 January 1991; "Product Warnings Unheard," *San Jose Mercury News*, 13 April 1990.

[7] "A U.S. Report Spurs Community Action by Revealing Polluters," *Wall Street Journal*, 15 January 1991; "EPA Study Hits Chemical Plants' Toxic Emissions," *Journal of Commerce*, 16 January 1990; "U.S. to Sue 15 Firms Over Pollution," *Los Angeles Times* , 18 January 1990; "Pesticide Export Reform Act Tries to Break the Circle of Poison," *In These Times*, 15 May 1990; "The Poison Trail," *Los Angeles Times*, 23 September 1990.

[8] "Coal Company Admits Safety Test Fraud," *New York Times*, 19 January 1991; "ARCO Agrees to Pay Record OSHA Fine for Explosion," *AFL-CIO News*, 21 January 1991; "Lockheed to Pay Full $1.49 Million in Safety Penalties," *Los Angeles Times*, 1 July 1989; "Chevron Blaze Brings Huge Fine," *Oakland Tribune*, 27 September 1989; "Oversight of Workplace Hazards," *In These Times*, 25 April 1990; "Prosecutors Go After Employers for On-the-Job Deaths, Injuries," *San Francisco Chronicle*, 27 August 1990.

[9] "Chrysler Signs Accord with NAACP on Hiring Practices," *Los Angeles Times*, 12 July 1989; "Ruling May Curb Harrassment," *Los Angeles Times*, 5 February 1991; "Efforts Fail to Advance Women's Jobs," *Washington Post*, 20 February 1990; "Few Women, Minorities at the Top," *Washington Post*, 14 August 1990; "Nude Pictures Are Ruled Sexual Harrassment," *The New York Times*, 25 January 1991.

that officers and directors of corporations make unethical use of their funds or engage in unethical operations.[10] And tragic dilemmas arise when the values and policies of an organization conflict with the employee's own aims and values.[11] The organization, for example, might insist on a production schedule that the manager is afraid will result in defective and perhaps dangerous products. Or the organization might ask the manager to investigate its employees in a way that the manager thinks is an invasion of their right to privacy. Or the employee may find himself or herself in an organization whose practices seem inimical to the best interests of the people the organization serves. Again, a real case may best illustrate the dilemma.

For one week, Kate Simpson had been working for the Atlanta branch of Lawton Medical Financing, Inc. (a small investment banking firm specializing in loans to medical groups).[12] Besides the two secretaries, the Atlanta branch consisted of three professionals: Kate, who planned on returning to graduate business school in six months and who was hired to help out in whatever capacity was needed; David Moore, an intelligent, affable, and energetic senior vice president who combined a pragmatic business streak with a strong moral sense; and Bill Hillman, a youngish vice president, who had been transferred from New York to the Atlanta branch four months before and who was outspoken about his intent to make Atlanta his permanent home. On Wednesday before leaving town, David had asked Kate to help him advise a hospital in Nashville that wanted to choose a consultant to study the purchase of a new facility. She was to review the proposals of the four consultants who were submitting bids. On Friday, when David returned, they were to meet with the hospital's board of directors to advise them on the proposals. Of the three bids she had received by Thursday noon, the one by Roberts and Company had emerged as the best study for the least amount of money:

> I happened to go into Bill Hillman's office and found him on the phone talking to Thomas Rice, the fourth consultant whose office was in the same building, and whose bid was due in a few hours. Bill was about to hang up as I entered: "Fine, Tom. You owe me one now," he was saying, "but don't worry about it. Good luck getting the thing cranked out by five." Bill looked up and saw me as he slid a copy of the Roberts and Company proposal into an envelope. "Tom Rice really likes to run it down to the wire," he said. "Tom's just finishing their hospital

[10] "Shareholders Exert Moral Pressure," *San Jose Mercury*, 4 April 1984; "The Corporate Raider of the '90s: Big Business," *Wall Street Journal*, 4 December 1990; "Shareholders at 54 Firms Face Environmental Code Proposal," *Washington Post*, 18 December 1990; "Disney, Raider to Pay Investors for 'Greenmail'," *Los Angeles Times*, 13 July 1989.

[11] "From Database to Blacklist," *Christian Science Monitor*, 1 August 1990; "Workers' Privacy Seen As Eroding," *San Jose Mercury News*, 19 December 1990; "Genetic Job-Testing Raises Fears," *Contra Costa Times*, 20 August 1990; Douglas J. Lincoln, Milton M. Pressley, and Taylor Little, "Ethical Beliefs and Personal Values of Top Level Executives," *Journal of Business Research*, 10 (1982): 475–87; "Overdriven Execs: Some Middle Managers Cut Corners to Achieve High Corporate Goals," *Wall Street Journal*, 8 November 1979.

[12] These materials are based on a case prepared by Cara F. Jonassen as a basis for class discussion rather than to illustrate either effective or ineffective handling of an administrative situation. The names of the individuals and the companies involved have been changed. With the permission of the author, Cara F. Jonassen.

> proposal. I told him we'd let him glance at Robert's version of the thing. Why don't you run it upstairs for him? You can wait and make sure we get it back." As I headed for the elevator I was furious with Bill for having placed me in the position of carrying a competitor's bid to Thomas Rice. But I had only a few moments to decide what I should do.

Thus, the ethical dilemmas that business organizations often present for their managers are not trivial. Nor are they avoidable. We cannot live without our business organizations because we cannot live without the large-scale production that these organizations make possible. We have no choice but to face the ethical issues raised by our business institutions and attempt to deal with them.

This text directly addresses the moral dilemmas that managers of modern business organizations must face. This does not mean that it is designed to give moral advice to people in business nor that it is aimed at persuading people to act in certain "moral" ways. The main purpose of the text is to provide a deeper knowledge of the nature of ethical principles and concepts and an understanding of how these apply to the moral problems encountered in business. This type of knowledge and understanding should help managers see their way through the moral dilemmas that confront them in their business lives.

These first two chapters will introduce the reader to some basic ethical principles and methods of reasoning that can be used to analyze moral issues in business. The following chapters will then apply these principles and methods to the kinds of moral dilemmas we have been discussing. We begin in this chapter by discussing three preliminary topics: (1) the nature of business ethics, (2) moral reasoning, and (3) moral responsibility. Once these notions have been clarified, we will devote the next chapter to a discussion of three basic approaches to business ethics.

1.1 THE NATURE OF BUSINESS ETHICS

In a now-classic study of the ethics of business managers, Raymond Baumhart asked more than a hundred businessmen, "What does *ethical* mean to you?" Typical of their replies were the following:[13]

> —Before coming to the interview, to make sure that I knew what we would talk about, I looked up *ethics* in my dictionary. I read it and can't understand it. I don't know what the concept means. . . .
>
> —*Ethical* is what my feelings tell me is right. But this is not a fixed standard, and that makes problems.
>
> —*Ethical* means accepted standards in terms of your personal and social welfare; what you believe is right. But what confuses me . . . is the possibility that I have

[13] Raymond Baumhart, *An Honest Profit: What Businessmen Say About Ethics in Business* (New York: Holt, Rinehart and Winston, 1968), pp. 11–12; for an update of the Baumhart study see Steven N. Brenner and Earl A. Molander, "Is the Ethics of Business Changing?" *Harvard Business Review*, 55, no. 1 (January-February 1977); 57–71.

been misguided, or that somebody else has been poorly educated. Maybe each of us thinks he knows what is ethical, but we differ. How can you tell who is right then?

Fifty percent of the businessmen Baumhart interviewed defined "ethical" as "what my feelings tell me is right"; 25 percent defined it in religious terms as what is "in accord with my religious beliefs"; and 18 percent defined "ethical" as what "conforms to 'the golden rule'."[14] Yet feelings are a notoriously inadequate basis on which to make decisions of *any* sort, and religious authority and the "golden rule" have been rather devastatingly criticized as inadequate foundations for ethical claims.[15] What then do "ethics" and "ethical" mean?

In popular usage the term "ethics" has a variety of different meanings. One of the meanings often given to it is: "the principles of conduct governing an individual or a group."[16] We use the term "personal ethics," for example, to refer to the rules by which an individual lives his or her personal life, and we use the term "accounting ethics" to refer to the code that guides the professional conduct of accountants.

Ethicians, however, use the term "ethics" to refer primarily to a theoretical study, just as chemists use the term "chemistry" to refer to a theoretical study of the properties of the elements and their compounds.[17]

The subject matter of ethics, however, differs in an important way from the subject matter of a natural science like chemistry. Whereas the natural sciences are concerned with a study of physical objects, ethics is concerned with the moral judgments involved in moral decisions. Suppose, for example, that I am trying to decide whether to lie on my income tax, and part of what makes me hesitant about lying is my belief that lying is wrong. Then my decision is a moral decision (that is, a decision that raises moral issues) and the judgment that lying is wrong is the moral judgment involved in this decision.

To understand what a moral judgment is, we must begin by understanding what "normative judgments" are, since moral judgments are special kinds of normative judgments.

Normative Judgments

Normative judgments are claims that state or imply that something is good or bad, right or wrong, better or worse, ought to be or ought not to be. Normative judgments, therefore, express values: They indicate a person's favorable or unfavorable attitude toward some state of affairs.[18] The following are examples of normative judgments:

[14] *Ibid.*, p. 13.

[15] See, for example, James Rachels' criticisms of religious authority and feeling as the basis of ethical reasoning in *The Elements of Moral Philosophy* (New York: McGraw-Hill, Inc., 1986), pp. 25–38 and 39–52; Craig C. Lundberg criticizes the golden rule in "The Golden Rule and Business Management: Quo Vadis?" *Journal of Economics and Business* 20 (January 1968): 36–40.

[16] "Ethic," *Webster's Third New International Dictionary, Unabridged* (Springfield, MA: Merriam-Webster Inc., 1986), p. 780. Similar definitions can be found in any recent dictionary.

[17] Fred Feldman, *Introductory Ethics* (Englewood Cliffs, NJ: Prentice Hall, 1978), pp. 9–15.

[18] C. E. Harris, Jr., *Applying Moral Theories* (Belmont, CA: Wadsworth Publishing Company, 1986), pp. 7–8.

The Mona Lisa is a beautiful painting.
Your office is tastefully furnished.
These figures are mistaken.
You made the wrong investment.
Free enterprise is the best economic system.
Pornography should be illegal.
Price-fixing is unfair.
Labor unions violate management's rights.
You have an obligation to keep your word.
You should add eggs after the flour.

Because normative judgments express values, they usually carry some implications concerning the kind of conduct with which humans should respond to a situation. If I claim that a certain novel is "good," for example, I am implying that people should seek it, buy it, or read it. Normative judgments, therefore, are "action guiding": They usually are intended to influence human behavior in the present or in the future.

Nonnormative judgments, on the other hand, are value-neutral.[19] They describe, name, define, report, and make predictions concerning a certain state of affairs. They are not, however, intended to assert that the state of affairs is good or bad, right or wrong. Nonnormative judgments are not meant to imply a favorable or unfavorable attitude toward a given state of affairs, nor are they usually intended to guide human action with respect to that state of affairs. The following statements are examples of nonnormative judgments:

The Mona Lisa is an Italian painting.
Your office is furnished with a desk and a chair.
These figures do not match the auditor's.
Your investment lost money.
Free enterprise means different things to different people.
Pornography is illegal in certain states.
Many Americans believe that price-fixing is unfair.
Labor unions frequently disagree with management.
Most people believe a person should keep his or her word.
The recipe says the eggs should be added after the flour.

Of course, in certain contexts some of these "nonnormative statements" can be used to express normative judgments. When I say, for example, "Your investment lost money," I may intend this to mean, "You made the wrong investment." Some statements are ambiguous: They can be interpreted as either normative or nonnormative, depending on what the statement is taken to imply or is intended to imply in the context in which it is uttered. To determine whether a statement

[19] William K. Frankena, *Ethics*, 2nd ed. (Englewood Cliffs, NJ: Prentice Hall, 1973), p. 4.

is normative or nonnormative, one must determine whether it is merely meant to *describe* a certain state of affairs, or whether it is also meant to *prescribe* certain behavior vis-à-vis that state of affairs. Normative judgments are "prescriptive," whereas nonnormative judgments are simply "descriptive."

Moral Judgments

Ethics does not study all normative judgments, only those that are concerned with what is *morally* right and wrong, or *morally* good and bad. To understand what this means, it may help to see that normative terms such as "right" and "wrong" or "good" and "bad" are generally applied on the basis of some explicit or implicit standards or criteria.[20] The standards may be *legal*, as when we judge that it is legally wrong to drive on the left side of a street because a state law prohibits this; or the standards may be *grammatical*, as when we judge that it is grammatically right to end sentences with prepositions because English grammar now permits this usage; or the standards may be *aesthetic*, as when we judge that *Moby Dick* is aesthetically good because it meets the aesthetic standards of art critics.

When something is judged to be *morally* right or wrong, or *morally* good or bad, the underlying standards on which the judgment is based are *moral* standards. Moral standards include both specific moral norms and more general moral principles. Moral norms are standards of behavior that require, prohibit, or allow certain specific kinds of behavior.[21] Prohibitions against lying, stealing, injuring, and so on, are all moral norms. Moral principles, on the other hand, are much more general standards that are used to evaluate the adequacy of our social policies and institutions as well as of individual behavior.[22] Examples of such principles would include principles of *rights*, which evaluate policies, institutions, and behavior in terms of the protection they provide for the interests and freedoms of individuals; principles of *justice*, which evaluate policies, institutions, and behavior in terms of how equitably they distribute benefits and burdens among the members of a group; and principles of *utility*, which evaluate policies, institutions, and behavior in terms of the net social benefits they produce. These three kinds of principles will be fully discussed in the next chapter.

When, then, does a decision raise ethical issues or when does it "involve" ethical issues? A decision raises (or involves) ethical issues when there is a question concerning whether or not the decision violates any moral standards. Analysis may show, of course, that the decision is perfectly consistent with all relevant

[20] This common view may be found in writers as diverse as Kurt Baier, *Moral Point of View*, abr. ed. (New York, Random House, Inc., 1965), pp. 8–26; and R. M. Hare, *The Language of Morals* (New York: Oxford University Press, 1964), pp. 111–26.

[21] On the nature and development of norms see Arnold Birenbaum and Edward Sagarin, *Norms and Human Behavior* (New York: Praeger Publishers, Inc., 1976), pp. 1–29; and Muzafer Sherif, *The Psychology of Social Norms* (New York: Octagon Books, Inc., 1965), pp. 89–112.

[22] Sometimes moral principles also seem to be used to evaluate the moral worth of *persons* and of *intentions*. We can safely ignore these uses, however, because the evaluation of actions seems to be more basic: a "morally good" person is one who regularly *does* what is morally right, and a "good intention" is an intention to *do* what is morally right.

moral standards: To say that a decision raises ethical issues does not mean that the decision is *immoral*, only that there is some reason to examine more closely whether it does or does not conform to some moral standard.

Moral Standards

How, exactly, are moral standards different from other kinds of standards? Although there is some controversy concerning precisely what the distinguishing characteristics of moral standards are, the following features are most often pointed to as some of their more important distinguishing characteristics, and should thus give us a picture of moral standards clear enough for our purposes.

First, moral standards deal with matters that are (or are thought to be) of serious consequence to our human well-being.[23] That is, they are concerned with behavior that can seriously injure or seriously benefit human beings (or that is believed to be capable of having these consequences). The moral norm prohibiting price-fixing, for example, rests on the belief that price-fixing imposes serious injuries upon consumers; whereas the moral principle that employees have a moral right to collective bargaining rests on the belief that this right protects a critical interest of employees. The moral norms against lying, rape, enslavement, murder, theft, child abuse, assault, slander, fraud, and so on, all plainly deal with forms of behavior that can cause serious injury to human beings. Thus the *seriousness* of moral standards sets them off from standards that deal with matters that are not as critically connected to our well-being, such as grammatical standards or rules of etiquette.

Second, moral standards cannot be established or changed by the decisions of particular authoritative bodies.[24] Laws and company codes for example, can be established and changed by the decisions of a legislature or of enfranchised voters and by the decisions of a company board of directors, respectively. Moral standards are not made up by particular bodies, nor does their validity rest on the particular decisions of particular persons. The validity of moral standards rests, instead, on the adequacy of the reasons that are taken to support and justify them, and so long as these reasons are adequate the standards remain valid.

Third, and perhaps most strikingly, moral standards are supposed to override self-interest.[25] That is, if a person has a moral obligation to do something, then the person is supposed to do it even if it is not in the person's own interests to do so. This is an obvious feature of the moral norms we commonly accept, such as the negative prohibitions on stealing, lying, and cheating, as well as the positive injunctions to be honest and to keep one's promises. We are supposed to adhere to these common moral norms even when (especially when?) contravening these norms would advance our own self-interest. A certified public accountant working

[23] H. L. A. Hart, *The Concept of Law* (London: Oxford University Press, 1961), pp. 84–85. See also Charles Fried, *An Anatomy of Values* (Cambridge: Harvard University Press, 1970), pp. 91–142.

[24] See Baier, *Moral Point of View*, p. 88.

[25] The point is made in Michael Scriven, *Primary Philosophy* (New York: McGraw-Hill Book Company, 1966), pp. 232–33.

for a corporation, for example, is commonly assumed to recognize that the accountant has an ethical duty to refrain from "knowingly misrepresent[ing] facts" (rule 102 of the AICPA Code of Professional Ethics) even when misrepresentation would make the boss look good and thereby lead to the accountant's career advancement. (None of this means, obviously, that it is always unacceptable to act on self-interest, only that it is unacceptable when one's act is morally wrong.)

Fourth, moral standards are based on impartial considerations.[26] The fact, for example, that my business will benefit from a bribe and that yours will lose from it, is irrelevant to whether or not bribery is morally wrong. Recent philosophers have expressed this point by saying that moral standards are based on "the moral point of view," that is, a point of view that does not evaluate standards according to whether or not they advance the interests of a particular individual or group, but that goes beyond personal interests to a "universal" standpoint in which everyone's interests are impartially counted as equal.[27] Other philosophers have made the same point by saying that moral standards are based on the kinds of impartial reasons that an "ideal observer" or an "impartial spectator" would accept, or that in deciding moral matters "each counts for one and none for more than one."[28]

Last, moral standards are associated with special emotions and a special vocabulary.[29] For example, if I act contrary to a moral standard, I will normally feel guilty, ashamed, or remorseful; I will characterize my behavior as "immoral" or "wrong" and I will feel bad about myself and experience a loss of self-esteem. On the other hand, if I see others acting contrary to a moral standard I accept, I will normally feel indignation or resentment or even disgust toward those persons; I will say that they are not "living up" to their "moral obligations" or their "moral responsibilities" and I will esteem them less.

Moral Standards and Society

We may gain a better understanding of moral standards if we note some of the important social functions they can serve. The members of a society typically adhere to a system of moral standards—a system, that is, of general ethical principles and related moral norms. The moral system of a society forbids certain behavior as wrong (such as, lying or stealing) and enjoins certain behavior as right (helping others, keeping one's promises). These moral standards serve several important functions, but two deserve special mention.[30]

First, a society's system of moral standards will identify situations in which

[26] See, for example, Rachels, *Elements of Moral Philosophy*, pp. 9–10.

[27] Baier, *Moral Point of View*, p. 107.

[28] The point is made in Peter Singer, *Practical Ethics* (New York: Cambridge University Press, 1979), pp. 10–11.

[29] Richard B. Brandt, *A Theory of the God and the Right* (New York: Oxford University Press, 1979), pp. 166–69.

[30] An important but perhaps obvious point should be made here: Neither of these functions is being offered as a *justification* of moral standards. They are simply intended to illustrate two important services that moral standards must be capable of performing.

each person must restrain his or her self-interest to secure a system of conduct that is mutually advantageous to everyone.[31] To more easily understand this function of moral standards, we can begin by noticing that it is not uncommon for a group of persons to find that self-interested (noncooperative self-seeking) behavior is not always in each person's best interests. Take, for example, an army that is under attack. Suppose that if every soldier selflessly remains at his post, the army can easily turn back the attack; but if large numbers of soldiers desert, the attackers will slaughter the army and then catch and kill the deserters; and if only a few soldiers desert, the deserters will make it home safely while the rest will eventually be overcome. In such a situation, self-interest would tell every soldier that he should desert his post and be one of the few to escape safely to his home. But if every soldier tries to advance his private interests in this way, all of them will be killed. Thus, self-interested behavior here is not in every soldier's best interests. Paradoxically, the best interests of each soldier will be served only if each of them acts selflessly and remains at his post.

Although a society is not an army under attack (at least not usually), self-interested behavior within a society is, as with an army, not always in its members' best interests. In particular, a society whose members regularly cooperate in advancing socially beneficial goals even when this requires setting aside their immediate private interests, whose members leave each individual free to pursue his or her basic interests, and whose members share benefits and burdens in ways that are perceived as "fair" and "just," is a society that will have a much greater chance of surviving and flourishing than a society whose members act differently. In the first place, cooperation in advancing socially beneficial goals will produce a greater store of goods for all. In the second place, each individual will benefit from the respect shown for his or her interests when others leave the individual free to pursue those interests in peace and security. And in the third place, fairness and justice will provide the stability without which societies cannot long survive. The best interests of all members of a society will be served, therefore, if they do not always act out of self-interest. Just as the soldiers of an army under attack will survive only if each of them selflessly remains at his post, so will the members of a society also gain several major advantages (not the least of which is survival!) if each of its members selflessly restrains his or her self-interest and cooperates with others in the ways just described.

A major function of a society's moral standards is the prescription of specific ways in which the members of a society are to cooperate with each other, leave each other free, and deal fairly with each other. When everyone internalizes these moral standards and adheres to them in his or her conduct with others, the result is a productive, secure, and stable system of conduct that is in everyone's mutual

[31] This, too, is commonplace. See J. L. Mackie, *Ethics: Inventing Right and Wrong* (New York: Penguin Books, 1977), pp. 105–24. Recently there has been renewed interest in the idea that moral standards enable us to overcome the problems of noncooperative self-interested behavior that are exemplified in the text with the "army that is under attack." These problems, which are generally discussed as "prisoner's dilemma" problems, were discussed by Thomas Hobbes in the seventeenth century (see the preface to this textbook, where some significant points are made concerning Hobbes and this textbook). Two recent approaches to morality from this perspective are David Gauthier, *Morals by Agreement* (Oxford: Clarendon Press, 1986) and Robert Frank, *Passions Within Reason* (New York: W. W. Norton & Company, 1988).

best interests. Bankers, creditors, and consumers, for example, generally accept the moral norm of honesty in the business communications that pass between them millions of times each day, even when they have nothing to gain; and each of them in turn must depend upon everyone else's general acceptance of that norm. If dishonesty became a general practice in these daily business communications, our system of communication would collapse and our business system would fall with it. The norm of honesty is an internalized moral standard by which people generally restrain their self-interest and thereby cooperate to secure a system of communication that is in everyone's mutual best interests.

A second social function that moral standards serve is that they enable the resolution of social conflicts by providing publicly acceptable justifications for actions and policies.[32] To understand this second major function of moral standards, it will help if we begin by noting how *prudential claims* differ from *moral claims.* Prudential claims are based on self-interest: They take into account only the interests (desires, needs, aims) of the individual.[33] Moral claims, as we noted, are based on standards that go beyond a particular person's self-interests.

In any group of people, one or more persons often will want to do something beneficial to their self-interest but not to that of the others, that they will not be able to do unless they can persuade the others to let them do it or help them do it. As the owner of a factory, for example, I may want to burn coal that produces a high level of pollution. I will then have to find some way of persuading those other people upon whom the pollution will fall to allow me to do what I want. Or I may have to do a job that I cannot do alone and will have to find some way of persuading others to help me.

In situations of this sort, in which a person must persuade others to gain an end, prudential reasons will not be of much help. Other people will be persuaded only if I show them that the action is justified from a point of view that takes everyone's interests into account, not just my own. Moral standards provide such publicly acceptable considerations. By showing that I am morally entitled to carry out an action or that others are morally obligated to help me, I will be showing that my action is part of a system of conduct from which everyone benefits. As the owner of a pollution-generating factory, for example, I might claim that I have a moral right to generate pollution in my plant by virtue of the property rights I possess over that factory. And if it is clear that in the long run the individual's interests will best be protected by the recognition of people's property rights, then I will have succeeded in showing that my action is part of a system of conduct from which everyone benefits. By basing my position on moral standards I am, in effect, trying to justify my action from a point of view that impartially takes everyone's interests into account, and consequently from a point of view that is publicly acceptable.

It may be useful for us to summarize the discussion up to now. Ethics, we have been saying, is the study of a particular group of normative judgments: those judgments that are concerned with what is morally right and wrong, or

[32] See John Rawls, *A Theory of Justice* (Cambridge: Harvard University Press, Belknap Press, 1971), pp. 4, 133, 582; see also Sir Patrick Devlin, *The Enforcement of Morals* (New York: Oxford University Press, 1965), pp. 6–10.

[33] David P. Gauthier, *Practical Reasoning* (Oxford: The Clarendon Press, 1963), pp. 18–23; Marcus G. Singer, *Generalization in Ethics* (New York: Alfred A. Knopf, Inc., 1961), p. 220.

morally good and bad. Judgments of moral right and wrong are based on standards that (1) deal with serious human injuries and benefits, (2) are not laid down by authoritative bodies, (3) override self-interest, (4) are based on impartial considerations, and (5) are associated with special emotions. Such standards can serve two important ends: When internalized they can help establish mutually beneficial systems of conduct, and they can provide publicly acceptable justifications for actions or policies.

Ethics differs from other inquiries such as the social sciences, which also study values.[34] Anthropologists and sociologists, for example, may study the moral beliefs of a particular village culture. In doing so, they attempt to develop accurate descriptions of the moral beliefs of that culture and perhaps even to formulate a descriptive theory about their structure. As anthropologists or sociologists, however, it is not their aim to determine whether or not these moral views are correct or incorrect. Ethics, on the other hand, is a study of moral standards whose explicit purpose is to determine as far as possible whether a given moral judgment is more or less correct. Whereas the sociologist asks, "Do Americans believe that bribery is wrong?" the ethician asks, "Is bribery wrong?" The ethician, then, is concerned with developing adequate *prescriptive* claims and theories, whereas an anthropological or sociological study of morality aims at being *descriptive*.

Business Ethics

This characterization of ethics has been intended to convey an idea of what the study of ethics encompasses. Our concern here, however, is not with ethics in general but with a particular field of ethics: *business* ethics.

Business ethics is a specialized study of moral right and wrong. It concentrates on how moral standards apply particularly to business policies, institutions, and behavior. A brief description of the nature of business institutions should make this clearer.

A society consists of people who have common ends and whose activities are organized by a system of institutions designed to achieve these ends. That men, women, and children have common ends is obvious. There is the common end of establishing, nurturing, and protecting family life; that of producing and distributing the materials on which human life depends; that of restraining and regularizing the use of force; that of organizing the means for making collective decisions; and that of creating and preserving cultural artifacts such as art, knowledge, and technology. The members of a society will achieve these ends by establishing the relatively fixed patterns of activity that we call "institutions": familial, economic, legal, political, and educational institutions.

The most significant institutions within contemporary societies are probably economic institutions. These are designed to achieve two ends: (1) production of the goods and services the members of society want and need, and (2) distribution of these goods and services to the various members of society. Thus, economic institutions determine who will carry out the work of production, how that work

[34] See Frankena, *Ethics*, p. 4.

will be organized, what resources that work will consume, and how its products and benefits will be distributed among society's members.

Business enterprises are the primary economic institutions through which people in modern societies carry on the tasks of producing and distributing goods and services. They provide the fundamental structures within which the members of society combine their scarce resources—land, labor, capital, and technology—into usable goods, and they provide the channels through which these goods are distributed in the form of consumer products, employee salaries, investors' return, and government taxes. Mining, manufacturing, retailing, banking, marketing, transporting, insuring, constructing, and advertising are all different facets of the productive and distributive processes of our modern business institutions.

The most significant kinds of modern business enterprises are corporations: organizations that the law endows with special legal rights and powers. Today large corporate organizations dominate our economies. In 1990 General Motors had sales of $126 billion, held assets valued at $173 billion, and employed more than 775,000 workers; Exxon Corporation's net revenues were $106 billion, its assets were valued at more than $83 billion, and it employed more than 104,000 workers.[35] Of the world's 190 nations, only a handful (Canada, France, West Germany, Italy, Japan, United States, Soviet Union, United Kingdom) had government budgets larger than these companies' sales revenues, and only about thirty nations had more workers engaged in manufacturing than General Motors did. About half of America's combined industrial profits and earnings are in the hands of about a hundred corporations, each of which has assets worth $1 billion or more. The 195,000 smaller industrial firms with assets of less than $10 million control only about 10 percent of the nation's industrial assets and profits. As reported in *Fortune* magazine's annual summary, the 500 largest American industrial corporations in 1989 had combined sales of $2.16 trillion, combined profits of $105 billion, combined assets of $2.29 trillion, and a combined labor force of 12.5 million employees.[36] These 500 corporations account for about 65 percent of all industrial sales, 80 percent of all industrial profits, 80 percent of all industrial assets, and about 75 percent of all industrial employees. Yet they comprise only about .2 percent of the total number of industrial firms operating in the United States.

The business corporation in its present form is a relatively new kind of institution (as institutions go): Although it developed from the sixteenth-century "joint stock company," most of its current characteristics were acquired during the nineteenth century. Modern corporations are organizations that the law treats as immortal fictitious "persons" who have the right to sue and be sued, own and sell property, and enter into contracts, all in their own name. As an organization, the modern corporation consists of (1) stockholders who contribute capital and who own the corporation but whose liability for the acts of the corporation is limited to the money they contributed, (2) directors and officers who administer

[35] See *Fortune*, 22 April 1991; these figures are drawn from an advance of publication notice cited in "Recession Nips at Top U.S. Companies," *San Jose Mercury News*, 2 April 1991, p. 5E.

[36] *Fortune*, 23 April 1990, p. 392.

the corporation's assets and who run the corporation through various levels of "middle managers," and (3) employees who provide labor and who do the basic work related directly to the production of goods and services. To cope with their complex coordination and control problems, the officers and managers of large corporations adopt formal bureaucratic systems of rules that link together the activities of the individual members of the organization so as to achieve certain outcomes or "objectives." So long as the individual follows these rules, the outcome will be achieved even if the individual does not know what it is and does not care about it.

Corporate organizations pose major problems for anyone who tries to apply moral standards to business activities: Can we say that the acts of these organizations are "moral" or "immoral" in the same sense that the actions of human individuals are? And can we say that these organizations are "morally responsible" for their acts in the same sense that human individuals are? Or must we agree that it makes no sense to apply moral terms to organizations? In a recent case, for example, the Justice Department charged E. F. Hutton Corporation with operating an elaborate fraud in which employees wrote overdrafts on bank accounts that allowed E. F. Hutton to derive interest earnings that rightly belonged to the banks. Critics afterward claimed that the Justice Department should have charged the individual managers of E. F. Hutton, not the corporation, since "Corporations don't commit crimes, people do."[37] Can moral notions like "responsibility," "wrongdoing," and "obligation" be applied to corporations, or are individual people the only real moral agents?

Two views have emerged in response to this problem. At one extreme is the view of those who argue that since the rules that tie organizations together allow us to say that corporations "act"[38] as individuals and that they have "intended objectives" for what they do, we can also say that they are "morally responsible" for their actions and that their actions are "moral" or "immoral" in exactly the same sense that a human being's are. The major problem with this view is that organizations do not seem to "act" or "intend" in the same sense that individual humans do and organizations differ from human beings in morally important ways: Organizations feel neither pain nor pleasure and they cannot act except through human beings. At the other extreme is the view of philosophers who hold that it makes no sense to hold business organizations "morally responsible" or to say

[37] "Corporate Criminals or Criminal Corporations?" *Wall Street Journal*, 19 June 1985; "Who Pays for Executive Sins?" *New York Times*, 4 March 1984.

[38] For the first view see Peter A. French, *Collective and Corporate Responsibility* (New York: Columbia University Press, 1984); Kenneth E. Goodpaster and John B. Matthews, Jr., "Can a Corporation Have a Conscience?" *Harvard Business Review*, 60 (1982): 132–41; Thomas Donaldson, "Moral Agency and Corporations," *Philosophy in Context*, 10 (1980): 51–70; David T. Ozar, "The Moral Responsibility of Corporations," in *Ethical Issues in Business*, Thomas Donaldson and Patricia Werhane, eds. (Englewood Cliffs, NJ: Prentice Hall, 1979), pp. 294–300. For the second see John Ladd, "Morality and the Ideal of Rationality in Formal Organizations," *The Monist*, 54, no. 4 (1970): 488–516, and "Corporate Mythology and Individual Responsibility," *The International Journal of Applied Philosophy*, 2, no. 1 (Spring 1984): 1–21; Patricia H. Werhane, "Formal Organizations, Economic Freedom and Moral Agency," *Journal of Value Inquiry*, 14 (1980): 43–50. The author's own views are more fully developed in Manuel Velasquez, "Why Corporations Are Not Morally Responsible for Anything They Do," *Business & Professional Ethics Journal*, 2, no. 3 (Spring 1983): 1–18; also similar to the author's views are those in Michael Keeley, "Organizations as Non-Persons," *Journal of Value Inquiry*, 15 (1981): 149–55.

that they have "moral" duties. These philosophers argue that business organizations are like machines whose members must blindly and undeviatingly conform to formal rules that have nothing to do with morality. Consequently it makes no more sense to hold organizations "morally responsible" for failing to follow moral standards than it makes to criticize a machine for failing to act morally. The major problem with this second view is that, unlike machines, at least some of the members of organizations usually know what they are doing and are free to choose whether to follow the organization's rules or even to change these rules. When an organization's members collectively, but freely and knowingly, pursue immoral objectives it ordinarily makes perfectly good sense to say that the actions they perform for the organization are "immoral" and that the organization is "morally responsible" for this immoral action.

Which of these two extreme views is correct? Perhaps neither. The underlying difficulty with which both views are trying to struggle is this: Although we say that corporate organizations "exist" and "act" like individuals, they obviously are not *human* individuals. Yet our moral categories are designed to deal primarily with individual humans who feel, reason, and deliberate, and who act on the basis of their own feelings, reasonings, and deliberations. So how can we apply these moral categories to corporate organizations and their "acts"? We can see our way through these difficulties only if we first see that corporate organizations and their acts depend on human individuals: Organizations are composed of human individuals and they act only when these individuals choose to act.

Since corporate acts originate in the choices and actions of human individuals, it is these individuals who must be seen as the *primary* bearers of moral duties and moral responsibility: Human individuals are responsible for what the corporation does because corporate actions flow wholly out of their choices and behaviors. If a corporation acts wrongly, it is because of what some individual or individuals in that corporation chose to do; if a corporation acts morally, it is because some individual or some group in that corporation chose to have the corporation act morally.

Nonetheless, it makes perfectly good sense to say that a corporate organization has "moral" duties and that it is "morally responsible" for its acts. But organizations have moral duties and are morally responsible in a *secondary* sense: A corporation has a moral duty to do something only if some of its members have a moral duty to make sure it is done, and a corporation is morally responsible for something only if some of its members are morally responsible for what happened (that is, they acted with knowledge and freedom, topics that we will discuss later).

The central point that we must constantly keep before our eyes as we aim at analyzing the ethics of business activities and that we must not let the fiction of "the corporation" obscure is that human individuals underlie the corporate organization and that, consequently, these human individuals are the primary carriers of moral duties and moral responsibilities. This is not to say, of course, that the human beings who make up a corporation are not influenced by the corporation and its structure. Corporate policies, corporate culture, corporate norms, and corporate design can and do have an enormous influence on the choices, beliefs, and behaviors of corporate employees. But these corporate realities are like the furniture of the world the corporate employee inhabits. They provide the subject matter of the employee's choices, the obstacles around which the employee might have to maneuver, and the instruments that help the employee act. But these corporate realities do not make the employee's choices for him or her and so they are not responsible for his or her actions.

Business organizations are embedded in a larger society. They are, in the jargon of the social sciences, a "subsystem" that is part of a larger "social system." As such, business does not, cannot, exist without the tacit consent of that larger system. Through their laws the citizens of the larger system allow a business organization to exist by granting it the rights, powers, privileges, protections, and benefits which they believe the organization will need if it is to achieve the purpose for which it is created. Business organizations are part of the basic structure of society, and the moral standards that serve to ensure a stable, productive, and secure society by restraining the self-interest of its members in mutually beneficial ways must also apply to the members of business organizations.

Business ethics is a study of how these moral standards apply to the conduct of individuals involved in these organizations through which modern societies produce and distribute goods and services. Business ethics, in other words, is a form of applied ethics. It includes not only the analysis of moral principles and norms, but also attempts to apply the conclusions of this analysis to particular kinds of behavior: the behavior of people in business institutions.

The Multinational Corporation and Ethics

Most large corporations today are multinationals: firms that maintain manufacturing, marketing, service, or administrative operations in several "host" countries. In fact, virtually all of the 500 largest U.S. industrial corporations maintain operations in more than one nation. Because they operate in several different nations, such corporations face a number of ethical issues that deserve special mention.

With a worldwide presence, multinational corporations tend to be very large, tend to draw capital, raw materials and human labor from wherever in the world they are cheap and available, and tend to assemble and market their products in whatever nations offer manufacturing advantages and open markets. Dow Chemical Company, for example, which is headquartered in Midland, Michigan, operates 179 manufacturing plants in 31 countries. In 1989 these plants employed more than 62,100 workers of almost every nationality and produced more than 2,000 chemical products including numerous plastics, generic chemicals, agricultural fertilizers and pesticides, and dozens of consumer goods, including Saran Wrap, Cepacol mouthwash, Spray 'N Wash stain remover, Freezloc wrap, Fantastik cleaner, and Seldane antihistamine. Raw materials for these products came from all over the world, and the finished products, whose sales produced more than $17 million of revenues, were predominantly marketed in countries outside the United States. Dow Company's CEO and 10 of its 22-member management committee were born in foreign countries and 17 members of this top management committee have worked abroad.

The fact that multinationals operate in more than one country produces ethical dilemmas for their managers that managers of firms limited to a single country do not face. First, because the multinational has operations in more than one country, it sometimes has the ability to shift its operations out of any country that becomes inhospitable and relocate in another country that offers it cheaper labor, less stringent laws, or other favorable treatment. This ability to shift its operations sometimes enables the multinational to escape the social controls that a single nation might attempt to impose on the multinational and can allow the multinational to play one country against another. Environmental laws, for example, which can ensure that domestic companies operate in the responsible manner that a country deems right for its people, may not be effective constraints on a multinational that can simply move—or threaten to move—to a country without such laws. Again, union rules that can ensure fair treatment of workers or decent wages may be ineffective against a multinational that can go—or threaten to go—anywhere in the world to look for workers. Thus, the managers of multinationals are sometimes confronted with the dilemma of choosing between the economic needs and interests of their business on the one hand, and the local needs and interests of their host country on the other.

Governments, however, are not completely powerless, and many have developed highly effective means of controlling the multinationals they allow within their borders. For example, once a multinational invests in a foreign country and starts a profitable operation, it becomes a hostage of the local government, because that government can threaten to confiscate all or part of the multinational's local investment and profits. If its investment is large or if it depends heavily on the foreign profits, the multinational will find it difficult to disagree with any demands of the local government, including ethically questionable demands such as the South African government's demand that companies in effect discriminate against local black minorities. This situation creates additional moral dilemmas for multinational managers: that of either refusing to do what they believe is wrong and risking their business investment or saving their business by going along with what they believe is an unethical practice. Moreover, the objectives of the governments of different countries can result in conflicting demands on the multinational. A multinational, for example, may have invested heavily in South Africa in the past and may now find itself pressured by the U.S. government to eliminate all discriminatory practices in its South African subsidiaries and simultaneously commanded by the South African government to maintain discriminatory practices in its South African operations. Or Mexico can require a Dow Chemical subsidiary in Mexico to export more and import less, at the same time that the governments of Brazil, Korea, Europe, and elsewhere are also telling their Dow Chemical subsidiaries to export more and import less.

Another set of dilemmas is created by the fact that because the multinational operates plants in several countries, it can sometimes transfer raw materials, goods, and capital among its plants in different countries at terms that enable it to escape taxes and fiscal obligations that companies limited to a single nation must bear. Suppose, for example, that a multinational manufactures goods in plants in nation H, where taxes on profits are high, by using raw materials from one of its mines in nation L, where taxes are low. And suppose that it ships the manufactured goods to its stores in a third country, S, where taxes are low and where the goods are ultimately marketed. Clearly, the multinational will want to maximize its profits at its mine and store in the low-tax country L and S, and minimize its profits at its plant in high-tax country H. To accomplish this, it will have its mine in country L sell raw materials to its plant in country H at high, inflated prices; this increases profits at its mine in low-tax country L while reducing profits at its plant in high-tax country H. Then it will have its plant in country H sell its finished goods to its store in country S at low, deflated prices. This will further reduce its profits in high-tax country H, while increasing its profits in low-tax country S. Because the multinational is thus able to set the prices for the materials it transfers and exchanges among its network of plants and operations, it can, in effect, transfer income, expenses, and profits to whatever country it chooses, always seeking the most favorable tax treatment it can. Thus, the managers of a multinational often are faced with the choice of whether or not they will escape from carrying the share of the tax burden that a local regime believes is morally just. Local governments, of course, will try to control such practices by imposing regulations on the multinational's pricing policies, but such regulations are difficult to frame and even more difficult to enforce.

Yet another group of dilemmas faced by multinationals is created by the fact that because they operate in several countries, they often have the opportunity to transfer a new technology or set of products from a more developed country into nations that are less developed. The multinational wants to carry out the transfer, of course, because it perceives an opportunity for profit, and the host country wants and allows the transfer because it perceives these technologies and products as keys to its own development. However, the transfer of new technologies and products into a developing country can create risks when the country is not ready to assimilate them. A chemical company, for example, may import a new toxic pesticide into a developing agrarian nation whose farm workers are neither knowledgeable about nor able to protect themselves against the injuries it will inflict on their health when they apply the foreign-made pesticide by hand to their plants. Yet if the chemical company refuses to supply the pesticide, the local government may object that it is withholding a technology that it judges to be critically needed by its farmers. Or the advertising campaigns of a food company can motivate consumers in Third World nations to spend their meager food budgets on "foods" such as carbonated soft drinks, sweets, or cigarettes that provide few or no nutritional benefits and that may impose some long-range health costs. Yet, again, the local government may object if the food company holds back some foods that it makes available to consumers of other "advanced" nations. Thus the managers of multinationals are often faced with the dilemma of choosing between the benefits that both the company and its host country can derive from a product or technology transfer, and the risks and hazards that such transfers can produce.

Finally, because the multinational operates in different nations, and because countries have different national standards, it is often faced with the quandary of deciding which of these different norms and standards it should implement in its many operations. For example, when a nation headquartered in a highly developed country such as the United States operates in a less developed nation such as Trinidad, should it pay workers U.S. wages or the lower wages prevalent among Trinidad businesses? Should it use U.S. workplace safety standards for its workers or the lower standards prevalent among Trinidad businesses? If it uses U.S. wages and U.S. safety standards, the result may be that it unfairly draws the best workers away from local Trinidad businesses that cannot afford to do the same. If it uses the wages and safety standards prevalent in Trinidad, it may in effect be exploiting workers.

Thus, multinationals, because they operate in many different countries, are faced with a number of unique ethical dilemmas. Their presence in different countries may allow them to escape the taxes and other legal and social constraints through which local governments seek to control their activities. Because they operate in countries at different levels of development and with different standards and norms, they must determine which risks and which standards are ethically appropriate for a given country. And because their foreign operations become hostage to the governments of their host countries, they must choose whether to go along with the many conflicting and sometimes morally questionable demands of these governments or risk losing some or all of their foreign investment.

Three Objections

Occasionally people object to the view that ethical standards should be applied to the behavior of people in business organizations. Persons involved in business, they claim, should single-mindedly pursue the financial interests of their firm and not sidetrack their energies or their firm's resources into "doing good works." Three different kinds of arguments are advanced in support of this view.

First, some have argued that in perfectly competitive free markets, the pursuit of profit will by itself ensure that the members of society are served in the most socially beneficial ways.[39] For, in order to be profitable, each firm has to produce only what the members of society want and has to do this by the most efficient means available. The members of society will benefit most, then, if managers do not impose their own values on a business but instead devote themselves to the single-minded pursuit of profit, and thereby devote themselves to producing efficiently what the members of society themselves value.

Arguments of this sort conceal a number of assumptions that require a much lengthier discussion than we can provide at this stage. Since we will examine many of these claims in greater detail in the chapters that follow, we will here only note some of the more questionable assumptions on which the argument rests.[40] First, most industrial markets are not "perfectly competitive" as the argument assumes, and to the extent that firms do not have to compete they can maximize profits in spite of inefficient production. Second, the argument assumes that any steps taken to increase profits will necessarily be socially beneficial, when in fact several ways of increasing profits actually injure society: allowing harmful pollution to go uncontrolled, deceptive advertising, concealing product hazards, fraud, bribery, tax evasion, price-fixing, and so on. Third, the argument assumes that by producing whatever the *buying* public wants (or values), firms are producing what all the members of society want, when in fact the wants of large segments of society (the poor and the disadvantaged) are not necessarily met because they cannot participate fully in the marketplace. Fourth, the argument is essentially making a normative judgment ("managers *should* devote themselves to the single-minded pursuit of profits") on the basis of some assumed but unproved

[39] See, for example, the long discussion of these issues in LaRue Tone Hosmer, *The Ethics of Management*, 2nd ed. (Homewood, IL: Richard D. Irwin, Inc., 1991), pp. 34–55.

[40] For these and other criticisms see Alan H. Goldman, "Business Ethics: Profits, Utilities, and Moral Rights," *Philosophy and Public Affairs*, 9, no. 3 (Spring 1980): 260–86.

moral standards ("people *should* do whatever will benefit those who participate in markets"). Thus, although the argument tries to show that ethics does not matter, it can do this only by itself assuming an unproven moral standard that at least appears mistaken.

A second kind of argument sometimes advanced to show that business managers should single-mindedly pursue the interests of their firms and should ignore ethical considerations is embodied in what Alex C. Michales calls the "loyal agent's argument."[41] The argument can be paraphrased as follows:

> *As a loyal agent of his or her employer, the manager has a duty to serve his or her employer as the employer would want to be served (if the employer had the agent's expertise).*
>
> *An employer would want to be served in whatever ways will advance his or her self-interests.*
>
> *Therefore, as a loyal agent of his or her employer, the manager has a duty to serve his or her employer in whatever ways will advance the employer's self-interests.*

The argument can be, and has often been, used to justify a manager's unethical or illegal conduct. The officer of a corporation, for example, may plead that although he engaged in certain illegal or unethical conduct (say, price-fixing), he should be excused because he did it not for himself but in order to protect the best interests of his company, or its shareholders, or its workers. The "loyal agent's argument" underlies this kind of excuse. More generally, if we replace "employer" with "government" and "manager" with "officer," we get the kind of argument that Nazi officers used after World War II to defend their involvement in Hitler's morally corrupt government.

The loyal agent's argument relies on several questionable assumptions. First, the argument tries to show, again, that ethics does not matter by assuming an unproven moral standard ("the manager *should* serve his or her employer in whatever way the employer wants to be served"). But there is no reason to assume that this moral standard is acceptable as it stands, and some reason to think that it would be acceptable only if it were suitably qualified (for example, "the manager should serve his or her employer in whatever *moral* way the employer wants to be served"). Second, the loyal agent's argument assumes that there are no limits to the manager's duties to serve the employer, when in fact such limits are an express part of the legal and social institutions from which these duties arise. An "agent's" duties are defined by what is called "the law of agency," that is, the law that specifies the duties of persons ("agents") who agree to act on behalf of another party and who are authorized by the agreement so to act. Lawyers, managers, engineers, stockbrokers, and so on, all act as "agents" for their employers in this sense. By freely entering an agreement to act as someone's agent, then, a person accepts a legal (and moral) duty to serve the client loyally, obediently,

[41] Alex C. Michales, "The Loyal Agent's Argument," in *Ethical Theory and Business*, Tom L. Beauchamp and Norman E. Bowie, eds. (Englewood Cliffs, NJ: Prentice Hall, 1979), pp. 338–48. See also Milton Friedman, "The Social Responsibility of Business is to Increase Its Profits," *New York Times Magazine*, 13 (September 1970).

and in a confidential manner as specified in the law of agency.[42] But the law of agency states that "in determining whether or not the orders of the [client] to the agent are reasonable . . . business or professional ethics are to be considered," and "in no event would it be implied that an agent has a duty to perform acts which are illegal or unethical."[43] The manager's duties to serve his employer, then, are limited by the constraints of morality, since it is with this understanding that his duties as a loyal agent are defined. Third, the loyal agent's argument assumes that if a manager agrees to serve a firm, then this agreement automatically justifies whatever the manager does on behalf of the firm. But this assumption is false: Agreements to serve other people do not automatically justify doing wrong on their behalf. For example, it is clearly wrong for me to kill an innocent person to advance my own interests. Suppose that one day I enter an agreement to serve your interests and that later it turns out that your interests require that I kill an innocent person for you. Does the agreement now justify my killing the innocent person? Obviously it does not, because agreements do not change the moral character of wrongful acts. If it is morally wrong, then, for a manager to do something out of self-interest, it is also morally wrong for him to do it in the interests of his company even though he has agreed to serve the company. The assumptions of the loyal agent's argument, then, are mistaken.

A third kind of objection is sometimes made against bringing ethics into business. This is the objection that to be ethical it is enough for business people merely to obey the law: Business ethics is essentially obeying the law. When an accountant, for example, was asked to prepare a "business ethics" report for the Board of Directors of 7-Eleven Stores, his report excluded evidence suggesting that a manager was trying to bribe New York tax officials. When asked why the alleged bribery attempt was excluded from a report that should have included any "unethical" behavior, he replied that he left it out because it did not seem to be an "illegality," implying that "unethical" and "illegal" are the same.[44]

It is wrong, however, to see law and ethics as identical. It is true that some laws require behavior that is the same as the behavior required by our moral standards. Examples of these are laws that prohibit murder, rape, theft, fraud, and so on. In such cases, law and morality coincide and the obligation to obey such laws is the same as the obligation to be moral. But law and morality do not always coincide. Some laws have nothing to do with morality because they do not involve serious matters. These include parking laws, dress codes, and other laws covering similar matters. Other laws may even violate our moral standards so that they are actually contrary to morality. Our own pre–Civil War slavery laws, for example, required us to treat slaves like property, and the laws of Nazi Germany required antisemitic behavior. The laws of present-day South Africa require businesses to discriminate against blacks in ways that most people would say are clearly immoral. And, as we saw, when hundreds died in Bhopal, India, Union Carbide was accused of immorally neglecting safety although it had

[42] See Phillip I. Blumberg, "Corporate Responsibility and the Employee's Duty of Loyalty and Obedience: A Preliminary Inquiry," in *The Corporate Dilemma: Traditional Values Versus Contemporary Problems*, Dow Votaw and S. Prakash Sethi, eds. (Englewood Cliffs, NJ: Prentice Hall, 1973), pp. 82–113.

[43] Quoted in *Ibid.*, p. 86.

[44] "The Complex Case of the U.S. vs. Southland," *Business Week*, 21 November 1983.

carefully followed all local laws. Thus it is clear that ethics is not simply following the law.

This does not mean, of course, that ethics has nothing to do with the law.[45] Our moral standards are sometimes incorporated into the law when enough of us feel that a moral standard should be enforced by the pressures of a legal system; and laws, on the other hand, are sometimes criticized and eliminated when it becomes clear that they blatantly violate our moral standards. Our moral standards against bribery in business, for example, were incorporated into "The Foreign Corrupt Practices Act," and only a few decades ago it became clear that laws permitting job discrimination—like earlier laws permitting slavery—were blatantly unjust and had to be eliminated. Moreover, most people hold that all citizens have a general ethical obligation to obey the law so long as it does not require clearly unjust behavior. Tragically, this means that terrible conflicts can arise when the law requires or allows something that the businessperson believes is immoral. Dr. Grace Pierce, for example, worked for Ortho Pharmaceutical Corporation developing a drug that contained an ingredient that in her medical judgment carried unnecessary carcinogenic risks for consumers. Ortho company managers, she claimed, exerted "pressures" on her to develop the drug, pointing out that use of the ingredient was in no way illegal and that she had a legal obligation to the company to work on the drug. "I was on the spot," she said. "I had to get with it or get out." Faced with a terrible conflict between what she felt was ethical and what was legal, she ultimately quit her job. In her mind, it was obvious that ethics is not the same as legality.

1.2 MORAL REASONING

The last section defined ethics in terms of the moral standards on which moral judgments are based. We will turn in this section to examine the processes by which these moral standards are linked to moral judgments. We begin by describing how a person's ability to employ moral standards develops and then we turn to describing the reasoning processes in which these moral standards are employed.

Moral Development and Virtue

Individuals are not born with an ability to understand and apply moral standards. Just as people's physical, emotional, and cognitive abilities develop as they mature, so also their ability to deal with moral issues develops as they move through their lives. Aristotle, an early Greek thinker who proposed one of the most influential theories of ethics in the West, argued that our moral abilities, which he called "virtues" or morally good "habits," develop only through training and repetition. Just as individuals develop other kinds of practical abilities through practice and repetition, so also, he argued, humans acquire their moral abilities when they are taught and habituated by their families and communities to think, feel, and behave in morally appropriate ways. Courage, temperance, generosity,

[45] See John Finnis, *Natural Law and Natural Rights* (Oxford: Clarendon Press, 1980), pp. 295–350; John Rawls, *A Theory of Justice* (Cambridge, MA: Harvard University Press, 1971), pp. 108–14; Alan Donagan, *The Theory of Morality* (Chicago: University of Chicago Press, 1977), pp. 108–11.

self-control, honesty, sociability, modesty, and fairness or justice, are all virtues that he discussed and that he held were acquired through this kind of habituation. Although the development of these virtues requires time and effort, once they are acquired virtuous behavior comes easily and naturally.

Recently, a large number of thinkers have returned to Aristotle's views, claiming that we should put greater stress on the development of the moral abilities that he called "the virtues." Those who have advanced this claim hold that contemporary ethics places too much emphasis on *action*—what people should and should not *do*—and that much more attention must be paid to people's *character*—what a human being should *be*. Some have gone so far as to argue that we should not waste time on other aspects of ethics but should concentrate solely on trying to understand and develop the virtues that make a person a morally decent human being. Although few ethicists have accepted this extreme view, a large number have nevertheless begun to devote considerable energy to analyzing human virtue, and some have produced important analyses of the moral virtues that professional managers should develop such as perseverance, public-spiritedness, integrity, veracity, fidelity, benevolence, and humility.[46]

Recent work in psychology has clarified the exact steps through which people move as their moral abilities develop and mature. Just as there are identifiable stages of growth in physical development, so the ability to make reasoned moral judgments also develops in identifiable stages. As children we are simply told what is right and what is wrong, and we obey unthinkingly so as to avoid punishment: The child's adherence to moral standards is essentially based on self-interest. As we mature into adolescence, these moral standards are gradually internalized. We begin to understand their implications more clearly, and we follow them because they advance the well-being of people we know and to whom we feel attached: Adherence to moral standards is now essentially based on loyalty to family, friends, and nation. It is only as rational and experienced adults that we finally acquire the ability to critically reflect upon the moral standards bequeathed to us by our families, peers, culture, or religion. We then begin to rationally evaluate these moral standards and their consequences, and to revise them where they are inadequate, inconsistent, or biased toward particular groups: Morality is now essentially based on universal standards that impartially take into account the interests of all persons.

The psychologist Lawrence Kohlberg, for example, has concluded on the basis of over twenty years of research that there is a sequence of six identifiable stages in the development of a person's ability to deal with moral issues. Kohlberg

[46] Aristotle's views on virtue are easily accessible in any of the numerous translations of his ethical treatise, *Nicomachean Ethics*, such as the one found in W. D. Ross, ed., *The Works of Aristotle Translated Into English*, 12 vols. (Oxford: Oxford Press, 1908–1952); for a useful collection of essays on contemporary research on virtue theory, see Christina Hoff Sommers, ed., *Vice and Virtue in Everyday Life* (New York: Harcourt Brace Jovanovich, Publishers, 1985); for earlier treatments of the virtues see Peter Geach, *The Virtues* (Cambridge, Cambridge University Press, 1977), and J. D. Wallace, *Virtues and Vices* (Ithaca, NY: Cornell University Press, 1978). The view that ethics should consist of a study of the virtues is proposed by Alisdair MacIntyre, *After Virtue* (Notre Dame, IN: University of Notre Dame Press, 1981). An interesting analysis of the virtues of professional managers is found in William F. May, "Professional Ethics: Setting, Terrain, and Teacher," in *Ethics Teaching in Higher Education*, Daniel Callahan and Sissela Bok, eds. (New York: Plenum, 1980), pp. 205–41; see also Clarence C. Walton, *The Moral Manager* (Cambridge, MA: Ballinger Publishing Company, 1988).

grouped these stages of moral development into three levels, each containing two stages, the second of which is the more advanced and organized form of the general perspective of each level. The sequence of six stages can be summarized as follows:[47]

LEVEL ONE: PRECONVENTIONAL STAGES

At these first two stages, the child is able to respond to rules and social expectations and can apply the labels "good," "bad," "right," and "wrong." These rules, however, are seen as something external imposed on the self. Right and wrong are interpreted in terms of the pleasant or painful consequences of actions or in terms of the physical power of those who set the rules. The child sees situations only from his or her own point of view, and since the child does not yet have the ability to identify with others to any great extent, the primary motivation is self-interest.

Stage One: Punishment and Obedience Orientation.

At this stage the physical consequences of an act wholly determine the goodness or badness of that act. The child's reasons for doing the right thing are to avoid punishment or to defer to the superior physical power of authorities. There is little awareness that others have needs and desires similar to one's own.

Stage Two: Instrument and Relativity Orientation.

At this stage right actions are those that can serve as instruments for satisfying the child's own needs or the needs of those for whom the child cares. The child is now aware that others have needs and desires similar to his or her own and begins to defer to them in order to get them to do what he or she wants.

LEVEL TWO: CONVENTIONAL STAGES

Maintaining the expectations of one's own family, peer group, or nation is seen as valuable in its own right, regardless of the consequences. The person does not merely conform to expectations but exhibits loyalty to the group and its norms. The person is now able to see situations from the point of view of others in the group and assumes that everyone is similar. The person is motivated to conform to the group's norms and subordinates the needs of the individual to those of the group.

[47] This summary is based on Lawrence Kohlberg, "Moral Stages and Moralization: The Cognitive-Developmental Approach," in Thomas Lickona, ed., *Moral Development and Behavior: Theory, Research, and Social Issues* (New York: Holt, Rinehart and Winston, 1976), pp. 31–53; other papers collected in Lickona's book survey the literature both in support of and critical of Kohlberg. For a more recent and superb overview of the research and literature on Kohlberg and his relevance to teaching, see Edward J. Conry and Donald R. Nelson, "Business Law and Moral Growth," *American Business Law Journal*, vol. 27, no. 1 (Spring 1989), pp. 1–39. Kohlberg's work is built on the theories of Piaget; see Jean Piaget, *The Moral Judgment of the Child*, Marjorie Grabain, trans. (New York: The Free Press, 1965).

Stage Three: Interpersonal Concordance Orientation.

Good behavior is living up to what is expected by those for whom one feels loyalty, affection, and trust, such as family and friends. Right action is conformity to what is generally expected in one's role as a good son, daughter, brother, friend, etc. Doing what is right is motivated by the need to be a "good person" in one's own eyes and in the eyes of others.

Stage Four: Law and Order Orientation.

Right and wrong are determined by loyalty to one's own nation. Laws are to be upheld except where they conflict with other fixed social duties. The person is now able to see other people as parts of a larger social system that defines individual roles and obligations, and he or she can separate the norms generated by this system from his or her interpersonal relationships and motives.

LEVEL THREE: POSTCONVENTIONAL, AUTONOMOUS, OR PRINCIPLED STAGES

At these stages the person no longer simply accepts the values and norms of the groups to which he or she belongs. Instead the person now tries to see situations from a point of view that impartially takes everyone's interests into account. The person questions the laws and values that society has adopted and redefines them in terms of self-chosen universal moral principles that can be justified to any rational individual. The proper laws and values are those to which any reasonable person would be motivated to commit himself or herself, whatever place the person holds in society and whatever society he or she belongs to.

Stage Five: Social Contract Orientation.

The person is aware that people hold a variety of conflicting personal views and opinions, and emphasizes fair ways of reaching consensus by agreement, contract, and due process. The person believes that all values and norms are relative and that, apart from this democratic consensus, all should be tolerated.

Stage Six: Universal Ethical Principles Orientation.

Right action is defined in terms of universal principles chosen because of their logical comprehensiveness, their universality, and their consistency. These ethical principles are not concrete like the ten commandments but abstract universal principles dealing with justice, society's welfare, the equality of human rights, respect for the dignity of individual human beings, and with the idea that persons are ends in themselves and must be treated as such. The person's reasons for doing right are based on a commitment to these moral principles, and the person sees them as the criteria for evaluating all other moral rules and arrangements including democratic consensus.

Kohlberg's theory is important because it helps us understand in detail how individuals develop their moral capacities or "virtues" through the internalization of the moral standards prevalent in their communities. It also reveals how we become increasingly sophisticated and critical in our use and understanding of these moral standards. Kohlberg's theory, however, has been subjected to a number of criticisms, the most significant of which arises from the work of Carol Gilligan, a psychologist who suggests that although Kohlberg's theory correctly identifies the stages through which men pass as they develop, it fails to adequately trace out the pattern of development of women.[48] Because most of Kohlberg's subjects were male, Gilligan argued, his theory failed to take into account the patterns of moral thinking of women.

Gilligan suggests that men tend to deal with moral issues in terms of impersonal, impartial, and abstract moral rules, exemplified by the principles of justice and rights that Kohlberg says are characteristic of postconventional thinking. Women, however, tend to see themselves as part of a network of relationships with family and friends, and when they encounter moral issues they are concerned with sustaining these relationships and with avoiding hurt to others. For women morality is primarily a matter of caring and being responsible for others with whom one is involved in personal relationships, and not a matter of adhering to impartial and impersonal rules. Moral development for women is marked by progress toward more adequate ways of caring and being responsible for oneself and others. In her theory, the earliest or "preconventional" level of moral development for women is marked by caring only for oneself. Women move to a second or "conventional" level when they internalize conventional norms about caring for others to the neglect of oneself. And they move to the "postconventional" or most mature level when, having become critical of the conventional norms they had earlier accepted, they come to achieve a balance between caring for others and caring for oneself.

Although recent research has tended to show that male and female moral development does not differ in the ways that Gilligan suggested, that same research has tended to support the claim that Gilligan has identified an approach or "perspective" toward moral issues that is both different from the approach that Kohlberg emphasizes and that is prevalent in our moral thinking. Both men and women sometimes approach moral issues from the perspective of impartial and impersonal moral rules, and sometimes from the perspective of care and responsibility in relationships. It is too early to tell how these two perspectives are related, and the development of the "care perspective" that Gilligan describes is still in its infancy.[49]

[48] See Carol Gilligan, *In a Different Voice*: *Psychological Theory and Women's Development* (Cambridge, MA: Harvard University Press, 1982).

[49] Among the studies that have failed to find significant gender differences in moral reasoning are Robbin Derry, "Moral Reasoning in Work Related Conflicts," in *Research in Corporate Social Performance and Policy*, William Frederick, ed., vol. 9 (Greenwich, CT: JAI, 1987), pp. 25–49; Freedman, Robinson, & Freedman, "Sex Differences in Moral Judgment? A Test of Gilligan's Theory," *Psychology of Women Quarterly*, vol. 37 (1987); Thoma, "Estimating Gender Differences in the Comprehension and Preference of Moral Issues" (unpublished manuscript cited in Conry and Nelson and available from the Center for the Study of Ethical Development, University of Minnesota); for some recent studies that explore the two different perspectives see Eva Feder Kittay and Diana T. Meyers, eds., *Women and Moral Theory* (Totowa, NJ: Rowman and Littlefield, 1987). An attempt to work out an ethic of care is Nell Noddings, *Caring*: *A Feminine Approach to Ethics and Moral Education* (Berkeley, CA: University of California Press, 1984).

For our purposes, what is important to note is that both Kohlberg and Gilligan agree that there are stages of growth in our moral development. Both also agree that moral development moves from a preconventional stage focused on self-interest, through a conventional stage in which we uncritically accept the conventional moral standards of those around us, and on to a mature stage in which we learn to critically and reflectively examine the conventional moral standards we earlier accepted and to fashion more adequate standards of our own.

Kohlberg and Gilligan also agree that the stages of moral development are sequential. That is, people do not enter a later stage until they have passed through each of the earlier ones. Progress through the stages, however, is not inevitable. A person may never reach the later stages, but may remain stuck at one of the earlier stages throughout life. Kohlberg has argued, in fact, that much of the American population does not reach the later stages, but remains at a conventional level of development throughout adulthood.

One of the purposes of studying ethics is to develop one's ability to deal with moral issues. In terms of the older moral tradition of Aristotle, the purpose is to develop the virtues. In terms of Lawrence Kohlberg's developmental sequence, the study of ethics should enable the individual to acquire the more critical understanding of "right" and "wrong" that characterize the later postconventional stages of moral development. One of the central aims of the study of ethics, therefore, is the stimulation of this moral development.

This is an important point, and one that should not be lost upon the reader. The text and cases that follow are designed to be read and discussed with others in order to stimulate in ourselves the kind of moral development that we have been discussing. Intense interaction and discussion of moral issues with others develop our ability to move beyond a simple acceptance of the moral standards we may have uncritically absorbed from family, peers, organization, nation, or culture. By discussing, analyzing, and criticizing the moral judgments we and others make, we come to acquire the habits of thinking that are needed to develop and determine for ourselves a set of moral principles to which we can reasonably assent. We can get a clearer idea of these processes by looking more closely at the nature of moral reasoning.

Moral Reasoning

The terms "moral reasoning" and "ethical reasoning" refer to the reasoning process by which human behaviors, institutions, or policies are judged to be in accordance with or in violation of moral standards. Moral reasoning always involves two essential components: (1) an understanding of what moral standards require or prohibit and (2) evidence or information that shows that a particular policy, institution, or behavior has the kinds of features that these moral standards require or prohibit. Here is an illustration of moral reasoning whose author is offering us his reasons for claiming that American social institutions are unjust:

> The nonwhite . . . live in American society, fight for American society in disproportionate numbers and contribute cheap labor to American society, thereby enabling others to live disproportionately well. But the nonwhite . . . do not share in the benefits of the American society in which they live and for which they fight and to which they contribute. 41 percent of Negroes fall below the poverty line as compared

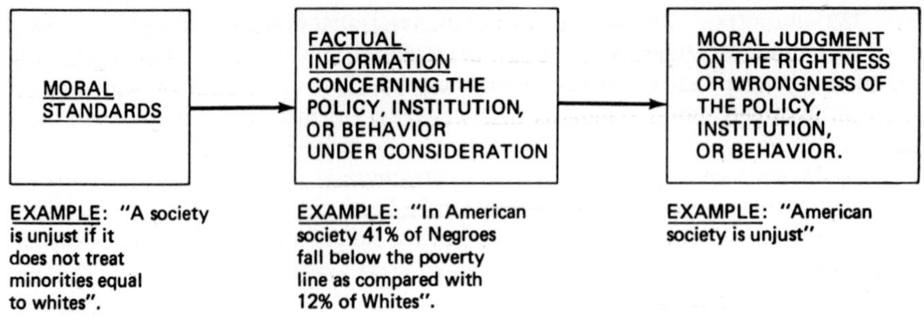

FIGURE 1-1

> with 12 percent of whites. Infant mortality is three times as high among nonwhite babies as among white. Whereas, Negroes make up 11 percent of the nation's work force, they have but 6 percent of the nation's technical and professional jobs, 3 percent of the managerial jobs and 6 percent of jobs in skilled trades. Discrimination which prevents people from gettting out of their society what they contribute is unjust.[50]

In this example, the author has in mind a moral standard which he sets out at the end of the paragraph: "Discrimination which prevents people from getting out of their society what they contribute is unjust." The rest of the paragraph is devoted to citing evidence to show that American society exhibits the kind of discrimination proscribed by this moral principle. The author's moral judgment that American society is unjust, then, is based on a chain of reasoning that appeals to a moral standard and to evidence that American society has the features condemned by this standard. Schematically, then, moral or ethical reasoning usually has the kind of structure indicated in Figure 1.1.[51]

In many cases, one or more of the three components involved in a person's moral reasoning will not be expressed. More often than not, in fact, people will fail to make explicit the moral standards on which their moral judgments are based. A person might say, for example: "American society is unjust because it allows 41 percent of Negroes to fall below the poverty line as compared with 12 percent of whites." Here the unspoken moral standard on which the judgment "American society is unjust" is based is something like "A society is unjust if it does not treat minorities equal to the majority." And the disproportionate number of Negroes that fall below the poverty line is being cited as evidence that minorities in America are not treated equally to the white majority. The main reason that moral standards are often not made explicit is that they are generally presumed to be obvious. People put more of their efforts into producing evidence that a given policy, institution, or action conforms to, or violates, their unexpressed standards than they put into identifying or explaining the moral standards on which their judgments rely. Failure to make one's moral standards explicit leaves one vulnerable to all the problems created by basing critical decisions on unexamined assumptions: The assumptions may be inconsistent, they may have no rational

[50] Edward J. Stevens, *Making Moral Decisions* (New York: Paulist Press, 1969), pp. 123–25.

[51] For a fuller discussion of this approach see Stephen Toulmin, Richard Rieke, and Allan Janik, *An Introduction to Reasoning* (New York: Macmillan Inc., 1979), pp. 309–37.

basis, and they may lead the decision-maker into unwittingly making decisions with undesirable consequences. We saw at the end of the last section two arguments that tried to show that managers should not be ethical but both of which were based on assumed moral standards that were unacceptable once they were made explicit.

To uncover the implicit moral standards on which a person's moral judgments are based, one has to retrace the person's moral reasoning back to its bases. This involves asking (1) What factual information does the person accept as evidence for this moral judgment? and (2) What moral standards are needed to relate this factual information (logically) to the moral judgment?[52] For example, suppose I judge that capital punishment is morally wrong. And suppose that I base my judgment on the factual evidence that capital punishment occasionally results in the death of innocent people. Then, in order to relate this factual information to my judgment, I must accept the general moral principle: Whatever occasionally results in the death of innocent people is morally wrong. This general moral principle is needed if there is to be a (logical) connection between the factual information ("capital punishment occasionally results in the death of innocent people") and the moral judgment that is based on this fact ("capital punishment is morally wrong"). Without the moral principle, the factual information would have no logical relation to the judgment and would therefore be irrelevant.

The moral standards on which adults base their moral judgments will usually be much more complex than this simple example suggests. Developed moral standards (as we will see) incorporate qualifications, exceptions, and restrictions that limit their scope. Also they may be combined in various ways with other important standards. But the general method of uncovering unexpressed moral standards remains roughly the same whatever their complexity: One asks what general standards relate a person's factual evidence to his or her moral judgments.

It is to be hoped that this account of ethical reasoning has not suggested to the reader that it is always easy to separate factual information from moral standards in a piece of moral reasoning; nothing could be further from the truth. In practice, the two are sometimes intertwined in ways that are difficult to disentangle. And there are several theoretical difficulties in trying to draw a precise line separating the two.[53] Although the difference between the two is usually clear enough for practical purposes, the reader should be aware that sometimes they cannot be clearly distinguished.

Analyzing Moral Reasoning

There are various criteria that ethicians use to evaluate the adequacy of moral reasoning. First and primarily, moral reasoning must be *logical.* The analysis of moral reasoning requires that the logic of the arguments used to establish a moral judgment be rigorously examined, that all the unspoken moral and factual assumptions be made explicit, and that both assumptions and premises be displayed and subjected to criticism.

[52] See Richard M. Hare, *Freedom and Reason* (New York: Oxford University Press, 1965), pp. 30–50; 86–111.

[53] The difficulties are discussed in John R. Searle, *Speech Acts* (New York: Cambridge University Press, 1969), pp. 182–88.

Second, the factual evidence cited in support of a person's judgment must be *accurate*, it must be *relevant*, and it must be *complete*.[54] For example, the illustration of moral reasoning quoted above cites several statistics ("Whereas Negroes make up 11 percent of the nation's work force, they have but 6 percent of the nation's technical and professional jobs, 3 percent of . . .") and relationships ("The nonwhite contribute cheap labor which enables others to live disproportionately well") that are claimed to exist in America. If the moral reasoning is to be adequate, these statistics and relationships must be *accurate*: They must rest on reliable statistical methods and on well-supported scientific theory. In addition, evidence must be *relevant*: It must show that the behavior, policy, or institution being judged has precisely those characteristics that are proscribed by the moral standards involved. The statistics and relationships in the illustration of moral reasoning given above, for instance, must show that some people are "prevented from getting out of [American] society what they contribute," the precise characteristic that is condemned by the moral standard cited in the illustration. And evidence must be *complete*: It must take into account all relevant information and must not selectively advert only to the evidence that tends to support a single point of view.

Third, the moral standards involved in a person's moral reasonings must be *consistent*. They must be consistent with each other and with the other standards and beliefs the person holds.[55] Inconsistency between a person's moral standards can be uncovered and corrected by examining situations in which these moral standards require incompatible things. Suppose that I believe that (1) it is wrong to disobey an employer whom one has contractually agreed to obey, and I also believe that (2) it is wrong to help someone who is endangering innocent people's lives. Then suppose that one day my employer insists that I work on a project that might result in the deaths of several innocent people. The situation now reveals an inconsistency between these two moral standards: I can either obey my employer and avoid disloyalty, or I can disobey him and avoid helping endanger people's lives, but I cannot do both.

When inconsistencies between one's moral standards are uncovered in this way, one (or both) of the standards must be modified. In the example above I might decide, for instance, that orders of employers have to be obeyed *except* when they threaten human life. Notice that in order to determine what kinds of modifications are called for, one has to examine the *reasons* one has for accepting the inconsistent standards and weigh these reasons to see what is more important and worth retaining and what is less important and subject to modification. In the example above, for instance, I may have decided that the reason that employee loyalty is important is that it safeguards property but that the reason why the refusal to endanger people is important is that it safeguards human life. And human life, I then decide, is more important than property. This sort of criticism and adjustment of one's moral standards is an important part of the process through which moral development takes place.

[54] An excellent and compact account of these features may be found in Lawrence Habermehl; "The Susceptibility of Moral Claims to Reasoned Assessment," in *Morality in the Modern World*, Lawrence Habermehl, ed. (Belmont, CA.: Dickenson Publishing Co., Inc., 1976), pp. 18–32.

[55] *Ibid.*

There is another kind of consistency that is perhaps even more important in ethical reasoning. Consistency also refers to the requirement that one must be willing to accept the consequences of applying one's moral standards consistently to all persons in similar circumstances.[56] This "consistency requirement" can be phrased as follows:

> *If I judge that a certain person is morally justified (or unjustified) in doing A in circumstances C, then I must accept that it is morally justified (or unjustified) for any other person*
> *(a) to perform any act relevantly similar to A*
> *(b) in any circumstances relevantly similar to C.*

I must, that is, apply the same moral standards to one situation that I applied to another one that was relevantly similar. (Two situations are "relevantly similar" when all those factors that have a bearing on the judgment that an action is right or wrong in one situation are also present in the other situation.) For example, suppose that I judge that it is morally permissible for me to fix prices because I want the high profits. Then if I am to be consistent, I must hold that it is morally permissible for my *suppliers* to fix prices when they want high profits. If I am not willing to consistently accept the consequences of applying to other similar persons the standard that price-fixing is morally justified for those who want high prices, then I cannot rationally hold that the standard is true in my own case.

The consistency requirement is the basis of an important method of showing that a given moral standard must be modified or rejected: the use of "counterexamples" or "hypotheticals." If a moral standard is inadequate or unacceptable, we can often show it is inadequate by showing that its implications in a certain hypothetical example are unacceptable. For instance, suppose someone should advance the claim that we ought always to do only what will benefit ourselves—that is, that we *ought* to act only egoistically. We might want to attack this view by proposing the hypothetical example of an individual who is made happy only when she does what will benefit *others* and *not* herself. According to the egoistic standard, this individual *ought* to do only what will make her unhappy! And this, we might want to hold, is clearly unacceptable. The egoist, of course, may want to modify his view (by saying "What I *really* meant by 'benefit ourselves' was . . ."), but that is another story. The point is that hypothetical "counterexamples" can be used effectively to show that a moral standard must be rejected or at least modified.

Moral Reasoning and Ethical Relativism

We discussed earlier some of the unique ethical issues confronted by international businesses. There is one important issue, however, that is inevitably encountered when applying ethical standards to businesses that operate in different societies and about which something must be said: the issue of ethical relativism.

Ethical relativism is the theory that, because different societies have different ethical beliefs, there is no way of determining whether an action is morally right

[56] See Marcus G. Singer, *Generalization in Ethics* (New York: Alfred A. Knopf, Inc., 1961), p. 5; Hare, *Freedom and Reason*, p. 15; Frankena, *Ethics*, p. 25.

or wrong other than by asking whether the people of this or that society believe it is morally right or wrong. Or, to put it another way: Ethical relativism is the view that there are no ethical standards that are universally true or correct for the people of all societies; instead, something is right for the people of a particular society if they believe it is right, and wrong if they believe it is wrong. The people of certain Arab societies, for example, are said to believe that business bribery is morally acceptable, although Americans believe it is immoral. The ethical relativist will conclude that while it is wrong for an American to bribe in America, it is not wrong for such Arabs to bribe in their own society. The businessperson who operates in several different countries, then, and who encounters societies with many different moral beliefs will be advised by the theory of ethical relativism that in one's moral reasoning one should always follow the moral standards prevalent in whatever society one finds oneself. After all, since moral standards differ and since there are no other criteria of right and wrong, the best one can do is to follow the old adage "When in Rome, do as the Romans do."

Clearly, there are numerous practices that are judged immoral by some societies that other societies have deemed morally acceptable, including polygamy, abortion, infanticide, slavery, homosexuality, racial and sexual discrimination, genocide, patricide, and the torture of animals. But critics of the theory of ethical relativism have pointed out that it does not follow that there are no universal moral standards. Critics of ethical relativism have argued, in fact, that there are certain moral standards that the members of any society must accept if that society is to survive and if its members are to interact with each other effectively. Thus, all societies have norms against injuring or killing other members of the society, norms about using language truthfully when communicating with members of one's society, and norms against taking the personal goods of other members of one's society. Moreover, many apparent moral differences among societies turn out upon closer examination to mask deeper underlying similarities. For example, anthropologists tell us that in some Eskimo societies it was morally acceptable for families to abandon their aged to die outdoors during times of hardship, while other societies felt they had a moral obligation to protect and nurture their aged at all times. Yet, upon closer examination, it can turn out that underlying the different practices of both kinds of societies is a belief in the same ethical standard: the moral duty of ensuring the long-term survival of the community. In their harsh environment, Eskimos may have had no way of ensuring their community's survival when food supplies ran short other than by abandoning their aged. Other communities ensured their long-term survival by protecting the elders who carried within them the knowledge and experience they needed.

Other critics of the theory of ethical relativism point out, moreover, that from the fact that different people have different moral beliefs, it does not follow that all moral beliefs are equally acceptable. When two people have different beliefs, all that follows is that one of them is probably wrong.

But perhaps the most telling criticisms against the theory of ethical relativism are those that point to the unacceptable consequences of the theory. If the theory of ethical relativism were true, then it would make no sense to criticize the practices of other societies so long as they conformed to their own standards. We could not say, for example, that the slavery of our pre–Civil War Southern societies was wrong, or that the discrimination practiced in the societies of the American

South before the 1950s was unjust, or that the Germans' treatment of Jews in the Nazi society of the 1930s was immoral. Moreover, if the theory of ethical relativism were correct, it would also make no sense—in fact it would be morally wrong—to criticize any of the moral standards or practices accepted by our own society. For if our society accepts that a certain practice—such as torturing animals—is morally right, then as members of this society, we too must accept that practice as morally right and it is immoral for us to tell others in our society to go against this belief, because right and wrong for us must be determined by the accepted standards of our society. Thus, the theory of ethical relativism implies that whatever the majority in our society believes about morality is automatically correct.

Thus, the fundamental problem with the theory of ethical relativism is that it holds that the moral standards of a society are the only criteria by which the actions of that society can be judged. The theory thus gives the moral standards of each society a privileged place that is above all criticism by members of that society or by anyone else. Clearly, this implication of the theory of ethical relativism indicates that the theory is mistaken. For we recognize that the moral standards of our own society as well as those of other societies can be mistaken. This recognition that our own moral standards as well as those of other societies might be wrong implies that the moral standards a society happens to accept are not the only criteria of right and wrong.

The ethical relativist correctly reminds us that different societies have different moral beliefs, and that we should not simply dismiss the moral beliefs of other cultures when they do not match our own. But the ethical relativist is wrong to conclude that all moral beliefs are equally acceptable, and wrong to conclude that the only criteria of right and wrong are the moral standards prevalent in a given society.

Moral Responsiblity

The discussion up to now has focused on reasoning that is aimed at judging whether an action (or policy or institution) is morally right or wrong. Moral reasoning, however, is sometimes directed at a related but different kind of judgment: determining whether a person is *morally responsible*, or culpable, for having done something wrong or for having wrongfully injured someone.[57] A judgment about a person's moral responsibility for a wrongful injury is a judgment about the extent to which the person deserves blame or punishment, or should pay restitution for the injury. If an employer, for example, deliberately injures the health of her employees, we would judge her "morally responsible" for those injuries. We are then saying she is to blame for those injuries, and perhaps that she deserves punishment and should compensate the victims.

People are not always morally responsible for their wrongful or injurious acts. A person, for example, may inflict an injury upon an innocent human being, but do so without knowing what he or she was doing (perhaps the person did it by accident). We would not hold the person morally responsible for that injury: What the person did was "wrong," but the person is *excused* by virtue of his or

[57] A person can also be morally responsible for good acts. But since we are concerned with determining when a person is excused from doing wrong, we will discuss moral responsibility only as it relates to wrongdoing and to being excused therefrom.

her ignorance. When, then, is a person morally responsible—or to blame—for having done something?

A person is morally responsible only for those acts and their foreseen injurious effects (1) which the person knowingly and freely performed or brought about and which it was morally wrong for the person to perform or bring about, or (2) which the person knowingly and freely failed to perform or prevent and which it was morally wrong for the person to fail to perform or prevent. Stefan Golab, for example, a fifty-nine-year-old Polish immigrant who spoke little English, died from cyanide poisoning after working for two months over open vats of fuming cyanide for Film Recovery Systems, a company that recovered silver from old film. Steven O'Neil, president of the company, together with Charles Kirschbaum, the plant supervisor, and Daniel Rodriguez, the plant foreman, in a landmark case, were judged responsible by a court for Golab's death on charges of murder.[58] The judgment was based on testimony that the managers maintained the hazardous working conditions knowing the life-threatening dangers of breathing the cyanide fumes, that they failed to warn or protect workers like Golab who could not read English, and that they had skull-and-crossbones warning symbols scraped off cyanide drums. Thus, they were held responsible for knowingly and freely maintaining the dangerous workplace and for defacing the pictorial warnings, both of which were wrongful actions. They were also held responsible for Golab's death since it was held that they "knew there was a strong probability of bodily harm" resulting from their actions.

One can also be morally responsible for failing to act or failing to prevent an injury if one's omission is free and knowledgeable and if one could and should have acted or could and should have prevented the injury. Several manufacturers of asbestos, for example, were recently judged responsible for the lung diseases suffered by some of their workers.[59] The judgment was based in part on the finding that the manufacturers had a special duty (a duty they were assigned by their position) to warn their workers of the known dangers of working with asbestos, but that they knowingly failed to perform this duty, and the lung diseases were a foreseen injury that they could have prevented had they acted as they had a duty to act.

There is wide agreement that two conditions completely eliminate a person's moral responsibility for causing a wrongful injury: (1) ignorance and (2) inability.[60] These are called "excusing" conditions because they fully excuse a person from being held responsible for something. If a person was ignorant of, or was unable to avoid, what he or she did, then that person did not act knowingly and freely and so cannot be blamed for what he or she did. Asbestos manufacturers, for

[58] "Job Safety Becomes a Murder Issue," *Business Week*, 6 August 1984; "3 Executives Convicted of Murder For Unsafe Workplace Conditions," *New York Times*, 15 June 1985; "Working Them to Death," *Time*, 15 July 1985; "Murder Case a Corporate Landmark," part I, *Los Angeles Times*, 15 September 1985; "Trial Makes History," part II, *Los Angeles Times*, 16 September 1985. Their conviction was later overturned.

[59] Jim Jubak, "They Are the First," *Environmental Action*, (February 1983); Jeff Coplon, "Left in the Dust," *Voice*, 1 March 1983; George Miller, "The Asbestos Cover-Up," *Congressional Record*, 17 May 1979.

[60] This agreement goes back to Aristotle, *Nicomachean Ethics*, Martin Ostwald, trans. (New York: The Bobbs-Merrill Company, 1962), bk. III, ch. 1.

example, have claimed that they did not know that conditions in their plants would cause lung cancer in their workers. If this is true, then it would be wrong to blame them for the diseases that resulted. Other asbestos manufacturers have said that they tried to prevent these diseases by trying to get their workers to wear protective masks and clothing but they were unable to enforce these protective measures because the workers refused to adhere to them. If these manufacturers truly tried everything they could to prevent these diseases but they were unable to do so because of circumstances they could not control, then again they are not morally responsible for these injurious effects.

It is important to understand exactly when ignorance and inability remove a person's responsibility. For ignorance and inability do not always excuse a person. One exception is when a person deliberately keeps himself ignorant of a certain matter precisely in order to escape responsibility. If an asbestos manufacturer, for example, told the company's doctors *not* to tell him the results of the medical examinations they carried out on his workers so that he would not be legally liable for leaving conditions in his factory unchanged, he would still be morally responsible for any injuries if the tests turned out positive. A second exception is when a person negligently fails to take adequate steps to become informed about a matter that is of known importance. A manager in an asbestos company, for example, who has reason to suspect that asbestos may be dangerous, but who fails to inform himself on the matter out of laziness, cannot later plead ignorance as an excuse.

A person may be ignorant either of the relevant facts or the relevant moral standards. For example, I may be sure that bribery is wrong (a moral standard) but may not have realized that in tipping a customs official I was actually bribing him into cancelling certain import fees (a fact). On the other hand, I may be genuinely ignorant that bribing government officials is wrong (a moral standard) although I know that in tipping the customs official I am bribing him into reducing the fees I owe (a fact).

Ignorance of *fact* generally eliminates moral responsibility completely for the simple reason that a person cannot be obligated to do something over which he or she has no control: moral obligation requires freedom.[61] Since people cannot control matters of which they are ignorant, they cannot have any moral obligations with respect to such matters, and their moral responsibility for such matters is consequently nonexistent. Negligently or deliberately created ignorance is an exception to this principle because such ignorance can be controlled. Insofar as we can control the extent of our ignorance, we become morally responsible for it and therefore also for its injurious consequences. Ignorance of the relevant *moral standards* generally also removes responsibility because a person is not responsible for failing to meet obligations of whose existence he or she is genuinely ignorant. However, to the extent that our ignorance of moral standards is the result of freely choosing not to ascertain what these standards are, to that extent we are responsible for our ignorance and for its wrongful or injurious consequences.

Inability can be the result of either internal or external circumstances that render a person unable to do something or unable to keep from doing something. A person may lack sufficient power, skill, opportunity or resources to act, or the

[61] See the discussion of this in Hare, *Freedom and Reason*, pp. 50–60.

person may be physically constrained or prevented from acting, or the person's mind may be psychologically impaired in a way that prevents the person from controlling his or her actions. A manager working under extremely stressful circumstances, for example, may be so tense that one day he is overcome by rage at a subordinate and genuinely is unable to control his actions toward that subordinate. Or an engineer who is part of a larger operating committee may find that she is unable to prevent the other committee members from making a decision that she feels will wrongfully injure other parties. Or an assembly-line worker with an undiagnosed malady may suffer muscle spasms that cause the assembly line to malfunction in a way that inflicts physical injuries on other workers around him. In all of these cases the person is not morally responsible for the wrong or the injury due to the person's inability to control events.

Inability eliminates responsibility because, again, a person cannot have any moral obligation to do (or forbear from doing) something over which the person has no control. Insofar as circumstances render a person unable to control his or her actions or unable to prevent a certain injury, it is wrong to blame the person.

In addition to the two *excusing* conditions (ignorance and inability) that completely remove a person's moral responsibility for a wrong, there are also several *mitigating* factors that can lessen a person's moral responsibility depending on how serious the wrong is. Mitigating factors include (1) circumstances that leave a person *uncertain* but not altogether unsure about what he or she is doing (these affect the person's knowledge); (2) circumstances that make it *difficult* but not impossible for the person to avoid doing it (these affect the person's freedom); and (3) circumstances that minimize but do not completely remove a person's *involvement* in an act (these affect the degree to which the person actually caused or helped to cause the wrongful injury). These can lessen a person's responsibility for wrongdoing depending upon a fourth factor: the seriousness of the wrong. To clarify these we can discuss each of them in turn.

First, circumstances can produce *uncertainty* about a variety of matters. A person may be fairly convinced that doing something is wrong, yet may still be doubtful about some important *facts*, or may have doubts about the *moral standards* involved, or doubts about how *seriously wrong* the action is. For example, an office worker who is asked to carry proprietary information to a competitor might feel fairly sure that doing so is wrong yet may also have some genuine uncertainty about how serious the matter is. Such uncertainties can lessen a person's moral responsibility for a wrongful act.

Second, a person may find it *difficult* to avoid a certain course of action because he or she is subjected to threats or duress of some sort or because avoiding that course of action will impose heavy costs on the person. Middle managers, for example, are sometimes intensely pressured or threatened by their superiors to reach unrealistic production targets or to keep certain health information secret from workers or the public, although it is clearly unethical to do so.[62] If the pressures on managers are great enough, we generally hold, then their responsibility is correspondingly diminished. Although they are to blame for the wrong, their blame is mitigated (those who knowingly and freely impose pressures on subordi-

[62] "Overdriven Execs: Some Middle Managers Cut Corners to Achieve High Corporate Goals," *Wall Street Journal*, 8 November 1979.

nates that can be expected to issue in wrongful acts are also responsible for those wrongful acts).

Third, a person's responsibility can also be mitigated by circumstances that diminish the person's *active involvement* in the act that caused or brought about an injury. An engineer may contribute to an unsafe product, for example, by knowingly drawing up the unsafe design and thus being actively involved in causing the future injuries. On the other hand, the engineer may be aware of the unsafe features in somebody else's design, but passively stand by without doing anything about it because "that's not my job." In such a case the engineer is not actively involved in causing any future injuries. In general, the less my actual actions contribute to the outcome of an act, the less I am morally responsible for that outcome (depending, however, on the seriousness of the act). However, if a person has a special (an officially assigned) duty to report or try to prevent certain wrongdoings, then that person is morally responsible for acts he or she refrains from reporting or trying to prevent even if the person is not otherwise involved in the act. An accountant, for example, who has been hired to report any fraudulent activity she observes cannot plead diminished responsibility for a fraud she knowingly failed to report by pleading that she did not actively carry out the fraudulent act. In such cases, where a person has a special (explicitly assigned) duty to prevent an injury, freely and knowingly *failing* to prevent it is wrong, and one is responsible for it (along with the other guilty party or parties) if one should and could have prevented it but did not.

Fourth, the extent to which these three mitigating circumstances can diminish a person's responsibility for a wrongful injury depends upon how *serious* the wrong is. For example, if doing something is very seriously wrong, then even heavy pressures and minimal involvement may not substantially reduce a person's responsibility for the act. If my employer, for example, threatens to fire me unless I sell a used product that I know will kill someone, it would be wrong for me to obey him even though loss of a job will impose some heavy costs on me. On the other hand, if only a relatively minor matter is involved, then the threat of a job loss might substantially mitigate my responsibility. In determining one's moral responsibility for a wrongful act, therefore, one must judge one's uncertainties, the pressures to which one is subjected, and the extent of one's involvement, and weigh these against the seriousness of the wrong. Obviously, such judgments are often extremely difficult and tragically painful to make.

It may be helpful to summarize here the essential points of this discussion of an individual's moral responsibility for a wrong or an injury. First, an individual is morally responsible for those wrongful acts he performs (or wrongly omits) and for those injurious effects he brings about (or wrongly fails to prevent) when this is done knowingly and freely. Second, moral responsibility is completely eliminated (excused) by ignorance and inability. Third, moral responsibility for a wrong or an injury is mitigated by (1) uncertainty, (2) difficulty, and (3) minimal involvement (although failure to act does not mitigate if one has a specifically assigned duty to prevent that kind of wrong), but the extent to which these lessen one's responsibility depends upon (4) the seriousness of the wrong or the injury: The greater the seriousness, the less the first three factors mitigate.

Before leaving this topic we should note that critics have contested whether all of the mitigating factors above really affect a person's responsibility. Some have claimed that evil may never be done no matter what personal pressures are exerted on a person.[63] Other critics have claimed that I am as responsible when I refrain from stopping a wrong as I am when I perform the wrong myself, since passively *allowing* something to happen is morally no different from actively *causing* it to happen.[64] If these critics are correct, then mere passive involvement in making something happen does not mitigate moral responsibility. Although neither of these criticisms seems to be correct, the reader should make up his or her own mind on the matter. Discussing all the issues the criticisms raise would take us too far afield.

Corporate Responsibility

Within the modern corporation, responsibility for a corporate act is often distributed among a number of cooperating participants. Corporate acts normally are brought about by several actions or omissions of many different people all cooperating together so that their concatenated actions and omissions jointly produce the corporate act. One team of managers, for example, may design a car, another team test it, and a third team build it; one person orders, advises, or encourages something and others act on these orders, advice, or encouragement; one group knowingly defrauds buyers and another group knowingly but silently enjoys the resulting profits; one person contributes the means, and another person accomplishes the act; one group does the wrong and another group conceals it. The variations on cooperation are endless.

Who is morally responsible for such jointly produced acts? The traditional view is that those who knowingly and freely did what was necessary to produce the corporate act are each morally responsible.[65] On this view, situations in which a person needs the actions of others to bring about a wrongful corporate act are no different in principle from situations in which a person needs certain external circumstances in order to commit a wrong. For example, if I want to shoot an innocent person, I must rely on my gun going off (an external circumstance). And if I want to defraud the stockholders of a corporation I must rely on others to do their part in the fraud. In both cases I can bring about the wrongful injury only by relying on something or someone other than myself. But in both cases, if I am knowingly and freely trying to bring about the fraud, then I am equally morally responsible for the wrongful injury. Bringing about a wrongful act by acting with others, then, does not differ in a morally significant way from deliberately bringing about a wrongful act with the help of inanimate instruments: the person is fully responsible for the wrong or the injury even if this responsibility is shared with others. So if, for example, as a member of the board of directors of a corporation, with full knowledge and complete freedom, I act on insider

[63] Alan Donagan, *The Theory of Morality* (Chicago: University of Chicago Press, 1977), pp. 154–57, 206–7.

[64] Singer, *Practical Ethics*, p. 152.

[65] See W. L. LaCroix, *Principles for Ethics in Business* (Washington, DC: University Press of America, 1976), pp. 106–7; Thomas M. Garrett, *Business Ethics*, 2nd ed. (Englewood Cliffs, NJ: Prentice Hall, 1986), pp. 12–13; Henry J. Wirtenberger, S. J., *Morality and Business* (Chicago: Loyola University Press, 1962), pp. 109–14; Herbert Jone, *Moral Theology*, Urban Adelman, trans. (Westminster, MD: The Newman Press, 1961), p. 236.

information to vote for some stock options that will benefit me but unfairly injure the other stockholders, then I am morally responsible for the wrongful corporate act of the board even if I share this responsibility with other members of the board. By my vote I was trying to bring about the illegal corporate act and I did so knowingly and freely.

Critics of this traditional view of the individual's responsibility for corporate acts have claimed that when an organized group, such as a corporation, acts together, their corporate act may be described as the act of the group and, consequently, the corporate group and not the individuals who make up the group must be held responsible for the act.[66] For example, we normally credit the manufacture of a defective car to the corporation that made it and not to the individual engineers involved in its manufacture; and the law typically attributes the acts of a corporation's managers to the corporation itself (so long as the managers act within their authority) and not to the managers as individuals. Traditionalists, however, can reply that, although we sometimes attribute acts to corporate groups, this linguistic and legal fact does not change the moral reality behind all such corporate acts: Individuals had to carry out the particular actions that brought about the corporate act. Since individuals are morally responsible for the known and intended consequences of their free actions, any individual who knowingly and freely joins his actions together with those of others, intending thereby to bring about a certain corporate act, will be morally responsible for that act.[67]

More often than not, however, employees of large corporations cannot be said to have "knowingly and freely joined their actions together" to bring about a corporate act or to pursue a corporate objective. Employees of large-scale organizations follow bureaucratic rules that link their activities together to achieve corporate outcomes of which the employee may not even be aware. The engineers in one department may build a component with certain weaknesses, for example, not knowing that another department plans to use that component in a product that these weaknesses will render dangerous. Or employees may feel pressured to conform to company rules with whose corporate outcomes they may not agree but which they feel they are not in a position to change. A worker on an assembly line, for example, may feel he has no choice but to stay at his job even though he knows that the cars he and others help to build are dangerous. Obviously, then, a person working within the bureaucratic structure of a large organization is not necessarily morally responsible for every corporate act he or she helps to bring about. If I am working as a secretary, a clerk, or a janitor in a corporation, or if I become a stockholder in a corporation, then my actions may help the officers of the corporation commit a fraud. But if I know nothing about the fraud or if I am in no way able to prevent it (for example, by reporting it) then I am not morally responsible for the fraud. Here, as elsewhere, the excusing factors of

[66] Peter A. French, "Corporate Moral Agency," in *Ethical Theory and Business*, Tom L. Beauchamp and Norman E. Bowie, eds. (Englewood Cliffs, NJ: Prentice Hall, 1979), pp. 175–86; see also Christopher D. Stone, *Where the Law Ends* (New York: Harper & Row, Publishers, Inc., 1975), pp. 58–69, for the legal basis of this view.

[67] See Manuel Velasquez, "Why Corporations Are Not Morally Responsible for Anything they Do," *Business & Professional Ethics Journal*, 2, no. 3 (Spring 1983): pp. 1–18; see also the two commentaries on this article appearing in the same journal by Kenneth E. Goodpaster, *ibid.*, 2, no. 4, pp. 100–103, and Thomas A. Klein, *ibid.*, 3, no. 2, pp. 70–71.

ignorance and inability—which are endemic to large-scale bureaucratic corporate organizations—will completely eliminate a person's moral responsibility.

Moreover, depending on the seriousness of the act, the mitigating factors of uncertainty, difficulty, and minimal involvement can also diminish a person's moral responsibility for a corporate act. Sometimes employees in a corporation go along with a wrongful corporate act although they know (to some extent) that it is wrong and although they have the ability (to some extent) to withdraw their cooperation: They unwillingly go along because of pressures placed on them. Traditional moralists have argued that a person's responsibility for unwillingly cooperating with others in a wrongful act should be determined by weighing the various factors that *mitigate* individual responsibility. That is, one must weigh the seriousness of the wrongful act against the uncertainty, the difficulty, and the degree of involvement that were present (but, again, those who have a moral duty to prevent a wrong cannot plead that their omission constitutes "minimal involvement"). The more seriously wrong a corporate act is, the less my responsibility is mitigated by uncertainty, pressures, and minimal involvement.

Subordinates' Responsibility

In a corporation employees often act on the basis of the orders of their superiors. Corporations usually have a hierarchical structure of authority in which orders and directives pass from those higher in the structure to a variety of agents in lower levels. A vice president tells several middle managers that they must reach certain production goals and the middle managers try to attain them. A plant manager tells her foremen to close down a certain line and the foremen do it. An engineer tells a clerk to write up a certain report and the clerk does it. Who is morally responsible when a superior orders a legitimate subordinate to carry out an act that both of them know is wrong?

People sometimes suggest that when a subordinate acts on the orders of a legitimate superior, the subordinate is absolved of all responsibility for that act: Only the superior is morally responsible for the wrongful act even though the subordinate was the agent who carried it out. A short while ago, for example, the managers of a National Semiconductor plant allegedly ordered their employees to write up a government report that falsely stated that certain computer components sold to the government had been tested for defects.[68] Some employees objected, but when the managers allegedly insisted, the employees complied with their orders. When the falsified reports were discovered the managers argued that only the corporation as a whole or the managers as a group should be held responsible for the falsified reports. The employees were not morally responsible because the employees were simply agents who were following orders.

It is clearly mistaken, however, to think that an employee who freely and knowingly does something wrong is absolved of all responsibility when he or she is "following orders." Moral responsibility requires merely that one act freely and knowingly and it is irrelevant that one's wrongful act is that of freely and knowingly choosing to follow an order. For example, if I am ordered by my superior to murder a competitor and I do so, I can hardly later claim that I am

[68] David Sylvester, "National Semi May Lose Defense Jobs," *San Jose Mercury News*, 31 May 1984.

totally innocent because I was merely "following orders." The fact that my superior ordered me to perform what I knew was an immoral act in no way alters the fact that in performing that act I knew what I was doing and I freely chose to do it anyway. As we noted when discussing the "loyal agent's argument," there are limits to an employee's obligation to obey his or her superior: an employee has no obligation to obey an order to do what is immoral. Of course, a superior can put significant economic pressures on an employee and such pressures can *mitigate* the employee's responsibility but they do not totally eliminate it.

Thus, when a superior orders an employee to carry out an act that both of them know is wrong, the employee is morally responsible for that act if he or she carries it out. Is the superior also morally responsible? Obviously the superior is also morally responsible since in ordering the employee the superior is knowingly and freely bringing about the wrongful act through the instrumentality of the employee. The fact that a superior uses a human being to bring about the wrongful act does not change the fact that the superior brought it about.

1.3 SUMMARY

This chapter has developed the idea that ethics is the study of judgments concerned with moral right and wrong, that is, with judgments based on moral standards. The first section of the chapter clarified this idea by explaining what moral standards are and by describing the kinds of social functions they serve. The second section turned to explaining in detail how moral standards form the basis of moral judgments, that is, to explaining what moral reasoning is. We first described how a person's capacity to engage in moral reasoning develops and then outlined the general structure that moral reasoning usually has. We ended by describing several methods by which moral reasoning can be analyzed and corrected and by explaining how moral responsibility is determined.

The discussion, however, has not yet developed any specific standards for distinguishing right from wrong. That is the burden of the next chapter, which will describe three kinds of standards that are commonly employed in moral reasoning: utilitarian moral standards, standards concerned with moral rights, and standards of justice.

QUESTIONS FOR REVIEW AND DISCUSSION

1. Define the following concepts: ethics, normative judgment, moral judgment, moral norm, moral principle, moral standard, prudential claim, business ethics, preconventional morality, conventional morality, autonomous morality, moral reasoning, consistency requirement, ethical relativism, moral responsibility.
2. "Ethics is a purely private matter." Discuss this statement.
3. "Ethics has no place in business." Discuss.
4. "Kohlberg's views on moral development show that the more morally mature a person becomes, the more likely he is to obey the moral norms of his society." Comment.

CASES FOR DISCUSSION

The Air Force Brake

On June 28, 1967, Ling-Temco-Vought (LTV) Aerospace Corporation contracted to purchase 202 aircraft brakes from B. F. Goodrich for the A7D, a new plane that Ling-Temco-Vought was constructing for the Air Force. B. F. Goodrich, a tire manufacturer, agreed to supply the brakes for less than $70,000. According to Mr. Vandivier, a Goodrich employee who worked on this project, Goodrich had submitted this "absurdly low" bid to LTV because it badly wanted the contract.[1] Even if Goodrich lost money on this initial contract, the Air Force afterwards would be committed to buying all future brakes for the A7D from B. F. Goodrich.

Besides a low price, the Goodrich bid carried a second attractive feature: The brake described in its bid was small; it contained only four disks (or "rotors") and would weigh only 106 pounds. Weight was of course an important factor for Ling-Temco-Vought, since the lighter the Air Force plane turned out to be, the heavier the payload it could carry.[2]

The four-rotor brake was designed primarily by John Warren, an engineer who had been with Goodrich for seven years. As senior project engineer, Warren was directly in charge of the brake. Working under him was Searle Lawson, a young man of twenty-six who had graduated from engineering school only one year earlier. Warren made the original computations for the brake and drew up the preliminary design.

Using Warren's design, Lawson was to build a prototype of the four-rotor brake and test it in the Goodrich laboratories. By simulating the weight of the A7D plane and its landing speed, Lawson was to ensure that the brake could "stop" the plane fifty-one consecutive times without any changes in the brake lining. If the brake "qualified" under this indoor laboratory test, it would then be mounted on airplanes and tested by pilots in flight. Kermit Vandivier, though not an engineer, was to write up the results of these laboratory qualifying tests and submit them as the laboratory report prior to the test flights.

Upon testing the prototype of Warren's four-rotor brake in simulated "landings" in the laboratory, Lawson found that high temperatures built up in the brake and the linings "disintegrated" before they made the required fifty-one consecutive stops.[3]

> Ignoring Warren's original computations, Lawson made his own, and it didn't take him long to discover where the trouble lay—the brake was too small. There simply was not enough surface area on the disks to stop the aircraft without generating the excessive heat that caused the linings to fail. . . . Despite the evidence of the abortive tests and Lawson's careful computations, Warren rejected the suggestion that the four-disk brake was too light for the job. Warren knew that his superior had already told LTV, in rather glowing terms, that the preliminary tests on the A7D brake were very successful. . . . It would [also] have been difficult for Warren

[1] Kermit Vandivier, "Why Should My Conscience Bother Me?" *In the Name of Profit* (Garden City, NY: Doubleday & Co., Inc., 1972), p. 4.

[2] *Ibid.*

[3] *Ibid.*

> to admit not only that he had made a serious error in his calculations and original design but that his mistake had been caught by a green kid, barely out of college. (Statement of Mr. Vandivier)[4]

Lawson decided to go over Warren's head to Warren's supervisor, Robert Sink. The supervisor, however, deciding to rely on the judgment of Warren who was known to be an experienced engineer, told Lawson to continue with the tests as Warren had directed.

Dejected, Lawson returned to the laboratory and over the next few months tried twelve separate times to get the brake to pass the "fifty-one-stop" qualifying tests, using various different lining materials for the brakes. To no avail: The heat inevitably burnt up the linings. By April 1968, Lawson was engaged in a thirteenth attempt to qualify the brakes.

> On the morning of April 11, Richard Gloor, who was the test engineer assigned to the A7D project, came to me and told me he had discovered that sometime during the previous twenty-four hours instrumentation used to record brake pressure had *deliberately* been miscalibrated so that while the instrumentation showed that a pressure of 1,000 pounds per square inch had been used to conduct brake stops numbers forty-six and forty-seven . . . , 1,100 pounds per square inch had actually been applied to the brakes. Maximum pressure available on the A7D is 1,000 pounds per square inch. Mr. Gloor further told me he had questioned instrumentation personnel about the miscalibration and had been told they were asked to do so by Searle Lawson. (Statement of Mr. Vandivier)[5]

The thirteenth series of tests also ended in failure and the results could not be used to qualify the brake. Mr. Vandivier, however, was anxious to ascertain why Lawson had asked to have the instruments miscalibrated:

> I subsequently questioned Lawson who admitted he had ordered the instruments miscalibrated at the direction of a superior. . . . Mr. Lawson told me that he had been informed by . . . Mr. Robert Sink, project manager at Goodrich, . . . and Mr. Russell Van Horn, project manager at Goodrich that "Regardless of what the brake does on test, we're going to qualify it." (Statement of Mr. Vandivier)[6]

Lawson then undertook the fourteenth and final attempt to qualify the brake. To ensure that the four-rotor brake passed the fifty-one-stop tests, Mr. Vandivier later testified, several procedures were used that violated military performance criteria.

> After each stop, the wheel was removed from the brake, and the accumulated dust was blown out. During each stop, pressure was released when the brake had decelerated to 10 miles per hour [and allowed to coast to a stop]. By these and other irregular procedures, the brake was nursed along. (Statement of Mr. Vandivier)[7]

[4] *Ibid.*, pp. 8–9.

[5] U.S., Congress, *Air Force A-7D Brake Problem: Hearing before the Subcommittee on Economy in Government of the Joint Economic Committee*, 91st Congress, 1st session, 13 August 1969, p. 2. Hereafter cited as "Brake Hearing."

[6] *Ibid.*, p. 3.

[7] *Ibid.*, p. 4.

When the fourteenth series of test stops was completed, Lawson asked Vandivier to help him write up a report on the brake indicating the brake had been qualified.

> I explained to Lawson that . . . the only way such a report could be written was to falsify test data. Mr. Lawson said he was well aware of what was required, but that he had been ordered to get a report written regardless of how or what had to be done . . . [He] asked if I would help him gather the test data and draw up the various engineering curves and graphic displays that are normally included in a report. (Statement of Mr. Vandivier)[8]

Kermit Vandivier had to make up his mind whether to participate in writing up the false report.

> [My] job paid well, it was pleasant and challenging, and the future looked reasonably bright. My wife and I had bought a home . . . If I refused to take part in the A7D fraud, I would have to either resign or be fired. The report would be written by someone anyway, but I would have the satisfaction of knowing I had had no part in the matter. But bills aren't paid with personal satisfaction, nor house payments with ethical principles. I made my decision. The next morning I telephoned Lawson and told him I was ready to begin the qualification report. (Statement of Mr. Vandivier)[9]

Mr. Lawson and Mr. Vandivier worked on the curves, charts, and logs for the report for about a month, "tailoring" the pressures, values, distances, and times "to fit the occasion." During that time, Mr. Vandivier frequently discussed the tests with Mr. Russell Line, the senior executive for his section, a respected and well-liked individual.

> Mr. Line . . . advised me that it would be wise to just do my work and keep quiet. I told him of the extensive irregularities during testing and suggested that the brake was actually dangerous and if allowed to be installed on an aircraft, might cause an accident. Mr. Line said he thought I was worrying too much about things which did not really concern me. . . . I asked Mr. Line if his conscience would hurt him if such a thing caused the death of a pilot, and this is when he replied I was worrying about too many things that did not concern me and advised me to "do what you're told." (Statement of Mr. Vandivier)[10]

Eventually, Mr. Vandivier's superiors also insisted that he write up the entire report and not just the graphs and charts. Mr. Vandivier complied and on June 5, 1968 the qualifying report was finally issued.

1. Were any moral issues involved in Mr. Vandivier's decision to write up the final qualifying report? Explain.
2. In your judgment, is it morally right or morally wrong for a person in Mr. Vandivier's situation to write up a false report as he did? Formulate the moral standards on which your judgment is based. Do your standards meet the consistency requirement (that is, would you be willing to apply the same standards in other similar situations)?

[8] *Ibid.*, p. 5.

[9] Vandivier, "Why Should My Conscience Bother Me?," p. 4.

[10] *Brake Hearing*, pp. 5 and 6.

3. At which of Kohlberg's levels would you place Mr. Vandivier? Mr. Lawson? Mr. Warren? Mr. Line? Yourself? Explain each of your answers.
4. In your opinion, would Mr. Vandivier be morally responsible for any "accidents" that resulted when pilots tested the brake? Explain your answer. Would this responsibility be shared with any others? Explain.

National Semiconductor's Microchips

On June 3, 1980 the computers in the North American Aerospace Defense Command bunker deep underground Cheyenne Mountain in Colorado sounded an alarm: Two missiles had just been launched from Soviet nuclear submarines and were heading toward the United States. Strategic Air Command officers monitoring the terminals immediately notified their superiors. The alert was passed on and waiting B-52 bombers carrying nuclear warheads were prepared for takeoff. Eighteen seconds later tensions increased in the underground bunker when the terminals indicated that the number of Soviet missiles had increased from 2 to 22. Then the number increased to 222, then 2,222, then 22,222, and kept increasing regularly in increments of 2. By the time the computers were reporting over 2 million incoming missiles, the officers knew they had a computer malfunction.[1]

After calling off the B-52 alert, NORAD inspectors worked around the clock for three days until they tracked down the malfunction to a single defective semiconductor "chip" in a portion of the computer that converts incoming information into messages for transmission. Semiconductor chips are minute bits of silicon no bigger than a soapflake on which microscopic electronic circuits are etched. Miniaturization has allowed manufacturers to pack millions of connected transistors and other components onto the tiny chips so that a single chip can contain the equivalent of a computer that formerly had to be housed in several large rooms. Such semiconductor chips are found in virtually all electronic components in use today, both by the military and by civilians. They constitute the heart of every computer and calculator and are used in satellite communications, missile guidance systems, radar systems on airplanes, video games, the space shuttle, and in a variety of industrial applications.

There is a sharp distinction, however, between the semiconductors manufactured for commercial applications (such as video games and home computers) and those produced for highly sensitive military purposes (such as the U.S. nuclear warning and weapons systems or in satellite communications). Semiconductors made for sensitive purposes are required by the government to undergo a lengthy, costly, and rigorous period of testing to ensure that each one will work perfectly, while commercial-grade semiconductors undergo much shorter and less rigorous tests. The higher-grade military chips must be examined under microscopes for the most minute cracks or nicks; they are alternately frozen in refrigerators and then baked in ovens at 125 degrees centigrade for hundreds of hours; they are whirled in centrifuges and immersed in various gases and liquids to test for leaks; and they are periodically run through a variety of electrical trials to gauge how well they are standing up to each test. At each step in this testing process, moreover,

[1] David Sylvester, "The Day 2 Million Soviet Missiles 'Attacked' the U.S.," *San Jose Mercury News*, 3 June 1984, p. 13A.

the government requires workers to fill out lengthy forms testifying that all tests were carried out as mandated by the Department of Defense and that the chips met all the standards set by the Department of Defense. Lower-grade commercial semiconductors are not required to meet such rigorous standards. Whereas commercial chips, for example, are baked in a "burn-in" oven test for only forty-eight hours, the higher-grade military chips may have to undergo a "burn-in" test of 240 hours at much higher temperatures. As a result, only 30 to 60 percent of the commercial chips are rejected, while the rejection rate for the higher-grade chips is 60 to 75 percent.[2]

TABLE 1.1 Defense Electronics Supply Center—List of Firms Suspended from Qualified Products List

COMPANY	PROBLEM	REMOVED	REINSTATED
Fairchild Camera and Instrument Corp. (South Portland, Ore.)	On Sept. 29, 1980, the company disclosed that it was not conducting electrical testing on all of its semiconductors	Feb. 13, 1981	April 6, 1981
Fairchild Camera and Instrument Corp. (Mountain View, Calif.)	Problems were reported in electrical testing performance	June 1, 1981	June 15, 1981
Fairchild Camera and Instrument Corp. (Mountain View, Calif.)	Electrical testing problems were not yet corrected	June 25, 1981	Oct. 2, 1981
Raytheon Co. (Mountain View, Calif.)	A federal audit revealed 30 quality deficiencies	May 28, 1981	June 22, 1981
National Semiconductor Corp. (Santa Clara, Calif.)	Electrical testing performance was unacceptable	Feb. 11, 1982	May 14, 1982
Advanced Micro Devices, Inc. (Sunnyvale, Calif.)	Test records were found to be inconsistent with official records of chip testing	Sept. 20, 1982	June 7, 1983
Precision Monolithics, Inc. (Santa Clara, Calif.)	Some chips were not processed to required military standards	Mar. 1, 1983	April 12, 1983
Fairchild Camera and Instrument Corp. (Mountain View, Calif.)	Burn-in testing was found to be too short and electrical testing violations were reported	Jan. 20, 1984	Mar. 14, 1984

Source: Defense Electronics Supply Center, Dayton, Ohio. Reprinted in *San Jose Mercury News*, 4 June 1984, p. 6A.

[2] David Sylvester, "The 91 Steps to a Fail-safe Chip," *San Jose Mercury News*, 4 June 1984, p. 6A.

Because of the sensitive nature of the uses to which high-grade semiconductor chips are put, the government has naturally been concerned that all tests be properly carried out on the chips manufacturers supply. At various times the government has in fact removed certain manufacturers of computer chips from the Defense Electronics Supply Center's list of firms allowed to sell to the military (see Table 1.1) because it felt that tests were not properly conducted. As Table 1.1 indicates, however, manufacturers have been suspended only for short periods of time. The reason is simple. Only a relatively small number of firms can manufacture the semiconductor chips that the military must have. Without the chips many Defense Department projects would come to a standstill:

> A lot of people depend on those parts. That's always a consideration on our part—we try to get them back on [the Qualified Products List] as quickly as possible. Some of these [semiconductor] companies are the only suppliers of these products. So [to suspend them for more than a few months] is a very tough decision. (Statement of Steven Stromp, spokesman for the Defense Electronics Supply Center)[3]

Penalties for failing to test semiconductors fully were thus relatively mild, consisting for the most part of nothing more than temporary removal from the Qualified Products List. On March 6, 1984, however, criminal charges were brought against National Semiconductor Corporation, for "routinely" skipping burn-in tests "in order to speed production and speed delivery" of the chips and "lying to the government in a three-year scheme involving thousands of improperly tested computer parts sold to military contractors.[4] National Semiconductor, located in the "Silicon Valley" of Santa Clara, California, pleaded guilty to seventeen counts of mail fraud and twenty-three counts of making false statements to the government and agreed to pay $1.75 million in civil and criminal penalties because of its failure to adequately test some 26 million chips from 1978 to 1981 and for falsifying test reports. Investigators working on the case said that the improperly tested chips were now in use in a wide range of aerospace and military equipment and their locations were virtually impossible to track down:

> These devices are on our ships and planes scattered throughout the world. We could not find a reliable and effective method to make a determination where they are. . . . The system is too complex. . . . I find it pretty scary. . . . In a worst-case scenario, there could be some harmful effects. (Statement of government investigator)[5]

Founded in Connecticut in 1959, National began operations manufacturing transistors. Described as an initially "genteel" company that kept losing money, National's style changed abruptly when Charles E. Sporck took over as president and chief executive officer in 1967.[6] Before coming to National, Sporck had been a highly successful manager at Fairchild, where he was one of the first to use the technique of shipping company-produced components to Asia to be assembled by

[3] *San Jose Mercury News*, 4 June 1984, p. 6A.

[4] "National Semi Pleads Guilty to Scheme," *San Jose Mercury News*, 7 March 1984, p. 1.

[5] *Ibid.*

[6] Kathryn Harris, "Chips Maker Feels Attack on Four Sides," *Los Angeles Times*, 4 April 1982, p. B1.

cheap labor. Described by journalists as ''aggressive,'' ''decisive,'' ''hard-charging,'' ''tough,'' and ''blunt,'' Sporck brought an aggressive, informal, entrepreneurial style to the fledging company.[7] In seventeen years he transformed National from a $7 million per year maker of transistors operating out of Connecticut with 600 employees, into a $1.6 billion per year manufacturer of integrated semiconductor chips headquartered in California's booming ''Silicon Valley'' and commanding a worldwide labor force of 40,000.[8]

National's expansion, however, was not entirely smooth. Disaster struck the company in 1977 when competition from Japan, combined with strikes, technical problems, and poor controls, resulted in losses in its consumer products division that cut earnings almost in half. About the same time there developed a steady exodus of talented and ''fiercely autonomous'' managers who abandoned the company in frustration because they did not see eye-to-eye with Sporck's autocratic style. Insiders reported that several top managers did not like Sporck's ''table-pounding'' at meetings, nor the extent to which he got involved in everyday pricing decisions and kept control of production and marketing decisions.[9] Bad luck struck again in February 1982 when the government briefly removed National from its Qualified Products List for the sale of high-grade microchips on the grounds that National had not followed proper testing procedures. Matters worsened toward the end of 1982 when a nationwide recession hit the semiconductor industry particularly hard, leading to several quarters of losses and declining earnings through early 1983. By 1984, however, the country was coming out of the recession and orders for semiconductors began to boom once again. Soon National had recovered from its setbacks and was once again enjoying record profits. Then, in March 1984, National was indicted on the charges of failing to properly test its high-grade military microchips and of lying to the government about these improper procedures. The company was accused of falsifying records to cover its failure to complete burn-in tests that should have involved running electricity through the chips while they were baked in ovens for 160 hours. The company conceded that it had frequently cut the test periods to forty-eight hours.

The systematic omission of required tests and the falsification of records allegedly took place only during 1979 and 1981 when the chips were in such high demand that there were intense pressures to take shortcuts as the company fell farther and farther behind in its attempts to meet contract schedules. During this period, according to San Jose newspaper reporters:

> Management-level officials at National approved the formation of a 10- to 12-member employee team that worked full time for periods up to 10 weeks fabricating testing-verification documents [to be] reviewed by Defense Department inspectors. . . . A [National] supervisor . . . said two National officials who were her bosses once directly approved her unit's falsification of testing records. She also said she and her colleagues at National had used the identities of employees who already had

[7] *Wall Street Journal*, ''National Semiconductor Forces Out Top Finance Aides in Clash of Styles,'' 17 July 1981.

[8] See Harris, ''Chips Maker Feels Attack on Four Sides''; Peter J. Schuyten, ''To Clone a Computer,'' *New York Times*, 4 February 1979, p. 1; Bro Uttal, ''The Animals of Silicon Valley,'' *Fortune*, 12 January 1981, pp. 92–96.

[9] ''Behind the Exodus at National Semiconductor,'' *Business Week*, 21 September 1981, pp. 95–102.

> left the firm to backdate and fabricate testing-verification documents for government inspectors from 1979 to 1981. (Statement of *San Jose Mercury News* reporters David Willman and David Sylvester)[10]

According to employees who had been working for National at the time, the alleged falsification of records was well known within the company:

> I'd say that over 100 employees had to know. To say that dozens participated would be a very conservative estimate . . . Just about everybody in production control knew about it who had been there for six months . . . I would borrow my gals' [identification] stamps [and] tell them, "You don't know I'm using your stamp." Yeah, we did make it up. There was a lot of documentation I personally dummied up. . . . When I realized how deeply things were being falsified, I just couldn't believe it. . . . I asked, "How did things get the way they were?" Nobody seemed to be able to give me a good answer. . . . [But] I had a lot of confidence in the reliability of the parts. I never thought we were selling bad chips to anyone. (Statements of anonymous former employee)[11]

The employees involved claimed they were told to gather whatever testing information was available and, when none was available, to simply make up dates and times and write them into the record books that would be turned over to the government when the chips were delivered. However, not everyone went along. Officials in the National plant in Singapore refused to falsify their records. National employees in the United States were allegedly told to go over the Singapore records and alter them before submitting them to the government.

According to insiders any cheating on tests and the falsification of records were due to pressures to meet contract deadlines and to save money. Omitting the costly tests is estimated to have saved National several million dollars. In addition several company officials, including president of the company Charles Sporck, maintained that other companies were also cheating and that the microchips were all reliable anyway and did not need more than the forty-eight hours of tests they were given. Not everyone agreed with this sanguine view. Government investigators pointed out that cheating on semiconductor tests increases the risks of a military disaster since defective chips could affect the operations of our nuclear warning and weapons systems. Said one government agent, "We're talking about national security and we're talking about lives. . . . You could have a missile that would end up in Cleveland instead of the intended target."[12]

Although the corporation was indicted on criminal charges, no criminal charges were brought against any individuals in the company. According to U.S. attorney Joseph Russoniello, "The fact that persons in lower-level functions may have failed to report" the testing shortcuts, was not significant enough to merit prosecution.[13] Criminal prosecution would have been merited only if officials at the level of company president or the board of directors were known to have

[10] David Willman and David Sylvester, "How Tests Were Faked at National," *San Jose Mercury News*, 3 June 1984, p. 1.

[11] David Willman and David Sylvester, "2 Workers Tried to Stop the Cheating," *San Jose Mercury News*, 3 June 1984, p. 12A, and "How Tests were Faked at National."

[12] David Willman, "DCIS: The Pentagon's Sleuth Against Fraud," *San Jose Mercury News*, 4 June 1984, p. 7A.

[13] *San Jose Mercury News*, 3 June 1984, p. 13A.

participated. Moreover, officials of the company refused to provide the names of any individuals involved in the alleged cheating and falsification.

Three months after the indictment, however, the Department of Defense announced that it was not satisfied with the fact that only the corporation as a whole was held responsible for the fraud.[14] On May 30, 1984, the Department notified National Semiconductor that it was undertaking steps to bar National from all future military contracts because of the company's refusal to name the individuals involved in the fraud. The Department of Defense's own investigation had uncovered the names of seven individuals that it alleged to have been among those involved in the fraud, and these individuals were also notified that they would be barred from all future government work.

The position of the Department of Defense was that it had to have some assurance that the individual perpetrators of the fraud were no longer in positions within the company where they might repeat the same testing short-cuts and falsification of documents. According to Karl Kabeisman, counsel for the Department of Defense, the Department had to know the individuals responsible for the fraud and where those people were in order to determine whether National could now serve as a reliable supplier. "My concern," said Kabeisman, "is simply that a corporation acts only through its employees and officers."[15]

National Semiconductor, however, vigorously contested these claims and held that responsibility for the fraud should be attributed to the corporation as a whole and not to any particular individuals in the corporation. In a public statement, company president Charles Sporck made the point quite clear:

> We totally disagree with the [Defense Department's] proposal. We have repeatedly stated that we accept responsibility as a company and we steadfastly continue to stand by that statement. (Statement of Charles Sporck)[16]

Linda Baker, an official company spokesperson, repeated the same sentiments in a public statement avowing that the company would not divulge the name of any individual involved in the fraud and that the company as a whole would stand behind any individual accused by the government. She said, "We will see [our people] are not harmed. Any National employee will be supported by the company. We feel it's a company responsibility, a matter of ethics."[17]

1. List the moral issues that you believe are raised by the events in this case, and explain why these issues are *moral* issues and not *merely* political, economic, strategic, financial, or other sorts of issues.
2. In your judgment, what parties were morally responsible for whatever cheating and falsification of records took place? Were there any excusing or mitigating factors involved? Explain. If in the future military personnel should lose their lives because of the failure of chips that were not adequately tested, what parties, if any, are morally responsible for the deaths? Explain your answer.

[14] David Sylvester, "National Semi May Lose Defense Jobs," *San Jose Mercury News*, 31 May 1984, p. 1.

[15] *Ibid.*

[16] *Ibid.*

[17] *Ibid.*

3. Comment on the refusal of Charles Sporck to give the names of the individuals involved to the Defense Department. In your judgment was his refusal morally justified? Formulate the moral standards on which your judgment is based. Do your standards meet the consistency requirement? Comment on his final statement and on the final statement of Linda Baker. Do you agree that only the "company," and not any individuals in the company, should have been held responsible for whatever cheating and falsification of records took place? Explain your answer.

Eberhard Faber, Inc.

Eberhard Faber, Inc. is a closely held family company founded in 1849 by Eberhard Faber. In 1975 the company's revenues totaled about $30 million. The majority stock of the company was held in a trust of which Mrs. Julia Faber was the income beneficiary. Other family members held minority interests in the firm. Its basic product line consisted of stationary and school supplies: pencils, erasers, rubber bands, felt markers, adhesives, type cleaners, visual-aid panels, and other items. Headquartered in Pennsylvania, the company had wholly owned subsidiaries in Germany and Canada, partnerships in Venezuela and Colombia, and licensees in Argentina, Brazil, El Salvador, Peru, Syria, Turkey, and the Philippines.

In 1971 the Company was reorganized after several years of poor performance.[1] The pencil market, upon which the company depended for 40 percent of its revenues, was chronically depressed and subject to price wars. Attempts to diversify had been unsuccessful. An eleven-week strike in 1969 hurt sales and reduced profit margins substantially. The years 1969 and 1970 were both years of loss. In 1970 a management consultant firm recommended a reorganization and a change of management. On June 8, 1971, the Board of Directors acted on this recommendation and named Eberhard Faber (the fourth) as chief executive officer. Substantial budget trimming and a reduction of inventories eventually stemmed the losses and turned the company around.

In April 1976, at a quarterly meeting of the board of directors, Mr. Faber introduced a new proposal under which Eberhard Faber, Inc. would allow a pencil company "in a Third World country" to use the Faber name and would supply it with managerial expertise and equipment. In return, Eberhard Faber, Inc. would acquire an equity position (about 30%) in the company. This acquisition would significantly increase Eberhard Faber Inc.'s book value and would provide a "pretty good profit." Mr. Eberhard Faber had worked several months on the deal and strongly urged its adoption. There was one problem with the deal, however:

> The management of the pencil company had cheerfully confessed to me that they were paying off the government of their country in order to do business. . . . From the standpoint of ethics, I viewed the proposal as a straight exchange of know-how and our name for stock in a company that needed to conserve its cash for expansion. The ethical practices of the company's management seemed to me as irrelevant as they would if it was simply buying merchandise from us. Besides, although the laws of the country in question prohibit bribery, it is a common and accepted practice there. . . . (Statement of Eberhard Faber)[2]

[1] Eberhard Faber, "What Happened When I Gave Up the Good Life and Became President," *Fortune*, December, 1971.

[2] Eberhard Faber, "How I Lost Our Great Debate About Corporate Ethics," *Fortune*, November 1976, pp. 182,186.

Nonetheless, one of the directors, Tony Carey, questioned the ethics of acquiring stock in a company that was engaged in government payoffs. Mr. Faber countered that Carey's reasoning seemed to be based on guilt-by-association and he argued that they would not become unethical simply because they owned stock in an unethical company.

> [One director] pressed on me whether we couldn't be paid cash instead of stock. That distinction seemed ethically irrelevant to me. [Another] director raised the possibility of a new sales company being set up to handle the payoffs, leaving us free to participate in the manufacturing company—which would be clear. There was a chorus of nos to this idea. (Statement of Eberhard Faber)[3]

The April meeting ended with a vote to hold off on the deal until the problem could be worked out. After the meeting, Eberhard Faber discussed the issue with several persons outside the company. All of the people with whom he consulted insisted that they would be making a "foolish mistake" if they did not enter the deal. Although the U.S. government was discussing legislation that would make it illegal for American companies to bribe foreign officials, they pointed out, it was not concerned about foreign companies bribing their own officials nor was there any concern about American companies owning stock in such companies.

At the next board meeting in June, Mr. Faber again brought up the proposal, arguing that refusing the deal would not be in the stockholders' best interests and that this was a most serious criticism of a director. He also pointed out that the firm's legal counsel had determined that the deal would not involve any illegalities and the IRS had informally reported a similar opinion.

Led by Tony, however, several members of the Board held that the issues of "legal or tax exposure" were not relevant. What was at issue was the ethics of taking an equity position in a firm that was paying bribes to its own government officials. After a heated discussion, Eberhard Faber called for a vote on his proposal.

QUESTIONS

1. In your judgment, did the Faber decision to acquire an equity position in the Third World pencil company involve any ethical issues? Explain.
2. Mr. Faber suggests that it may be morally permissible for the management of the Third World company to engage in bribery because "although the laws of the country in question prohibit bribery, it is a common and accepted practice there." Formulate the moral standard(s) on which Mr. Faber's suggested judgment is based. Comment on whether this moral standard satisfies the consistency requirement.
3. In your judgment, would the board members of Eberhard Faber, Inc. become morally responsible for the actions of the Third World pencil company if Eberhard Faber Inc. took an equity position in the pencil company? Explain and justify your position.
4. How would you vote on the proposal at the end of the June meeting? Explain and justify your vote.

[3] *Ibid.*

2

ETHICAL PRINCIPLES IN BUSINESS

INTRODUCTION

Several years ago members of Congress proposed that the federal government should be granted sole power to confer corporate status on businesses. Such "federal chartering" of businesses, they claimed, would strengthen the government's ability to regulate corporate activities and to eliminate corporate abuses. During a congressional hearing called to examine this proposal, the following exchange took place between Senator Durkin, who favored the proposal, and a witness who was testifying against the proposal:[1]

Senator Durkin:

> Good morning, ladies and gentlemen. We are beginning an inquiry that, in my opinion, is crucial to the well-being of our people and the country. How do we control and hold accountable huge institutions? To what extent do we profit from these organizations, and to what extent is each of us limited or harmed by their actions? DuPont allegedly [suppressed] price competition among retailers of its Lucite brand paint. I wonder how much more it cost somebody to paint his house because of DuPont's alleged price-fixing! We have, over the last few years, begun to appreciate

[1] U.S. Congress, Senate, *Hearings Before the Committee on Commerce on Corporate Rights and Responsibilities*, 94th Congress, 2nd session, June 1976, pp. 1, 4, 6, 9, 11, 14.

> the real costs of some industrial activities of the past [that] affect our health and environment. The federal response to these problems has been to look at one problem at a time. [But] why not consolidate the hundreds of federal laws and regulations into concise constitutional principles in a single document [on federal chartering]?

Witness:

> Mr. Chairman, I am here today to present for your consideration my views on why the proposal for federal chartering of corporations should be rejected. A corporation is created by a voluntary contractual agreement between individuals seeking to promote their own financial self-interest. Corporations are created and sustained by freedom of association and contract, and the source of these freedoms is individual rights. As long as you are not wronging anybody else, you have the right to combine with others for any purpose, and the state has no right to monitor, or restrict, or [define] the form of [a] contractual arrangement. I have rights as an individual, and I delegate them to the Congress to make laws in accordance with standards of justice and for the protection of individual rights.

The conclusions of Senator Durkin and the witness were essentially moral judgments. They were not debating whether the law allows federal chartering nor were they debating whether federal chartering is constitutional. Instead, they were judging whether it would be right to *create* a federal chartering law. Their judgments appealed to three basic kinds of moral standards by which we evaluate the moral adequacy of our laws, institutions, and activities: utilitarianism, rights, and justice.

Senator Durkin, for example, argued in favor of federal chartering of businesses by claiming that it would diminish the social costs associated with certain corporate abuses. His argument was an implicit appeal to what is called a "utilitarian" standard of morality; a moral principle, that is, that claims that something is right to the extent that it diminishes social costs and increases social benefits. The witness, on the other hand, argued against federal chartering by claiming that it would violate the "rights of individuals" and be contrary to "standards of justice." These arguments were also appeals to moral standards. Individual rights are based on moral principles that indicate the areas in which the freedom of individuals must be respected, while justice is based on moral principles that identify equitable ways of distributing benefits and burdens among the members of a society.

These three kinds of moral principles constitute three of the most important types of ethical standards studied by moral philosophers. Each kind of principle employs distinctive moral concepts, and each one emphasizes aspects of moral behavior that are neglected or at least not emphasized by the others. The purpose of this chapter is to explain each of these three approaches to moral judgments by describing the kinds of concepts and information that each standard employs.

2.1 UTILITARIANISM: SOCIAL COSTS AND BENEFITS

In 1983 the Council on Environmental Quality urged the use of cost-benefit analysis when selecting air pollution standards for "particulates" (airborne particles):

> The Clean Air Act requires that . . . air quality standards be set at a level of air quality that protects public health with an adequate margin of safety. [Different] standards for particulates may be specified by particle size (e.g., all particles or only small particles), by [maximum] allowable concentrations [of particles], and by averaging times (e.g., annual daily averages or specific 24-hour averages). Various . . . standards may achieve the same level of health protection but at differing costs. The Environmental Protection Agency recently analyzed the benefits and costs of various standards for controlling particulate matter [by] . . . identifying and quantifying both the health and nonhealth benefits, [including] . . . Health effects (mortality, Acute Morbidity, Chronic Morbidity), Soiling, and Materials Damages. . . . Table 2.1 summarizes the aggregate benefits [and costs] of . . . alternative standards. . . . [This] analysis indicates that standard "F" will generate net benefits (total benefits less costs) of $13–$26 billion.[2]

Following out the logic of its cost-benefit analysis, the Council on Environmental Quality concluded that standard "F" in Table 2.1 was preferable to the other alternatives because it would produce the most net benefits for society.

TABLE 2.1 Benefits and Costs of Six Alternative Particulate Standards

SPECIFICATIONS OF SIX ALTERNATIVE STANDARDS			COSTS AND BENEFITS	
DIAMETER OF PARTICLES CONTROLLED	MAXIMUM AVERAGE NUMBER OF PARTICLES ALLOWED PER DAY DURING THE ENTIRE YEAR (PER CUBIC METER)	MAXIMUM AVERAGE NUMBER OF PARTICLES ALLOWED IN ANY SINGLE 24-HOUR DAY (PER CUBIC METER)	ESTIMATED TOTAL BENEFITS (MINIMUM AND MAXIMUM IN BILLIONS OF 1980 DOLLARS)	ESTIMATED TOTAL COSTS (IN BILLIONS OF 1980 DOLLARS)
A. less than 10 microns	70	250	$ 8.2–$15.7	$ .50
B. less than 10 microns	55	250	$11.5–$21.8	$ .93
C. less than 10 microns	55	200	$11.9–$22.5	$ .95
D. less than 10 microns	55	150	$13.9–$26.3	$1.26
E. less than 10 microns	48	183	$14.1–$26.6	$1.32
F. all diameters	75	260	$14.4–$27.0	$1.08

Source: Council on Environmental Quality, *Environmental Quality, 1983* (Washington, DC: U.S. Government Printing Office, 1984), p. 182.

[2] Council on Environmental Quality, *Environmental Quality, 1983* (Washington, DC: U.S. Government Printing Office, 1984), pp. 181, 182, 186.

The cost-benefit analysis used by the Council on Environmental Quality is a version of what has traditionally been called "utilitarianism." "Utilitarianism" is a general term for any view that holds that actions and policies should be evaluated on the basis of the benefits and costs they will impose on society. In any situation, the "right" action or policy is the one that will produce the greatest net benefits or the lowest net costs (when all alternatives have only net costs).

The Council on Economic Quality restricted "costs" and "benefits" to *economic* costs and benefits (such as medical costs, loss of income, and damage to buildings) and these were measured in monetary terms. But the "benefits" of an action may include any desirable goods (pleasures, health, lives, satisfactions, knowledge, happiness) produced by the action, and "costs" may include any of its undesirable evils (pain, sickness, deaths, dissatisfaction, ignorance, unhappiness). The inclusive term used to refer to the net benefits of any sort produced by an action is "utility;" hence, the name *utilitarianism* for any theory that advocates selection of that action or policy that maximizes benefits (or minimizes costs).

Many business analysts assume that the best way of evaluating the ethical propriety of a business decision—or any other decision—is by relying on utilitarian cost-benefit analysis.[3] The "socially responsible" course for a business to take is the one that will produce the greatest net benefits for society or impose the lowest net costs. Several government agencies (like the Council on Environmental Quality), many legal theorists, numerous moralists, and a variety of business analysts advocate utilitarianism.[4] We will begin our discussion of ethical principles by examining this popular approach.

Traditional Utilitarianism

Jeremy Bentham (1748–1832) is generally considered the founder of traditional utilitarianism.[5] Bentham sought an objective basis for making value judgments that would provide a common and publicly acceptable norm for determining social policy and social legislation. The most promising way of reaching such an objective ground of agreement, he believed, is by looking at the various policies a legislature could enact and comparing the beneficial and harmful consequences of each. The right course of action from an ethical point of view would be to choose the policy that would produce the greatest amount of utility. Summarized, the utilitarian principle holds that

[3] Thomas A. Klein, *Social Costs and Benefits of Business* (Englewood Cliffs, NJ: Prentice Hall, 1977).

[4] Among the more well known utilitarian moralists are Peter Singer, *Practical Ethics* (London: Cambridge University Press, 1979) and Richard B. Brandt, *A Theory of the Good and the Right* (New York: Oxford University Press, 1979).

[5] Jeremy Bentham, *The Principles of Morals and Legislation* (Oxford, 1789); Henry Sidgwick, *Outlines of the History of Ethics*, 5th ed. (London, 1902), traces the history of utilitarian thought to Bentham's predecessors. Some modern expositions of utilitarian thought may be found in Michael D. Bayles, ed., *Contemporary Utilitarianism* (Garden City, NY: Doubleday & Co., Inc., 1968); J. J. C. Smart and Bernard Williams, *Utilitarianism: For and Against* (London: Cambridge University Press, 1973); Amartya Sen and Bernard Williams, eds., *Utilitarianism and Beyond* (New York: Cambridge University Press, 1982); and Harlan B. Miller and William H. Williams, eds., *The Limits of Utilitarianism* (Minneapolis: University of Minnesota Press, 1982).

An action is right from an ethical point of view if and only if the sum total of utilities produced by that act is greater than the sum total of utilities produced by any other act the agent could have performed in its place.

The utilitarian principle assumes that we can somehow measure and add the quantities of benefits produced by an action and subtract from them the measured quantities of harm the action will have, and thereby determine which action produces the greatest total benefits or the lowest total costs. That is, the principle assumes that all the benefits and costs of an action can be measured on a common numerical scale and then added or subtracted from each other.[6] The satisfactions that an improved work environment imparts to workers, for example, might be equivalent to five hundred positive units of utility, while the resulting bills that arrive the next month might be equivalent to seven hundred negative units of utility. So the total combined utility of this act (improving the work environment) would be two hundred units of *negative* utility.

When the utilitarian principle says that the right action for a particular occasion is the one that produces more utility than any other possible action, it does not mean that the right action is the one that produces the most utility for the person performing the action. Rather, an action is right if it produces the most utility for *all* persons affected by the action (including the person performing the action).[7] Nor does the utilitarian principle say that an action is right so long as its benefits outweigh its costs. Rather, utilitarianism holds that in the final analysis only one action is right: that one action whose net benefits are greatest by comparison to the net benefits of all other possible alternatives. A third misunderstanding is to think that the utilitarian principle requires us to consider only the direct and immediate consequences of our actions. Instead, both the immediate and all foreseeable future costs and benefits that each alternative will provide for each individual must be taken into account as well as any significant indirect effects.

Consequently, to ascertain what I ought to do on a particular occasion I must do three things: First, I must determine what alternative actions or policies are available to me on that occasion. When evaluating air pollution standards, for example, the Council on Environmental Quality identified six alternatives it could impose, as indicated in Table 2.1. Second, for each alternative action I must estimate the direct and indirect benefits and costs that the action would produce for each and every person affected by the action in the foreseeable future. In Table 2.1, for example, the Council on Environmental Quality estimated the total benefits that each standard would produce for every person in the United States who would benefit from the decrease in pollution associated with that standard. The table also aggregates the estimated total costs that various persons would have to pay if the standard were adopted, including the costs of installing and maintaining industrial air pollution control devices. In making these estimates the council included all the direct and indirect effects it could foresee for the next ten years. Third, the alternative that produces the greatest sum total of utility must be chosen as the ethically appropriate course of action. The Council on En-

[6] Henry Sidgwick, *Methods of Ethics*, 7th ed. (Chicago: University of Chicago Press, 1962), p. 413.

[7] John Stuart Mill, *Utilitarianism* (Indianapolis: The Bobbs-Merrill Co., Inc., 1957), p. 22.

vironmental Quality in our example reviewed the estimates given in Table 2.1, compared them all, and concluded that the greatest net benefits lay with standard "F."

Utilitarianism is in many respects an attractive theory. For one thing, it matches fairly nicely the views that we tend to advocate when discussing the choice of government policies and public goods. Most people will agree, for example, that when the government is trying to determine on which public projects it should spend tax monies, the proper course of action would be for it to adopt those projects that objective studies show will provide the greatest benefits for the members of society at the least cost. And this, of course, is just another way of saying that the proper government policies are those that would have the greatest measurable utility for people or, in the words of a famous slogan, those that will produce "the greatest good for the greatest number."

Utilitarianism also seems to fit in rather neatly with the intuitive criteria that people employ when discussing moral conduct.[8] When people explain, for example, why they have a moral obligation to perform some action, they will often proceed by pointing to the benefits or harms the action will impose upon human beings. Moreover, morality requires that one impartially take everyone's interest equally into account. Utilitarianism meets this requirement insofar as it takes into account the effects actions have on everyone and insofar as it requires one to impartially choose the action with the greatest net utility regardless of who gets the benefits.

Utilitarianism also has the advantage of being able to explain why we hold that certain types of activities are generally morally wrong (lying, adultery, killing), while others are generally morally right (telling the truth, fidelity, keeping one's promises). The utilitarian can say that lying is generally wrong because of the costly effects lying has on our human welfare. When people lie to each other, they are less apt to trust each other and to cooperate with each other. And the less trust and cooperation, the more our welfare declines. On the other hand, telling the truth is generally right because it strengthens cooperation and trust, and thereby improves everyone's well-being. In general, then, it is a good rule of thumb to tell the truth and to refrain from lying. Traditional utilitarians would deny, however, that any kinds of actions are always right or always wrong. They would deny, for example, that dishonesty or theft is necessarily always wrong. If in a certain situation more good consequences would flow from being dishonest than from any other act a person could perform in that situation, then, according to traditional utilitarian theory, dishonesty would be morally right in that particular situation.

Utilitarian views have also been highly influential in economics.[9] A long line of economists, beginning in the nineteenth century, argued that economic behavior could be explained by assuming that human beings always attempt to maximize their utility and that the utilities of commodities can be measured by the prices people are willing to pay for them. With these and a few other simplifying

[8] Richard Brandt, *Ethical Theory* (Englewood Cliffs, NJ: Prentice Hall, 1959), p. 386; see also Dan W. Brock, "Utilitarianism," in *And Justice for All*, Tom Regan and Donald Van DeVeer, eds. (Totowa, NJ: Rowman and Littlefield, 1982), pp. 217–40.

[9] For example, William Stanley Javons, *Theory of Political Economy* (1871); Alfred Marshall, *Principles of Economics* (1890); Cecil Arthur Pigou, *Wealth and Welfare* (1912); for a contemporary defense of utilitarianism in economics, see J. A. Mirrlees, "The Economic Uses of Utilitarianism," in *Utilitarianism and Beyond*, Sen and Williams, eds., pp. 63–84.

assumptions (such as the use of indifference curves), economists were able to derive the familiar supply and demand curves of sellers and buyers in markets and explain why prices in a perfectly competitive market gravitate toward an equilibrium. More importantly, economists were also able to demonstrate that a system of perfectly competitive markets would lead to a use of resources and to price variations that would enable consumers to maximize their utility (defined in terms of Pareto optimality) through their purchases.[10] On utilitarian grounds, therefore, these economists concluded that such a system of markets is better than any other alternative.

As we noted in the introduction, utilitarianism is also the basis of the techniques of economic cost-benefit analysis.[11] This type of analysis is used to determine the desirability of investing in a project (like a dam, a factory, or a public park) by figuring whether its present and future economic benefits outweigh its present and future economic costs. To calculate these costs and benefits, discounted monetary prices are estimated for all the effects the project will have on the present and future environment and on present and future populations. Carrying out these sorts of calculations is not always an easy matter, but various methods have been devised for determining the monetary prices of even such intangible benefits as the beauty of a forest (for instance, we might ask how much people pay to see the beauty of a similar privately owned park). If the monetary benefits of a certain public project exceed the monetary costs and if the excess is greater than the excess produced by any other feasible project, then the project should be undertaken. In this form of utilitarianism the concept of utility is restricted to monetarily measurable economic costs and benefits.

Finally, we can note that utilitarianism fits nicely with a value that many people prize: efficiency. Efficiency can mean different things to different people, but for many it means operating in such a way that one produces the most one can with the resources at hand. That is, an efficient operation is one that produces a desired output with the lowest resource input. Such efficiency is precisely what utilitarianism advocates since it holds that one should always adopt that course of action that will produce the greatest benefits at the lowest cost. If we read "desired output" in the place of "benefits," and "resource input" in place of "cost," utilitarianism implies that the right course of action is always the most efficient one.

Problems of Measurement

One major set of problems with utilitarianism is centered on the difficulties encountered when trying to measure "utility."[12] One problem is this: How can

[10] See Paul Samuelson, *Foundations of Economic Analysis* (Cambridge: Harvard University Press, 1947). A system is "Pareto optimal" if no one in the system can be made better off without making some other person worse off; an "indifference curve" indicates the quantities of one good a person would willingly trade for given quantities of another good.

[11] E. J. Mishan, *Economics for Social Decisions: Elements of Cost-Benefit Analysis* (New York: Praeger Publishers, Inc., 1973), pp. 14–17. See also E. J. Mishan, ed., Cost-Benefit Analysis, 3rd. (London: Cambridge University Press, 1982).

[12] See, for example, Wesley C. Mitchell, "Bentham's Felicific Calculus," in *The Backward Art of Spending Money and Other Essays* (New York: Augustus M. Kelley, Inc., 1950), pp. 177–202; but see the replies to these measurement objections in Paul Weirch, "Interpersonal Utility in Principles of Social Choice," *Erkenntnis*, 21 (November 1984): 295–318.

the utilities different actions have for different people be measured and compared as utilitarianism requires? Suppose you and I would both enjoy getting a certain job: How can we figure out whether the utility you would get out of having the job is more or less than the utility I would get out of having it? Each of us may be sure that he or she would benefit most from the job, but since we cannot get into each other's skin, this judgment has no objective basis. Since comparative measures of the values things have for different people cannot be made, the critics argue, there is no way of knowing whether utility would be maximized by giving me the job or giving you the job. And if we cannot know which actions will produce the greatest amounts of utility, then we cannot apply the utilitarian principle.

A second problem is that some benefits and costs seem intractible to measurement. How, for example, can one measure the value of health or life?[13] Suppose that installing an expensive exhaust system in a workshop will eliminate a large portion of certain carcinogenic particles that workers might otherwise inhale. And suppose that as a result some of the workers probably will live five years longer. How is one to calculate the value of those years of added life, and how is this value to be quantitatively balanced against the costs of installing the exhaust system?

A third problem is that because many of the benefits and costs of an action cannot be reliably predicted, they also cannot be adequately measured.[14] The beneficial or costly consequences of basic scientific knowledge, for example, are notoriously difficult to predict. Yet suppose that one has to decide how much to invest in a research program that will probably uncover some highly theoretical, but not immediately usable, information about the universe. How is the future value of that information to be measured, and how can it be weighed against either the present costs of funding the research or the more certain benefits that would result from putting the funds to an alternative use, such as adding a new wing to the local hospital or building housing for the poor?

Yet a fourth problem is that it is unclear exactly what is to count as a "benefit" and what is to count as a "cost."[15] This lack of clarity is especially problematic with respect to social issues that are given significantly different evaluations by different cultural groups. Suppose a bank must decide, for example, whether to extend a loan to the manager of a local pornographic theater or to the manager of a bar that caters to homosexuals. One group of people may see the increased enjoyment of pornography connoisseurs or the increased enjoyment of homosexuals as *benefits* accruing to society. Another group, however, may see these as harmful and hence as *costs*.

[13] For a discussion of this problem see Michael D. Bayles, "The Price of Life," *Ethics*, 89, no. 1 (October 1978): 20–34; Jonathan Glover, *Causing Death and Saving Lives* (New York: Penguin Books, 1977); Peter S. Albin, "Economic Values and the Value of Human Life," in *Human Values and Economic Policy*, Sidney Hook, ed. (New York: New York University Press, 1967).

[14] G. E. Moore, *Principia Ethica*, 5th ed. (Cambridge: Cambridge University Press, 1956), p. 149.

[15] Alastair MacIntyre, "Utilitarianism and Cost-Benefit Analysis: An Essay on the Relevance of Moral Philosophy to Bureaucratic Theory," in *Values in the Electric Power Industry*, Kenneth Syre, ed. (Notre Dame, IN: University of Notre Dame Press, 1977).

The critics of utilitarianism contend that these measurement problems undercut whatever claims utilitarian theory makes to providing an objective basis for determining normative issues. These problems have become especially obvious in debates over the feasibility of corporate social audits.[16] Although business firms have been increasingly pressured to produce an "audit" or report measuring the social costs and benefits resulting from their business activities,[17] their efforts have been stymied by their inability to place quantitative measures on their various programs,[18] and by differences of opinion over what should be counted as a benefit. The only way of resolving these problems is by arbitrarily accepting the valuations of one social group or another. But this in effect bases utilitarian cost-benefit analysis on the subjective biases and tastes of that group.

Utilitarian Replies to Measurement Objections

The defender of utilitarianism has an array of replies ready to counter the measurement objections enumerated above.

First, the utilitarian may argue that, although utilitarianism ideally requires accurate quantifiable measurements of all costs and benefits, this requirement can be relaxed when such measurements are impossible.[19] Utilitarianism merely insists that the consequences of any projected act be expressly stated with as much clarity and accuracy as is humanly possible, and that all relevant information concerning these consequences be presented in a form that will allow them to be systematically compared and impartially weighed against each other. Expressing this information in quantitative terms will facilitate such comparisons and weighings. But where quantitative data are unavailable, one may legitimately rely on shared and common-sense judgments of the comparative values things have for most people. We know, for example, that by and large cancer is a greater injury than a cold, no matter who has the cancer and who has the cold; similarly, a steak has a greater value as food than a peanut, no matter whose hunger is involved.

The utilitarian can also point to several common-sense criteria that can be used to determine the relative values that should be given to various categories of goods. One criterion, for example, depends on the distinction between "intrin-

[16] David H. Blake, William C. Frederick, and Mildred S. Myers, "Measurement Problems in the Social Audit," in *Ethical Theory and Business*, Tom L. Beauchamp and Norman E. Bowie, eds. (Englewood Cliffs, NJ: Prentice Hall, 1979), pp. 246–52; an excellent review of the literature is contained in Task Force on Corporate Social Performance, *Corporate Social Reporting in the United States and Western Europe* (Washington, DC: U.S. Government Printing Office, 1979), pp. 2–36; see also the more accessible Harold L. John, *Disclosure of Corporate Social Performance: Survey, Evaluation and Prospects* (New York: Praeger Publishers, Inc., 1979).

[17] Raymond A. Bauer and Dan H. Fenn, Jr., *The Corporate Social Audit* (New York: Sage Publications, Inc., 1972), pp. 3–14.

[18] John J. Corson and George A. Steiner, *Measuring Business's Social Performance: The Corporate Social Audit* (New York: Committee for Economic Development, 1974), p. 41; Thomas C. Taylor, "The Illusions of Social Accounting," *CPA Journal*, 46 (January 1976), 24–28; Manuel A. Tipgos, "A Case against the Social Audit," *Management Accounting* (August 1976), pp. 23–26.

[19] Tom L. Beauchamp, "Utilitarianism and Cost-Benefit Analysis: A Reply to MacIntyre," in *Ethical Theory*, Beauchamp and Bowie, eds., pp. 276–82, and Herman B. Leonard and Richard J. Zeckhauser, "Cost-Benefit Analysis Defended," *QQ-Report from the Center for Philosophy and Public Policy*, 3, no. 3 (Summer 1983): 6–9.

sic'' and ''instrumental'' goods.[20] Instrumental goods are things that are considered valuable only because they lead to other good things. A painful visit to the dentist, for example, is only an instrumental good (unless I happen to be a masochist): It is desired only as a means to health. Intrinsic goods, however, are things that are desirable independently of any other benefits they may produce. Thus, health is an intrinsic good: It is desired for its own sake. (Many things, of course, have both intrinsic and instrumental value. I may go skiing, for example, both because skiing is a means to health and because I enjoy skiing for itself.) Now it is clear that intrinsic goods take priority over instrumental goods. Under most circumstances, for example, money, which is an instrumental good, must not take priority over life and health, which have intrinsic values.

A second common-sense criterion that can be used to weigh goods turns on the distinction between needs and wants.[21] To say that someone *needs* something is to say that without it he or she will be harmed in some way. People's ''basic'' needs consist of their needs for things without which they will suffer some fundamental harm such as injury, illness, or death. Among a person's basic needs are the food, clothing, and housing required to stay alive; the medical care and hygienic environment required to remain healthy; and the security and safety required to remain free from injury. On the other hand, to say that a person *wants* something is to say that the person desires it: The person believes it will advance his or her interests in some way. A need, of course, may also be a want: If I know I need something then I may also want it. Many wants, however, are not needs but simply desires for things without which the individual would not suffer any fundamental harm. I may want something simply because I enjoy it, even though it is a luxury I could as well do without. Desires of this sort that are not also needs are called ''mere wants.'' In general, satisfying a person's basic needs is more valuable than satisfying his or her mere wants. If people do not get something for which they have a basic need, they may be injured in a way that makes it impossible for them to enjoy the satisfaction of any number of mere wants. Since the satisfaction of a person's basic needs makes possible not only the intrinsic values of life and health but also the enjoyment of most other intrinsic values, satisfaction of the basic needs has a value that is greater than that of satisfying mere wants.

But these common-sense methods of weighing goods are only intended to aid us in situations where quantitative methods fail. In actual fact the consequences of many decisions are relatively amenable to quantification, the convinced utilitarian will claim. This constitutes the utilitarian's second major reply to the measurement objections outlined above.

The most flexible method of providing a common quantitative measure for the benefits and costs associated with a decision, the utilitarian may hold, is in

[20] See Amitai Etzioni and Edward W. Lehman, ''Dangers in 'Valid' Social Measurements,'' *Annals of the American Academy of Political and Social Sciences*, 373 (September 1967): 6; also William K. Frankena, *Ethics*, 2nd ed. (Englewood Cliffs, NJ: Prentice Hall, 1973), pp. 80–83.

[21] See Kenneth Arrow, *Social Choice and Individual Values*, 2nd ed. (New York: John Wiley & Sons, Inc., 1951), p. 87; and Norman E. Bowie, *Towards a New Theory of Distributive Justice* (Amherst: The University of Massachusetts Press, 1971), pp. 86–87.

terms of their monetary equivalents.[22] Basically this implies that the value a thing has for a person can be measured by the price the person is willing to pay for it. If a person will pay twice as much for one thing as for another, then that thing has exactly twice the value of the other for that person. In order to determine the average values items have for a group of people, then, one need merely look at the average prices given to those items when everyone is allowed to bid for them on open markets. In short, market prices can serve to provide a common quantitative measure of the various benefits and costs associated with a decision. In general, to determine the value of a thing one need merely ask what it sells for on an open market. If the item does not sell on an open market, then one can ask what similar items are selling for.

The use of monetary values also has the advantage of allowing one to take into account the effects of the passage of time and the impact of uncertainty.[23] If the known monetary costs or benefits lie in the future, then their present values can be determined by discounting them at the appropriate rate of interest. If the monetary costs or benefits are only probable and not certain, then their expected values can be computed by multiplying the monetary costs or benefits by the appropriate probability factor.

A standard objection against using monetary values to measure all costs and benefits is that some goods, in particular health and life, cannot be priced. The utilitarian may argue, however, that not only is it possible to put a price on health and life but that we do so almost daily. Anytime people place a limit on the amount of money they are willing to pay to reduce the risk that some object poses to their lives, they have set an implicit price on their own lives. For example, suppose that people are willing to pay $5.00 for a piece of safety equipment that will reduce the probability of their being killed in an auto accident from .00005 to .00004, but they are unwilling to pay any more than that. Then, in effect, they have implicitly decided that .00001 of a life is worth $5, or in other words, that a life is worth $500,000. Such pricing is inevitable and necessary, the utilitarian may hold, so long as we live in an environment in which risks to health and life can be lowered only by giving up (trading off) other things that we may want and on which we set a clear price.

Finally, the utilitarian may say, where market prices are incapable of providing quantitative data for comparing the costs and benefits of various decisions, other sorts of quantitative measures are available.[24] Should people disagree, for example, as they often do, over the harmful or beneficial aspects of various sexual activities, then sociological surveys or political votes can be used to measure the intensity and extensiveness of people's attitudes. Economic experts can also provide informed judgments of the relative quantitative values of various costs and benefits. Thus the utilitarian will grant that the problems of measurement encountered by utilitarianism are real enough. But they are at least partially soluble by the various methods enumerated above. There are, however, other criticisms of utilitarianism.

[22] See, for example, the techniques enumerated in Mishan, *Economics for Social Decisions.*

[23] *Ibid.*, pp. 118–24 and 141–44.

[24] E. Bruce Frederickson, "Noneconomic Criteria and the Decision Process," *Decision Sciences*, 2, no. 1 (January 1971): 25–52.

Problems with Rights and Justice

The major difficulty with utilitarianism, according to some critics, is that it is unable to deal with two kinds of moral issues: those relating to *rights*[25] and those relating to *justice*.[26] That is, the utilitarian principle implies that certain actions are morally right when in fact they are unjust or they violate people's rights. Some examples may serve to indicate the sort of difficult "counter-examples" critics pose for utilitarianism.

First, suppose that your uncle had an incurable and painful disease, so that as a result he was quite unhappy but does not choose to die. Although he is hospitalized and will die within a year, he continues to run his chemical plant. Because of his own misery he deliberately makes life miserable for his workers and has insisted on not installing safety devices in his chemical plant, although he knows that as a result one worker will certainly lose his life over the next year. You, his only living relative, know that on your uncle's death you will inherit his business and will not only be wealthy and immensely happy, but also intend to prevent any future loss of life by installing the needed safety devices. You are cold-blooded, and correctly judge that you could secretly murder your uncle without being caught and without your happiness being in any way affected by it afterwards. If it is possible for you to murder your uncle without in any way diminishing anyone else's happiness, then according to utilitarianism you have a moral obligation to do so. By murdering your uncle, you are trading his life for the life of the worker, and you are gaining your happiness while doing away with his unhappiness and pain: The gain is obviously on the side of utility. However, the critics of utilitarianism claim, it seems quite clear that the murder of your uncle would be a gross violation of his right to life. Utilitarianism has led us to approve an act of murder that is an obvious violation of an individual's most important right.

Second, utilitarianism can also go wrong, according to the critics, when it is applied to situations that involve social justice. Suppose, for example, that the fact that they are paid subsistence wages forces a small group of migrant workers to continue doing the most undesirable agricultural jobs in an economy but produces immense amounts of satisfaction for the vast majority of society's members, since they enjoy cheap vegetables and savings that allow them to indulge other wants. Suppose also that the amounts of satisfaction thereby produced, when balanced against the unhappiness and pain imposed upon the small group of farm workers, results in a greater net utility than would exist if everyone had to share the burdens of farm work. Then, according to the utilitarian criterion, it would be morally right to continue this system of subsistence wages for farm workers. Yet to the critics of utilitarianism, a social system that imposes such unequal sharing of burdens is clearly immoral and offends against justice. The great benefits the system may have for the majority does not justify the extreme burdens that it imposes on a small group. The shortcoming this counter-example reveals is that utilitarianism allows benefits and burdens to be distributed among the members of society in any way whatsoever, so long as the total amount of benefits is

[25] Bowie, *Towards a New Theory of Distributive Justice*, pp. 20–22.
[26] *Ibid.*, pp. 22–24.

maximized. But in fact, some ways of distributing benefits and burdens (like the extremely unequal distributions involved in the counter-example) are unjust, regardless of how great the store of benefits such distributions produce. Utilitarianism looks only at how much utility is produced in a society and fails to take into account how that utility is distributed among the members of society.

Utilitarian Replies to Objections on Rights and Justice

To deal with the sorts of counter-examples that critics of traditional utilitarianism have offered, utilitarians have recently proposed an important and influential alternative version of utilitarianism called "rule-utilitarianism."[27] The basic strategy of the rule-utilitarian is to limit utilitarian analysis to the evaluations of moral rules. According to the rule-utilitarian, when trying to determine whether a particular *action* is ethical, one is never supposed to ask whether that particular action will produce the greatest amount of utility. Instead, one is supposed to ask whether the action is required by the correct moral rules that everyone should follow. If the action is required by such rules, then one should carry out the action. But what are the "correct" moral rules? It is only this second question, according to the rule-utilitarian, that is supposed to be answered by reference to maximizing utility. The correct moral rules are those that would produce the greatest amount of utility if everyone were to follow them. An example may make this clear.

Suppose I am trying to decide whether or not it is ethical for me to fix prices with a competitor. Then, according to the rule-utilitarian, I should not ask whether this particular instance of price-fixing will produce more utility than anything else I can do. Instead, I should first ask myself: What are the correct moral rules with respect to price-fixing? Perhaps I might conclude, after some thought, that the following list of rules includes all the candidates:

1. Managers are never to meet with competitors for the purpose of fixing prices.
2. Managers may always meet with competitors for the purpose of fixing prices.
3. Managers may meet with competitors for the purpose of fixing prices when they are losing money.

Which of these three is the correct moral rule? According to the rule-utilitarian, the correct moral rule is the one that would produce the greatest amount of utility for everyone affected. Let us suppose that after analyzing the economic effects of price-fixing, I conclude that within our economic and social circumstances people would benefit much more if everyone followed rule 1 than if everyone followed rule 2 or 3. If this is so, then rule 1 is the correct moral rule concerning price-fixing. Now that I know what the correct moral rule on price-fixing is, I can go on to ask a second question: Should I engage in this particular act of fixing prices? To answer this second question I only have to ask: What is required by the correct moral rules? As we have already noted, the correct rule is to never fix prices.

[27] S. E. Toulmin, *An Examination of the Place of Reason in Ethics* (Cambridge: Cambridge University Press, 1950), ch. 11; J. Rawls, "Two Concepts of Rules," *Philosophical Review*, 64 (1955): 3–32; J. O. Ormson, "The Interpretation of the Philosophy of J. S. Mill," *Philosophical Quarterly*, 3 (1953): 33–40.

Consequently, even if on this particular occasion, fixing prices actually would produce more utility than not doing so, I am, nonetheless, ethically obligated to refrain from fixing prices because this is required by the rules from which everyone in my society would most benefit.

The theory of the rule-utilitarian, then, has two parts, which we can summarize in the following two principles:

I. An action is right from an ethical point of view if and only if the action would be required by those moral rules that are correct.

II. A moral rule is correct if and only if the sum total of utilities produced if everyone were to follow that rule is greater than the sum total utilities produced if everyone were to follow some alternative rule.

Thus, according to the rule-utilitarian, the fact that a certain action would maximize utility on one particular occasion does not show that it is right from an ethical point of view.

For the rule-utilitarian, the flaw in the counter-examples that the critics of traditional utilitarianism offer is that in each case the utilitarian criterion is applied to particular actions and not to rules. Instead, the rule-utilitarian would urge, we must use the utilitarian criterion to find out what the correct moral *rule* is for each counter-example, and then evaluate the particular actions involved in the counter-example only in terms of this rule. Doing this will allow utilitarianism to escape the counter-examples undamaged.

The counter-example involving the rich uncle and the murderous heir, for example, is a situation that deals with killing a sick person. In such situations, the rule-utilitarian might argue, it is clear that a moral rule that forbids killing without the due process of law will, in the long run, have greater utility for society than other kinds of rules. Such a rule, therefore, is the correct one to apply to the case. It would be wrong for the heir to kill his uncle because doing so would violate a correct moral rule and the fact that murder would on this particular occasion maximize utility is irrelevant.

The case dealing with subsistence wages, the rule-utilitarian would argue, should be treated similarly. It is clear that a rule that forbade unnecessary subsistence wages in societies would in the long run result in more utility than a rule which allowed them. Such a rule would therefore be the correct rule to invoke when asking whether practicing "wage slavery" is morally permissble, and the practice would then be rejected as ethically wrong even if it would maximize utility on a particular occasion.

The ploy of the rule-utilitarian, however, has not satisfied the critics of utilitarianism, who have pointed out an important difficulty in the rule-utilitarian position: According to its critics, rule-utilitarianism is traditional utilitarianism in disguise.[28] These critics argue that rules that allow (beneficial) exceptions will

[28] See David Lyons, *Forms and Limits of Utilitarianism* (Oxford: Oxford University Press, 1965). Some ethicians hold, however, that act utilitarianism and rule utilitarianism are not really equivalent; see Thomas M. Lennon, "Rules and Relevance: The Act Utilitarianism-Rule Utilitarianism Equivalence Issue," *Idealistic Studies: An International Philosophical Journal*, 14, (May 1984): 148–58.

produce more utility than rules that do not allow any exceptions. But once a rule allows these exceptions, the critics claim, it will allow the same injustices and violations of rights that traditional utilitarianism allows. Some examples may help us see more clearly what these critics mean. The critics claim that if a rule allows people to make an exception whenever an exception will maximize utility, then it will produce more utility than it would if it allowed no exceptions. For example, more utility would be produced by a rule which says "People are not to be killed without due process *except when doing so will produce more utility than not doing so*," than would be produced by a rule that simply says "People are not to be killed without due process." The first rule will *always* maximize utility, while the second rule will maximize utility only *most* of the time (because the second rule rigidly requires due process even when it would be more beneficial to dispense with due process). Since the rule-utilitarian holds that the "correct" moral rule is the one that produces more utility, he must hold that the correct moral rule is the one which allows exceptions when exceptions will maximize utility. But once the exception clause is made part of the rule, the critics point out, then applying the rule to an action will have exactly the same consequences as applying the traditional utilitarian criterion directly to the action since the utilitarian criterion is now part of the rule. In the case of the sick uncle and murderous heir, for example, the rule that "People are not to be killed without due process except when doing so will produce more utility than not doing so," will now allow the heir to murder his uncle exactly as traditional utilitarianism did before. Similarly, more utility would be produced by a rule that says, "Subsistence wages are prohibited *except in those situations where they will maximize utility*," than would be produced by a rule that simply says, "Subsistence wages are prohibited." So the rule that allows exceptions will be the "correct" one. But this "correct" rule will now allow the society we described earlier to institute wage slavery, exactly as traditional utilitarianism did. Rule-utilitarianism, then, is a disguised form of traditional utilitarianism and the counter-examples that set difficulties for one seem to set similar difficulties for the other.

Many rule utilitarians do not admit that rules produce more utility when they allow exceptions. Since human nature is weak and self-interested, they claim, humans would take advantage of any allowable exceptions and this would leave everyone worse off. Other utilitarians refuse to admit that the counter-examples of the critics are correct. They claim that if killing a person without due process really would produce more utility than all other feasible alternatives, then all other alternatives must have greater evils attached to them. And if this is so, then killing the person without due process really would be morally right. Similarly, if in certain circumstances subsistence wages really are the least (socially) injurious means to employ in getting a job done, then in those circumstances subsistence wages are morally right exactly as utilitarianism implies.

There are two main limits to utilitarian methods of moral reasoning, therefore, although the precise extent of these limits is controversial. First, utilitarian methods are difficult to use when dealing with values that are difficult and perhaps impossible to measure quantitatively. Second, utilitarianism by itself seems to deal inadequately with situations that involve rights and justice, although some have tried to remedy this deficiency by restricting utilitarianism to the evaluation of rules. To clarify our ideas on these issues, the next two sections will examine methods of moral reasoning that explicitly deal with the two moral issues on which utilitarianism seems to fall short: rights and justice.

2.2 RIGHTS

In May 1984, Coca-Cola executives began meeting with Guatemalan union leaders who had forcibly occupied a Coca-Cola plant in Guatemala.[29] Local owners of the plant complained that the workers were violating their "property rights." Workers responded that union organizers had suffered six years of "serious violations of human rights and labor union rights," including the kidnaping and murder of several union leaders and continual threats. Five years earlier, stockholders of Coca-Cola Company, alarmed by the growing violence, had submitted the following resolution at their shareholders' meeting:

> Be it resolved that the shareholders request the Board of Directors of Coca-Cola to develop . . . a code of minimum labor standards required of its franchise bottlers and the procedures for their enforcement by the Company.
> In preparing this code, the Board should consider the following principles recognized by most employer associations and governments:
> A. The right of workers to organize and operate their own associations or unions without interference from management in the adoption of rules, election of officers, administration of affairs and determination of programs;
> B. The right of each individual worker to belong to such association or union without discrimination in employment, task assignment, or promotion;
> C. The right of such associations or unions to negotiate collective agreements and grievance procedures for and on behalf of the members, and to represent their members before management wherever disputes arise;
> D. The right of such associations or unions to join others to form regional or national organizations, and international trade union bodies. (Excerpt from Coca-Cola Company 1979 proxy statement)[30]

Coca-Cola's board of directors opposed the resolution and it was voted down. A similar resolution the following year was also opposed and defeated. Finally, on July 10, 1984 Coca-Cola executives announced that they had reached a labor union settlement with the Guatemala workers.

The concept of a "right" obviously appears in many of the moral arguments and moral claims invoked in business discussions. Employees, for example, argue that they have a "right to equal pay for equal work"; managers assert that unions violate their "right to manage"; investors complain that taxation violates their "property rights"; consumers claim that they have a "right to know." Moreover, public documents often employ the notion of a right. The American Constitution itself enshrines a long "Bill of Rights," defined largely in terms of the duties the federal government has to not interfere in certain areas of its citizens' lives.

[29] "Guatemala Unions Watch Plant Feud," *New York Times,* 10 July 1984; see also, Robert Morris, "Coca-Cola and Human Rights in Guatemala," *The Corporate Examiner* (November 1980), pp. 3A-3D; Jim Wilson, "Union Fights Coke," *Democratic Left* (March/April 1984).

[30] Investor Responsibility Research Center, "Minimum Labor Standards: The Coca-Cola Company, 1979 Analysis Z," 16 April 1979, p. Z-11; see also Investor Responsibility Research Center, "Human Rights Policy: Coca-Cola Co., 1980 Analysis W," 11 April 1980.

The Declaration of Independence was based on the idea that "all men . . . are endowed by their Creator with certain unalienable rights . . . among these are life, liberty, and the pursuit of happiness." In 1948 the United Nations adopted a "Universal Declaration of Human Rights," which claimed that "all human beings" are entitled, among other things, to:

> the right to own property alone as well as in association with others . . .
>
> the right to work, to free choice of employment, to just and favorable conditions of work, and to protection against unemployment . . .
>
> the right to just and favorable remuneration ensuring for [the worker] and his family an existence worthy of human dignity . . .
>
> the right to form and to join trade unions . . .
>
> the right to rest and leisure, including reasonable limitation of working hours and periodic holidays with pay . . .

The concept of a right and the correlative notion of duty, then, lie at the heart of much of our moral discourse. This section is intended to provide an understanding of these concepts and of some of the major kinds of ethical principles and methods of analysis that underlie their use.

The Concept of a Right

In general, a right is an individual's entitlement to something.[31] A person has a right when that person is entitled to act in a certain way or is entitled to have others act in a certain way toward him or her. The entitlement may derive from a *legal* system that permits or empowers the person to act in a specified way or that requires others to act in certain ways toward that person; the entitlement is then called a "legal right." The American Constitution, for example, guarantees all citizens the "right to freedom of speech" and commercial statutes specify that each party to a valid contract has a "right" to whatever performance the contract requires from the other person. Legal rights are limited, of course, to the particular jurisdiction within which the legal system is in force.

Entitlements can also derive from a system of *moral* standards independently of any particular legal system. The "right to work," for example, is not guaranteed by the American Constitution, but many argue that this is a right that all human beings possess. Such rights, which are called "moral rights" or "human rights," are based on moral norms and principles that specify that all human beings are permitted or empowered to do something or are entitled to have something done for them. Moral rights, unlike legal rights, are usually thought of as being universal insofar as they are rights that all human beings of every nationality possess to an equal extent simply by virtue of being human beings. Unlike legal rights, moral

[31] H. J. McCloskey, "Rights," *The Philosophical Quarterly*, 15 (1965): 115–27; several book-length discussions of rights are available including Alan R. White, *Rights* (Oxford: Clarendon Press, 1984), Samuel Stoljar, *An Analysis of Rights* (New York: St. Martin's Press, 1984), and Henry Shue, *Basic Rights* (Princeton: Princeton University Press, 1981); for a review of the literature on rights see R. Martin and J. W. Nickel, "Recent Work on the Concept of Rights," *American Philosophical Quarterly*, 17, no. 3 (July 1980): 165–80; an outstanding historical account of the evolution of the concept of a right is Richard Tuck, *Natural Rights Theories, Their Origin and Development* (New York: Cambridge University Press, 1979).

rights are not limited to a particular jurisdiction. If humans have a moral right not to be tortured, for example, then this is a right that human beings of every nationality have regardless of the legal system under which they live.

Rights are powerful devices whose main purpose is that of enabling the individual to choose freely whether to pursue certain interests or activities and of protecting those choices. But in our ordinary discourse we use the term "right" to cover a variety of situations in which individuals are enabled to make such choices in very different ways. First, we sometimes use the term "right" to indicate the mere *absence of prohibitions* against pursuing some interest or activity. For example, I have a "right" to do whatever the law or morality does not positively forbid me to do. In this weak sense of a "right" the enabling and protective aspects are minimal. Secondly, we sometimes use the term "right" to indicate that a person is *authorized or empowered* to do something either to secure the interests of others or to secure his own interests. An army or police officer, for example, acquires legal rights of command over subordinates which enable him to pursue the security of others, while a property owner acquires legal property rights which enable her to do as she wishes with the property. Third, the term "right" is sometimes used to indicate the *existence of prohibitions or requirements* on others which enable the individual to pursue certain interests or activities. For example the American Constitution is said to give citizens the right to free speech because it contains a prohibition against government limits on speech, and federal law is said to give citizens the right to an education because it contains a requirement that each state must provide free public education for all its citizens.[32]

The most important moral rights—and those that will concern us in this chapter—are rights which *impose prohibitions or requirements* on others and which thereby enable individuals to choose freely whether to pursue certain interests or activities. These moral rights (we will mean these kinds of rights when we use the term "moral rights") identify those activities or interests that the individual is empowered to pursue, or must be left free to pursue, or must be helped to pursue, as he or she chooses; and they protect the individual's pursuit of those interests and activities within the boundaries specified by the rights. These kinds of moral rights have three important features that define these enabling and protective functions.

First, moral rights are tightly correlated with duties.[33] This is because one person's moral right generally can be defined—at least partially—in terms of the moral duties other people have toward that person. To have a moral right necessarily implies that others have certain duties toward the bearer of that right. My moral

[32] For a more technical but now widely accepted classification of legal rights see Wesley Hohfeld, *Fundamental Legal Conceptions* (New Haven: Yale University Press, 1919, rpt. 1964), pp. 457–84.

[33] There are different ways of characterizing the relation between rights and duties, not all of them equally sound. For example, some authors claim that a person is granted rights only if the person accepts certain duties toward the community which grants those rights. Other authors claim that all my rights can be defined wholly in terms of the duties of others. Both of these claims are probably mistaken, but neither claim is being advanced in this paragraph. The view of this paragraph is that moral rights of the kind identified in the previous paragraph always can be defined *at least in part* in terms of duties others have twoard the bearer of the right. To have a moral right of this kind always implies that others have certain moral duties toward me; but it does *not* follow that if others have those duties, then I have the corresponding right. Thus the claim is that the imposition of certain correlative moral duties on others is a necessary but not sufficient condition for one's possession of a moral right.

right to worship as I choose, for example, can be defined in terms of the moral duties other people have to not interfere in my chosen form of worship. And the moral right to a suitable standard of living can be defined in terms of the duty that governments (or some other agents of society) have to ensure a suitable standard of living for their citizens. Duties, then, are generally the other side of moral rights: If I have a moral right to do something, then other people have a moral duty not to interfere with me when I do it; and if I have a moral right to have someone do something for me, then that other person (or group of persons) has a moral duty to do it for me. Thus, moral rights impose correlative duties on others, either duties of noninterference or duties of positive performance.

In some cases, the correlative duties imposed by a right may fall not on any specific individual but on all the members of a group. If a person, for example, has the "right to work" (a right mentioned in the United Nations' Universal Declaration of Human Rights), this does not necessarily mean that any specific employer has a duty to provide that person with a job. Rather, it means that all the members of society, through their public agencies, have the duty of ensuring that jobs are available to workers.

Second, moral rights provide individuals with autonomy and equality in the free pursuit of their interests.[34] That is, a right identifies activities or interests which people must be left free to pursue or not pursue as they themselves choose (or must be helped to pursue as they freely choose) and whose pursuit must not be subordinated to the interests of others except for special and exceptionally weighty reasons. If I have a right to worship as I choose, for example, then this implies that I am free to worship if and as I personally choose, and that I am not dependent on anyone's permission in order to worship. It also implies that I cannot generally be forced to stop worshipping on the grounds that society will gain more benefits if I am kept from worshipping: The gains of others do not generally justify interference with a person's pursuit of an interest or an activity when that pursuit is protected by a moral right. To acknowledge a person's moral right, then, is to acknowledge that there is an area in which the person is not subject to my wishes and in which the person's interests are not subordinate to mine. There is an area, in short, within which we stand as autonomous equals.

Thirdly, moral rights provide a basis for justifying one's actions and for invoking the protection or aid of others.[35] If I have a moral right to do something, then I have a moral justification for doing it. Moreover, if I have a right to do something, then others have no justification for interfering with me. On the contrary, others are justified in restraining any persons who try to prevent me from exercising my right or others may have a duty to aid me in exercising my right. When a stronger person helps a weaker one defend his or her rights, for example, we generally acknowledge that the act of the stronger person was justified.

Because moral rights have these three features, they provide bases for making moral judgments that differ substantially from utilitarian standards.[36] First, moral rights express the requirements of morality from the point of view of the *individual*

[34] See Richard Wasserstrom, "Rights, Human Rights, and Racial Discrimination," *The Journal of Philosophy*, 61 (29 October 1964): 628–41.

[35] *Ibid.*, p. 62.

[36] See Ronald Dworkin, "Taking Rights Seriously," in *Taking Rights Seriously*, Ronald Dworkin, ed. (Cambridge: Harvard University Press, 1978), pp. 184–205.

while utilitarianism expresses the requirements of morality from the point of view of *society as a whole.* Moral standards concerned with rights indicate what is due to the individual from others and they promote the individual's welfare and protect the individual's choices against encroachment by society. Utilitarian standards promote society's aggregate utility, and they are indifferent to the individual's welfare except insofar as it affects this social aggregate. Second, rights limit the validity of appeals to social benefits and to numbers. That is, if a person has a right to do something, then it is wrong for anyone to interfere, even though a large number of people might gain much more utility from such interference. If I have a right to life, for example, then it is morally wrong for someone to kill me, even if many others would gain much more from my death than I will ever gain from living. And if the members of a minority group have a right to free speech then the majority must leave the minority free to speak, even if the majority is much more numerous and intensely opposed to what the minority will say.

Although rights generally override utilitarian standards, they are not immune from all utilitarian considerations: If the utilitarian benefits or losses imposed on society become great enough, they might be sufficient to breach the protective walls the right sets up around a person's freedom to pursue his or her interests. In times of war or major public emergencies, for example, it is generally acknowledged that civil rights may legitimately be restricted for the sake of "the public welfare." And the property rights of factory owners may be restricted in order to prevent pollution that is imposing major damages on the health of others. The more important is the interest protected by a right, the larger the utilitarian tradeoffs must be: Rights erect higher walls around more important interests, and so the level of social benefits or costs needed to breach the walls must be greater.

Negative and Positive Rights

A large group of rights called "negative rights" is distinguished by the fact that its members can be defined wholly in terms of the duties others have to *not* interfere in certain activities of the person who holds a given right.[37] For example, if I have a right to privacy, this means that every other person, including my employer, has the duty not to intervene in my private affairs. And if I have a right to use, sell, or destroy my personal business assets, this means that every other person has the duty not to prevent me from using, selling, or destroying my business property as I choose.

On the other hand, "positive rights" do more than impose negative duties. They also imply that some other agents (it is not always clear who) have the *positive* duty of providing the holder of the right with whatever he or she needs to freely pursue his or her interests.[38] For example, if I have a right to an adequate standard of living, this does not mean merely that others must not interfere: It also means that if I am unable to provide myself with an adequate income, then I must be provided with such an income (perhaps by the government). Similarly, the right to work, the right to an education, the right to adequate health care,

[37] Feinberg, *Social Philosophy,* pp. 59–61.
[38] *Ibid.*

and the right to social security are all rights that go beyond noninterference to also impose a positive duty of providing people with something when they are unable to provide it for themselves.

Positive rights were not emphasized until the twentieth century. Negative rights were often employed in the seventeenth and eighteenth centuries by writers of manifestos (like the Declaration of Independence and the Bill of Rights), who were anxious to protect individuals against the encroachments of monarchical governments. Positive rights became important in the twentieth century when society increasingly took it upon itself to provide its members with the necessities of life that they were unable to provide for themselves. The United Nations declaration, for example, is influenced by this trend when it provides for the rights "to food, clothing, housing, and medical care." The change in the meaning of the phrase "the right to life" is another indication of the rising importance of positive rights. Whereas the eighteenth century interpreted the "right to life" as the negative right to not be killed (this is the meaning the phrase has in the Declaration of Independence), the twentieth century has reinterpreted the phrase to refer to the positive right to be provided with the minimum necessities of life.

Much of the debate over moral rights has concentrated on whether negative or positive rights should be given priority. So-called "conservative" writers, for example, have claimed that government efforts should be limited to enforcing negative rights and not expended on providing positive rights.[39] This is the crux of the debate over whether government efforts should be restricted to protecting property and securing law and order (that is, protecting people's negative rights) or whether government should in addition provide the needy with jobs, job training, housing, medical care, and other welfare benefits (that is, provide for people's positive rights). So-called "liberal" authors, on the other hand, hold that positive rights have as strong a claim to being honored as negative rights and that, consequently, government has a duty to provide for both.[40]

Contractual Rights and Duties

Contractual rights and duties (sometimes called "special" rights and duties or "special obligations") are the limited rights and correlative duties that arise when one person enters an agreement with another person.[41] For example, if I contract to do something for you, then you are entitled to my performance: You acquire a contractual *right* to whatever I promised, and I have a contractual *duty* to perform as I promised.

Contractual rights and duties are distinguished, first, by the fact that they attach to *specific* individuals and the correlative duties are imposed only on other *specific* individuals. If I agree to do something for you, everyone else does not thereby acquire new rights over me, nor do I acquire any new duties toward

[39] See, for example, Milton Friedman, *Capitalism and Freedom* (Chicago: The University of Chicago Press, 1962), p. 22–36; Friedrich Hayek, *The Road to Serfdom* (Chicago: The University of Chicago Press, 1944), pp. 25–26.

[40] Peter Singer, "Rights and the Market," in *Justice and Economic Distribution*, John Arthur and William Shaw, eds. (Englewood Cliffs, NJ: Prentice Hall, 1978), pp. 207–21.

[41] H. L. A. Hart, "Are There Any Natural Rights," *Philosophical Review*, 64 (April 1955): 185.

them. Secondly, contractual rights arise out of a specific transaction between particular individuals. Unless I actually make a promise or enter some other similar arrangement with you, you do not acquire any contractual rights over me.

Thirdly, contractual rights and duties depend on a publicly accepted system of rules that define the transactions that give rise to those rights and duties.[42] Contracts, for example, create special rights and duties between people only if these people recognize and accept a system of conventions that specifies that by doing certain things (such as signing a paper) a person undertakes an obligation to do what he or she agrees to do. When a person goes through the appropriate actions, other people know that person is putting himself or herself under an obligation because the publicly recognized system of rules specifies that such actions count as a contractual agreement. And because the publicly recognized system obligates or requires the person to do what he or she says, or suffer the appropriate penalties, everyone understands that the person can be relied on to keep the contract and that others can act in accordance with this understanding.

Without the institution of contract and the rights and duties it can create, modern business societies could not operate. Virtually every business transaction at some point requires one of the parties to rely on the word of the other party to the effect that the other party will pay later, will deliver certain services later, or will transfer goods of a certain quality and quantity. Without the social institution of contract, individuals in such situations would be unwilling to rely on the word of the other party, and the transactions would never take place. The institution of contracts provides a way of ensuring that individuals keep their word, and this in turn makes it possible for business society to operate. Employers, for example, acquire contractual rights to the services of their employees in virtue of the work contract that employees enter, and sellers acquire contractual rights to the future cash that credit buyers agree to give them.

Contractual rights and duties also provide a basis for the special duties or obligations that people acquire when they accept a position or a role within a legitimate social institution or an organization. Married parents, for example, have a special duty to care for the upbringing of their children; doctors have a special duty to care for the health of their patients; and managers have a special duty to care for the organization they administer. In each of these cases, there is a publicly accepted institution (such as a familial, medical, or corporate institution) that defines a certain position or role (such as parent, doctor, or manager) upon which the welfare of certain vulnerable persons (such as the parent's children, the doctor's patients, the manager's corporate constituencies) depends. Society attaches to these institutional roles special duties of caring for these vulnerable dependents and of protecting them from injury, duties that the person who enters the role knows he or she is expected to fulfill. When a person freely enters the role knowing what duties society attaches to the acceptance of the role, that person in effect enters an agreement to fulfill those duties. The existence of a system of contractual obligations ensures that individuals fulfill these agreements by laying on them the public obligations that all agreements carry. As a result, these familial, medical, and corporate institutions can continue to exist and their vulnerable members are protected against harm. We should recall here that a person's institutional duties

[42] J. R. Searle, *Speech Acts* (Cambridge: The University Press, 1969), pp. 57–62.

are not unlimited. In the first chapter we noted that as a "loyal agent," the manager's duties to care for the corporation are limited by the ethical principles that govern any person. Similarly, a doctor cannot murder other people in order to obtain vital organs for the patients whom he or she has a duty to care for.

What kind of ethical rules govern contracts? The system of rules that underlies contractual rights and duties has traditionally been interpreted as including several moral constraints:[43]

1. Both of the parties to a contract must have full knowledge of the nature of the agreement they are entering.
2. Neither party to a contract must intentionally misrepresent the facts of the contractual situation to the other party.
3. Neither party to the contract must be forced to enter the contract under duress or coercion.
4. The contract must not bind the parties to an immoral act.

Contracts that violate one or more of these four conditions have traditionally been considered void.[44] Below we shall discuss the basis of these sorts of conditions.

A BASIS FOR MORAL RIGHTS: KANT

How do we know that people have rights? This question can be answered in a fairly straightforward way when it is asked about legal rights: A person has certain legal rights because the person lives within a legal system that guarantees those rights. But what is the basis of moral rights?

Utilitarians have suggested that utilitarian principles can provide a satisfactory basis for moral rights: People have moral rights because the possession of moral rights maximizes utility. It is doubtful, however, that utilitarianism can serve as an adequate basis for moral rights. To say that someone has a moral right to do something is to say that he or she is entitled to do it regardless of the utilitarian benefits it provides for others. Utilitarianism cannot easily support such a nonutilitarian concept.

A more satisfactory foundation for moral rights is provided by the ethical theory developed by Immanuel Kant (1724–1804). Kant in fact attempts to show that there are certain moral rights and duties that all human beings possess, regardless of any utilitarian benefits that the exercise of those rights and duties may provide for others.

Kant's theory is based on a moral principle that he calls the "categorical imperative" and that requires that everyone should be treated as a free person equal to everyone else. That is, everyone has a moral right to such treatment, and everyone has the correlative duty to treat others in this way. Kant provides at least two ways of formulating this basic moral principle; each formulation serves as an explanation of the meaning of this basic moral right and correlative duty.

[43] Thomas M. Garrett, *Business Ethics*, 2nd ed. (Englewood Cliffs, NJ: Prentice Hall, 1986), pp. 88–91.

[44] *Ibid.*, p. 75. See also John Rawls, *A Theory of Justice* (Cambridge: Harvard University Press, The Belknap Press, 1971), pp. 342–50.

The First Formulation of Kant's Categorical Imperative

Kant's first formulation of the categorical imperative goes like this: "I ought never to act except in such a way that I can also will that my maxim should become a universal law."[45] A "maxim" for Kant is the reason a person in a certain situation has for doing what he or she plans to do. And a maxim would "become a universal law" if every person in a similar situation chose to do the same thing for the same reason. Kant's first version of the categorical imperative, then, comes down to the following principle:

> *An action is morally right for a person in a certain situation if and only if the person's reason for carrying out the action is a reason that he or she would be willing to have every person act on, in any similar situation.*

An example may help to clarify the meaning of Kant's principle. Suppose that I am trying to decide whether to fire an employee because I do not like the employee's race. According to Kant's principle, I must ask myself whether I would be willing to have an employer fire any employee whenever the employer does not like the race of his or her employee. In particular, I must ask myself whether I would be willing to be fired myself should my employer not like my race. If I am not willing to have everyone act in this way, even toward me, then it is morally wrong for me to act in this way toward others. A person's reasons for acting, then, must be "reversible": One must be willing to have all others use those reasons even against oneself. There is an obvious similarity, then, between the categorical imperative and the so-called "golden rule": "Do unto others as you would have them do unto you."

Kant points out that sometimes it is not even possible to *conceive* of having everyone act on a certain reason, much less be *willing* to have everyone act on that reason.[46] For example, suppose that I am considering breaking a contract because it has committed me to do something I do not want to do. Then I must ask whether I would be willing to have everyone break any contract that one did not want to keep. But it is impossible to even conceive of everyone making and then breaking contracts in this way since if everyone knew that any contract could be broken, then people would cease making contracts altogether (what possible purpose would they serve?) and contracts would no longer exist. Consequently, since it is impossible to conceive of everyone making and breaking contracts in this way, it is also impossible for me to be willing to have everyone act like this (how can I want something I cannot even conceive?). It would be wrong, therefore, for me to break a contract simply because I do not want to keep it. A person's reasons for acting, then, must also be universalizable: It must be possible, at least in principle, for everyone to act on those reasons.

The first formulation of the categorical imperative, then, incorporates two criteria for determining moral right and wrong: universalizability and reversibility.

UNIVERSALIZABILITY: The person's reasons for acting must be reasons that everyone *could* act on at least in principle.

[45] Immanuel Kant, *Groundwork of the Metaphysics of Morals*, H. J. Paton, trans. (New York: Harper & Row, Publishers, Inc., 1964), p. 70.

[46] *Ibid.*, p. 91.

REVERSIBILITY: The person's reasons for acting must be reasons that he or she would be *willing* to have all others use, even as a basis of how they treat him or her.

This formulation of Kant's categorical imperative is attractive for a number of reasons, not the least of which is that it seems to capture some fundamental aspects of our moral views. Frequently, for example, we say to a person who has done something wrong or who is about to do something wrong: How would you like it if he did that to you? or How would you like it if you were in her place?, thereby invoking something like reversibility. Or we may ask, What if everybody did that? and thereby invoke universalizability.

Unlike the principle of utilitarianism, Kant's categorical imperative focuses on a person's interior motivations and not on the consequences of one's external actions. Moral right and wrong, according to Kantian theory, are distinguished not by what a person accomplishes, but by the reasons the person has for what he tries to do.[47] Kant argues that to the extent that a person performs an action merely because it will advance the person's own future interests or merely because the person finds the action pleasurable, the action "has no moral worth." A person's action has "moral worth" only to the degree that it is *also* motivated by a sense of "duty," that is, a belief that it is the right way for people to behave. And, Kant claims, to be motivated by a sense of "duty" is to be motivated by reasons that I wish everyone would act upon. Consequently, my action has "moral worth" (that is, it is morally right) only to the extent that it is motivated by reasons that I would be willing to have every person act on. Hence the categorical imperative.[48]

The Second Formulation of Kant's Categorical Imperative

The second formulation Kant gives of the categorical imperative is this: "Act in such a way that you always treat humanity, whether in your own person or in the person of any other, never simply as a means, but always at the same time as an end."[49] Or, never treat people *only* as means, but always also as ends.

What Kant means by "treating humanity as an end" is that I should treat each human being as a being whose existence as a free rational person should be promoted. For Kant this means two things: (1) respecting each person's freedom by treating people only as they have freely consented to be treated beforehand and (2) developing each person's capacity to freely choose for him or herself the aims he or she will pursue.[50] On the other hand, to treat a person only as a means is to use the person only as an instrument for advancing my own interests and involves neither respect for, nor development of, the person's capacity to choose freely. Kant's second version of the categorical imperative can be expressed in the following principle:

[47] *Ibid.*, p. 62.

[48] *Ibid.*, pp. 64–70.

[49] *Ibid.*, p. 96.

[50] See Fred Feldman, *Introductory Ethics* (Englewood Cliffs, NJ: Prentice Hall, 1978), pp. 119–28; and Rawls, *A Theory of Justice*, pp. 179–80.

An action is morally right for a person if and only if in performing the action, the person does not use others merely as a means for advancing his or her own interests, but also both respects and develops their capacity to choose freely for themselves.

This version of the categorical imperative implies that human beings each have an equal dignity that sets them apart from things like tools or machines and that is incompatible with their being manipulated, deceived, or otherwise unwillingly exploited to satisfy the self-interests of another. The principle in effect says that people should not be treated as objects incapable of free choice. By this principle, an employee may legitimately be asked to perform the unpleasant (or even dangerous) tasks involved in a job if the employee freely consented to take the job knowing that it would involve these tasks. But it would be wrong to subject an employee to health risks *without the employee's knowledge.* In general, deception, force, and coercion fail to respect people's freedom to choose and are therefore immoral (unless, perhaps, a person first freely consented to have force used against himself or herself).

Kant argues that making fraudulent contracts by deceiving others is wrong and that deliberately refraining from giving others help when they need it is also wrong. By deceiving a person into making a contract that that person would not otherwise freely choose to make, I fail to respect that person's freedom to choose and merely use the person to advance my own interests. And by failing to lend needed and easily extended help to another person, I limit what that person is free to choose to do.

The second formulation of the categorical imperative, according to Kant, is really equivalent to the first.[51] The first version says that what is morally right for me must be morally right for others: Everyone is of equal value. If this is so, then no person's freedom should be subordinated to that of others so that the person is used merely to advance the interests of others. And since I myself am of value, I cannot sacrifice myself to mere self-interest. And this, of course, is what the second version of the categorical imperative requires. Both formulations come down to the same thing: People are to treat each other as free and equal in the pursuit of their interests.

Kantian Rights

A large number of authors have held that the categorical imperative (in one or the other of its formulations) explains why people have moral rights.[52] As we have seen, moral rights identify interests that individuals must be left free to pursue as they autonomously choose (or which we must help them pursue as they choose) and whose free pursuit must not be subordinated to our own interests. And that is precisely what both formulations of Kant's categorical imperative

[51] Kant, *Groundwork*, p. 105.

[52] See, for example, A. K. Bierman, *Life and Morals: An Introduction to Ethics* (New York: Harcourt Brace Jovanovich, Inc., 1980), pp. 300–301; Charles Fried, *Right and Wrong* (Cambridge: Harvard University Press, 1978), p. 129; Dworkin, *Taking Rights Seriously*, p. 198; Thomas E. Hill, Jr., "Servility and Self-Respect," *The Monist*, 57, no. 1 (January 1973): 87–104; Feinberg, *Social Philosophy*, p. 93; Gregory Vlastos, "Justice and Equality," p. 48 in *Social Justice*, Richard Brandt, ed. (Englewood Cliffs, NJ: Prentice Hall, 1964), pp. 31–72.

require in holding that people must be respected as free and equal in the pursuit of their interests. In short, moral rights identify the specific major areas in which persons must deal with each other as free equals, and Kant's categorical imperative implies that persons should deal with each other in precisely this way. The categorical imperative, however, cannot by itself tell us what particular moral rights human beings have. In order to know what particular rights human beings have, one first must know what interests humans have and must know whether there are good reasons for giving the free pursuit of one interest, rather than another, the protected status of a right (clearly, not all interests can be turned into rights, since interests can conflict with each other). For example, to establish that humans have a right to free speech, one has to show that freedom to say what one chooses is critically important to human beings and that it is more important than the free pursuit of other conflicting interests that humans may have (such as an interest in repressing ideas that we find distasteful, offensive, or disturbing). Insofar as free speech is critically important, humans must leave each other equally free to speak as they choose: Everyone has a moral right to freedom of speech. But insofar as free speech conflicts with another human interest that can be shown to be of equal or greater importance (such as our interest in not being libeled or defamed), the right to freedom of speech must be limited.

Although later chapters will present various arguments in support of several particular rights, it might be helpful here to give a rough sketch of how some rights have been plausibly defended on the basis of Kant's two formulations of the categorical imperative. First, human beings have a clear interest in being helped by being provided with the work, food, clothing, housing, and medical care they need to live on when they cannot provide these for themselves. Suppose we agree that we would not be willing to have everyone (especially ourselves) deprived of such help when it is needed, and that such help is necessary if a person's capacity to choose freely is to develop and even survive.[53] If so, then no individual ought to be deprived of such help. That is, human beings have *positive rights* to the work, food, clothing, housing, and medical care they need to live on when they cannot provide these for themselves and when these are available.

Second, human beings also have a clear interest in being free from injury or fraud and in being free to think, associate, speak, and live privately as they choose. Suppose we agree that we would be willing to have everyone be free of the interference of others in these areas, and that interference in these areas fails to respect a person's freedom to choose for him or herself.[54] If so, then everyone ought to be free of the interference of others in these areas. That is, human

[53] For a similar argument based on Kant's first formulation of the categorical imperative see Marcus Singer, *Generalization in Ethics* (New York: Alfred A. Knopf, Inc., 1961), pp. 267–74; for one based on Kant's second formulation see Alan Donagan, *The Theory of Morality* (Chicago: The University of Chicago Press, 1977), p. 85; also see I. Kant, *Metaphysical Elements of Justice* (New York: Bobbs-Merrill Co., Inc., 1965), pp. 91–99.

[54] See Alan Gewirth, *Reason and Morality* (Chicago: The University of Chicago Press, 1978), who argues for these rights (p. 256) on the basis of a principle that, although different from Kant's first formulation in some important respects, is nonetheless very much like it: "Every agent must claim that he has rights to freedom and well-being for the reason that he is a prospective purposive agent . . . it follows, by the principle of universalizability, that all prospective purposive agents have rights to freedom and well-being" (p. 133); Donagan, *The Theory of Morality*, pp. 81–90, argues for these on the basis of Kant's second formulation.

beings have these *negative rights*: the right to freedom from injury or fraud, the right to freedom of thought, freedom of association and freedom of speech, and the right to privacy.

Third, as we have seen, human beings have a clear interest in preserving the institution of contracts. Suppose we agree that we would end up dropping the institution of contracts (which we are unwilling to do) if everyone stopped honoring their contracts or if everyone had to honor even contracts that were made under duress or without full information; and suppose we agree that we show respect for people's freedom by honoring the contracts they freely make with us and by leaving them free and fully informed about any contracts they make with us.[55] If so, then everyone ought to honor his or her contracts and everyone ought to be fully informed and free when making contracts. That is, human beings have a *contractual right* to what they have been promised in contracts, and everyone also has a right to be left free and fully informed when contracts are made.

Each of the rights just described has been sketched in barest outline, and each one requires a great deal more in the way of qualifications, adjustments with other (conflicting) interests, and full supporting arguments. Crude as it is, however, the list provides some idea of how Kant's categorical imperative might be used in establishing positive rights, negative rights, and contractual rights.

Problems with Kant

In spite of the attractiveness of Kant's theory, critics have argued that, like utilitarianism, it has its limitations and inadequacies. A first problem that critics have traditionally pointed out is that Kant's theory is not precise enough to always be useful. One difficulty lies in trying to determine whether or not one would (as the first formulation requires) "be willing to have everyone follow" a certain policy. Although the general thrust of this requirement is usually clear, it sometimes leads to problems. For example, suppose I am a murderer: Would I then be willing to have everyone follow the policy that all murderers should be punished? In a sense I would be willing to, since I would want to be protected from other murderers, but in another sense I would not be willing, since I do not want to be punished myself; which sense is correct?[56] It is also sometimes difficult to determine whether or not (as the second formulation states) one person is using another "merely as a means." Suppose, for example, that an employer pays only minimum wages to her employees and refuses to install the safety equipment they want, yet she says she is "respecting their capacity to freely choose for themselves" because she is willing to let them work elsewhere if they choose. Is she then treating them merely as means or also as ends? Critics complain that they cannot answer

[55] See Singer, *Generalization in Ethics,* pp. 255–57, for a discussion of how Kant's first formulation provides a basis for the obligation to keep one's promises and for truthfulness in the making of promises; see Donagan, *Theory of Morality* pp. 90–94, for a discussion of the same subject in terms of the second formulation.

[56] See Jonathan Harrison, "Kant's Examples of the First Formulation of the Categorical Imperative," in *Kant, A Collection of Critical Essays*, Robert Paul Wolff, ed. (Garden City, NY: Doubleday & Co., Inc., 1967), pp. 228–45; see also in the same work, the reply by J. Kemp and the counterreply by J. Harrison, both of which focus on the meaning of "is willing."

such questions because Kant's theory is too vague.[57] There are cases, then, where the requirements of Kant's theory are unclear.

Second, some critics claim that, although we might be able to agree on the kinds of interests that have the status of moral rights, there is substantial disagreement concerning what the *limits* of each of these rights are and concerning how each of these rights should be balanced against other conflicting rights.[58] And Kant's theory does not help us resolve these disagreements. For example, we all agree that everyone should have a right to associate with whomever one wants, as well as a right not to be injured by others. But how should these rights be balanced against each other when a certain association of people begins to injure others? Suppose the loud music of a group of trombone players, for example, disturbs others; or suppose a corporation (which is an association of people) pollutes the air and water on which the health of others depends. Kant's categorical imperative does not tell us how the conflicting rights of these persons should be adjusted to each other: Which right should be limited in favor of the other?

A defender of Kant, however, can counter this second kind of criticism by holding that Kant's categorical imperative is not intended to tell us how conflicting rights should be limited and adjusted to each other. To decide whether one right should be curtailed in favor of a second right one has to examine the relative importance of the *interests* that each right protects. What arguments can be given to show, for example, that a corporation's interest in financial gains is more or less important than the health of its neighbors? The answer to this question will determine whether or not a corporation's right to use its property for financial gains should be limited in favor of its neighbors' right not to have their health injured. All that Kant's categorical imperative is meant to tell us is that everyone must have equal moral rights and that everyone must show as much respect for the protected interests of others as he or she wants others to show for his or her own. It does not tell us what interests people have, nor what their relative importance is.

A third group of criticisms that have been made of Kant's theory is that there are counter-examples which show that the theory sometimes goes wrong. Most counter-examples to Kant's theory focus on the criteria of universalizability and reversibility.[59] Suppose that an employer can get away with discriminating against blacks by paying them lower wages than whites for the same work. And suppose also that he is so fanatical in his dislike of blacks that he is willing to accept the proposition that if his own skin were black, employers should also disciminate against him. Then, according to Kant's theory, the employer would be acting morally. But this, according to the critics, is wrong, since discrimination is obviously immoral.

Defenders of a Kantian approach to ethics, of course, would reply that it is the critics, not Kant, who are mistaken. If the employer genuinely and conscien-

[57] Fred Feldman, *Introductory Ethics*, pp. 123–28; Robert Paul Wolff, *The Autonomy of Reason* (New York: Harper Torch Books, 1973), p. 175.

[58] For example, J. B. Mabbott, *The State and the Citizen* (London: Arrow, 1958), p. 57–58.

[59] Feldman, *Introductory Ethics*, pp. 116–17.

tiously would be willing to universalize the principles on which he is acting, then the action is in fact morally right for him.[60] For us, who would be unwilling to universalize the same principle, the action would be immoral. We may also find that it would be morally right for us to impose sanctions on the employer to make him stop discriminating. But, insofar as the employer is trying to remain true to his own universal principles, he is acting conscientiously and, therefore, in a moral manner.

THE LIBERTARIAN OBJECTION: NOZICK

Some important views on rights that are different from the ones we just sketched have been proposed recently by several "libertarian philosophers."

Libertarian philosophers go beyond the general presumption that freedom from human constraint is usually good, to claim that such freedom is necessarily good and that all constraints imposed by others are necessarily evil except when needed to prevent the imposition of greater human constraints. The American philosopher Robert Nozick, for example, claims that the only basic right that every individual possesses is the negative right to be free from the coercion of other human beings.[61] This negative right to freedom from coercion, according to Nozick, must be recognized if individuals are to be treated as distinct persons with separate lives, each of whom has an equal moral weight that may not be sacrificed for the sake of others. The only circumstances under which coercion may be exerted upon a person is when it is necessary to keep him or her from coercing others.

According to Nozick, prohibiting people from coercing others constitutes a legitimate "moral" constraint that rests on "the underlying Kantian principle that individuals are ends and not merely means; they may not be sacrificed or used for achieving of other ends without their consent."[62] Thus Nozick seems to hold that Kant's theory supports his own views on freedom.

Nozick goes on to argue that the negative right to freedom from the coercion of others implies that people must be left free to do what they want with their own labor and with whatever products they manufacture by their labor.[63] And this in turn implies that people must be left free to acquire property, to use it in whatever way they wish, and to exchange it with others in free markets (so long as the situation of others is not thereby harmed or "worsened"). Thus, the libertarian view that coercive restrictions on freedom are immoral (except when needed to restrain coercion itself) is also supposed to justify the free use of property, freedom of contract, the institution of free markets in which individuals can ex-

[60] For example, Richard M. Hare, *Freedom and Reason* (New York: Oxford University Press, 1965), who uses Kant's first formulation (p. 34), defends himself against the example of the "fanatic" in this way.

[61] Robert Nozick, *Anarchy, State, and Utopia* (New York: Basic Books, Inc., Publishers, 1974), p. ix.

[62] *Ibid.*, pp. 30–31.

[63] *Ibid.*, p. 160; see also pp. 160–62.

change goods as they choose without government restrictions, and the elimination of taxes for social welfare programs. But there is no basis for any *positive* rights nor for the social programs they might require.

Nozick and other libertarians, however, pass too quickly over the fact that the freedom of one person necessarily imposes constraints upon other persons. Such constraints are inevitable, since when one person is granted freedom, other persons must be constrained from interfering with that person. If I am to be free to do what I want with my property, for example, other people must be constrained from trespassing on it and from taking it from me. Even the "free market system" that Nozick advocates depends on an underlying system of coercion: for I can "sell" something only if I first "own" it, and ownership depends essentially on an enforced (coercive) system of property laws. Consequently, since granting a freedom to one person necessarily imposes constraints on others, it follows that if constraints require justification, then freedom will likewise always require justification.

The same point can be made in a different way. Because there are many different kinds of freedoms, the freedom one group of agents is given to pursue some of its interests will usually restrict the freedom other agents have to pursue other conflicting interests. For example, the freedom of corporations to use their property to pollute the environment as they want can restrict the freedom of individuals to breathe clean air whenever they want. And the freedom of employees to unionize as they want can conflict with the freedom of employers to hire whatever nonunion workers they want. Consequently, allowing one kind of freedom to one group entails restricting some other kind of freedom for some other group: A decision in favor of the freedom to pursue one interest implies a decision against the freedom to pursue another kind of interest. This means that we cannot argue in favor of a certain kind of freedom by simply claiming that constraints are always evil and must always be replaced by freedom. Instead, an argument for a specific freedom must show that the interests that can be satisfied by that kind of freedom are somehow better or more worth satisfying than the interests that other opposing kinds of freedoms could satisfy. Neither Nozick nor other libertarians supply such arguments.

Moreover, it is not obvious that Kantian principles can support libertarian views like that of Nozick. Kant holds, as we saw, that the dignity of each person should be respected and that each person's capacity to choose freely should be developed. Because we have these duties to each other, government coercion is legitimate whenever it is needed to ensure that the dignity of citizens is being respected or when it is needed to secure the full development of people's capacity to choose. And this, as Kant argues, means that government may legitimatel[y] place limits on the use of property and on the making of contracts and impo[se] market restrictions and compulsory taxes when these are needed to care for t[he] welfare or development of persons "who are not able to support themselves." We have no reason to think that only negative rights exist. People can also h[ave] positive rights and Kant's theory supports these as much as it supports nega[tive] rights.

[64] Kant, *The Metaphysical Elements of Justice*, p. 93.

2.3 JUSTICE AND FAIRNESS

On Friday, December 9, 1977, a Senate subcommittee heard the testimony of several workers who had contracted "brown lung" disease by breathing cotton dust while working cotton mills in the south.[65] Brown lung is a chronic disabling respiratory disease with symptoms similar to asthma and emphysema and is a cause of premature death. The disabled workers were seeking a federal law that would facilitate the process of getting disability compensation from the cotton mills, similar to federal laws covering "black lung" disease contracted in coal mines.

Senator Strom Thurmond:

> A number of people have talked to me about this and they feel that if the federal government enters the field of black lung, it should enter the field of brown lung; and if those who have suffered from black lung are to receive federal consideration, then it seems fair that those who have suffered from brown lung receive federal consideration. . . . If our [state's cotton mill] workers have been injured and have not been properly compensated, then steps should be taken to see that is done. We want to see them treated fairly and squarely and properly, and so we look forward to . . . the testimony here today.

Mrs. Beatrice Norton:

> I started in the mill when I was fourteen years old and I had to get out in 1968 . . . I worked in the dust year after year, just like my mother. I got sicker and sicker . . . [In 1968 I] suddenly had no job, no money, and I was sick, too sick to ever work in my life again . . . State legislators have proven in two successive essions that they are not going to do anything to help the brown lung victims, so ıw we come to you in Washington and ask for help. We've waited a long time, ł many of us have died waiting. I don't want to die of injustice.

Ellison:

> ınd worked for twenty-one years [in the mill] in Spartanburg, and he worked tiest parts of the mill, the opening room, the cardroom, and cleaning the ›ning ducts . . . In the early sixties he started having trouble keeping up use of his breathing. In 1963 his bossman told him that he had been a but wasn't worth a damn anymore, and fired him . . . He had no ›thing to live on and we had to go on welfare to live . . . My husband ıd hard and lost his health and many years of pay because of the ˜ that [the mill] threw him away like so much human garbage after

ıate, *Brown Lung: Hearing Before a Subcommittee of the Committee on* ˜, 1st Session. 9 December 1977, pp. 3, 52, 53, 54, 59, and 60.

> he couldn't keep up his job because he was sick from the dust. We are not asking for handouts; we want what is owed to my husband for twenty-five years of hard work.

Disputes among individuals in business are often interlaced with references to "justice" or to "fairness." This is the case, for example, when one person accuses another of "unjustly" discriminating against him or her, or of showing "unjust" favoritism toward someone else, or of not taking up a "fair" share of the burdens involved in some cooperative venture. Resolving disputes like these requires that we compare and weigh the conflicting claims of each of the parties and strike a balance between them. Justice and fairness are essentially comparative. They are concerned with the comparative treatment given to the members of a group when benefits and burdens are distributed, when rules and laws are administered, when members of a group cooperate or compete with each other, and when people are punished for the wrongs they have done or compensated for the wrongs they have suffered. Although the terms "justice" and "fairness" are used almost interchangeably, we tend to reserve the word "justice" for matters that are especially serious, although some authors have held that the concept of fairness is more fundamental.[66]

Standards of justice are generally taken to be more important than utilitarian considerations.[67] If a society is unjust to some of its members, then we normally condemn that society, even if the injustices secure more utilitarian benefits for everyone. If we think that slavery is unjust, for example, then we condemn a society that uses slavery, even if slavery makes that society more productive. Greater benefits for some cannot justify injustices for others. Nonetheless, we also seem to hold that if the social gains are sufficiently large, a certain level of injustice may legitimately be tolerated.[68] In countries with extreme deprivation and poverty, for example, we seem to hold that some degree of equality may be traded off for major economic gains that leave everyone better off.

But standards of justice do not generally override the moral rights of individuals. Part of the reason for this is that, to some extent, justice is based on individual moral rights. The moral right to be treated as a free and equal person, for example, is part of what lies behind the idea that benefits and burdens should be distributed equally.[69] More important, however, is the fact that, as we saw, a moral right identifies interests people have, the free pursuit of which may not be subordinated to the interests of others except where there are special and exceptionally weighty reasons. This means that, for the most part, the moral rights of some individuals cannot be sacrificed merely in order to secure a somewhat better distribution of

[66] John Rawls, "Justice as Fairness," *The Philosophical Review*, 67 (1958); 164–94; R. M. Hare, "Justice and Equality," in *Justice and Economic Distribution*, Arthur and Shaw, eds., p. 119.

[67] Rawls, *A Theory of Justice*, pp. 3–4.

[68] See, for example, Rawls, *A Theory of Justice*, p. 542; and Joel Feinberg, "Rawls and Intuitionism," pp. 114–16 in *Reading Rawls*. Norman Daniels, ed. (New York: Basic Books, Inc., Publishers, n.d.), pp. 108–24; and T. M. Scanlon, "Rawls' Theory of Justice," pp. 185–91 in *ibid.*, pp. 160–205.

[69] See, for example, Vlastos, "Justice and Equality."

benefits for others. Yet correcting extreme injustices may justify restricting some individuals' rights. Property rights, for example, might be legitimately redistributed for the sake of justice. We will discuss trade-offs of this sort more fully after we have a better idea of what justice means.

Issues involving questions of justice and fairness are usually divided into three categories. *Distributive justice*, the first and basic category, is concerned with the fair distribution of society's benefits and burdens. In the 1977 brown lung hearings, for example, Senator Thurmond pointed out that if federal law helped workers afflicted by black lung, then it was only "fair" that it also help workers afflicted by brown lung. *Retributive justice*, the second category, refers to the just imposition of punishments and penalties upon those who do wrong: A "just" penalty is one that in some sense is deserved by the person who does wrong. Retributive justice would be at issue, for example, if we were to ask whether it would be fair to penalize cotton mills for causing brown lung disease among their workers. *Compensatory justice*, the third category, concerns the just way of compensating people for what they lost when they were wronged by others: A just compensation is one that in some sense is proportional to the loss suffered by the person being compensated (such as loss of livelihood). During the brown lung hearings, for example, both Mrs. Norton and Mrs. Ellison claimed that, in justice, they were owed compensation from the cotton mills because of injuries inflicted by the mills.

This section examines each of these three kinds of justice separately. The section begins with a discussion of a basic principle of distributive justice (equals should be treated as equals) and then examines several views on the criteria relevant to determining whether or not two persons are "equal." The section then turns to a brief discussion of retributive justice and ends with a discussion of compensatory justice.

Distributive Justice

Questions of distributive justice arise when different people put forth conflicting claims on society's benefits and burdens and all the claims cannot be satisfied.[70] The central cases are those where there is a scarcity of benefits—such as jobs, food, housing, medical care, income, and wealth—as compared to the numbers and the desires of the people who want these goods. Or (the other side of the coin) there may be too many burdens—unpleasant work, drudgery, substandard housing, health injuries of various sorts—and not enough people willing to shoulder them. If there were enough goods to satisfy everyone's desires and enough people willing to share society's burdens, then conflicts between people would not arise and distributive justice would not be needed.

When people's desires and aversions exceed the adequacy of their resources, they are forced to develop principles for allocating scarce benefits and undesirable burdens in ways that are just and that resolve the conflicts in a fair way. The development of such principles is the concern of distributive justice.

The fundamental principle of distributive justice is that equals should be

[70] Rawls, *A Theory of Justice*, pp. 126–30.

treated equally and unequals, unequally.[71] More precisely, the fundamental principle of distributive justice may be expressed as follows:

> *Individuals who are similar in all respects relevant to the kind of treatment in question should be given similar benefits and burdens, even if they are dissimilar in other irrelevant respects; and individuals who are dissimilar in a relevant respect ought to be treated dissimilarly, in proportion to their dissimilarity.*

If, for example, Susan and Bill are both doing the same work for me and there are no relevant differences between them or the work they are doing, then in justice I should pay them equal wages. But if Susan is working twice as long as Bill and if length of working time is the relevant basis for determining wages on the sort of work they are doing, then, to be just, I should pay Susan twice as much as Bill. Or, to return to our earlier example, if the federal government rightly helps workers who have suffered from black lung and there are no relevant differences between such workers and workers who have suffered from brown lung, then, as Senator Thurmond said, it is "fair that those who have suffered from brown lung [also] receive federal consideration."

This fundamental principle of distributive justice, however, is purely formal.[72] It is based on the purely logical idea that we must be consistent in the way we treat similar situations. And the principle does not specify the "relevant respects" that may legitimately provide the basis for similarity or dissimilarity of treatment. Is race, for example, relevant when determining who should get what jobs? Most of us would say no, but then what characteristics are relevant when determining what benefits and burdens people should receive? We will turn now to examine different views on the kinds of characteristics that may be relevant when determining who should get what. Each of these views provides a "material" principle of justice—that is, a principle that gives specific content to the fundamental principle of distributive justice.

Justice as Equality: Egalitarianism

Egalitarians hold that there are no relevant differences among people that can justify unequal treatment.[73] According to the egalitarian, all benefits and burdens should be distributed according to the following formula:

> *Every person should be given exactly equal shares of society's benefits and burdens.*

Egalitarians base their view on the proposition that all human beings are equal in some fundamental respect and that, in virtue of this equality, each person has an

[71] William K. Frankena, "The Concept of Social Justice," in *Social Justice*, Brandt ed., pp. 1–29; C. Perelman, *The Idea of Justice and the Problem of Argument* (New York: Humanities Press, Inc., 1963), p. 16.

[72] Feinberg, *Social Philosophy*, pp. 100–102; Perelman, *Idea of Justice*, p. 16.

[73] Christopher Ake, "Justice as Equality," *Philosophy and Public Affairs*, 5, no. 1 (Fall 1975): 69–89.

equal claim to society's goods.[74] And this, according to the egalitarian, implies that goods should be allocated to people in equal portions.

Equality has, of course, appeared to many as an attractive social ideal and inequality, as a defect. "All men are created equal," says our Declaration of Independence, and the ideal of equality has been the driving force behind the emancipation of slaves, the prohibition of indentured servitude, the elimination of racial, sexual, and property requirements on voting and holding public office, and the institution of free public education. Americans have long prided themselves on the lack of overt status consciousness in their social relations.

In spite of their popularity, however, egalitarian views have been subjected to heavy criticisms. One line of attack has focused on the egalitarian claim that all human beings are equal in some fundamental respect.[75] Critics claim that there is *no* quality that all human beings possess in precisely the same degree: Human beings differ in their abilities, intelligence, virtues, needs, desires, and in all their other physical and mental characteristics. If this is so, then human beings are unequal in all respects.

A second set of criticisms argues that the egalitarian ignores some characteristics that should be taken into account in distributing society's goods: need, ability, and effort.[76] If everyone is given exactly the same things, critics point out, then the lazy person will get as much as the industrious one, even though the lazy one does not deserve as much. If everyone is given exactly the same, then the sick person will get only as much as healthy ones, even though the sick person needs more. If everyone is given exactly the same, the handicapped person will have to do as much as talented persons, even though the handicapped person has less ability. And if everyone is given exactly the same, then individuals will have no incentives to exert greater efforts in their work; as a result, society's productivity and efficiency will decline. Since the egalitarian formula ignores all these facts, and since it is clear that they should be taken into account, critics allege, egalitarianism must be mistaken.

Some egalitarians have tried to strengthen their position by distinguishing two different kinds of equality: political equality and economic equality.[77] *Political equality* refers to an equal participation in, and treatment by, the means of controlling and directing the political system. This includes equal rights to participate in the legislative process, equal civil liberties, and equal rights to due process. *Economic equality,* on the other hand, refers to equality of income and wealth and equality of opportunity. The criticisms leveled against equality, according to some egalitarians, apply only to economic equality and not to political equality. Although everyone will concede that differences of need, ability, and effort may justify some inequalities in the distribution of income and wealth, everyone will also

[74] Kai Nielsen, "Class and Justice" in *Justice and Economic Distribution*, Arthur and Shaw, eds., pp. 225–45; see also Gregory Vlastos, *Justice and Equality*. Vlastos interprets "equality" in a much different sense than I do here.

[75] Bernard Williams, "The Idea of Equality," in *Philosophy and Society*, 2nd series, Laslett and Runciman, ed. (London: Blackwell, 1962), pp. 110–31.

[76] Feinberg, *Social Philosophy*, 109–11.

[77] See Bowie, *A New Theory of Distributive Justice*, pp. 60–64.

agree that political rights and liberties should not be unequally distributed. Thus, the egalitarian position may be correct with respect to political equality, even if it is mistaken with respect to economic equality.

Other egalitarians have claimed that even economic equality is defensible if it is suitably limited. Thus, they have argued that every person has a right to a minimum standard of living and that income and wealth should be distributed equally until this standard is achieved for everyone.[78] The economic surplus that remains after everyone has achieved the minimum standard of living can then be distributed unequally according to need, effort, etc. A major difficulty that this limited type of economic egalitarianism must face, however, is specifying what it means by "minimum standard of living." Different societies and different cultures have different views as to what constitutes the necessary minimum to live on. A relatively primitive economy will place the minimum at a lower point than a relatively affluent one. Nonetheless, most people would agree that justice requires that affluent societies satisfy at least the basic needs of their members and not let them die of starvation, exposure, or disease.

Justice Based on Contribution: Capitalist Justice

Some writers assume that a society's benefits should be distributed according to what each individual contributes to that society. The more a person contributes to a society's pool of economic goods, for example, the more that person is entitled to take from that pool; the less an individual contributes, the less that individual should get. Quite simply:

> *Benefits should be distributed according to the contribution each individual makes to achieving the aims of his or her group (the firm, society, humanity, etc.).*

The main question raised by this view of distributive justice is how the "contribution" of each individual is to be measured.

One long-lived tradition has held that contributions should be measured in terms of *work effort*. The more effort people put forth in their work, the greater the share of benefits to which they are entitled. This is the assumption behind the "Puritan ethic," which held that every individual had a religious obligation to work hard at his "calling" (the career to which God summons each individual) and that God justly rewards hard work with wealth and success, while He justly punishes laziness with poverty and failure.[79] In the United States this Puritan ethic has evolved into a secularized "work ethic" which places a high value on

[78] See D. D. Raphael, "Equality and Equity," *Philosophy*, 21 (1946): 118–32. See also, Bowie, *A New Theory of Distributive Justice*, pp. 64–65.

[79] See Francis X. Sutton, Seymour E. Harris, Carl Kaysen, and James Tobin, *The American Business Creed* (Cambridge: Harvard University Press, 1956), pp. 276–78; the classic source is Max Weber, *The Protestant Ethic and the Spirit of Capitalism*, Talcott Parsons, trans. (London: 1930); see also, Perry Miller, *The New England Mind: From Colony to Province* (Cambridge: Harvard University Press, 1953), pp. 40–52.

individual effort and which assumes that, whereas hard work does and should lead to success, loafing is and should be punished.[80]

But there are many problems with using effort as the basis of distribution.[81] First, to reward a person's efforts without any reference to whether the person produces anything worthwhile through these efforts is to reward incompetence and inefficiency, Secondly, if we reward people solely for their efforts and ignore their abilities and relative productivity, then talented and highly productive people will be given little incentive to invest their talent and productivity in producing goods for society. As a result, society's welfare will decline.

A second important tradition has held that contributions should be measured in terms of *productivity*: The better the quality of a person's contributed product, the more he or she should receive. ("Product" here should be interpreted broadly to include services rendered, capital invested, commodities manufactured, and any type of literary, scientific, or aesthetic works produced.)[82] A major problem with this second proposal is that it ignores people's needs. Handicapped, ill, untrained, and immature persons may be unable to produce anything worthwhile; if people are rewarded on the basis of their productivity, the needs of these disadvantaged groups will not be met. But the main problem with this second proposal is that it is difficult to place any objective measure on the value of a person's product, especially in fields like the sciences, the arts, entertainment, athletics, education, theology, and health care. And who would want to have their products priced on the basis of someone else's subjective estimates?

In order to deal with the last difficulty above, some authors have assumed that the value of a person's product should be determined by the market forces of supply and demand.[83] The value of a product would then depend not on its intrinsic value but upon the extent to which it is both relatively scarce and is viewed by consumers as desirable. Unfortunately, this method of measuring the value of a person's product still ignores people's needs. Moreover, to many people market prices are an unjust method of evaluating the value of a person's product precisely because markets ignore the intrinsic values of things. Markets, for example, reward entertainers more than doctors. Also, markets often reward a person who through pure chance has ended up with something (an inheritance, for example) that is scarce and that people happen to want. This, to many, seems the height of injustice.

Justice Based on Needs and Abilities: Socialism

Since there are probably as many kinds of socialism as there are socialists, it is somewhat inaccurate to speak of "the" socialist position on distributive justice.

[80] See A. Whitner Griswold, "Three Puritans on Prosperity," *The New England Quarterly*, 7 (September 1934): 475–88; see also Daniel T. Rodgers, *The Work Ethic in Industrial America* (Chicago: The University of Chicago Press, 1978).

[81] John A. Ryan, *Distributive Justice*, 3rd ed. (New York: The Macmillan Co., 1941), pp. 182–83; Nicholas Rescher, *Distributive Justice* (New York: The Bobbs-Merrill Co., Inc., 1966), pp. 77–78.

[82] Rescher, *Distributive Justice*, pp. 78–79; Ryan, *Distributive Justice*, pp. 183–85.

[83] Rescher, *Distributive Justice*, pp. 80–81; Ryan, *Distributive Justice*, pp. 186–87.

Nonetheless, the dictum proposed first by Louis Blanc (1811–1882) and then by Karl Marx (1818–1883) and Nikolai Lenin (1870–1924) is traditionally taken to represent the "socialist" view on distribution: "From each according to his ability, to each according to his needs."[84] The socialist principle, then, can be paraphrased as follows:

> *Work burdens should be distributed according to people's abilities, and benefits should be distributed according to people's needs.*

This "socialist" principle is based first on the idea that people realize their human potential by exercising their abilities in productive work.[85] Since the realization of one's full potentiality is a value, work should be distributed in such a way that a person can be as productive as possible, and this implies distributing work according to ability. Second, the benefits produced through work should be used to promote human happiness and well-being. And this means distributing them so that people's basic biological and health needs are met, and then using what is left over to meet people's other nonbasic needs. But perhaps most fundamental to the socialist view is the notion that societies should be communities in which benefits and burdens are distributed on the model of a family. Just as able family members willingly support the family, and just as needy family members are willingly supported by the family, so also the able members of a society should contribute their abilities to society by taking up its burdens while the needy should be allowed to share in its benefits.

There is something to be said for the socialist principle: Needs and abilities certainly should be taken into account when determining how society's benefits and burdens should be distributed. Most people would agree, for example, that we should make a greater contribution to the lives of cotton mill workers with brown lung disease who have greater needs than to the lives of healthy persons who have all they need. Most people would also agree that individuals should be employed in occupations for which they are fitted and that this means matching each person's abilities to his or her job as far as possible. Vocational tests in high school and college, for example, are supposed to help students find careers that match their abilities.

However, the socialist principle has also had its critics. First, opponents have pointed out that under the socialist principle there would be no relation between the amount of effort a worker puts forth and the amount of remuneration she receives (since remuneration depends on need, not on effort). Consequently, opponents conclude, workers would not be motivated to put forth any work efforts

[84] Karl Marx, *Critique of the Gotha Program* (London: Lawrence and Wishart, Ltd., 1938), pp. 14 and 107; Louis Blanc, *L'Organization du Travail* (Paris, 1850) cited in D. O. Wagner, *Social Reformers* (New York: The Macmillan Co., 1946), p. 218; Nikolai Lenin, "Marxism on the State," pp. 76–77; on the question whether Marx had a theory of distributive justice, see Ziyad I. Husami, "Marx on Distributive Justice," in *Marx, Justice, and History*, Marshall Cohen, Thomas Nagel, and Thomas Scanlon, eds. (Princeton: Princeton University Press, 1980), pp. 42–79.

[85] Marx, *Critique of the Gotha Program*; see also John McMurtry, *The Structure of Marx's World View* (Princeton: Princeton University Press, 1978), ch. I.

at all, knowing that they will receive the same whether they work hard or not. The result will be a stagnating economy with a declining productivity.[86] Underlying this criticism is a deeper objection, namely that it is unrealistic to think that entire societies could be modeled on familial relationships. Human nature is essentially self-interested and competitive, the critics of socialism hold; and so, outside the family, people cannot be motivated by the fraternal willingness to share and help that is characteristic of families. Socialists have usually replied to this charge by arguing that human beings are taught to be self-interested and competitive by modern social and economic institutions that inculcate and encourage competitive and self-interested behavior, but that they are not that way by nature. By nature, humans are born into families where they instinctively value helping each other. If these instinctive and "natural" attitudes continued to be nurtured instead of being eradicated, humans would continue to value helping others even outside the family. The debate on what kinds of motivations human nature is subject to is still largely unsettled.

A second objection that opponents of the socialist principle have urged is that if the socialist principle were enforced, it would obliterate individual freedom.[87] Under the socialist principle, the occupation each person entered would be determined by the person's abilities and not by his or her free choice. If a person has the ability to be a university teacher but wants to be a ditch-digger, the person will have to become a teacher. Similarly, under the socialist principle, the goods a person gets will be determined by the person's needs and not by his or her free choice. If a person needs a loaf of bread but wants a bottle of beer, he or she will have to take the loaf of bread. The sacrifice of freedom is even greater, the critics claim, when one considers that in a socialist society some central government agency has to decide what tasks should be matched to each person's abilities and what goods should be allotted to each person's needs. The decisions of this central agency will then have to be imposed on other persons at the expense of their freedom to choose for themselves. The socialist principle substitutes paternalism for freedom.

Justice as Freedom: Libertarianism

The last section discussed libertarian views on moral rights; libertarians also have some clear and related views on the nature of justice. The libertarian holds that no particular way of distributing goods can be said to be just or unjust apart from the free choices individuals make. Any distribution of benefits and burdens is just if it is the result of individuals freely choosing to exchange with each other the goods each person already owns. Robert Nozick, a leading libertarian, suggests this principle as the basic principle of distributive justice:

> *From each according to what he chooses to do, to each according to what he makes for himself (perhaps with the contracted aid of others) and what others choose to do for him and choose to give him of what they've been*

[86] Bowie, *A New Theory of Distributive Justice*, pp. 92–93. See also Norman Daniels, "Meritocracy," in *Justice and Economic Distribution*, Arthur and Shaw, eds., pp. 167–78.

[87] Bowie, *ibid.*, pp. 96–98.

> *given previously (under this maxim) and haven't yet expended or transferred.*[88]

Or, quite simply, "From each as they choose, to each as they are chosen." For example, if I choose to write a novel or choose to carve a statue out of a piece of driftwood, then I should be allowed to keep the novel or the statue if I choose to keep it. Of, if I choose, I should be allowed to give them away to someone else or to exchange them for other objects with whomever I choose. In general, people should be allowed to keep everything they make and everything they are freely given. Obviously, this means it would be wrong to tax one person (that is, take the person's money) in order to provide welfare benefits for someone else's needs.

Nozick's principle is based on the claim (which we have already discussed) that every person has a right to freedom from coercion that takes priority over all other rights and values. The only distribution that is just, according to Nozick, is one that results from free individual choices. Any distribution that results from an attempt to impose a certain pattern on society (for instance, imposing equality on everyone or taking from the have's and giving to the have-not's) will therefore be unjust.

We have already noted some of the problems associated with the libertarian position. The major difficulty is that the libertarian enshrines a certain value—freedom from the coercion of others—and sacrifices all other rights and values to it, without giving any persuasive reasons why this should be done. Opponents of the libertarian view argue that other forms of freedom must also be secured, such as freedom from ignorance and freedom from hunger. These other forms of freedom in many cases override freedom from coercion. If a man is starving, for example, his right to be free from the constraints imposed by hunger is more important than the right of a satisfied man to be free of the constraint of being forced to share his surplus food. In order to secure these more important rights, society may impose a certain pattern of distribution, even if this means that in some cases some people will have to be coerced into conforming to the distribution. Those with surplus money, for example, may have to be taxed to provide for those who are starving.

A second related criticism of libertarianism claims that the libertarian principle of distributive justice will generate unjust treatment of the disadvantaged.[89] Under the libertarian principle, a person's share of goods will depend wholly on what the person can produce through his or her own efforts or what others choose to give the person out of charity (or some other motive). But both of these sources may be unavailable to a person through no fault of the person. A person may be ill, handicapped, unable to obtain the tools or land needed to produce goods, too old or too young to work, or otherwise incapable of producing anything through his or her own efforts. And other people (perhaps out of greed) may refuse to provide that person with what he or she needs. According to the libertarian principle, such a person should get nothing. But this, say the critics of libertarianism, is

[88] Robert Nozick, *Anarchy, State, and Utopia*, p. 160.

[89] Rawls, *A Theory of Justice*, pp. 65–75.

surely mistaken. If people through no fault of their own happen to be unable to care for themselves, their survival should not depend on the outside chance that others will provide them with what they need. Each person's life is of value and consequently each person should be cared for, even if this means coercing others into distributing some of their surplus to the person.

Justice as Fairness: Rawls

The discussions above have suggested several different considerations that should be taken into account in the distribution of society's benefits and burdens: political and economic equality, a minimum standard of living, needs, ability, effort, and freedom. What is needed, however, is a comprehensive theory capable of drawing these considerations together and fitting them together into a logical whole. John Rawls provides one approach to distributive justice that at least approximates this ideal of a comprehensive theory.[90]

John Rawls's theory is based on the assumption that conflicts involving justice should be settled by first devising a fair method for choosing the principles by which the conflicts will be resolved. Once a fair method of choosing principles is devised, the principles we choose by using that method should serve us as our own principles of distributive justice.

Rawls proposes two basic principles that, he argues, we would select if we were to use a fair method of choosing principles to resolve our social conflicts.[91] The principles of distributive justice that Rawls proposes can be paraphrased by saying that the distribution of benefits and burdens in a society is just if and only if:

1. *each person has an equal right to the most extensive basic liberties compatible with similar liberties for all, and*
2. *social and economic inequalities are arranged so that they are both*
   a. *to the greatest benefit of the least advantaged persons, and*
   b. *attached to offices and positions open to all under conditions of fair equality of opportunity.*

Rawls tells us that principle 1 is supposed to take priority over principle 2 should the two of them ever come into conflict. And within principle 2, part b is supposed to take priority over part a.

Principle 1 is called the "principle of equal liberty." Essentially it says that each citizen's liberties must be protected from invasion by others and must be equal to those of others. These basic liberties include the right to vote, freedom of speech and conscience and the other civil liberties, freedom to hold personal property, and freedom from arbitrary arrest.[92] If the principle of equal liberty is correct, then it implies that it is unjust for business institutions to invade the privacy of employees, to pressure managers to vote in certain ways, to exert undue influence on political processes by the use of bribes, or to otherwise violate

[90] *Ibid.*, pp. 577–87.
[91] *Ibid.*, pp. 298–303.
[92] *Ibid.*, p. 61.

the equal political liberties of society's members. According to Rawls, moreover, since our freedom to make contracts would diminish if we were afraid of being defrauded or were afraid that contracts would not be honored, the principle of equal liberty also prohibits the use of force, fraud, or deception in contractual transactions and requires that just contracts should be honored.[93] If this is true, then contractual transactions with customers (including advertising) ought morally to be free of fraud, and employees have a moral obligation to render the services they have justly contracted to their employer.

Part a of principle 2 is the "difference principle." It assumes that a productive society will incorporate inequalities, but it then asserts that steps must be taken to improve the position of the most needy members of society, such as the sick and the disabled unless such improvements would so burden society that they make everyone, including the needy, worse off than before.[94] Rawls claims that the more productive a society is, the more benefits it will be able to provide for its least advantaged members. Since the difference principle obliges us to maximize benefits for the least advantaged, this means that business institutions should be as efficient in their use of resources as possible. If we assume that a market system like ours is most efficient when it is most competitive, then the difference principle will in effect imply that markets should be competitive and that anticompetitive practices like price-fixing and monopolies are unjust. In addition, since pollution and other environmentally damaging "external effects" consume resources inefficiently, the difference principle also implies that it is wrong for firms to pollute.

Part b of principle 2 is the "principle of fair equality of opportunity." It says that everyone should be given an equal opportunity to qualify for the more privileged positions in society's institutions.[95] This means not only that job qualifications should be related to the requirements of the job (thereby prohibiting racial and sexual discrimination), but that each person must have access to the training and education needed to qualify for the desirable jobs. A person's efforts, abilities and contribution would then determine his or her remuneration.

The principles that Rawls proposes are quite comprehensive and bring together the main considerations stressed by the other approaches to justice that we have examined. But Rawls not only provides us with a set of principles of justice, he also proposes a general method for evaluating in a fair way the adequacy of any moral principles. The method he proposes consists of determining what principles a group of rational self-interested persons would choose to live by if they knew they would live in a society governed by those principles but they did not yet know what each of them would turn out to be like in that society.[96] We might ask, for example, whether such a group of rational self-interested persons would choose to live in a society governed by a principle that discriminates against blacks when none of them knows whether he himself or she herself will turn out to be a black person in that society. The answer, clearly, is that such a racist principle would be rejected and consequently, according to Rawls, the racist princi-

[93] *Ibid.*, pp. 108–14 and 342–50.

[94] *Ibid.*, pp. 75–83 and 274–84.

[95] *Ibid.*, pp. 83–90.

[96] *Ibid.*, pp. 17–22.

ple would be unjust. Thus, Rawls claims that a principle is a morally justified principle of justice if and only if the principle would be acceptable to a group of rational self-interested persons who know they will live in a society governed by the principles they accept but who do not yet know what sex, race, abilities, religion, interests, social position, income, or other particular characteristics each of them will possess in that future society.

Rawls refers to the situation of such an imaginary group of rational persons as the "original position," and he refers to their ignorance of any particulars about themselves as the "veil of ignorance."[97] The purpose and effect of decreeing that the parties to the original position do not know what particular characteristics each of them will possess is to ensure that none of them can protect his or her own special interests. Because they are ignorant of their particular qualities, the parties to the original position are forced to be fair and impartial and to show no favoritism toward any special group: They must look after the good of all.

According to Rawls, the principles that the imaginary parties to the original position accept will *ipso facto* turn out to be morally justified.[98] They will be morally justified because the original position incorporates the Kantian moral ideas of reversibility (the parties choose principles that will apply to themselves), of universalizability (the principles must apply equally to everyone), and of treating people as ends (each party has an equal say in the choice of principles). The principles are further justified, according to Rawls, because they are consistent with our deepest considered intuitions about justice. The principles chosen by the parties to the original position match most of the moral convictions we already have and where they do not, according to Rawls, we would be willing to change them to fit Rawls's principles once we reflect on his arguments.

Rawls goes on to claim that the parties to the original position would in fact choose his (Rawls's) principles of justice, that is, the principle of equal liberty, the difference principle, and the principle of fair equality of opportunity.[99] The principle of equal liberty would be chosen because the parties will want to be free to pursue their major special interests whatever these might be. Since in the original position each person is ignorant of what special interests he or she will have, everyone will want to secure a maximum amount of freedom so that he or she can pursue whatever interests he or she has upon entering society. The difference principle will be chosen because all parties will want to protect themselves against the possibility of ending up in the worst position in society. By adopting the difference principle, the parties will ensure that even the position of the most needy is cared for. And the principle of fair equality of opportunity will be chosen, according to Rawls, because all parties to the original position will want to protect their interests should they turn out to be among the talented. The principle of fair equality of opportunity ensures that everyone has an equal opportunity to advance through the use of his or her own abilities, efforts, and contributions.

If Rawls is correct in claiming that the principles chosen by the parties to the original position are morally justified, and if he is correct in arguing that his own principles would be chosen by the parties to the original position, then it

[97] *Ibid.*, pp. 136–42.

[98] *Ibid.*, pp. 46–53.

[99] The core of the argument is at *ibid.*, pp. 175–83, but parts may also be found at pp. 205–9; 325–32; 333–50; 541–48.

follows that his principles are in fact morally justified to serve as our own principles of justice. These principles would then constitute the proper principles of distributive justice.

Critics, however, have objected to various parts of Rawls's theory.[100] Some have argued that the original position is not an adequate method for choosing moral principles. According to these critics, the mere fact that a set of principles is chosen by the hypothetical parties to the original position tells us nothing about whether the principles are morally justified. Other critics have argued that the parties to the original position would not choose Rawls's principles at all. Utilitarians, for example, have argued that the hypothetical parties to the original position would choose utilitarianism and not Rawls's principles. Still other critics have claimed that Rawls's principles are themselves mistaken. Rawls's principles, according to these critics, are opposed to our basic convictions concerning what justice is.

In spite of the many objections that have been raised against Rawls's theory, his defenders still claim that the advantages of the theory outweigh its defects. For one thing, they claim, the theory preserves the basic values that have become embedded in our moral beliefs: freedom, equality of opportunity, and a concern for the disadvantaged. Secondly, the theory fits easily into the basic economic institutions of Western societies: It does not reject the market system, work incentives, nor the inequalities consequent on a division of labor. Instead, by requiring that inequalities work for the benefit of the least advantaged and by requiring equality of opportunity, the theory shows how the inequalities that attend the division of labor and free markets can be compensated for and thereby made just. Thirdly, the theory incorporates both the communitarian and the individualistic strains that are intertwined in Western culture. The difference principle encourages the more talented to use their skills in ways that will rebound to the benefit of fellow citizens who are less well off, thereby encouraging a type of communitarian or "fraternal" concern.[101] Yet the principle of equal liberty leaves the individual free to pursue whatever special interests the individual may have. Fourthly, Rawls's theory takes into account the criteria of need, ability, effort, and contribution. The difference principle distributes benefits in accordance with need, while the principle of fair equality of opportunity in effect distributes benefits and burdens according to ability and contribution.[102] And fifthly, the defenders of Rawls argue, there is the moral justification that the original position provides. The original position is defined so that its parties choose impartial principles that take into account the equal interests of everyone, and this, they claim, is the essence of morality.

Retributive Justice

Retributive justice concerns the justice of blaming or punishing persons for doing wrong. Philosophers have long debated the justification of blame and punish-

[100] See the articles collected in *Reading Rawls*, Daniels, ed.; see also Brian Barry, *The Libal Theory of Justice* (Oxford: Clarendon Press, 1973); Robert Paul Wolff, *Understanding Rawls* (Princeton: Princeton University Press, 1977).

[101] Rawls, *A Theory of Justice*, pp. 105–8.

[102] *Ibid.*, p. 276.

ment, but we need not enter these debates here. More relevant to our purposes is the question of the conditions under which it is just to punish a person for doing wrong.

The first chapter discussed two major conditions under which a person could not be held morally responsible for what he or she did: ignorance and inability. These two conditions are also relevant to determining the justice of punishing or blaming someone for doing wrong: If people do not know or freely choose what they are doing, then they cannot justly be punished or blamed for it. For example, if the cotton mill owners mentioned at the beginning of this section did not know that the conditions in their mills would cause brown lung disease, then it would be unjust to punish them when it turns out that their mills caused this disease.

A second condition of just punishments is certitude that the person being punished actually did wrong. Many firms, for example, use more or less complex systems of "due process" that are intended to ascertain whether the conduct of employees was really such as to merit dismissal or some other penalty.[103] Penalizing an employee on the basis of flimsy or incomplete evidence is rightly considered an injustice.

Third, just punishments must be consistent and proportioned to the wrong. Punishment is consistent only when everyone is given the same penalty for the same infraction; punishment is proportioned to the wrong when the penalty is no greater in magnitude than the harm that the wrongdoer inflicted.[104] It is unjust, for example, for a manager to impose harsh penalties for minor infractions of rules, or to be lenient toward favorites but harsh toward all others. If the purpose of a punishment is to deter others from committing the same wrong or to prevent the wrongdoer from repeating the wrong, then punishment should not be greater than what is consistently necessary to achieve these aims.

Compensatory Justice

Compensatory justice concerns the justice of restoring to a person what the person lost when he or she was wronged by someone else. We generally hold that when one person wrongfully harms the interests of another person, the wrongdoer has a moral duty to provide some form of restitution to the person he or she wronged. If, for example, I destroy someone's property or injure him bodily, I will be held morally responsible for paying him damages.

There are no hard and fast rules for determining how much compensation a wrongdoer owes the victim. Justice seems to require that the wrongdoer as far as possible should restore whatever he or she took and this would usually mean that the amount of restitution should be equal to the loss the wrongdoer knowingly inflicted on the victim. Yet some losses are impossible to measure. If I maliciously

[103] On the relation between justice and due process see David Resnick, "Due Process and Procedural Justice," in *Due Process*, J. Roland Pennock and John W. Chapman, eds. (New York: New York University Press, 1977), pp. 302–10; employee due process procedures are discussed in Maurice S. Trotta and Harry R. Gudenberg, "Resolving Personnel Problems in Non-union Plants," in *Individual Rights in the Corporation*, Alan F. Westin and Stephen Salisbury, eds. (New York: Pantheon Books, Inc., 1980), pp. 302–10.

[104] On the relation between justice and consistency in the application of rules see Perelman, *The Idea of Justice*, pp. 36–45; proportionality in punishment is discussed in John Kleinig, *Punishment and Desert* (The Hague: Martinus Nijoff, 1973), pp. 110–33; and C. W. K. Mundle, "Punishment and Desert," *Philosophical Quarterly*, IV (1954): 216–28.

injure someone's reputation, for example, how much restitution should I make? Some losses, moreover, cannot be restored at all: For can the loss of life or the loss of sight be compensated? In cases of this sort, where the injury is such that full restoration of the loss is not possible, we seem to hold that the wrongdoer should at least pay for the material damages the loss inflicts upon the injured person and his or her immediate family.

Traditional moralists have argued that a person has a moral obligation to compensate an injured party only if three conditions are present:[105]

1. *The action that inflicted the injury was wrong or negligent. For example, if by efficiently managing my firm I undersell my competitor and run her out of business, I am not morally bound to compensate her since such competition is neither wrongful nor negligent; but if I steal from my employer, then I owe him compensation, or if I fail to exercise due care in my driving, then I owe compensation to those whom I injure.*
2. *The person's action was the real cause of the injury. For example, if a banker loans a person money and the borrower then uses it to cheat others, the banker is not morally obligated to compensate the victims; but if the banker defrauds a customer, the customer must be compensated.*
3. *The person inflicted the injury voluntarily. For example, if I injure someone's property accidentally and without negligence, I am not morally obligated to compensate the person. (I may, however, be* legally *bound to do so depending on how the law chooses to distribute the social costs of injury.)*

The most controversial forms of compensation undoubtedly are the "preferential treatment" programs that attempt to remedy past injustices against groups. If a racial group, for example, has been unjustly discriminated against for an extended period of time in the past and its members consequently now hold the lowest economic and social positions in society, does justice require that members of that group be compensated by being given special preference in hiring, training, and promotion procedures? Or would such special treatment itself be a violation of justice by violating the principle of equal treatment? Does justice legitimize quotas even if this requires turning down more highly qualified nonminorities? These are complex and involved questions that we will not be able to answer at this point. We will return to them in a later chapter.

2.4 SUMMARY: UTILITY, RIGHTS, AND JUSTICE

The last three sections have described the three main kinds of moral standards that today lie at the basis of most of our moral judgments and that force us to bring distinctive kinds of considerations into our moral reasonings. Utilitarian standards must be used when we do not have the resources for attaining everyone's objectives, so we are forced to consider the net social benefits and social costs

[105] Henry J. Wirtenberger, S.J., *Morality and Business* (Chicago: Loyola University Press, 1962), pp. 109–19; see also Herbert Jone, *Moral Theology*, Urban Adelman, trans. (Westminster, MD: The Newman Press, 1961), pp. 225–47.

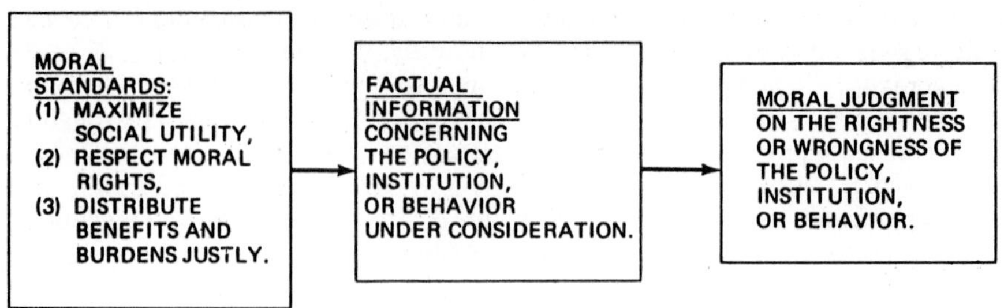

FIGURE 2.1

consequent on the actions (or policies or institutions) by which we can attain these objectives. When these utilitarian considerations are employed, the person must bring into his or her moral reasoning measurements, estimates, and comparisons of the relevant benefits and costs. Such measurements, estimates, and comparisons constitute the information on which the utilitarian moral judgment is based.

Our moral judgments are also partially based on standards that specify how individuals must be treated or respected. These sorts of standards must be employed when our actions and policies will substantially affect the welfare and freedom of specifiable individuals. Moral reasoning of this type forces consideration of whether the behavior respects the basic rights of the individuals involved and whether the behavior is consistent with one's agreements and special duties. These sorts of considerations require information concerning how the behavior affects the basic needs of the humans involved, the freedom they have to choose, the information available to them, the extent to which force, coercion, manipulation, or deception are used upon them, and the tacit and explicit understandings with which they entered various roles and agreements.

And third, our moral judgments are also in part based on standards of justice that indicate how benefits and burdens should be distributed among the members of a group. These sorts of standards must be employed when evaluating actions whose distributive effects differ in important ways. The moral reasoning on which such judgments are based will incorporate considerations concerning whether the behavior distributes benefits and burdens equally or in accordance with the needs, abilities, contributions, and free choices of people as well as with the extent of their wrongdoing. These sorts of considerations in turn rely on comparisons of the benefits and burdens going to different groups (or individuals) and comparisons of their relative needs, efforts, etc.

Our morality therefore contains three main kinds of moral considerations, each of which emphasizes certain morally important aspects of our behavior, but no one of which captures all the factors that must be taken into account in making moral judgments. Utilitarian standards consider only the aggregate social welfare but ignore the individual and how that welfare is distributed. Moral rights consider the individual but discount both aggregate well-being and distributive considerations. Standards of justice consider distributive issues but they ignore aggregate social welfare and the individual as such. These three kinds of moral considerations do not seem to be reducible to each other yet all three seem to be necessary parts of our morality. That is, there are some moral problems for which utilitarian considerations are decisive, while for other problems the decisive considerations are either the rights of individuals or the justice of the distributions involved. This suggests that moral reasoning should incorporate all three kinds of moral considerations, even though only one or the other may turn out to be relevant or decisive in a particular situation. One simple strategy for ensuring that all three kinds of considerations are incorporated into one's moral reasoning is to inquire systematically into the utility, rights, and justice involved in a given moral judgment as in Figure 2.1. One might, for example, ask a series of questions about an action that one is considering: (1) Does the action, as far as possible, maximize social benefits and minimize social injuries? (2) Is the action consistent with the moral rights of those whom it will affect? (3) Will the action lead to a just distribution of benefits and burdens?

Bringing together different moral standards in this way, however, requires that one keep in mind how they relate to each other. As we have seen, moral rights identify areas in which other people generally may not interfere even if they can show that they would derive greater benefits from such interference. Generally speaking, therefore, standards concerned with moral rights have greater weight than either utilitarian standards or standards of justice. And standards of justice are generally accorded greater weight than utilitarian considerations.

But these relationships hold only in general. If a certain action (or policy or institution) promises to generate sufficiently large social benefits or to prevent sufficiently large social harm, the enormity of these utilitarian consequences may justify limited infringements of the rights of some individuals. Moreover, sufficiently large social costs and benefits may also be significant enough to justify some departures from standards of justice; and the correction of large and widespread injustices may be important enough to justify limited infringements on some individual rights.

We have at this time no comprehensive moral theory capable of determining precisely when utilitarian considerations become "sufficiently large" to outweigh narrow infringements on a conflicting right or standard of justice, or when considerations of justice become "important enough" to outweigh infringements on conflicting rights. Moral philosophers have been unable to agree on any absolute rules for making such judgments. There are, however, a number of rough criteria that can guide us in these matters. Suppose, for example, that only by invading my employees' right to privacy (with hidden cameras and legal on-the-job phone taps) will I be able to stop the continuing theft of several life-saving drugs that some of them are clearly stealing. How can I determine whether the utilitarian benefits are here "sufficiently large" to justify infringing on their right? First, I might ask whether the *kinds* of utilitarian values involved are clearly more important than the *kinds* of values protected by the right (or distributed by the standard of justice). The utilitarian benefits in the present example, for instance, include the saving of human life, while the right to privacy protects (let us suppose) the values of freedom from shame and blackmail and of freedom to live one's life as one chooses. Considering this I might decide that human life is here clearly the more important kind of value. Second, I might then ask whether the more important kind of value also involves substantially more people. For example, since the recovered drugs will (we assume) save several hundred lives, while the invasion of privacy will affect only a dozen people, the utilitarian values do involve substantially more people. Third, I can ask whether the actual injuries sustained by the persons whose rights are violated (or to whom an injustice is done) will be minor.

For example, suppose that I can ensure that my employees suffer no shame, blackmail, or restriction on their freedom as a result of my uncovering information about their private lives (I intend to destroy all such information). Then it would appear that they will not be injured in any major way by my invasion of their privacy.

There are, then, rough criteria that can guide our thinking when it appears that in a certain situation utilitarian considerations might be sufficiently important to override conflicting rights or standards of justice; and similar criteria can be used to determine whether in a certain situation considerations of justice should override an individual's rights. But these criteria remain rough and intuitive. They lie at the edges of the light that ethics can shed on moral reasoning.

MORAL PRINCIPLES IN INTERNATIONAL CONTEXTS

We noted in Chapter One that multinational corporations operate in foreign host countries whose laws or government decrees, common practices, levels of development, and cultural understandings are sometimes much different from those of their home country. These differences, we argued, do not provide adequate justification for the theory of ethical relativism. But how should the moral principles of utilitarianism, rights, and justice be applied in foreign countries that differ in so many ways from our own?[106]

For example, the laws and decrees of government that the managers of Dow Chemical Company find prevalent in the company's home country, the United States, are very different from those they confront in Mexico and other host countries. Legal safety standards regulating worker exposure to workplace toxins and other hazards are quite explicit and stringent in the United States while they are vague, lax, or altogether lacking in Mexico. Consumer product safety and labeling laws, which require careful quality controls, rigorous product tests, and warnings of risk for end users in the United States, are very different in Mexico, which allows lower levels of quality control, much less testing of products, and fewer warnings directed at end users. The environmental pollution laws of the U.S.

[106] Business ethics in the international arena is a topic that is not well developed in the literature on business ethics. The best book on this topic, and one from which my discussion here draws heavily, is that of Thomas Donaldson, *The Ethics of International Business* (New York: Oxford University Press, 1989). See also Raymond Vernon, "Ethics of Transnationalism," *Society* (March/April 1987), pp. 53–56; W. Michael Hoffman, Ann E. Lange, and David A. Fedo, eds., *Ethics and the Multinational Enterprise* (New York: University Press of America, 1986); Henry Shue, "Transnational Transgressions," in Tom Regan, ed., *Just Business: New Introductory Essays in Business Ethics* (New York: Random House, 1984), pp. 271–91; Richard T. DeGeorge, *Business Ethics*, 3rd ed. (New York: Macmillan Publishing Company, 1990), pp. 399–426; and Lee Preston, "The Evolution of Multinational Public Policy Toward Business: Codes of Conduct," in Lee Preston, ed., *Research in Corporate Social Performance and Policy: Volume 10* (Greenwich, CT: JAI Press, 1988). An older but still useful compendium of the ethical issues multinationals face is Thomas N. Gladwin and Ingo Walter, *Multinationals Under Fire: Lessons in the Management of Conflict* (New York: John Wiley & Sons, 1980). Two classic accounts of multinational issues that reach rather different conclusions are Richard J. Barnet and Ronald E. Muller, *Global Reach: The Power of the Multinational Corporations* (New York: Simon and Schuster, 1974), and Raymond Vernon, *Storm Over the Multinationals: The Real Issues* (Cambridge, MA: Harvard University Press, 1977).

government are strict and set at very high levels, while those of Mexico are virtually nonexistent. Moreover, the very legitimacy of government decrees differs from country to country, since governments differ in the extent to which they are truly representative of the needs and aspirations of their people. While the government of the United States is deficient in many respects, it is to a relatively high degree responsive to the needs of American citizens. Not so the governments of other nations such as the former government of Haiti that was notoriously corrupt and that consistently promoted the interests and wealth of a small group of government elites at the expense of the needs of the general population.

Common practices can also differ markedly among nations. Whereas all forms of bribery of government personnel are considered wrong in the United States, many forms of petty bribery of lower level government personnel are not only openly engaged in in Mexico: They are universally accepted there as standard practices even if officially frowned upon. Nepotism and sexism, while all condemned in the United States, are accepted as a matter of course in some Arab business environments. Manufacturing wages of $2 an hour without benefits are accepted as common practice in Jamaica, while manufacturing wages in the United States average close to $12 an hour plus benefits.

Multinationals also often operate in countries at very different levels of development.[107] Some countries have very high levels of technological, social, and economic resources available, while the resources of other countries in these and other areas are quite undeveloped. Technological sophistication, unions, financial markets, unemployment insurance, social security, and public education are widespread in more developed nations but are virtually unknown in Third World countries. Dow Chemical, for example, periodically has been accused of introducing pesticides, whose safe use requires a literate worker with access to technologically sophisticated protective gear, into developing nations whose uneducated laborers are ill prepared to handle such pesticides safely. Again, the Swiss company, Nestle Corporation has been accused of marketing powdered infant formula, whose safe use requires a literate consumer who has a clean supply of water available, in less developed nations where illiterate mothers have used unsanitary water to mix and dilute the formula, which they have fed to their babies, many of whom have subsequently died.

Most strikingly, the cultural practices of nations may differ so radically that the same action may mean something very different in two different cultures. In the United States, for example, it would be considered a lie for a company to provide the government with income statements that would understate the company's actual earnings for tax purposes. In some periods of Italy's history, however, it was accepted as a matter of course that all businesses would understate their annual earnings by one third when they reported their tax liability to the government at the end of the year. Knowing this, the government would automatically inflate each company's income statements by one third and levy taxes on this more accurate estimate, which companies willingly paid. Thus, because of a cultural practice that was known to both the business community and the government, Italian companies did not actually lie to their government when they understated

[107] The importance of singling out issues of development is a point made by Thomas Donaldson in *op. cit.*, pp. 102–3.

their income: What looked like a lie to an outsider was, in the cultural context, a clearly understood signal of a company's true income.

When confronted with a foreign context, in which laws and government decrees, prevailing practices, levels of development, and cultural understandings are very different from those of the manager's home country, what should the manager of a multinational do? For example, when operating in a foreign country, should the manager of the multinational adopt the practices of its home country or those prevalent in the host country? Some have claimed that when operating in less developed countries, multinationals from more developed home countries should always follow those practices prevalent in the more developed country, which set higher or more stringent standards.[108] But this claim ignores the fact that introducing practices that have evolved in a highly developed country into one that is less developed may produce more harm than good, a violation of utilitarian standards of ethics. For example, if an American company operating in Mexico pays local workers U.S. wages, it may draw all the skilled workers away from local Mexican companies that cannot afford to pay the same high salaries. As a consequence, Mexico's efforts to develop local companies may be crippled, while havoc is wreaked in local labor markets. Again, if American companies operating in Mexico are required to operate in Mexico according to the more costly wage, consumer, environmental, and safety standards prevalent in the United States, they will have no reason to invest in Mexico, and Mexico's development will be retarded. Precisely because they need and want foreign investment and technology, the governments of many less developed nations, genuinely interested in advancing the interests of their people, have insisted on less costly standards that can attract foreign companies. Thus it is clear that local conditions, particularly developmental conditions, must at least be considered when determining whether or not to import practices from a developing country into a less developed one, and that it is a mistake to accept the blanket claim that one must always adopt the "higher" practices of the more developed home country.

Some have gone to the opposite extreme and argued that multinationals should always follow local practices, whatever they might be, or that they should do whatever the local government wants, since it is the representative of the people. Yet it is also clear that it is often as unethical to go along with local practices or government requirements as it sometimes is to oppose them. The lower environmental standards of Mexico, for example, may be so low that they permit pollution levels that cripple the health of or even kill those living near chemical plants, producing flagrant violations of these people's basic human rights. Or the apartheid policies of the South African government may require levels of discrimination against South African blacks that are deep violations of justice. Or, again, the self-interest of government elites in Haiti may lead them to support policies that enrich them while harming the citizens they are supposed to represent. So the blanket claim that local practices should always be adopted is also mistaken.

It is clear, then, that while local laws or government decrees, common practices, levels of development, and cultural understandings all must be taken into account when evaluating the ethics of business policies and actions in a foreign

[108] Arnold Berleant, "Multinationals and the Problem of Ethical Consistency," *Journal of Business Ethics*, vol. 3 (August 1982), pp. 185–95.

country, the local status quo cannot simply be adopted without question by the multinational manager but must still be subjected to ethical analysis. What factors should be considered when evaluating the ethics of an action or policy in a foreign context? The foregoing discussion suggests that the following questions should be asked about any corporate action or policy under consideration by a company operating in a foreign country:

1. *What does the corporate policy or action really mean in the context of the local culture? When viewed in terms of its local cultural meaning, is the policy or action ethically acceptable, or does it violate the ethical standards of utilitarianism, rights, and justice to such an extent that it should not be undertaken?*
2. *Taking into account the nation's level of technological, social, and economic development and what its government is doing to promote this development, does the corporate policy or action produce consequences that are ethically acceptable from the point of view of utilitarianism, rights, and justice? Can the more stringent legal requirements or practices common in more developed nations be implemented without damage to the host country and its development, and in context would such implementation be more consistent with the ethical standards of utilitarianism, rights, and justice?*
3. *If the corporate action or policy is allowed or required by the laws or the decrees of the local government, does this government truly represent the needs of all its people? Does the corporate action or policy nevertheless violate any fundamental rights, standards of justice, or utilitarian standards? If it does, and if the action or policy is legally required to do business in the host country, then is the ethical violation significant enough to require withdrawal from that country?*
4. *If the corporate action or policy involves a local common practice that is morally questionable by home country standards (such as sexual discrimination or bribery of government personnel), is it possible to conduct business in the host country without engaging in the practice?*[109] *If not, then does the practice violate fundamental rights, standards of justice, or utilitarian standards, to a degree significant enough to require withdrawal from that country?*

Asking these questions, of course, will not automatically solve all the ethical dilemmas encountered in international contexts. The questions, however, indicate the kinds of issues that must be considered when applying ethical principles in international contexts.

QUESTIONS FOR REVIEW AND DISCUSSION

1. Define the following concepts: utilitarianism, utility, intrinsic good, instrumental good, basic need, mere wants, rule-utilitarianism, rights, legal rights, moral rights,

[109] This is a suggestion of Thomas Donaldson in *op. cit.*, pp. 104–5.

negative rights, positive rights, contractual rights, categorical imperative (both versions), the libertarian view on rights, distributive justice, the fundamental (or formal) principle of distributive justice, material principle of justice, egalitarian justice, capitalist justice, socialist justice, libertarian justice, justice as fairness, principle of equal liberty, difference principle, principle of fair equality of opportunity, the "original position," retributive justice, compensatory justice.

2. A student incorrectly defined utilitarianism this way: "Utilitarianism is the view that so long as an action provides me with more measurable economic benefits than costs, the action is morally right." Identify all of the mistakes contained in this statement.
3. In your view, does utilitarianism provide a more objective standard for determining right and wrong than moral rights do? Explain your answer fully. Does utilitarianism provide a more objective standard than principles of justice? Explain.
4. "Every principle of distributive justice, whether that of the egalitarian, or the capitalist, or the socialist, or the libertarian, or of Rawls, in the end is illegitimately advocating some type of equality." Do you agree or disagree? Explain.

CASES FOR DISCUSSION

The Ford Motor Car

Ford Motor Company is the second largest producer of automobiles. With annual sales of over six million cars and trucks worldwide, it has revenues of over $30 billion per year. In 1976 Ford's net worth was $7.7 billion and its income after taxes was over $983 million.[1]

During the early 1960s Ford's market position was being dangerously eroded by competition from domestic and foreign subcompacts, especially Volkswagens. Lee Iacocca, president of Ford, determined to regain Ford's share of the market by having a new subcompact, the Pinto, in production by 1970. Design on the subcompact automobile began in 1968. Mr. Iacocca conceived the project whose objective was to build a car at or below 2,000 pounds to sell for no more than $2,000.[2] The feasibility study for the Pinto was conducted under the supervision of Mr. Robert Alexander, Vice President of Car Engineering. Ford's Product Planning Committee—whose members included Mr. Iacocca, Mr. Alexander, and Mr. Harold MacDonald, Ford's Group Vice President of Car Engineering—approved the Pinto's concept and made the decision to go forward with the project. During the course of the project, regular product review meetings were held which were chaired by Mr. MacDonald and attended by Mr. Alexander. As the project approached actual production, the engineers responsible for the components of the project "signed off" to their immediate supervisors who in turn "signed off" to their superiors and so on up the chain of command until the entire project was approved for public release by Vice Presidents Alexander and MacDonald and ultimately by Mr. Iacocca.[3]

[1] *Grimshaw v. Ford Motor Co.*, App., 174 Cal. Rptr. 348, p. 388; here and below all statements with citations to the *Grimshaw* case are restatements of the allegations described as findings of fact by the court in the *Grimshaw* case.

[2] *Grimshaw v. Ford Motor Co.*, App., 174 Cal. Rptr. 348, p. 360.

[3] *Grimshaw v. Ford Motor Co.*, App., 174 Cal. Rptr. 348, p. 361.

Although the normal preproduction testing and development of an automobile takes about forty-three months, the Ford teams managed to bring the Pinto to the production stage in a little over two years. Because the Pinto was a rush project, styling preceded engineering and dictated engineering design to a greater degree than usual. Among other things, the Pinto's styling required that the gas tank be placed behind the rear axle, leaving only nine or ten inches of "crush space" between the rear axle and rear bumper. In addition, the differential housing had an exposed flange and a line of exposed bolt heads that were sufficient to puncture a gas tank driven forward against the differential upon rear impact.[4]

Among the reports forwarded up the chain of command by Ford's engineers were several describing the results of crash tests conducted on early prototypes of the Pinto.[5] These tests were later described in court as follows:

> These prototypes as well as two production Pintos were crash tested by Ford to determine, among other things, the integrity of the fuel system in rear-end accidents. . . . Prototypes struck from the rear with a moving barrier at 21-miles-per-hour caused the fuel tank to be driven forward and to be punctured, causing fuel leakage. . . . A production Pinto crash tested at 21-miles-per-hour into a fixed barrier caused the fuel neck to be torn from the gas tank and the tank to be punctured by a bolt head on the differential housing. In at least one test, spilled fuel entered the driver's compartment . . .[6]

In a crash stray sparks could ignite any spilling gasoline and engulf the car in flames. According to Mr. Harley Copp, then a Ford engineer and executive in charge of the crash testing program, the test results were forwarded to the highest level of Ford's management.[7] Other test results conducted by Ford showed that when rubber bladders were installed in the tank or when the fuel tank was installed above rather than behind the rear axle, test vehicles could pass the 20-mile-per-hour rear impact test.

Nonetheless, the company went on with production of the Pinto as designed, since it met all applicable federal safety standards then in effect and was comparable in safety to other cars then being produced. Moreover, a later Ford company study released by J. C. Echold, director of automotive safety for Ford, claimed that an improved design that would have rendered the Pinto and other similar cars less likely to burst into flames on collision would not be cost-effective for society. Entitled "Fatalities Associated with Crash Induced Fuel Leakage and Fires," the Ford study (which was intended to counter the prospect of stiffer government regulations on gasoline tank design) showed that the costs of the design improvement ($11 per vehicle) far outweighed its social benefits:

> The total benefit is shown to be just under $50 million, while the associated cost is $137 million. Thus the cost is almost three times the benefits, even using a number of highly favorable benefit assumptions.

[4] *Grimshaw v. Ford Motor Co.*, App., 174 Cal. Rptr. 348, p. 360.
[5] *Grimshaw v. Ford Motor Co.*, App., 174 Cal. Rptr. 348, p. 361.
[6] *Grimshaw v. Ford Motor Co.*, App., 174 Cal. Rptr. 348, p. 360.
[7] *Grimshaw v. Ford Motor Co.*, App., 174 Cal. Rptr. 348, p. 361.

Benefits:

Savings	—	180 burn deaths, 180 serious burn injuries, 2,100 burned vehicles.
Unit cost	—	$200,000 per death, $67,000 per injury, $700 per vehicle.
Total Benefits	—	180 × ($200,000) plus 180 × ($ 67,000) plus 2,100 × ($ 700) = $49.15 million

Costs:

Sales	—	11 million cars, 1.5 million light trucks
Unit Cost	—	$11 per car, $11 per truck
Total Costs	—	11,000,000 × ($11) plus 1,500,000 × ($11) = $137 million

[From memorandum attached to statement of J. C. Echold][8]

Ford's estimate of the number of deaths, injuries, and vehicles that would be lost as a result of fires from fuel leakage were based on statistical studies. The $200,000 value attributed to the loss of life was based on a study of the National Highway Traffic Safety Administration, which broke down the estimated social costs of a death as follows:[9]

Component	**1971 Costs**
Future Productivity Losses	
Direct	$132,000
Indirect	41,300
Medical Costs	
Hospital	700
Other	425
Property Damage	1,500
Insurance Administration	4,700
Legal and Court	3,000
Employer Losses	1,000
Victim's Pain and Suffering	10,000
Funeral	900
Assets (Lost Consumption)	5,000
Miscellaneous Accident Cost	200
Total per Fatality:	$200,725

At an April 1971 product review meeting chaired by Mr. MacDonald and attended by Mr. Alexander, those present received and discussed a report containing

[8] Ralph Drayton, "One Manufacturer's Approach to Automobile Safety Standards," *CTLA News*, VIII, no. 2 (February 1968): 11.

[9] Mark Dowie, "Pinto Madness," *Mother Jones* (September/October 1977), p. 28.

much the same materials as those later incorporated into the study entitled "Fatalities Associated with Crash Induced Fuel Leakage and Fires."[10]

On May 28, 1972, Mrs. Lily Gray was driving a six-month-old Pinto on Interstate 15 near San Bernardino, California. In the car with her was Richard Grimshaw, a thirteen-year-old boy. Mrs. Gray was a unique person. She had adopted two girls, worked forty hours a week (earning $20,000 a year), was den-mother for all the teenagers in the neighborhood, sold refreshments at the Bobby Sox games, and had maintained a happy marriage of twenty-two years.

Mrs. Gray stopped in San Bernardino for gasoline, got back onto the freeway (Interstate 15) and proceeded toward her destination at sixty to sixty-five miles per hour. As she approached the Route 30 off-ramp, where traffic was congested, she moved from the outer fast lane to the middle lane of the freeway. Shortly after this lane change, the Pinto suddenly stalled and coasted to a halt in the middle lane. A car traveling immediately behind the Pinto was able to swerve and pass it. But the driver of a 1962 Ford Galaxie was unable to avoid colliding with the Pinto. Before impact the Galaxie had been braked to a speed of from twenty-eight to thirty-seven miles per hour.

At the moment of impact, the Pinto caught fire and its interior burst into flames. The crash had driven the Pinto's gas tank forward and punctured it against the flange on the differential housing. Fuel spraying into the passenger compartment immediately ignited. By the time the Pinto came to rest, both occupants had suffered serious burns. When they tumbled from the Pinto, their clothing was almost completely burned off. Mrs. Gray died a few days later. Although badly disfigured, Grimshaw managed to survive with severe burns over 90 percent of his body. He subsequently underwent over seventy painful operations and skin grafts and would have to undergo additional surgeries over the next ten years. He lost portions of several fingers on his left hand and portions of his left ear, while his face required many skin grafts from various parts of his body.[11] As of 1978, at least fifty-three persons had died in accidents involving Pinto fires and many more had been severely burnt.[12]

1. Using the Ford figures given in the memo calculate the probability that a vehicle would be involved in a burn death (that is, the number of burn deaths divided by the total number of cars and trucks sold). In your opinion, is there a limit to the amount that Ford should have been willing to invest in order to reduce this figure to zero? If your answer is yes, then determine from your answer what price you place on life and compare your price to the government's. If your answer is no, then discuss whether your answer implies that no matter how much it would take to make such cars, automakers should make cars completely accident-proof.
2. In your opinion, was the management of Ford morally responsible for Mrs. Gray's "burn death"? Explain. Was there something wrong with the utilitarian analysis Ford management used? Explain. Would it have made any difference from a moral point of view if Ford management had informed its buyers of the risks of fire? Explain.

[10] *Grimshaw v. Ford Motor Co.*, App., 174 Cal. Rptr. 348, pp. 369–70.

[11] *Grimshaw v. Ford Motor Co.*, App., 174 Cal. Rptr. 348, p. 359.

[12] "Ford Fights Pinto Case: Jury Gives 128 Million," *Auto News*, 13 February 1978, pp. 3, 44.

3. Suppose that you were on Mr. J. C. Echold's staff and before the Pinto reached the production stage you were assigned the task of writing an analysis of the overall desirability of producing and marketing the Pinto as planned. One part of your report is to be subtitled "ethical and social desirability." What would you write in this part?

A South African Investment

In April 1977, the Interfaith Center on Corporate Responsibility announced that some of its subscribing members owned stock in Texaco, Inc. and in Standard Oil Co. of California (SoCal), and that these members would introduce shareholders' resolutions at the next annual stockholders' meeting of Texaco and SoCal that would require that these companies and their affiliates terminate their operations in South Africa. The effort to get Texaco and SoCal out of South Africa was primarily directed and coordinated by Tim Smith, project director of the Interfaith Center on Corporate Responsibility. The stockholders' resolution that Tim Smith would have the Interfaith shareholders introduce at the annual meetings of Texaco and SoCal read as follows:

> Whereas in South Africa the black majority is controlled and oppressed by a white minority that comprises 18 percent of the population;
> Whereas South Africa's apartheid system legalizes racial discrimination in all aspects of life and deprives the black population of their most basic human rights, such as, Africans cannot vote, cannot collectively bargain, must live in racially segregated areas, are paid grossly discriminatory wages, are assigned 13 percent of the land while 87 percent of the land is reserved for the white population;
> Whereas black opposition to apartheid and black demands for full political, legal, and social rights in their country has risen dramatically within the last year;
> Whereas widespread killing, arrests, and repression have been the response of the white South African government to nationwide demonstrations for democratic rights;
> Whereas Prime Minister Vorster has openly declared his intention to maintain apartheid and deny political rights to South African blacks;
> Whereas we believe that U.S. business investments in the Republic of South Africa, including our company's operations, provide significant economic support and moral legitimacy to South Africa's apartheid government;
> Therefore be it resolved: that the shareholders request the Board of Directors to establish the following as corporate policy:
>
> > "Texaco [and Standard Oil of California] and any of its subsidiaries or affiliates shall terminate its present operations in the Republic of South Africa as expeditiously as possible unless and until the South African government has committed itself to ending the legally enforced form of racism called apartheid and has taken meaningful steps toward the achievement of full political, legal, and social rights for the majority population (African, Asian, colored)."

The resolution was occasioned by the fact that Texaco and SoCal were the joint owners of Caltex Petroleum Co. (each owns 50 percent of Caltex), an affiliate that operates oil refineries in South Africa and that in 1973 was worth about $100 million. In 1975 Caltex announced that it was planning to expand its refinery plant in Milnerto, South Africa, from a capacity of 58,000 barrels a day to an increased capacity of 108,000 barrels a day. The expansion would cost $135 million and would increase South Africa's *total* refining capacity by 11 percent. Caltex would be obliged by South African law to bring in at least $100 million of these investment funds from outside the country.

The management of Texaco and SoCal were both opposed to the resolution that would have required them to pull out of South Africa and to abandon their Caltex expansion plans, which, by some estimates, promised an annual return of 20 percent on the original investment. They therefore recommended that stockholders vote against the resolution. The managements of both Texaco and SoCal argued that Caltex was committed to improving the economic working conditions of its black employees and that their continued presence in South Africa did not constitute an "endorsement" of South Africa's "policies." The commitment of Caltex to improving the condition of its employees was evidenced, the companies claimed, by its adherence to the 1977 "Sullivan principles."

Early in 1977, Caltex was one of several dozen corporations that had adopted a code of conduct drafted by the Reverend Dr. Leon Sullivan, a civil rights activist who is a minister of Philadelphia's large Zion Baptist Church. The Code was based on these six principles that the corporations affirmed for their plants:[1]

I. Nonsegregation of the races in all eating, comfort, and work facilities.
II. Equal and fair employment practices for all employees.
III. Equal pay for all employees doing equal or comparable work for the same period of time.
IV. Initiation of and development of training programs that will prepare, in substantial numbers, blacks and other nonwhites for supervisory, administrative, clerical, and technical jobs.
V. Increasing the number of blacks and other nonwhites in management and supervisory positions.
VI. Improving the quality of employees' lives outside the work environment in such areas as housing, transportation, schooling, recreation, and health facilities.

> These companies agree to further implement these principles. Where implementation requires a modification of existing South African working conditions, we will seek such modification through appropriate channels.

The code had been approved by the South African government since the principles were to operate within "existing South African working conditions," that is, within South African laws. South African laws requiring separate facilities and South African laws prohibiting blacks from becoming apprentices, for example, would continue to apply where in force.[2] Also, the principle of equal pay for equal work would probably require few changes where blacks and whites did not have equal work.

Caltex, however, was apparently committed to improving the economic position of its workers. It had moved 40 percent of its 742 black workers into refinery jobs formerly held by whites, although most blacks had remained in the lower

[1] Jack Magarrell, "U.S. Adopts Stand on Apartheid: Backed on Many Campuses," *The Chronicle of Higher Education*, 12 March 1979.

[2] See Herman Nickel, "The Case for Doing Business in South Africa," *Fortune*, 19 June 1968, p. 72.

six job categories (a total of 29 had moved into the top four white-collar and skilled categories).[3] The company had also kept its wages well above the averages determined in studies conducted by the South African University of Port Elizabeth. A basic argument that Texaco and SoCal advanced in favor of remaining in South Africa, then, was that their continued presence in South Africa advanced the economic welfare of blacks.

> Texaco believes that continuation of Caltex's operations in South Africa is in the best interests of Caltex's employees of all races in South Africa. . . . In management's opinion, if Caltex were to withdraw from South Africa in an attempt to achieve political changes in that country, as the proposal directs, . . . such withdrawal would endanger prospects for the future of all Caltex employees in South Africa regardless of race. We are convinced that the resulting dislocation and hardship would fall most heavily on the nonwhite communities. In this regard, and contrary to the implications of the stockholders' statement, Caltex employment policies include equal pay for equal work and the same level of benefit plans for all employees as well as a continuing and successful program to advance employees to positions of responsibility on the basis of ability, not race. [Statement of Texaco management][4]

It is undeniable that the presence of foreign corporations in South Africa had helped to improve the real earnings of black industrial workers. Between 1970 and 1975, black incomes in Johannesburg rose 118 percent, while between 1975 and 1980 black per capita income was expected to rise 30 percent. In addition, the gap between black and white incomes in South Africa had narrowed. Between 1970 and 1976, the gap in industry narrowed from 1:5.8 to 1:4.4; in construction from 1:6.6 to 1:5.2; and in the mining sector from 1:19.8 to 1:7.7.[5] If the flow of foreign investment came to a halt, however, the South African normal yearly growth rate of 6 percent would drop to about 3 percent and the results would undoubtedly hit blacks the hardest.[6] Unemployment would rise (American companies employ 60,000 blacks), and whatever benefits blacks had gained would be lost.

Tim Smith and the Interfaith stockholders were aware of these facts. The basic issue for them, however, was not whether Caltex adhered to the six Sullivan principles or whether its presence in South Africa improved the economic position of blacks:

> The issue in South Africa at this time is black political power; it is not slightly higher wages or better benefits or training programs, unless these lead to basic social change. As one South African church leader put it, "These [six] principles attempt to polish my chains and make them more comfortable. I want to cut my chains and cast them away." . . . We must look not just at wages but at the transfer of technology, the taxes paid to South Africa, the effect of U.S. foreign policy, and the provision of strategic products to the racist government. If these criteria become part of the "principles" of U.S. investors, it should be clear that on balance many of the corpora-

[3] Investor Responsibility Research Center, *Analysis E Supplement No. 9*, 7 April 1977, p. E 114.

[4] *Texaco Proxy Statement*, 1977, item 3.

[5] Nickel, "Doing Business in South Africa," p. 64.

[6] *Ibid.*, p. 63.

> tions strengthen and support white minority rule. This form of support should be challenged, and American economic complicity in apartheid ended. [Statement of Tim Smith][7]

In short, the issue was one of human rights. The white South African government was committed to denying blacks their basic rights, and the continued presence of American companies supported this system of white rule.

> Nonwhites in South Africa are rightless persons in the land of their birth. . . . [The black African] has no rights in "white areas." He cannot vote, cannot own land, and may not have his family with him unless he has government permission. . . . The two major black political parties have been banned and hundreds of persons detained for political offenses . . . strikes by Africans are illegal, and meaningful collective bargaining is outlawed. . . . by investing in South Africa, American companies inevitably strengthen the status quo of [this] white supremacy. . . . The leasing of a computer, the establishment of a new plant, the selling of supplies to the military—all have political overtones. . . . And among the country's white community, the overriding goal of politics is maintenance of white control. In the words of Prime Minister John Vorster during the 1970 election campaign: "We are building a nation for whites only. Black people are entitled to political rights but only over their own people—not my people." [Statement of Tim Smith][8]

There was no doubt that the continuing operations of Caltex provided some economic support for the South African government. South African law required oil refineries in South Africa to set aside a percentage of their oil for government purchase. In 1975, about 7 percent of Caltex's oil sales went to the government of South Africa. As a whole, the South African economy relied on oil for 25 percent of its energy needs. Moreover, Caltex represented almost 11 percent of the total U.S. investment in South Africa. If Caltex closed down its operations in South Africa, this would certainly have had great impact on the economy, especially if other companies then lost confidence in the South African economy and subsequently also withdrew from South Africa. Finally, Caltex also supported the South African government through corporate taxes.

At each of the Texaco and SoCal shareholders' meetings held in May, 1977, the resolutions of the Interfaith Center on Corporate Responsibility received less than 5 percent of the shares voted. The Caltex plant in South Africa completed its expansion as planned. But conditions in South Africa continued to deterioriate for the oil industry.

In 1978, the OPEC nations announced that all of their members had at last unanimously agreed to embargo oil shipments to South Africa. Concerned about the increasingly sensitive vulnerability of its strategic oil supplies, the South African government, now under the leadership of Prime Minister P. W. Botha, responded by tightening its regulation of the oil industry. The National Supplies Procurement Act was strengthened to give the government authority to force foreign-owned companies to produce strategically important petroleum products. The Act also

[7] Timothy Smith, "Whitewash for Apartheid from Twelve U.S. Firms," *Business and Society Review*, Summer 1977, pp. 59, 60.

[8] Timothy Smith, "South Africa: The Churches vs. the Corporations," *Business and Society Review*, 1971, pp. 54, 55, 56.

prohibited oil companies from restricting sales of oil products to any credit-worthy customers, including any branch of government. And the Official Secrets Act made it a crime for anyone within South Africa to release any information whatsoever on the petroleum industry or the operations of any oil enterprise.

Because it was important that foreign companies remain in South Africa, however, the government became more receptive to the lobbying efforts of American companies. Business lobbying efforts were instrumental in the 1979 repeal of laws that had denied legal status to unions for Africans and of laws that hindered Africans from being trained or promoted for skilled jobs. Starting in the early 1980s, American businesses began lobbying for the repeal of the hated "influx control laws" (laws requiring black Africans within white South Africa to carry a "pass book" detailing their residence and employer and prohibiting non-employed black Africans from remaining in white South Africa for longer than seventy-two hours) and for granting blacks some form of political representation in the South African government. Several of the social aspects of apartheid (such as the "Immorality Act" which made interracial sexual intercourse a criminal offense until 1985 and the "petty apartheid laws" which required enforced segregation of the races) were eventually lifted or attenuated.

Although the 1977 defeat of their resolution was diasppointing, antiapartheid activists determined to press on with their battle. In May 1983, activists introduced another shareholder resolution to be considered at the Texaco and SoCal shareholders' meetings, this time asking that Caltex not sell petroleum products to the police or military of South Africa. The managers of both Texaco and SoCal objected to the resolution, claiming that this new resolution asked them to violate the laws of South Africa. According to the managers, South Africa's National Supplies Procurement Act gave the South African government the authority to require any business to supply it with goods. Moreover, the Price Control Act of 1964 also gave the government the authority to prohibit companies from placing restrictions on the sale of their goods. The South African government had exercised this authority, the managers said, when it earlier had "directed Caltex to refrain from imposing any conditions or reservations of whatever nature in respect to the use, resale, or further distribution of petroleum products and, also, from refusing to sell except subject to such conditions."[9] Consequently, they held, the resolution in effect asked them to commit a serious crime: "It would be a crime under South Africa's law were Caltex-South Africa to undertake a commitment to not supply petroleum products for use by the South African military or any other branch of the South African government."[10] The Securities and Exchange Commission (SEC), which regulates the submission of shareholders' resolutions, agreed with the companies. The SEC therefore allowed SoCal to remove the resolution from its proxy ballots on the grounds that the resolution might be asking the company to do something illegal. Although Texaco was allowed to do the same, Texaco managers decided to let the resolution be voted upon by its shareholders.

At the May, 1983 shareholders' meetings, the resolution received the support of 7.4 percent of the Texaco shares voted, an unusually high level of support, but not sufficient to require the company to implement the resolution.

[9] Investor Responsibility Research Center, Inc., *Corporate Activity in South Africa*, 1984, Analysis G, supplement no. 2, April 10, 1984.

[10] *The Corporate Examiner*, vol. 14, no. 5, 1985, p. 2.

Encouraged by the gradually increasing levels of shareholder support their resolutions were drawing, the anti-apartheid forces were more determined than ever to press on with their efforts. In June, 1983, Bishop Desmond Tutu, a moderate black South African religious leader, had outlined four principles that he urged foreign companies in South Africa to follow. Foreign companies, he said, should tell the government of South Africa that they would remain in the country only if they were permitted to (1) ensure their black workers could live with their families, (2) recognize black labor unions, (3) oppose influx control over labor, and (4) enforce fair labor practices and invest in black education. These four principles, activists felt, went beyond the Sullivan principles because they required companies to work for change *outside* the company. Consequently, in 1984, and again in 1985, they brought a resolution before the shareholders of Texaco and SoCal (now renamed "Chevron") that read as follows:

> WHEREAS, the system of apartheid assigns the non-white majority of South Africa to perpetual and enforced inferiority by excluding them from full participation in the social and economic system and political processes by which their lives are controlled, thus effectively denying them their economic and political rights;
> WHEREAS, laws such as the Group Areas Act which assigns 87% of the land to 16% of the population and the various influx control laws which regulate the movement of blacks within the country form the basic legal structure of apartheid;
> WHEREAS, Texaco Inc. [and Chevron], through Caltex, is one of the largest U.S. investors in South Africa, with assets of approximately 300 million;
> WHEREAS, Caltex is engaged in South Africa, through subsidiaries in refining crude oil, manufacturing and blending lubricants, and marketing petroleum products, including retail gasoline sales. Caltex holds an estimated 20 percent share of the petroleum market in South Africa. The oil industry plays an extremely strategic role in South Africa today, and oil is deemed a "munition of war" under South African Law;
> WHEREAS, the operations of Caltex in South Africa are subject to the National Supplies Procurement Act No. 89 of 1970, and the Price Control Act No. 25 of 1964. Caltex has been given a directive under these laws that it may not refuse to supply petroleum products to any credit-worthy South African citizen or organization, and the Government has power to demand the supply and delivery of such products. The South African Government has directed Caltex to refrain from imposing any conditions or reservations of whatever nature in respect of the use, resale or further distribution of petroleum products. Caltex cannot impose any restrictions on its sales to the military or police;
> WHEREAS, the size of Texaco's investment, strategic role in the economy, and sales to the military and police in South Africa invest Texaco with special social responsibility for the impact of its operations in South Africa;
> WHEREAS, Texaco has stated that "We believe our affiliate is making an important positive contribution to improving economic and social opportunities for its present and future employees";
> WHEREAS, Bishop Tutu, General Secretary of the South African Council of Churches, recently outlined several conditions of the investment which would enable Caltex and other U.S. companies to make such a "positive contribution to improving economic and social opportunities," these conditions include:
>
> 1. House the workforce in family-type accomodations as family units near the place of work of the breadwinner.
> 2. Recognizing black trade unions as long as they are representative.
> 3. Recognizing the right of the worker to sell labor wherever the best price can

be obtained, calling for labor mobility, and opposing any ultimate implementation of influx control, and

4. Enforcing fair labor practices and investing massively in black education and training.

RESOLVED, Shareholders request the Board of Directors to:

1. Implement and/or increase activity on each of the four Tutu conditions and report to shareholders annually how the Company's presence is, on balance, a positive influence for improving the quality of life for non-white South Africans; Or,
2. If the South African Government does not within 24 months take steps to rescind the Group Areas Act and the influx control laws as steps toward the dismantling of apartheid, begin the process of withdrawal from South Africa.

Although the resolutions failed in both years, they were again supported by a surprisingly large number of votes. By the end of 1985, it was clear that South Africa was at a crisis point and that the pressure on companies would continue.[11] Hundreds of blacks had been killed in the unrest that had erupted in September 1984 when a new constitution had established a three-part government with representation for whites, Indians, and coloreds, but not for blacks. In 1985 martial law was imposed on the country. Freed from the fear of civil restraints, the police brutally abused blacks. Thousands were imprisoned without charges, dozens were shot and killed in "incidents." Black townships assigned as living areas for blacks in white South Africa became dangerous "no go" areas for whites. The press and television were banned from photographing "any public disturbance." The economy was undergoing a severe recession. Sporadic black boycotts of white businesses broke out. Black unemployment climbed to 35 percent, while the costs of basic goods and services rose sharply. In an effort to show that black Africans were not completely disenfranchised, Prime Minister Botha had earlier established elected community councils to govern the black townships. But in most townships council members were forced to resign under pressure from other blacks who held that the councils were a cover for the basic fact that blacks still had no political rights in the three-part government that had been imposed on them.

Several major Western nations imposed economic sanctions against South Africa, and Western banks began to refuse to renew loans to private companies as they came due. The South African government responded by imposing a moratorium on the repayment of its foreign debt on September 1, 1985. The government also announced that foreign companies wishing to sell their assets in South Africa would have to be paid in "financial rands," special currency that could not be converted into a foreign currency unless another foreign investor wanted to buy the South African assets. It thus became more difficult for firms to leave South Africa.

1. In your judgment, were the possible utilitarian benefits of building the Caltex plant in 1977 more important than the possible violations of moral rights and of justice that may be involved? Justify your answer fully by identifying the possible benefits

[11] Investor Responsibility Research Center, Inc., *U.S. Corporate Activity in South Africa*, 1986 Analysis B, 28 January 1986.

and the possible violations of rights and justice that you believe may be associated with the building of the plant, and explaining which you think are more important.

2. If you were a stockholder in Texaco or Standard Oil (now named Chevron), how do you believe you ought to vote on the three kinds of stockholder's resolutions that were proposed (the first asking Caltex to terminate its operations, the second asking Caltex not to sell to the military or police of South Africa, and the third asking Caltex to implement the Tutu principles)? Justify each of your answers fully.
3. What kind of responses should the *managers* of Texaco and SoCal have made to each of the three resolutions? Justify your answer fully.
4. In your judgment, does the management of a company have any responsibilities (i.e., duties) beyond ensuring a high return for its stockholders? Should the management of a company look primarily to the law and to the rate of return on its investment as the ultimate criteria for deciding what investments it should make? Why or why not?

Asbestos in Industry

Clarence Borel began working as an installer of industrial insulation in 1936, a job that necessarily exposed him to heavy concentrations of asbestos dust. Among the insulating materials with which he worked were asbestos products manufactured by Johns-Manville Corporation and other asbestos companies. At the end of a day working with asbestos materials, Borel's clothes would be covered with the dangerous dust:

> You just move them just a little and there is going to be dust, and I blowed this dust out of my nostrils by handfuls at the end of the day, trying to use water too, I even used Mentholatum in my nostrils to keep some of the dust from going down in my throat, but it is impossible to get rid of all of it. Even your clothes just stay dusty continually unless you blow it off with an air hose . . . I knew the dust was bad, but we used to talk [about] it among the insulators, [about] how bad was this dust, could it give you TB, could it give you this, and everyone was saying no, that dust don't hurt you, it dissolves as it hits your lungs . . . There was always a question, you just never knew how dangerous it was. I never did know really. If I had known, I would have gotten out of it. (Statement of Clarence Borel)[1]

But Borel did not ''get out of it.'' Shortly after making the statement above, Borel died of a form of lung cancer known as mesothelioma that had been caused by asbestosis.

Asbestosis is a scarring of the lung tissue that has been associated with 10 percent of the deaths among asbestos workers. The onset of asbestosis is usually gradual, becoming noticeable only when a period of ten to thirty years elapses after the initial exposure. During this period the worker will feel, and will be diagnosed as, healthy. Once inhaled, however, asbestos fibers can remain permanently in the lungs, causing a tissue reaction that progresses slowly and apparently irreversibly. By the time the disease is diagnosable, a decade or more has elapsed since the date of the injurious exposure; each exposure to asbestos dust can cause additional tissue changes. The disease gradually makes breathing so difficult that

[1] *Borel* v. *Fiberboard Paper Products Corporation, et al.*, 493 F. 2d 1076 (1973), p. 1082.

victims become pulmonary cripples incapable of any exertion, even climbing stairs. Ten percent of all asbestosis victims die as a result of secondary lung complications. Mesothelioma is a highly malignant and particularly painful cancer of the chest linings that is associated exclusively with asbestos exposure and is usually fatal within a year after symptoms appear. People with such lung cancers become suddenly emaciated, after having been vigorous, productive individuals. Like asbestosis, mesotheliomas take two or more decades to appear, and during these years the future victim will feel and be diagnosed as normal. Many cancers caused by current work with asbestos will not appear until the year 2000. Studies have shown that cigarette smoking and earlier lung disease can substantially increase a person's risk of contracting lung cancer from asbestos exposure.

Asbestos is a grayish white fibrous mineral that is heat resistant and possesses remarkable strength and flexibility. These qualities have rendered it virtually irreplaceable in our society as an electrical and heat insulator. Over three thousand products commonly found in homes and factories contain asbestos, including electrical insulation, fireproofing, brakedrums, filters, acoustical tiles, potholders, and so on. As a result, about 4 million workers (and innumerable consumers) have been exposed to heavy concentrations of asbestos in the United States alone since the 1940s. Today between 1.5 and 2.5 million U.S. workers are employed in environments with significant asbestos exposure. Since about 35 percent of heavily exposed asbestos workers are killed by asbestos-related diseases, about 1.5 million of these workers will die as victims of asbestos exposure over the next three decades.[2]

Johns-Manville is the largest producer of asbestos fiber in the United States. In 1979 it had sales of $168.2 million worth of asbestos fibers, plus sales of several million more dollars worth of asbestos paper and textiles, asbestos cement, and asbestos cement products. The company conducts mining and manufacturing operations in the United States, Canada, and twelve other countries. Johns-Manville was incorporated in New York in 1926 and has been dealing in asbestos products since the 1920s. Net sales in 1979 were $2.28 billion, up from $.58 billion in 1970. Total (pretax) profits in 1979 were $217.8 million, up from $55.6 million in 1970. Today Johns-Manville employs about 32,500 workers.

It is difficult to say when Johns-Manville first became aware of the danger of asbestosis. The first medical reference to asbestos-related diseases among American workers appeared in 1918, in a monograph published by the U.S. Bureau of Labor Statistics. This paper noted that insurance company records showed increased mortality among asbestos workers and commented that these companies were now reluctant to insure them. During the period 1924–1929 a series of medical studies of asbestosis among textile factory workers appeared in British journals. These reports stimulated Johns-Manville to commission two studies on the effects of asbestos. The first of these studies, which Dr. Leroy V. Gardner carried out at the Saranac Laboratory in New York, was part of a series of experiments on animals that continued for several years. On November 20, 1936, Mr. Brown,

[2] U.S. Congress, House, *Asbestos-related Occupational Diseases: Hearings before the Subcommittee on Compensation, Health, and Safety of the Committee on Education and Labor*, 94th Congress, 2nd session, 23 and 24 October; 13 and 14 November 1978, pp. 132–35. Hereafter cited as "Asbestos Hearings."

head of the legal department of Johns-Manville, wrote to Dr. Gardner clarifying the terms of their agreement to sponsor these animal studies:

> It is our further understanding that the results obtained will be considered the property of those who are advancing the required funds, who will determine to what extent and in what manner they shall be made public. In the event it is deemed desirable that the results be made public, the manuscript of your study will be submitted to us for approval prior to publication.[3]

Eventually, Dr. Gardner dropped from the study.

The second study, a health survey of asbestos workers that Dr. A. J. Lanza carried out for the asbestos industry, was ready for publication in 1934. Mr. Hobart, a private attorney, was asked to review Lanza's article for the industry before it was published. On December 15, Mr. Hobart wrote to Mr. Brown (head of Johns-Manville's legal department) saying that the Lanza report should be changed before publication. In particular, any comparisons between asbestosis and silicosis (a recognized occupational disease) should be eliminated. The letter read, in part, as follows:

> And if it is the policy of Johns-Manville to oppose any [legislative] bill that attempted to include asbestos as compensable, it would be very helpful to have an official report to show that there is a substantial difference between asbestosis and silicosis, and, by the same token, it would be troublesome if an official report should appear from which the conclusion might be drawn that there is very little, if any, difference between the two diseases.[4]

On December 21, Mr. Brown sent these and other requests for changes to Dr. Lanza in a letter that read, in part, as follows:

> I trust that you will give his [Hobart's] comments and suggestions, as well as those mentioned in my letter of December 10th, your most serious consideration. I am sure that you understand fully that no one in our organization is suggesting for a moment that you alter by one dot or title any scientific facts or inevitable conclusions revealed or justified by your preliminary survey. All we ask is that all of the favorable aspects of the survey be included and that none of the unfavorable be unintentionally pictured in darker tones than the circumstances justify. I feel confident we can depend upon you and Dr. McConnell to give us this "break."[5]

The Lanza report was published in 1935, with a few (but not all) of the changes for which Johns-Manville had asked.[6] The essence of the article was not changed: of 126 randomly sampled asbestos workers employed three years or more, 106 had abnormal lung findings.[7]

[3] *Ibid.*, p. 31.

[4] *Ibid.*, pp. 28–29.

[5] *Ibid.*, pp. 29 and 643.

[6] *Ibid.*, 643.

[7] A. J. Lanza et al., "Effects of the Inhalation of Asbestos on the Lungs of Asbestos Workers," *Public Health Reports*, 4 January, 1935, pp. 1–12.

The number of employees who were beginning to succumb to asbestosis had started to pose a problem for asbestos manufacturers, since some of these employees or their survivors were now suing for compensation. A 1935 memorandum from Mr. Brown (of Johns-Manville) reported on an industry meeting held on January 15, 1935, at which the participants had discussed their emerging problems with asbestosis-afflicted workers and had also discussed strategies for dealing with these problems. The memo read in part:

> It appeared that among the problems common to all industry were the following:
>
> 1. The menace of ambulance-chasing lawyers in combination with unscrupulous doctors. The uncertainties surrounding diagnosis of any of the various forms of pneumoconiosis are so many that a question of fact is presented in every case. Expert testimony can be produced by both plaintiff and defendant, and . . . the jury is not likely to favor the opinion of the experts produced by the employers. . . .
> 2. One of the speakers stated that "the strongest bulwark against future disaster for industry is the enactment of properly drawn occupational disease legislation." Such legislation would (a) eliminate the jury and empower a medical board to pass upon the existence of the disease and the extent of the disability; (b) eliminate the shyster lawyer and the quack doctor, since fees would be strictly limited by law.[8]

By the latter 1930s, several dozen articles had been published suggesting that, although asbestosis was caused by inhaling asbestos dust, the danger might be controlled by maintaining a low level of exposure. An extensive study by the U.S. Public Health Service published in 1938, in fact, suggested that daily exposure to asbestos dust concentrations of up to five million particles per cubic foot of air would be safe as a "tentative standard."[9] The first large-scale survey of asbestos insulation applicators (as opposed to workers in asbestos mines and factories) was published by Dr. Fleisher and others in 1946. The authors examined large numbers of insulation applicators, 95 percent of whom had worked in eastern Navy shipyards for less than ten years, and found only three cases of asbestosis. They concluded that "asbestos covering of naval vessels is a relatively safe operation," especially since the measured exposures to asbestos dust for the insulation workers were with one exception below what the 1938 U.S. Public Health Service study had proposed as a tentative standard of safety.[10]

In 1947, the American Conference of Governmental Industrial Hygienists recommended that employers use the 1938 proposed standard and limit the work environment to no more than five million particles of asbestos dust per cubic foot of air. Nearly all workers, it suggested, could be repeatedly exposed to these concentrations day after day without adverse effect. Except for this recommendation, the government did very little about asbestosis during the next several years: Regulations were few and government inspections and supervision were infrequent.

[8] *Asbestos Hearings*, pp. 94–95.

[9] W. C. Dressen, et al., "A Study of Asbestosis in the Asbestos Textile Industry," *Public Health Bulletin*, no. 241 (1938).

[10] W. E. Fleisher, et al., "A Health Survey of Pipe Covering Operations in Constructing Naval Vessels," *Journal of Industrial Hygiene and Toxicology*, January 1946.

Johns-Manville itself did not conduct any more major tests to determine the hazards of its products.

By the early 1960s, several more reports had been published indicating that the incidence of asbestos-related disease was now climbing at an alarming rate. Then, in 1965, I. J. Selikoff and his colleagues published a definitive study on asbestosis entitled "The Occurrence of Asbestosis Among Insulation Workers in the United States."[11] The authors examined 1,522 members of an insulation workers union and found that 44 percent of those who had been exposed to asbestos for ten to nineteen years had asbestosis; 73 percent of those who had been exposed twenty to twenty-nine years had it; 87 percent of those who had been exposed thirty to thirty-nine years had it; and 94 percent of those exposed more than 40 years had the disease. The authors concluded that "asbestosis and its complications are significant hazards among insulation workers."

Two years before Dr. Selikoff's study was officially published the substance of his findings had been announced at asbestos industry meetings.[12] Johns-Manville became concerned and, in 1964, for the first time, the company fixed the following warning labels on its asbestos products:

> This product contains asbestos fiber. Inhalation of asbestos in excessive quantities over long periods of time may be harmful. If dust is created when this product is handled, avoid breathing the dust. If adequate ventilation control is not possible, wear respirators approved by the U.S. Bureau of Mines for pneumoconiosis-producing dusts.[13]

Johns-Manville did not feel that more warning than this was necessary. According to Dr. Paul Kotin, senior vice-president for health, safety, and environment for Johns-Manville Corporation:

> Johns-Manville was aware of the fact [that] asbestos exposure was potentially a hazard, and Johns-Manville certainly made no secret of the fact it was a hazard. . . . Johns-Manville had the responsibility of informing the people [to whom] it was selling the material [and] . . . it did this. . . . Now, whether Johns-Manville had the responsibility for going to the work site of the insulation manufacturers anymore than the Bayer Corporation has for going into my home when I take an aspirin [is another matter]. Rather, it suffices [to say] . . . in its ads, "avoid excessive use" or, now, "use only as directed." (Statement of Dr. Kotin in 1977)[14]

Clarence Borel never worked for Johns-Manville. Instead, Borel worked for a building contractor who employed him to install asbestos insulation that Johns-Manville (and other firms) had manufactured. Shortly before he died, however, Borel argued that Johns-Manville should be held responsible for his sickness and should pay him compensation. He claimed that the manufacturer knew that asbestos was dangerous and had a duty to inform the final users of its asbestos products that inhaling the dust could be fatal. Johns-Manville also had had a

[11] I. J. Selikoff, et al., "The Occurrence of Asbestosis Among Insulation Workers in the United States, *Annals of the New York Academy of Science*, 132 (1965); 139–55.

[12] *Asbestos Hearings*, pp. 50 and 51.

[13] *Borel* v. *Fiberboard Paper Products*, p. 1104.

[14] *Asbestos Hearings*, p. 116.

duty, he claimed, to test asbestos products more thoroughly in order to ascertain the dangers involved in their use.[15]

Johns-Manville, however, held that Clarence Borel's own employer should have warned him of the dangers of asbestos, or that Borel should have protected himself against the asbestos dust by wearing a mask (or by asking his employer to furnish ventilating blowers), since, in his own words, he "knew the dust was bad."[16] Johns-Manville also claimed that the manufacturers of the asbestos products that Borel handled were not responsible for Borel's disease and death because manufacturers did not know enough about asbestosis during the period in which Borel probably contracted the disease. And last, Johns-Manville claimed, there was no way of knowing whether Borel's disease had been caused by Johns-Manville's products or by asbestos from the products of other manufacturers that Borel had also handled.

Before he died, Borel was asked about the use of respirators. He replied that they were not furnished by his employers during his early work years. Although respirators were later made available on some jobs, insulation workers were not required to wear them and had to make a special request if they wanted one. According to Borel, when respirators were furnished, they were uncomfortable, could not be worn in hot weather, and "you can't breathe with the respirator." Borel further claimed that no respirator in use during his working life could prevent the inhalation of asbestos dust.

Eventually, Borel's estate was awarded $79,436.24 in a verdict that was later upheld by a federal appeals court. But Borel's suit was merely the first of a flood of lawsuits Manville would have to face. In 1977, 445 Texas workers sued for asbestos-related injuries, eventually settling for $20 million.[17] By the middle of 1982 more than 15,000 workers and family members had sued Manville for exposure to asbestos, and 500 new lawsuits were being filed each month. Average settlements were costing the company $40,000—half for the plaintiff and half for medical and legal costs.[18] In interviews for *Environmental Action* and *Village Voice*, Ted Kowalski, a victim of asbestosis who began working for Manville in 1947 and whose wife also has asbestosis, describes his situation and that of fellow workers and their family members who had asbestos-related diseases as follows:

> There's Ronnie, her husband died of mesothelioma; she never worked there, she has it. There's Sue, her husband died from mesothelioma. She has it. Carol has it; her husband Steve is very sick. She's been diagnosed as having asbestosis. . . . I could go on and on. . . . I started off working in the shipping department loading box cars. I was a carton maker in the finishing department. And I was a bandsaw operator. I worked on a crusher. Every job you worked on was dusty. . . . The sun would shine in through the skylight. It was like millions of tiny crystals that would float around. They'd fall in your coffee . . . and you'd drink the stuff . . . We sat down, a bunch of us to eat our lunch and the stuff was there falling. . . . I brought it home on my clothing. My children used to call me 'Daddy the snowman'. . . . They never said you had to wear one [a respirator]. You'd ask for one [when the old one got clogged] and they'd say, 'Geez, what did you do with the other

[15] *Borel* v. *Fiberboard Paper Products*, p. 1086.

[16] *Ibid.*, p. 1091.

[17] "Manville Move Brings Asbestos Battle to Head in Courts and Congress," *Los Angeles Times*, August 27, 1982.

[18] Jim Jubak, "They Are the First," *Environmental Action*, February 1983, p. 12.

one?'. . . . When we were hired, they should have said, 'Hey, there's a risk involved. Do you want to take it with the risk?' And you'd have had the option to say no. . . . [In 1981] on my wife's birthday, my son Teddy had some chest pains. He went to the doctor, and she diagnosed my son as asbestosis. He pulled up to the house. My wife asked, 'How you made out?' and he had tears in his eyes. . . . They didn't tell us, so I carried the disease home to my family. . . . They knew and they didn't tell us. They lied. . . . I pray as I did in the past, each day, and I pray that those who did what they did to us will be punished. (Statement of Ted Kowalski, aged 54)[19]

To cope with the asbestos suits, Manville Corporation filed for protection under Chapter 11 bankruptcy laws on August 26, 1982, which allow a company to reorganize while continuing to operate but which freezes all claims and lawsuits against it. The move astonished the financial and legal community since this was the first time a financially healthy company used bankruptcy to protect itself against future financial problems. Although its financial condition was very strong (with sales of $22 billion, profits of $60.3 million, and a net worth of $1.1 billion in 1981) and it faced no immediate threat of insolvency, Manville's Chief Executive, John McKinnery, claimed that at least 32,000 more suits eventually would be brought against it and settling these future suits would exceed its net worth.[20]

Filing Chapter 11 [bankruptcy] does not mean that the Company is going out of business or that its assets will be liquidated. Thousands of asbestos-health lawsuits are the problem! . . . We're overwhelmed by 16,500 lawsuits . . . with many more projected. The federal government has refused to admit its responsibility to its shipyard workers. Congress has failed to act to provide compensation for claimants. Chapter 11 is the only orderly way for the Company to handle the litigation and treat everybody fairly. . . . To avoid Chapter 11, we would have had to strangle the Company slowly, by deferring maintenance and postponing capital expenditures. We would also have had to cannibalize our good businesses just to keep going. . . . We believe Chapter 11 is the best way to permit the Company to operate normally, providing jobs and useful products, despite all the litigation. Most important, I want to keep our employee's morale up. They've done a bang-up job to keep Manville lean and competitive. . . . The Chapter 11 filing automatically stops all lawsuits pending against us. New lawsuits are also automatically stopped. We hope to establish an effective system to handle these claims in Chapter 11. . . . The largest group now suing us consists of shipyard workers claiming recently manifested injury from asbestos exposure during wartime service, 40 years ago. . . . Over the years, Johns-Manville Corporation's former insurance broker bought insurance coverage for it totaling hundreds of millions of dollars. Right now, however, only one company is paying, and it pays only a small part of each claim. . . . Now, when we need the coverage, with one exception, the insurance companies are reneging. . . . We need an effective, practical national system which delivers maximum payments to injured workers, minimizes the costs of delivering those payments and withholds payments to those with no disability. . . . We had one suit from a plaintiff with doubtful asbestosis who . . . received . . . one and a quarter million dollars. . . . We have seen others totally disabled or in fact dead who

[19] Jim Jubak, "They Are the First," *Environmental Action*, February 1983, pp. 9–14; and Jeff Coplon, "Left in the Dust," *Village Voice*, pp. 1–34.

[20] "Asbestos Maker Files for Bankruptcy, Cites Lawsuits," *Los Angeles Times*, 27 August, 1982, p. 1.

> received no award. . . . This type of toxic tort litigation is an intolerable gambling exercise for both plaintiff and defendant. (Statement of John A. McKinney)[21]

The bankruptcy filing had the immediate effect of freezing all asbestos suits and of ensuring that no new claims could be filed against the company after six months. Filing for bankruptcy also moved all cases then in progress out of state and federal courts which allow both trial by jury and imposition of punitive damages, and into federal bankruptcy court where nonjury trials are standard and where punitive damages are not allowed. Also as a result of the bankruptcy petition, payment on all suits would have to wait until after all secured creditors (such as banks and suppliers) were paid in full, and then they would be paid from whatever assets remained.[22] The bankruptcy filing came under intense fire from critics, who called it a "scam" and who argued it was nothing more than an effort to escape its obligations to the victims.[23]

When large numbers of asbestos lawsuits began to be filed, Manville and other asbestos companies formed the Asbestos Compensation Coalition to lobby Congress to pass legislation that would limit workers' right to sue or that would establish a trust fund to compensate victims with the government putting up half the funds and the companies the other half. Lobbyists for the companies contended that since about half of the suing workers had been injured while working in government shipyards during World War II and the Korean war, the government should pay part of the bill. On September 9, 1982, J. Paul McGrath, Assistant Attorney General of the Department of Justice announced the government's position on the asbestos suits:

> The government's position in the pending asbestos litigations is that it has no tort liability to the victims of asbestos-related diseases. If such victims were exposed to asbestos while they were government employees, then they may be compensated through the Federal Employees Compensation Act. If they were not government employees, then they must look to other workmen's compensation schemes or to litigation against their employer or others for compensation. (statement of J. Paul McGrath)[24]

On July 18, Manville Corporation sued the U.S. government for some of the costs of the asbestos suits. Company lawyers claimed:

> The government knew what was going on in the shipyards. The Navy permitted gross overexposure to asbestos fibers. . . . [A confidential 1941 memo written by the Navy chief of preventive medicine to the service's surgeon general said,] "We are having a considerable amount of work done in asbestos and from my observations,

[21] "Despite Strong Business, Litigation Forces Manville to File for Reorganization," advertisement, *Wall Street Journal*, 27 August 1982, p. 29.

[22] Edward Greer, "Going 'Bankrupt' To Flee the Public," *The Nation*, 16 October 1982, pp. 360–62.

[23] "Manville bankruptcy Scam Under Fire," *The Dispatcher* (published by the International Longshoreman's and Workingman's Union), June 3, 1983; "Manville Thriving in Bankruptcy, Shielded From Asbestos Lawsuits," *New York Times*, 25 August 1983.

[24] Department of Justice, "Statement of J. Paul McGrath Assistant Attorney General Civil Division, Before the Education and Labor Committee Subcommittee on Labor Standards, House of Representatives, Concerning Manville and UNR Bankruptcy, on September 9, 1982"; see also "Government Disavows Any Asbestos Liability," *New York Times*, September 10, 1982.

> I am certain that we are not protecting the men as we should.". . . In its World War II shipbuilding program, the government failed to adhere to the recommended U.S. Public Health Service safety standard, thus causing shipyard workers to be exposed to excessive concentrations of asbestos. . . . Moreover, the government kept knowledge of these excessive exposures confidential. These acts of the United States led to the occurrence of asbestos-related disease in workers who were employed in shipyards during World War II. These workers or their representatives have sued Johns Manville and others to recover damages allegedly incurred as a result of asbestos-related disease although those damages were in fact caused by acts of the United States and not Johns Manville." (Statement of Manville Lawyers)[25]

On July 19, upon receiving word that Manville Corporation intended to sue the federal government for the costs involved in settling the asbestos suits, Assistant Attorney General J. Paul McGrath issued another public statement again setting out the government's position on the suits:

> I have been advised that the Manville Corporation publicly announced today its intent to file yet another suit against the United States in its five year unsuccessful campaign in the press, media, legislature and the courts to shift responsibility for injuries due to exposure to its asbestos products from the corporation to the shoulders of the taxpayers . . . Manville's position . . . is that the taxpayers should bear the burden of any corporate liability because Manville and its predecessor corporations were serving the war effort by meeting the demand of the military for asbestos products. Such a theory ignores the fact that Manville, as a publicly owned corporation was in the business for the profit of its shareholders and was not a public service organization. Indeed, one searches the record in vain for any indication that public welfare, rather than maximization of corporate profit, motivated corporate decisions. As demonstrated in cases tried to date, Manville developed and introduced its asbestos products into the stream of commerce and work sites all over the country. It spurred demand for its products and maintained this demand by withholding vital information about the risks associated with asbestos. Having promoted the use of asbestos products with great corporate success and profit, Manville now, from the haven of bankruptcy court, contends that the taxpayer ought to pay Manville's creditors. Manville's theory has no foundation in reality or in the law and will not justify a shifting of corporate responsibility to the taxpayer. (Statement of Assistant Attorney General J. Paul McGrath)[26]

Judge Burton Lifland of the New York Bankrupty court gave Manville Corporation until February 22, 1983 to present to his court a reorganization plan detailing how the company would reorganize its assets and operations and how it would repay its credit and asbestos claims. In January 1983, G. Earl Parker, a Manville senior vice president charged with developing the reorganization plan, described some of the reorganization proposals it was considering. The proposals included provisions limiting the number of asbestos claims the company would pay and the amount of compensation it would provide each claimant. The company would have no responsibility for any additional claims from asbestos victims that might become aware of their diseases in the future. Compensation would be funded partly by the company (analysts suggested Manville was thinking of paying around

[25] "Asbestos Firm Sues U.S.," *San Jose Mercury*, Wednesday, July 20, 1983, p. 8A.

[26] Department of Justice, Press Release, July 19, 1983.

$500 million), partly by the federal government, and partly by its insurance carriers. These proposals assumed that the bankruptcy court would pressure the government and the insurance carriers into paying part of the asbestos claims. In addition, the proposal would include a provision for binding arbitration in cases where the company or the claimant disagreed over how much compensation was due.[27]

The suggested proposals were not acceptable to lawyers for the asbestos victims. Consequently, Manville managers asked for and received a 90-day extension on the time granted to file a reorganization plan. On May 12, 1983, the company presented a document to the court proposing that the corporation be split into two companies.[28] Manville Two would take over all of the corporation's nonasbestos operations and subsidiaries and its assets would be totally immune from liability for any asbestos injuries. Manville One would include all asbestos operations and all asbestos suits would have to be paid from its assets. Manville Two would make periodic cash payments to Manville One. Asbestos victims would be compensated either on the basis of a "no-fault" schedule that set compensation payments at certain fixed levels, or on the basis of negotiations that would ultimately be arbitrated by the bankruptcy court. No punitive damage claims would be allowed on either basis.

Attorneys for the asbestos victims and Judge Lifland sharply criticized the plan. Judge Lifland protested that the plan "doesn't advance things. It runs counter to a solution. I haven't seen any numbers here." Asbestos attorneys called the plan an "outrageous rehash" and said "it's another footdragging attempt." Judge Lifland instructed Manville's lawyer: "I am giving you two weeks to come up with something we can work with."[29]

By summer of 1985, however, the company still had not come up with a plan that was acceptable to all parties. Then, on Friday August 2, 1985, Manville announced that the company board of directors had approved a reorganization plan which had also been approved by Leon Silverman, a court-appointed lawyer representing future asbestos claimants; Mr. Rosenber, a lawyer representing current asbestos plaintiffs, also announced his approval of the "general outlines" of the plan.[30] The proposal would establish a trust fund that would assume all liability for present and future asbestos injuries through the next 25 years. The trust would start off with $815 million in cash, including $315 million in currently settled insurance proceeds, $300 million in cash or future insurance settlements, and $200 million in cash or short-term receivables. Manville would pay $75 million a year into the fund for the final 22 years of the fund, and up to 20 percent of Manville's annual profits could go into the fund after the fourth year if needed. In addition the trust would receive 50 percent of Manville's outstanding common stock, giving the trust a controlling interest in the company that would ensure that future payments are made as agreed. The plan put no limits on the amount of compensation victims could receive from the trust. Manville's continuing opera-

[27] "Manville Plans to Seek Strict Limit On Its Liability for Asbestos Claims," *The Wall Street Journal*, January 27, 1983.

[28] "Manville Unveils Outline of a Plan to Reorganize," *The Wall Street Journal*, May 13, 1983.

[29] *Ibid.*

[30] "Breakthrough Plan Advances at Manville," *New York Times*, 2 August 1985; "Manville OKs Huge Asbestos Settlement," *San Jose Mercury News*, 3 August 1985.

tions would be shielded by court order from asbestos-health liabilities. No mention was made of government contributions to the fund.

1. Identify all the moral issues that you think are involved in this case. Explain why you believe the issues you identify count as *moral* issues.
2. In your opinion, was Johns-Manville *corporation* morally responsible for Clarence Borel's condition? Were individual *managers* morally responsible, and if so which ones? Identify the factors that in your opinion are decisive in making the corporation or given individuals morally responsible or that were decisive in absolving them from the responsibility. Explain why these factors are decisive. Was the moral responsibility for Clarence Borel's condition shared by any other parties in the case (such as government officials)? Explain. Were Johns-Manville or its managers morally responsible for the asbestos-related injuries of other workers? Did the financial burden of the hundreds of liability suits extinguish or mitigate this responsibility?
3. Should greater penalties have been levied against Johns-Manville or its managers? Explain. In your view, was the final resolution of the case morally acceptable? Who should ultimately have paid for the asbestos injuries: the corporation, its stockholders, U.S. citizens, Johns-Manville managers, the injured parties, the U.S. government? Explain. If the costs should have been shared, in what proportions do you feel they should have been allocated to the various parties? Should there be legally imposed limits on the amount of compensation victims or their estates should be allowed to seek?
4. In your view, what moral duties, if any, did Johns-Manville as a corporation (or any other corporate or individual parties in the case) have that should have been carried out. Formulate the moral standards on which your view is based. Do your standards meet the consistency requirement?

Wage Differences at Robert Hall

Robert Hall Clothes, Inc., owns a chain of retail stores that specializes in clothing for the family.[1] One of the chain's stores is located in Wilmington, Delaware.

The Robert Hall store in Wilmington has a department for men's and boys' clothing and another department for women's and girls' clothing. The departments are physically separated and are staffed by different personnel: Only men are allowed to work in the men's department and only women in the women's department. The personnel of the store were sexually segregated because the store's managers felt that the frequent physical contact between clerks and customers would embarrass both and would inhibit sales unless they were of the same sex.

The clothing in the men's department is generally of a higher and more expensive quality than the clothing in the women's department. Competitive factors may account for this: There are fewer men's stores than women's stores. Because of these differences in merchandise, the store's profit margin on the men's clothing was higher than its margin on the women's clothing. As a result, the men's depart-

[1] Information for this case is drawn entirely from *Hodgson v. Robert Hall Clothes, Inc.*, 473 F. 2nd 589, cert. denied, 42 U.S.L.W. 3198 (9 October 1973) and 326 F. Supp. 1264 (D. Del. 1971).

TABLE 2.2

YEAR	MEN'S DEPARTMENT			WOMEN'S DEPARTMENT		
	SALES	GROSS PROFIT	% PROFIT	SALES	GROSS PROFIT	% PROFIT
1963	$210,639	$ 85,328	40.5	$177,742	$58,547	32.9
1964	178,867	73,608	41.2	142,788	44,612	31.2
1965	206,472	89,930	43.6	148,252	49,608	33.5
1966	217,765	97,447	44.7	166,479	55,463	33.3
1967	244,922	111,498	45.5	206,680	69,190	33.5
1968	263,663	123,681	46.9	230,156	79,846	34.7
1969	316,242	248,001	46.8	254,379	91,687	36.4

ment consistently showed a larger dollar volume in gross sales and a greater gross profit, as is indicated in Table 2.2.

Because of the differences shown in Table 2.2, women personnel brought in lower sales and profits per hour. In fact, male salespersons brought in substantially more than the females did (Tables 2.3 and 2.4).

As a result of these differences in the income produced by the two depart-

TABLE 2.3

YEAR	MALE SALES PER HOUR	FEMALE SALES PER HOUR	EXCESS M OVER F
1963	$38.31	$27.31	40%
1964	40.22	30.36	32%
1965	54.77	33.30	64%
1966	59.58	34.31	73%
1967	63.14	36.92	71%
1968	62.27	37.20	70%
1969	73.00	41.26	77%

TABLE 2.4

YEAR	MALE GROSS PROFITS PER HOUR	FEMALE GROSS PROFITS PER HOUR	EXCESS M OVER F
1963	$15.52	$ 9.00	72%
1964	16.55	$ 9.49	74%
1965	23.85	11.14	114%
1966	26.66	11.43	134%
1967	28.74	12.36	133%
1968	29.21	12.91	127%
1969	34.16	15.03	127%

TABLE 2.5

YEAR	MALE EARNINGS PER HOUR	FEMALE EARNINGS PER HOUR	EXCESS M OVER F
1963	$2.18	$1.75	25%
1964	2.46	1.86	32%
1965	2.67	1.80	48%
1966	2.92	1.95	50%
1967	2.88	1.98	45%
1968	2.97	2.02	47%
1969	3.13	2.16	45%

ments, the management of Robert Hall paid their male salespersons more than their female personnel. (Management learned in 1973 that it was entirely legal for them to do this if they wanted.) Although the wage differences between males and females were substantial, they were not as large as the percentage differences between male and female sales and profits. Over the years, Robert Hall set the wages given in Table 2.5. The management of Robert Hall could argue that their female clerks were paid less because the commodities they sold could not bear the same selling costs that the commodities sold in the men's department could bear. On the other hand, the female clerks argued, the skills, sales efforts, and responsibilities required of male and female clerks were "substantially" the same.

1. In your judgment, do the managers of the Robert Hall store have any ethical obligations to change their salary policies? If you do not think they should change, then explain why their salary policy is ethically justified; if you think they should change, then explain why they have an obligation to change and describe the kinds of changes they should make. Would it make any difference to your analysis if instead of two departments in the same store, it involved two different Robert Hall stores, one for men and one for women? Would it make a difference if two stores (one for men and one for women) owned by different companies were involved? Explain each of your answers in terms of the relevant ethical principles upon which you are relying.
2. Suppose that there were very few males applying for clerks' jobs in Wilmington, while females were flooding the clerking job market. Would this competitive factor justify paying males more than females? Why? Suppose that 95 percent of the women in Wilmington who were applying for clerks' jobs were single women with children who were on welfare, while 95 percent of the men were single with no families to support. Would this "need" factor justify paying females more than males? Why? Suppose for the sake of argument that men were better at selling than women; would this justify different salaries?
3. If you think the managers of the Robert Hall store should pay their male and female clerks equal wages because they do "substantially the same work," then do you also think that ideally each worker's salary should be pegged to the work he or she individually performs (such as by having each worker sell on commission)? Why? Would a commission system be preferable from a utilitarian point of view considering the substantial bookkeeping expenses it would involve? From the point of view of justice? What does the phrase "substantially the same" mean to you?

Part Two

THE MARKET AND BUSINESS

American business transactions are for the most part carried out within market structures. Businesses acquire supplies, raw materials, and machinery in industrial markets; they go to labor markets to find workers; they transfer their finished products to retailers in wholesale markets; and the final transfer to consumers is made in retail markets. The next two chapters examine the ethical aspects of these market activities. Chapter Three discusses the morality of the market system as a whole: How is it justified and what are its shortcomings from an ethical point of view? Chapter Four discusses the ethics of various market practices. There the emphasis is no longer on the ethics of the market system considered as a whole, but on the ethics of particular practices within the market system: price-fixing, manipulation of supply, price discrimination, bribery, and market concentration.

3

THE BUSINESS SYSTEM

INTRODUCTION

The American economy during the 1980s and on into the 1990s suffered severely turbulent shocks, partly as a result of the United States' declining ability to compete with other nations. The economy suffered from declining productivity (for example, in the textile, automobile, and steel industries), persistently high unemployment, increasing international competition (especially from the Japanese), rising trade deficits of astronomical proportions, repeated economic recessions (in the early 1980s and early 1990s), and rising poverty rates. By the 1990s foreign nations had become dominant in several segments of the high-technology and information industries the United States had pioneered. As Figure 3.1 shows, for example, the U.S. share of the international market in computer components known as "DRAMS" has shrunk from 100 percent to less than 20 percent, while the Japanese have increased their share from nothing to almost 80 percent. These challenges to America's international economic leadership have sparked a national debate on the need for a "new industrial policy" that will strengthen domestic industries so that they can compete more vigorously abroad.[1]

[1] Among the many books written on the subject are Gar Alperovitz and Jeff Faux, *Rebuilding America* (New York: Pantheon Books, 1984); George C. Lodge, *Perestroika for America: Restructuring Business-Government Relations for World Competitiveness* (Boston, MA: Harvard Business School Press, 1990); Stephen S. Cohen and John Zysman, *Manufacturing Matters: The Myth of the Post Industrial Economy* (New York: Basic Books, 1987); Robert B. Reich, *The Next American Frontier* (New York: Times Books, 1983); Robert Reich, *The Work of Nations*, (New York: Alfred A. Knopf, Inc., 1991).

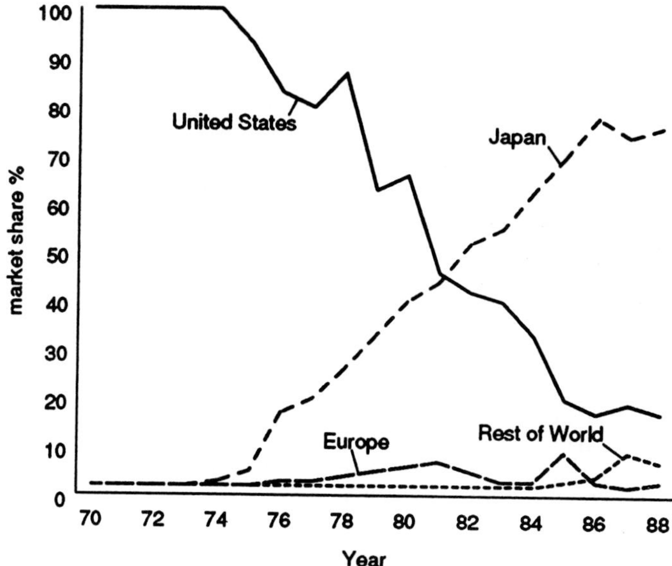

FIGURE 3.1 World Production of DRAMS by Region

Source: Dataquest, PREL '88.

Proponents of industrial policy have repeatedly urged the government to adopt coherent economic measures to help declining industries and their workers adjust to new economic conditions, and to nurture and protect newly emerging technological industries until they are strong enough to compete abroad. Proposals have included the passage of laws to restrict foreign imports; the development of planning agencies in which business, government, and labor representatives can negotiate coherent industrial plans; and the creation of public financial institutions to oversee direct loans to selected industries. Only these kinds of coordinating mechanisms, it has been argued, can deal with the economic problems posed by rising competition from other countries, by declining industries, and by unemployment. The economist Ray Marshall, for example, testifying during one of several congressional hearings on these issues, said:

> The solutions to economic problems should be built on a sensible division of labor between government, the market, and mechanisms that promote cooperative problem solving. And I would give heavy weight to the latter, because I think it's one of the main disadvantages the United States faces relative to other countries. While the market can be a marvel of promoting short-run efficiency, it cannot solve larger problems. It cannot prevent recession, inflation, or create open and fair trade and competition. Markets by themselves cannot protect the environment, promote equal opportunities and adequate income for our people, foster our long-run basic research and innovation, and insure the national security. Indeed, without government intervention to preserve competitive conditions, markets would be less effective than they are. While we must rely primarily on market forces, there can be little doubt about the need for positive government partnership with the private sector in addressing important national problems. There is an important range of problems, particularly in fighting inflation and in strengthening the international competitiveness of American

industry, that will not yield to the uncoordinated actions of either the public or private sector alone. Public and private partnership must be forged, establishing a new institution of governance.[2]

Opponents of these "industrial policy" proposals, however, hold that government should not intervene in the economy in this manner since such intervention is not a proper function of government. Many business people are especially antagonistic to the proposals, holding that in the long run free market competition would create stronger industries while government intervention would inevitably fail. Robert Anderson, chairman of Rockwell International Corporation, for example, testified at another congressional hearing:

> The full revitalization of the American economy . . . will occur only if those improvements contribute to increasing America's ability to compete in the new world we are in. . . . Given the emergence of a global marketplace, a turn inward [through protectionist limits on foreign imports] would be self-defeating in the long run. Our mandate must not be to punish or retard the competitive gains made by other nations, but to do a better job of competing ourselves. . . . Just as we must avoid the pitfall of protectionism, so we must avoid the peril of increased Government intervention into the activities of the private sector. If industrial policy simply means centralized Government planning, count us out. Such a course would be inconsistent with our historic free market traditions and counterproductive in this new era.[3]

The controversy over "industrial policy" is in fact only an episode in a great and centuries-long debate over the American business system: Should government regulate and coordinate the activities of business firms, or should business firms be left free to pursue their own interests within unregulated markets? Should the business system be a "planned" economy, or should it be a "free market" economy? The arguments Marshall and Anderson advanced are clear examples of the two opposing viewpoints on this critical issue. One side argues that *unregulated* market systems are defective because they cannot deal with the problems of recession, inflation, ensuring open and fair trade and competition, the environment, equal opportunities, poverty, the need to foster long-run basic research and innovation, and ensuring national security. The other side argues that *regulation* is defective because it violates the right to freedom and leads to an inefficient allocation of resources. This chapter examines these arguments for and against free markets and government regulation.

Ideologies

In analyzing these arguments on free markets and government, we will, in effect, be analyzing what sociologists refer to as "ideologies." An ideology is a

[2] Joint Economic Committee, *The Unemployment Crisis and Policies for Economic Recovery, Hearings Before the Joint Economic Committee of the Congress of the United States*, 97th Congress, 2nd session, October 15, 20, and November 24, 1982 (Washington, DC: U.S. Government Printing Office, 1983), p. 34.

[3] House Committee on Banking, Finance, and Urban Affairs, *Industrial Policy, Hearings Before the Subcommittee on Economic Stabilization of the Committee on Banking, Finance and Urban Affairs of the House of Representatives*, 98th Congress, 1st session, part I, June 9, 14, 21, 22, 28, and 30, 1983 (Washington, DC: U.S. Government Printing Office, 1983), p. 12.

system of normative beliefs shared by members of some social group. The ideology expresses the group's answers to questions about human nature (such as, are human beings motivated only by economic incentives?), about the basic purpose of our social institutions (as, what is the purpose of government? of business? of the market?), about how societies actually function (as, are markets free? does big business control government?), and about the values society should try to protect (as, freedom? productivity? equality?). A *business* ideology, then, is a normative system of beliefs on these matters, but specifically one that is held by business groups such as managers.

The importance of analyzing business ideologies is obvious: A business person's ideology often determines the business decisions he or she makes, and through these decisions the ideology influences the person's behavior. The businessperson's ideology, for example, will color the person's perceptions of the groups with whom he or she has to deal (employees, government officials, the poor, competitors, consumers); it will encourage the person to give in to certain pressures from these groups (perhaps even to support them) and to oppose others; it will make him or her look upon some actions as justified and legitimate and look on other actions (both those of the person and those of other groups) as unjustified and illegitimate. If a person's ideology is never examined, it will nonetheless have a deep and pervasive influence on the person's decision-making, an influence that may go largely unnoticed and that may derive from what is actually a false and ethically objectionable ideology.

In a widely read analysis of the business ideologies that tend to dominate in American society, and of the need to make these ideologies more appropriate for the highly competitive environment in which U.S. businesses now operate, George Lodge, of the Harvard Business School, identified two important ideologies: "individualistic" and "communitarian."

> In an individualistic society, the role of government is limited. Its fundamental purposes are to protect property, enforce contracts, and keep the marketplace open so that competition among firms may be as vigorous and as free as possible. Government is essentially separate from business. It intervenes in the affairs of business only when the national health and safety are involved. Intervention thus hinges on crisis—epidemics, pollution, economic disaster, war—and is temporary, an exception to the normal state of individual and business autonomy. . . . An individualistic society is inherently suspicious of government, anxious about centralized power, and reluctant to allow government to plan, especially over the long term.
>
> The role of government in a communitarian society is quite different. Here, government is prestigious and authoritative, sometimes authoritarian. Its function is to define the needs of the community over the long as well as the short term, and to see that those needs are met (although not necessarily through its offices). It sets a vision for the community; it defines and ensures the rights and duties of community membership, and it plays a central role in creating—sometimes imposing consensus to support the direction in which it decides the community should move. Consensus-making often requires coercion of one sort or another, which may occur in either a centralized or decentralized fashion, flowing down from an elite or up from the grass roots. Communitarian societies may be hierarchical or egalitarian. . . .
>
> To oversimplify, among the so-called capitalist countries, the United States has tended traditionally to be the most individualistic, Japan the most communitarian. Other nations can be placed somewhere along the continuum between these two

> extremes. Germany is more communitarian than the United Kingdom, but still less so than Japan. France is a complex mix. . . . Mikhail Gorbachev's USSR may, with luck, move out of its dark ages to a more Japanese-like version of communitarianism. . . .
>
> Traditional Western economics is rooted in individualism, holding that free trade among independent firms unconstrained by the hand of government results in the best outcome for all concerned. Firms benefit from their country's natural endowments or its comparative advantage.
>
> The dramatic success of Japan and other Asian countries in the past twenty years, however, has called this ideology into question. These nations and their companies have benefited greatly by acting contrary to the tenets of individualism. Their governments and companies practice neither free trade nor free enterprise, as traditionally conceived, and they are quite prepared to restrict the freedom of the market when it serves their purposes.[4]

Lodge, like many others, is suggesting that businesspeople in the United States must change the individualistic ideology they espouse, because this individualistic ideology obstructs their ability to accept the many changes they must make if U.S. businesses are to regain their competitive edge in the world economy. The individualistic ideology that Lodge identifies incorporates various ideas drawn from the thinking of Adam Smith, John Locke, and other influential thinkers whose normative views we will examine and evaluate in this chapter. We discuss these ideas not only because of the significant influence they have on businesspeople's ideologies, but also because of the rising insistence with which many Americans are urging that these ideologies be adapted to the contemporary needs of business. It would be a valuable exercise for the reader to identify the ideology he or she holds and to examine and criticize its elements as he or she reads through this chapter.

Market Systems Versus Command Systems

Markets are meant to solve a fundamental economic problem that all societies face: that of coordinating the economic activities of society's many members.[5] Who will produce what goods for what people? Modern societies solve this problem in two main ways: by a *command* system or by a *market* system.[6]

In a command system, a single authority (a person or a committee) makes the decisions about what is to be produced, who will produce it, and who will get it. The authority then communicates these decisions to the members of the system in the form of enforcible commands or directives, and transfers between the members then take place in accordance with the commands. This is, for example, the way in which the internal economic activities of vertically integrated business corporations may be coordinated. In the integrated corporation, a manage-

[4] George C. Lodge, *Perestroika for America: Restructuring Business-Government Relations for World Competitiveness* (Boston, MA: Harvard Business School Press, 1990), pp. 15, 16, 17.

[5] Robert L. Heilbroner, *The Economic Problem*, 3rd ed. (Englewood Cliffs, NJ: Prentice Hall, 1972), pp. 14–28; see also Paul A. Samuelson, *Economics*, 9th ed. (New York: McGraw-Hill Book Company, 1973), pp. 17–18.

[6] See Charles E. Lindblom, *Politics and Markets* (New York: Basic Books Inc., Publishers, 1977), chapters 2, 3, 5, and 6 for a discussion contrasting these two abstractions, and for a subtle criticism of their adequacy.

ment group may decide what the various divisions will produce and what products each division will supply to the other divisions. These decisions are then communicated to the organization, perhaps in the form of a "budget." Command systems can also be extended to an entire economy. For five years during World War II, the United States and Great Britain both employed command systems to coordinate production among war-related industries.[7] And from 1928 to 1953 the Soviet Union imposed a series of plans upon its entire economy that told each firm exactly what labor and material resources it was to acquire, what goods it was to produce from these, and how it was to allocate its finished products among other firms and consumers.[8] The purpose of the USSR's "central planning system" was to industrialize the economy as rapidly as possible: Whereas in 1928 the Soviet Union was the fifth largest producer of industrial goods, it is now second after the United States.

The modern alternative to command is the "free market."[9] Within a free market system, individual firms—each privately owned and each desirous of making a profit—make their own decisions about what they will produce and how they will produce it. Each firm then exchanges its goods with other firms and with consumers at the most advantageous prices it can get. Price levels serve to coordinate production by encouraging investment in highly profitable industries and discouraging it in unprofitable ones.

Free market systems, in theory, are based on two main components: a private property system and a voluntary exchange system.[10] If a society is to employ a market system, it must maintain a system of property laws (including contract law) that will assign to private individuals the right to make decisions about the firms and commodities they own, and that reassigns these rights when individuals exchange their goods with each other. And, of course, a free market system cannot exist unless individuals are legally free to come together in "markets" to voluntarily exchange their goods with each other.

In a pure free market system, there would be no constraints whatsoever on the property one could own and what one could do with the property one owns, nor on the voluntary exchanges one could make. Slavery would be entirely legal, as would prostitution. There are, however, no pure market systems. Some things may not be owned (such as slaves), some things may not be done with one's own property (such as pollution), some exchanges are illegal (as children's labor), and some exchanges are imposed (as in taxation). Such limitations on free markets are, of course, intrusions of a command system: Government concern for the public welfare leads it to issue directives concerning which goods may or may not be produced or exchanged. The result is government regulation of one form or another.

[7] George Dalton, *Economic Systems and Society: Capitalism, Communism, and the Third World* (New York: Penguin Books, 1974), pp. 122–24; Otis L. Graham, Jr. *Toward a Planned Society: From Roosevelt to Nixon* (New York: Oxford University Press, 1976), pp. 69–86.

[8] *Ibid.*, pp. 121–31.

[9] Lindblom, *Politics and Markets*, p. 33.

[10] Milton Friedman, *Capitalism and Freedom* (Chicago: The University of Chicago Press, 1962), p. 14; see also, John Chamberlain, *The Roots of Capitalism* (New York: D. Van Nostrand Company, 1959), pp. 7–42.

Since the eighteenth century, debates have raged over whether government commands should intervene in the market or whether market systems should remain free of all government intervention.[11] Should economies be partially or wholly coordinated by a government-authored command system? Or should private property rights and free exchanges be allowed to operate with few or no restrictions? The debate over industrial policy is essentially a debate over these issues.

Two main arguments are usually advanced in favor of the free market system. The first argument, which originated with John Locke, is based on a theory of moral rights that employs many of the concepts we examined in the second section of Chapter Two. The second, which was first clearly proposed by Adam Smith, is based on the utilitarian benefits free markets provide to society, an argument that rests on the utilitarian principles we discussed in the first section of Chapter Two. A third important but opposing argument is that of Karl Marx, who held that capitalist systems promote injustice. All of these arguments are examined in what follows.

3.1 FREE MARKETS AND RIGHTS: JOHN LOCKE

One of the strongest cases for an unregulated market derives from the idea that human beings have certain "natural rights" that only a free market system can preserve. The two natural rights that free markets are supposed to protect are the right to freedom and the right to private property. Free markets are supposed to preserve the right to freedom insofar as they enable each individual to voluntarily exchange goods with others free from the coercive power of government. And they are supposed to preserve the right to private property insofar as each individual is free to decide what will be done with what he or she owns without interference from government.

John Locke (1632–1704), an English political philosopher, is generally credited with developing the idea that human beings have a "natural right" to liberty and a "natural right" to private property.[12] Locke argued that if there were no governments, human beings would find themselves in a "state of nature." In this state of nature each man would be the political equal of all others and would be perfectly free of any constraints other than the "law of nature," that is, the moral principles that God gave to humanity and that each man can discover by the use of his own God-given reason. As he puts it, in a state of nature all men would be in

> A *state of perfect freedom* to order their actions and dispose of their possessions and persons as they think fit, within the bounds of the law of nature, without asking leave, or depending upon the will of any other man. A *state* also *of equality,* wherein all the power and jurisdiction is reciprocal, no one having more than another . . . without subordination or subjection [to another] . . . But . . . the *state of nature*

[11] Joseph Schumpeter, *A History of Economic Analysis* (New York: Oxford University Press, 1954), pp. 370–72 and 397–99. For a treatment of 20th-century controversies see Graham, *Toward a Planned Society*.

[12] The literature on Locke is extensive; see Richard I. Aaron, *John Locke*, 3rd ed. (London: Oxford University Press, 1971), pp. 352–76 for bibliographic materials.

> has a law of nature to govern it, which obliges everyone: and reason, which is that law, teaches all mankind, who will but consult it, that being all equal and independent, no one ought to harm another in his life, health, liberty, or possessions.[13]

The law of nature, according to Locke, "teaches" each man that he has a right to liberty and that, consequently, "no one can be put out of this [natural] estate and subjected to the political power of another without his own consent."[14] The law of nature also informs us that each man has rights of ownership over his own body, his own labor, and the products of his labor and that these ownership rights are "natural," that is, they are not invented or created by government nor are they the result of a government grant:

> Every man has a *property* in his own *person*: This nobody has a right to but himself. The *labor* of his body, and the *work* of his hands, we may say, are properly his. Whatsoever then he removes out of the state that nature has provided and left it in, he has mixed his *labor* with, and joined to it something that is his own, and thereby makes it his property. . . . [For] this *labor* being the unquestionable property of the laborer, no man but he can have a right to what that [labor] is once joined to, at least where there is enough, and as good, left in common for others.[15]

The state of nature, however, is a perilous state, in which individuals are in constant danger of being harmed by others, "for all being kings as much as he, every man his equal, and the greater part no strict observers of equity and justice, the enjoyment of the property he has in this state is very unsafe, very insecure."[16] Consequently, individuals inevitably organize themselves into a political body and create a government whose primary purpose is to provide the protection of their natural rights that is lacking in the state of nature. Since the citizen consents to government "only with an intention . . . to preserve himself, his liberty and property . . . the power of the society or legislature constituted by them can never be supposed to extend farther" than what is needed to preserve these rights.[17] Government, that is, cannot interfere with any citizen's natural right to liberty and natural right to property except insofar as such interference is needed to protect one person's liberty or property from being invaded by others.

Although Locke himself never explicitly used his theory of natural rights to argue for free markets, several twentieth-century authors have employed his theory for this purpose.[18] Friedrich A. Hayek, Murray Rothbard, Gottfried Dietze, Eric Mack, and many others claim that each person has the right to liberty and to property which Locke credited to every human being and that, consequently, government must leave individuals free to exchange their labor and their property as

[13] John Locke, *Two Treatises of Government*, rev. ed., Peter Laslett, ed. (New York: Cambridge University Press, 1963), pp. 309, 311.

[14] *Ibid.*, p. 374.

[15] *Ibid.*, p. 328–29.

[16] *Ibid.*, p. 395.

[17] *Ibid.*, p. 398.

[18] C. B. Macpherson, however, argues that Locke was attempting to establish the morality and rationality of a capitalist system; see his *The Political Theory of Possessive Individualism: Hobbes to Locke* (Oxford: The Clarendon Press, 1962).

they voluntarily choose.[19] Only a free private enterprise exchange economy in which government stays out of the market and in which government protects the property rights of private individuals allows for such voluntary exchanges. The existence of the Lockean rights to liberty and property, then, implies that societies should incorporate private property institutions and free markets.

Criticisms of Lockean Rights

Criticisms of the Lockean defense of free markets have focused on three of its major weaknesses: (1) the assumption that individuals have the "natural rights" Locke claimed they have, (2) the conflict between these negative rights and positive rights, and (3) the conflict between these Lockean rights and the principles of justice.

First, then, the Lockean defense of free markets rests on the unproven assumption that people have rights to liberty and property that take precedence over all other rights. If humans do not have the overriding rights to liberty and property, then the fact that free markets would preserve the rights does not mean a great deal. Neither Locke nor his twentieth-century followers, however, has provided the arguments needed to establish that human beings have such "natural" rights. Locke himself merely asserted that "reason . . . teaches all mankind, who will but consult it" that these rights exist.[20] Instead of arguing for these rights, therefore, Locke had to fall back on the bare assertion that the existence of these rights is "self-evident": all rational human beings are supposed to be able to intuit that the alleged rights to liberty and to property exist. Unfortunately, many rational human beings have tried and failed to have this intuition.[21]

Second, even if human beings have a natural right to liberty and property, it does not follow that this right must override all other rights. The right to liberty and property is a "negative" right in the sense we defined in Chapter Two. But as we saw there, negative rights can conflict with people's positive rights. The negative right to liberty, for example, may conflict with someone else's positive right to food, medical care, housing, or clean air. Why must we believe that in such cases the negative right has greater priority than the positive right? Critics argue, in fact, that we have no reason to believe that the rights to liberty and property are overriding. Consequently we also have no reason to be persuaded by the argument that free markets must be preserved because they protect this alleged right.[22]

The third major criticism of the Lockean defense of free markets is based

[19] Friedrich A. Hayek, *The Road to Serfdom* (Chicago: University of Chicago Press, 1944); Murray N. Rothbard, *For a New Liberty* (New York: Collier Books, 1978); Gottfried Dietz, *In Defense of Property* (Baltimore: The Johns Hopkins Press, 1971); Eric Mack, "Liberty and Justice," in *Justice and Economic Distribution*, eds. John Arthur and William Shaw (Englewood Cliffs, NJ: Prentice Hall, 1978), pp. 183–93; John Hospers, *Libertarianism* (Los Angeles: Nash, 1971); T. R. Machan, *Human Rights and Human Liberties* (Chicago: Nelson-Hall, 1975).

[20] Locke, *Two Treatises*, p. 311; for a fuller treatment of Locke's views on the law of nature, see John Locke, *Essays on the Law of Nature*, W. von Leyden, ed. (Oxford: The Clarendon Press, 1954).

[21] William K. Frankena, *Ethics*, 2nd ed. (Englewood Cliffs, NJ: Prentice Hall, 1973), pp. 102–5.

[22] For versions of this argument see Lindblom, *Politics and Markets*, pp. 45–51.

TABLE 3.1 Distribution of Income and Wealth in American Society

INCOME GROUP	FAMILY INCOME RANGE (1989)	PERCENTAGE OF TOTAL INCOME (1989)	PERCENTAGE OF TOTAL WEALTH (1973)	PERCENTAGE OF INCOME FROM PROPERTY (1962)	PERCENTAGE OF STOCK DIVIDENDS (1962)
Richest Fifth	$53,711 and up	46.8	76	65	82
Fourth Fifth	35,351–53,710	24.0	15.5	11	4
Middle Fifth	23,001–35,350	15.8	6.2	10	9
Second Fifth	12,097–23,000	9.5	2.1	8	4
Poorest Fifth	0–12,096	3.8	.2	4	2

Sources: First and second columns from the left are drawn from U.S. Bureau of the Census, Current Population Reports, Series P-60, No. 168, *Money Income and Poverty Status in the United States: 1989*; third column is from Executive Office of the President: Office of Management and Budget, *Social Indicators, 1973* (Washington, DC: U.S. Government Printing Office, 1973); fourth and fifth columns from Jonathan Turner and Charles E. Starnes, *Inequality: Privilege and Power in America* (Pacific Palisades, CA: Goodyear Publishing Co., 1976).

on the idea that free markets create unjust inequalities.[23] In a free market economy a person's productive power will be proportioned to the amount of labor or property he or she already possesses. Those individuals who have accumulated a great deal of wealth and who have access to education and training will be able to accumulate even more wealth by purchasing more productive assets. And individuals who own no property, who are unable to work or who are unskilled (such as the handicapped, the infirm, the poor, the aged) will be unable to buy any goods at all without help from the government. As a result, without government intervention the gap between the richest and the poorest will widen until large disparities of wealth emerge. Unless government intervenes to adjust the distribution of property that results from "free markets," large groups of citizens will remain at a subsistence level while others grow ever wealthier.

To prove their point, critics cite the high poverty levels and large inequalities of "capitalist" nations like the United States. In 1989, for example, during a period of economic expansion that increased the wealth of the richest Americans, 31.5 million Americans or about 12.8 percent of the population continued living

[23] Arthur M. Okun, *Equality and Efficiency* (Washington, DC: The Brookings Institution, 1975), pp. 1–4; see also Paul Baron and Paul Sweezy, *Monopoly Capitalism* (New York: Monthly Review, 1966), ch. 10; Frank Ackerman and Andrew Zimbalist, "Capitalism and Inequality in the United States," in *The Capitalist System*, 2nd ed., Richard C. Edwards, Michael Reich, Thomas E. Weisskopf, eds. (Englewood Cliffs, NJ: Prentice Hall, 1978), pp. 297–307; Jonathan H. Turner and Charles E. Starnes, *Inequality: Privilege & Poverty in America* (Pacific Palisades, CA: Goodyear Publishing Company, Inc., 1976), pp. 44–45, 134–38.

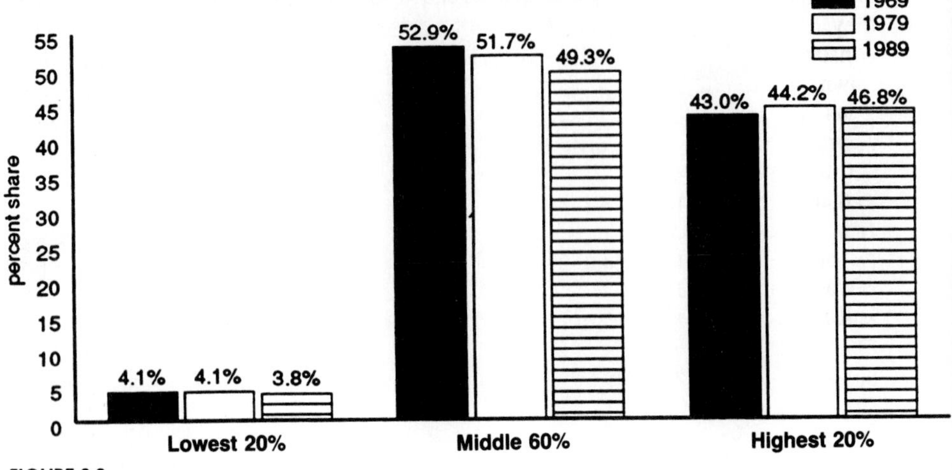

FIGURE 3.2

Source: U.S. Bureau of the Census, Current Population Reports, Series P-60, No. 168.

in poverty (as defined by the Council of Economic Advisors).[24] During the 1980s, between 250,000 and 750,000 were estimated to be homeless and living in the streets each year. In 1989 one out of every five American children under the age of 18 was poor. On the other hand, the top 1 percent of the population holds one fourth of all U.S. personal wealth, controls more than half of all of America's stocks, and owns 60 percent of its wealth in bonds.[25] Critics also point to the highly unequal distribution of income and wealth among each fifth of the population that has emerged each time researchers have investigated the American population, as Table 3.1 summarizes. Moreover, as Figure 3.2 indicates, this inequality has continued to increase, as those families who rank among the richest 20 percent of the population have acquired an ever larger share of income, while the other 80 percent have less and less to divide among themselves.

3.2 THE UTILITY OF FREE MARKETS: ADAM SMITH

The second major defense of unregulated markets rests on the utilitarian argument that unregulated markets and private property will produce greater benefits than any amount of regulation could. In a system with free markets and private property,

[24] For these and other data on poverty in America, see U.S. Bureau of the Census, Current Population Reports, Series P-60, No. 168, *Money Income and Poverty Status in the United States: 1989 (Advance Data from the March 1990 Current Population Survey* (Washington, DC: U.S. Government Printing Office, 1990)).

[25] Lars Osberg, *Economic Inequality in the United States* (New York: M. E. Sharpe, Inc., 1984), p. 41.

buyers will seek to purchase what they want for themselves at the lowest prices they can find. It will therefore pay private businesses to produce and sell what consumers want and to do this at the lowest possible prices. To keep their prices down, private businesses will try to cut back on the costly resources they consume. Thus, the free market, coupled with private property, ensures that the economy is producing what consumers want, that prices are at the lowest levels possible, and that resources are efficiently used. The economic utility of society's members is thereby maximized.

Adam Smith (1723–1790), the "father of modern economics," is the originator of this utilitarian argument for the free market.[26] According to Smith, when private individuals are left free to seek their own interests in free markets, they will inevitably be led to further the public welfare by an "invisible hand":

> By directing [his] industry in such a manner as its produce may be of the greatest value, [the individual] intends only his own gain, and he is in this, as in many other cases, led by an invisible hand to promote an end that was no part of his intention . . . By pursuing his own interest he frequently promotes that of society more effectively than when he really intends to promote it.[27]

The "invisible hand," of course, is market competition. Every producer seeks to make his living by using his private resources to produce and sell those goods that he perceives people want to buy. In a competitive market a multiplicity of such private businesses must all compete with each other for the same buyers. To attract customers, therefore, each seller is forced not only to supply what consumers want, but to drop the price of his goods as close as possible to "what it really costs the person who brings it to market."[28] And to increase his profits each producer must pare his costs, thereby reducing the resources he consumes. The competition produced by a multiplicity of self-interested private sellers, then, serves to lower prices, conserve resources, and make producers respond to consumer desires. Motivated only by self-interest, private businesses are led to serve society. As Smith put the matter in a famous passage:

> It is not from the benevolence of the butcher, the baker, and the brewer that we expect our dinner, but from their regard for their own self-interest. We address ourselves not to their humanity, but to their self-love, and never talk to them of our own necessities, but of their advantages.[29]

Smith also argued that a system of competitive markets will allocate resources efficiently among the various industries of a society.[30] For when the supply of a certain commodity is not enough to meet the demand, buyers will bid the price

[26] See S. Hollander, *The Economics of Adam Smith* (Toronto: University of Toronto Press, 1973).

[27] Adam Smith, *An Inquiry into the Nature and Causes of the Wealth of Nations* [1776] (New York: The Modern Library, n.d.), p. 423.

[28] *Ibid.*, p. 55.

[29] *Ibid.*, p. 14.

[30] *Ibid.*, pp. 55–58.

of the commodity upward until it rises above what Smith called the "natural price" (that is, the price that just covers the costs of producing the commodity including the going rate of profit obtainable in other markets). Producers of that commodity will then reap profits higher than those available to producers of other commodities. The higher profits will induce producers of those other products to switch their resources into the production of the more profitable commodity. As a result, the shortage of that commodity disappears and its price will sink back to its "natural" level. Conversely, when the supply of a commodity is greater than the quantity demanded, its price will fall, inducing its producers to switch their resources into the production of other, more profitable commodities. The fluctuating prices of commodities in a system of competitive markets, then, forces producers to allocate their resources to those industries where they are most in demand and to withdraw resources from industries where there is an oversupply of commodities. The market, in short, allocates resources so as to most efficiently meet consumer demand, thereby promoting social utility.

The best policy of a government that hopes to advance the public welfare, therefore, is to do nothing: to let each individual pursue his or her self-interest in "natural liberty."[31] Any interventions into the market by government can only serve to interrupt the self-regulating effect of competition and reduce its many beneficial consequences.

In the early twentieth century, the economists Ludwig von Mises and Friedrich A. Hayek supplemented Smith's market theories by an ingenious argument.[32] They argued that not only does a system of free markets and private ownership serve to allocate resources efficiently, but it is in principle impossible for the government or any human being to allocate resources with the same efficiency. Human beings cannot allocate resources efficiently because they can never have enough information nor calculate fast enough to coordinate in an efficient way the hundreds of thousands of daily exchanges required by a complex industrial economy. In a free market, high prices indicate that additional resources are needed to meet consumer demand, and they motivate producers to allocate their resources to those consumers. The market thereby allocates resources efficiently from day to day through the pricing mechanism. If a human agency were to try to do the same thing, von Mises and Hayek argued, the agency would have to know from day to day what things each consumer desired, what materials each producer would need to produce the countless things consumers desired, and would then have to calculate how best to allocate resources among interrelated producers so as to enable them to meet consumer desires. The infinite quantity of detailed bits of information and the astronomical number of calculations that such an agency would need, von Mises and Hayek claimed, were beyond the capacity of any human beings. Thus, not only do free markets allocate goods efficiently, but it is quite impossible for government planners to duplicate their performance.

[31] *Ibid.*, p. 651.

[32] Friedrich A. Hayek, "The Price System as a Mechanism for Using Knowledge," and Ludwig von Mises, "Economic Calculation in Socialism," both in *Comparative Economic Systems: Models and Cases*, Morris Bornstein, ed. (Homewood, IL: Richard D. Irwin, Inc., 1965), pp. 39–50 and 79–85.

Criticisms of Adam Smith

Critics of Smith's classic utilitarian argument in defense of free markets and private property have attacked it on a variety of fronts. The most common criticism is that the argument rests on unrealistic assumptions.[33] Smith's arguments assume, first, that the impersonal forces of supply and demand will force prices down to their lowest levels because the sellers of products are so numerous and each enterprise is so small that no one seller can control the price of a product. This assumption was perhaps true enough in Smith's day, when the largest firms employed only a few dozen men and a multitude of small shops and petty merchants competed for the consumer's attention. But today many industries and markets are completely or partially monopolized, and the small firm is no longer the rule. In these monopolized industries where one or a few large enterprises are able to set their own prices, it is no longer true that prices necessarily move to their lowest levels. The monopoly power of the industrial giants enables them to keep prices at artificially high levels and to keep production at artificially low levels.

Second, critics claim, Smith's arguments assume that all the resources used to produce a product will be paid for by the manufacturer and that the manufacturer will try to reduce these costs in order to maximize his profits. As a result, there will be a tendency toward a more efficient utilization of society's resources. But this assumption is also proved false when the manufacturer of a product consumes resources for which he or she does not have to pay and on which he or she therefore does not try to economize. For example, when manufacturers use up clean air by polluting it, or when they impose health costs by dumping harmful chemicals into rivers, lakes, and seas, they are using up resources of society for which they do not pay. Consequently, there is no reason for them to attempt to minimize these costs and social waste is the result. Such waste is a particular instance of a more general problem that Smith's analysis ignored. Smith failed to take into account the external effects that business activities often have on their surrounding environment. Pollution is one example of such effects, but there are others, such as the effects on society of introducing advanced technology, the psychological effects increased mechanization has had on laborers, the harmful effects that handling dangerous products has on the health of workers, and the economic shocks that result when natural resources are depleted for short-term gains. Smith ignored these external effects of the firm and assumed that the firm is a self-contained agent whose activities affect only itself and its buyers.

Third, critics claim, Smith's analysis wrongly assumes that every human being is motivated only by a "natural" and self-interested desire for profit. Smith assumes that in all his dealings a person "intends only his own gain." Human nature follows the rule of "economic rationality": Give away as little as you can in return for as much as you can get. Since a human being "intends only his own gain" anyway, the best economic arrangement will be one that recognizes this "natural" motivation and allows it free play in competitive markets that force self-interest to serve the public interest. But this theory of human nature, critics have claimed, is clearly false. First, human beings regularly show a concern

[33] These criticisms can be found in any standard economic textbook, but see especially, Frank J. B. Stilwell, *Normative Economics* (Elmsford, NY: Pergamon Press, 1975).

for the good of others and constrain their self-interest for the sake of the rights of others. Even when buying and selling in markets the constraints of honesty and fairness affect our conduct. Second, the critics claim, it is not necessarily "rational" to follow the rule "give away as little as you can for as much as you can get." In numerous situations everyone is better off when everyone shows concern for others, and it is then rational to show such concern. Third, socialist critics have argued, if human beings often behave like "rational economic men," this is not because such behavior is natural, but because the widespread adoption of competitive market relations forces humans to relate to each other as "rational economic men." The market system of a society *makes* humans selfish and this widespread selfishness then makes us think the profit motive is "natural." But in actual fact human beings are born with a natural tendency to show concern for other members of their species (in their families, for example).

As for the argument of von Mises and Hayek that human planners cannot allocate resources efficiently, the examples of French, Dutch, and Swedish planning have demonstrated that planning is not quite as impossible as von Mises and Hayek imagined.[34] Moreover, the argument of von Mises and Hayek was answered on theoretical grounds by the socialist economist Oskar Lange who demonstrated that a "central planning board" could efficiently allocate goods in an economy without having to know everything about consumers and producers and without engaging in impossibly elaborate calculations.[35] All that is necessary is for the central planners to receive reports on the sizes of the inventories of producers, and price their commodities accordingly. Surplus inventories would indicate that lowering of prices was necessary, while inventory shortages would indicate that prices should be raised. By setting the prices of all commodities in this way, the central planning board could create an efficient flow of resources throughout the economy.

The Keynesian Criticism

The most influential criticism of Adam Smith's classical assumptions came from John Maynard Keynes (1883–1946), an English economist.[36] Smith assumed that without any help from the government, the automatic play of market forces would ensure full employment of all economic resources including labor. If some resources are not being used, then their costs will drop and entrepreneurs will be induced to expand their output by using these cheapened resources. The purchase of these resources will in turn create the incomes that will enable people to buy the products made from them. Thus, all available resources will be used and demand will always expand to absorb the supply of commodities made from them (a relationship which is now called "Say's Law"). Since Keynes, however, economists have argued that without government intervention, the demand for goods

[34] See Vaclav Holesovsky, *Economic Systems, Analysis, and Comparison* (New York: McGraw-Hill Book Company, 1977), chs. 9 and 10.

[35] Oskar Lange, "On the Economic Theory of Socialism," in *Comparative Economic Systems*, Bornstein, ed., pp. 86–94.

[36] The standard work on Keynes is Alvin H. Hansen, *A Guide to Keynes* (New York: McGraw-Hill Book Company, 1953).

may not be high enough to absorb the supply. The result will be rising unemployment and a slide into economic depression.

Keynes argued that the total demand for goods and services is the sum of the demand of three sectors of the economy: households, businesses, and government.[37] The aggregate demand of these three sectors may be less than the aggregate amounts of goods and services supplied by the economy at the full employment level. This mismatch between aggregate demand and aggregate supply will occur when households prefer to save some of their income in liquid securities instead of spending it on goods and services. When, as a consequence, aggregate demand is less than aggregate supply, the result will be a contraction of supply. Businesses will realize they are not selling all their goods, so they will cut back on production and thereby cut back on employment. As production falls, the incomes of households will also fall, but the amounts households are willing to save will fall even faster. Eventually, the economy will reach a stable point of equilibrium at which demand once again equals supply but at which there is widespread unemployment of labor and other resources.

Government, according to Keynes, can influence the propensity to save that lowers aggregate demand and creates unemployment. Government can prevent excess savings through its influence on interest rates and it can influence interest rates by regulating the money supply: The higher the supply of money the lower the rates at which it will be lent. Second, government can directly affect the amount of money households have available to them by raising or lowering taxes. And third, government spending can close any gap between aggregate demand and aggregate supply by taking up the slack in demand from households and businesses (and, incidentally, creating inflation).

Thus, contrary to Smith's claims, government intervention in the economy is a necessary instrument for maximizing society's utility. Free markets alone are not necessarily the most efficient means for coordinating the use of society's resources. Government spending and fiscal policies can serve to create the demand needed to stave off unemployment. These views were the kernels of "Keynesian economics."

Keynes's views, however, have themselves fallen on hard times. During the 1970s, the United States (and other Western economies) were confronted with the simultaneous occurrence of inflation and unemployment. The standard Keynesian analysis would lead us to believe that these two should not occur together: Increased government spending, although inflationary, should serve to enlarge demand and thereby alleviate unemployment. However, during the 1970s the standard Keynesian remedy for unemployment (increased government spending) had the expected effect of creating increasing inflation but did not cure unemployment.

Various diagnoses have been offered for the apparent failure of Keynesian economics to deal with the twin problems of inflation and unemployment.[38] John

[37] John Maynard Keynes, *The General Theory of Employment, Interest, and Money* (London: Macmillan & Co., Ltd., 1936). For an accessible summary of Keynes's views, see his article, "The General Theory of Employment," *Quarterly Journal of Economics*, 51 (September 1937): 209–23.

[38] For a nontechnical review of some of these approaches see Walter Guzzardi, Jr., "The New Down-to-Earth Economics," *Fortune*, 31 December 1978, pp. 72–79.

Hicks, a former Keynesian enthusiast, for example, has suggested that in many industries today prices and wages are no longer determined by market forces as Keynes assumed: They are, instead, set by producers and unions.[39] The ultimate effect of this price-setting is continuing inflation in the face of continued unemployment. Whether this analysis of Hicks' is correct or not, it is at least clear that we can no longer rely so heavily on Keynes to support economic planning.

The Utility of Survival of the Fittest: Social Darwinism

Nineteenth-century social Darwinists added a new twist to utilitarian justifications of free markets by arguing that free markets have beneficial consequences over and above those which Adam Smith identified. They argued that economic competition produces human progress. The doctrines of social Darwinism were named after Charles Darwin (1809–1882), who argued that the various species of living things were evolving as the result of the action of an environment that favored the survival of some things while destroying others: "This preservation of favorable individual differences and variations, and the destruction of those which are injurious, I have called natural selection or the survival of the fittest."[40] The environmental factors that resulted in the "survival of the fittest" were the competitive pressures of the animal world. As a result of this competitive "struggle for existence," Darwin held, species gradually change, since only the "fittest" survive to pass their favorable characteristics on to their progeny.

Even before Darwin published his theories, the philosopher Herbert Spencer (1820–1903) and other thinkers had already begun to suggest that the evolutionary processes that Darwin described were also operative in human societies. Spencer claimed in *Social Statics* that just as competition in the animal world ensures that only the fittest survive, so free competition in the economic world ensures that only the most capable individuals survive and rise to the top. The implication is that

> Inconvenience, suffering, and death are the penalties attached by Nature to ignorance as well as to incompetence and are also the means of remedying these. Partly by weeding out those of lowest development, and partly by subjecting those who remain to the never-ceasing discipline of experience, Nature secures the growth of a race who shall both understand the conditions of existence, and be able to act up to them.[41]

Those individuals whose aggressive business dealings enable them to succeed in the competitive world of business are the "fittest" and therefore the best. And just as survival of the fittest ensures the continuing progress and improvement of an animal species, so the free competition that enriches some individuals and reduces others to poverty will result in the gradual improvement of the human race. Government must not be allowed to interfere with this stern competition

[39] John Hicks, *The Crisis in Keynesian Economics* (Oxford: Basil Blackwell, 1974), p. 25.

[40] Charles Darwin, *The Origin of Species by Means of Natural Selection* (New York: D. Appleton and Company, 1883), p. 63.

[41] Herbert Spencer, *Social Statics, Abridged and Revised* (New York: D. Appleton and Company, 1893), pp. 204–5; for an account of Spencerism in America see Richard Hofstadter, *Social Darwinism in American Thought* (Boston: Beacon Press, 1955).

since this would only impede progress. In particular, government must not lend economic aid to those who fall behind in the competition for survival. For if these economic misfits survive, they will pass on their inferior qualities and the human race will decline.

It was easy enough for later thinkers to revise Spencer's views so as to rid them of their apparent callousness. Modern versions of Spencerism hold that competition is good not because it destroys the weak individual, but because it weeds out the weak *firm*. Economic competition ensures that the "best" business firms survive and, as a result, the economic system gradually improves. The lesson of modern social Darwinism is the same: Government must stay out of the market because competition is beneficial.

The shortcomings of Spencer's views were obvious even to his contemporaries.[42] Critics were quick to point out that the skills and traits that help individuals and firms advance and "survive" in the business world are not necessarily those which will help humanity survive on the planet. Advancement in the business world might be achieved through a ruthless disregard for other human beings. The survival of humanity, on the other hand, may well depend on the development of cooperative attitudes and on the mutual willingness of people to help each other.

The basic problem underlying the views of the social Darwinist, however, is the fundamental normative assumption that "survival of the fittest" means "survival of the best." That is, whatever results from the workings of nature is necessarily good. The fallacy, which modern authors call the "naturalistic fallacy," implies, of course, that whatever happens naturally is always for the best. It is a basic failure of logic, however, to infer that what *is* necessarily *ought* to be or that what nature creates is necessarily for the best.

3.3 MARXIST CRITICISMS

Karl Marx (1818–1883) is undoubtedly the harshest and most influential critic of the inequalities that private property institutions and free markets are accused of creating.[43] Writing at the height of the Industrial Revolution, Marx was an eyewitness of the wrenching and exploitative effects that industrialization had upon the laboring peasant classes of England and Europe. In his writings he detailed the suffering and misery that capitalism was imposing upon its workers: exploitative working hours; pulmonary diseases and premature deaths caused by unsanitary

[42] See the essays collected in R. J. Wilson, *Darwinism and the American Intellectual* (Homewood, IL: The Dorsey Press, 1967); see also Donald Fleming, "Social Darwinism," in *Paths of American Thoughts*, Arthur Schlesinger, Jr. and Morton White, eds. (Boston: Houghton Mifflin Company, 1970), pp. 123–46.

[43] The current revival of interest in Marx has resulted in a number of excellent studies: David McLellan, *Karl Marx: His Life and Thought* (New York: Harper and Row Publishers, Inc., 1973); John McMurtry, *The Structure of Marx's World-View* (Princeton: Princeton University Press, 1978); Anthony Cutler, Barry Hindess, Paul Hirst, and Arthur Hussain, *Marx's Capital and Capitalism Today* (London: Routledge and Kegan Paul, 1977); Ernest Mandel, *An Introduction to Marxist Economic Theory* (New York: Pathfinder Press, 1970); Shlomo Avineri, *The Social and Political Thought of Karl Marx* (New York: Cambridge University Press, 1968); Robert Heilbroner, *Marxism: For and Against* (New York: W. W. Norton & Co., Inc., 1980).

factory conditions; seven-year-olds working twelve to fifteen hours a day; thirty seamstresses working thirty hours without a break in a room made for ten people.[44]

Marx claimed, however, that these instances of worker exploitation were merely symptoms of the underlying extremes of inequality that capitalism necessarily produces. According to Marx, capitalist systems offer only two sources of income: sale of one's own labor and ownership of the means of production (buildings, machinery, land, raw materials). Since workers cannot produce anything without access to the means of production, they are forced to sell their labor to the owner in return for a wage. The owner, however, does not pay workers the full value of their labor, only what they need to subsist. The difference ("surplus") between the value of their labor and the subsistence wages they receive is retained by the owner and is the source of the owner's profits. Thus the owner is able to exploit workers by appropriating from them the surplus they produce, using as leverage his ownership of the means of production. As a result, those who own the means of production gradually become wealthier, and workers become relatively poorer. Capitalism promotes injustice.

Alienation

The living conditions that capitalism imposed on the lower working classes contrasted sharply with Marx's view of how human beings should live. Marx held that human beings should be enabled to realize their human nature by freely developing their potential for self-expression and by satisfying their real human needs.[45] In order to develop their capacity for expressing themselves in what they make and in what they do, people should be able to engage in activities that develop their productive potential and should have control over what they produce. To satisfy their needs they must know what their real human needs are and be able to form satisfying social relationships. In Marx's view, capitalism "alienated" the lower working classes by neither allowing them to develop their productive potential nor satisfying their real human needs.

According to Marx, capitalist economies produce four forms of "alienation" in workers, that is, four forms of "separation" from what is essentially theirs.[46] First, capitalist societies give control of the worker's products to others. The objects that the worker produces by his labor are taken away by the capitalist employer and used for purposes that are antagonistic to the worker's own interests. As Marx wrote:

> The life that he has given to the object sets itself against him as an alien and hostile force . . . Labor certainly produces marvels for the rich, but it produces privation for the worker. It produces palaces, but hovels for the worker. It produces beauty, but deformity for the worker. It replaces human labor with machines, but it casts

[44] For these and other illustrations cited by Marx see his *Capital*, vol. I., Samuel Moore and Edward Aveling, trans. (Chicago: Charles H. Kerr & Company, 1906), pp. 268–82.

[45] McMurtry, *Structure of Marx's World-View*, pp. 19–37.

[46] Karl Marx, "Estranged Labor," in *The Economic and Philosophic Manuscripts of 1844*, Martin Milligan, trans., Dirk Struik, ed. (New York: International Publishers, 1964) pp. 106–19.

> some of the workers back into a barbarous kind of work and turns others into machines. It produces intelligence, but also stupidity and cretinism for the workers.[47]

Second, capitalism alienates the worker from his own activity. Labor markets force him into earning his living by accepting work that he finds dissatisfying, unfulfilling, and that is controlled by someone else's choices. Marx asks:

> What constitutes the alienation of laboring? That working is *external* to the worker, that it is not part of his nature and that, consequently, he does not fulfill himself in his work, but denies himself, has a feeling of misery rather than well-being, does not develop freely his mental and physical energies but is physically exhausted and mentally debased . . . its alien character is clearly shown by the fact that as soon as there is no physical or other compulsion it is avoided like a plague . . . it is not his own work but work for someone else.[48]

Third, capitalism alienates people from themselves by instilling in them false views of what their real human needs and desires are. Marx describes this alienation from one's own true self in a graphic portrait of the principles of the capitalist economist:

> [His] principal thesis is the renunciation of life and of human needs. The less you eat, drink, buy books, go to the theater or to balls, or to the public house, and the less you think, love, theorize, sing, paint, play, etc., the more you will be able to save and the greater will become your treasure which neither moth nor dust will corrupt—your capital. The less you are, the less you express your life, the more you have, the greater is your alienated life, and the greater is the saving of your alienated being.[49]

And, fourth, capitalist societies alienate human beings from each other by separating them into antagonistic and unequal social classes.[50] According to Marx, capitalism divides humanity into a "proletariat" laboring class and a "bourgeois" class of owners and employers: "Society as a whole is more and more splitting up into two great hostile camps, into two great classes directly facing each other: bourgeoisie and proletariat."[51]

Capitalist ownership and unregulated markets, then, necessarily produce inequalities of wealth and power: a "bourgeois" class of owners who own the means of production and who accumulate ever greater amounts of capital; and a "proletariat" class of workers who must sell their labor to subsist and who are alienated from what they produce, from their own work, from their own human needs, and from their fellow human beings. Although private property and free markets may secure the "freedom" of the wealthy owner class, they do so by creating an alienated laboring class. And such alienation is unjust.

[47] *Ibid.*, pp. 108–9.

[48] *Ibid.*, pp. 110–11.

[49] *Ibid.*, p. 150.

[50] *Ibid.*, p. 116.

[51] Karl Marx and Friedrich Engels, *Manifesto of the Communist Party* (New York: International Publishers, 1948), p. 9.

The Real Purpose of Government

The actual function that governments have historically served, according to Marx, is that of protecting the interests of the ruling economic class. It may be a popular belief that government exists to protect freedom and equality and that it rules by consent (as Locke suggested), but in fact, such beliefs are ideological myths which hide the reality of the control the wealthiest class exercises over the political process. To back up his claim Marx offered a breathtakingly comprehensive analysis of society, which we can only sketch here.

Every society, according to Marx, can be analyzed in terms of its two main components: its *economic substructure*, and its *social superstructure*.[52] The economic substructure of a society consists of the materials and social controls that society uses to produce its economic goods. Marx refers to the materials (land, labor, natural resources, machinery, energy, technology) used in production as the "forces of production." Societies during the Middle Ages, for example, were based on agricultural economies in which the forces of production were primitive farming methods, manual labor, and hand tools. Modern societies are based on an industrial economy that uses assembly-line manufacturing techniques, electricity, and factory machinery.

The social controls used in producing goods (that is, the social controls by which society organizes and controls its workers) Marx called the "relations of production." There are, Marx suggests, two main types of relations of production: (1) control based on *ownership* of the materials used to produce goods and (2) control based on *authority* to command. In medieval society, for example, the feudal lords controlled their serfs through (1) the ownership the lords exercised over the manor farms on which the serfs worked and (2) the legal authority the lords exercised over their serfs who were legally bound to live on the manor lands and to obey the lord of the manor. In modern industrial society, capitalist owners control their factory laborers because (1) the capitalists own the machinery on which laborers must work if they are to survive and (2) the laborer must enter a wage contract by which he gives the owner (or his manager) the legal authority to command him. According to Marx, a society's relations of production define the main classes that exist in that society. In medieval society, for example, the relations of production created the ruling class of lords and the exploited serf class, while in industrial society the relations of production created the capitalist class of owners (whom Marx called the "bourgeoisie") and the exploited working class of wage-earners (whom Marx called the "proletariat").

Marx also claims that the *kinds* of relations of production a society adopts depends on the *kinds* of forces of production that society has. That is, the methods a society uses to produce goods determine the way that society organizes and controls its workers. For example, the fact that medieval society had to depend on manual farming methods to survive forced it to adopt a social system in which a small class of lords organized and directed the large class of serfs who provided the manual labor society needed on its farms. Similarly, the fact that modern society depends on mass production methods has forced us to adopt a social system

[52] The classic expression of this distinction is Karl Marx, *A Contribution to the Critique of Political Economy*, N. I. Stone, ed. (New York: The International Library Publishing Co., 1904), pp. 11–13.

in which a small class of owners accumulates the capital needed to build large factories, and in which a large class of workers provides the labor these mechanized factory assembly-lines require. In short, a society's forces of production determine its relations of production, and these relations of production then determine its social classes.

So much for the economic substructure: What is the "social superstructure" of a society and how is it determined? A society's superstructure consists of its government and its popular ideologies. And, Marx claims, the ruling class created by the economic substructure will inevitably control this superstructure. That is, the members of the ruling class will control the government and ensure that it uses its force to protect their privileged position; and, at the same time, they will popularize those ideologies that justify their position of privilege. Medieval kings, for example, were selected from the class of lords and they enforced feudal law, even while the lords helped spread the ideology that their noble status was justified because of the aristocratic blood that ran in their veins. Similarly, in modern societies, Marx suggested, the class of owners is instrumental in the selection of government officials and the government then enforces the property system on which the wealth of this class depends; moreover, the ownership class, through its economists and its popularizing writers, inculcates the ideologies of free enterprise and of respect for private property, both of which support their privileged positions. Modern government, then, is not created by "consent," as Locke had claimed, but by a kind of economic determination.

According to Marx, a society's government and its ideologies are designed to protect the interests of its ruling economic classes. These classes, in turn, are created by the society's underlying relations of production, and these relations of production in their turn are determined by the underlying forces of production. In fact, Marx claimed, all major historical changes are ultimately produced by changes in society's forces of production: Economic or "material" forces determine the course of history, as they determine the functions of government. As new material forces of production are found or invented (such as the steam engine or the assembly line), the old forces are pushed out of the way (as water-power and hand-crafts), and society reorganizes itself around the newly fashioned economic methods of production. New legal structures and social classes are created (as the corporation and the managerial class) and the old legal structures and social classes are demolished (as the manor and the aristocracy). Great "ideological" battles took place for men's minds during these periods of "transformation," but the new ideas always triumph: History always follows the lead of the newest forces of production. This Marxist view of history as determined by changes in the economic methods by which humanity produces the materials on which it must live is now generally referred to as "historical materialism."

Immiseration of Workers

Marx also claimed that so long as production in modern economies is not planned but is left to depend on private ownership and free markets, the result could only be a series of related disasters that would all tend to harm the working class. This claim rested on his analysis of two basic features of modern capitalism.[53]

[53] See McMurtry, *Structure of Marx's World-View*, pp. 72–89.

First, in modern capitalist systems productive assets (factories, land, technology, etc.) are privately controlled by self-interested owners, each of whom seeks to increase his assets by competing in free markets against other self-interested owners. Second, in modern capitalist systems, commodities are mass produced in factories by a highly organized group of laborers who, if they are to live, must work on the modern factory assembly lines controlled by the self-seeking owners. Such economic systems, in which self-interested owners *compete* in free markets while their organized workers *combine* to produce massive amounts of goods, Marx argues, is a "contradiction" that will inevitably generate three tendencies that collectively leave the worker in a "miserable" state. First, such societies will exhibit an increasing concentration of industrial power in a relatively few hands.[54] As self-interested private owners struggle to increase the assets they control, little businesses will gradually be taken over by larger firms that will keep expanding in size. As time passes, Marx predicted, the small businessman will become less important and the owners of a few large firms will come to control the bulk of society's markets and assets. The rich, that is, will get richer.

Second, capitalist societies will experience repeated cycles of economic downturns or "crises."[55] Since the production of workers is highly organized, the firm of each owner can produce large amounts of surplus. And since owners are self-interested and competitive, each one will try to produce as much as he can in his firm without coordinating his production with that of other owners. As a result, firms will periodically produce an oversupply of goods. These will flood the market, and a depression or a recession will result as the economy slows down to absorb the surplus.

Third, Marx argues, the position of the worker in capitalist societies will gradually worsen.[56] This gradual decline will result from the self-interested desire of capitalist owners to increase their assets at the expense of their workers. This self-interest will lead owners to replace workers with machines, thereby creating a rising level of unemployment, which society will be unable to curb. Self-interest will also keep owners from increasing their workers' wages in proportion to the increase in productivity that mechanization makes possible. The combined effects of increased concentration, of cyclic crises, of rising unemployment, and of declining relative compensation are what Marx refers to as the "immiseration" of the worker. The solution to all these problems, according to Marx, is collective ownership of society's productive assets and the use of central planning to replace unregulated markets.[57]

Marx's theory has, of course, been subjected to intense and detailed criticism. The most telling criticism is that the immiseration of workers that he predicted has not in fact occurred. Workers in capitalist countries are much better off now than their fathers were a century ago. Nonetheless, contemporary Marxist writers point out that many of Marx's predictions have turned out correct. Factory workers today continue to find their work alienating insofar as it is dehumanizing, meaning-

[54] Marx, *Capital*, vol. I, pp. 681–89.

[55] Marx, *Capital*, vol. II, pp. 86–87.

[56] Marx, *Capital*, vol. I, pp. 689 ff.

[57] Marx and Engels, *Manifesto*, p. 30.

less, and lacking in personal satisfaction.[58] Unemployment, inflation, recessions, and other "crises" continue to plague our economy.[59] Advertisements incessantly attempt to instill in us desires for things that we do not really need.[60] And inequality and discrimination persist.[61]

The Replies

Proponents of the free market have traditionally answered the criticisms that free markets generate injustices by arguing that the criticisms wrongly assume that justice means either equality or distribution according to need. This assumption is unprovable, they claim.[62] There are too many difficulties in the way of establishing acceptable principles of justice. Should distributive justice be determined in terms of effort, or ability, or need? These questions cannot be answered in any objective way, they claim, so any attempt to replace free markets with some distributive principle will, in the final analysis, be an imposition of someone's subjective preferences upon the other members of society. And this, of course, will violate the (negative) right every individual has to be free of the coercion of others.

Other defenders of free markets argue that justice can be given a clear meaning but one which supports free markets. Justice really means distribution according to contribution.[63] When markets are free and functioning competitively, some have argued, they will pay each worker the value of his or her contribution because each person's wage will be determined by what the person adds to the output of the economy. Consequently, they argue, justice *requires* free markets.

A third kind of reply that free market proponents have made to the criticism that markets generate unjust inequalities is that, although inequalities may be endemic to private ownership and free markets, the benefits that private ownership and free markets make possible are more important.[64] The free market enables resources to be allocated efficiently without coercion, and this is a greater benefit than equality.

Thus the persuasiveness of the argument that unregulated markets should

[58] See *Work in America: Report of the Special Task Force to the Secretary of Health, Education and Welfare* (Cambridge, MA: MIT Press, 1973).

[59] See Thomas E. Weisskopf, "Sources of Cyclical Downturns and Inflation" and Arthur MacEwan, "World Capitalism and the Crisis of the 1970s," in *The Capitalist System*, 2nd ed., Richard C. Edwards, Michael Reich, and Thomas E. Weisskopf, eds. (Englewood Cliffs, NJ: Prentice Hall, 1978); pp. 441–61.

[60] Herbert Marcuse, *One Dimensional Man* (Boston: Beacon Press, 1964), pp. 225–46.

[61] Frank Ackerman and Andrew Zimbalist, "Capitalism and Inequality in the United States," in *The Capitalist System*, Edwards, Reich, Weisskopf, eds., pp. 297–307; and Michael Reich, "The Economics of Racism," in *ibid.*, pp. 381–88.

[62] Irving Kristol, "A Capitalist Conception of Justice," in *Ethics, Free Enterprise and Public Policy*, Richard T. DeGeorge and Joseph A. Pickler, eds. (New York: Oxford University Press, 1978), p. 65; see also H. B. Acton, *The Morals of Markets* (London: Longman Group Limited, 1971), pp. 68–72.

[63] John Bates Clark, *The Distribution of Wealth* (New York: The Macmillan Co., 1899), pp. 7–9, 106–7; for a critique of this argument, see Okun, *Equality and Efficiency*, pp. 40–47.

[64] Milton Friedman, *Capitalism and Freedom*, pp. 168–72.

be supported because they are efficient and protect the right to liberty and property depends, in the end, on the importance attributed to several ethical factors. How important are the rights to liberty and to property as compared to a just distribution of income and wealth? How important are the negative rights of liberty and property as compared to the positive rights of needy workers and of those who own no property? And how important is efficiency as compared to the claims of justice?

3.4 CONCLUSION: THE MIXED ECONOMY

The debate for and against free markets and private property still rages on. While critics continue to point to their defects, proponents continue to praise their virtues. It is inevitable, perhaps, that the controversy has led many economists to advocate retention of market systems and private ownership but modification of their workings through government regulation so as to rid them of their most obvious defects. The resulting amalgam of government regulation, partially free markets, and limited property rights is appropriately referred to as the "mixed economy."[65]

Basically, a mixed economy retains a market and private property system but relies heavily on government policies to remedy their deficiencies. Government transfers (of private income) are used to get rid of the worst aspects of inequality by drawing money from the wealthy in the form of income taxes and distributing it to the disadvantaged in the form of welfare. Minimum wage laws, safety laws, union laws, and other forms of labor legislation are used to protect workers from exploitation. Monopolies are regulated, nationalized, or outlawed. Government monetary and fiscal policies attempt to ensure full employment. And government regulatory agencies police firms to ensure they do not engage in socially harmful behavior.

How effective are these sorts of policies? A comparison of the American economy with other economies that have gone much further down the road toward implementing the policies of a "mixed economy" may be helpful. Sweden, West Germany, Denmark, Japan, and Switzerland are all highly regulated nations with mixed economies. The MIT economist Lester G. Thurow has made the following comparisons of the United States with these nations.[66] In terms of per capita GNP, the United States has been surpassed by Sweden, Switzerland, Denmark, Norway, and West Germany. Yet the United States has greater inequality in the distribution of income than these countries. The top 10 percent of all U.S. households, for example, receive fifteen times as much income as the bottom 10 percent, whereas in Sweden the ratio is seven times, in West Germany it is eleven times, and in Japan it is ten times. Although inequality in the U.S. is comparatively high, productivity has been on a comparative decline. During the 1970s, Sweden's productivity growth rate was 11 percent more than ours, and Japan's was 25 percent more than ours.

Although these brief comparisons do not tell the whole story, they indicate at least that a mixed economy may have some advantages. Moreover, if we compare

[65] See, for example, Paul Samuelson, *Economics*, 9th ed. (New York: McGraw-Hill Book Company, 1973), p. 845.

[66] Lester C. Thurow, *The Zero-Sum Society* (New York: Basic Books, Inc., 1980), pp. 3–9.

the performance of the U.S. economy at different periods in its history, the same conclusion is indicated. *Prior* to the intrusion of government regulation and social welfare programs, the *highest* per capita growth rate in GNP that the United States experienced during a single decade was the 22 percent rate of growth that occurred between 1900 and 1910. Yet during the decade of the 1940s, when the U.S. economy was run as a command wartime economy, the growth rate in per capita GNP climbed to 36 percent (the highest ever), and during the decade of the 1960s, when the United States introduced its major social welfare programs, the per capita GNP growth rate was at a 30 percent level. Again, these comparisons do not tell the whole story but they suggest that the "mixed economy" is not altogether a bad thing.

The desirability of the policies of the mixed economy also continues to be subject to the same debates that swirl around the concepts of free markets, private property, and government intervention. Since 1980 these debates have begun to focus on the "productivity crisis" that the United States is currently undergoing.[67] During the two decades between 1948 and 1968, worker output per hour increased at a rate of 3.2 percent each year; between 1968 and 1973 the annual rate of increase slipped to 1.9 percent; and from 1973 to 1979 it averaged only .7 percent.[68] Some have blamed this crisis on government intervention in the marketplace. According to these critics, environmental legislation and worker health laws have forced companies to invest heavily in "nonproductive" pollution-control equipment and in worker safety and have thereby drained off capital that should have been used to upgrade or replace inefficient plants and machines. Others have argued that much of the problem can be traced to the short-term strategies of business managers who have been reluctant to invest in risky research and development and in retooling programs that might hurt their short-run profit picture, and who have been more interested in expanding their companies through mergers and acquisitions that create no new value.[69]

Defenders of free markets have been greatly encouraged by what some have called the "complete abandonment" of Marxism in several formerly Communist nations, particularly the U.S.S.R. On September 24, 1990, the Soviet legislature voted to switch to a free market economy and to scrap seventy years of Communist economics that had led to inefficiencies and consumer shortages. Then, during the summer of 1991, the Communist party itself was outlawed after party leaders botched an attempt to take over the Soviet government. The Soviet Union fragmented and its reorganized states discarded their radical Marxist-Leninist ideologies in favor of world views that incorporated both socialist and capitalist elements. The new nations embarked on experimental attempts to integrate private property and free markets into their still heavily socialist economies.

These historic Communist reforms, however, have not really signaled the "complete abandonment" of socialism. Without exception all of these reforms have been aimed at moving Communist systems toward economies that are based

[67] See "The Productivity Crisis," *Newsweek*, 8 September 1980, pp. 50–69, especially the debate between Friedman and Samuelson capsulized on pp. 68–69.

[68] "The Reindustrialization of America," *Business Week*, 30 June 1980, p. 65.

[69] For analyses of these viewpoints see James Fallows, "American Industry, What Ails It, How to Save It," *The Atlantic*, September 1980, pp. 35–50.

on the best features of both socialist and free market ideologies. They have, in short, been aimed at moving the Communist countries toward the same ideology of the mixed economy that dominates Western Capitalist nations. The debate today in the formerly Communist world as in the Capitalist world is over the best mix of government regulation, private property rights, and free markets.

Followers of Smith and of Locke continue to insist that the level of government intervention tolerated by the mixed economy does more harm than good. Their opponents continue to counter that in our mixed economy government favors business interests and that allowing businesses to set their own policies exacerbates our economic problems. On balance, however, it appears that the mixed economy comes closest to combining the utilitarian benefits of free markets with the respect for human rights and for justice that are the characteristic strengths of planned economies.

QUESTIONS FOR REVIEW AND DISCUSSION

1. Define the following: ideology, individualistic ideology, communitarian ideology, command economy, free market system, private property system, state of nature, natural rights, Locke's natural right to property, surplus value, alienation, bourgeois, proletariat, economic substructure, social superstructure, forces of production, relations of production, historical materialism, immiseration of workers, invisible hand, natural price, natural liberty, aggregate demand, aggregate supply, Keynesian economics, survival of the fittest, social Darwinism, naturalistic fallacy, mixed economy, productivity crisis.
2. Contrast the views of Locke, Marx, Smith, Keynes, and Spencer on the nature and proper functions of government and on its relationship to business. Which views seem to you to provide the most adequate analysis of contemporary relations between business and government? Explain your answer fully.
3. "Locke's views on property, Smith's views on free markets, and Marx's views on capitalism obviously do not hold true when applied to the organizational structure and the operations of modern corporations." Comment on this statement. What reforms, if any, would Locke, Smith, and Marx advocate with respect to current corporate organization and performance?
4. "Equality, justice, and a respect for rights are characteristics of the American economic system." Would you agree or disagree with this statement? Why?
5. "Free markets allocate economic goods in the most socially beneficial way and ensure progress." To what extent is this statement true? To what extent do you think it is false?

CASES FOR DISCUSSION

The Chrysler Loan

On July 31, 1979, John Riccardo, chairman of Chrysler Corporation, announced that Chrysler had lost $207.1 million in the second quarter of 1979. A quarter earlier, Chrysler had lost $53.8 million. Analysts were predicting that by the end of the year Chrysler's losses would total $400 to $600 million, more than double the previous year's deficit of $204.6 million. To continue operating, Riccardo said, the company was forced to request $1 billion in cash from the federal government.[1]

Chrysler Corporation is the nation's third largest automobile manufacturer. In 1978 Chrysler posted sales of $16,340,700,000 and employed 250,000 workers. It ranked as the tenth-largest industrial firm in the United States and as the fourteenth largest in the world. If the company failed the effects would be widespread.

Many analysts blamed Chrysler's problems on its own management's mistakes.[2] During the 1960s, Lynn Townsend, Chrysler's chairman at that time, had attempted to expand into overseas markets by investing in several European companies which were failing: Sima in France and Rootes Motors in Britain. These investments further hurt the company by draining off cash funds that the company later needed for its operations at home. Then throughout the 1970s, Chrysler repeatedly miscalculated consumer demand. In 1971, when both GM and Ford introduced their subcompact models, Chrysler chose to redesign its big cars because large cars promised higher profit margins. The large Chrysler cars came on the market in 1973, the year the Arab oil embargo shifted the market away from large gas guzzlers towards the kinds of small cars that Ford and GM were marketing. In 1976 Chrysler finally began to market a line of compact cars (the Volare and Aspen) but by that time consumers had begun to turn away from small cars toward large cars again. In 1978 Chrysler repeated its mistake: In that year it announced production of large New Yorker and St. Regis model cars. By the time these large cars were rolling off the assembly lines, gasoline shortages had forced consumers to return to small cars. By mid-year 1979, Chrysler's share of the market had dropped to about 11.8 percent (the lowest level since 1962), and its inventories of unsold large cars had climbed to eighty thousand units, for which it was paying $2 million per week in storage costs. Moreover, Chrysler could sell only a limited number of its highly popular four-cylinder subcompacts (Omnis and Horizons) because contracts negotiated with suppliers two years before had locked it into a low production schedule. This series of miscalculations was clearly reflected in Chrysler's earnings during the 1970s, which are indicated in Table 3.2. The losses posted by Chrysler had led Moody's investors service and Standard & Poor's to rate Chrysler as a riskier and more speculative investment. This in turn forced Chrysler to pay higher interest rates when borrowing money and made borrowing more difficult.

Chrysler management claimed that its financial problems were the result of government regulations. Arthur Laffer, a well-known economist, prepared a Chrysler-sponsored study that argued that the nation's safety, fuel-efficiency, and pollution requirements had hit Chrysler harder than GM and Ford. Although all three automakers had to spend roughly similar amounts in developing the technology to meet government standards, the two larger companies were able to spread these fixed costs over more units than Chrysler. According to the study the fixed costs of complying with government regulations came to $620 per car for Chrysler as compared to $340 per car for GM. John Riccardo, Chrysler's chairman, argued his company's case as follows:

[1] "Chrysler Drives for a Tax Break," *Time*, 16 July 1979, p. 55.

[2] *Fortune*, 27 August 1979, pp. 30–31.

TABLE 3.2 Chrysler Revenues and Income

YEAR	TOTAL REVENUES (IN MILLIONS)	NET INCOME AFTER TAXES (IN MILLIONS)
1971	$ 7,999	$ 84
1972	9,759	220
1973	11,774	255
1974	10,971	(52)*
1975	11,598	(207)
1976	15,538	328
1977	16,708	125
1978	13,618	(205)
1979	12,002	(1,097)
1980	9,225	(1,710)
1981	10,822	(476)
1982	10,045	(69)
1983	13,240	302
1984	19,573	1,469
1985	21,260	1,629

* Parentheses indicate losses

Source: *Standard & Poor's Stock Reports*, April 1980 and April 1986.

> Because of the hundreds of millions committed for new plants and new products, and the hundreds of millions invested to meet regulations, Chrysler faces a temporary shortage of funds. Chrysler has no choice but to seek temporary assistance from the heavy burden regulation places on us. We want equity restored to the competitive system because the system is anticompetitive as it stands now. We're not asking for a handout, a bail-out, or welfare. Chrysler is asking for temporary assistance for 1979 and 1980 equal to the cost of meeting government regulations for those two years. [Statement of John Riccardo][3]

Chrysler's management also pointed out that if Chrysler did not get the financial aid it was seeking, there was a high probability that the company would go bankrupt and that this would have a disastrous effect on American society. A Congressional Budget Office study concluded that if Chrysler were to shut down, 360,000 workers would immediately be out of jobs, and "ripple effects" would put an equal number out of work in other parts of the economy.[4] Some areas would be hit harder than others; unemployment in Detroit could hit 16 percent while some small company towns in the midwest might have to shut down completely.[5] A Department of Transportation study argued that unemployment

[3] Advertisement, *San Jose Mercury*, 21 August 1979, p. 8B.

[4] "Chrysler's Crisis Bailout," *Time*, 20 August 1979, p. 41.

[5] Peter Bohr, "Chrysler's Pie-in-the-Sky Plan for Survival," *Fortune*, 22 October 1979, p. 50.

compensation combined with losses in personal and corporate taxes could cost city, state, and federal governments up to $16 billion by 1982.[6] John Riccardo stressed these reasons in his pleas for government aid:

> [To] turn our back on 140 thousand of our own employees would be irresponsibility. To close the doors in fifty-two American communities in which Chrysler is a major factor of the local economy would be irresponsibility. To deny employment to the 150 thousand people who work for the dealers who sell Chrysler products would be irresponsibility. To curtail the income of the hundreds of thousands who supply goods and services to Chrysler would be irresponsibility. . . . A Congressional Budget Office study shows that people with jobs at Chrysler, or jobs that depend on Chrysler, contribute 11 billion dollars each year in tax revenues to our country. Without those jobs they would be collecting 2 billion dollars instead in unemployment benefits. [Statement of John Riccardo][7]

In addition, $1.1 billion of the pension benefits Chrysler had set up for its workers were unfunded. Of this, $250 million was uninsured and these benefits would be lost to its workers if the company were to shut down.

In September of 1979, John Riccardo resigned as chairman of Chrysler, stating that he was too "closely associated with the past management of a troubled company" and that his continued presence at Chrysler might "hinder the final passage of our request" for federal aid.[8] He was succeeded by Lee A. Iacocca, who had been serving as president of the company. Lee Iacocca's views on Chrysler's problems and the necessity of government aid essentially coincided with the views of his predecessor:

> Government regulation . . . is a massive cost burden. It has increased our expenditures to over double the size they would normally be . . . I don't blame regulation for all of Chrysler's problems . . . I think half of all of Chrysler's problems were tough management mistakes . . . I think that the other half is regulation . . . Free enterprise, laissez-faire free enterprise died a while back. . . . If Chrysler should fail, the country would lose 500,000 to 600,000 jobs in the short term, and probably 200,000 to 300,000 jobs in the long term, many of them to overseas companies . . . Either we get $1 billion or in 12 months [the government] will have to spend $2.7 billion . . . in welfare payments [and] supplemental unemployment benefits. [Statements of Lee Iacocca][9]

The claims Chrysler's management was making on its behalf were not accepted by all observers. *Fortune Magazine*, for example, pointed out that "[Chrysler] does not explain why so many foreign automakers, smaller than Chrysler, have managed to meet the same [government] standards and earn a profit."[10]

[6] *Ibid.*

[7] Advertisement, *San Jose Mercury*, 21 August 1979, p. 8B.

[8] *Facts on File*, 21 September 1979, p. 699.

[9] United States Senate, *Chrysler Corporation Loan Guarantee Act of 1979, Hearings Before the Committee on Banking, Housing, and Urban Affairs, United States Senate, ninety-sixth Congress, first session*, (Washington, DC: U.S. Government Printing Office, 1979), pp. 609, 641, 611, 666.

[10] *Fortune*, 27 August 1979, p. 30.

Fortune Magazine also argued that Chrysler's real costs of meeting government regulations (which *Fortune* estimated at $137 million in 1979) did not begin to account for the staggering $1 billion loss that Chrysler projected for 1979.

The basic objections against giving government aid to Chrysler, however, were ideological: Government aid to businesses, critics held, is contrary to the basic principles of a free enterprise system in which firms are financed and managed, not by the government, but by private individuals. Thomas Murphy, chairman of GM, for example, opposed government aid because "federal assistance shouldn't violate the fundamental principles of the American system of free enterprise. . . . I don't think that's in accordance with what really made this country great."[11] Senator William Proxmire argued that "you just can't have a free-enterprise system without failures. Are we going to guarantee businessmen against their own incompetence by eliminating any incentive for avoiding the specter of bankruptcy?"[12] Jack Meany, president of Norris Industries, urged that "the right solution is to let the natural forces take place. In general, I don't think the government should underwrite private enterprise's failures. If we do that, we aren't going to have private enterprise."[13] *Business Week* editorialized that unless companies were allowed to fail, the "discipline" of market forces "simply vanishes"; that the loan would give Chrysler an "unfair advantage" over other car makers; that it would set a "dangerous precedent"; and that it would put the government on the "expensive" course of "futilely" pumping money into failing enterprises for the sake of saving jobs.[14]

Milton Friedman, an economist and an enthusiastic advocate of free enterprise also attacked the idea of government aid to Chrysler. If Chrysler should be forced to shut down, he argued:

> No doubt many related enterprises will suffer losses, along with Chrysler stockholders, but that is a risk they knowingly run in order to be able to enjoy profits. . . . If Chrysler is not bailed out, the facilities worth using would be taken over by people who would be risking their money in the belief that they can make more effective and productive use of them than Chrysler's present management. In the process, they would create new jobs. If Chrysler is bailed out, it will cost the taxpayer money. The cost may be hidden in the form of loan guarantees, but it is real, nonetheless. It includes the possible loss if Chrysler cannot repay the loan. It includes also the slightly higher interest rate that the government will have to pay because it has increased its liabilities. Bailing out Chrysler will not change the total amount of capital available to the economy. But it will divert capital to Chrysler from other more productive uses. . . . The private-enterprise economic system is often described as a profit system. That is a misnomer. It is a profit and *loss* system. If anything, the loss part is even more vital than the profit part. That is where it differs most from a government-controlled system. . . . This system produced the remarkable growth in the productivity of the U.S. economy during the past two centuries. Our increasing rejection of this system in favor of a government-controlled economy is

[11] *Wall Street Journal*, 6 August 1979.

[12] *Newsweek*, 13 August 1979, p. 55.

[13] *Wall Street Journal*, 17 September 1979, p. 1.

[14] *Business Week*, 20 August 1979, p. 132.

> a major reason why productivity in recent years has gone into reverse. [Statement of Milton Friedman][15]

Other economists attacked this approach as doctrinaire. Paul Samuelson, for example, wrote:

> [The] hard-boiled consistent advocate of laissez-faire will say: "let the losers bite the dust. Ours is a profit-and-loss system" . . . this kind of answer can be given without really thinking about the matter or knowing any facts . . . [It] means accepting a particular set of understood dogmas and sticking with them through thick or thin . . . Then there are the pragmatists . . . They say we must think about the workers who will be thrown out of jobs and about the merchants who will thereby lose business in a cumulative chain of lost spending and responding . . . My own counsel is to go very slow in weighing the Chrysler petition. Let's ascertain all the key facts first. [Statement of Paul Samuelson][16]

And John Kenneth Galbraith in his inimitable style dryly predicted that in the end ideological objections would give way to corporate interests:

> This request, one cannot doubt, will be granted. Even the finest and firmest free enterprise principles, we know, can be bent as needed to pecuniary and corporate need. And government handouts, however debilitating to the poor, have never been thought inimical to the wealthy. However, . . . if, as taxpayers, we are to invest one billion dollars in Chrysler, could we not be accorded an appropriate equity or ownership position? This is thought a reasonable claim by people who are putting up capital. And . . . in this high noon of the great conservative revolt, could we not ask that all corporations and all corporate executives that approve, or acquiesce by their silence in this expansive new public activity, refrain most scrupulously from any more of this criticism of big government? [Statement of John Kenneth Galbraith][17]

Chrysler's request for government aid was supported by its smooth and experienced lobbying efforts.[18] The Chrysler lobby team was headed by former congressman Joe Waggoner, Jr., of Louisiana, a once-influential member of the House Ways and Means Committee. The team also included Thomas Hale Boggs, Jr., son of the late majority leader of the House, and Ernest Christian, Jr., former legislative counsel in the Nixon administration. Waggoner, Boggs, and Christian had all maintained significant contacts in Washington. By September over a dozen of the sixty lawyers in Boggs's law firm were busy contacting Democratic congressmen, while Christian and others rallied Republican support. Moreover, while still chairman, Riccardo had spent long hours with Michigan's two Democratic senators, Donald Riegle and Carl Levin, and with Detroit mayor Coleman Young, all of

[15] Milton Friedman, "Chrysler: Are Jobs the Issue?" *Newsweek*, 10 September 1979, p. 66.

[16] Paul Samuelson, "Judging Corporate Handouts," *Newsweek*, 13 August 1979, p. 58.

[17] "Letters to the Editor," *Wall Street Journal*, 13 August 1979.

[18] See *Fortune*, 27 August 1979, pp. 30–31; and *Wall Street Journal*, 6 September 1979, p. 1.

whom subsequently also pleaded Chrysler's cause both locally and in Washington. In early June, Chrysler had stepped up its efforts by mobilizing a lobby consisting of dealers, suppliers, and the United Auto Workers. All were urged to contact their congressmen in order to "let them know how important Chrysler's business is." Before his retirement, Riccardo himself was spending four and five days a week in Washington visiting federal officials and congressmen, including Treasury Secretary G. William Miller, Rep. Henry Reuss, chairman of the House Banking Committee, Rep. Al Ullman, chairman of the House Ways and Means Committee, and Senator Russell B. Long, chairman of the Finance Committee. These, together with the governors of several midwestern states in which major Chrysler plants were located, all helped to further Chrysler's request for aid.

Chrysler's efforts eventually paid off.[19] On August 9, 1979, President Carter rejected Chrysler's initial request for $1 billion in cash as an advance against future tax credits but offered to extend Chrysler a federal loan guarantee. On September 15, Chrysler submitted a request for $1.2 billion in federal loan guarantees and was again turned down by the Carter administration with the admonition that any such request "would have to be well below $1 billion." But on November 1, the Carter administration reversed its position and offered Chrysler a $1.5 billion federal loan guarantee on condition that Chrysler raise an additional $1.5 billion of new unguaranteed capital and on condition that the government (the treasury secretary) be given the authority to change Chrysler's management if it failed to exercise "reasonable business judgment." Five days earlier, Chrysler had agreed to give Douglas A. Fraser, president of the United Auto Workers, a position on its board of directors in return for several wage concessions that the union had granted Chrysler. Thus, both government and labor would now exercise a measure of authority over Chrysler's management. Chrysler accepted the government offer and the plan was subsequently ratified by Congress in the closing days of December 1979.

The aid bill approved by Congress in December set up a government "loan guarantee board" with substantial control over Chrysler's affairs. The board could require the company to close plants, to drop existing automobile models, to cut spending for future products, to desist from acquiring new subsidiaries, or from selling off old ones; it could veto contracts over $10 million, it could inspect all Chrysler records, and it could place government personnel on Chrysler's board of directors to gain a majority. Almost all of Chrysler's assets were put up as collateral to the government. In case of bankruptcy, the federal government would end up owning the company and its assets.

When the Chrysler Loan Guarantee Act was passed by Congress, Chrysler managers forecast that 1980 losses would be about $482 million, but that the company would make profits in 1981 of about $383 million. This prediction was based on their estimates of the results of cutting about $1 billion from the company's fixed costs, selling off all foreign operations (except those in Canada and Mexico), and getting union wage concessions totaling $462.5 million. Unfortunately, the company's estimates proved drastically mistaken.

Chrysler took its first $500 million of guaranteed loans on June 24, 1980,

[19] See *Facts on File*, 7 September 1979, p. 662; 21 September 1979, p. 699; 9 November 1979, p. 845.

and a second installment of $300 million on July 31. But the infusion of new cash did not prevent the company's position from deteriorating. By early 1980 foreign car makers had taken over almost 30 percent of the U.S. car market, providing stiff competition for all U.S. automakers. Soaring interest rates for new car loans made buyers hesitant to purchase new cars (65 percent of all new cars are sold on credit). High inflation rates made auto production costs climb so that in the space of eighteen months domestic car makers were forced to raise car prices by 30 percent, thereby further discouraging buyers. By April 1980, with the prime interest rate at 20 percent, with production costs still climbing, with heavy foreign competition, and with customers unwilling to buy from a car maker that might be out of business tomorrow, car sales at Chrysler came almost to a standstill.

To make matters worse, Chrysler managers now made a costly error. During the summer and fall of 1980, just as Chrysler introduced its new 1981 models, interest rates stabilized and began to drop (to 13 percent). Unfortunately, Chrysler miscalculated what customers wanted and did not take advantage of the opportunity. Instead of bringing cost-conscious customers a wide range of low-priced cars with few options, Chrysler managers opted to send into their showrooms a large number of high-priced cars loaded down with expensive options. Customers refused to buy. As managers scrambled to correct their mistake by supplying more stripped-down, low-priced models, the prime interest rate once again shot upward, hitting 18.5 percent by the end of the year. By the time Chrysler got the right models into the showrooms, it was too late: High interest rates once again made consumers reluctant to buy.

It was clear by early December 1980 that Chrysler would once again suffer record losses. On Wall Street investors began to worry that the automaker would soon go bankrupt. Chrysler by now had spent all of the $800 million in guaranteed loans that it had drawn down in June and July, and the company's financial condition was as bad as it had ever been. It was clear already that 1980 would be even worse than 1979, and there was no longer any hope that 1981 would be profitable.

Once again Iacocca was forced to ask for concessions and new loans to keep the company going. The United Auto Workers union was asked to accept a $622 million pay freeze on cost-of-living adjustments, and other employees were asked for $161 million in pay freezes. Suppliers were asked to cut their prices by 5 percent for a $36 million saving. The company pledged to cut its operating budget over the next five years by $3 billion through further layoffs and postponement of several programs. And the Chrysler Loan Guarantee Board handed over another $400 million in new loans, raising the total to $1.2 billion.

By now Chrysler was on the way to becoming a completely changed company. Its workforce had been reduced by 40 percent, and more plants were certain to close in the future. Its overseas plants were closed or sold off. No longer was it producing large gas guzzlers: 80 percent of its cars were small four-cyclinder models and the most fuel-efficient small models were getting 50 mpg on the highway. In 1979 the company had made only ten cars per employee; by now the number was moving toward twenty cars per worker. And the company had introduced strict quality control standards to compete with the Japanese. Where buyers earlier had complained bitterly of car quality, by 1981 80 percent said they were satisfied with the quality of their Chrysler cars.

Nevertheless, in 1981 Chrysler still lost $476 million. But that was the turnaround year. The following year the automaker reported net operating losses of only $69 million, although the company's annual report showed a profit of $170 million as a result of the sale of some of its remaining nonessential assets. The next year, 1983, was the first year of clear operating profits for Chrysler.

On July 13, 1983, Lee Iacocca announced that Chrysler profits had finally enabled the company to finish paying off all of the $1.2 billion in government-guaranteed loans. One year later, bankers were describing the company as "an attractive client," and in November 1984, Standard & Poor's raised the company's debt rating from BB to an investment grade BBB. Chrysler had finally emerged from the throes of disaster.

1. As far as possible, identify the real factors (social, organizational, political, economic, managerial, etc.) that, in your view, explain the difficulties Chrysler was experiencing in July 1979. Identify the factors (social, organizational, political, etc.) that, in your view, resulted in the passage of the Chrysler Loan Act in December 1979. Which of the various analyses of government and economics (that is, Locke's, Smith's, Marx's, etc.) studied in the chapter provide the best understanding of the events that led to the difficulties of July 1979, and of the events that led to the passage of the Loan Act in December. Explain your answers.
2. Define, compare, and contrast the ideological views implied by the statements of each of the parties quoted in the case study. How did those ideological views influence the kinds of policy recommendations each party made? What elements of the philosophies examined in the chapter appear in these ideological views?
3. In your opinion, should the Chrysler loans have been made? From an ethical point of view, was it desirable to grant the loans? Was it desirable to give the government a say in the running of a private business corporation? Was it desirable to give the union a say in the running of a business? Justify your answer fully in terms of the utilities, the rights, and the justice factors involved. Does the fact that Chrysler eventually paid off the loans make a difference as to whether the loans should have been made in the first place?
4. How would Marx analyze the events in the case?

Humboldt County Private Enterprise

Mack Barber (not his real name) owns forty acres of rolling wooded land in Humboldt County in California. He uses it to grow marijuana.

Mr. Barber is in his early forties, married, and holds degrees from two universities. For several years he held a responsible position working for an engineering firm. Several years ago he gave it all up, "dropped out," and he and his wife, Rebecca, moved to the woods of Humboldt, and began to grow a few plants of marijuana for their own use. Eventually they decided to go into the business of producing marijuana, as many of their neighbors were doing in response to the depressed economic conditions of the area (unemployment was running as high as 22 percent).

> Like me, most of the growers raised marijuana just for their own use until four years ago when the word got out and it became so profitable people grew it to sell.

> . . . What's happened is a lot of good people have become independent of the welfare system because of this crop. . . . A good year for me would be 20 pounds. A nice, comfortable year is 10 to 15 pounds. [Statement of Mack Barber][1]

The particular kind of marijuana—"sinsemilla"—grown by Mr. Barber sells for from $1,000 to $2,500 a pound, depending on market supply and demand factors. The plants are germinated indoors in January or February, transplanted outdoors in April, and harvested in September and October. The climate in Humboldt County is particularly favorable for growing sinsemilla. Sinsemilla is a seedless form of marijuana that produces unusual amounts of tetrahydrocannabinol, the mild hallucinogenic that gives marijuana its desirable qualities and that makes Humboldt County marijuana one of the most sought-after varieties of marijuana. Humboldt sinsemilla is known to be exported and marketed in Alaska, New York, southern California, and Florida, the four corners of the United States.[2]

Experts estimate that the marijuana industry brought $300 million into Humboldt County in 1979 alone. By comparison, the second largest agricultural commodity (hay) brought in only $7 million. Only timber and possibly fishing are larger industries. As the marijuana business grew from a few small plots in 1975 and became a multimillion-dollar industry in 1979, the employment picture in Humboldt County also improved dramatically. The jobless rate declined from a high of 22 percent in 1975 to about 9 percent in 1979. Many observers believe this decline was brought about by the absorption of several thousand persons into the marijuana industry.[3]

The marijuana industry of Humboldt County has created a considerable stir. Because of its economic importance and because large numbers of people believe they should not be prohibited from smoking marijuana if they freely choose to, Humboldt County supervisors have often discouraged police efforts to restrict marijuana growers by voting against funding for such efforts. As one supervisor put it:

> Some responsible businessmen think it (the marijuana industry) is very important to the economy. You know: people who sell cars, hardware, fencing and garden tools. [Statement of county supervisor][4]

Or, as a woman resident put it: "There are people who feel very strongly that this is their [rightful] living." Many other residents also felt that if the farmers wanted to use their private property to grow and sell marijuana, that was their right.

The sheriff's department, however, has tried to step up its efforts to enforce California law, which prohibits growing or selling marijuana. During harvest season, the sheriff's department flies over the county in airplanes and helicopters to locate marijuana farms. Once a farm is located, the department "raids" it, confis-

[1] Ed Pope, "Grower Brings New Life to Land," *San Jose Mercury*, 21 October 1979, p. 3A.

[2] Ed Pope, "Harvest Tension Grows for Pot Farmers," *San Jose Mercury*, 26 November 1979, p. 12A.

[3] Ed Pope, "Marijuana is Cash Crop for North Coast Farmers," *San Jose Mercury*, 21 October 1979, p. 3A.

[4] *Ibid.*

cates and destroys the marijuana farmer's crop, and destroys his watering system. Many residents see this as an unfortunate use of the county's very limited public resources.

Robert Cogan, an attorney for some of the farmers, sees these raids as ways of suppressing the political impact of the predominantly left-wing farmers:

> The raids take away their source of income; they will reduce the growers' participation in the upcoming election, prevent them from spending money in the campaign and financially backing their candidates and make them withdraw even further from this society . . . [The average marijuana farmer only] makes between $5,000 and $10,000 off any crop he harvests and he is lucky if he brings in more than one of every five crops he plants. [Statement of Robert Cogan][5]

In addition, of course, the raids restrict supply, thereby making it more difficult and expensive for users of marijuana to obtain what they want.

1. How would Marx analyze the events recounted in the case? How would Smith analyze these events? How would Locke analyze these events? To what extent, if at all, are these analyses correct?
2. In your view, should government prohibit economic activities like growing and selling marijuana? Why or why not? What sorts of business activities should government prohibit; what sort should it not prohibit? Justify your position fully. Identify the ideology implied by your position.
3. From an ethical point of view, what recommendations would you make to the various parties involved in the case? Explain your recommendations in terms of the utilities, the rights, and the just or unjust distributions involved.

[5] *Ibid.*

4

ETHICS IN THE MARKETPLACE

INTRODUCTION

Consider the following recent news stories:

> Eight Chrysler, Plymouth, Dodge, and Jeep-Eagle dealers were indicted for planning to fix prices at a tent sale that had been scheduled for September 1989. . . . Chrysler dealer James Koken, president of Main Street Chrysler-Plymouth of Avon, New York, has been fined $1,000 and sentenced to 200 hours of community service. . . .[1]
>
> Three record companies agreed to pay a total of $11.2 million to settle a price-fixing lawsuit. . . RCA agreed to pay $4.9 million, Polygram $3.5 million and Capital-EMI $2.8 million. . . . Earlier, two other companies that own record concerns, CBS Inc. and MCA Inc., settled the suit for $4.3 million and $1.7 million respectively. The federal suit . . . charged eight record companies with conspiring to "fix, raise and maintain" the price of records and tapes.[2]
>
> Twenty-two states last week filed suit charging [Sandoz Pharmaceutical Co.] with antitrust violations and price-fixing. . . . The suits, filed in U.S. District Court in New York, claim that Sandoz's distribution arrangement for [the anti-schizophrenic drug Clozaril], which required the purchase of a blood monitoring system from Baxter Healthcare Corp.'s. Caremark division, is illegal and has inflated the price

[1] *Automotive News*, 31 December 1990, p. 11.

[2] *Wall Street Journal*, 17 April 1985, p. 28.

of Clozaril. Sandoz charges patients $8,944 per year for the drug, including the monitoring system. Some 7,100 people are receiving the medication.[3]

Since 1985, state attorneys general have filed or investigated at least 70 antitrust cases in the healthcare industry, according to the preliminary results of a recent study. . . . Of those cases, 34 involved allegations of illegal group boycotts or concerted efforts by competitors against a third party. Seventeen cases involved allegations of price fixing; eleven cases involved allegations of anticompetitive mergers; and eight cases involved various other suspected antitrust violations.[4]

Abbott Laboratories, American Home Products, and Bristol-Myers Squibb, the US' top three producers of infant formula, have been charged with conspiring to drive up the price of infant formula. Formula prices rose 155.4% between 12/79 and 12/89, vs a 36.4% price rise for milk and a 50.8% rise in overall grocery prices. The three companies named in the suit . . . control over 95% of the US infant formula market.[5]

Best Buy Co. [a discount retailer] has filed a complaint against Onkyo U.S.A. charging antitrust violations. According to Best Buy general counsel Elliot Kaplan, Onkyo pulled its lines from all stores in late August, at least partly because of displeasure with the low prices charged by Best Buy . . . The retailer claims that Onkyo "fixed, set and stabilized . . . resale prices at artificially high levels" and was "most upset about Best Buy's 'price cutting.' "[6]

If free markets are justified, it is because they allocate resources and distribute commodities in ways that are just, that maximize the economic utility of society's members, and that respect the freedom of choice of both buyers and sellers. These moral aspects of a market system depend crucially on the competitive nature of the system. If firms join together and use their combined power to fix prices, to drive out competitors with unfair practices, or to earn monopolistic profits at the expense of consumers, the market ceases to be competitive and the results are injustice, a decline in social utility, and a restriction of people's freedom of choice.

In view of the key role of competition in the American economy, both factually and from a normative point of view, it is surprising that anticompetitive practices are so common. A report on New York Stock Exchange companies showed that 10 percent of the companies had been involved in antitrust suits during the previous five years.[7] A survey of major corporate executives indicated that 60 percent of those sampled believed that many businesses engage in price-fixing.[8] In 1975 and 1976 alone over sixty major firms were prosecuted by federal agencies for anticompetitive practices. This chapter examines such practices, the underlying rationales for prohibiting them, and the moral values that market competition is meant to achieve.

Before studying the ethics of anticompetitive practices it is essential that

[3] *Modern Healthcare*, 31 December 1990, p. 10.

[4] *Modern Healthcare*, 17 December 1990, p. 41.

[5] *New York Times*, 5 January 1991, p. 21.

[6] *Discount Store News*, 17 September 1990, p. 3.

[7] Sharen D. Knight, ed., *Concerned Investors Guide, NYSE Volume 1983* (Arlington, VA: Resource Publishing Group, Inc., 1983), pp. 24–25.

[8] Ralph Nader and Mark J. Green, "Crime in the Suites," *New Republic*, 29 April 1972, pp. 17–21.

one have a precise understanding of the complex meaning of market competition. We all have, of course, an intuitive understanding of competition: It is a rivalry between two or more parties trying to obtain something that only one of them can possess. Competition exists in political elections, in football games, on the battlefield, and in courses in which grades are distributed "on the curve." Market competition, however, involves more than mere rivalry between two or more firms. To get a clearer idea of the nature of market competition we will examine three abstract models describing three degrees of competition in a market: perfect competition, pure monopoly, and oligopoly. We will examine, also, the ethical issues raised by each type of competition.

4.1 PERFECT COMPETITION

A market is any forum in which people come together for the purpose of exchanging ownership of goods or money. Markets can be small and very temporary (two friends trading clothes can constitute a tiny transient market) or quite large and relatively permanent (the oil market spans several continents and has been operating for decades).

A perfectly competitive free market is one in which no buyer or seller has the power to significantly affect the prices at which goods are being exchanged.[9] Perfectly competitive free markets are characterized by the following seven features:

1. There are numerous buyers and sellers, none of whom has a substantial share of the market.
2. All buyers and sellers can freely and immediately enter or leave the market.
3. Every buyer and seller has full and perfect knowledge of what every other buyer and seller is doing, including knowledge of the prices, quantities, and quality of all goods being bought and sold.
4. The goods being sold in the market are so similar to each other that no one cares from whom each buys or sells.
5. The costs and benefits of producing or using the goods being exchanged are borne entirely by those buying or selling the goods and not by any other external parties.
6. All buyers and sellers are utility maximizers: each tries to get as much as possible for as little as possible.
7. No external parties (such as the government) regulate the price, quantity, or quality of any of the goods being bought and sold in the market.

The first two features are the basic characteristics of a "competitive" market since they ensure that buyers and sellers are roughly equal in power and none can force the others to accept his terms. The seventh feature is what makes a market qualify as a "free" market: It is one that is free of any externally imposed regulations on price, quantity, or quality. (So-called "free" markets, however, are not necessarily free of all constraints, as we will see.)

In addition to these seven characteristics, free competitive markets also need

[9] The elementary account that follows can be found in any standard economics textbook, for instance, Paul A. Samuelson, *Economics*, 11th ed. (New York: McGraw-Hill Book Company, 1980), pp. 52–62.

an enforceable private property system (otherwise buyers and sellers would not have any "ownership rights" to exchange), an underlying system of contracts (which allows buyers and sellers to forge agreements that transfer ownership), and an underlying system of production (that generates goods or services whose ownership can be exchanged).

In a perfectly competitive free market the price buyers are willing to pay for goods rises when fewer goods are available, and these rising prices induce sellers to provide greater quantities of goods. On the other hand, as more goods are made available, prices tend to fall and these falling prices lead sellers to decrease the quantities of goods they provide. These fluctuations produce a striking outcome: In a perfectly competitive market prices and quantities always move toward what is called the "equilibrium point." *The equilibrium point is the point at which the amount of goods buyers want to buy exactly equals the amount of goods sellers want to sell, and at which the highest price buyers are willing to pay exactly equals the lowest price sellers are willing to take.* At the equilibrium point every seller finds a willing buyer and every buyer finds a willing seller. Moreover, this surprising result of perfectly competitive free markets has an even more astonishing outcome: It satisfies the three moral criteria of justice, utility, and rights. That is, perfectly competitive free markets achieve a certain kind of justice, they satisfy a certain version of utilitarianism, and they respect certain kinds of moral rights.

Why do perfectly competitive markets achieve these three surprising moral outcomes? The well-known supply and demand curves can be used to explain the phenomenon. Our explanation will proceed in two stages. First, we will see why perfectly competitive free markets always move toward the equilibrium point. Then we will see why markets that move toward equilibrium in this way achieve these three moral outcomes.

Equilibrium in Perfectly Competitive Markets

A *demand* curve is a line on a graph indicating the value that consumers (or buyers) place on goods as different quantities of those goods are made available to them. As we mentioned above, the fewer the goods available to consume, the higher the price buyers put on them, so the demand curve slopes down to the right. In the imaginary curve in Figure 4.1, for example, buyers will pay $1 per basket of potatoes if 600 tons of potatoes are available for their consumption, but they are willing to pay as much as $5 per basket if only 100 tons of potatoes can be purchased.

Notice that the demand curve slopes downward to the right, indicating that consumers are willing to pay less for each unit of a good as more of those units become available: The value of potatoes falls for consumers as more potatoes become available. Why is this? This phenomenon is explained by a principle we will assume human nature always follows, the so-called "principle of diminishing marginal utility." The principle of diminishing marginal utility states that each additional item a person consumes is less satisfying than each of the earlier items the person consumed: the more we consume, the less we get from consuming more. The second pizza a person eats at lunch, for example, is much less satisfying than the first one; the third will be substantially less tasty than the second; while the fourth may be positively disgusting. Because of the principle of diminishing

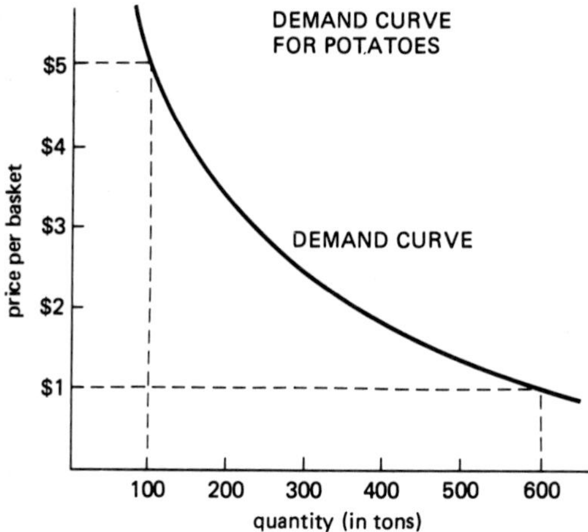

FIGURE 4-1

marginal utility, the more goods consumers purchase in a market, the less satisfying additional goods are to them and the less value they place on each additional good. Thus, the buyer's demand curve slopes downward to the right because the principle of diminishing marginal utility ensures that the value of goods diminishes for the buyer as quantities increase.

The demand curve thus indicates the value consumers place on, say, each basket of potatoes, as more baskets become available to them. Consequently, if prices rose above their demand curve, buyers would see themselves as losers, that is, as paying out more in costs than the value of what they were gaining in return. At any point below the demand curve they would see themselves as winners, that is, as paying out less in costs than what they get in return. ("Costs" here refer to whatever other satisfactions the consumer had to forgo in order to pay for the commodity.) So when prices rise *above* the demand curve, buyers will tend to leave the market and invest their resources in other markets. But if prices fall *below* the demand curve, new buyers will tend to flock into the market since they perceive an opportunity to increase their satisfactions at a low cost.

Now let us look at the other side of the market: the supply side. A *supply* curve is a line on a graph indicating the prices producers or sellers must charge to cover the costs of supplying given amounts of a commodity. The higher the price per unit, the more units sellers can supply, so the curve slopes upward to the right. In the example curve traced in Figure 4.2, for example, farmers can provide only 100 tons of potatoes if potatoes will sell at only $1 per basket; but they can supply 500 tons if their potatoes will sell at $4 per basket.

At first sight it may seem odd that producers or sellers must charge higher prices when they are producing large volumes than when producing in small quantities. We are accustomed to thinking that it costs less to produce goods in large quantities than in small quantities. But the increasing costs of production are explained by a principle that we will call the "principle of increasing marginal costs." This principle states that after a certain point, each additional item the seller produces costs him more to produce than earlier items. Why? Because of an unfortunate feature of our physical world: Its productive resources are limited. A producer will use the best and most productive resources to make his first few

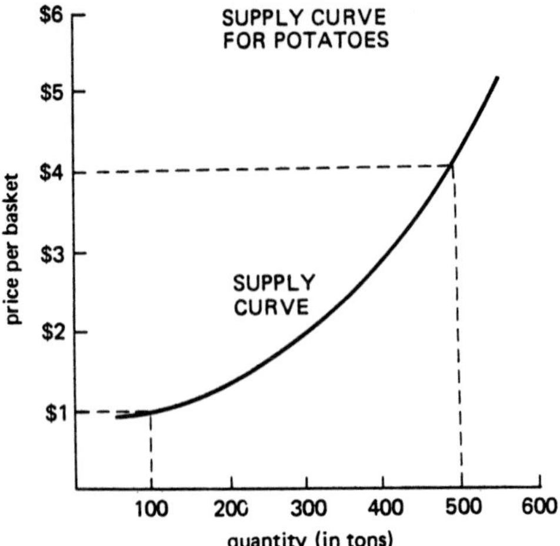

FIGURE 4-2

goods and at this point his costs will indeed decline as he expands his production. A potato grower farming in a valley, for example, will begin by planting the level fertile acres in the floor of the valley where the more acreage he plants the more his costs per unit decline. But as the farmer continues to expand his farm he eventually runs out of these highly productive resources and must turn to using less productive land. As the potato farmer uses up the acreage on the floor of the valley, he is forced to start planting the sloping and less fertile land at the edges of the valley which may be rocky and may require more expensive irrigation. If he continues increasing his production he will eventually have to start planting the land on the mountainsides and his costs will rise even higher. Eventually the farmer reaches a situation where the more he produces, the more it costs him to produce each unit because he is forced to use increasingly unproductive materials. The predicament of the potato farmer illustrates the principle of increasing marginal costs: After a certain point added production always entails increasing costs per unit. And that is the situation illustrated by the supply curve. The supply curve rises upward to the right because it pictures the point at which sellers must begin to charge more per unit to cover the costs of supplying additional goods.

The supply curve, then, indicates how much producers must charge per unit in order to cover the costs of producing increasing amounts of a commodity. The curve represents, therefore, the minimum price producers can accept without sustaining losses. (''Costs'' here include not only the costs of labor, materials, distribution, etc., but also the ''normal'' profits sellers must make to motivate them to invest their resources in producing the commodity and to forgo the opportunity of making profits by investing in other markets.) For this reason, when prices fall below the supply curve, producers see themselves as losers: They are receiving less than the costs they must pay to produce the commodity. Consequently, if prices fall *below* the supply curve, producers will tend to leave the market and invest their resources in other, more profitable markets. On the other hand, if prices rise *above* the supply curve, then new producers will come crowding into the market, attracted by the opportunity to invest their resources in a market where they can derive higher profits than in other markets.

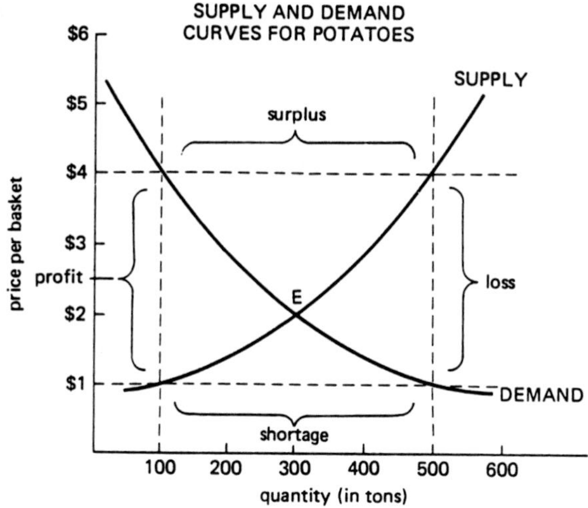

FIGURE 4-3

Sellers and buyers, of course, trade in the same markets, so their respective supply and demand curves can be superimposed on the same graph. Typically, when this is done, the supply and demand curves will meet and cross at some point. The point at which they meet is the point at which the price buyers are willing to pay for a certain amount of goods exactly matches the price sellers are willing to accept for that same amount (that is, the "equilibrium price"). This point of intersection, as indicated in Figure 4.3, where the point, "E," at which the supply and demand curves meet, is the so-called "point of equilibrium" or "equilibrium price." It is at $2 on the graph.

We mentioned that in a perfectly competitive free market, prices, the amounts supplied, and the amounts demanded will all tend to move toward the point of equilibrium. Why does this happen? Notice in Figure 4.3 that if the *prices* of potatoes rise above the point of equilibrium, say to $4 per basket, producers will supply more goods (500 tons) than at the equilibrium price level (300 tons). But at that high price, consumers will purchase fewer goods (only 100 tons) than at the equilibrium price. The result will be a surplus of unsold goods (500 − 100 = 400 tons of unsold potatoes). To get rid of their unsold surplus, sellers will be forced to lower their prices and decrease production. Eventually, equilibrium prices and amounts will be reached.

On the other hand, if the price drops below the point of equilibrium in Figure 4.3, say to $1 per basket, then producers will start supplying less than consumers want at that price. The result will be an excessive demand and shortages will appear. Subsequently, prices will rise and the rising prices will attract more producers into the market, thereby raising supplies. Eventually, again, equilibrium will reassert itself.

Notice also what happens in Figure 4.3 if the *amount* being supplied, say 100 tons, for some reason is less than the equilibrium amount. The cost of supplying such an amount ($1 per basket) is much less than what consumers are willing to pay ($4 per basket) for that same amount. Consequently, prices will rise to the level the consumer is willing to pay ($4), and the difference ($3) will be abnormally high profits. The high profits, however, will attract outside producers into the market, thereby increasing the amounts supplied and bringing about a corresponding decrease in the price consumers are willing to pay for the increased amounts of goods that become available. Gradually, the amounts supplied will increase to the equilibrium point, and prices will drop to equilibrium prices.

The opposite happens if the amount being supplied, say 500 tons, is for some reason more than the equilibrium amount. Under these circumstances sellers will have to lower their prices to the very low levels that consumers are willing to pay for such large amounts. At such low price levels, the producers will leave the market to invest their resources in other, more profitable markets, thereby lowering the supply, raising the price, and once again reestablishing equilibrium levels.

At this point the reader may be trying to think of an industry that fits the description of perfect competition we have just given. The reader will have some difficulty finding one. Only a few agricultural markets, such as grain markets and potato markets, come close to embodying the six features that characterize a perfectly competitive market.[10] The fact is that the model of perfect competition is a theoretical construct of the economist which does not exist. But although the model does not describe real markets, it does provide us with a clear understanding of the advantages of competition and an understanding of why it is desirable to keep markets as competitive as possible.

Morality in Perfectly Competitive Markets

As we have seen, perfectly competitive free markets incorporate forces that inevitably drive all buyers and sellers toward the so-called "point of equilibrium." In doing so they achieve three major moral values: (1) they lead buyers and sellers to exchange their goods in a way that is perfectly just (in a certain sense of "just"), (2) they maximize the utility of buyers and sellers by leading them to allocate, use, and distribute their goods with perfect efficiency, and (3) they bring about these achievements in a way that respects buyers' and sellers' right of free consent. As we examine each of these moral achievements, it is important to keep in mind that they are characteristics *only* of the perfectly competitive free market, that is, *of markets that have the seven features we listed above.* Markets that fail to have one or the other of these features do not necessarily achieve these three moral values.

To understand why perfectly competitive free markets lead buyers and sellers to make exchanges that are perfectly just we can begin by recalling the capitalist meaning of justice described in Chapter Two. According to the *capitalist* criterion of justice benefits and burdens are distributed justly when each person receives in return the exact value of the contribution he or she made to an enterprise: Fairness is getting paid fully, in return for what one contributes. It is this form of justice (and only this form) that is perfectly achieved in perfectly competitive free markets.

Perfectly competitive free markets embody perfect capitalist justice because such markets necessarily converge on the equilibrium point and *the equilibrium*

[10] Daniel B. Suits, "Agriculture," in *The Structure of American Industry*, 5th ed., Walter Adams, ed. (New York: Macmillan Inc., 1977), pp. 1–39.

point is the one (and only) point at which buyers and sellers each receive the exact value of what they contribute. Why is this true? Recall that the consumer's demand curve indicates the value consumers place on goods at each different level of consumption. So if prices (and quantities) rise above the consumer's demand curve, the consumer unfairly has to pay sellers more for goods than what he feels those goods (in those quantities) are worth. If prices (and quantities) fall below the consumer's demand curve, the consumer unfairly pays sellers less than what the consumer knows those goods (in those quantities) are worth to him. Thus, from the standpoint of the value the consumer places on different quantities of goods, the price is fair (that is, the price exactly equals the value the consumer places on the goods) only if it falls somewhere on the consumer's demand curve.

On the other hand, the seller's supply curve indicates the value the seller places on goods insofar as it indicates what it cost him to produce those goods at different levels of production. Consequently, if prices (and quantities) fall below the seller's supply curve, consumers are unfairly shortchanging the seller since they are paying him less than it cost him to produce those goods in those quantities. And if prices rise above the seller's supply curve, the seller is unfairly shortchanging the consumers since he is charging them more than what the seller knows those goods are worth in terms of what they cost to produce in those quantities. Thus, from the standpoint of the value the seller places on goods, the price is fair (that is, the price exactly equals the value the seller places on the goods) only if it falls somewhere on the seller's supply curve.

Obviously, there is only a single point at which the price and quantity of a commodity lies both on the buyer's demand curve (and is thus fair from the standpoint of the value the buyer places on the goods) and on the seller's supply curve (and is thus fair from the standpoint of the value the seller places on the goods): the equilibrium point. Thus, the equilibrium point is the one and only point at which prices are perfectly just both from the buyer's and the seller's point of view. When prices or quantities deviate from the equilibrium point, either the buyer or the seller is unjustly being shortchanged: One or the other has to pay more than the value placed on those goods in those quantities.

The perfectly competitive market thus continually—almost magically—reestablishes a perfect capitalist justice for its participants by continually leading them to buy and sell goods at the one quantity and the one price at which each receives the exact value of what he contributes, whether this value is calculated from the buyer's or the seller's point of view.[11]

In addition to establishing a form of justice perfectly and continuously, competitive markets also maximize the utility of buyers and sellers by leading them to allocate, use, and distribute their goods with perfect efficiency. A market is

[11] The reader may recall that one of the major criticisms leveled at the capitalist conception of justice is that it says people should be paid the exact value of the things they contribute, yet it gives no criterion for determining the "value" of a thing. Since different people place different values on things, this indeterminacy seems to make the capitalist conception of justice hopelessly vague: A price that is "just" in terms of the value one person places on a thing, may be "unjust" in terms of the value another person places on that same thing. However, the values given to things by perfectly competitive markets are just from every participant's point of view since at the point of equilibrium all participants (both buyers and sellers) place the same value on commodities and prices converge on this uniquely just value.

perfectly efficient when goods are allocated, used, and distributed in a way that produces the highest level of satisfaction possible from these goods. A system of perfectly competitive markets achieves such efficiency in three main ways.[12]

First, a perfectly competitive market system motivates firms to invest resources in those industries where consumer demand is high and to move resources away from industries where consumer demand is low. Resources will be attracted into markets where high consumer demand creates shortages that raise prices above equilibrium, and they will flee markets where low consumer demand leads to surpluses that lower prices below equilibrium. The perfectly competitive market system allocates resources efficiently in accordance with consumer demands and needs: The consumer is "sovereign" over the market.

Second, perfectly competitive markets encourage firms both to minimize the amount of resources consumed in producing a commodity and to use the most efficient technology available. Firms are motivated to use resources sparingly because they will want to lower their costs and thereby increase their profit margin. Moreover, in order not to lose buyers to other firms, each firm will reduce its profits to the lowest levels consistent with the survival of the firm. The perfectly competitive market encourages an efficient use of the seller's resources as well.

Third, perfectly competitive markets distribute commodities among buyers in such a way that all buyers receive the most satisfying bundle of commodities they can purchase, given the commodities available to them and the money they can spend on these commodities. For when faced by a system of perfectly competitive markets, each buyer will buy up those proportions of each commodity that correspond with the buyer's desire for the commodity when weighed against the buyer's desires for other commodities. And when buyers have completed their buying they will each know that they cannot improve on their purchases by trading their goods with other consumers, since all consumers can buy the same goods at the same prices. Thus, perfectly competitive markets enable consumers to attain a level of satisfaction upon which they cannot improve given the constraints of their budgets and the range of available goods. An efficient distribution of commodities is thereby achieved.

Finally, perfectly competitive markets establish capitalist justice and maximize utility in a way that respects buyers' and sellers' negative rights. First, in a perfectly competitive market, buyers and sellers are free (by definition) to enter or leave the market as they choose. That is, individuals are neither forced into nor prevented from engaging in a certain business, provided they have the expertise and the financial resources required.[13] Perfectly competitive markets thus embody the negative right of freedom of opportunity. Second, in the perfectly competitive free market, all exchanges are fully voluntary. That is, participants are not forced to buy or sell anything other than what they freely and knowingly consent to buy or sell. For in a competitive free market all participants have full and complete knowledge of what they are buying or selling and no external agency (such as the government) forces them to buy or sell goods they do not want at prices they

[12] See Robert Dorfman, *Prices and Markets*, 2nd ed. (Englewood Cliffs, NJ: Prentice Hall, 1972), pp. 170–226.

[13] Russell G. Warren, *Antitrust in Theory and Practice* (Columbus, OH: Grid, Inc., 1975), pp. 58–59.

do not choose in quantities they do not desire.[14] Moreover, buyers and sellers in a perfectly competitive free market are not forced to pay for goods that others enjoy. For in a perfectly competitive free market, by definition, the costs and benefits of producing or using goods are borne entirely by those buying or selling the goods and not by any other external parties. Free competitive markets thus embody the negative right of freedom of consent. Third, no single seller or buyer so dominates the perfectly competitive free market that he is able to force the others to accept his terms or go without.[15] In a perfectly competitive market, industrial power is decentralized among numerous firms so that prices and quantities are not dependent on the whim of one or a few businesses. In short, perfectly competitive free markets embody the negative right of freedom from coercion.

Thus, perfectly competitive free markets are, in three important respects, "perfectly" moral: (1) They perfectly and continuously establish a capitalist form of justice; (2) they maximize utility in the form of market efficiency; and (3) they respect certain important negative rights of buyers and sellers.

Several cautions are in order, however, when interpreting these moral features of perfectly competitive free markets. First, perfectly competitive free markets do not establish other forms of justice. Since they do not respond to the needs of those outside the market or those who have little to exchange, for example, they cannot establish a justice based on needs. Moreover, perfectly competitive free markets impose no restrictions on how much wealth each participant accumulates relative to the others, so they ignore egalitarian justice and may incorporate large inequalities. Second, competitive markets maximize the utility of those who can participate in the market given the constraints of each participant's budget. But this does not mean that society's total utility is necessarily maximized. For the bundle of goods distributed to each individual by a competitive market system depends ultimately on that individual's ability to participate in the market and on how much that individual has to spend in the market. But this way of distributing goods may not produce the most satisfaction for everyone in society. Society's welfare might be increased, for example, by giving more goods to those who cannot participate in the market because they have nothing to exchange (perhaps they are too poor, too old, too sick, too disabled, or too young to have anything to trade in markets); or the overall welfare might be increased by distributing more goods to those who have only a little to spend or by limiting the consumption of those who can spend a lot. Third, although free competitive markets establish certain negative rights for those within the market, they may actually diminish the positive rights of those outside (those, for example, who cannot compete) or of those whose participation is minimal. People who have the money to participate in markets may consume goods (such as food or educational resources) that people outside the market, or those with very little money, need in order to develop and exercise their own freedom and rationality. Thus, although perfectly competitive free markets secure capitalist justice, although they maximize economic utility, and respect certain negative rights, they largely do this only for those who have the means (the money or the goods) to participate fully in those markets, and

[14] Milton Friedman, *Capitalism and Freedom* (Chicago: The University of Chicago Press, 1962), p. 14.

[15] Warren, *Antitrust*, pp. 76–77.

they necessarily ignore the needs, the utility, and the rights of those who are left out of the marketplace.

Finally, and most importantly, we should note that the three values of capitalist justice, utility, and negative rights are produced by free markets *only if they embody the seven conditions that define perfect competition.* If one or more of these conditions are not present in a given real market, then the claim can no longer be made that these three values are present. As we will see in the remainder of this chapter—and, in fact, throughout the rest of this book—this is the most crucial limitation of free market morality. For real markets are *not* perfectly competitive and consequently they do not achieve the three moral values that characterize perfect competition. In spite of this critical limitation, however, the perfectly competitive free market provides us with a precise idea of how economic exchanges in a market economy should be structured if relationships among buyers and sellers are to secure the three moral achievements we indicated above. We will turn next to see what happens when some of the defining characteristics of perfect competition are absent.

4.2 MONOPOLY COMPETITION

What happens when a free market (that is, one without government intervention) ceases to be perfectly competitive? We will begin to answer this question in this section by examining the opposite extreme of a perfectly competitive market: the free (unregulated) monopoly market. We will then examine some less extreme varieties of noncompetition.

We noted earlier that a perfectly competitive market is characterized by seven conditions. In a monopoly, two of these conditions are not present.[16] First, instead of "numerous sellers, none of whom has a substantial share of the market," the monopoly market has only one seller and that single seller has a substantial (100 percent) share of the market. Second, instead of being a market that other sellers "can freely and immediately enter or leave," the monopoly market is one that other buyers cannot enter. Instead, there are barriers to entry such as patent laws, which give only one seller the right to produce a commodity, or high capitalization costs, which make it too expensive for a new seller to start a business in that industry.

The classic and standard example of a monopoly is the market in aluminum that developed during the first few decades of this century.[17] Alcoa (the Aluminum Company of America) held the patents for the production of virgin aluminum in the United States until 1909, by which time it was firmly entrenched as the sole domestic producer of aluminum. Moreover, although its patents ran out in 1909, other manufacturers were never able to enter successfully into the production of aluminum because their start-up costs would have been too high and they lacked

[16] Again, any standard economics textbook can be consulted for these elementary ideas, for example, H. Robert Heller, *The Economic System* (New York: Macmillan Inc., 1972), p. 109.

[17] See Douglas F. Greer, *Industrial Organization and Public Policy* (New York: Macmillan, Inc. 1984), pp. 189–91. Note, however, that some researchers challenge this traditional approach to the Alcoa Case, for example, Dominick T. Armentano, *Antitrust and Monopoly, Anatomy of a Policy Failure* (New York: John Wiley & Sons, Inc. 1982), pp. 100–12.

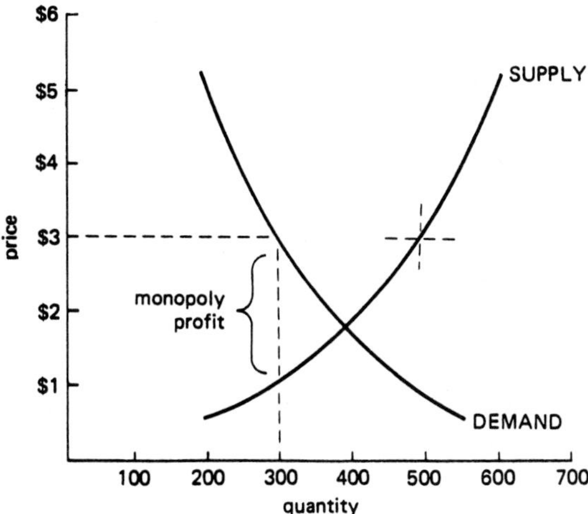

FIGURE 4-4

Alcoa's experience, trade connections, and trained personnel. Alcoa remained the sole domestic producer of virgin aluminum until the 1940s when it was successfully prosecuted under the Sherman Antitrust Act. For similar reasons, Western Electric emerged during the 1960s as the sole monopoly producer of certain telephone products.

Monopolies can also be created through mergers. At the turn of the century, for example, the leading oil refineries merged into a "holding company" (then called "Standard Oil," now named "Exxon") which acquired monopoly control over oil refining. The monopoly was broken up into thirty-four separate companies when the Supreme Court charged the company with monopolization in 1911. And a policy of forced mergers during the closing decades of the nineteenth century enabled the American Tobacco Company to absorb all the major cigarette manufacturing companies in the United States so that by the turn of the century the combine controlled the American cigarette market. In 1911 the company was ordered broken up into several smaller firms.

Monopoly markets, then, are those in which a single firm is the only seller in the market and which new sellers are barred from entering. A seller in a monopoly market, therefore, can control the prices of the available goods. Figure 4.4 illustrates the situation in a monopoly market: The monopoly firm is able to fix its output at a quantity that is less than equilibrium and at which demand is so high that it allows the firm to reap an excess "monopoly profit" by charging prices that are far above the supply curve and above the equilibrium price. A monopoly seller, for example, can set prices above their equilibrium level at, say, $3. By limiting supply to only those amounts buyers will purchase at the monopolist's high prices (300 units), the monopoly firm can ensure that it sells all its products, and that it will reap substantial profits from its business. The monopoly firm will, of course, calculate the price–amount ratios that will secure the highest total profits (that is, the profit-per-unit multiplied by the number of units), and will then fix its prices and production at those levels. At the turn of the century, for example, American Tobacco Company, which earlier had managed to acquire a monopoly in the sale of cigarettes, was making profits equal to about 56 percent of its sales.

If entry into the market were open, of course, these excess profits would draw other producers into the market, resulting in an increased supply of goods and a drop in prices until equilibrium was attained. In a monopoly market, where entry is closed or prohibitive, this does not happen and prices remain high.

Monopoly Competition: Justice, Utility, and Rights

How well does a free monopoly market succeed in achieving the moral values that characterize perfectly competitive free markets? Not well. Unregulated monopoly markets can fall short of the three values of capitalist justice, economic efficiency, and respect for negative rights that perfect competition achieves.

The most obvious failure of monopoly markets lies in the high prices they enable the monopolist to charge and the high profits they enable him to reap, a failure that violates capitalist justice.[18] Why do the high prices and profits of the monopolist violate capitalist justice? Capitalist justice says that each person should receive the exact value of the contribution he or she makes. As we saw, the equilibrium point is the one (and only) point at which buyers and sellers each receive in return the exact value of what each contributes to the other, whether this value is determined from the buyer's or the seller's point of view. In a monopoly market, however, prices for goods are set above the equilibrium level, and quantities are set at less than the equilibrium amount. As a result, the seller charges the buyer far more than the goods are worth (from his own seller's point of view) since he charges far more than it cost him to make those goods. Thus, the high prices the seller forces the buyer to pay are unjust and these unjustly high prices are the source of the seller's excess profits.

A monopoly market also results in a decline in the efficiency with which it allocates and distributes goods. First, the monopoly market allows resources to be used in ways that will produce shortages of those things buyers want and cause them to be sold at higher prices than necessary. The high profits in a monopoly market indicate a shortage of goods but because other firms are blocked from entering the market, their resources cannot be used to make up the shortages indicated by the high profits. This means that the resources of these other firms are deflected into other nonmonopoly markets that already have an adequate supply of goods. Shortages, therefore, continue to exist. Moreover, the monopoly market allows the monopoly firm to set its prices well above costs, instead of forcing the firm to lower its prices to cost levels. The result is an inflated price for the consumer, a price that the consumer is forced to accept because the absence of other sellers has limited his or her choices. These excess profits absorbed by the monopolist are resources that are not needed to supply the amounts of goods the consumer is getting.

Second, monopoly markets do not encourage suppliers to use resources in ways that will minimize the resources consumed to produce a certain amount of a commodity. A monopoly firm is not encouraged to reduce its costs and is therefore not motivated to find less costly methods of production. Since profits are high

[18] Of course, it is conceivable that the managers of a monopoly firm may be motivated by altruism to forgo potential profits and fix their prices at a low equilibrium level, that is, the level that just covers their costs. But we will assume that in the absence of any external regulatory agencies (such as the government), monopolists are utility maximizers like everyone else in a market and therefore seek to maximize their profits.

anyway, there is little incentive for it to develop new technology that might reduce costs or that might give it a competitive edge over other firms for there are no other competing firms.

Third, a monopoly market allows the seller to introduce price differentials that block consumers from putting together the most satisfying bundle of commodities they can purchase given the commodities available and the money they can spend. Since everyone must buy from the monopoly firm, the firm can set its prices so that some buyers are forced to pay a higher price for the same goods than others. The monopoly firm, for example, can adjust its prices so that those consumers who have a greater desire for its goods must pay a higher price for the same goods than those consumers who have a lesser desire for them. As a consequence, those who have the greater desire now buy less, and those who have the lesser desire now buy more, than either would buy at an equal price. The result is that some consumers are no longer able to purchase the most satisfying bundle of goods they could buy.

Monopoly markets also embody restrictions on the negative rights that perfectly free markets respect. First, monopoly markets by definition are markets that other sellers are not free to enter. Second, monopoly markets enable the monopoly firm to force on its buyers goods that they may not want, in quantities they may not desire. The monopoly firm, for example, can force consumers to purchase commodity X only if they also purchase commodity Y from the firm. Third, monopoly markets are dominated by a single seller whose decisions determine the prices and quantities of a commodity offered for sale. The monopoly firm's power over the market is absolute.

A monopoly market, then, is one that deviates from the ideals of capitalist justice, economic utility, and negative rights. Instead of continually establishing a just equilibrium, the monopoly market imposes unjustly high prices upon the buyer and generates unjustly high profits for the seller. Instead of maximizing efficiency, monopoly markets provide incentives for waste, misallocation of resources, and profit-gouging. Instead of respecting negative rights of freedom, monopoly markets create an inequality of power that allows the monopoly firm to dictate terms to the consumer. The producer then replaces the consumer as "sovereign" of the market.

4.3 OLIGOPOLISTIC COMPETITION

Few industries are monopolies. Most major industrial markets are not dominated by a single firm, but, more usually, by as many as four firms or more. Such markets lie somewhere on the spectrum between the two extremes of the perfectly competitive market with innumerable sellers and the pure monopoly market with only one seller. Market structures of this "impure" type are referred to collectively as "imperfectly competitive markets," of which the most important kind is the "oligopoly."[19]

In an oligopoly, two of the seven conditions that characterize the purely competitive market are once again not present. First, instead of many sellers,

[19] See Samuelson, *Economics*, pp. 462–63, 481–84.

TABLE 4.1 Market Shares of Largest Firms by Product—1982

PRODUCT	PERCENT OF MARKET CONTROLLED BY LARGEST FIRMS		HERFINDAHL-HIRSCHMAN INDEX
	4 LARGEST	8 LARGEST	
Canned Meats	74	94	NA
Canned Milk	74	94	2114
Canned Baby Food	100	100	NA
Cat Food	84	93	2222
Canned Beer	80	97	2046
Bottled Beer	81	92	2600
Soft Drink Bases	90	95	NA
Concentrated Coffee	95	98	NA
Tea	86	92	NA
Fine Cotton Goods	83	NA	NA
Wool Fabrics	79	92	NA
Plywood	81	99	2025
Water Beds	78	95	2106
Sanitary Napkins	98	NA	NA
Disposable Diapers	96	100	NA
Milk Cartons	96	99	NA
Paper Cups	83	93	2074
Clothes Patterns	94	99	2838
Greeting Cards	88	93	2660
Checkbooks	92	97	NA
Nylon Fibers	94	NA	NA
Household Detergents	79	90	27351
Table Glasses	84	92	2008
Glass Fiber	93	99	NA
Copper	92	99	2483
Optic Cable	87	85	NA
Vacuum Jugs	93	NA	NA
Calculators	90	99	NA
Dublicating Machines	91	99	2630
Refrigerators	90	99	2253
Washing Machines	93	NA	NA
Electric Lamps	90	96	2954
Home Radios	77	89	NA
Magnetic Tapes	99	NA	2710
TV Picture Tubes	90	99	2458
Batteries	87	92	NA
Spark Plugs	97	99	NA
Motor Vehicles	92	97	NA
Motorcycles	80	87	2166
Electronic Games & Toys	87	99	2388

Source: U.S. Bureau of the Census, 1982 Census of Manufacturers, Concentration Ratios in Manufacturing, Table 6. The Herfindahl-Hirschman index is a measure of market concentration calculated by squaring the individual market share (in percent) of each of the firms in the market and adding the squares together.

there are only a few significant sellers. That is, most of the market is shared by a relatively small number of large firms that together can exercise some influence on prices. The share each firm holds may be somewhere between 25 percent and 90 percent of the market, and the firms controlling this share may range from two to fifty, depending on the industry. Second, other sellers are not able to freely enter the market. Although more than one seller is present in an oligopoly market, new sellers find it difficult to break into the industry. This may be due to the prohibitively high costs of starting a business in that industry, it may be due to long-term contracts which have tied all the buyers to the firms already in the industry, or it may be due to enduring loyalties created by brand-name advertising.

Oligopoly markets which are dominated by a few (four) large firms are said to be "highly concentrated." Examples of such oligopoly markets are not hard to find since they include many of the largest manufacturing industries. Table 4.1 lists several highly concentrated U.S. industries, as indicated by the large share of the market that the four biggest firms control.

The firms that dominate the highly concentrated American industries tend, by and large, to be among the largest corporations in the United States. Table 4.2 lists several major corporations dominant in various oligopoly industries during the 1970s, together with the approximate percentage of the markets controlled by these firms. As the reader can see, these include many of the most well known and largest American firms operating in several of the most basic American industries.

Although oligopolies can form in a variety of ways, the most common causes

TABLE 4.2 Leading Dominant Firms in Oligopoly Industries, 1976

FIRM	MARKETS	AVERAGE MARKET SHARE	BARRIERS TO ENTRY
General Motors	Autos, locomotives, buses	55%	High
IBM	Computers, typewriters	65	High
Western Electric	Telecommunication equipment	95	High
General Electric	Heavy electrical equipment	50	High
Eastman Kodak	Photographic supplies	65	Medium
Xerox	Copying equipment	75	High
Procter & Gamble	Detergents, toiletries	50	Medium
Boeing	Aircraft	45	High
McDonnell-Douglas	Aircraft	45	High
United Aircraft	Aircraft engines	60	Medium
Coca-Cola	Flavoring syrups	50	Medium
Campbell Soup	Canned soups	80	Medium
Gillette	Razors, toiletries	65	Medium
Kellogg	Dry cereals	45	Medium
Times-Mirror	Newspaper	70	High
New York Times	Newspaper	75	High

Source: William G. Shepherd, *The Economics of Industrial Organization* (Englewood Cliffs, NJ: Prentice-Hall, Inc., 1979), p. 206.

of an oligopolistic market structure are horizontal mergers.[20] A horizontal merger is simply the unification of two or more companies that were formerly competing in the same line of business. If enough companies in a competitive industry merge, the industry can become an oligopoly composed of a few very large firms. During the 1950s, for example, the 108 competing banks in Philadelphia began to merge, until by 1963 the number of bank firms had been reduced to 42.[21] The Philadelphia National Bank emerged as the second largest bank (as a result of nine mergers) and the Girard Bank emerged as the third largest (as a result of six mergers). In the early 1960s, the Philadelphia National Bank and the Girard Bank proposed to merge into a single firm. If the merger had been approved (it was stopped through legal action), the two banks together would have controlled well over a third of the banking activities of metropolitan Philadelphia.

How do oligopoly industries affect the market? Because a highly concentrated oligopoly has a relatively small number of firms, it is relatively easy for the managers of these firms to join forces and act as a unit. By explicitly or tacitly agreeing to set their prices at the same levels and to restrict their output accordingly, the oligopolists can function much like a single giant firm. This uniting of forces, together with the barriers to entry that are characteristic of oligopoly industries, can result in the same high prices and low supply levels characteristic of monopoly markets. As a consequence, oligopoly markets, like monopolies, can fail to exhibit just profit levels, can generate a decline in social utility, and can fail to respect basic economic freedoms. It has been shown, for example, that generally the more highly concentrated an oligopoly industry is, the higher the profits it is able to extract.[22] Studies also have estimated that the overall decline in utility due to inefficient allocation of resources by highly concentrated oligopoly industries ranges between .5 percent and 4.0 percent of the nation's gross national product or between $10 billion and $80 billion per year.[23]

Explicit Agreements

Prices in an oligopoly can be set at profitable levels through explicit agreements that restrain competition. The managers of the few firms operating in an oligopoly can meet and jointly agree to fix prices at a level much higher than what each would be forced to take in a perfectly competitive market. The greater the degree of market concentration present in an industry, the fewer the managers that have to be brought into such a price-fixing agreement, and the easier it is for them to come to an agreement, as Table 4.3 suggests. Such agreements, of course, reproduce the effects of a monopoly and consequently curtail market justice, market efficiency, and market rights as defined in the first section of this chapter.

If the justice, freedom, and social utility that competitive markets achieve

[20] See George J. Stigler, "Monopoly and Oligopoly by Merger," *The American Economic Review* 40 (Proceedings of the American Economic Association, 1950): 23–34.

[21] Warren, *Antitrust*, p. 271.

[22] The numerous studies confirming this relationship are surveyed in Douglas F. Greer, *Industrial Organization and Public Policy*, 2nd ed. (New York: Macmillan, Inc. 1984), pp. 407–14; Greer also critically evaluates the few studies that seem to show no such relationship.

[23] Greer, *Industrial Organization*, pp. 416–17.

TABLE 4.3 Selected Price-Fixing Conspiracies in U.S. Industries, 1961–1970

MARKET	GEOGRAPHICAL SCOPE	PERCENT OF MARKET CONTROLLED BY FOUR LARGEST FIRMS	NUMBER OF CONSPIRATORS	THEIR SHARE OF SALES	NUMBER OF FIRMS IN MARKET
Wrought steel wheels	National	85%	7	100%	5
Bed springs	National	61	10		20
Metal library shelving	National	60	7	78	9
Self-locking nuts	National	97	4	97	6
Refuse collection	Local		86		102
Steel products	Regional	66	5	72	
Gasoline	Regional	49	12		
Milk	Local	90	11	80	13
Concrete pipe	Regional	100	4	100	4
Drill jig bushings	National	56	9	82	13
Linen supplies	Local	49	31	90	
Plumbing fixtures	National	76	7	98	15
Class rings	Regional	100	3	90	5
Tickets	Regional	78	9	91	10
Athletic equipment	Local	90	6	100	6
Dairy products	Regional	95	3	95	13
Vending machines	Local	93	6	100	6
Ready-mix concrete	Local	86	9	100	9
Carbon steel sheets	National	59	10		
Liquid asphalt	Regional	56	20	95	

Source: William G. Shepherd, *The Economics of Industrial Organization* (Englewood Cliffs, NJ: Prentice-Hall, Inc., 1979), p. 306.

are important values for society, then it is crucial that the managers of oligopoly firms refrain from engaging in practices that restrict competition. Only if markets function competitively will they exhibit the justice, freedom, and utility that justify their existence. These beneficial aspects of a free market will be reaped by society only so long as monopoly firms refrain from engaging in collusive arrangements that do away with competition and reproduce the effects of monopoly markets. In particular, the following sorts of market practices have been identified as unethical:

Price-Fixing When firms are operating in an oligopoly market, it is easy enough for their managers to meet secretly and agree to set their prices at artificially high levels. This is straightforward price-fixing. In 1978, for example, several managers of firms manufacturing paper bags used for packaging foods, coffee, and other goods were fined for getting together and conspiring to fix the prices of those paper bags.[24] The managers worked for Continental Group, Inc., Chase Bag Co., American Bag and Paper Corp., and Harley Corp., four of the dominant firms in paper bag markets.

Manipulation of Supply Firms in an oligopoly industry might agree to limit their production so that prices rise to levels higher than those that would result from free competition. When hardwood manufacturers met periodically in trade associations early in this century, they would often agree on output policies that would secure high profits.[25] The American Column and Lumber Company was eventually prosecuted under the Sherman Antitrust law to force it to desist from this practice. Such a "manipulation of supply" would also result in market shortages.

Exclusive Dealing Arrangements A firm institutes an exclusive dealing arrangement when it sells to a buyer on condition that the buyer will not purchase any products from certain other sellers. During the 1940s, for instance, American Can Company would lease its can closing machines (at very low prices) only to those customers who agreed not to purchase any cans from Continental Can Company, its major competitor.[26]

Tying Arrangements A firm enters into a tying arrangement when it sells a buyer a certain commodity only on condition that the buyer agrees to purchase certain other commodities from the firm. Chicken Delight, for example, franchises home delivery and pick-up food stores whose major product is chicken cooked in a special mix. In 1970, Chicken Delight would sell a franchise license

[24] "Paper Companies Get Heavy Fines for Price-Fixing," *Wall Street Journal*, 21 September 1978, p. 2. For an analysis of price-fixing see Jeffrey Sonnenfeld and Paul R. Lawrence, "Why do Companies Succumb to Price-Fixing?", *Harvard Business Review*, 56, no. 4 (July-August 1978): 145–57.

[25] Almarin Phillips, *Market Structure, Organization, and Performance* (Cambridge: Harvard University Press, 1962), pp. 138–60.

[26] Warren, *Antitrust*, pp. 233–35.

to a person only if the person also agreed to purchase a certain number of cookers, fryers, and other supplies.[27] The firm was subsequently forced to stop the practice through legal action.

Retail Price Maintenance If a manufacturer sells to retailers only on condition that they all charge the same set retail prices for its goods, it is engaging in "retail price maintenance." Eastman Kodak Company, for example, until stopped by the Federal Trade Commission, used to establish the prices at which retailers had to sell its "Kodachrome" and "Magazine Cine-Kodak Film."[28] Retail price maintenance dampens competition between retailers and removes from the manufacturer the competitive pressure to lower prices and cut costs.

Price Discrimination To charge different prices to different buyers for identical goods or services is to engage in price discrimination. Price discrimination was used by Continental Pie Company during the 1960s in an attempt to undersell Utah Pie Company, which had managed to take away much of the Salt Lake City business of Continental Baking Company. For several years, Continental sold its pies to Salt Lake City customers at prices substantially lower than those it charged for the same goods sold to customers in other areas. The Supreme Court found such pricing practices "predatory." Price differences should be based on true differences in the cost of manufacturing, packaging, marketing, transporting, or servicing goods.

Why do businesspeople engage in such anticompetitive practices? In a detailed study of several companies whose employees had been implicated in price-fixing arrangements, researchers Sonnenfeld and Lawrence found that several industry and organizational factors tended to lead to price-fixing including the following:[29]

A Crowded and Mature Market When large numbers of new entrants or declining demand create overcapacity in a market, the resulting decline in revenues and profits creates pressures on middle-level managers. They may respond by allowing, encouraging, and even ordering their sales teams to engage in price-fixing.

Job-order Nature of Business If orders are priced individually so that pricing decisions are made frequently and at low levels of the organization, collusion among low-level salespeople is more likely.

Undifferentiated Products When the product offered by each company in an industry is so similar to those of other companies that they must compete on price alone by continually reducing prices, salespeople come to feel that the only way to keep prices from collapsing is by getting together and fixing prices.

[27] *Ibid.*, pp. 218–19.

[28] *Ibid.*, pp. 161–62.

[29] Jeffrey Sonnenfeld and Paul R. Lawrence, "Why Do Companies Succumb To Price-Fixing?" in Kenneth R. Andrews, ed., *ethics in Practice* (Boston, MA: Harvard Business School Press, 1989), pp. 71–83.

Culture of the Business When an organization's salespeople feel that price-fixing is a common practice and is desired, condoned, accepted, rationalized, and even encouraged by the organization, price-fixing is more likely. Top managers should counter this through personal example and through consistent communication of a commitment to ethical practices, and through development of a code of ethics that explicitly addresses price-fixing in clear detail, that is backed by sanctions, and that is checked through regular corporate audits.

Personnel Practices When managers are evaluated and rewarded solely or primarily on the basis of profits and volume, so that bonuses, commissions, advancement and other rewards are dependent on these objectives, they will come to believe that the company wants them to achieve these objectives regardless of the means. Compensation should be based on other factors, and the organization should strive to instill in employees a professional pride in the company's adherence to ethics.

Pricing Decisions When organizations are decentralized so that pricing decisions are pushed down into the hands of a lower part of the organization, price-fixing is more likely to happen. Price decisions should be made at higher organizational levels.

Trade Associations Allowing salespeople to meet with competitors in trade association meetings will encourage them to talk about pricing and to begin to engage in price-setting arrangements with their counterparts in competing firms. Salespeople should be prohibited from meeting with competitors.

Corporate Legal Staff When legal departments fail to provide guidance to sales staff until after a problem has occurred, price-fixing problems will be more likely. The legal staff should regularly provide one-on-one training in the legal aspects of price-fixing for those who make pricing and sales decisions.

The failure of top managers to deal with these industry and organizational factors can put significant pressures on individuals who are otherwise striving to do what is best for a company. One chief executive officer describes the pressures that an irresponsible management can place on young new salespeople:

> I think we are particularly vulnerable where we have a salesman with two kids, plenty of financial demands, and a concern over the security of his job. There is a certain amount of looseness to a new set of rules. He may accept questionable practices feeling that he may just not know the system. There are no specific procedures for him to follow other that what other salesmen tell him. At the same time, he is in an industry where the acceptance for his product and the level of profitability are clearly dropping. Finally, we add to his pressures by letting him know who will take his job from him if he doesn't get good price and volume levels. I guess this will bring a lot of soul-searching out of an individual.[30]

[30] *Ibid.*, p. 75.

Tacit Agreements

Although most of the forms of explicit market agreements enumerated above are illegal, the more common types of price-setting in oligopolies are accomplished through some unspoken form of cooperation against which it is difficult to legislate. How does this take place? The managers of the major firms in an oligopoly can learn by hard experience that competition is not in their personal financial interests. Price-cutting competition, they find, will only lead to minimal profits. The firms in an oligopoly, therefore, may each come to the conclusion that cooperation is in the best interests of all. Each firm may then reach the independent conclusion that they will all benefit if, when one major firm raises its prices, all other firms set their prices at the same high levels. Through this process of "price-setting," all the major firms will retain their share of the market and they will all gain by the higher price. Since the 1930s, for example, the major tobacco companies have charged identical list prices for cigarettes. When one company decides it has a reason to raise or lower its cigarette prices, the other companies will always follow suit within a short period of time. The officials of these companies, however, have made no explicit agreement to act in concert; without ever having talked the matter over among themselves, each realizes that all will benefit so long as they continue to act in a unified fashion. In 1945, incidentally, the Supreme Court found the dominant cigarette companies guilty of tacit collusion, but the companies reverted to identical pricing after the case was settled.

To coordinate their prices, some oligopoly industries will recognize one firm as the industry's "price leader."[31] Each firm will tacitly agree to set its prices at the levels announced by the price leader, knowing that all other firms will also follow its price leadership. Since each oligopolist knows it will not have to compete with another firm's lower prices, it is not forced to reduce its margin of profit to the levels to which open competition would reduce them. There need be no overt collusion involved in this form of price-setting, only an unspoken understanding that all firms will follow the price leadership of the dominant firm and will not engage in the price-lowering tactics of competition.

Whether prices in an oligopoly market are set by explicit agreements or by implicit understandings, it is clear that social utility declines to the extent that prices are artificially raised above the levels that would be set by a perfectly competitive market. Consumers must pay the unjust prices of the oligopolists, resources are no longer efficiently allocated and used, and the freedom of both consumers and potential competitors diminishes.

Bribery

When used to secure the sale of a product, political bribery can also introduce diseconomies into the operations of markets. This is a form of market defect that received a great deal of public attention during the late 1970s when it was discovered that a sizable group of companies had attempted to land contracts with overseas governments by paying bribes to various government officials. Lockheed Aircraft

[31] Jesse W. Markham, "The Nature and Significance of Price Leadership," *The American Economic Review*, 41 (1951): 891–905.

Corporation, for example, paid several million dollars to government officials in Saudi Arabia, Japan, Italy, and Holland in order to influence aircraft sales in those countries.[32]

When bribes are used to secure the purchase of a commodity, the net effect is a decline in market competition.[33] The product of the briber no longer competes equally with the product of other sellers on the basis of its price or its merits. Instead, the bribe serves as a barrier to prevent other sellers from entering the briber's government market. Because of the bribe, the government involved buys only from the firm who supplies the bribe and the briber becomes in effect a monopoly seller.

If a briber succeeds in preventing other sellers from receiving equal entry into a government market, it becomes possible for the briber to engage in the inefficiencies characteristic of monopolies. The bribing firm can impose higher prices, engage in waste, and neglect quality and cost controls since the monopoly secured by the bribe will secure a sizable profit without need of making the price or quality of its products competitive with those of other sellers.

Bribes used to secure the sale of products by shutting out other sellers differ, of course, from bribes used for other purposes. An official may insist on being paid to perform his or her legal duties on behalf of a petitioner as when, for example, a customs officer asks for a "tip" to expedite the processing of an import permit. Or a government official may offer to lower a costly tariff in return for an under-the-table payment. The previous analysis would not apply to bribes of this sort, which are being used for a purpose other than to erect market barriers.

In determining the ethical nature of payments used for purposes other than to shut out other competitors from a market, the following considerations are relevant:

1. Is the offer of a payment initiated by the payer (the one who pays the money) or does the payee (the one who receives the money) demand the payment by threatening injury to the payer's interests? In the latter case, the payment is not a bribe but a form of extortion and if the threatened injury is large enough, the payer may not be morally responsible for his or her act, or the moral responsibility may at least be diminished.
2. Is the payment made to induce the payee to act in a manner that violates his or her official sworn duty to act in the best interests of the public, or is the payment made to induce the payee to perform what is already his or her official duty? If the payee is being induced to violate his or her official duty, then the payer is cooperating in an immoral act since the payee has entered an agreement to fulfill these duties.
3. Are the nature and purpose of the payment considered ethically unobjectionable in the local culture? If a form of payment is a locally accepted public custom *and* there is a proportionately serious reason for making the payment (it is not intended to erect a market barrier nor to induce an official to violate his or her public duties), then it would appear to be ethically permissible on utilitarian grounds. (It might, however, constitute a legal violation of the Foreign Corrupt Practices Act of 1977.)

[32] Willard F. Mueller, "Conglomerates: A Nonindustry," [pp. 442–81] in *The Structure of American Industry*, Adams, ed., p. 459.

[33] Neil H. Jacoby, Peter Nehemkis, and Richard Fells, *Bribery and Extortion in World Business* (New York: Macmillan Inc., 1977), p. 183.

4.4 OLIGOPOLIES AND PUBLIC POLICY

It is the high degree of market concentration in oligopoly industries that places a great deal of economic power in the hands of a small number of firms and that enables them to collude, overtly or tacitly. It is not clear, however, how great this economic power is or how much it is used. Some authors have argued that the economic power held by oligopoly corporations is actually quite small and insufficient to affect society, while others have claimed that several social factors inhibit the use of this power. One's opinion of what, if anything, should be done about the high degree of market concentration in oligopoly industries depends largely on one's views concerning the extent and the use of oligopoly power.

The Do-Nothing View

Some observers hold that nothing should be done about the economic power held by oligopoly corporations because that power is actually not as large as it may first appear. Several reasons have been given to support this claim. First, it is argued that, although competition *within* industries has declined, it has been replaced by competition *between* industries with substitutable products.[34] The steel industry, for example, is now in competition with the aluminum and cement industries. Consequently, although there may be a high degree of market concentration in a single industry like steel, a high level of competition is still maintained by its relation to other competing industries.

Second, as John Kenneth Galbraith has argued, the economic power of any large corporation may be balanced and restrained by the "countervailing power" of other large corporate groups in society.[35] Government and unions, for example, both restrain the power of big businesses. And although a business corporation may have a large share of an industrial market, it is faced by buyers that are equally large and equally powerful. A large steel company, for example, must sell to equally large automobile companies. This balance of power between large corporate groups, Galbraith claims, effectively reduces the economic power any one corporate giant can exert.

The Antitrust View

Other observers are less sanguine about the economic power exerted by oligopoly corporations. They argue that prices and profits in concentrated industries are higher than they should be. The solution, they argue, is to reinstate competitive pressures by forcing the large companies to divest themselves of their holdings, thereby breaking them up into smaller firms.

Clearly, the antitrust view is based on a number of assumptions. J. Fred Weston has summarized the basic propositions on which this view is based as follows:

[34] See J. M. Clarm, "Toward a Concept of Workable Competition," *American Economic Review*, 30 (1940): 241–56.

[35] John Kenneth Galbraith, *American Capitalism: The Concept of Countervailing Power*, rev. ed. (Cambridge, MA: The Riverside Press, 1956), pp. 112–13.

1. If an industry is not atomistic with many small competitors, there is likely to be administrative discretion over prices.
2. Concentration results in recognized interdependence among companies, with no price competition in concentrated industries.
3. Concentration is due mostly to mergers, for the most efficient scale of operation is not more than 3 to 5 percent of the industry. A high degree of concentration is unnecessary.
4. There is a positive correlation between concentration and profitability that gives evidence of monopoly power in concentrated industries—the ability to elevate prices and the persistence of high profits. Entry does not take place to eliminate excessive profits.
5. Concentration is aggravated by product differentiation and advertising. Advertising is correlated with higher profits.
6. There is oligopolistic coordination by signaling through press releases or other means.[36]

On the basis of these assumptions, proponents of the antitrust view reach the conclusion that by breaking up large corporations into smaller units, higher levels of competition will emerge in those industries that are currently highly concentrated. The result will be a decrease in explicit and tacit collusion, lower prices for consumers, greater innovation, and the increased development of cost-cutting technologies that will benefit us all.

The Regulation View

A third group of observers holds that oligopoly corporations should not be broken up because their large size has beneficial consequences that would be lost if they were forced to decentralize.[37] In particular, they argue, mass production and mass distribution of goods can be carried out only by using the highly centralized accumulation of assets and manpower that the large corporation makes possible. Moreover, the concentration of assets allows large firms to take advantage of the economies made possible by large-scale production in large plants. These savings are passed on to consumers in the form of cheaper and more plentiful products.

Although firms should not be broken up, it does not follow that they should not be regulated. According to this third view, concentration gives large firms an economic power that allows them to fix prices and engage in other forms of behavior that are not in the public interest. To ensure that consumers are not harmed by large firms, regulatory agencies and legislation should be set up to restrain and control the activities of large corporations.

Some observers, in fact, advocate that where large firms cannot be effectively controlled by the usual forms of regulation, then regulation should take the form of nationalization. That is, the government should take over the operation of firms

[36] J. Fred Weston, "Big Corporations: The Arguments For and Against Breaking Them Up," *Business and Its Changing Environment*, proceedings of a conference held by the Graduate School of Management at UCLA, July 24–August 3, 1977, pp. 232–33; see also John M. Blair, *Economic Concentration: Structure, Behavior, and Public Policy* (New York: Harcourt Brace Jovanovich, 1972).

[37] J. A. Schumpeter, *Capitalism, Socialism, and Democracy* (New York: Harper, 1943), pp. 79 ff.

in those industries where only public ownership can ensure that firms operate in the public interest.

Other advocates of regulation, however, argue that nationalization is itself not in the public interests.[38] Public ownership of firms, they claim, inevitably leads to the creation of unresponsive and inefficient bureaucracies. Moreover, publicly owned enterprises are not subject to competitive market pressures and this results in higher prices and higher costs.

Which of these three views is correct: the do-nothing view, the antitrust view, or the regulation view? Readers will have to decide this issue for themselves, since at the moment there does not appear to be sufficient evidence to answer this question unequivocably. Whichever of these three views the reader may find most persuasive, it is clear that the social benefits generated by free markets cannot be secured unless the managers of firms maintain competitive market relationships between themselves. The ethical rules prohibiting collusion are at bottom rules meant to ensure that markets are structured competitively. These rules may be voluntarily followed or legally enforced. They are justified insofar as society is justified in pursuing the utilitarian benefits, justice, and the rights to freedom that competitive markets can secure.

QUESTIONS FOR REVIEW AND DISCUSSION

1. Define the following concepts: perfect competition, demand curve, supply curve, equilibrium point, monopoly competition, oligopolistic competition, price-fixing, manipulation of supply, tying arrangements, retail price maintenance, price discrimination, price-setting, price leadership, extortion, countervailing power, do-nothing view on oligopoly power, antitrust view on oligopoly power, regulation view on oligopoly power.
2. "From an ethical point of view big business is always bad business." Discuss the pros and cons of this statement.
3. What kind of public policy do you think the United States should have with respect to business competition? Develop moral arguments to support your answer (that is, arguments which show that the kinds of policies you favor will advance the public welfare, or that they will secure certain important rights, or that they will ensure certain forms of justice).
4. In your judgment, should an American company operating in a foreign country in which collusive price-fixing is not illegal obey the U.S. laws against collusion? Explain your answer.

CASES FOR DISCUSSION

General Electric Prices

Clarence Burke began working for the heavy-equipment division of General Electric as soon as he graduated from college in 1926. Clarence was an energetic, hard-driving, and tenacious person and looked forward to a promising career at

[38] L. Von Mises, *Planned Chaos* (New York: Foundations for Economic Education, 1947).

GE. The heavy electrical equipment division at GE was the oldest part of the company, around which the rest had been built, and it still accounted for a quarter of its sales. Moreover, GE dominated the heavy electrical equipment markets: It held 40 to 45 percent of the heavy equipment markets, followed by Westinghouse who held 30 to 35 percent, then Allis-Chalmers and Federal Pacific who held 10 percent apiece. By the 1950s, the combined sales of these companies would average $1,750,000,000 per year in the heavy electrical equipment markets alone.[1]

Long before Clarence Burke began working for GE, the company was involved in a series of antitrust suits that continued through the 1940s. These suits are summarized in Table 4.4. In November 1946, as a response to these suits, GE formulated an antitrust directive which stated that it "is the policy of this company to conform to the antitrust laws." The directive (which came to be known as "directive 20.5") was repeatedly revised and filled out until it eventually read:

Directive Policy on the Compliance by the Company and its Employees with the Antitrust Laws No. 20.5

> It is the policy of the company to comply strictly in all respects with the antitrust laws. There shall be no exception to this policy nor shall it be compromised or qualified by any employee acting for or on behalf of the company. No employee shall enter into any understanding, agreement, plan, or scheme, express or implied, formal or informal, with any competitor, in regard to prices, terms or conditions of sale, production, distribution, territories, or customers; nor exchange or discuss with a competitor prices, terms, or conditions of sale, or any other competitive information; nor engage in any other conduct that in the opinion of the company's counsel violates any of the antitrust laws.[2]

Every manager was periodically asked to indicate in writing that he was adhering to the policy. The standard written letter the manager would sign stated:

> I have received a copy of directive policy general No. 20.5, dated ______. I have read and understood this policy. I am observing it and will observe it in the future.[3]

The letter was not signed under oath, of course, nor was a manager responsible to his or her immediate local superior for adhering to the policy. The letter was sent out from GE's central offices, and was returned to the central offices by mail. Any disciplinary action taken to enforce the directive also had to originate at the home office.

In 1945 Clarence Burke was promoted to Sales Manager of GE's distribution transformer department. Here he worked under H. L. "Buster" Brown, general manager in charge of sales for all transformer departments. In July 1945, a month

[1] U.S. Congress, Senate, *Administered Prices: Hearings before the Subcommittee on Antitrust and Monopoly of the Committee on the Judiciary*, 87th Congress, 1st session, May—June, 1961, p. 17111. Hereafter cited as "Administered Prices."

[2] *Ibid.*, p. 17120.

[3] *Ibid.*, p. 16737.

TABLE 4.4 General Electric Antitrust Suits

TITLE OF CASE	DATE	COMMENT
General Electric Co., et al.	1911	Price-fixing conspiracy in electric lamps enjoined Oct. 12, 1911.
General Electric Co., et al.	1924	Electric lamp price-fixing conspiracy; Nov. 23, 1926, dismissed.
Radio Corp. of America, et al.	1930	Consent decree Mar. 7, 1932, enjoined activities in conspiracy to monopolize radio communication and apparatus.
Corning Glass Works, et al.	1940	Glass bulb cartel; Sept. 9, 1941, nolo contendere; fines in case totaled $47,000.
General Electric Co., et al.	1940	Conspiracy to fix prices in hard metal compositions and tools and dies made therefrom; dismissed Jan. 6, 1949.
General Electric Co., et al.	1941	Jan. 19, 1949, court held GE had monopolized incandescent lamp industry; Aug. 6, 1953, court enjoined illegal practices and ordered patents dedicated to public.
General Electric Co., et al.	1941	Cartel found guilty Oct. 18, 1948, of price-fixing, division of markets, and production limitation in hard metal alloys, tools and dies, fines in case totaled $56,000.
General Electric Co., et al.	1942	Consent decree Mar. 26, 1954, canceled foreign and domestic agreements in fluorescent electric lamp cartel and ordered compulsory royalty-free licensing of patents.
Line Material Co., et al.	1945	Decree Oct. 4, 1948, enjoined activities in price-fixing conspiracy in drop-out fuse cutouts.
General Electric Co., et al.	1945	Consent decree, Oct. 6, 1953, enjoined activities in electrical equipment cartel and required nonexclusive reasonable royalty patent licenses.

TABLE 4.4 (continued)

TITLE OF CASE	DATE	COMMENT
Electrical Apparatus Export Association, et al.	1945	Consent decree Mar. 12, 1947, enjoined price-fixing and market allocations and other activities of electrical equipment cartel.
General Cable Corp.	1947	Consent decree Aug. 25, 1948, enjoined present and future cartel patent pooling, and price-fixing agreements in high-tension cable and accessories.
General Electric Co., et al.	1948	Nov. 4, 1949, nolo contendere; fines in case totaled $40,000; electrical switches and equipment price-fixing conspiracy.
General Electric Co., et al.	1948	Consent decree Nov. 14, 1949, enjoined activities in electrical switches and equipment price-fixing conspiracy.
General Electric Co., et al.	1948	May 27, 1952, nolo contendere; fines in case totaled $78,000; monopoly in street-lighting equipment.
General Electric Co., et al.	1948	Consent decree May 27, 1952, enjoined customer allocation and price-fixing street-lighting equipment.

Source: U.S. Congress, Senate, ADMINISTERED PRICES: HEARINGS BEFORE THE SUBCOMMITTEE ON ANTITRUST AND MONOPOLY OF THE COMMITTEE ON THE JUDICIARY, 87th CONGRESS FIRST SESSION, May–June, 1961, p. 17688.

after Clarence entered his new position as department sales manager, his superior, Mr. Brown, told him he would be expected to attend the regularly scheduled meetings of the National Electrical Manufacturers Association in Pittsburgh, meetings which were also attended by the sales managers of the other three or four major producers of electrical equipment. Conversations at the meetings gradually began to turn to prices and soon the managers were making informal agreements to quote "an agreed upon price" to all their customers. Clarence Burke went along and accepted the practice, especially after the managers were assured by "Buster" Brown that the company's antitrust directive did not refer to the sorts of informal agreements they were making: The only agreements that were illegal, according to Brown, were those which "gouged the public." Several years later Clarence Burke recalled that he and others had "understood" that what they were doing was what the company wanted.[4]

[4] Richard Austin Smith, "The Incredible Electrical Conspiracy," *Fortune*, April 1961, p. 136.

Clarence Burke was not the only GE manager who moved into price-fixing arrangements with the other major electrical companies. By the late 1950s, W. W. Ginn, a GE vice-president, was meeting with competitors to fix prices for power transformers; Frank Stehlik, a GE general manager, was meeting to fix prices for power switchgear assemblies; W. F. Oswalt, another general manager, was fixing industrial control equipment prices; and G. L. Roark, a GE marketing manager, was fixing prices for power switching equipment. In fact, as later investigations showed, the managers of all the principal companies manufacturing heavy electrical equipment (General Electric, Westinghouse, Allis-Chalmers, and Federal Pacific) were meeting regularly to set prices for their products.[5] Throughout the late 1940s, Clarence Burke was gradually introduced to the details of a practice that was accepted in the entire industry, as well as in his own company:

> I was taught [the techniques] by my superiors back as far as 1945, who took me to meetings with them and told me that, instead of showing Pittsburgh [the place of the meetings] in your expense account, let's all show so-and-so. . . . From then on it was just inbred in me. . . . I ascertained that it [was the usual way to act] because my superiors at Pittsfield were doing it and asking me to do it. So it was their practice. [Statement of C. Burke][6]

In 1950, the general manager of GE's switchgear division, R. F. Tinnerholm, offered to move Clarence Burke to the more prestigious position of sales manager in a department of GE's switchgear division:

> I was offered the position of manager of sales of the specialty transformer division in Fort Wayne, Indiana, and I accepted and I went there on February 1, 1950. . . . They wanted to replace the manager of marketing. . . . Walter F. Rauber, I think his name is; they had determined to replace him, and since I had had switchgear experience and had had large apparatus experience, they determined that I was a logical replacement for Mr. Rauber. . . . I was interviewed [by] . . . R. F. Tinnerholm, who was then manager of the switchgear division. . . . Mr. Tinnerholm . . . spelled it out very clearly: Mr. Rauber (to use his words as I remember it) was so "religious" that, since he had signed this slip of paper saying that he would observe policy 20.5, he would not talk with competitors. So he was "not broad enough for the job" and they would expect me to be "broad enough" to hold down that job. [Statement of Clarence Burke][7]

Part of what had led many managers to adopt price-fixing were the pressures they felt on them to meet corporate goals. Clarence Burke recalled several years later that the general manager of GE's switchgear division always insisted on a "reach budget," that is, a budget that increased the percent of net profit to sales over what it had been the year before. Burke claimed that he and the other managers felt that if they wanted to "get ahead" and have the "good will" of their superiors,

[5] *New York Times*, 7 February 1961, p. 26.

[6] *Administered Prices*, pp. 16772–73.

[7] *Ibid.*, p. 16736.

they would have to attain these goals; and the only way to attain these, they felt, was to get together with their competitors.[8]

The price-fixing agreements that the four main electrical switchgear companies entered into in 1950, according to Burke, were intended to "stabilize" prices and to ensure at the same time that each company retained its share of the market. Managers of the four companies met in a hotel room at least once a month and arranged to take turns submitting the lowest bids for upcoming contracts so that GE would wind up with 45 percent of the jobs, Westinghouse with 35 percent, Allis-Chalmers with 10 percent, and Federal Pacific with 10 percent. These were the approximate percentages of the market that each company had controlled before the agreements.

A major fear of the companies was that without the agreements, they might be forced into what Burke termed "a ruinous cutthroat competition." That fear seemed to be borne out in 1954 when GE decided to withdraw from the price-fixing meetings. The result was a financial downturn for the industry, as each company rushed to undersell the others, until prices were being cut by as much as 50 percent. After two years, the damaging effect of the price war led the four electrical companies to resort to fixing prices again in order to "restore stability" to the market:

> The latter part of 1953 [General Electric] served notice on the rest of the industry people that [we] would not meet with them any more. . . . Through 1954 there were no meetings . . . and that is when prices began to deteriorate gradually. . . . Prices began to get farther and farther off book until the latter part of 1954 they were about 15 percent off book. Then in January 1955 they really went down to the bottom, about 45 to 50 percent off book. . . . That summer—and I think it was June or July 1955—Mr. Burens [general manager of GE's switchgear division] asked me to come over to his office, and he told me that he had to start meeting with competition again. . . . And he said something to the effect that he had no other alternative. [Statement of Clarence Burke][9]

The meetings resumed until the winter of 1957 when Westinghouse decided to withdraw from the price-fixing agreements and the market once again went down. Within months prices fell by 60 percent. In the fall of 1958, however, the agreements were reestablished and prices moved back to their prior levels where they remained until the price-fixing meetings were finally ended in 1960. General Electric's profits during the years of these price-fixing agreements are indicated in Table 4.5.[10]

Clarence Burke was not entirely unconcerned about his involvement in the price-fixing agreements. His reflections turned on what he saw as the effects of these agreements:

> I will have to say that we did not charge everything [the market could bear]. Our purpose in meeting with competitors was not to dig the customers or anything. It was just to get what was a fair market value and would produce a fair profit for the industry and would keep the industry healthy. And I think if you will look over the

[8] Smith, "Incredible Electrical Conspiracy," p. 172.

[9] *Administered Prices*, p. 16740.

[10] *Ibid.*, p. 17743.

TABLE 4.5 Net Profit and Rate of Return on Stockholders' Equity, and Profit in Percent of Sales, 1940 and 1947–60 for General Electric Company

YEAR	NET PROFIT AFTER TAXES	RATE OF RETURN	PROFIT IN PERCENT OF SALES
	THOUSANDS	PERCENT	PERCENT
1940	$ 56,494	17.1	......
1947	101,221	22.5	6.6
1948	131,594	25.4	7.1
1949	129,946	21.8	7.0
1950	177,722	26.6	8.0
1951	133,699	18.7	5.1
1952	165,181	18.4	5.5
1953	174,128	18.5	4.9
1954	204,482	20.9	6.1
1955	209,055	19.7	6.0
1956	213,837	19.4	5.2
1957	247,972	21.1	5.7
1958	243,050	19.4	5.9
1959	280,348	20.6	6.4
1960	200,165	13.6	4.8

Source: U.S. Congress, Senate, ADMINISTERED PRICES: HEARINGS BEFORE THE SUBCOMMITTEE ON ANTITRUST AND MONOPOLY OF THE COMMITTEE ON THE JUDICIARY, 87th CONGRESS, FIRST SESSION, May–June, 1961, p. 17743.

> records of the industry during that period, you will see that it did not make any huge profits. General Electric Company's maximum was less than 6 cents on the sales dollar. We were not meeting for the purpose of getting the most that the traffic could bear. It was to get a value for our product . . . I knew I violated the technicalities of the law. I salved my own conscience by saying I was not violating the spirit of the law. Because I was not establishing prices that would gouge the public, and I thought the spirit of the law was to prevent you from establishing abnormal prices, from making huge profits. [Statement of Clarence Burke][11]

In June 1960 a federal grand jury indicted the companies and managers involved in the price-fixing agreements. Clarence Burke was granted immunity in return for his willingness to testify against the other companies and managers. Seven executives of the companies pleaded guilty and were sentenced to jail; thirty-eight other managers were fined, and fines were brought against the companies. Although Clarence Burke was not prosecuted by the government he was fired by GE:

> [The vice president of relations services] gave me this talk about how it would be to my advantage to resign from the General Electric Company. . . . They made it very clear that this had nothing to do with disciplinary action on 20.5 or because we pleaded guilty in the antitrust case. It was just the fact that because of the

[11] *Ibid.*, pp. 16745 and 16790.

adverse publicity that had been received, that they would never put me in a position that my talents warranted. Therefore I would be better off if I resigned. . . . I asked him what the alternative to resigning was, and he said, "Well, if you don't resign you are off the payroll at 5 o'clock today." And that was between 4:30 and 5. [Statement of Clarence Burke][12]

Between 1960 and 1963, a pattern of strong competition emerged in many of the markets that had been subject to the price-fixing agreements. Prices fell by 15 to 20 percent.[13] Then, in May 1963, General Electric published a pricing system that (as internal GE documents later revealed) it hoped would once again make it possible for the industry to set prices, but this time without entering into explicit collusion. The pricing system which GE published stated that (1) all of its book prices would be published, (2) all bids and discounts would be exactly 76 percent of book prices, (3) if GE offered any buyer a lower discount, it would be contractually (hence legally) bound to penalize itself, because it publicly guaranteed every customer that it would apply any lower discounts retroactively on all sales of the preceding six months, (4) all sales and orders would be published. Westinghouse immediately adopted the same pricing system, and the managers of the two firms now coordinated their prices by using public communications and public penalties instead of the secret methods that had sent some of them to jail in 1961. This pricing system continued at least until 1976.[14]

1. Where would you estimate the equilibrium price was during the price-fixing schemes (at 10 percent below the list or "book" price? 30 percent? 60 percent?). Identify the conditions within GE and within the industry which encouraged the price-fixing schemes.
2. Evaluate the price-fixing scheme from an ethical point of view (your evaluation should describe the effects of the scheme on society's welfare, on the moral rights of society's members, and on the distribution of benefits and burdens within society). In your judgment, did Clarence Burke act wrongly? Why? Was he morally responsible for his actions? Why?
3. Why was GE's written policy on antitrust ineffective? In his book *White Collar Crime*, Edwin Sutherland hypothesized that "criminal behavior [in business] is learned in association with those who define such behavior favorably and in isolation from those who define it unfavorably. . . . As a part of the process of learning practical business, a young man with idealism and thoughtfulness for others is inducted into white collar crime" (pp. 234 and 240). To what extent was this hypothesis verified in the case of GE? What implications, if any, does this have for moral responsibility within GE? Within any business?
4. Apart from their legality, did the price-setting scheme set up in 1963 differ in any morally relevant ways from the earlier price-fixing schemes?
5. What internal policies might have changed GE's moral climate? What public policies might have changed the industry's practices?

[12] *Ibid.*, p. 16785.

[13] *Ibid.*, p. 17093.

[14] William G. Shepherd and Clair Wilcox, *Public Policies Toward Business*, 6th ed. (Homewood, IL.: Richard D. Irwin, Inc., 1979), p. 215.

A Japanese Bribe

In July of 1976, Kukeo Tanaka, former prime minister of Japan, was arrested on charges of taking bribes ($1.8 million) from Lockheed Aircraft Company to secure the purchase of several Lockheed jets. Tanaka's secretary and several other government officials were arrested with him. The Japanese public reacted with angry demands for a complete disclosure of Tanaka's dealings. By the end of the year, they had ousted Tanaka's successor, Takeo Miki, who was widely believed to have been trying to conceal Tanaka's actions.

In Holland that same year, Prince Bernhard, husband of Queen Juliana, resigned from three hundred positions he held in government, military, and private organizations. The reason: He was alleged to have accepted $1.1 million in bribes from Lockheed in connection with the sale of 138 F-104 Starfighter jets.

In Italy, Giovani Leone, president in 1970, and Aldo Moro and Mariano Rumor, both prime ministers, were accused of accepting bribes from Lockheed in connection with the purchase of $100 million worth of aircraft in the late 1960s. All were excluded from government.

Scandinavia, South Africa, Turkey, Greece, and Nigeria were also among the fifteen countries in which Lockheed admitted to having handed out payments and at least $202 million in "commissions" since 1970.

Lockheed Aircraft's involvement in the Japanese bribes was revealed to have begun in 1958 when Lockheed and Grumman Aircraft (also an American firm) were competing for a Japanese Air Force jet aircraft contract. According to the testimony of Mr. William Findley, a partner in Arthur Young & Co. (auditors for Lockheed), Lockheed in 1958 engaged the services of Yoshio Kodama, an ultra right-wing war criminal and reputed underworld figure with strong political ties to officials in the ruling Liberal Democratic Party. With Kodama's help, Lockheed secured the government contract. Seventeen years later, it was revealed that the CIA had been informed at the time (by an American embassy employee) that Lockheed had made several bribes while negotiating the contract.[1]

In 1972, Lockheed again hired Kodama as a consultant to help secure the sale of its aircraft in Japan. Lockheed was desperate to sell planes to any major Japanese airline since it was scrambling to recover from a series of financial disasters. Cost overruns on a government contract had pushed Lockheed to the brink of bankruptcy in 1970. Only through a controversial emergency government loan guarantee of $250 million in 1971 did the company narrowly avert disaster. Mr. A. Carl Kotchian, president of Lockheed from 1967 to 1975, was especially anxious to make the sales since the company had been unable to get as many contracts in other parts of the world as it had wanted.

> This bleak situation all but dictated a strong push for sales in the biggest untapped market left—Japan. This push, if successful, might well bring in revenues upwards of $400 million. Such a cash inflow would go a long way towards helping to restore Lockheed's fiscal health, and it would, of course, save the jobs of thousands of the firm's employees. [Statement of Mr. Kotchian][2]

[1] James Post, *Corporate Behavior and Social Change* (Reston, VA: Reston Publishing Co., 1978), p. 207.

[2] A. Carl Kotchian, "The Payoff: Lockheed's 70-Day Mission to Tokyo," *Saturday Review*, 9 July 1977, p. 8.

Kodama eventually succeeded in engineering a contract for Lockheed with All-Nippon Airways, even beating out McDonnell Douglas, which was actively competing with Lockheed for the same sales. To ensure the sale, Kodama asked for and received from Lockheed about $9 million during the period from 1972 to 1975. Much of the money allegedly went to then prime minister Kukeo Tanaka and other government officials, who were supposed to intercede with All-Nippon Airlines on behalf of Lockheed.

According to Mr. Carl Kotchian, "I knew from the beginning that this money was going to the office of the prime minister."[3] He was, however, persuaded that by paying the money, he was sure to get the contract from All-Nippon Airways. The negotiations eventually netted over $1.3 billion in contracts for Lockheed.

In addition to Kodama, Lockheed had also been advised by Toshiharu Okubo, an official of the private trading company, Marubeni, which acted as Lockheed's official representative. Mr. A. Carl Kotchian later defended the payments, which he saw as one of many "Japanese business practices" that he had accepted on the advice of his local consultants. The payments, the company was convinced, were in keeping with local "business practices."[4]

> Further, as I've noted, such disbursements *did not violate American laws*. I should also like to stress that my decision to make such payments stemmed from my judgment that the (contracts) . . . would provide Lockheed workers with jobs and thus redound to the benefit of their dependents, their communities, and stockholders of the corporation. I should like to emphasize that the payments to the so-called "high Japanese government officials" were all requested by Okubo and were *not brought up from my side*. When he told me "five hundred million yen is necessary for such sales," from a purely ethical and moral standpoint I would have declined such a request. However, in that case, I would *most certainly* have sacrificed commercial success. . . . [If] Lockheed had not remained competitive by the rules of the game as then played, we would not have sold [our planes]. . . . I knew that if we wanted our product to have a chance to win on its own merits, we had to follow the functioning system. [Statement of A. Carl Kotchian][5]

In August 1975 investigations by the United States government led Lockheed to admit it had made $22 million in secret payoffs.[6] Subsequent Senate investigations in February 1976 made Lockheed's involvement with Japanese government officials public.[7] Japan subsequently canceled their billion dollar contract with Lockheed.

In June 1979 Lockheed pleaded guilty to concealing the Japanese bribes from the government by falsely writing them off as "marketing costs."[8] The Internal Revenue Code states in part, "No deduction shall be allowed . . . for any payment made, directly or indirectly, to an official or employee of any govern-

[3] *Ibid.*

[4] "Lockheed Says It Paid $22 Million to Get Contracts," *Wall Street Journal*, 4 August 1975.

[5] Kotchian, "The Payoff," p. 12.

[6] *Wall Street Journal*, *op. cit.*

[7] "Payoffs: The Growing Scandal, *Newsweek*, 23 February 1976.

[8] "Lockheed Pleads Guilty to Making Secret Payoffs," *San Francisco Chronicle*, 2 June 1979.

ment . . . if the payment constitutes an illegal bribe or kickback.''[9] Lockheed was not charged specifically with bribery because the U.S. law forbidding bribery was not enacted until 1978. Lockheed pleaded guilty to four counts of fraud and four counts of making false statements to the government. Mr. Kotchian was not indicted, but under pressure from the board of directors, he was forced to resign from Lockheed. In Japan, Kodama was arrested along with Tanaka.

1. Explain fully the effects that payments like those which Lockheed made to the Japanese have on the structure of a market.
2. In your view, were Lockheed's payments to the various Japanese parties ''bribes'' or ''extortions''? Explain your response fully.
3. In your judgment, did Mr. A. Carl Kotchian act rightly from a moral point of view? (Your answer should take into account the effects of the payments on the welfare of the societies affected, on the rights and duties of the various parties involved, and on the distribution of benefits and burdens among the groups involved.) In your judgment, was Mr. Kotchian morally responsible for his actions? Was he, in the end, treated fairly?
4. In its October 27, 1980, issue, *Business Week* argued that every corporation has a ''corporate culture,''—that is, a set of values that set a pattern for its employees' activities, opinions, and actions, and which are instilled in succeeding generations of employees (pp. 148–60). Describe, if you can, the ''corporate culture'' of Lockheed and relate that culture to Mr. Kotchian's actions. Describe some strategies for changing that culture in ways that might make foreign payments less likely.

[9] Internal Revenue Code 1975, Section 162C.

Part Three

BUSINESS AND ITS EXTERNAL EXCHANGES

Ecology and Consumers

The process of producing goods forces businesses to engage in exchanges and interactions with two main external environments: the natural environment and a consumer environment. It is from the natural environment that business ultimately draws the raw materials which it transforms into its finished products. These finished products are then externally promoted and sold to consumers. The natural environment therefore provides the raw material input of business while the consumer environment absorbs its finished output.

The next two chapters explore the ethical issues raised by these exchanges and interactions. Chapter Five discusses the two basic problems related to the natural environment: pollution and resource depletion. Chapter Six discusses several consumer issues, including product quality and advertising.

5

ETHICS AND THE ENVIRONMENT

INTRODUCTION

Modern industry has provided us with a material prosperity unequaled in our history. It has also created unparalleled environmental threats to ourselves and to future generations. The very technology that has enabled us to manipulate and control nature has also polluted our environment and has rapidly depleted our natural resources. Each year more than 150 million tons of pollutants were pumped into the air we breathe, more than 41 million tons of toxic wastes are produced, and 15 million gallons of pollutants are dumped into the nation's waterways. The total energy consumption of the United States each year is equivalent to about 13 million barrels of oil. Each U.S. citizen annually accounts for the consumption of 1,300 pounds of metal and 18,500 pounds of other minerals.

Although the nation has made significant progress in controlling certain types of pollution and in conserving energy, significant environmental problems still remain, especially at an international level. A decade ago a three-year government study projected a pessimistic future:

> If present trends continue, the world in 2000 will be more crowded, more polluted, less stable ecologically, and more vulnerable to disruption than the world we live in now. Serious stresses involving population, resources, and environment are clearly visible ahead. Despite greater material output, the world's people will be poorer in many ways than they are today . . .
>
> During the 1990s world oil production will approach geological estimates of maxi-

mum production capacity, even with rapidly increasing petroleum prices. . . . For the one-quarter of humankind that depends primarily on wood for fuel, the outlook is bleak. Needs for fuelwood will exceed available supplies by about 25 percent before the turn of the century.

Significant losses of world forests will continue over the next 20 years as demand for forest products and fuelwood increases. . . . The world's forests are now disappearing at the rate of 18–20 million hectares a year (an area half the size of California) . . .

Serious deterioration of agricultural soils will occur worldwide, due to erosion, loss of organic matter, desertification, salinization, alkalinization, and waterlogging. Already, an area of cropland and grassland approximately the size of Maine is becoming barren wasteland each year, and the spread of desert-like conditions is likely to accelerate.

Atmospheric concentrations of carbon dioxide and ozone-depleting chemicals are expected to increase at rates that could alter the world's climate and upper atmosphere significantly by 2050. Acid rain from increased combustion of fossil fuels (especially coal) threatens damage to lakes, soils, and crops. Radioactive and other hazardous materials present health and safety problems in increasing numbers of countries.

Extinctions of plant and animal species will increase dramatically. Hundreds of thousands of species—perhaps as many as 20 percent of all species on earth—will be irretrievably lost as their habitats vanish, especially in tropical forests. . . .

The world will be more vulnerable both to natural disaster and to disruptions from human causes. Most nations are likely to be still more dependent on foreign sources of energy in 2000 than they are today. Food production will be more vulnerable to disruptions of fossil fuel energy supplies and to weather fluctuations as cultivation expands to more marginal areas. The loss of diverse germ plasm in local strains and wild progenitors of food crops, together with the increase of monoculture, could lead to greater risks of massive crop failures. Larger numbers of people will be vulnerable to higher food prices or even famine when adverse weather occurs. The world will be more vulnerable to the disruptive effects of war. The tensions that could lead to war will have multiplied. . . .

[T]he best evidence now available—even allowing for the many beneficial effects of technological developments and adoptions—suggests that by 2000 the world's human population may be within a few generations of reaching the entire planet's carrying capacity. . . . The U.S. National Academy of Sciences' report, *Resources and Man* . . . concluded that a world population of 10 billion "is close to (if not above) the maximum that an *intensively managed* world might hope to support with some degree of comfort and individual choice.". . . If the fertility and mortality rates projected for 2000 were to continue unchanged into the twenty-first century, the world's population would reach 10 billion by 2030. Thus anyone with a present life expectancy of an additional 50 years could expect to see the world population reach 10 billion. This same rate of growth would produce a population of nearly 30 billion before the end of the twenty-first century. . . . [These] population projections assume extensive policy changes and developments to reduce fertility rates. Without the assumed policy changes, the projected rate of population growth would be still more rapid. . . .

The time for action to prevent this outcome is running out. Unless nations collectively and individually take bold and imaginative steps toward improved social and economic conditions, reduced fertility, better management of resources, and protection of the environment, the world must expect a troubled entry into the twenty-first century.[1]

[1] Council on Environmental Quality, *The Global 2000 Report to the President*, vol. 1, (Washington, DC: U.S. Government Printing Office, 1980), pp. 1, 2, 3, 39.

So intractable and difficult are the problems raised by these environmental threats, that many observers believe that they cannot be solved. William Pollard, a physicist, for example, despairs of our being able to deal adequately with these problems:

> My own view is that [mankind] will not do so until he has suffered greatly and much that he now relies upon has been destroyed. As the earth in a short few decades becomes twice as crowded with human beings as it is now, and as human societies are confronted with dwindling resources in the midst of mounting accumulations of wastes, and a steadily deteriorating environment, we can only foresee social paroxysms of an intensity greater than any we have so far known. The problems are so varied and so vast and the means for their solutions so far beyond the resources of the scientific and technological knowhow on which we have relied that there simply is not time to avoid the impending catastrophe. We stand, therefore, on the threshold of a time of judgment more severe, undoubtedly, than any mankind has ever faced before in history.[2]

Environmental issues, then, raise large and complicated ethical and technological questions for our business society. What is the extent of the environmental damage produced by present and projected industrial technology? How large a threat does this damage pose to our welfare? What values must we give up in order to halt or slow such damage? Whose rights are violated by pollution and who should be given the responsibility of paying for the costs of polluting the environment? How long will our natural resources last? What obligations do firms have to future generations to preserve the environment and conserve our resources?

This chapter explores these environmental issues. It begins with an overview of various technical aspects of environmental resource use. This is followed by a discussion of the ethical basis of environmental protection. The final sections discuss two controversial issues: our obligations to future generations and the prospects for continued economic growth.

5.1 THE DIMENSIONS OF POLLUTION AND RESOURCE DEPLETION

Environmental damage inevitably threatens the welfare of human beings as well as of plants and animals. Threats to the environment come from two sources: pollution and resource depletion. Pollution refers to the undesirable and unintended contamination of the environment by the manufacture or use of commodities. Resource depletion, on the other hand, refers to the consumption of finite or scarce resources. In a certain sense, pollution is really a type of resource depletion, since contamination of air, water, or land diminishes their beneficial qualities. But for purposes of discussion, we will keep the two issues distinct.

[2] William G. Pollard, "The Uniqueness of the Earth," in *Earth Might Be Fair*, Ian G. Barbour. ed. (Englewood Cliffs, NJ: Prentice Hall, 1972), pp. 95–96; see also Robert L. Heilbroner, *An Inquiry into the Human Prospect, Updated for the 1980s* (New York: W. W. Norton & Company, Inc., 1980).

Air Pollution

Air pollution is not new—it has been with us since the industrial revolution introduced the world to the belching factory smokestack. But the costs of air pollution increased exponentially as industrialization expanded. Today, air pollutants affect vegetation, decreasing agricultural yields and inflicting losses on the timber industry; they deteriorate exposed construction materials through corrosion, discoloration, and rot; and they are hazardous to health and life, raising medical costs and lessening the enjoyment of living.[3]

Studies have indicated that air pollution in the form of carbon dioxide may have potentially disastrous long-range effects on climate through the creation of a "greenhouse effect" that threatens to trap heat in the atmosphere and raise temperatures worldwide. When carbon dioxide is released into the atmosphere by the burning of fossil fuels such as coal, it absorbs solar energy that would otherwise be reflected back into space, thereby increasing the temperature of the world. Since the beginning of the industrial era, the amount of carbon dioxide in the atmosphere has increased by 25 percent. Recent measurements at Mauna Loa, Hawaii, indicate that currently carbon dioxide is increasing at the rate of 1.4 percent a year and that this rate accelerates each passing year.[4] Average global temperatures are now .5°C higher than our earliest reliable records and are expected to rise by 1.5° to 4.5°C during the next century. This is expected to expand the world's deserts; melt the polar ice caps, causing sea levels to rise and flood coastal lands; make several species of plants and animals extinct, disrupt farming; and increase the severity of respiratory diseases.[5] If coal is once again widely used, the temperature of the globe may rise faster and these effects may be felt as early as 2020.[6]

Of even more serious concern and potentially more disastrous is the gradual breakdown of ozone gas in the stratosphere above us caused by the release of chlorofluorocarbons, or CFCs, into the air. A layer of ozone in the lower stratosphere screens all life on earth from harmful ultraviolet radiation. This ozone layer, however, is destroyed by CFC gases, which are used in aerosol cans, refrigerators, air conditioners, industrial solvents, and industrial foam blowers. When released into the air, CFC gasses rise and in 7 to 10 years they reach the stratosphere, where they destroy ozone molecules and where they remain for 75 to 130 years, continuing all the while to break down additional ozone molecules. Average global atmospheric concentrations of CFC-11 and CFC-12 (two kinds of CFC gases) are increasing annually at rates of about 5 percent each, while concentrations of CFC-

[3] John R. Holum, *Topics and Terms in Environmental Problems* (New York: John Wiley & Sons, Inc., 1977), pp. 16–17; the most important study of the health effects of air pollution remains Lester Lave and Eugene Seskind, *Air Pollution and Human Health* (Baltimore: Johns Hopkins University Press, 1977); for a review of the literature see A. Myrick Freeman, III, *Air and Water Pollution Control* (New York: John Wiley & Sons, Inc., 1982), pp. 36–85.

[4] Council on Environmental Quality, *Environmental Trends* (Washington, DC: U.S. Government Printing Office, 1989), pp. 62–63.

[5] John Gribbin, *Future Weather and the Greenhouse Effect* (New York: Delacorte Press/Eleanor Friede, 1982). Tim Beardsley, "Getting Warmer?" *Scientific American*, July 1988: 32.

[6] Siegenthaler and H. Oeschger, "Predicting Future Atmospheric Carbon Dioxide Levels," *Science*, 199 (1978): 388–95.

113 and CFC-22 are increasing even more rapidly at annual rates of 10 and 11 percent, respectively. Some data indicate that the ozone layer may already have shrunk by about 2.5 percent, a level that had not been expected to be reached until next century. Studies predict that the shrinking of the ozone layer and the subsequent increase of ultraviolet rays will cause several hundred thousand new cases of skin cancer and may cause considerable destruction of the 75 percent of the world's major crops that are sensitive to ultraviolet light. Other studies caution that the plankton that float on the surface layers of the earth's oceans and on which the entire food chain of the world's oceans ultimately depends, is sensitive to ultraviolet light and may suffer mass destruction. Recent international agreements to which the United States is a party have pledged to gradually phase out the use of CFC gases during the next decade. But scientists warn that even if the use of CFC gases were immediately halted, CFC levels in the atmosphere would still continue their dangerous upward climb, because those gases already released will continue to rise upward for another decade and will persist for perhaps a century.[7]

Less catastrophic but highly worrisome air pollution threats are the 2.4 billion pounds of airborne toxic substances that are released annually into the nation's atmosphere, including phosgene, a nerve gas used in warfare, and methyl isocyanate, which killed more than 2,000 Indians in Bhopal. In addition, the chemical brew released into the air annually includes 235 million pounds of carcinogens such as benzene and formaldehyde, and 527 million pounds of such neurotoxins as toluene and trichloroethylene. Although levels of other "conventional" forms of air pollutants have been decreasing during the last decade, toxics have not. The Environmental Protection Agency estimated in 1989 that 20 of the more than 329 toxics released into the air alone cause more than 2,000 cases of cancer each year and that living near chemical plants raises a person's chances of cancer to more than 1 in 1,000. Exceptionally high cancer rates have been found near plants in several states including West Virginia and Louisiana.

Acid rain is a still little-understood but very real threat to the environment. Acid rain forms when nitrogen and sulfur oxides in the air combine with water vapor in clouds to form nitric acid and sulfuric acid, which is then carried down with the rainfall. The acidic rainfall—sometimes as acidic as vinegar—is thought to kill fish in lakes and rivers and to destroy large areas of forest. Acid rain has now become a major international problem. Much of Canada, the northeastern part of the United States, West Germany, and the Netherlands have suffered from acid rain and many researchers fear that future emissions will devastate the world's forests.[8]

The most prevalent forms of air pollution, however, are the gases and particulates spewed out by autos, coal and oil fuels, and by industrial processes. The

[7] Council on Environmental Quality, *Environmental Trends*, p. 63; Barry Meier, "Ozone Demise Quickens Despite '78 Ban on Spray Propellant; New Curbs Debated," *Wall Street Journal*, 13 August 1986, p. 21; "Ozone Industry Is Getting Its Head Out of the Clouds," *Business Week*, 13 October 1986, pp. 110–114.

[8] For readable and informal overviews of the problem see Thomas Pawlick, *A Killing Rain* (San Francisco: Sierra Club Books, 1984); Jon R. Luoma, *Troubled Skies, Troubled Waters* (New York: The Viking Press, 1984); Sandra Postel, "Protecting Forests from Air Pollution and Acid Rain," in *State of the World, 1985*, Lester Brown et al., eds. (New York: W. W. Norton & Company, Inc., 1985), pp. 97–123.

effects of these pollutants were recognized more than two decades ago when a report of the Department of Health, Education and Welfare summarized them as follows:

> At levels frequently found in heavy traffic, carbon monoxide produces headaches, loss of visual acuity, and decreased muscular coordination.
>
> Sulfur oxides, found wherever coal and oil are common fuels, corrode metal and stone and, at concentrations frequently found in our larger cities, reduce visibility, injure vegetation, and contribute to the incidence of respiratory diseases and to premature death.
>
> Besides their contribution to photochemical smog, described below, nitrogen oxides are responsible for the whiskey-brown haze that not only destroys the view in some of our cities, but endangers the takeoff and landing of planes. At concentrations higher than those usually experienced, these oxides can interfere with respiratory function and, it is suspected, contribute to respiratory disease. They are formed in the combustion of all types of fuel.
>
> Hydrocarbons are a very large class of chemicals, some of which, in particle form, have produced cancer in laboratory animals, and others of which, discharged chiefly by the automobile, play a major role in the formation of photochemical smog.
>
> Photochemical smog is a complex mixture of gases and particles manufactured by sunlight out of the raw materials—nitrogen oxides and hydrocarbons—discharged to the atmosphere chiefly by the automobile. Smog, whose effects have been observed in every region of the United States, can severely damage crops and trees, deteriorate rubber and other materials, reduce visibility, cause the eyes to smart and the throat to sting, and, it is thought, reduce resistance to respiratory disease.
>
> Particulate matter not only soils our clothes, shows up on our window sills, and scatters light to blur the image of what we see, it acts as a catalyst in the formation of other pollutants, it contributes to the corrosion of metals, and, in proper particle size, can carry into our lungs irritant gases which might otherwise have been harmlessly dissipated in the upper respiratory tract. Some particulates contain poisons whose effects on man are gradual, often the result of the accumulation of years.[9]

What was not known twenty years ago, and what more recent long-range studies have indicated is that the deterioration of lung function in human beings caused by their chronic exposure to air pollution, whether it be auto smog or industrial smokestack emissions, is long-lasting and often irreversible. Some of the 2,500 subjects in the studies suffered as much as 75 percent loss of lung capacity during a ten-year period of living in Los Angeles communities—a region with dangerously high levels of air pollution—leaving them vulnerable to respiratory disease, emphysema, and impairment of their stamina. Damage to the still-developing lungs of children was especially problematic.[10]

The major sources of air pollution are automobiles and industrial smokestacks. In 1981, auto emissions accounted for 47 percent of all air pollutants, mostly in the form of carbon monoxide, a toxic gas. In congested urban areas such as Los

[9] Quoted in *No Deposit-No Return*, Huey D. Johnson, ed. (Reading, MA: Addison-Wesley Publishing Co., Inc., 1970), pp. 166–67.

[10] Bad Air's Damage to Lungs Is Long-lasting, Study Says," *San Jose Mercury News*, 29 March 1991, p. 1f.

TABLE 5.1 Quantities and Major Sources of Air Pollution in 1987 (in millions of tons)

	Transportation	Power Production	Industrial Processes	Solid Waste Disposal	Miscellaneous
Caron monoxide	40.7	7.2	4.7	1.7	7.1
Sulfur oxides	.9	16.4	3.1	.0	.0
Volatile organic compounds	6.0	2.3	8.3	.6	2.4
Particulates	1.4	1.8	2.5	.3	1.0
Nitrogen oxides	8.4	10.3	.6	.1	.1
Lead	3.0	.5	2.0	2.6	.0

Source: U.S. Environmental Protection Agency, *National Air Pollutant Emission Estimates, 1940–1947,* March 1989.

Angeles, estimates of the proportion of air pollution caused by automobiles rise to as much as 70 percent.

Industrial pollution is derived principally from power plants and from plants that refine and manufacture basic metals. Electrical power plants that depend on fossil fuels such as oil, coal, or natural gas throw tons of sulfur oxides, nitrogen oxides, and ashes into the air. When taken into the lungs, sulfur oxides form sulfuric acid, which damages the linings of the lungs and causes emphysema and bronchitis. Sulfur oxides have also been found to be a major factor in infant deaths, and particulates have been implicated in deaths from pneumonia and

FIGURE 5-1. Emissions of Selected Pollutants in the United States, 1950–87

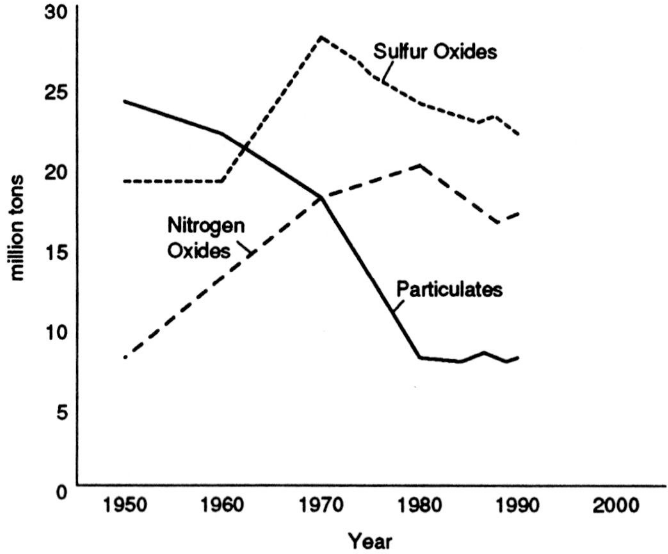

Source: Environmental Protection Agency

influenza.[11] As mentioned earlier, sulfur oxides and nitrogen oxides also produce acid rain. Copper refineries and smelters produce large quantities of copper oxides and ash, while steel, nickel, cement, and chemical plants produce a variety of airborne particulates. The major sources of air pollutants for 1987 are summarized in Table 5.1.

The last decade has seen considerable improvement in air quality, largely as a result of environmental legislation enacted during the 1970s. Figure 5.1 indicates the quantities of various air pollutants emitted before and since 1970, the year Congress passed the Clean Air Act. As the figure indicates, emissions of some major air pollutants (such as particulates) have been reduced since that time by more than half, a remarkable record of success for this piece of environmental regulation. Emissions of at least one major hazardous air pollutant—nitrogen oxides—however, have hardly declined. And, as the figure indicates, substantial amounts of pollutants are still being spewed into the air we breathe.

The costs of air pollution are high. It is estimated that without environmental controls, air pollution damages in 1978 would have amounted to an additional $23.3 billion in costs.[12] These additional costs would have included health damages (both deaths and sickness) of $17 billion; soiling and cleaning bills of $3 billion; damages to vegetation and external materials equal to $1 billion; and declines in property values of $2.3 billion. An earlier study by the Environmental Protection Agency estimated that in 1968 the *total* costs of air pollution were $16.5 billion in 1968 dollars (about $61.9 billion in 1990 dollars).[13] Studies have indicated that if the concentrations of sulfur oxides over our major cities were cut in half from their 1960 levels this would add an average of one year to the lives of each of its residents.[14] If air pollution in urban areas were reduced to the levels of rural regions with clean air, the death rates for asthma, bronchitis, and emphysema would drop by about 50 percent;[15] and deaths from heart disease would drop by about 15 percent.[16] Reduction in air pollution since 1970 now saves about 14,000 lives per year.[17]

Water Pollution

The contamination of water sources is an old problem, one that has been with us since civilization began using water to dispose of its wastes and sewage. Water pollutants today, however, are much more diverse, consisting not only of

[11] See Philip E. Graves, Ronald J. Krumm, and Daniel M. Violette, "Issues in Health Benefit Measurement," in *Environment Policy, Volume II*, George S. Tolley, Philip E. Graves, and Alan S. Cohen, ed. (Cambridge, MA: Harper & Row, Publishers, Inc.: 1982).

[12] A. Myrick Freeman, III, *Air and Water Pollution Control, A Benefit-Cost Assessment* (New York: John Wiley & Sons, Inc., 1982), p. 128; see also Allen V. Kueese, *Measuring the Benefits of Clean Air and Water*, (Washington, DC: Resources for the Future, 1984).

[13] U.S. Environmental Protection Agency, "The Challenge of the Environment: A Primer on EPA's Statutory Authority," in *A Managerial Odyssey: Problems in Business and Its Environment*, Arthur Elkins and Dennis W. Callaghan, eds. (Reading, MA: Addison-Wesley Publishing Co., Inc., 1975), p. 252.

[14] Lester Lave and Eugene Seskind, *Air Pollution and Human Health* (Baltimore: Johns Hopkins University Press, 1977).

[15] *Ibid.*, pp. 723–33.

[16] *Ibid.*

[17] Freeman, *Air and Water Pollution Control*, p. 69.

organic wastes but also including dissolved salts, metals, and radioactive materials, as well as suspended materials such as bacteria, viruses, and sediments. These can impair or destroy aquatic life, threaten human health, and foul the water. Water pollutants enter surface water or underground water basins either from a single or "point" source, such as a pipe or a well carrying sewage or industrial wastes, or they enter from a diffused or "nonpoint" source covering a large area, such as crop pesticides or animal wastes carried in rainwater or runoff.[18]

Salt brines from mines and oil wells, as well as mixtures of sodium chloride and calcium chloride used to keep winter roads clear of snow, all eventually drain into water sources where they raise the saline content.[19] The high saline levels in ponds, lakes, and rivers kill whatever fish, vegetation, or other organisms inhabit them. Highly salinated water also poses major health hazards when it finds its way into city water supplies and is drunk by persons afflicted with heart disease, hypertension, cirrhosis of the liver, or renal disease.

Water drainage from coal mining operations contains sulfuric acid as well as iron and sulfate particles. Continuous-casting and hot-rolling mills employ acids to scrub metals, and these acids are then rinsed off with water. The acidic water from these sources is sometimes flushed into streams and rivers. The high acid levels produced in waterways by these practices are lethal to most organisms living within the aquatic environment.[20]

Organic wastes in water are comprised in large part of untreated human wastes and sewage, but a substantial amount is also derived from industrial processing of various food products, from the pulp and paper industry, and from animal feedlots.[21] Organic wastes that find their way into water resources are consumed by various types of bacteria, which in the process deplete the water of its oxygen. The oxygen-depleted water then becomes incapable of supporting fish life and other organisms.

Phosphorus compounds also contaminate many of our water sources.[22] Phosphorus compounds are found in cleansing detergents used both domestically and industrially, in fertilizers used for agricultural purposes, and in untreated human and animal sewage. Lakes with high concentrations of phosphorus give rise to explosive expansions of algae populations that choke waterways, drive out other forms of life, deplete the water of its oxygen, and severely restrict water visibility.

Various inorganic pollutants pose serious health hazards when they make their way into water used for drinking and eating purposes. Mercury has been finding its way into fresh water supplies and the oceans, put there by runoff from the combustion of fossil fuels, by past pulp mill uses of mercury-based fungicides, and by the use of certain pesticides.[23] Mercury is transformed into organic com-

[18] Council on Environmental Quality, *Environmental Trends*, p. 31.

[19] Richard H. Wagner, *Environment and Man*, 2nd ed. (New York: W. W. Norton & Co., Inc., 1974), p. 99.

[20] X. M. Mackenthun, *The Practice of Water Pollution* (Washington, DC: U.S. Government Printing Office, 1969), ch. 8.

[21] Wagner, *Environment*, pp. 102–7.

[22] J. H. Ryther, "Nitrogen, Phosphorus, and Eutrophication in the Coastal Marine Environment," *Science*, 171, no. 3975 (1971): 1008–13.

[23] L. J. Carter, "Chemical Plants Leave Unexpected Legacy for Two Virginia Rivers," *Science*, 198 (1977): 1015–20; J. Holmes, "Mercury Is Heavier Than You Think," *Esquire*, May 1971; T. Aaronson, "Mercury in the Environment," *Environment*, May 1971.

pounds by microorganisms and becomes increasingly concentrated as it moves up the food chain to fish and birds. When consumed by humans, these compounds can cause brain damage, paralysis, and death. The Allied Chemical Company was recently found to be discharging large quantities of kepone into Virginia's James River.[24] Kepone is a chlorine compound that is toxic to fish life and causes nerve damage, sterility, and possibly cancer in humans. Cadmium from zinc refineries, from the agricultural use of certain fertilizers, and from battery manufacturers, also makes its way into water sources, where it becomes concentrated in the tissues of fish and shellfish.[25] Cadmium causes a degenerate bone disease that cripples some victims and kills others; it induces severe cramps, vomiting, and diarrhea, and it produces high blood pressure and heart disease. A few years ago, Reserve Mining Company was found to be depositing asbestos-contaminated wastes in the waters of Lake Superior, which provides the drinking supply of several towns.[26] Asbestos fibers may cause cancer of the gastrointestinal tract.

Heat is also a water pollutant.[27] Water is used as a coolant in various industrial manufacturing processes and by the electrical power industry, a major heat polluter. Transferring heat into water raises the water's thermal energy to levels that decrease its ability to hold the dissolved oxygen that aquatic organisms require. In addition, the alternating rise and fall of temperatures prevents the water from being populated by fish, since most water organisms are adapted only to stable water temperatures.

Oil spills are a form of water pollution whose occurrence became more frequent as our dependence on oil increased. Since 1973 the number of oil pollution incidents reported has remained fairly constant, although the volume of oil spilled has been highly variable. Oil spills result from offshore drilling, discharges of sludge from oil tankers, and oil tanker accidents. In 1989, Exxon Corporation ran the supertanker *Valdez* aground in Alaska's Prince William Sound, spilling 240,000 barrels (a barrel is 42 gallons) of crude oil over 900 square miles within Prince William Sound.[28] Several years earlier two Standard Oil of California tankers collided in San Francisco Bay, spilling hundreds of thousands of gallons of oil along 50 miles of California coastlines; eight months later a Navy tanker spilled 230,000 gallons on the beaches of San Clemente, and the following month a Swedish tanker spilled 15,000 to 30,000 more gallons of oil into San Francisco Bay. The contamination produced by oil spills is directly lethal to sea life, including fish, seals, plants, and aquatic birds; it requires expensive cleanup operations for residents, and it imposes costly losses on nearby tourist and fishing industries. In 1985 about 11,000 oil spills, involving about 24 million gallons of oil, were recorded in and around U.S. waters.[29]

In the past, the oceans have been used as disposal sites for intermediate-

[24] F. S. Sterrett and C. A. Boss, "Careless Kepone," *Environment*, 19 (1977): 30–37.

[25] L. Friberg, *Cadmium in the Environment* (Cleveland, OH: C.R.C. Press, 1971).

[26] See Presson S. Shane, "Case Study—Silver Bay: Reserve Mining Company," in *Ethical Issues in Business*, Thomas Donaldson and Patricia H. Werhane, eds. (Englewood Cliffs, NJ: Prentice Hall, 1979), p. 358–61.

[27] C. T. Hill, "Thermal Pollution and Its Control," in *The Social Cost of Power Production* (New York: Macmillan Inc., 1975); J. R. Clark, "Thermal Pollution and Aquatic Life," *Scientific American*, March 1969.

[28] Sharon Begley, "Smothering the Waters," *Newsweek*, 10 April 1989.

[29] Council on Environmental Quality, *Environmental Quality, 1987–1988*, (Washington, DC: U.S. Government Printing Office, 1989).

and low-level radioactive wastes (which are more fully discussed below). Since the mid-1970s, oceanographers have found in seawater traces of plutonium, cesium, and other radioactive materials that have apparently leaked from the sealed drums in which radioactive wastes are disposed.[30] Coastal estuaries and marine sediments also have been found to contain unusually high concentrations of cadmium, chromium, copper, lead, mercury, and silver. High concentrations of PAHs or polycyclic aromatic hydrocarbons (chemicals given off by the burning of fossil fuels) have also been found in coastal waters such as those around Boston Harbor and Salem Harbor. PAHs cause mutations and cancers in some marine organisms and are acutely toxic to others. PCBs, or polychlorinated biphenyls, which were used as cooling fluids in electrical transformers, as lubricants, and as flame retardants until their production was completely banned in the United States in 1979, have become widespread in the environment and are gradually accumulating in the oceans, especially in coastal areas. Minute amounts of PCBs are deadly toxic to human beings and other life forms, and traces can engender a variety of toxic effects including reproductive failures, birth defects, tumors, liver disorders, skin lesions, and immune suppression. PCBs, which continue to be produced by other countries and which still are often improperly disposed of in the United States, are a cause of profound concern since they are persistent and they become increasingly concentrated as they move up the food chain.[31] Since 1976, parts of New York's Hudson River have been closed to fishing because of PCB contamination; in 1986 all fishing was totally banned.

Underground water supplies are also becoming more polluted. According to a recent government report, "Incidents of ground-water contamination—by organic chemicals, inorganic chemicals, radionuclides [radioactive wastes], or microorganisms—are being reported with increasing frequency and have now occurred . . . in every state in the nation.[32] The sources of contamination have included landfills, waste piles, legal and illegal dumps, and surface reservoirs. More than 50 percent of the population depends on underground water sources for drinking water. Underground water contaminants have been linked to cancers, liver and kidney diseases, and damage to the central nervous system. Unfortunately, exposure frequently occurs unknowingly over periods of years because contaminated groundwater is usually odorless, colorless, and tasteless.

How much does water pollution cost us, and what benefits might we expect from its removal? Unfortunately, there are few reliable estimates of the costs of water pollution, and some of these estimates are dated. In 1973 the Environmental Protection Agency estimated that the annual costs of water pollution in 1973 dollars are $10.1 billion per year (or about $29.57 billion per year in 1990 dollars).[33] More recent estimates of the additional annual costs that would have been incurred in 1985 without water pollution controls ranged from $18 billion to $.8 billion (in 1990 dollars from about $21.74 billion to $.96 billion).[34]

[30] D. Burnham, "Radioactive Material Found in Oceans," *New York Times*, 31 May 1976, p. 13.

[31] Council on Environmental Quality, *Environmental Trends*, p. 47.

[32] *Ibid.*

[33] H. T. Heintz, A. Hershaft, and G. Horak, *National Damages of Air and Water Pollution* (Washington, DC: Environmental Protection Agency, 1976).

[34] Freeman, *Air and Water Pollution Control*, p. 159.

Toxic Substances

Hazardous or toxic substances are substances that can cause an increase in mortality rates or an increase in irreversible or incapacitating illness, or that have other seriously adverse health or environmental effects. These include acidic chemicals, inorganic metals (such as mercury or arsenic), flammable solvents, pesticides, herbicides, phenols, explosives, and so on. (Radioactive wastes are also classified as hazardous substances, but these will be discussed separately below.) 2, 4, 5-T and Silvex, for example, are two widely used herbicides that contain dioxin—a deadly poison (one hundred times more deadly than strychnine) and a carcinogen. Until 1979 these herbicides were being sprayed on forests in Oregon, where they are believed to have led to an abnormal number of miscarriages in local women and to have caused a range of reproductive defects in animals. A second example: In the late 1970s, toxic chemicals buried by Hooker Chemical Company at sites near Niagara Falls, New York, were found to have leaked from the sites and to have contaminated the surrounding residential areas, including homes, schools, playing fields, and underground water supplies. The chemicals included dioxin, pesticides, carbon tetrachloride, and other carcinogenic or toxic chemicals that were suspected of having induced spontaneous abortions, nerve damage, and congenital malformations among families living nearby.[35]

The government estimates that over 58,000 different chemical compounds are currently being used in the United States and that their number is growing each year. Ten times more chemicals, many of them toxic, were being used in the mid-1980s than in 1970. Among the most common of the toxic chemicals produced by industry is acrylonitrile, which is used in the manufacture of plastics (used in appliances, luggage, telephones, and numerous common household and industrial products) and whose production is currently rising by 3 percent a year. Acrylonitrile is a suspected carcinogen, and it releases the toxic chemical hydrogen cyanide when plastic containing it is burned.[36]

Benzene is another common industrial toxic chemical used in plastics, dyes, nylon, food additives, detergents, drugs, fungicides, and gasoline. Benzene is a cause of anemia, bone marrow damage, and leukemia. Recent studies have shown that benzene workers are several times more likely than the general population to get leukemia.[37]

Vinyl chloride is another common industrial chemical used in the production of plastics, whose production is rising by 3 percent per year. Vinyl chloride, which is released in small amounts when plastic products deteriorate, causes liver damage, birth anomalies, liver, respiratory, brain, and lymph cancers, and bone damage. Cancer mortality for vinyl chloride workers is 50 percent higher than for the general population, and communities located around plants where it is used also have higher cancer rates than the general population.[38]

Phthalates are resins used in industry to produce model cement, paints, and

[35] For these and other similar examples, see Lewis Regenstein, *America the Poisoned* (Washington, DC: Acropolis Books, Ltd., 1982); "The Poisoning of America," *Time*, 22 September 1980, 58–69; "The Poisoning of America Continues," *Time*, 14 October, 1985, pp. 76–90.

[36] Council on Environmental Quality, Environmental Trends, p. 139.

[37] *Ibid.*, p. 140.

[38] *Ibid.*

finishes. They damage the central nervous system of humans and are toxic to fish and birdlife.

Although the health effects of some substances is now known, the toxicity of many others is unknown and difficult to determine. Many chemicals cause chronic diseases only after a long period following a person's first exposure to the chemical. For example, most human cancers caused by exposure to toxic chemicals take 15 to 30 years to show up, which makes it difficult to identify the original causes of the disease. Moreover, studies are expensive and take time, since rates of illness in large exposed populations must be compared to those of similar but unexposed groups over these long periods of time.

Solid Waste

Americans today produce more residential garbage than do the citizens of any other country in the world. Each year people living in America's cities produce more than 160 million tons of municipal solid waste, enough to fill a 145,000-mile-long convoy of 10-ton garbage trucks, more than half the distance to the moon,[39] or enough to fill the Astrodome in Houston more than twice daily for a year. Each person reading this book produces, on the average, almost 4 pounds of garbage a day. Only about 10 percent of residential wastes are recovered through recycling, a disappointingly low proportion that is due to the lack of financial backing for recycling operations, the small size of markets for recycled products, and toxic chemicals present in recyclable garbage.

While the amount of garbage we produce has been increasing each year, the facilities to handle it have decreased. In 1978 there were about 20,000 municipal garbage dumps in operation; by 1988 there were less than 6,000, and over a third of these will be filled during the 1990s, while others will be closed for safety reasons. Florida, Massachusetts, New Hampshire, and New Jersey are a few of the states that will close virtually all of there garbage dumps during this decade. Moreover, fewer and fewer dumps are opened. In the early 1970s, 300 to 400 new facilities were opened each year around the country; today that number has dropped to between 50 and 200.

City garbage dumps themselves are significant sources of pollution, containing toxic substances such as cadmium (from rechargeable batteries), mercury, lead (from car batteries and TV picture tubes), vanadium, copper, zinc, and PCBs (from refrigerators, stoves, engines, and appliances built before 1980). Only about one fourth of all city dumps test groundwater for possible contamination; less than 16 percent have insulating liners; only 5 percent collect polluting liquid wastes before they percolate into groundwater; less than half impose any restrictions on the kinds of liquid wastes that can be poured into them. Not surprisingly, almost one fourth of the sites identified in the Superfund National Priorities List as posing the greatest chemical hazards to public health and the environment are city dumps.[40]

The quantity of residential garbage Americans produce, however, is dwarfed by the quantities of solid waste produced through industrial, agricultural, and mining processes. While residential garbage, as mentioned above, is estimated at

[39] Council on Environmental Quality, *Environmental Quality Report, 1987–1988* (Washington, DC: U.S. Government Printing Office, 1989), p. 3.

[40] *Ibid.*

about 160 million tons a year, American industries generate over 7.6 billion tons of solid waste a year, while oil and gas producers generate 2 to 3 billion tons, and mining operations about 1.4 billion tons.[41] These wastes are dumped into some 220,000 industrial waste heaps, the vast majority of which are unlined surface dumps.

Thousands of abandoned dumps have been discovered containing hazardous wastes, most created by the chemical and petroleum industries.[42] The majority of hazardous waste sites are located in industrial regions. Altogether, about 80 percent of industrial wastes are estimated to have been deposited in ponds, lagoons, and landfills that are not secure.[43] Efforts begun in 1980 to indentify all uncontrolled hazardous sites had succeeded by 1986 in identifying over 24,000 uncontrolled hazardous sites. In many places wastes have been migrating out of the sites and seeping into the ground, where they have contaminated the water supplies of several communities. A sizable number of these required emergency action because they represented immediate threats. The costs of cleaning up these dumps have been estimated at between $28.4 billion and $55 billion.[44]

The net amounts of hazardous wastes currently being produced have been difficult to establish. In 1979 the Environmental Protection Agency estimated that 10 to 15 percent of the industrial wastes being produced each year were toxic, an estimated total of 15 million tons per year. But in 1984 the agency announced that nearly six times as much hazardous waste was being generated each year than it had previously estimated. New studies suggested that in 1981 alone, 290 million tons of toxic wastes were produced.[45]

Nuclear Wastes

Light-water nuclear reactors contain radioactive materials, including known carcinogens such as strontium 90, cesium 137, barium 140, and iodine 131. Extremely high levels of radiation from these elements can kill a person, lower dosages (especially if radioactive dust particles are inhaled or ingested) can cause thyroid, lung, or bone cancer and can cause genetic damage that will be transmitted to future generations. To this date nuclear plants have operated safely without any catastrophic release of large quantities of radioactive materials. Estimates of the probable risk of such a catastrophic accident are highly controversial, and considerable doubt has been cast on these probability estimates, especially since the accidents at Three Mile Island and Chernobyl.[46] Even without catastrophic accidents, however, small amounts of radioactive materials are routinely released into the environment during the normal operations of a nuclear plant and during the mining, processing, and transporting of nuclear fuels. The government has

[41] *Ibid.* p. 5.

[42] Council on Environmental Quality, *Environmental Trends*, p. 139.

[43] *Time*, 14 October 1985, p. 77.

[44] *Ibid.*

[45] Council on Environmental Quality, *Environmental Quality 1983*, (Washington, DC: U.S. Government Printing Office, 1984), p. 62.

[46] See U.S. Nuclear Regulatory Commission, "NRC Statement on Risk Assessment and the Reactor Safety Study Report in Light of the Risk Assessment Review Group Report," 18 January 1979.

estimated that between the years 1975 and 2000 at least one thousand people will die of cancer from these routine emissions; other estimates, however, place these figures at substantially higher levels.[47]

Plutonium is produced as a waste by-product in the spent fuel of light-water reactors. A 1,000-megawatt reactor, for example, will generate about 265 pounds (120 kilograms) of plutonium wastes each year that must be disposed of. Plutonium is a highly toxic and extremely carcinogenic substance. A particle weighing 10 millionths of a gram, if inhaled, can cause death within a few weeks. Twenty pounds, if properly distributed, could give lung cancer to everyone on earth. Plutonium is also the basic constituent of atomic bombs. As nuclear power plants proliferate around the world, therefore, the probability has increased that plutonium will fall into the hands of criminal terrorists or other hostile groups, who may use it to construct an atomic weapon or to lethally contaminate large populated areas.[48]

Nuclear power plant wastes are of three main types: high-level wastes, transuranic wastes, and low-level wastes.[49] High-level wastes emit gamma rays, which can penetrate all but the thickest shielding. These include cesium 137 and strontium 90—which both become harmless after about 1,000 years—and plutonium—which remains hazardous for 250,000 to 1,000,000 years. All of these are highly carcinogenic. Nuclear reactors have already produced about 612,000 gallons of liquid and 2,300 tons of solid high-level wastes each year. These wastes must be isolated from the environment until they are no longer hazardous. It is unknown at this time whether there is any safe and permanent method for disposing of these wastes.[50]

Transuranic wastes contain smaller quantities of the elements found in high-level wastes. These come from spent fuel processing and from various military weapons processes. Until recently, transuranic wastes were buried in shallow trenches. It has been discovered, however, that radioactive materials have been migrating out of these trenches, and they may eventually have to be exhumed and redisposed of at a cost of several hundred million dollars.[51]

Low-level wastes consist of the contaminated clothing and used equipment from reactor sites and of the tailings from mining and milling uranium. About 16 million cubic feet of these wastes have been produced at reactor sites, and an additional 500 million cubic feet of uranium tailings (about 140 million tons)

[47] U.S. Nuclear Regulatory Commission, "Final Generic Environmental Statement on the Use of Plutonium Recycle in Mixed Oxide Fuel in Light Water Cooled Reactors," NUREG-0002, vol. 1, August 1976.

[48] See Theodore B. Taylor and Mason Willrich, *Nuclear Theft: Risks and Safeguards* (Cambridge, MA: Ballinger Publishing Co., 1974).

[49] For a nontechnical review of the literature on nuclear waste products see Scott Fenn, *The Nuclear Power Debate* (Washington, DC: Investor Responsibility Research Center, 1980); see also William Ramsay, *Unpaid Costs of Electrical Energy* (Baltimore: Johns Hopkins University Press for Resources for the Future, 1978).

[50] Thomas O'Toole, "Glass, Salt Challenged as Radioactive Waste Disposal Methods," *The Washington Post*, 24 December 1978.

[51] U.S. General Accounting Office, GAO Report to Congress B–164052, "Cleaning Up the Remains of Nuclear Facilities—A Multibillion Dollar Problem," EMD–77–46 (Washington, DC: U.S. Government Printing Office, 1977), 16 June 1977.

have accumulated in the open at mine sites. About 10 million additional tons of mill tailings are produced each year. Uranium tailings continue to emit radioactive radon for several hundred thousand years. In addition, all nuclear plants (including equipment, buildings, and land) become low-level nuclear wastes themselves after an operating life of thirty to thirty-five years. The entire plant must then be decommissioned, and, since it remains radioactive for thousands of years, the dismantled plant and land site must be maintained under constant security for the next several centuries.[52]

More than one author has suggested that the safe disposal of nuclear wastes is soluble only if we assume that none of our descendants will ever accidentally drill into nuclear repositories or enter them during times of war, that records of their locations will be preserved for the next several centuries, that the wastes will not accidently flow together and begin reacting, that geological events, ice sheets, or other unforeseen earth movements never uncover the wastes, that our engineering estimates of the properties of metal, glass, and cement containers are accurate, and that our medical predictions concerning safe levels of radiation exposure prove correct.[53]

Depletion of Species

It is well known that human beings have depleted dozens of plant and animal species to the point of extinction. Since 1600 A.D., at least thirty-six species of mammals and ninety-four species of birds have become extinct.[54] Several more species, such as whales and salmon, today find themselves threatened by commercial predators. Forests are also being decimated by the timber industry. Between the years 1600 and 1900 half of the forested land area in the United States was cleared.[55] Experts estimate that the planet's rain forests are being destroyed at the rate of about one percent a year.[56] If present trends continue, total forest cover will decrease by 40 percent by the year 2000. The loss of forest habitats combined with the effects of pollution is expected to lead to the extinction of between half a million to two million species—15 to 20 percent of all species on earth—by the year 2000.[57]

Depletion of Fossil Fuels

Until the early 1980s, fossil fuels were being depleted at an exponentially rising rate. That is, the rate at which they were being used had doubled with the passage of a regular fixed time period. This type of "exponential depletion" is illustrated in Figure 5.2. Several early predictions of resource depletion assumed

[52] Sam H. Schurr, et al., *Energy in America's Future* (Baltimore: The Johns Hopkins University Press, 1979), p. 35.

[53] Ellen Winchester, "Nuclear Wastes," *Sierra*, July/August 1979.

[54] J. Fisher, N. Simon, and J. Vincent, *Wildlife in Danger* (New York: The Viking Press, 1969).

[55] C. S. Wong, "Atmospheric Input of Carbon Dioxide from Burning Wood," *Science*, 200 (1978): 197–200.

[56] G. M. Woodwell, "The Carbon Dioxide Question," *Scientific American*, 238 (1978): 34–43.

[57] Council on Environmental Quality, *The Global 2000 Report to the President*, p. 23.

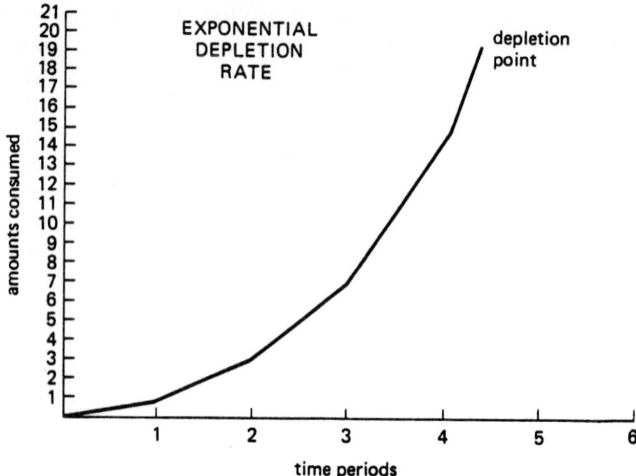

FIGURE 5-2

that fossil fuels would continue to be depleted at these exponentially rising rates. If continued, an exponentially rising rate of depletion would end with the complete and catastrophic depletion of the resource in a relatively short time.[58] Estimated world resources of coal would be depleted in about one hundred years, estimated world reserves of oil would be exhausted in about forty years, and estimated reserves of natural gas would last only about thirty years.[59]

As many researchers argue, however, our consumption of fossil fuels could not continue rising at historical exponential rates.[60] As reserves of any resource shrink, they become increasingly difficult, and therefore more costly, to extract.

FIGURE 5-3

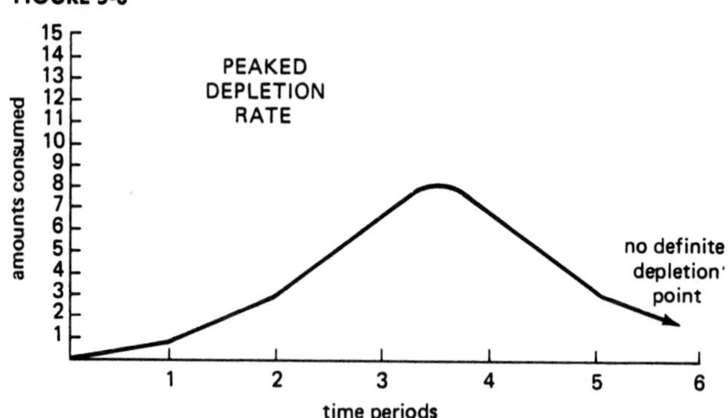

[58] An exponential rate of depletion is assumed in the Club of Rome report; Donella H. Meadows, Dennis L. Meadows, Jergen Randers, and William W. Behrens III, *The Limits to Growth* (New York: Universe Books, 1972).

[59] W. Jackson Davis, *The Seventh Year* (New York: W. W. Norton & Co., Inc., 1979), pp. 38–40; see also, U.S. Congress Office of Technology Assessment, *World Petroleum Availability: 1980–2000* (Washington, DC: U.S. Government Printing Office, 1980).

[60] M. K. Hubbert, "U.S. Energy Resources: A Review as of 1972," Document No. 93–40 (92–72) (Washington, DC: U.S. Government Printing Office, 1974).

Consequently, although the rates at which reserves are depleted may rise exponentially for a period, the rising costs of extraction eventually cause the rates to peak and then begin to decline, without complete depletion ever being attained. Figure 5.3 illustrates this type of "peaked depletion" rate, in which consumption of the resource gradually peters out as the resource becomes increasingly difficult to extract, rather than culminating in complete and sudden depletion within a relatively short period of time. Rising energy prices during the 1970s, in fact, led to drastic reductions in worldwide consumption of oil by 1980.[61] Although this lowered demand, coupled with the breakdown of OPEC, has led to a downward drift in oil prices during the early 1980s, many researchers agree that our consumption of fossil fuels will not return to the exponentially rising rates of earlier decades.[62]

If we assume that the rate at which we consume our resources is more adequately mirrored by the "peaked" model than by the "exponential" model, then fossil fuels would not be depleted within the short time frame predicted by earlier exponential growth models. The extraction of estimated reserves of coal will probably peak in about 150 years and then continue, but at a declining rate, for another 150 years; the extraction of estimated reserves of oil will probably peak in about forty years and then gradually decline; the extraction of estimated U.S. reserves of natural gas has already peaked (in 1975) and is expected to decline gradually over the next thirty or forty years.[63]

Depletion of Minerals

The depletion of mineral reserves, like the depletion of fossil fuels, can also be calculated either on the basis of an "exponential growth" model or on the basis of a "peaked growth" model. If earlier exponentially rising rates of depletion continued, then aluminum would be scheduled for exhaustion in the year 2003, copper in 1993, iron in 2025, lead in 1993, manganese in 2018, molybdenum in 2006, nickel in 2025, tungsten in 2000, and zinc in 1990.[64] Clearly, if these depletion schedules were correct, the economic consequences would be catastrophic, since running out of these essential minerals within these relatively short time frames would lead to a collapse of the numerous industries that rely on them. During the early 1970s many researchers believed that such an industrial and economic collapse was imminent. But further research has indicated that such catastrophic depletion schedules are mistaken.

As with fossil fuels, the rate at which minerals are depleted does not seem to continue to grow exponentially, but peaks and then declines as metals become rarer and more difficult to extract. If we use this "peaked" model analysis and restrict ourselves solely to presently known U.S. reserves, then it turns out that while the extraction rates of several important minerals in the United States have peaked, none have been completely depleted and all continue to be mined. We can speculate that by the year 2000, if there were no significant discoveries of

[61] *Time*, "Cheap Oil," 14 April 1986, pp. 62–78.

[62] See the overview of this issue in Barry B. Hughes, *World Futures* (Baltimore: The Johns Hopkins University Press, 1985), pp. 113–23.

[63] Davis, *The Seventh Year*, pp. 44–46; see also Schurr et al., *Energy in America's Future*, pp. 225–46, for more detailed estimates.

[64] *Ibid.*, p. 128.

new reserves, we would have exhausted perhaps 90 percent of our domestic aluminum reserves, 80 percent of our iron, 70 percent of our lead, 90 percent of our manganese, 80 percent of our mercury, 90 percent of our tungsten, and 70 percent of our zinc.[65] Any reserves remaining in the United States will be more difficult to extract, and we will probably be forced to turn increasingly to recycling, substitutes, and imports from world markets.

World sources, of course, are also limited, and the depletion rates of many of the world's supplies of minerals probably will also peak and then gradually decline as supplies become rarer and more difficult to mine.[66] The precise impact the limitations of world supplies will have on us are exceedingly difficult to predict. Mining technologies may continue to develop that will reduce the difficulty and costs of mineral extraction. This has, in fact, been the case for most minerals up to the present. Increased recycling may reduce the need for intensive mining of remaining mineral reserves. Substitutes may be found for many of the minerals whose supply is limited, and technological development may make many current uses of these minerals obsolete.

Still, the most exhaustive and thorough study to date of the world limits of a single mineral—copper—indicates that in the future copper and the other minerals will become increasingly scarce and expensive and that this scarcity will have a noticible economic impact on our societies.[67] The study, undertaken by Robert B. Gordon and others, indicates that the rate of extraction of the world's copper will rise rapidly over the next hundred years, peak in about the year 2100, and then slowly decline. Rich copper ores will be exhausted by about the year 2070, and thereafter copper must be mined from common rock, an expensive process that forces dramatic exponential rises of copper prices from about $2 per kilogram to $120 per kilogram, even with intense recycling and even assuming other materials can be substituted for all but a handful of the essential uses of copper. According to Gordon and his coauthors: "similar arguments can be raised for other metals, such as lead, zinc, tin, tungsten, and silver. . . . We have not made a complete analysis for any other scarce metal, but we strongly suspect that if we did a pattern of future use similar to that predicted for copper and would emerge."[68]

There are physical limits, then, to our natural resources: They cannot be exploited indefinitely. Eventually, they will peter out and the costs of extraction will rise exponentially. More plentiful substitute materials may be found for many of these resources, but it is likely that substitutes cannot be found for all of them. And whatever substitutes are developed will also be limited, so the day of reckoning will only be delayed.

5.2 THE ETHICS OF POLLUTION CONTROL

For centuries business institutions were able to ignore their impact on the natural environment, an indulgence created by a number of causes. First, business was

[65] *Ibid.*, pp. 131–132.

[66] Paul R. Portney, ed., *Current Issues in Natural Resource Policy* (Washington, DC: Resources for the Future, 1982), pp. 80–81.

[67] Robert B. Gordon, Tjalling C. Koopmans, William D. Nordhaus, Brian J. Skinner, *Toward A New Iron Age*? (Cambridge, MA: Harvard University Press, 1987).

[68] *Ibid.*, p. 153.

able to treat things like air and water as free goods—that is, as goods that no one owns and that each firm can therefore use without reimbursing anyone for their use. For several years, for example, a DuPont plant in West Virginia had been dumping 10,000 tons of chemical wastes each month into the Gulf of Mexico, until it was stopped in the 1970s. The waters of the Gulf provided a free dumping site for whose damages DuPont did not have to pay. Because such resources are not privately owned, they lack the protection that a private owner would normally provide, and businesses were able to ignore the damages they inflicted on them. Second, businesses have seen the environment as an *unlimited* good. That is, the "carrying capacity" of air and water is relatively large, and each firm's contribution of pollution to these resources is relatively small and insignificant.[69] The amount of chemicals DuPont was dumping into the Gulf, for example, might be relatively small compared to the size of the Gulf and the effects viewed as being negligible. When the effects of its activities are seen as so slight, a firm will tend to ignore these effects. However, when *every* firm reasons in this way, the combined "negligible" effects of each firm's activities may become enormous, and potentially disastrous. The carrying capacity of the air and water is soon exceeded and these "free" and "unlimited" goods rapidly deteriorate.

Of course, pollution problems are not rooted only in business activies. Pollution also results from the use that consumers make of products and from human waste products.[70] A primary source of air pollution, for example, is automobile use, and a primary source of water pollution is sewage. We are truly *all* polluters.[71] And since every human being pollutes, pollution problems have increased as our population has multiplied. The world's population grew from 1 billion in 1850 to 2 billion in 1930 to 5 billion in 1986, and will continue to grow to between 10 and 12 billion by 2040.[72] This population explosion has put severe strains on the air and water resources into which we dump our share of pollutants. These strains, moreover, have been aggravated by our tendency to concentrate our populations in urban centers. All over the world, urban areas are growing rapidly, and the high population densities urbanization has created multiplies the pollution burdens placed on air and water resources.[73]

The problems of pollution, then, have a variety of origins and their treatment requires a similarly variegated set of solutions. Our focus in what follows, however, will concentrate on a single range of problems: the ethical issues raised by pollution from commercial and industrial enterprises.

Ecological Ethics

The problem of pollution (and of environmental issues in general) is seen by some researchers as a problem that can best be framed in terms of our duty to

[69] The term is Garrit Hardin's; see his "The Tragedy of the Commons," *Science*, 162 No. 3859 (13 December 1968): 1243–48.

[70] Richard M. Stephenson, *Living with Tomorrow* (New York: John Wiley & Sons, Inc., 1981), pp. 205–8.

[71] *Ibid.*, p. 204.

[72] Hughes, *World Futures*, p. 56.

[73] Carl J. George and Daniel McKinely, *Urban Ecology: In Search of an Asphalt Rose* (New York: McGraw-Hill Book Company, 1974).

recognize and preserve the "ecological systems" within which we live.[74] An ecological system is an interrelated and interdependent set of organisms and environments, such as a lake—in which the fish depend on small aquatic organisms, which in turn live off of decaying plant and fish waste products.[75] Because the various parts of an ecological system are interrelated, the activities of one of its parts will affect all the other parts. And because the various parts are interdependent, the survival of each part depends on the survival of the other parts. Now business firms (and all other social institutions) are parts of a larger ecological system, "spaceship earth."[76] Business firms depend upon the natural environment for their energy, material resources, and waste disposal. And that environment in turn is affected by the commercial activities of business firms. The activities of eighteenth-century European manufacturers of beaver hats, for example, led to the wholesale destruction of beavers in the United States, which in turn led to the drying up of the innumerable swamp lands that had been created by beaver dams.[77] Unless businesses recognize the interrelationships and interdependencies of the ecological systems within which they operate, and unless they ensure that their activities will not seriously injure these systems, we cannot hope to deal with the problem of pollution.

The fact that we are only a part of a larger ecological system has led many writers to insist that we should recognize our moral duty to protect the welfare not only of human beings, but also of other *nonhuman parts* of this system.[78] This insistence on what is sometimes called "ecological ethics" or "deep ecology" is not based on the idea that the environment should be protected for the sake of human beings. Instead, ecological ethics are based on the idea that nonhuman parts of the environment deserve to be preserved *for their own sake*, regardless of whether this benefits human beings. Several supporters of this approach have formulated their views in a "platform" consisting of the following statements:

1. The well-being and flourishing of human and nonhuman life on Earth have value in themselves. . . These values are independent of the usefulness of the nonhuman world for human purposes.

[74] Barry Commoner, *The Closing Circle* (New York: Alfred A. Knopf, Inc., 1971), ch. 2.

[75] See Kenneth E. F. Watt, *Understanding the Environment* (Boston: Allyn & Bacon, Inc., 1982).

[76] Matthew Edel, *Economics and the Environment* (Englewood Cliffs, NJ: Prentice Hall, 1973); for the term "spaceship earth," see Kenneth Boulding, "The Economics of the Coming Spaceship Earth," in *Environmental Quality in a Growing Economy*, Henry Jarret ed. (Baltimore: Johns Hopkins Press for Resources for the Future, 1966).

[77] George Perkins, *Man and Nature* (1864) (Cambridge: Harvard University Press, 1965), p. 76.

[78] For discussions favoring this view as well as criticisms see the essays collected in Donald Scherer and Thomas Attig, eds., *Ethics and the Environment* (Englewood Cliffs, NJ: Prentice Hall, 1983); see also W. K. Frankena, "Ethics and the Environment," in *Ethics and Problems of the 21st Century*, K. E. Goodpaster and K. M. Sayre, eds. (Notre Dame, IN: University of Notre Dame Press, 1979), pp. 3–20; William T. Blackstone, "The Search for an Environmental Ethic," in *Matters of Life and Death*, Tom Regan, ed. (New York: Random House, Inc., 1980), pp. 299–335; an excellent and extensive annotated bibliography is provided by Mary Anglemyer, et al., *A Search for Environmental Ethics, An Initial Bibliography* (Washington, DC: Smithsonian Institution Press, 1980).

2. Richness and diversity of life forms contribute to the realization of these values and are also values in themselves.
3. Humans have no right to reduce this richness and diversity except to satisfy vital needs.
4. The flourishing of human life and cultures is compatible with a substantial decrease of the human population. The flourishing of nonhuman life requires such a decrease.
5. Present human interference with the nonhuman world is excessive and the situation is rapidly worsening.
6. Policies must therefore be changed. The changes in policies affect basic economic, technological, and ideological structures. The resulting state of affairs will be deeply different from the present.
7. The ideological change is mainly that of appreciating life quality . . . rather than adhering to an increasingly higher standard of living.
8. Those who subscribe to the foregoing points have an obligation directly or indirectly to participate in the attempt to implement the necessary changes.[79]

An "ecological ethic" is thus an ethic that claims that the welfare of at least some nonhumans is intrinsically valuable and that because of this intrinsic value, we humans have a duty to respect and preserve them. These ethical claims have significant implications for those business activities that affect the environment. In June 1990, for example, environmentalists successfully petitioned the U.S. Fish and Wildlife Service to bar the timber industry from logging potentially lucrative old-growth forests of northern California in order to save the habitat of the spotted owl, an endangered species.[80] The move was estimated to have cost the timber industry millions of dollars, to have lost workers as many as 36,000 lumber jobs, and to have raised the costs of consumer prices for fine wood products such as furniture and musical instruments. Throughout the 1980s members of the Sea Shepherd Conservation Society have sabotaged whale processing plants, sunk several ships, and otherwise imposed costs on the whaling industry.[81] Members of Earth First! have driven nails into randomly selected trees of forest areas scheduled to be logged so that power logging saws are destroyed when they bite into the spiked trees. Supporters of the view that animals have intrinsic value have also imposed substantial costs on cattle ranchers, slaughterhouses, chicken farms, fur companies, and pharmaceutical and cosmetic corporations that use animals to test chemicals.

There are several varieties of ecological ethics, some more radical and far-reaching than others. Perhaps the most popular version claims that in addition to human beings, other animals have intrinsic value and are deserving of our respect and protection. Some utilitarians have claimed, for example, that pain is an evil whether it is inflicted on humans or on members of other animal species. The pain of an animal must be considered as equal to the comparable pain of a human and it is a form of "specist" prejudice (akin to racist or sexist bias against members

[79] Quoted in Bill Devall, *Simple in Means, Rich in Ends, Practicing Deep Ecology* (Salt Lake City, UT: Peregrine Smith Books, 1988), pp. 14–15.

[80] Ted Gup, "Owl vs. Man," *Time*, 25 June 1990, pp. 56–62; Catherine Caufield, "A Reporter at Large: The Ancient Forest," *New Yorker*, 14 May 1990, pp. 46–84.

[81] Devall, *Simple in Means, Rich in Ends*, p. 138.

of another race or sex) to think that the duty to avoid inflicting pain on members of other species is not equal to our duty to avoid inflicting pain on members of our own species.[82]

Certain nonutilitarians have reached similar conclusions by a different route. They have claimed that the life of every animal "itself has value" apart from the interests of human beings. Because of the intrinsic value of its life each animal has certain "moral rights," in particular the right to be treated with respect.[83] Humans have a duty to respect this right although in some cases a human's right might override an animal's right.

Both the utilitarian and the rights arguments in support of human duties toward animals imply that it is wrong to raise animals for food in the crowded and painful circumstances in which agricultural business enterprises currently raise cows, pigs, and chickens; they also imply that it is wrong to use animals in painful test procedures as they are currently used in some businesses—for example, to test the toxicity of cosmetics.[84]

Broader versions of ecological ethics would extend our duties beyond the *animal* world to include plants. Thus, some ethicians have claimed that it is "arbitrary" and "hedonistic" to confine our duties to creatures that can feel pain. Instead, they urge, we should acknowledge that all living things including plants have "an interest in remaining alive" and that consequently they deserve moral consideration for their own sakes.[85] Other authors have claimed that not only living things but even a natural species, a lake, a wild river, a mountain, and even the entire "biotic community" has a right to have its "integrity, stability, and beauty" preserved.[86] If correct, these views would have important implications for businesses engaged in strip-mining or logging operations.

But these attempts to extend moral rights to nonanimals are highly controversial, and some authors have labeled them "incredible."[87] It is difficult, for example, to see why the *fact* that something *is* alive implies that it *should* be alive and

[82] Peter Singer, *Animal Liberation* (New York: Random House, Inc., 1975).

[83] Tom Regan, *The Case for Animal Rights* (Berkeley, CA: University of California Press, 1983); in a similar vein, Joel Feinberg argues that animals have interests and consequently have rights in "The Rights of Animals and Unborn Generations," in *Philosophy and Environmental Crisis*, William T. Blackstone, ed. (Athens, GA: University of Georgia Press, 1974).

[84] See William Aiken, "Ethical Issues in Agriculture," in *Earthbound: New Introductory Essays in Environmental Ethics*, Tom Regan, ed. (New York: Random House, Inc., 1984), pp. 247–88.

[85] Kenneth Goodpaster, "On Being Morally Considerable," *Journal of Philosophy*, 75 (1978): 308–25; see also Paul Taylor, "The Ethics of Respect for Nature," *Environmental Ethics*, 3 (1981): 197–218; Robin Attfield, "The Good of Trees," *The Journal of Value Inquiry*, 15 (1981): 35–54; and Christopher D. Stone, *Should Trees Have Standing? Toward Legal Rights for Natural Objects* (Boston: Houghton Mifflin, 1978).

[86] Aldo Leopold, "The Land Ethic," in *A Sand County Almanac* (New York: Oxford University Press, 1949), pp. 201–26; see also J. Baird Callicott, "Animal Liberation: A Triangular Affair," *Environmental Ethics*, 2, no. 4 (Winter 1980), pp. 311–38; John Rodman, "The Liberation of Nature?," *Inquiry*, 20 (1977): pp. 83–131; K. Goodpaster argues that the "biosphere" as a whole has moral value in "On Being Morally Considerable"; Holmes Rolston, III holds a similar position in "Is There an Ecological Ethic," *Ethics*, 85, 1975, pp. 93–109; for a variety of views on this issue see Bryan G. Norton, ed., *The Preservation of Species* (Princeton, NJ: Princeton University Press, 1986).

[87] W. K. Frankena, "Ethics and the Environment," in *Ethics and Problems of the 21st Century*, K. E. Goodpaster and K. M. Sayre, eds. (Notre Dame, IN: University of Notre Dame Press, 1979), pp. 3–20.

that we therefore have a *duty* to keep it alive; and it is difficult to see why the *fact* that a river or a mountain *exists,* implies that it *should* exist and that we have a *duty* to keep it in existence. Facts do not imply values in this easy way.[88] It is also controversial whether we can claim that animals have rights or intrinsic value.[89] But we do not have to rely on these unusual views to develop an environmental ethic. For our purposes, we need only examine two traditional approaches to environmental issues.[90] One is based on a theory of human rights, and the other is based on utilitarian considerations.

Environmental Rights and Absolute Bans

In an influential article, William T. Blackstone argued that the possession of a livable environment is not merely a *desirable* state of affairs, but something to which each human being has a *right.*[91] That is, a livable environment is not merely something that we would all like to have: It is something that others have a duty to allow us to have. They have this duty, Blackstone argues, because we each have a right to a livable environment, and our right imposes on others the correlative duty of not interfering in our exercise of that right. This is a right, moreover, which should be incorporated into our legal system.

Why do human beings have this right? According to Blackstone, a person has a moral right to a thing when possession of that thing is "essential in permitting him to live a human life (that is, in permitting him to fulfill his capacities as a rational and free being)."[92] At this time in our history, it has become clear that a livable environment is essential to the fulfillment of our human capacities. Consequently, human beings have a moral right to a decent environment, and it should become a legal right.

Moreover, Blackstone adds, this moral and legal right should override people's legal property rights. Our great and increasing ability to manipulate the environment has revealed that unless we limit the legal freedom to engage in

[88] For other criticisms of these arguments see Edward Johnson, "Treating the Dirt: Environmental Ethics and Moral Theory," in *Earthbound: New Introductory Essays in Environmental Ethics*, Tom Regan, ed. (New York: Random House, 1984), pp. 336–65; see also the discussion between Goodpaster and Hunt in W. Murray Hunt, "Are *Mere Things* Morally Considerable?," *Environmental Ethics*, 2, (1980): pp. 59–65, and Kenneth Goodpaster, "On Stopping at Everything: A Reply to W. M. Hunt," *Environmental Ethics*, 2, (1980): pp. 281–84.

[89] See, for example, R. G. Frey, *Interests and Rights: The Case Against Animals* (Oxford: Clarendon Press, 1980), and Martin Benjamin, "Ethics and Animal Consciousness," in *Ethics: Theory and Practice*, Manuel Velasquez and Cynthia Rostankowski, eds. (Englewood Cliffs, NJ: Prentice Hall, 1985).

[90] For a comprehensive treatment of the ethics of environmental issues, see Robin Attfield, *The Ethics of Environmental Concern* (New York: Columbia University Press, 1983); an older but still useful treatment of these issues is John Passmore, *Man's Responsibility for Nature* (New York: Charles Scribner's Sons, 1974).

[91] William T. Blackstone, "Ethics and Ecology," in *Philosophy and Environmental Crisis*, William T. Blackstone, ed. (Athens, GA: University of Georgia Press, 1974); see also his later article, "On Rights and Responsibilities Pertaining to Toxic Substances and Trade Secrecy," *The Southern Journal of Philosophy*, 16 (1978): 589–603.

[92] *Ibid.*, p. 31; see also, William T. Blackstone, "Equality and Human Rights," *Monist*, vol. 52, no. 4 (1968); and William T. Blackstone, "Human Rights and Human Dignity," in *Human Dignity*, Laszlo and Grotesky.

practices that destroy the environment, we shall lose the very possibility of human life and the possibility of exercising other rights, such as the right to liberty and to equality.

Several states have introduced amendments to their constitution that grant to their citizens an ''environmental right'' much like Blackstone advocates. Article One of the Constitution of Pennsylvania, for example, was amended a few years ago to read:

> The people have a right to clean air, pure water, and to the preservation of the natural scenic, historic, and aesthetic values of the environment. Pennsylvania's natural resources . . . are the common property of all the people, including generations yet to come. As trustee of these resources, the commonwealth shall preserve and maintain them for the benefit of all people.

To a large extent, something like Blackstone's concept of ''environmental rights'' is recognized in federal law. Section 101(b) of the National Environmental Policy Act of 1969, for example, states that one of its purposes is to ''assure for all Americans safe, healthful, productive, and aesthetically and culturally pleasing surroundings.'' Subsequent acts tried to achieve this purpose. The Water Pollution Control Act of 1972 required firms, by 1977, to use the ''best practicable technology'' to get rid of pollution (that is, technology used by several of the least polluting plants in an industry); the Clean Water Act of 1977 required that by 1984 firms must eliminate all toxic and nonconventional wastes with the use of the ''best available technology'' (that is, technology used by the one least polluting plant). The Air Quality Act of 1967 and the Clean Air Amendments of 1970 established similar limits to air pollution from stationary sources and automobiles, and provided the machinery for enforcing these limits. These federal laws did *not* rest on a utilitarian cost-benefit analysis. That is, they did not say that firms should reduce pollution so long as the benefits outweigh the costs; instead they simply imposed absolute bans on pollution regardless of the costs involved. Such absolute restrictions can best be justified by an appeal to people's rights.

Federal statutes in effect impose absolute limits upon the property rights of owners of firms, and Blackstone's arguments provide a plausible rationale for limiting property rights in these absolute ways for the sake of a human right to a clean environment. Blackstone's argument obviously rests on a Kantian theory of rights: Since humans have a moral duty to treat each other as ends and not as means, they have a correlative duty to respect and promote the development of another's capacity to freely and rationally choose for himself.

The main difficulty with Blackstone's view, however, is that it fails to provide any nuanced guidance on several pressing environmental choices. How much pollution control is really needed? Should we have an *absolute* ban on pollution? How far should we go in limiting property rights for the sake of the environment? What goods, if any, should we cease manufacturing in order to halt or slow environmental damage? Who should pay for the costs of preserving the environment? Blackstone's theory gives us no way of handling these questions because it imposes a simple and absolute ban on pollution.

This lack of nuance in the absolute rights approach is especially problematic when the costs of removing certain amounts of pollution are high in comparison to the benefits that will be attained. Consider the situation of a pulp business as reported by its president:

> Surveys conducted along the lower Columbia river since completion of primary treatment facilities at our mills show that water-quality standards are being met and that the river is being used for fishing, swimming, water supply and recreation. In all respects, therefore, the 1985 goals of the [Federal Water Pollution Control] act are presently being met [in 1975]. But the technical requirements of the act call for installation of secondary treatment facilities at our mills at Camas and Wauna. The cost will be about $20 million and will not result in any measurable improvement of water quality on the river. On the contrary, the total environmental effect will be negative. We calculate that it will take about 57 million kwh of electricity and nearly 8,000 tons of chemicals to operate these unnecessary facilities. Total power requirements will involve burning 90,000 bbl/yr of scarce oil, in turn creating 900,000 lb of pollutants at the generating source . . . Similar tradeoffs occur in the field of air-quality control technology. For example, moving from 98% to 99.8% removal of particulate matter requires four times as much purchased energy as it took to get from zero to 98% control.[93]

Also troubling is the possible impact that pollution abatement requirements may have on plant closings and jobs.[94] Some researchers have claimed that pollution control legislation costs as much as 160,000 jobs a year. But such estimates appear both highly inflated and unreliable. Between 1971 and 1981 the Environmental Protection Agency found only 153 plant closings that possibly could be attributed to environmental legislation and these closings accounted for only 32,611 jobs for an average of 3,200 jobs lost a year.[95] Although many, perhaps most, of the workers affected by these closings found other jobs, and although many new jobs have been created in companies that design, manufacture, and install pollution control devices, environmental legislation clearly has some potential for imposing costs on some workers.

Because of the difficulties raised by absolute bans, the federal government in the late 1970s and early 1980s began to turn to methods of pollution control that tried to balance the costs and benefits of controlling pollution and that did not impose absolute bans. Deadlines for compliance with the standards of the Clean Air Act were extended so that the costs of compliance could be more adequately dealt with. Companies were allowed to increase discharges of pollutants that are costly to control when they agreed to make equivalent reductions of pollutants that are cheaper to control.[96] Executive Order No. 12291, signed into law by President Reagan on February 17, 1981, required all new environmental regula-

[93] Quoted in Keith Davis and William C. Frederick, *Business and Society* (New York: McGraw-Hill Book Company, 1984), p. 403–4.

[94] Robert H. Haveman and Greg Christiansen, *Jobs and the Environment* (Scarsdale, NY: Work in America Institute, Inc., 1979), p.4.

[95] Richard Kazis and Richard L. Grossman, "Job Blackmail: It's Not Jobs or Environment," p. 260, in *The Big Business Reader*, Mark Green, ed. (New York: The Pilgrim Press, 1983), pp. 259–69.

[96] The Environmental Protection Agency's so-called "bubble policy," see *Time*, 17 December 1979, p. 71; and *Business Week*, 9 July 1984, p. 34.

tions to be subjected to cost-benefit analysis before they were implemented.[97] These new regulations are not based on the notion that people have absolute environmental rights, but on a utilitarian approach to the environment.

Utilitarianism and Partial Controls

Utilitarianism provides a way of answering the questions that Blackstone's theory of environmental rights leaves unanswered. A fundamentally utilitarian approach to environmental problems is to see them as market defects. If an industry pollutes the environment, the market prices of its commodities will no longer reflect the true cost of producing the commodities; the result is a misallocation of resources, a rise in waste, and an inefficient distribution of commodities. Consequently, society as a whole is harmed as its overall economic welfare declines.[98] Utilitarians therefore argue that individuals should avoid pollution because they should avoid harming society's welfare. The following paragraphs explain this utilitarian argument in greater detail, and explain the more nuanced approach to pollution that utilitarian cost-benefit analysis seems to provide.

Private Costs and Social Costs

Economists often distinguish between what it cost a private manufacturer to make a product and what the manufacture of that product cost society as a whole. Suppose, for example, that an electric firm consumes a certain amount of fuel, labor, and equipment to produce one kilowatt of electricity. The cost of these resources is its *private* cost: The price it must pay out of its own pocket to manufacture one kilowatt of electricity. But producing the kilowatt of electricity may also involve other ''external'' costs for which the firm does not pay.[99] When the firm burns fuel, for example, it may generate smoke and soot that settles on surrounding neighbors, who have to bear the costs of cleaning up the grime and of paying for any medical problems the smoke creates. From the viewpoint of society as a whole, then, the costs of producing the kilowatt of electricity include not only the ''internal'' costs of fuel, labor, and equipment for which the manufacturer pays, but also the ''external'' costs of clean-up and medical care that the neighbors pay. This *sum total* of costs (the private internal costs plus the neighbors' external costs) are the *social* costs of producing the kilowatt of electricity: the total price society must pay to manufacture one kilowatt of electricity. Of course, private costs and social costs do not always diverge as in this example: Sometimes

[97] For an analysis of the impact of this executive order, see the essays collected in V. Kerry Smith, ed., *Environmental Policy Under Reagan*'s *Executive Order* (Chapel Hill, NC: The University of North Carolina Press, 1984).

[98] There are a number of texts describing this approach. An elementary text is Tom Tietenberg, *Environmental and Natural Resource Economics*, (Glenview, IL: Scott, Foresman & Company, 1984); a more compact treatment is Edwin S. Mills, *The Economics of Environmental Quality* (New York: W. W. Norton & Co., Inc., 1978), ch. 3; for several viewpoints consult Robert Dorfman and Nancy Dorman, eds., *Economics of the Environment* (New York: W. W. Norton & Co., Inc., 1977).

[99] For a compact review of the literature on external costs, see E. J. Mishan, ''The Postwar Literature on Externalities: An Interpretative Essay,'' *Journal of Economic Literature*, 9, no. 1 (March 1971): 1–28.

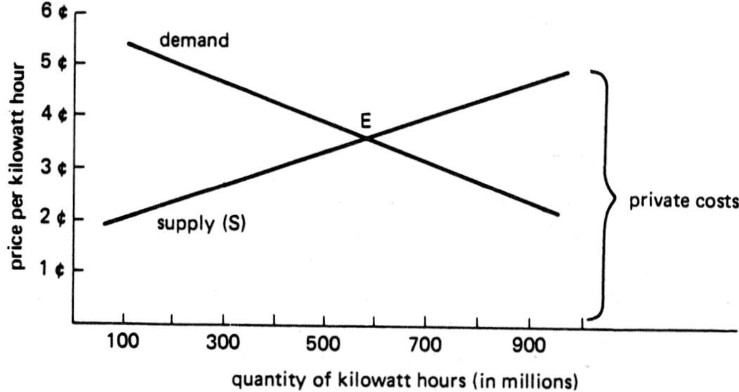

FIGURE 5-4

the two coincide. If a producer pays for *all* the costs involved in manufacturing a product, for example, or if manufacturing a product imposes no external costs, then the producer's costs and the total social costs will be the same.

Thus, when a firm pollutes its environment in any way, the firm's private costs are always *less* than the total social costs involved. Whether the pollution is localized and immediate, as in the neighborhood effects described in the example above, or whether the pollution is global and long-range as in the "hot-house" effects predicted to follow from introducing too much carbon dioxide into the atmosphere, pollution always imposes "external" costs—that is, costs for which the person who produces the pollution does not have to pay. Pollution is fundamentally a problem of this divergence between private and social costs.

Why should this divergence be a problem? It is a problem because when the private costs of manufacturing a product diverge from the social costs involved in its manufacture, markets no longer price commodities accurately; consequently, they no longer allocate resources efficiently. As a result, society's welfare declines. To understand why markets become inefficient when private and social costs diverge, let us suppose that the electrical power industry is perfectly competitive (it is not, but let us suppose it is).[100] Suppose, then, that market supply curve, S, in Figure 5.4 reflects the private costs producers must pay to manufacture each kilowatt of electricity. The market price will then be at the equilibrium point E, where the supply curve based on these private costs crosses the demand curve.

In the hypothetical situation in Figure 5.4, the curves intersect at the market price of 3.5 cents and at an output of 600 million kilowatt hours. But suppose that besides the private costs that producers incur in manufacturing electricity, the manufacture of electricity also imposes "external" costs on their neighbors in the form of environmental pollution. If these external costs were added to the private costs of producers, then a new supply curve, S′, would result that would take into account all the costs of manufacturing each kilowatt hour of electricity, as in Figure 5.5.

The new supply curve in Figure 5.5, S′, which is above the supply curve,

[100] Not only is the electrical power industry completely monopolized, but in the short run, at least, demand is relatively inelastic. Over the *long run* demand may have the more elastic characteristics we assume in the example.

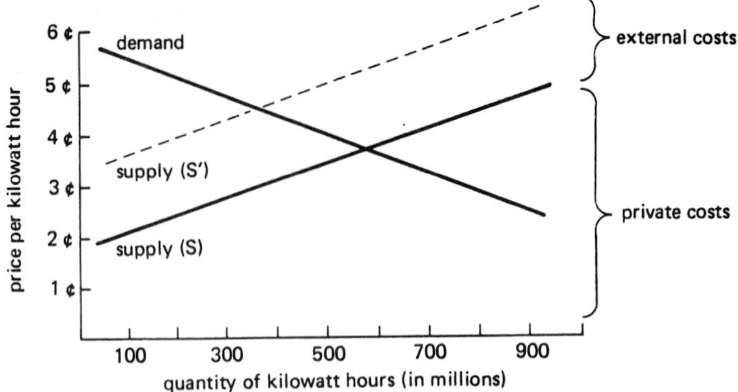

FIGURE 5-5

S (which includes only the manufacturers' private costs), shows the quantities of electricity that would be supplied if all the costs of producing the electricity were taken into account, and the prices that would have to be charged for each kilowatt hour if all costs were thus taken into account. As the new curve, S′, indicates, when all the costs are taken into account, the market price of the commodity, 4.5 cents, will be *higher,* and the output, 350 million kilowatt hours, will be *lower,* than when only private costs are incorporated. Thus, when *only* private costs are taken into account the electricity is *underpriced* and it is *overproduced.* And this in turn means that the electricity market is no longer allocating resources and distributing commodities so as to maximize utility. Three deficiencies, in particular, can be noted.

First, allocation of resources in markets that do not take all costs into account is not optimal, because from the point of view of society as a whole, more of the commodity is being produced than society would demand if society had available an accurate measure of what it is actually paying to produce the commodity. Since the commodity is being overproduced, more of society's resources are being consumed to produce the commodity than is optimal. The resources being consumed by overproduction of the commodity are resources that could be used to produce other commodities for which there would be greater demand if prices accurately reflected costs. Resources are thereby being misallocated.

Second, when external costs are not taken into account by producers, producers ignore these costs and make no attempt to minimize them. So long as the firm does not have to pay for external costs, it has no incentive to use technology that might decrease or eliminate them. Consequently, the resources being consumed by these external costs (such as clean air) are being unnecessarily wasted. There may be technologically feasible ways of producing the same commodities without imposing as many external costs, but the producer will make no attempt to find them.

Third, when the production of a commodity imposes external costs on third parties, goods are no longer efficiently distributed to consumers. External costs introduce effective price differentials into markets: Everyone does not pay equal prices for the same commodities. The neighbors who live near our imaginary electric plant, for example, pay not only the prices the plant charges everyone else for electricity, but also the costs the smoke from the burning fuel imposes on them in the form of extra cleaning bills, medical bills, painting bills, and so forth. Because they must pay for these extra external costs, of course, they have fewer funds to pay for their share of market commodities. Consequently, their share of goods is not proportioned to their desires and needs as compared to the shares of those who do not have to pay the extra external costs.

Pollution, then, imposes "external costs" and this in turn means that the private costs of production are less than the social costs. As a consequence, markets do not impose an optimal discipline on producers, and the result is a drop in social utility. Pollution of the environment, then, is a violation of the utilitarian principles that underlie a market system.

Remedies: The Duties of the Firm

The remedy for external costs, according to the utilitarian argument sketched above, is to ensure that the costs of pollution are internalized—that is, that they are absorbed by the producer and taken into account when determining the price of his goods.[101] In this way goods will be accurately priced, market forces will provide the incentives that will encourage producers to minimize external costs, and some consumers will no longer end up paying more than others for the same commodities.

There are various ways of internalizing the external costs of pollution. One way is for the polluting agent to pay to all of those being harmed, voluntarily or by law, an amount equal to the costs the pollution imposes on them. When Union Oil's drilling in the Santa Barbara channel on the California coast led to an oil spill, the total costs that the spill imposed on local residents and on state and federal agencies were estimated at about $16,400,000 (including costs of cleanup, containment, administration, damage to tourism and fishing, recreational and property damages, and loss of marine life). Union Oil paid about $10,400,000 of these costs voluntarily by paying for all cleanup and containment of the oil, and it paid about $6,300,000 in damages to the affected parties as the result of litigation.[102] Thus, the costs of the oil spill were "internalized," in part through voluntary action and in part through legal action. When the polluting firm pays those on whom its manufacturing processes impose costs, as Union Oil did, it is led to figure these costs into its own subsequent price determinations. Market mechanisms then lead it to come up with ways of cutting down pollution in order to cut down its costs. Since the Santa Barbara oil spill, for example, Union Oil and other petroleum firms have invested considerable amounts of money in developing methods to minimize pollution damage from oil spills.

A problem with this way of internalizing the costs of pollution, however, is that when several polluters are involved, it is not always clear just who is being damaged by whom. How much of the environmental damage caused by several polluters should be counted as damages to my property and how much should be counted as damages to your property, when the damages are inflicted on things such as air or public bodies of water, and for how much of the damage

[101] See E. J. Mishan, *Economics for Social Decisions* (New York: Praeger Publishers, Inc., 1973), pp. 85 ff., also E. J. Mishan, *Cost Benefit Analysis*, 3rd ed. (London: Allen & Unwin; 1982).

[102] S. Prakesh Sethi, *Up Against the Corporate Wall* (Englewood Cliffs, NJ: Prentice Hall, 1977), p. 21.

should each polluter be held responsible? Moreover, the administrative and legal costs of assessing damages for each distinct polluter and of granting separate compensations to each distinct claimant can become substantial.

A second remedy is for the polluter to stop pollution at its source by installing pollution-control devices. In this way, the external costs of polluting the environment are translated into the internal costs the firm itself pays to install pollution controls. Once costs are internalized in this way, market mechanisms again provide cost-cutting incentives and ensure that prices reflect the true costs of producing the commodity. In addition, the installation of pollution-control devices serves to eliminate the long-range and potentially disastrous worldwide effects of pollution.

Justice

This utilitarian way of dealing with pollution (that is, by internalizing costs) seems to be consistent with the requirements of distributive justice insofar as distributive justice favors equality. Observers have noted that pollution often has the effect of increasing inequality.[103] If a firm pollutes, its stockholders benefit because their firm does not have to absorb the external costs of pollution and this leaves them with greater profits, and those customers who purchase the firm's products also benefit because the firm does not charge them for all the costs involved in making the product. The *beneficiaries* of pollution, therefore, tend to be those who can afford to buy a firm's stock and its products. On the other hand, the external *costs* of pollution are borne largely by the poor.[104] Property values in polluted neighborhoods are generally lower, and consequently they are inhabited by the poor and abandoned by the wealthy. Pollution, therefore, may produce a net flow of benefits away from the poor and toward the well-off, thereby increasing inequality. To the extent that this occurs, pollution violates distributive justice. Internalizing the costs of pollution, as utilitarianism requires, would rectify matters by removing the burdens of external costs from the backs of the poor and placing them in the hands of the wealthy: the firm's stockholders and its customers. By and large, therefore, the utilitarian claim that the external costs of pollution should be internalized is consistent with the requirements of distributive justice.

We should note, however, that if a firm makes basic goods (food products, clothing, gasoline, automobiles) for which the poor must allocate a larger proportion of their budgets than the affluent, then internalizing costs may place a heavier burden on the poor than on the affluent, because the prices of these basic goods will rise. The poor may also suffer if the costs of pollution control rise so high that unemployment results (although current studies indicate that the unemployment effects of pollution-control programs are transitory and minimal).[105] There is some rudimentary evidence that tends to show that current pollution-control measures place greater burdens on the poor than on the wealthy.[106] This suggests the need to integrate distributional criteria into our pollution-control programs.

[103] See Mishan, "The Postwar Literature on Externalities," p. 24.

[104] William J. Baumal and Wallace E. Oates, *Economics, Environmental Policy, and the Quality of Life* (Englewood Cliffs, NJ: Prentice Hall, 1979), p. 177.

[105] *Ibid.*, pp. 180–82.

[106] *Ibid.*, pp. 182–84.

Internalizing external costs also seems to be consistent with the requirements of retributive and compensatory justice.[107] Retributive justice requires that those who are responsible for and who benefit from an injury should bear the burdens of rectifying the injury, while compensatory justice requires that those who have been injured should be compensated by those who injure them. Taken together, these requirements imply that (1) the costs of pollution control should be borne by those who cause pollution and who have benefited from pollution activities, while (2) the benefits of pollution control should flow to those who have had to bear the external costs of pollution. Internalizing external costs seems to meet these two requirements: (1) The costs of pollution control are borne by stockholders and by customers, both of whom benefit from the polluting activities of the firm, and (2) the benefits of pollution control flow to those neighbors who once had to put up with the firm's pollution.

Costs and Benefits

The technology for pollution control has developed effective but costly methods for abating pollution. Up to 60 percent of water pollutants can be removed through ''primary'' screening and sedimentation processes; up to 90 percent can be removed through more expensive ''secondary'' biological and chemical processes; and amounts over 95 percent can be removed through even more expensive ''tertiary'' chemical treatment.[108] Air pollution abatement techniques include the use of fuels and combustion procedures that burn more cleanly; mechanical filters that screen or isolate dust particles in the air; ''scrubbing'' processes that pass polluted air through liquids that remove pollutants; and chemical treatment that transforms gases into more easily removed compounds.[109]

It is possible, however, for a firm to invest *too much* in pollution control devices. Suppose, for example, that the pollution from a certain firm causes $100 worth of environmental damage, and suppose that the only device that can eliminate this pollution would cost the firm at least $1,000. Then, obviously, the firm should not install the device, for if it does so, the economic utility of society will decline: The costs of eliminating the pollution will be greater than the benefits society will reap, thereby resulting in a shrinkage of total utility.

How much should a firm invest in pollution control, then? Consider that the costs of controlling pollution and the benefits derived from pollution control are inversely related.[110] As one rises, the other falls. Why is this so? Think for a moment that if a body of water is highly polluted, it will probably be quite easy and consequently quite cheap to filter out a certain limited amount of pollutants. To filter out a few more pollutants, however, will require finer and therefore additional and more expensive filters. Costs will keep climbing for each additional level of purity desired, and getting out the last few molecules of impurities would require astronomically expensive additional equipment. However, getting out those last traces of impurities will probably not matter much to people and will therefore

[107] Mishan, ''The Postwar Literature on Externalities,'' p. 24.

[108] Mills, *Economics of Environmental Quality*, pp. 111–12.

[109] Frederick D. Sturdivant, *Business and Society* (Homewood, IL: Richard D. Irwin, Inc., 1977), p. 307.

[110] See Mills, *Economics of Environmental Quality*, pp. 83–91.

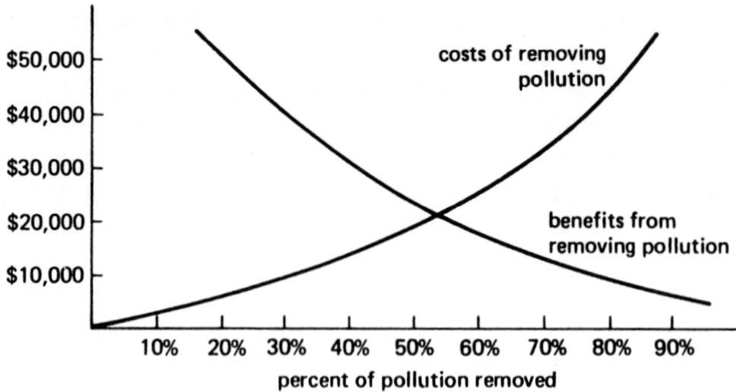

FIGURE 5-6

be unnecessary. At the other end of the scale, however, getting rid of the first gross amounts of pollutants will be highly beneficial to people: The costs of damages from these pollutants are substantial. Consequently, if we plot as curves on a graph the costs of removing pollution and the benefits of removing pollution (which are equivalent to the external costs removed) the result will be two intersecting curves as illustrated in Figure 5.6. What is the optimal amount of pollution control? Obviously, the point at which the two lines cross. At this point, the costs of pollution control exactly equal its benefits. If the firm invests additional resources in removing pollution, society's net utility will decline. Beyond this point, the firm should resort to directly or indirectly (that is, through taxes or other forms of social investment) paying society for the costs of polluting the environment.

To enable the firm to make such cost-benefit analyses, researchers have devised an array of theoretical methods and techniques for calculating the costs and benefits of removing pollution. These make use of estimates of consumer surplus, rents, market prices and "shadow prices," adjustment for "transfers," discounted future values, and recognition of risk factors.[111] Thomas Klein summarizes the procedures for cost-benefit analysis as follows:

1. Identify costs and benefits of the proposed program and the person or sectors incurring or receiving them. Trace transfers.
2. Evaluate the costs and benefits in terms of their value to beneficiaries and donors. The standard of measure is the value of each marginal unit to demanders and suppliers ideally captured in competitive prices. Useful refinements involve:
   a. Incorporating time values through the use of a discount rate.
   b. Recognizing risk by factoring possible outcomes according to probabilities and, where dependent, probability trees.
3. Add up costs and benefits to determine the net social benefit of a project or program.[112]

In order to avoid "erratic" and "costly" use of these procedures, Klein recommends that firms introduce a system of "social accounting" that "routinely mea-

[111] For a number of cases that apply these techniques, see Yusuf J. Ahmad, Partha Dasgupta, and Karl-Goran Maler, eds., *Environmental Decision-Making* (London: Hodder and Stoughton, 1984).

[112] Thomas A. Klein, *Social Costs and Benefits of Business* (Englewood Cliffs, NJ: Prentice Hall, 1977), p. 118.

sures, records, and reports external effects to management and other parties."[113]

It is at this point, however, that a fundamental difficulty in the utilitarian approach to pollution emerges. The cost-benefit analyses just described assume that the costs and benefits of reducing pollution can be accurately measured.[114] In some cases (limited and local in character) cost-benefit measurements are available: The costs and benefits of cleaning up the oil spilled by Union Oil at Santa Barbara, for example, were more or less measurable. But the costs and benefits of pollution removal are difficult to measure when they involve damages to human health and loss of life: What is the price of life?[115]

Measurement is also difficult when the effects of pollution are uncertain and, consequently, difficult to predict: What will be the effects of increasing the carbon dioxide content of our atmosphere by burning more coal, as the United States is now starting to do? In fact, perhaps the major problem involved in obtaining the measurements needed to apply cost-benefit analysis to pollution problems is the problem of estimating and evaluating *risk* (that is, the probability of future costly consequences).[116] Many new technologies carry with them unknown degrees of risk to present and future generations. The use of nuclear technology, for example, involves some probability of damages to health and loss of life for present and future generations: There are the risks of health damages from mining and the use and disposal of radioactive materials, plus the risks of sabotage and of a proliferation of the materials used in atomic weapons. But there are insurmountable obstacles in the way of measuring these risks accurately. We cannot use trial and error (a usual method for learning what the probabilities of an event are) to learn the risk, for example, of a nuclear accident, since the lesson would obviously be too costly and some of the health effects of radioactivity would not appear until decades after it is too late to correct them. Moreover, the mathematical models that we must rely on to measure risk in the absence of trial and error learning are not useful when all the possible things that can go wrong with a technology are not known. Human error, carelessness, and malice have been involved in most nuclear mishaps. The human factor is notoriously impossible to predict, and therefore impossible to incorporate into a measurement of the risks associated with using nuclear power. Moreover, even if the numerical risk associated with a new technology were known, it is unclear how much weight it should be given in a social cost-benefit analysis. Imagine, for example, that society currently accepts with some indifference a .01 risk of death associated with driving. Does it then follow that society also should be indifferent to accepting a .01 risk

[113] *Ibid.*, p. 119; the literature on social accounting for business firms is vast; see U.S. Department of Commerce, *Corporate Social Reporting in the United States and Western Europe* (Washington, DC: U.S. Government Printing Office, 1979); Committee on Social Measurement, *The Measurement of Corporate Social Performance* (New York: American Institute of Certified Public Accountants, Inc., 1977).

[114] See Boyd Collier, *Measurement of Environmental Deterioration* (August, TX: Bureau of Business Research, The University of Texas at Austin, 1971).

[115] See Michael D. Boyles, "The Price of Life," *Ethics*, 89, no. 1 (October 1978): 20–34; for other problems with using cost-benefit analysis in environmental areas, see Mark Sagoff, "Ethics and Economics in Environmental Law," in Regan, ed., *Earthbound*, pp. 147–78, and Rosemarie Tong, *Ethics in Policy Analysis* (Englewood Cliffs, NJ: Prentice Hall, 1986), pp. 14–29.

[116] Much of the material in this and the following paragraphs is based on the superb analysis in Robert E. Goodwin, "No Moral Nukes," *Ethics*, 90, no. 3 (April 1980): 417–49.

of death from the introduction of a certain new technology? Obviously not, because risk is cumulative: The new technology will *double* society's risk of death to .02, and while society may be indifferent to carrying a .01 risk of death, it may find a .02 risk unacceptable. Knowing the risk of a certain costly future event does not, then, necessarily tell us the value that society will place on that risk once it is added to the other risks society already runs. And, to make matters worse, individuals differ substantially in their aversion to risk: Some individuals *like* to gamble while others find it extremely distasteful.

The almost insurmountable problems involved in getting accurate pollution measurements are illustrated by the few federal estimates of the *benefits* produced by pollution control activities.[117] The present financial *costs* of pollution control are fairly easy to obtain by examining reports on expenditures for pollution equipment. Total 1978 expenditures for pollution control, including government and private expenditures, were $46.7 billion.[118] But the *benefits* associated with these expenditures have never been accurately measured. The federal government estimated that the annual benefits from air pollution control alone were approximately $21.4 billion in 1978, and earlier studies had estimated the annual benefits of water pollution control alone would be $12.3 billion by 1978.[119] But these estimates are based on exceedingly unreliable methodologies and deliberately omit many of the effects of pollution, especially long-range global effects such as the effects of carbon dioxide build-up and ozone depletion, as well as the health benefits from the elimination of chemical contamination in drinking water.

The problems involved in getting accurate measurements of the benefits of pollution control are also illustrated by the difficulties businesses have encountered in trying to construct a ''social audit'' (a report of the social costs and social benefits of the firm's activities). Those who advocate that a corporation should measure and report the social impacts of its activities have been forced to ''recognize that the goal of measuring all impacts of all actions upon all conditions and all publics, using standard techniques and units, considerably exceeds current capabilities and that compromises and modifications are inevitable.''[120] Due to this inability to measure benefits, so-called ''social audits'' are usually nothing more than qualitative descriptions of what a firm is doing. But without definite quantitative measurements of the benefits deriving from its attempts to reduce pollution, a firm has no way of knowing whether its efforts are cost-effective from a social point of view.

These failures of measurement pose significant technical problems for utilitarian approaches to pollution. In addition, the use of utilitarian cost-benefit analysis is sometimes based on assumptions that are inconsistent with people's moral rights. Advocates of utilitarian cost-benefit analysis sometimes assume that if the benefits of a certain technology or manufacturing process ''clearly'' outweigh its costs,

[117] Council on Environmental Quality, *Environmental Quality*, eighth annual report (Washington DC: U.S. Government Printing Office, 1979), pp. 323–25.

[118] Council on Environmental Quality, *Environmental Quality—1979*, p. 667.

[119] *Ibid.*, p. 655.

[120] Committee on Social Measurement, *The Measurement of Corporate Social Performance*, p. 31.

then it is morally permissible to impose the process on unwilling citizens. A recent government report, for example, makes the following recommendations:

> Because nuclear problems are such highly emotional issues and becoming even more so, as evidenced by the states that have indicated an unwillingness to permit nuclear waste disposal within their boundaries, it may be impossible to get the public and political support necessary for a given state to accept nuclear waste. Ultimately, if state approval for waste repository sites cannot be obtained within an established time, the federal government might have to mandate selections. While such action would not be easy it may be necessary if the waste problem is to be solved in a reasonable time.[121]

But recommendations of this type seem to violate the basic moral right that underlies democratic societies: Persons have a moral right to be treated only as they have consented to be treated beforehand (see Chapter Two, second section). If people have not consented to take on the costs of a technology (and indicate this unwillingness, for example, through local legislation, hearings, or opinion surveys), then their moral right of consent is violated when these costs are imposed on them anyway. Using only cost-benefit analysis to determine whether a new technology or manufacturing process should be used, then, ignores the question of whether the costs involved are *voluntarily* accepted by those who must bear them, or whether they are unilaterally *imposed* on them by others.

It should be noted that although the right of consent seems to imply that decisions concerning pollution control always should be left in the hands of the ordinary citizen, this implication is not necessarily correct. For people can give their informed consent to a risky project only if they have an adequate understanding of the project and its attendant risks. But contemporary technology is often so complex that even experts disagree when estimating and assessing the risks it may involve (scientists disagree wildly, for example, over the safety of using nuclear power). So it may be impossible for ordinary citizens to understand and assess the risks that a certain polluting technology will impose on them, and, consequently, it may be impossible, in principle, for them to give their informed consent to it.

In view of all the problems raised by utilitarian approaches to pollution, it may be that alternative approaches are more adequate. In particular, it may be that the absolute bans on pollution which are still incorporated in many federal laws, and the rights theory on which these absolute bans rest, are, for the present at least, a more adequate approach to pollution issues than utilitarianism. Alternatively, some writers have suggested that when risks cannot be reliably estimated it is best to choose only those projects that carry no risk of irreversible damages. For example, if there is a probability that the pollution from a certain technology may bring about catastrophic consequences that will continue to plague us forever, then the technology should be rejected in favor of other technologies that will not close off our options in the same permanent way. Others suggest that when risks cannot be assessed, we should, in justice, identify those who are most vulnerable and who would have to bear the heaviest costs if things should go wrong,

[121] U.S. General Accounting Office, *The Nation's Nuclear Waste* (Washington, DC: U.S. Government Printing Office, 1979), p. 12. For a criticism of this kind of policy analysis see Tong, *Ethics in Policy Analysis*, pp. 39–54.

and then take steps to ensure that they are protected. Future generations and children, for example, should be protected against our polluting choices. Finally, others suggest that when risks cannot be measured, the only rational procedure is to first assume that the worst will happen and then choose the option that will leave us best off when the worst happens (this is the so-called "maximum rule" of probability theory). It is unclear which of these alternative approaches should be adopted when utilitarian cost-benefit analysis fails.

5.3 THE ETHICS OF CONSERVING DEPLETABLE RESOURCES

"Conservation" refers to the saving or rationing of natural resources for later uses. Conservation, therefore, looks primarily to the future: to the need to limit consumption now in order to have resources available for tomorrow.

In a sense, pollution control is a form of conservation. Pollution "consumes" pure air and water, and pollution control "conserves" them for the future. But there are basic differences between the problems of pollution and the problems of *resource depletion* that makes the term "conservation" more applicable to the latter problems than to the former. With some notable exceptions (such as nuclear wastes), most forms of pollution affect present generations and their control will benefit present generations. The depletion of most scarce resources, however, lies far in the future, and the effects of their depletion will be felt primarily by posterity, and not by present generations. Consequently, our concern over the depletion of resources is primarily a concern for *future* generations and for the benefits that will be available to them. For this reason, conservation is more applicable to the problems of resource depletion than to those of pollution.[122] Moreover (again with notable exceptions), pollution is a problem concerned primarily with "renewable" resources, insofar as air and water can be "renewed" by ceasing to dump pollutants into them and allowing them time to recover. Tomorrow's supply, therefore, will be created anew over and over if we take the proper precautions. Resource depletion, however, is concerned with finite, nonrenewable resources. And the only store of a finite, nonrenewable resource that will be around tomorrow is that which is left over from today. Conservation, therefore, is the only way of ensuring a supply for tomorrow's generations.

Resource depletion forces two main kinds of questions on us, then: First, why ought we to conserve resources for future generations, and second, how much should we conserve?

Rights of Future Generations

It might appear that we have an obligation to conserve resources for future generations because they have an equal right to the limited resources of this planet. And if future generations have an equal right to the world's resources, then by depleting these resources, we are taking what is actually theirs and violating their equal right to these resources.

[122] Passmore, *Man's Responsibility for Nature*, p. 74.

A number of writers, however, have claimed that it is a mistake to think that future generations have rights.[123] It is a mistake, consequently, to think that we should refrain from consuming natural resources because we are taking what future generations have a right to. Three main reasons have been advanced to show that future generations cannot have rights.

First, future generations cannot intelligently be said to have rights because they do not now exist and may never exist.[124] I may be able to *think* about future people, but I cannot hit them, punish them, injure them, or treat them wrongly. Future people exist only in the imagination, and imaginary entities cannot be acted upon in any way whatsoever except in imagination. Similarly, we cannot say that future people possess things now, when they do not yet exist to possess or have them. Since there is a possibility that future generations may never exist, they cannot "possess" rights.

Second, if future generations did have rights, then we might be led to the absurd conclusion that we must sacrifice our entire civilization for their sake.[125] Suppose that each of the infinite number of future generations had an equal right to the world's supply of oil. Then we would have to divide the oil equally among them all, and our share would be a few quarts at the most. We would then be put in the absurd position of having to shut down our entire Western civilization in order that each future person might be able to possess a few quarts of oil.

Third, we can say that someone has a certain right only if we know that he or she has a certain interest which that right protects. The purpose of a right, after all, is to protect the interests of the right-holder. But we are virtually ignorant of what interests future generations will have. What wants will they have? The men and women of the future may be genetically fabricated to order, with desires, pleasures, and needs vastly different from our own. What kinds of resources will future technology require for supplying their wants? Science might come up with technologies for creating products from raw materials that we have in abundance—minerals in sea water, for example—and might find potentially unlimited energy sources such as nuclear fusion. Moreover, future generations might develop cheap and plentiful substitutes for the scarce resources that we now need. Since we are uncertain about these matters, we must remain ignorant about the interests future generations will want to protect (who could have guessed eighty years ago that uranium rocks would one day be considered a "resource" in which people would have an interest?). Consequently, we are unable to say what rights future people might have.[126]

[123] Martin Golding, "Obligations to Future Generations," *Monist*, 56, no. 1 (1972): 85–99; Richard T. DeGeorge, "The Environment, Rights, and Future Generations," in *Ethics and Problems of the 21st Century*, K. E. Goodpaster and K. M. Sayre, eds., pp. 93–105.

[124] DeGeorge, "The Environment, Rights, and Future Generations," pp. 97–98.

[125] *Ibid.*

[126] Martin Golding, "Obligations to Future Generations," *Monist*, 56, no. 1 (1972); Gregory Kavka argues, however, that full knowledge of the needs of future people is not required to accord them moral standing in "The Futurity Problem," in Ernest Partridge, *Responsibilities to Future Generations* (New York: Prometheus Books, 1981), pp. 109–22; see also Annette Baier, "For the Sake of Future Generations," in *Earthbound*, Regan, ed. pp. 214–46.

If these arguments are correct, then to the extent that we are uncertain what future generations will exist or what they will be like, they do not have any rights. It does not follow, however, that we have no obligations to any future generations since our obligations may be based on other grounds.

Justice to Future Generations

John Rawls argues that while it is unjust to impose disproportionately heavy burdens on present generations for the sake of future generations, it is also unjust for present generations to leave nothing for future generations. To determine a just way of distributing resources between generations, he suggests, the members of each generation should put themselves in the "original position" and, without knowing what generation they belong to, they should

> . . . ask what is reasonable for members of adjacent generations to expect of one another at each level of (historical) advance. They should try to piece together a just savings schedule by balancing how much at each stage (of history) they would be willing to save for their immediate descendants against what they would feel entitled to claim of their immediate predecessors. Thus imagining themselves to be parents, say, they are to ascertain how much they would set aside for their children by noting what they would believe themselves entitled to claim of their own parents.[127]

In general, Rawls claims, this method of ascertaining what earlier generations in justice owe to later generations will lead to the conclusion that what justice demands of us is merely that we hand to the next generation a situation no worse than we received from the generation before us:

> Each generation must not only preserve the gains of culture and civilization, and maintain intact those just institutions that have been established, but it must also put aside in each period of time a suitable amount of real capital accumulation. . . . (It should be kept in mind here that capital is not only factories, and machines, and so on, but also the knowledge and culture, as well as the techniques and skills, that make possible just institutions and the fair value of liberty.) This . . . is in return for what is received from previous generations that enables the later ones to enjoy better life in a more just society.[128]

Justice, then, requires that we hand over to our immediate successors a world that is not in worse condition than the one we received from our ancestors.[129]

This conclusion is supported also by some utilitarian reasoning. Robin Att-

[127] John Rawls, *A Theory of Justice* (Cambridge: Harvard University Press, 1971), p. 289.

[128] *Ibid.*, pp. 285 and 288.

[129] Among authors who favor Rawls in their treatment of our obligations to future generations are R. and V. Routley, "Nuclear Energy and Obligations to the Future," *Inquiry*, 21 (1978): 133–79; K. S. Shrader-Frechette, *Nuclear Power and Public Policy* (Dordecht, Boston and London: Reidel, 1980); F. Patrick Hubbard, "Justice, Limits to Growth, and an Equilibrium State," *Philosophy and Public Affairs*, 7 (1978): 326–45; Victor D. Lippit and Koichi Hamada, "Efficiency and Equity in Intergenerational Distribution," in *The Sustainable Society*, ed. Dennis Clark Pirages (New York and London: Praeger Publishers, Inc., 1977), pp. 285–99. Each of these authors, however, introduces modifications into Rawls's position.

field, a utilitarian, for example, argues that utilitarianism favors what he calls the "Lockean principle" that "each should leave enough and as good for others."[130] Attfield interprets this principle to mean that each generation must leave for future generations a world whose "output capacity" is no less than that generation received from previous generations.[131] That is, each generation must leave the world no less productive than they found it. Attfield suggests that leaving the world with the same "output capacity" does not necessarily mean leaving the world with the same resources. Instead, maintaining the same level of output can be achieved either through conservation, recycling, or technological innovation.

Other utilitarians have reached slightly different but otherwise similar conclusions by relying on other basic utilitarian principles. Utilitarians have argued that each generation has a duty to maximize the future beneficial consequences of its actions and to minimize their future injurious consequences.[132] However, utilitarians have claimed, these future consequences should be "discounted" (given less weight) in proportion to their uncertainty and to their distance in the future.[133] Together, these utilitarian principles imply that we at least have an obligation to avoid those practices whose harmful consequences for the generation that immediately follows us are certain to outweigh the beneficial consequences our own generation derives from them. Our responsibility for more distant future generations, however, is diminished, especially insofar as we are unable to foresee what effects our present actions will have on them because we do not know what needs or technology they will have.

Unfortunately, we cannot rely on market mechanisms (that is, price rises) to ensure that scarce resources are conserved for future generations.[134] The market registers only the effective demands of present participants and the actual supplies presently being made available. The needs and demands of future generations, as well as the potential scarcities that lie far in the future, are so heavily "discounted" by markets that they hardly affect prices at all.[135] William Shepherd and Clair Wilcox provide a summary of the reasons that the private choices represented in markets and market prices fail to take into account the future scarcity of resources:

1. *Multiple access* If a resource can be used by several separate extractors, then the shared access will invariably lead the resource to be depleted too fast. . . . As with several people with straws in one milkshake, each owner's private interest is in taking it out as fast as possible. . . .
2. *Time preferences and myopia* Firms often have short time horizons, under the stress of commercial competition. This may underrepresent the legitimate interests of future generations. . . .

[130] Attfield adopts this "Lockean principle" from G. Kavka, *ibid.*

[131] Attfield, *The Ethics of Environmental Concern*, pp. 107–10.

[132] J. Brenton Stearns, "Ecology and the Indefinite Unborn," *Monist*, 56, no. 4 (October 1972): 612–25; Jan Narveson, "Utilitarianism and New Generations," *Mind*, 76 (1967): 62–67.

[133] Robert Scott, Jr., "Environmental Ethics and Obligations to Future Generations," in *Obligations to Future Generations*, R. I. Sikora and Brian Barry, eds. (Philadelphia: Temple University Press, 1978), pp. 74–90; but see Kavka, *ibid.*, who argues against discounting.

[134] Passmore, *Man's Responsibility for Nature*, p. 85.

[135] Joan Robinson, *Economic Philosophy* (London: Penguin Books, 1966), p. 115.

3. *Inadequate forecasting* Present users may simply fail to foresee future developments. This may reflect a lack of sufficient research interest and ability to discern future changes. . . .
4. *Special influences* Specific taxes and other incentive devices may encourage overly rapid use of resources. . . .
5. *External effects* There are important externalities in the uses of many resources, so that private users ignore major degrees of pollution and other external costs. . . .
6. *Distribution* Finally, private market decisions are based on the existing pattern of distribution of wealth and income. As resource users vote with their dollars, market demand will more strongly reflect the interests and preferences of the wealthy.[136]

The only means of conserving for the future, then, appear to be voluntary (or politically enforced) policies of conservation.

In practical terms, Rawls's view implies that while we should not sacrifice the cultural advances we have made, we should adopt voluntary or legal measures to conserve those resources and environmental benefits that we can reasonably assume our immediate posterity will need if they are to live lives with a variety of available choices comparable, at least, to ours. In particular, this would mean that we should preserve wildlife and endangered species; that we should take steps to ensure that the rate of consumption of fossil fuels and of minerals does not continue to rise; that we should cut down our consumption and production of those goods that depend on nonrenewable resources; that we should recycle nonrenewable resources; that we should search for substitutes for materials that we are too rapidly depleting.

Several General Motors programs provide illustrations of the kinds of business policies that can embody these principles. A recent General Motors "social audit" included the following description of its energy saving programs:

> GM conservation efforts reduce the amount of energy used to build each vehicle by over 22 percent. Although some of these savings result from higher production volume, 16 percent comes directly from conservation programs. . . . Plant engineering and development groups are focusing on projects to reduce the energy used in [those operations which require the most energy]. Some examples:
> —A pilot coal-gasification system has been installed at the Saginaw Steering Gear Division to evaluate the effectiveness of coal gas, both as a basic industrial fuel and for heat treating and paint drying.
> —Methane gas from municipal wastes is being investigated as a potential supplemental fuel for operations which now must exclusively use natural gas.
> —Several programs are underway to improve the energy efficiency of the melting cupolas in iron foundries. . . .
> —Improved exhaust-air filtration systems being developed will remove particulates and allow recirculation of warm air into a plant, reducing the need to heat make-up air.[137]

[136] William G. Shepherd and Clair Wilcox, *Public Policies Toward Business*, 6th ed. (Homewood, IL: Richard D. Irwin, Inc., 1979), pp. 524–25.

[137] *1979 General Motors Public Interest Report* (New York: General Motors Corp., 1979), pp. 52—53.

Economic Growth?

But to many observers conservation measures fall far short of what is needed. Several writers have argued that if we are to preserve enough scarce resources that future generations can maintain their quality of life at a satisfactory level, we shall have to change our economies substantially, particularly by scaling down our pursuit of economic growth. E. F. Schumacher, for example, claims that the industrialized nations will have to convert from growth-oriented capital-intensive technologies to much more labor-intensive technologies in which humans do work machines now do.[138] Others argue that economic systems will have to abandon their goal of steadily increasing production, and put in its place the goal of decreasing production until it has been scaled down to "a steady state"—that is, a point at which "the total population and the total stock of physical wealth are maintained constant at some desired levels by a 'minimal' rate of maintenance throughout (that is, by birth and death rates that are equal at the lowest feasible level, and by physical production and consumption rates that are equal at the lowest feasible level)."[139] The conclusion that economic growth must be abandoned if society is to be able to deal with the problems of diminishing resources has been challenged.[140] But it is at least arguable that adherence to continual economic growth promises to degrade the quality of life of future generations.[141]

The arguments for this claim are simple, stark, and highly controversial. If the world's economies continue to pursue the goal of economic growth, the demand for depletable resources will continue to rise. But since world resources are finite, at some point supplies will simply run out. At this point, if the world's nations are still based on growth economies, we can expect a collapse of their major economic institutions (that is, of manufacturing and financial institutions, communication networks, the service industries) which in turn will bring down their political and social institutions (that is, centralized governments, education and cultural programs, scientific and technological development, health care).[142] Living standards will then decline precipitously in the wake of widespread starvation and political dislocations. Various scenarios for this sequence of events have been constructed, all of them more or less speculative and necessarily based on uncertain assumptions.[143] The most famous of these are the studies of the Club of Rome

[138] E. F. Schumacher, *Small Is Beautiful* (London: Blond and Briggs, Ltd., 1973).

[139] Herman E. Daly, ed., *Toward A Steady-state Economy* (San Francisco: W. H. Freeman & Company, Publishers, 1974), p. 152; see also Herman E. Daly, *Steady-State Economics* (San Francisco; W. H. Freeman & Company, Publishers, 1977); Herman E. Daly, ed., *Economics, Ecology, and Ethics* (San Francisco: W. H. Freeman & Company, Publishers, 1980); Robert L. Stirers, *The Sustainable Society: Ethics and Economic Growth* (Philadelphia: Westminster Press, 1976), and Lester R. Brown, *Building a Sustainable Society* (New York: W. W. Norton & Co., Inc., 1981).

[140] See, for example, Wilfred Beckerman, *In Defense of Economic Growth* (London: Jonathan Cape, 1974); Rudolph Klein, "The Trouble with Zero Economic Growth," *New York Review of Books* (April 1974); Julian L. Simon, *The Ultimate Resource* (Princeton, NJ: Princeton University Press, 1981).

[141] E. J. Mishan, *The Economic Growth Debate: An Assessment* (London: George Allen & Unwin Ltd., 1977).

[142] See Heilbroner, *An Inquiry into the Human Prospect, Updated for the 1980s*.

[143] Several of these scenarios are reviewed in James Just and Lester Lave, "Review of Scenarios of Future U.S. Energy Use," *Annual Review of Energy*, 4 (1979): 501–36; and in Hughes, *World Futures*.

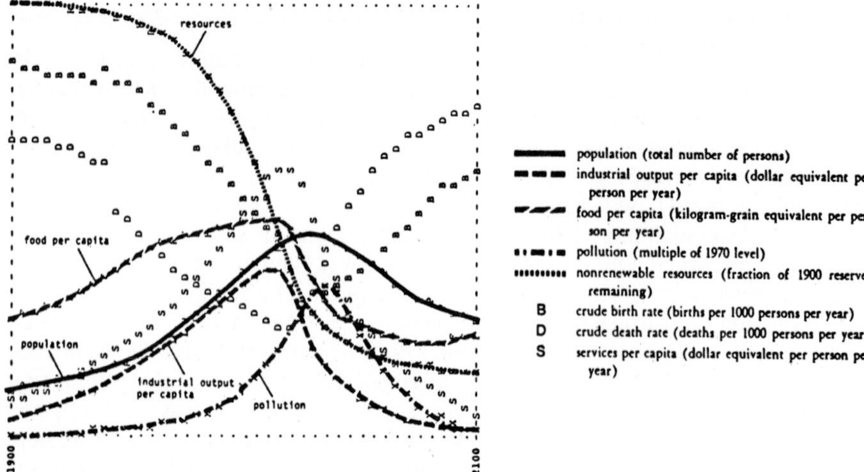

The "standard" world model run assumes no major change in the physical, economic, or social relationships that have historically governed the development of the world system. All variables plotted here follow historical values from 1900 to 1970. Food, industrial output, and population grow exponentially until the rapidly diminishing resource base forces a slowdown in industrial growth. Because of natural delays in the system, both population and pollution continue to increase for some time after the peak of industrialization. Population growth is finally halted by a rise in the death rate due to decreased food and medical services.

FIGURE 5.7 is from Donella H. Meadows et al., THE LIMITS TO GROWTH (New York: Universe Books, 1974), pp. 123–24. Reprinted by permission of Universe Books.

which has projected on computers the results of continuing the economic growth patterns of the past, in the face of declining resources.[144] Later studies came to similar conclusions.[145] Figure 5.7 reproduces one of the original computer projections of the Club of Rome.

In the computer-based graph of Figure 5.7, the horizontal axis represents time, so that as we run from the year A.D. 1900 at the left, to the year A.D. 2100 at the right, we see what will happen to the world's population, industrial output, food, pollution levels, nonrenewable resources, and so on, as time passes. During the first half of the 1900s, population, output, food, and services continue to grow while death rates, birth rates, and resources decline. At some point after 1950, however, a catastrophic collapse of output and services occurs as resources run out. Population continues to rise, but a climbing death rate and declining food supply soon brings it down. The decline in industrial output causes a decline in pollution, but food supplies, industrial output, and population by 2100 are below 1900 levels. "We can thus say with some confidence that, under the assumption of no major change in the present system, population and industrial growth will certainly stop within the next century at the latest."[146]

The assumptions on which these doomsday scenarios are based have been

[144] Meadows, Meadows, Randers, and Behrens, *The Limits to Growth* (New York: Universe Books, 1974).

[145] See, for example, Council on Environmental Quality, *The Global 2000 Report*.

[146] *Ibid.*, p. 132.

TABLE 5.3 Per Capita GNP (1980) and Energy Consumption for Twenty-Four Most Populated Nations

	GNP PER CAPITA ($)	ENERGY CONSUMPTION PER CAPITA (IN KILOGRAMS OF COAL EQUIVALENTS)
United States	11,360	10,410
West Germany	13,590	5,727
France	11,730	4,351
Japan	9,890	3,494
United Kingdom	7,920	4,942
Italy	6,480	3,318
Spain	5,350	2,539
Poland	3,900	5,586
Soviet Union	4,550	5,595
Brazil	2,050	761
Mexico	2,130	1,770
Turkey	1,460	737
South Korea	1,520	1,422
China	290	602
Philippines	720	316
Nigeria	1,010	144
Thailand	670	371
Egypt	580	496
Indonesia	420	220
Pakistan	300	218
India	240	191
Burma	180	63
Bangladesh	120	46
Ethiopia	140	29

Source: Figures based on G. T. Korian, THE NEW BOOK OF WORLD RANKINGS (New York: Facts on File, 1984), pp. 98 and 226.

repeatedly criticized and "debunked."[147] The computer programs and underlying equations on which the predictions are based make controversial and highly uncertain assumptions about future population growth rates, the absence of future increases in output per unit of input, our inability to find substitutes for depleted resources, and the ineffectiveness of recycling. These assumptions can all be challenged. Although future generations will certainly have fewer of the natural resources on which we depend, we cannot be sure exactly what impact this will have on them. Certainly the impact will not be as catastrophic as the prognostications of the Club of Rome indicated.[148] But we also cannot assume that the impact

[147] H. S. D. Cole, Christopher Freeman, Marie Jahoda, and K. L. R. Pavitt, eds., *Models of Doom: A Critique of the Limits to Growth* (New York: Universe Books, 1973); William Nordhaus, "World Dynamics: Measurement Without Data," *Economic Journal*, 83 (December 1973): 1156–83; Herman Kahn, William Brown, and Leon Martel, *The Next 200 Years* (New York: William Morrow & Company, Inc., 1976); Charles Maurice and Charles W. Smithson, *The Doomsday Myth* (Stanford: Hoover Institution Press, 1984); and Piers Blaikie, "The Use of Natural Resources in Developing and Developed Countries," in R. J. Johnston and P. J. Taylor, *A World in Crisis* (Cambridge, MA: Basil Blackwell, 1989), pp. 125–150.

[148] In a more recent study, the Club of Rome has moderated its predictions; see, Donella H. Meadows et al., *The Limits to Growth*, 2nd ed. (New York: Universe Books, 1974).

TABLE 5.4 World Energy Production and Consumption (1972)

REGION	% OF WORLD SUPPLIES PRODUCED	% OF WORLD SUPPLIES CONSUMED	PER CAPITA CONSUMPTION (IN KILOGRAMS OF COAL)	PER CAPITA SURPLUS (+) OR DEFICIT (−) (IN KILOGRAMS OF COAL)
North America	30.7	35.9	11,531	−1,210
Caribbean America	4.3	2.1	1,227	+1,560
Other America	1.1	1.7	759	− 290
Western Europe	7.8	19.4	4,000	−2,250
Middle East	16.2	1.3	857	+9,330
Far East	3.5	7.6	482	− 270
Oceana	1.2	1.2	4,275	− 60
Africa	5.8	1.8	363	+ 860
Communist Countries	29.4	29.0	1,800	+ 70

Source: United Nations, WORLD ENERGY SUPPLIES, 1969–1972 (New York: United Nations, 1974).

will be entirely benign.[149] Given the extreme uncertainties in this situation, at the very least a commitment to conservation seems to be in order. Whether a wholesale transformation of our economy is also necessary if civilization is to survive is a difficult and disturbing question that we may soon have to face.

Just as troubling are the moral questions raised by the distribution of dwindling energy supplies among the world's peoples. As is well known, and as the data in Table 5.3 confirm, the United States is the world's richest nation and the highest consumer of energy. The 6 percent of the world's population that lives within the United States consumes 35 percent of the world's annual energy supplies, while the 50 percent of the world's people who inhabit less developed nations must get along with about 8 percent of its energy supplies. Each person in the United States, in fact, consumes fifteen times more energy than a native South American, twenty-four times more than a native Asian, and thirty-one times more than a native African.

The high energy consumption rates of Americans are not paralleled by similarly high rates of energy production. As the data in Table 5.4 indicate, United States energy consumption is subsidized by other countries, in particular by the Caribbean, the Middle East, and Africa. That is, there is a net flow of energy *out of* these less-consuming populations and *into* the high-consumption population of the United States. Moreover, Americans use much of the energy supplies available to them for inessentials (unneeded products, unnecessary travel, household comforts, and conveniences) while the more frugal nations tend to use their supplies to meet basic needs (food, clothing, housing).

In view of the approaching scarcity of energy resources, these comparisons cannot help but raise the question of whether a high-consumption nation is morally

[149] Heilbroner, *The Human Prospect.*

justified in continuing to appropriate for its own use the nonrenewable energy resources of other more frugal nations that are too week economically to use these resources or too weak militarily to protect them. Any attempt to answer this question obviously requires a detailed inquiry into the nature of the world's social, economic, and political systems, an inquiry which is beyond the scope of this book. The question, however, is one that events may also soon force us to face.[150]

QUESTIONS FOR REVIEW AND DISCUSSION

1. Define the following concepts: pollution, toxic substance, nuclear wastes, exponential depletion, peaked depletion, free good, unlimited good, ecological system, ecological ethic, right to a livable environment, absolute ban, private costs, social costs, external costs, to internalize costs, cost-benefit analysis, risk, social audit, right of consent, conservation, rights of future generations, justice toward future generations, multiple access, time preference, doomsday scenario, high-consumption nation.
2. Define the main forms of pollution and resource depletion and identify the major problems associated with each form.
3. Compare and contrast the views of (a) an ecological ethic, (b) Blackstone's ethic of environmental rights, and (c) a utilitarian ethic of pollution control. Which view seems to you to be the more adequate? Explain your answer.
4. Do you agree with the claims that (1) future generations have no rights, and (2) the future generations to which we have obligations actually include only the generation which will immediately succeed us? Explain your answer. If you do not agree with these claims, then state your own views and provide arguments to support them.
5. In your judgment, should the major decisions on pollution and resource depletion (especially energy policy) be made by government experts? By scientific experts? By everyone? Provide moral arguments in support of your judgment.
6. "Any pollution law is unjust because it necessarily violates people's right to liberty and right to property." Discuss.
7. In their book *Energy Future,* R. Strobaugh and D. Yergin claim that in the debate over nuclear power "the resolution of differing opinions over how to deal with uncertainty, over how much risk is acceptable or how safe is safe enough—all require judgments in which values play as large a role as scientific facts" (p. 100). Discuss this claim.

CASES FOR DISCUSSION

Monarchs and Townspeople

In 1979, Synertex, a semiconductor company with headquarters in Sunnyvale, California, applied for a permit to build a $40 million research and manufacturing

[150] On the link between environmental resource use and the uneven distribution of world wealth see Willy Brandt, *North-South: A Program for Survival* (Cambridge: MIT Press, 1980).

plant in Santa Cruz, California.[1] The plant was to be located across the street from Natural Bridges State Park.

Natural Bridges State Park contains a grove of eucalyptus trees which, for several centuries, has served as a major wintering site for the Monarch butterfly. Park rangers estimated that each winter 95,000 of the large black and orange Monarchs settled on the eucalyptus trees concentrated in the few acres of the small park. So many of the bright-colored butterflies would land on the trees that their branches would bend and often break from their weight. The Monarch butterflies migrated several hundred miles each year to reach the park where they remained from November to March. Up to two thousand tourists visit the park on weekends to see the butterflies. A few other sites on the California coast also serve as wintering grounds for the world-famous butterfly, but none is as popular or as well known.

The environmental report which Synertex had to make before its request for a permit would be considered concluded that operations at the plant would pose an unknown degree of risk for the butterflies. The plant would sometimes release into the air small amounts of hydrocarbons as well as sulfur and nitrogen oxides, and these would be blown in the direction of the park by prevailing winds 20 percent of the time. Although the fumes would be 99 percent diluted by the time they reached the butterfly groves, "there is no available data" on the effects these diluted fumes would have on the butterflies.

Since the plant would employ 350 to 400 workers, most townspeople strongly supported granting the permit. Synertex believed the site was ideal in view of the availability of needed labor, as well as the material and geographical resources the site provided. Synertex also believed that the risk to the butterflies was virtually nil and was willing to hire a biologist to monitor the effects its operations had on the butterflies. The firm was unwilling, however, to guarantee that it would shut down its $40 million plant if the butterflies were affected by its operations.

1. Discuss the costs and benefits of building the Synertex plant. In your judgment, did the benefits outweigh the costs? Explain.
2. Who should have the right to make the final decision in the Synertex case? Local townspeople? Tourists? State government? The federal government? Synertex management? Explain your answers.
3. Do wildlife issues differ in any important ways from pollution issues or from issues concerning the depletion of energy resources?

The Ozone Threat: Managing with Uncertainty

In June 1974, two California chemists, Mario J. Molina and F. S. Roland, announced that chlorofluorocarbons (CFCs) being added to the atmosphere might decrease the ozone layer surrounding the earth by 10 percent within the next fifty to eighty years.[1] Since the ozone layer about 15 miles above the earth's surface shields the earth from the sun's harmful ultraviolet rays, the decrease in ozone

[1] This case is based entirely on Ken Peterson, "It's Butterflies vs. Industry," *San Jose Mercury*, 25 October 1979, pp. 1A and 24A.

[1] "Fluorocarbons and Ozone: New Predictions Ominous," *Science News*, 5 October 1974.

might allow these rays to reach the earth and induce skin cancer in humans. An earlier study in 1973 had predicted that a mere 5 percent decrease in ozone might produce at least 8,000 extra cases of skin cancer per year.[2] In addition, the 1973 study had speculated that increased solar radiation could damage the plankton in the oceans that produce much of the world's oxygen and might destroy many other plant and animal species. Other researchers suggested that an increase in solar radiation might lead to widespread climatic changes, including melting of polar ice, a consequent rise in sea levels and a flooding of coastal cities.[3]

Two months later, in September 1974, two more scientists, R. Cicerone and R. Stolarski, published a new computer study in *Science* that predicted a 10 percent decrease in the ozone layer by 1990. Fears increased when a third major prediction in October 1974 found that if CFCs continued to be added to the atmosphere at current rates, then by 1995, 40 percent of the ozone layer would be gone.[4]

All of these studies pointed out that much of the chlorofluorocarbon gas that was entering the ozone layer came from the propellents used in aerosol spray cans. When released from the can, the gas ($CFCl_3$) floats up into the stratosphere, where ultraviolet light from the sun causes the gas to release free chlorine atoms. A single chlorine molecule then acts as a catalyst to make tens of thousands of ozone molecules (O_3) break down into simple oxygen molecules (O_2). Whereas ozone filters out ultraviolet light, oxygen does not. The small amounts of CFC gas being used as propellents in deodorant sprays, hair sprays, perfume sprays, and so on, then, could destroy vast amounts of ozone once it reached the stratosphere.

In August 1975 government researchers reported that various atmospheric and laboratory experiments strongly confirmed the ozone depletion theory postulated by Rowland and Molina. Balloon samples indicated that CFCs had found their way into the stratosphere "in the predicted amounts" and that they were being broke down "as predicted and at the rates predicated by theory." Balloon tests also indicated that free chlorine atoms were being produced in the stratosphere as the ozone depletion theory predicted would happen.[5]

The DuPont Company was the largest producer of the one billion pounds of fluorocarbons (valued at $450 million) manufactured in the United States in 1974. By itself it accounted for about 50 percent of the CFC market, the rest being shared by five other manufacturers. In addition, DuPont was constructing a new $100 million chlorofluorocarbon plant in Corpus Christi which, when completed, would be the largest such plant in the world. DuPont was, therefore, highly concerned by the threat of a ban.[6]

DuPont management quickly moved to meet the threat. DuPont's research director, Ray McCarthy, pointed out that the ozone depletion theory had not yet

[2] "The Effects of Ozone Depletion," *Science*, 4 October 1974.

[3] "Fluorocarbon—Use Limit Urged by Panel to Avoid Cancer Risks, Climate Changes," *The Wall Street Journal*, 14 September 1976.

[4] "Fluorocarbons and Ozone: New Predictions Ominous."

[5] Jeffrey A. Tannenbaum, "Theory that Aerosols Deplete Ozone Shield is Attracting Support," *Wall Street Journal*, 3 December 1975.

[6] Walter Sullivan, "Federal Ban Urged on Spray-can Propellants," *New York Times*, 21 November 1974.

been fully established and large research gaps still remained. It was entirely possible that the computer models employed by the theories were mistaken, that the chlorine atoms found in the stratosphere had sources other than CFCs, and that the speculations concerning the effects of ozone depletion were exaggerated. McCarthy and other scientists claimed that it would be at least three to six years before proper proof of the theory was obtained. "I hope," McCarthy said, "that the measurements now planned and under way will prove effective in unequivocally providing information on reaction of chlorine in the stratosphere. If not, we will seek other methods which will give us that unequivocal proof."[7] Research should continue, but no regulations should be imposed until the necessary research had been completed.

> All we have are assumptions. Without experimental evidence, it would be an injustice if a few claims—which even the critics agree are hypotheses—were to be the basis of regulatory or consumer reaction. [Statement of Raymond L. McCarthy][8]

Other researchers, however, urged haste, since, if the ozone depletion theory was right, then there was little time left before its consequences would be almost irreversible. Ralph Cicerone, one of the authors of the ozone depletion theory, argued

> Decision-makers do not have much room to hedge their bets . . . whatever the effects of fluorocarbons will be, the full impact will not be felt for a decade after release and it will persist for many decades. . . . Complete scientific proof to everyone's satisfaction will take years, so we are faced with a benefit-risk analysis. I have come to the reluctant conclusion that the risks are greater than the benefits and the evidence is already strong. [Statement of Ralph Cicerone][9]

DuPont lobbied to prevent the passage of legislation that would ban the chlorofluorocarbons. In ten out of the fourteen states which had introduced CFC bills by the middle of 1975, the bills were defeated or tabled, in part as a result of industry lobbies.[10] When New York State succeeded in passing a bill banning CFCs unless proved safe, Raymond McCarthy of DuPont complained that "the bill gives the industry the real but impossible task of providing that something will never happen."[11]

To ensure that CFCs would not be banned, DuPont embarked on an extensive advertising campaign conveying their side of the story: The ozone depletion theory was backed by little evidence. The chairman of the board of DuPont published the following statement in several major newspapers:

> The current controversy centers around the theory [of ozone depletion]. On one side are scientists, theorists, and some legislators who contend that these useful, inert gases, breaking down into chlorine, will lead eventually to an unnatural amount

[7] Janet Weinberg, "Ozone Verdict: ON Faith or Fact," *Science News*, 17 May 1975, p. 324.

[8] "Industry Doubts Threat to Ozone," *New York Times*, 2 November 1974.

[9] *Ibid.*, p. 324.

[10] Steven Greenhouse, "Aerosol Feels the Ozone Effect," *New York Times*, 22 June 1975.

[11] *Ibid.*

> of ozone depletion. On the other side are scientists, researchers, and the aerosol industry who maintain there is not persuasive evidence to support this recently proposed theory of ozone depletion. And, they say, even if the theory has elements of correctness, other chemicals, reactions, and processes might be primarily responsible. Why, they ask, should an industry be prejudged and useful fluorocarbon products be destroyed before any answers are found? . . . As the world's leading supplier of fluorcarbon propellants, DuPont has an obvious stake in the outcome of the controversy. As a corporation we are committed to making products safely, and to supplying safe products to our customers. We have publicly announced that, should reputable evidence show that some fluorocarbons cause a health hazard through depletion of the ozone layer, we are prepared to stop production of the offending compounds. To date there is no experimental evidence to support the contention that . . . [these] compounds have caused a depletion of the ozone layer. . . . Nor will there be any hard answers until some hard facts are produced. In the meantime, aerosol products suffer under a cloud of presumed guilt, and other fluorocarbon-dependent industries are seriously threatened. We believe this is unfair. The "ban now-find out later" approach thrust upon an $8 billion segment of industry in this issue, both in the headlines and in many legislative proposals, is a disturbing trend. Businesses can be destroyed before scientific facts are assembled and evaluated; and many might never recover, even though these facts may vindicate them. Except where available evidence indicated that there may be immediate and substantial danger to health or environment, the nation cannot afford to act on this and other issues before the full facts are known. [Statement of Irving S. Shapiro, chairman of the board, DuPont][12]

In a surprising development, in 1976, Roland and Molina announced that their original calculations may have been mistaken because chemical interactions in the stratosphere were more complex than they had thought. Reactions with other compounds, they reported, may slow down CFC's ability to deplete the ozone, so their earlier estimates of the rate of ozone destruction may have been overstated.[13] The National Academy of Sciences, taking this new information into account, issued a report in September 1976 that concluded that global ozone losses produced by CFCs should be revised downward to a probable 7 percent during the next fifty years, although actual depletion could be anywhere between 2 and 20 percent.

Congress, uncertain what to do, decided in 1977 not to pass legislation directly banning CFCs, but instead voted to give federal regulatory agencies the authority to regulate CFC emissions if agency officials decided that these "may reasonably be anticipated to endanger public health or welfare."[14] On March 15, 1978, the heads of the Food and Drug Administration, the Environmental Protection Agency, and the Consumer Product Safety Commission announced that they had reached a joint decision to place a federal ban on all "nonessential" use of CFCs in the United States. The ban outlawed the use of chlorofluorocarbons in 98 percent of all aerosol sprays, but allowed their use to continue as coolants in refrigerators, air conditioners, in the manufacture of foams and solvents, and to clean electronic

[12] "The Ozone Layers vs the Aerosol Industry: DuPont Wants to See Them Both Survive," advertisement, *New York Times*, 30 June 1975.

[13] See Paul Brodeur, "Annuals of Chemistry: In the Face of Doubt," *The New Yorker*, 9 June 1986.

[14] See Douglas G. Cogan, *Stones in a Glass House: CFCs and Ozone Depletion* (Washington, DC: Investor Responsibility Research Center Inc., 1988), p. 32.

parts, uses which together accounted for about 50 percent of the fluorocarbons being produced before the ban. Also, the ban permitted the sale of fluorocarbon sprays already manufactued until April 1979 and put no restrictions on foreign sales of CFCs. Canada, Norway, and Sweden passed similar bans, but other nations did not follow.

In November 1979, the National Academy of Sciences announced that its researchers had found that the ozone layer was actually being depleted at twice the 7.6 percent rate it had finally accepted as probable in 1976.[15] According to the academy's National Research Council's panel on stratospheric chemistry, current uses of fluorocarbon chemicals "will result in ozone depletion that is calculated to reach 16.5 percent, half of which will occur over the next thirty years." The revised estimates were the results of improved atmospheric tests and improved mathematical models that had been used in a study done for the Environmental Protection Agency. These improved techniques also narrowed the range of uncertainty of the predictions to one chance out of twenty that the predictions could be wrong. In addition, the report warned of sharp increases in human skin cancer rates and of widespread destruction to food crops, ocean phytoplankton, and other sea organisms that provided the basic support of the marine food chain.

However, not everyone agreed with the Academy report. A committee of British scientists issued a study prepared for Britain's Department of the Environment in 1979 that concluded that although their computer models supported the findings of the Academy of Sciences, these models were nevertheless uncertain. Calling attention to the British study, DuPont officials argued that ozone depletion theories were all "based on a series of uncertain assumptions" and that "no ozone depletion has ever been detected, despite the most sophisticated analysis."[16] Industry leaders pointed out that in the United States alone, CFCs were essential to keeping food from rotting in 100 million home refrigerators, to transporting food unspoiled on 180,000 refrigerated trucks and 27,000 refrigerated railroad cars, to selling fresh food in 40,000 supermarkets and 180,000 food stores, and to keep food fresh in 250,000 restaurants. Indeed, American society as presently constituted could not feed itself if CFCs were to vanish overnight. An estimated $135 billion of equipment would become useless, and $28 billion worth of CFC-dependent economic activities would be destroyed.

Nevertheless, in March 1980, several European nations (including Canada, Denmark, the Netherlands, West Germany, Sweden, and Norway) convened in Norway and in April 1980 agreed that all major CFC-producing countries should decrease CFC production. Japan agreed to do the same in September 1980. And in the United States, on October 7, 1980, the Environmental Protection Agency announced plans to propose a "no-growth" policy on the manufacture of fluorocarbons.[17] Charles Masten, director of DuPont's freon products division, denounced the proposal as "unwarranted at this time." According to Mr. Masten new evidence had been found that cast doubt on the validity of the ozone theory.

[15] "Rate of Destruction Revised Upward for Earth's Ozone Layer," *San Jose Mercury*, 9 November 1979, p. 2F.

[16] *Ibid.*, p. 34.

[17] "EPA Wants to Halt Growth of Substances that Harm Ozone," *San Jose Mercury*, 8 October 1980, p. 17A.

With the election of Ronald Reagan and his promise to ''get government off the backs of the American people,'' however, all U.S. government efforts to control CFCs slowed to a halt. In response, DuPont in June 1980 decided to suspend its research on alternatives to CFCs, reasoning that there was no economic justification for investing in alternatives for which there was not yet a ready market. This decision seemed to receive some limited support when in March 1982 the National Academy of Sciences issued a third report revising its estimates of future ozone loss downward to between 5 and 9 percent, half of the levels predicted in its 1979 report. In 1983 officials at the EPA began talking privately about quietly withdrawing their 1980 plan to propose a ''no-growth'' policy for CFCs. A fourth report of the National Academy of Sciences in February 1984 again revised its estimates of global ozone loss due to CFCs downward, this time to only 2 to 4 percent, because of recent discoveries that reactions of methane and other atmospheric gases might generate ozone that would replace that destroyed by CFCs. While downgrading the ozone threat, however, the report issued an alarm about the growing concentrations of atmospheric carbon dioxide and its impact on atmospheric warning, or what has been called the ''greenhouse effect.''

In March 1985, representatives of twenty-one nations, including the United States, met in Vienna and agreed to cooperate in atmospheric research and monitoring of ozone levels. The United States, Canada, Norway, and Sweden supported a general worldwide CFC aerosol ban, but several other countries, including the members of the European Community, Japan, and the Soviet Union, were against such measures, and no agreement on curbing the use of CFCs was reached.

Then, in May 1985, Joseph Farman, a scientist from the British Antarctic Survey reported that detectors on the ground had for seven years been indicating the development each winter of a giant hole in the ozone layer over the Antarctic. Shortly thereafter, satellite observations confirmed the presence of the gigantic hole, the first frighteningly clear and direct evidence that the ozone layer was indeed breaking down at tremendously high rates: Observations in October 1985 indicated a loss of more than 50 percent of the ozone over the vast arctic region. The publicity given to the reports, coupled with a successful (in October 1985) lawsuit brought against the EPA by environmentalists who felt the EPA was moving too slowly, spurred the EPA into action, and on January 1986 it announced plans to regulate CFCs.

Industry reactions to the new discoveries and the EPA plans were protective. Speaking on behalf of the Alliance for Responsible CFC Policy, a group of CFC industry producers and users, chairman Richard Barnett downplayed the new observations, arguing that since ozone levels unexplainably returned to near normal over the Antarctic during springtime, it was still unclear what was going on in the stratosphere. In light of such uncertainties, he said, the CFC industry was being unfairly singled out for regulation. Moreover, he pointed out, even the models relied on by scientists pushing their ozone depletion theories suggested that there would be no significant change in total ozone for several decades.

DuPont decided to continue expanding its CFC production capacity in Japan, as it had announced it would do in 1985. Allied-Signal, the second-largest producer of CFCs, was reported to be planning to increase sales of CFCs to the expanding computer industry, which used CFCs to clean electronic parts. Other CFC producers continued with their plans to increase CFC production, especially in other parts of the world. DuPont and others, however, quietly decided to reactivate their research programs on alternatives to CFCs.

During the winter of 1986, a special scientific expedition to the Antarctic, funded in part by the chemical industry, once again recorded the return of the ozone hole in early September, its growth through the winter, and its gradual decrease and disappearance in early November. The scientists, reached no clear conclusions about its causes, but their report again alarmed people around the world.

Meanwhile, leaders of the CFC industry were changing their positions. On September 16, 1986, the Alliance for Responsible CFC Policy announced its support for "a reasonable global limit on the future rate of growth" of CFC production. On September 26, Joseph Glas, director of DuPont's Freon Products Division, released a letter to customers stating it was now DuPont's position that "it would be prudent to take further precautionary measures to limit the growth of CFCs worldwide."[18] However, DuPont and other U.S. producers lobbied hard against any federal legislation that would limit American production of CFCs until there were international agreements placing similar global limits on producers outside the United States.[19] The Reagan administration, through Interior Secretary Donald Hodel, suggested, moreover, that CFC reductions might not be necessary so long as people wore hats, sunglasses, and suntan lotion to ward off any increased ultraviolet rays.[20] Environmentalists pointed out that it would cost $10 billion a year to provide glasses, hats, and suntan lotion for every American, ten times what it would cost to freeze CFC production for a decade, and that this would still leave wildlife unprotected since "its very hard to get fish to wear sunscreen."[21]

Stung by reactions to its lack of support for CFC limits, the Reagan administration in June 1987 came out in favor of international limits of CFC production as supported by the CFC industry. In September 1987, delegates from sixty-four nations, including the United States, met in Montreal, Canada, to negotiate an international agreement on CFC production. On September 16, twenty-four of the nations attending, the United States among them, agreed to freeze CFC consumption at 1986 levels, beginning in 1989, and to cut consumption in half by 1996. A number of less developed nations, which account for about 15 percent of global consumption of CFCs, refused to go along with the agreement because of the critical role that CFCs play in their plans for economic development. Because of their refusal, and because of other exceptions to the agreements, global consumption of CFCs would be cut by only by about 35 percent by 1996, instead of the hoped-for goal of 50 percent reductions. Nevertheless, officials of KaiserTech and other CFC producers argued that the Montreal agreement would be "catastrophic" for their businesses.

Industry figures remained opposed to the complete termination of CFC pro-

[18] *Ibid.*, p. 50.

[19] Richard Barnett, "The U.S. Can't Do the Job All Alone," *New York Times*, November 16, 1986.

[20] Cass Peterson, "Administration Ozone Policy May Favor Sunglasses, Hats," *Washington Post*, 29 May 1987.

[21] Robert Taylor, "Advice on Ozone May Be: 'Wear Hats and Stand in the Shade,' " *Wall Street Journal*, 29 May 1987.

duction and, in fact, still urged gradual increases in production. Edwin E. Tuttle, chairman of Pennwalt, the third-largest U.S. manufacturer of CFCs, argued that ceasing production would "create economic chaos for the consumer," and "without far greater scientific justification . . . would . . . be irresponsible." Robert Traflet, president of Allied-Signal's Fluorine Products Division, assured Congress in May 1987 that "you'd feel very safe" with increased production rates of 3 percent a year. Elwood P. Blanchard, DuPont's executive vice president in charge of chemicals, suggested that annual production increases of 4 or 5 percent during the next 30 to 40 years would be tolerable and that ozone depletion should not "cause us concern" for "maybe a hundred years." EPA director Eileen Claussen, however, argued that "If CFC use continues to grow at 2.5 percent a year . . . the number of skin cancer cases in the United States would increase by 105 million and the number of early deaths by 2 million for those alive today and born through 2075." DuPont chairman, Richard Heckert, in a March 4 letter to Senator Stafford, stated that "scientific evidence does not point to the need for dramatic CFC emission reductions," and that suggestions that DuPont cease CFC production within a year were "unwarranted and counterproductive," since "there is no agreement within the scientific community on the potential health effects of any already observed ozone change."[22]

In the winter of 1987, the frightening ozone hole over the Antarctic was again observed, this time larger and deeper than ever before. Researchers flying through the hole discovered the presence of ice crystals that seemed to have been speeding up the reactions that were depleting the ozone over the Antarctic. In the United States, an international panel of more than 100 scientists brought together as the "Ozone Trends Panel," was conducting an exhaustive survey and reevaluation of all the scientific data available to date on ozone depletion. The panel issued a report on March 15, 1987, stating that ozone levels worldwide had fallen 1.7 percent between 1969 and 1985, and that wintertime ozone levels were dropping 3 to 5 percent all over the world and as much as 6.2 percent over northern latitudes. Moreover, the panel of 100 scientists concluded, the presence of chlorine monoxide radicals inside the Antarctic hole was clear evidence that CFCs, together with atmospheric climatic factors, were responsible for ozone depletion.[23]

The report sent a shock through DuPont executives who still held that there was little agreement within the scientific community about the ozone threat. Three days after the report was issued, DuPont's executive committee gathered at company headquarters in Wilmington, Delaware, to discuss the panel's findings. The committee closely questioned a DuPont staff scientist, Dr. Mack McFarland, who had served as a member of the panel, and Joseph Steed, a DuPont environmental manager, about the reliability of the report's findings. Both confirmed the report's conclusion that CFCs were the most likely cause of a worldwide decline in ozone to a level that had not been expected until early in the next century. Even if CFC production was cut by 50 percent by 1999, concentrations of CFC in the stratosphere would still climb to over five times the levels present the year the

[22] Cogan, *Stones in a Glass House*, pp. 71–74.

[23] Ozone Trends Panel, "Executive Summary" (Washington, DC: National Aeronatutics and Space Administration, Feb. 8, 1988); see also, Philip Shabecoff, "Study Shows Significant Decline in Ozone Layer," *New York Times*, 16 March 1988.

Antarctic ozone hole had first appeared. After intense discussions, the six-person committee came to the conclusion that DuPont would stop manufacturing CFCs by around the turn of the century. Six days later, on March 24, the committee announced the company's new CFC phase-out policy to the 2,000 employees involved in CFC production and to the press. DuPont's sales of CFCs that year were to total $600 million, or 2 percent of its revenues, and contribute $35 million to its profits. On the day of the announcement, DuPont's stock fell by $3.13. DuPont officials stated that it was not clear whether any of the substitutes the company was researching were commercially viable or environmentally safe, that all of them would cost two to five times more than CFCs, and that it was uncertain whether losses of CFC sales revenues could be replaced by sales of alternatives. Other CFC producers did not follow DuPont's lead, although Penwalt, the third-largest CFC producer, released a statement on the same day, urging that CFC production be stopped as soon as practical and committing itself to an eventual phase-out.

In December 1987, the EPA proposed regulations that would freeze CFC consumption in the United States at 1986 levels starting in 1989, and would reduce consumption by a further 50 percent by the end of the century, more or less in line with the Montreal agreements. The EPA estimated that the total social costs of its regulations would reach $27 billion by 2075, but that if it failed to act, the costs in cancer deaths, medical expenses, damage to crops, materials, the fishing industry, and the effects of rising sea levels would reach $6.5 trillion by 2075. Environmentalists criticized the EPA regulations, however, arguing that nothing short of a complete ban by the end of the century would be adequate. In 1989, twelve European Community nations agreed to a complete ban of all CFCs by the year 2000, a move that was endorsed by U.S. President Bush. In October 1990 Congress passed and President Bush signed the 1990 Clean Air Act, which required a complete end to the U.S. production of CFCs by the year 2000.

1990 world opinion and U.S. cooperation was partially due to the new records set by each of the ominous seasonal reappearances of the ozone hole over Antarctica in 1987, 1988, and 1989. While the 1988 hole was somewhat smaller than the record-breaking hole that developed in the winter of 1987, the 1989 hole broke all records. As early as August 1989, ozone within the hole had begun to decrease: The rate of ozone decline accelerated to about 1.5 percent per day during September, and by October 5, 1989, nearly half of the ozone over the Antarctic was gone. The hole has continued to reappear each year to this very day. Ozone-depleted air from the hole now migrates out of the Antarctica and is blown over other parts of the world. Ozone losses of 10 percent have been recorded over New Zealand, southern Australia, and other parts of the world.

Commenting on DuPont's change of heart in 1987, Senator Stafford of Vermont said simply, "I hope it isn't too late." Even if all CFC production were to stop tomorrow, the CFCs already released will continue to float upward and raise CFC concentrations in the stratosphere to one-and-a-half times present levels by the year 2000. They will remain there for 40 to 50 years, continuing their destruction of the ozone layer. Additional CFCs produced between now and the year 2000 will multiply and prolong this destruction. Further damage will be caused when inevitably each of us disposes or releases the CFC gases locked in the innards of each of our refrigerators, freezers, auto and home air conditioners, and the rigid foams insulating our walls. We have no idea how our world will change over the next fifty years.

1. Describe the strategies which DuPont's management used to respond to the ozone controversy before the 1978 ban. Identify the social costs and risks associated with these strategies and the populations that bore these costs and risks. Identify the social benefits deriving from these strategies and the groups that derived these benefits. In your judgment, did the social benefits outweigh the social costs and risks? Explain your answer fully.
2. Evaluate the moral quality of DuPont's strategies after 1978 in terms of (a) the utilitarian costs and benefits associated with those strategies as compared to other alternative strategies, (b) the moral rights of the various parties affected, and (c) the just or unjust way in which benefits and burdens were distributed among various populations by these strategies.
3. In view of the uncertainty and differences of opinion surrounding the theory of ozone depletion, were the strategies that DuPont adopted to respond to the controversy morally blameworthy? In your judgment, would DuPont be morally responsible for any health injuries that may result from the depletion of the ozone layer years later? Why?

Asarco and Jobs

The Asarco company copper smelter in Tacoma, Washington, with its 571-foot smokestack, had been famous for years for its contributions to the ripe "aroma of Tacoma." But the unpleasant odor was not the only thing the company contributed to the city's air. The smelter processed copper from ore with a high arsenic content, and some of this arsenic was vented into the air through the smokestack. During the previous decade the company had invested $40 million to reduce its arsenic emissions. However, on July 12, 1983, the Environmental Protection Agency (EPA), the federal agency charged with enforcing the nation's environmental laws, announced that the plant was still spewing 115 tons of arsenic into the air every year and that a new court ruling on federal regulations would require reductions of at least 25 percent. The arsenic, according to the EPA, was a carcinogenic for which there probably was no safe "threshold": even a tiny amount might cause cancer in some people. According to the EPA, the arsenic currently being emitted from the smelter was estimated to be producing about four lung cancers a year. The new standard would require the company to spend $4.5 million more on pollution control equipment that would reduce emissions of arsenic to a level that would produce about one lung cancer per year. In a statement issued at the time, Asarco officials announced that they intended to adhere to the new regulations and that the company was willing to spend the money required to bring its emissions into line with the new court-mandated standards.

The EPA also announced that the company even might be required by the EPA to reduce its arsenic emissions to zero. But according to its calculations reducing the emissions to a level that would completely eliminate all risk of cancer would require such an investment in pollution control that the smelter would no longer be economically viable. Since the smelter employed about 570 people and pumped about $20 million per year into the local economy, closing the smelter would have a substantial negative impact on Tacoma residents. However, the EPA announcement continued, in accord with a new policy of involving the public in its enforcement activities, it would give Tacoma residents a choice during hearings that would be held over the next several months: If Tacoma residents wanted, the EPA would require the smelter to completely eliminate its arsenic emissions although this would force the smelter to close down. The residents thus had a choice: Either they could choose to lose one additional person per year to death by cancer or they could choose to lose 570 jobs and $20 million.[1]

Opinions on the terrible choice posed by the EPA announcement varied widely. Tacoma's young mothers, like Ann Leask, 30, were frightened by the high arsenic levels that researchers had found in their children's hair: "[Cancer] is such an ugly way to die," she said as her eyes filled with tears, "It scares me to death to think we might have to contend with that with [our son] Ryan." Workers, such as Bill Powers, were skeptical of the EPA's estimates of the health risks involved: "I think it's a lot of baloney!"[2]

Ralph L. Henneback, chairman of Asarco, argued that the risk estimates of the EPA were exaggerated:

> We are convinced, based on studies of lung cancer incidence, that the risk of contracting lung cancer is no greater in Tacoma than in any other urban area . . . The proposed arsenic standards, it seems to me, reflect the realization that government regulators do not have at their disposal the means to protect us from all risks . . . The best we can do is reduce these risks to the lowest practicable level through the use of the best available technology. In cooperation with EPA we have been doing just that at our Tacoma plant and are well along on the installation of the technology specified in the proposed EPA arsenic regulations.[3]

The EPA admitted that some uncertainties surrounded their estimates of the health risks of the airborne arsenic. Doctor Sam Milham, head of the epidemiology section of the Washington State Department of Social and Health Services said that his own studies of lung cancer had failed to show any increase in the health risks of people living downwind from the smelter. EPA officials in Seattle themselves said that their data might be unreliable. The newly appointed head of the EPA, William D. Ruckelshous, defended his new policy of giving local communities a voice in determining whether an estimated (but uncertain) risk was acceptable: "For me to sit here in Washington and tell the people of Tacoma what is an acceptable risk would be at best arrogant and at worst inexcusable."[4]

1. Discuss the level of pollution prevention that, in your judgment, the Tacoma Asarco plant managers should have installed. Justify your position in terms of the utilitarian, rights, and justice perspectives that you believe apply to the case.
2. Discuss the ethics of the William D. Ruckelshous policy to allow the local community to decide whether to have the Tacoma plant shut down. In your judgment, is it possible for the community to make a "free" decision in the matter? If the EPA

[1] *San Francisco Chronicle*, 13 July 1983, pp. 1, 4.

[2] *San Jose Mercury News*, 2 November 1983, p. 16a.

[3] *New York Times*, 27 July 1983, "An EPA Cancer Risk Study Put in Perspective."

[4] *New York Times*, 12 July 1983, p. 1.

reserved this decision to itself, how should it have decided? Explain your answer. Explain how a process of "hearings" differs from a process of voting. In your judgment are hearings an appropriate method for determining whether the members of a community consent to a policy?

3. If you were a member of the Tacoma community, what would you have wanted the Asarco plant to do? Why?

emphasized the confidentiality that would be required from Johnson. Already, in his first two weeks, Johnson had been astonished by the number of sensitive discussions he was invited to sit in on.

6

THE ETHICS OF CONSUMER PRODUCTION AND MARKETING

INTRODUCTION

In April 1988, staff members of the Food and Drug Administration announced the results of a study that, they claimed, showed that the drug Accutane, a treatment for acne produced by Hoffman-La Roche, Inc., was being widely misused.[1] High doses of Accutane, they pointed out, can cause severe damage to fetuses and pregnant women, including birth defects and miscarriages. Yet their study, they claimed, showed that 52 percent of the women to whom Accutane had been administered had been pregnant at some point during their treatment. They estimated the drug was responsible for about 1,000 birth defects nationwide, 1,000 miscarriages, and thousands of voluntary abortions. Hoffman-La Roche charged that the study was "invalid" but agreed to impose future "restrictions" on uses of the drug.[2]

In 1985, Ethel Smith flicked on a Bic Corporation lighter to light her cigarette. It exploded in her hands, killing her and severely burning her husband. Earlier, Cynthia Littlejohn suffered severe burns about her torso that required seven painful skin grafts when a Bic lighter in her pocket spontaneously ignited and enveloped

[1] Michael Waldolz, "Study of Accutane and Birth Defects Stirs Debate on Use," *Wall Street Journal*, 25 April 1988, p. 4.

[2] Philip M. Boffey, "Maker of Drug for Acne Calls Birth-Defect Report 'Invalid,'" *New York Times*, 23 April 1988, pp. 1,9.

her in flames.[3] The company later confessed that its own tests showed that 1.2 percent of its lighters were faulty. Experts claimed that the defects could have been corrected for "a couple of pennies a lighter." Some 200 people a year, half of them children, are killed in lighter-related injuries.[4]

In March 1984, Christa Berlin was hospitalized with abdominal pain and fever. Twenty days later, she was dead. Her death was attributed to a pelvic abscess caused by the "Dalkon Shield," a birth control device inserted into her uterus that was produced by A. H. Robins Company, a pharmaceutical manufacturer.[5] As a result of using the birth control device, dozens of other women died similar deaths, thousands suffered the life-threatening infections known as pelvic inflammatory disease, some 10,000 suffered miscarriages, and hundreds gave birth prematurely to babies with congenital defects including blindness, cerebral palsy, and mental retardation.[6] Yet as early as 1973 the company had been aware of the deaths of six women associated with infected abortions.[7] A. H. Robins, however, continued to aggressively market the product until over 2.2 million women in the United States and 1 million women abroad were wearing them.

By 1986, all-terrain vehicles (ATVs) introduced in 1982 by Honda (with about 60 percent of the market), Kawasaki, Suzuki, and Yamaha had killed well over 600 people and injured 275,000, leaving many crippled for life. About half of the casualties inflicted by the three-wheeled motorcycles involved children.[8] Although concerned consumer advocates claimed that the machines incorporated design flaws that rendered them inherently unstable, that they were inappropriate for marketing to children, and that the companies should recall the risky three-wheelers, the companies continued to market the machines and refused to hear of a recall.

Americans are exposed daily to astonishingly high levels of risk from the use of consumer products. Each year thirty-four million people are injured in accidents involving consumer items; of these, 28,000 are killed and perhaps 100,000 are permanently disabled.[9] Product-related accidents are the major cause of death for people between the ages of one and thirty-six, outstripping the deaths caused by cancer or heart disease. The total cost of these injuries is estimated to be about $12 billion per year.[10]

But product injuries make up only one category of costs imposed on unwary

[3] Frederick D. Sturdivant and Heidi Vernon-Wortzel, *Business and Society: A Managerial Approach*, 4th ed. (Homewood, IL: Irwin, 1990), pp. 310–11.

[4] *Ibid.*

[5] Morton Mintz, "At Any Cost: Corporate Greed, Women, and the Dalkon Shield," in Stuart L. Hills, ed., *Corporate Violence: Injury and Death for Profit* (Totowa, NJ: Rowman & Littlefield, 1987), p. 37.

[6] *Ibid.*, p. 31.

[7] Rogene A. Buchholz, William D. Evans, and Robert A. Wagley, *Management Response to Public Issues* (Englewood Cliffs, NJ: Prentice Hall, 1989), p. 303.

[8] John R. Emshwiller, "All-Terrain Vehicles Spark Debate as User Deaths and Injuries Mount," *Wall Street Journal*, 11 February 1987, p. 29.

[9] Consumer Product Safety Commission, *1983 Annual Report*, part 1, (Washington, DC: U.S. Government Printing Office, 1983), p. 11.

[10] *Ibid.*

consumers. Consumers must also bear the costs of deceptive selling practices, of shoddy product construction, of products that immediately break down, and of warranties that are not honored. For example, a few years ago, the engine of Martha and George Rose's Chevrolet station wagon began missing and white smoke poured out of the tailpipe as she drove it six miles to work.[11] Two non-Chevrolet mechanics who then checked the car later testified that the radiator and cooling system were "in satisfactory condition," that the radiator "was not boiling over," and that the temperature light on the dashboard "was not burning." Upon taking the engine apart, a mechanic found that a hairline crack in the engine block had allowed water to enter the cylinder head, meaning that the car would need an expensive new engine. The engine was still under a "5-year or 50,000-mile" warranty, so the Roses thought the Chevrolet division of General Motors would bear the large costs of repairing what they concluded was an inherently defective engine block. However, when a Chevrolet service manager examined the dismantled car, he insisted that the problem was that the radiator thermostat had stuck shut so no coolant had reached the engine. Since the thermostat was only under a "12-month or 12,000-miles" warranty that had by then expired, and since, the Chevrolet manager claimed, the faulty thermostat had caused the engine to overheat and the engine block to crack, Chevrolet had no responsibility under the warranty. Moreover, the car had been torn down and worked on by unauthorized mechanics. Although the Roses pointed out that the other mechanics had found no evidence of overheating and that no Chevrolet mechanic had suggested replacing the thermostat at any of their regular maintenance servicings, the General Motors field manager and his superiors, both in New Orleans and in Detroit, refused to honor the warranty. Without the engine, the car that General Motors had sold them for $5000 was now worth only $600. Because they could not afford an attorney for a trial they might lose, the Roses could not file suit against General Motors.

The sales practices of Pacific Bell Telephone Company, which serves California telephone customers, provide another illustration of the difficulties that face consumers. On April 23, 1986, the Pacific Utilities Commission of California released a report stating that Pacific Bell service representatives were duping new telephone customers into buying expensive optional features by quoting a fee for new telephone service that included the expensive features, but without telling the new customer that the features were optional, that the consumer was being charged extra for them, and that basic service was available at a much cheaper monthly fee. A sales representative of the telephone company described the way that she approached a new customer calling to get a new telephone hook-up:

> I'm going to tell you that "You will get unlimited local calling, Touchtone service, our four, custom-calling services and a 20 percent discount in the Pacific Bell service area; the central office fee to turn the services on is $37.50 and I have all of these things available and its only $22.20 a month." Most customers will say, "That's fine." It really isn't a bad deal, but how many people know they don't have to buy all those things, that they can get basic service for $9.95? The company says, "People

[11] The facts summarized in this paragraph are drawn from Penny Addis, "The Life History Complaint Case of Martha and George Rose: 'Honoring the Warranty,' " in *No Access to Law*, Laura Nader, ed. (New York: Academic Press, Inc., 1980), pp. 171–89.

> should be intelligent enough to ask; why should it be PacBell's job to tell them?'' People who don't speak English, well, they end up with those services. Sometimes they call back and say, ''What is this? I didn't want this.'' [Pacific Telephone sales representative][12]

According to the Utilities Commission report, 65 percent of Pacific Bell's phone order centers did not quote the basic $9.95 monthly rate that allowed unlimited local calls, but instead quoted only a ''standard price'' which included extra features (such as a device that tells a customer another call is waiting, automatic forwarding of a call to another phone, equipment for three-way or conference calls, codes that automatically dial a preset number, and extra charges for call discounts at certain times or certain areas) that cost as much as $27.20 a month. The sales representatives pleaded that the company's marketing managers imposed stiff sales quotas on them and would put them on probation if they failed to meet the quotas. In one city, for example, they were expected to sell $197 to $238 worth of services each hour they spent on the telephone with customers. A Utilities Commission staff member remarked that ''Marketing management appears to be more concerned about generating revenues than they are about ethical and fair treatment of customers.''[13]

Consumers are also bombarded daily by an endless series of advertisements urging them to buy certain products. Although sometimes defended as sources of information, advertisements are also criticized on the grounds that they rarely do more than give the barest indications of the basic function a product is meant to serve and sometimes misrepresent and exaggerate its virtues. Economists argue that advertising expenditures are a waste of resources, while sociologists bemoan the cultural effects of advertising.[14]

This chapter examines various ethical issues raised by product quality and advertising. The first few sections discuss various approaches to consumer issues and the last sections deal with consumer advertising. We will begin with a focus on what is perhaps the most urgent issue: consumer product injuries and the responsibilities of manufacturers.

6.1 MARKETS AND CONSUMER PROTECTION

Consumer analysts point out that in 1986 alone there were more than 400,000 injuries requiring hospital treatment inflicted on youngsters and adults using toys, nursery equipment, and playground equipment; more than 292,000 people were mangled using home workshop equipment and over 200 of these were killed; 1,425,000 people needed emergency treatment for injuries involving home furnishings and over 1,000 of these injuries resulted in death; 2,722,000 more people

[12] Quoted in Ed Pope, ''PacBell's Sales Quotas,'' *San Jose Mercury News*, 24 April 1986, p. 1C; see also ''PacBell Accused of Sales Abuse,'' *San Jose Mercury News*, 24 April 1986, p. 1A; ''PacBell Offers Refund for Unwanted Services,'' *San Jose Mercury News*, 17 May 1986, p. 1A.

[13] *Ibid*, p. 134.

[14] Several of these criticisms are surveyed in Stephen A. Greyser, ''Advertising: Attacks and Counters,'' *Harvard Business Review*, 50 (10 March 1972): 22–28.

required treatment for injuries involving home construction materials that killed at least 1,500 of them.[15] Injuries from auto-related accidents average 70,000 each week; deaths average 1,000 per week; financial losses are estimated at $30 million per day.

Many people believe that consumers will be automatically protected from injury by the operations of free and competitive markets, and that neither governments nor businesspeople have to take special steps to deal with these issues. As we have seen in earlier chapters (particularly in Chapter Four), free markets promote an allocation, use, and distribution of goods that is, in a certain sense, just, respectful of rights, and efficiently productive of maximum utility for those who participate in the market. Moreover, in such markets, the consumer is said to be "sovereign." When consumers want and will willingly pay for something, sellers have an incentive to cater to their wishes. If sellers do not provide what consumers want, then sellers will suffer losses. But when sellers provide what consumers want, they will profit. As the author of a leading textbook on economics writes, "Consumers direct by their innate or learned tastes, as expressed in their dollar votes, the ultimate uses to which society's resources are channeled."[16]

In the "market" approach to consumer protection, consumer safety is seen as a good that is most efficiently provided through the mechanism of the free market whereby sellers must respond to consumer demands. If consumers want products to be safer, then they will indicate this preference in markets by willingly paying more for safer products and by showing a preference for manufacturers of safe products while turning down the goods of manufacturers of unsafe products. Producers will have to respond to this demand by building more safety into their products or they risk losing customers to competitors who cater to the preferences of consumers. Thus, the market ensures that producers respond adequately to consumers' desires for safety. On the other hand, if consumers do not place a high value on safety and demonstrate neither a willingness to pay more for safety nor a preference for safer products, then it is wrong to push increased levels of safety down their throats through government regulations that force producers to build more safety into their products than consumers demand. Such government interference, as we saw earlier, distorts markets, making them unjust, disrespectful of rights, and inefficient. It is just as wrong for businesspeople to decide on their own that consumers should have more protection than they are demanding, and to force on them costly safety devices that they would not buy on their own. Only consumers can say what value they place on safety, and they should be allowed to register their preferences through their free choices in markets and not be coerced by businesses or governments into paying for safety levels they may not want.

For example, an appliance selling for $100 may indicate that it will overheat if it is used for more than an hour and a half, while one selling for $400 may indicate that it can be run safely all day and night continuously. Some buyers will prefer the cheaper model, willingly trading the somewhat higher risk for the $300 cut in price, while others will prefer the more expensive one. If government

[15] National Safety Council, *Accident Facts, 1988 Edition* (Chicago, IL: National Safety Council, 1988), p. 95.

[16] Paul A. Samuelson and William D. Nordhaus, *Macroeconomics*, 13th ed. (New York: McGraw-Hill Book Company, 1989), p. 41.

regulations forced all appliance makers to make only the safer model, or if manufacturers voluntarily decided to make only the safer model, then consumers who do not feel that the increase in safety is worth $300 extra to them will be out of luck. If they cannot do without the appliance, they will be forced to pay the extra $300 even if they would have preferred spending it on something else that is more valuable to them. They are thus unjustly forced to pay money for something they do not want, and their resources are inefficiently wasted on something that produces little utility for anyone.

Critics to this market approach respond, however, that the benefits of free markets obtain with certainty only when markets have the seven characteristics that define them: (1) there are numerous buyers and sellers, (2) everyone can freely enter and exit the market, (3) everyone has full and perfect information, (4) all goods in the market are exactly similar, (5) there are no external costs, (6) all buyers and sellers are rational utility maximizers, and (7) the market is unregulated. Critics of the market approach to consumer issues argue that these characteristics are absent in consumer markets, focusing especially on characteristics (3) and (6).

Markets are efficient, critics point out, only if condition (3) obtains—that is, only if participants have full and perfect information about the goods they are buying. But obviously, consumers are frequently not well informed about the products they buy simply because the sophisticated consumer products on contemporary market shelves are too complex for anyone but an expert to be knowledgeable about them. Not surprisingly, manufacturers, who are knowledgeable about their products, might not voluntarily provide information about the safety levels or defective characteristics of their products to consumers. And, since gathering information is expensive, a consumer may not have the resources to acquire the information on his or her own by, for example, testing several competing brands to determine which provides the most safety for the cost.

In theory it would be possible for consumers who want information to turn to organizations such as the Consumers Union that make a business of acquiring and selling product information. That is, market mechanisms should create a market in consumer information if that is what consumers want. But for two reasons related to the nature of information, it is difficult for such organizations to cover their costs by selling information to consumers. First, as several economists have pointed out, once information is provided to one person who pays for it, it is easily leaked to many others who do not pay, especially in this age of photocopiers.[17] Since people know they can become "free riders" and acquire the information compiled by others without paying for it themselves, the number of people who willingly pay for the information is too small to allow the organization to cover its costs. Second, consumers are often unwilling to pay for information because they do not know what its value to them will be until after they get it and then they no longer need to pay for it since it is already in their possession. For example, a consumer may pay for the information contained in a research report and then find that he or she already knew what was in the report, or that it is about products other than those he or she wants to buy, or that it is irrelevant

[17] See Robert N. Mayer, *The Consumer Movement: Guardians of the Marketplace* (Boston: Twayne Publishers, 1989), p. 67; and Peter Asch, *Consumer Safety Regulation* (New York: Oxford University Press, 1988), p. 50.

information about those products. Since consumers cannot know in advance precisely what they are buying when they buy information, they are unwilling to pay the costs organizations must charge to gather the information.[18] Markets alone, then, are not able to support organizations that can provide consumers with the information they need. Instead, such organizations must rely on charitable contributions or on government grants.

A second criticism of the argument that free markets can deal with all consumer issues takes aim at characteristic (6) of free markets: the assumption that the consumer is a "rational utility maximizer." As one author put it, the consumer assumed by such arguments is "a budget-minded, rational individual, relentlessly pushing toward maximizing his satisfaction . . . [who is able] to think well ahead, to "wait," to consider. The consumer defined by the theory watches every penny."[19] More precisely, the "rational utility maximizer" that the consumer is assumed to be, is a person who has a well-defined and consistent set of preferences, and who is certain how his or her choices will affect those preferences.

Unfortunately, virtually all consumer choices are based on probability estimates we make concerning the chances that the products we buy will function as we think they will. And all the research available shows that we become highly inept, irrational, and inconsistent when we make choices based on probability estimates.

First, as is obvious to any observer, few of us are good at estimating probabilities. We typically underestimate the risks of personal life-threatening activities—such as driving, smoking, eating fried foods—and of being injured by the products we use, and we overestimate the probabilities of unlikely but memorable events such as tornados or attacks by grizzly bears in national parks.[20] Studies have shown that our probability judgments go astray for a number of reasons, including the following:

1. Prior probabilities are ignored when new information becomes available, even if the new information is irrelevant.
2. Emphasis on "causation" results in the underweighting of evidence that is relevant to probability but is not perceived as "causal."
3. Generalizations are made on the basis of small sample findings.
4. Belief is placed in a self-correcting but nonexistent "law of averages."
5. People believe that they exert control over purely chance events.[21]

Second, as a number of researchers have shown, people are irrational and inconsistent when weighing choices based on probability estimates of future costs or payoffs. For example, one set of researchers found that when people are asked to rank probable payoffs, they inconsistently will rank one payoff as being *both* better and worse than another. Another investigator found that when people were asked which of two probable payoffs they preferred, they would often say that they would pay *more* for the payoff that they *least* preferred. Yet another set of

[18] Peter Asch, *Consumer Safety Regulation*, p. 51.

[19] Lucy Black Creighton, *Pretenders to the Throne: The Consumer Movement in the United States* (Lexington, MA: Lexington Books, 1976), p. 85.

[20] Peter Asch, *Consumer Safety Regulation*, pp. 74, 76.

[21] *Ibid.*

studies found that in many cases, a majority of persons would prefer one probable payoff to another in one context, but reversed their preferences in a different context although the probable payoffs were identical in both contexts.[22]

On balance, then, it does not appear that market forces by themselves can deal with all consumer concerns for safety and freedom from risk. Market failures, characterized by inadequate consumer information and by irrationality in the choices of consumers, undercut arguments that try to show that markets alone can provide adequate consumer protection. Instead, consumers must be protected through the legal structures of government and through the voluntary initiatives of responsible businesspeople. We will turn, then, to examining several views about the responsibilities of businesses toward consumers, views that have formed the basis of many of our consumer laws and of increased calls for greater acceptance of responsibility for consumer protection on the part of business.

It is clear, of course, that part of the responsibility for consumer injuries must rest on consumers themselves. Individuals are often careless in their use of products. "Do-it-yourselfers" use power saws without guards attached or inflammable liquids near open flames. People often use tools and instruments that they do not have the skill, the knowledge, or the experience to handle.

But injuries also arise from flaws in product design, in the materials out of which products are made, or in the processes used to construct products. Insofar as manufacturing defects are the source of product-related injuries, consumer advocates claim, the duty of minimizing injuries should lie with the manufacturer. The producer is in the best position to know the hazards raised by a certain product and to eliminate the hazards at the point of manufacture. In addition, the producer's expertise makes the producer knowledgeable about the safest materials and manufacturing methods and enables him to build adequate safeguards into the design of the product. Finally, because the producer is intimately acquainted with the workings of the product, he or she can best inform the consumer on the safest way to use the product and on what precautions to be taken.

Where, then, does the consumer's duties to protect his or her own interests end, and where does the manufacturer's duty to protect consumers' interests begin? Three different theories on the ethical duties of manufacturers have been developed, each one of which strikes a different balance between the consumer's duty to himself or herself and the manufacturer's duty to the consumer: the contract view, the "due care" view, and the social costs view. The contract view would place the greater responsibility on the consumer, while the "due care" and social costs views place the larger measure of responsibility on the manufacturer. We will examine each of these views.

6.2 THE CONTRACT VIEW OF BUSINESS'S DUTIES TO CONSUMERS

According to the contract view of the business firm's duties to its customers, the relationship between a business firm and its customers is essentially a contractual relationship, and the firm's moral duties to the customer are those created by this

[22] For references to these studies see *ibid*, pp. 70–73.

contractual relationship.[23] When a consumer buys a product, this view holds, the consumer voluntarily enters into a ''sales contract'' with the business firm. The firm freely and knowingly agrees to give the consumer a product with certain characteristics and the consumer in turn freely and knowingly agrees to pay a certain sum of money to the firm for the product. In virtue of having voluntarily entered this agreement, the firm then has a duty to provide a product with those characteristics, and the consumer has a correlative right to get a product with those characteristics.

The contract theory of the business firm's duties to its customers rests on the view that a contract is a free agreement that imposes on the parties the basic duty of complying with the terms of the agreement. We examined this view earlier (Chapter Two) and noted the two justifications Kant provided for the view: A person has a duty to do what he or she contracts to do, because failure to adhere to the terms of a contract is a practice (1) that cannot be universalized, and (2) that treats the other person as a means and not as an end.[24] Rawl's theory also provides a justification for the view, but one that is based on the idea that our freedom is expanded by the recognition of contractual rights and duties: An enforced system of social rules that requires people to do what they contract to do will provide them with the assurance that contracts will be kept. Only if they have such assurance will people feel able to trust each other's word, and on that basis to secure the benefits of the institution of contracts.[25]

We also noted in Chapter Two that traditional moralists have argued that the act of entering into a contract is subject to several secondary moral constraints:

1. Both of the parties to the contract must have full knowledge of the nature of the agreement they are entering.
2. Neither party to a contract must intentionally misrepresent the facts of the contractual situation to the other party.
3. Neither party to a contract must be forced to enter the contract under duress or undue influence.

These secondary constraints can be justified by the same sorts of arguments that Kant and Rawls use to justify the basic duty to perform one's contracts. Kant, for example, easily shows that misrepresentation in the making of a contract cannot be universalized, and Rawls argues that if misrepresentation were not prohibited, fear of deception would make members of a society feel less free to enter contracts. But these secondary constraints can also be justified on the grounds that a contract cannot exist unless these constraints are fulfilled. For a contract is essentially a *free agreement* struck between two parties. Since an agreement cannot exist unless both parties know what they are agreeing to, contracts require full knowledge

[23] See Thomas Garrett and Richard J. Klonoski, *Business Ethics*, 2nd ed. (Englewood Cliffs, New Jersey: Prentice Hall, 1986), p. 88.

[24] Immanual Kant, *Groundwork of the Metaphysic of Morals*, H. J. Paton, ed. (New York: Harper & Row, Publishers, Inc., 1964), pp. 90, 97; see also, Alan Donagan, *The Theory of Morality* (Chicago: The University of Chicago Press), 1977, p. 92.

[25] John Rawls, *A Theory of Justice* (Cambridge: Harvard University Press, Belknap Press, 1971), pp. 344–50.

and the absence of misrepresentation. And since freedom implies the absence of coercion, contracts must be made without duress or undue influence.

The contractual theory of business's duties to consumers, then, claims that a business has four main moral duties: The basic duty of (1) complying with the terms of the sales contract, and the secondary duties of (2) disclosing the nature of the product, (3) avoiding misrepresentation, and (4) avoiding the use of duress and undue influence. By acting in accordance with these duties, a business respects the right of consumers to be treated as free and equal persons, that is, in accordance with their right to be treated only as they have freely consented to be treated.

The Duty to Comply

The most basic moral duty that a business firm owes its customers, according to the contract view, is the duty to provide consumers with a product that lives up to those claims that the firm expressly made about the product, which led the customer to enter the contract freely, and which formed the customer's understanding concerning what he or she was agreeing to buy. In the early 1970s, for example, Winthrop Laboratories marketed a painkiller that the firm advertised as "nonaddictive." Subsequently, a patient using the painkiller became addicted to it and shortly died from an overdose. A court in 1974 found Winthrop Laboratories liable for the patient's death because, although it had expressly stated that the drug was nonaddictive, Winthrop Laboratories had failed to live up to its duty to comply with this express contractual claim.[26]

As the above example suggests, our legal system has incorporated the moral view that firms have a duty to live up to the express claims they make about their products. The Uniform Commercial Code, for example, states in Section 2-314:

> Any affirmation of fact or promise made by the seller to the buyer that related to the goods and becomes part of the basis of the bargain creates an express warranty that the goods shall conform to the affirmation or promise.

In addition to the duties that result from the *express* claim a seller makes about the product, the contract view also holds that the seller has a duty to carry through on any *implied* claims he or she knowingly makes about the product. The seller, for example, has the moral duty to provide a product that can be used safely for the ordinary and special purposes for which the customer, relying on the seller's judgment, has been led to believe it can be used. The seller is morally bound to do whatever he or she knows the buyer understood the seller was promising, since at the point of sale sellers should have corrected any misunderstandings they were aware of.[27]

This idea of an "implied agreement" has also been incorporated into the law. Section 2-315 of the Uniform Commercial Code, for example, reads:

> Where the seller at the time of contracting has reason to know any particular purpose for which the goods are required and that the buyer is relying on the seller's skill

[26] *Crocker* v. *Winthrop Laboratories, Division of Sterling Drug, Inc.*, 514 Southwestern 2d 429 (1974).

[27] See Donagan, *Theory of Morality*, p. 91.

> or judgment to select or furnish suitable goods, there is . . . an implied warranty that the goods shall be fit for such purpose.

The express or implied claims that a seller might make about the qualities possessed by the product range over a variety of areas and are affected by a number of factors. Frederick Sturdivant classifies these areas in terms of four variables: "The definition of product quality used here is: the degree to which product performance meets predetermined expectation with respect to (1) reliability, (2) service life, (3) maintainability, and (4) safety."[28]

Reliability Claims of reliability refer to the probability that a product will function as the consumer is led to expect that it will function. If a product incorporates a number of interdependent components, then the probability that it will function properly is equal to the result of multiplying together each component's probability of proper functioning.[29] As the number of components in a product multiplies, therefore, the manufacturer has a corresponding duty to ensure that each component functions in such a manner that the total product is as reliable as he or she implicitly or expressly claims it will be. This is especially the case when malfunction poses health or safety hazards. The U.S. Consumer Product Safety Commission lists hundreds of examples of hazards from product malfunctions in its yearly report.[30]

Service Life Claims concerning the life of a product refer to the period of time during which the product will function as effectively as the consumer is led to expect it to function. Generally, the consumer implicitly understands that service life will depend on the amount of wear and tear to which one subjects the product. In addition, consumers also base some of their expectations of service life on the explicit guarantees the manufacturer attaches to the product.

A more subtle factor that influences service life is the factor of obsolescence.[31] Technological advances may render some products obsolete when a new product appears that carries out the same functions more efficiently. Or purely stylistic changes may make last year's product appear dated and less desirable. The contract view implies that a seller who knows that a certain product will become obsolete has a duty to correct any mistaken beliefs he or she knows buyers will form concerning the service life they may expect from the product.

Maintainability Claims of maintainability are claims concerning the ease with which the product can be repaired and kept in operating condition. Claims of maintainability are often made in the form of an express warranty. Whirlpool Corporation, for example, appended this express warranty on one of its products:

[28] Frederick D. Sturdivant, *Business and Society*, 3rd. ed. (Homewood, IL: Richard D. Irwin, Inc., 1985), p. 392.

[29] *Ibid.*, p. 393.

[30] U.S. Consumer Products Safety Commission, *1979 Annual Report* (Washington, DC: U.S. Government Printing Office, 1979), pp. 81–101.

[31] A somewhat dated but still incisive discussion of this issue is found in Vance Packard, *The Wastemakers* (New York: David McKay Co., Inc., 1960).

> During your first year of ownership, all parts of the appliance (except the light bulbs) that we find are defective in materials or workmanship will be repaired or replaced by Whirlpool free of charge, and we will pay all labor charges. During the second year, we will continue to assume the same responsibility as stated above except you pay any labor charges.[32]

But sellers often also imply that a product may be easily repaired even after the expiration date of an express warranty. In fact, however, product repairs may be costly, or even impossible, due to the unavailability of parts.

Product Safety Implied and express claims of product safety refer to the degree of risk associated with using a product. Since the use of virtually any product involves some degree of risk, questions of safety are essentially questions of *acceptable known levels* of risk. That is, a product is safe if its attendant risks are known and judged to be "acceptable" or "reasonable" by the *buyer* in view of the benefits the buyer expects to derive from using the product. This implies that the seller complies with his or her part of a free agreement if the seller provides a product that involves only those risks he or she says it involves, and the buyer purchases it with that understanding. The National Commission on Product Safety, for example, characterized "reasonable risk" in these terms:

> Risks of bodily harm to users are not unreasonable when consumers understand that risks exist, can appraise their probability and severity, know how to cope with them, and voluntarily accept them to get benefits they could not obtain in less risky ways. When there is a risk of this character, consumers have reasonable opportunity to protect themselves; and public authorities should hesitate to substitute their value judgments about the desirability of the risk for those of the consumers who choose to incur it. But preventable risk is not reasonable (a) when consumers do not know that it exists; or (b) when, though aware of it, consumers are unable to estimate its frequency and severity; or (c) when consumers do not know how to cope with it, and hence are likely to incur harm unnecessarily; or (d) when risk is unnecessary in that it could be reduced or eliminated at a cost in money or in the performance of the product that consumers would willingly incur if they knew the facts and were given the choice.[33]

Thus the seller of a product (according to the contractual theory) has a moral duty to provide a product whose use involves *no greater risks* than those the seller *expressly* communicates to the buyer or those the seller *implicitly* communicates by the implicit claims made when marketing the product for a use whose normal risk level is well known. If the label on a bottle, for example, indicates only that the contents are highly toxic ("Danger: Poison"), the product should not include additional risks from flammability. Or, if a firm makes and sells skis, use of the skis should not embody any unexpected additional risks other than the well-known risks which attend skiing (it should not, for example, involve the added possibility of being pierced by splinters should the skis fracture). In short,

[32] Quoted in address by S. E. Upton (vice-president of Whirlpool Corporation) to the American Marketing Association in Cleveland, OH: 11 December 1969.

[33] National Commission on Product Safety, *Final Report*, quoted in William W. Lowrance, *Of Acceptable Risk* (Los Altos, CA: William Kaufmann, Inc., 1976), p. 80.

the seller has a duty to provide a product with a level of risk which is no higher than he or she expressly or implicitly claims it to be, and which the consumer freely and knowingly contracts to assume.

The Duty of Disclosure

An agreement cannot bind unless both parties to the agreement know what they are doing and freely choose to do it. This implies that the seller who intends to enter a contract with a customer has a duty to disclose exactly what the customer is buying and what the terms of the sale are. At a minimum, this means the seller has a duty to inform the buyer of any facts about the product that would affect the customer's decision to purchase the product. For example, if the product the consumer is buying possesses a defect that poses a risk to the user's health or safety, the consumer should be so informed. Some have argued that sellers should also disclose a product's components or ingredients, its performance characteristics, costs of operation, product ratings, and any other applicable standards.[34]

Behind the claim that entry into a sales contract requires full disclosure is the idea that an agreement is free only to the extent that one knows what alternatives are available: Freedom depends on knowledge. The more the buyer knows about the various products available on the market and the more comparisons the buyer is able to make among them, the more one can say that the buyer's agreement is voluntary.[35]

The view that sellers should provide a great deal of information for buyers, however, has been criticized on the grounds that information is costly and therefore should itself be treated as a product for which the consumer should either pay or do without. In short, consumers should freely contract to purchase information as they freely contract to purchase goods, and producers should not have to provide it for them.[36] The problem with the criticism is that the information on which a person bases his or her decision to enter a contract is a rather different kind of entity from the product exchanged through the contract. Since a contract must be entered into freely, and since free choice depends on knowledge, contractual transactions must be based on an open exchange of information. If consumers had to bargain for such information, the resulting contract would hardly be free.

The Duty Not to Misrepresent

Misrepresentation, even more than the failure to disclose information, renders freedom of choice impossible. That is, misrepresentation is coercive: The person who is intentionally misled acts as the deceiver wants the person to act and not as the person would freely have chosen to act if he or she had known the truth. Since free choice is an essential ingredient of a binding contract, intentionally misrepresenting the nature of a commodity is wrong.

34 See Louis Stern, "Consumer Protection via Increased Information," *Journal of Marketing*, 31, no. 2 (April 1967).

35 Lawrence E. Hicks, *Coping with Packaging Laws* (New York: AMACOM, 1972). p. 17.

36 See the discussions in Richard Posner, *Economic Analysis of Law*, 2nd ed. (Boston: Little, Brown and Company, 1977), p. 83; and R. Posner, "Strict Liability: A Comment," *Journal of Legal Studies*, 2, no. 1 (January 1973): 21.

A seller misrepresents a commodity when he or she represents it in a way deliberately intended to deceive the buyer into thinking something about the product that the seller knows is false. The deception may be created by a verbal lie, as when a used model is described as "new," or it may be created by a gesture, as when an unmarked used model is displayed together with several new models. That is, the deliberate intent to misrepresent by false implication is as wrong as the explicit lie.

The varieties of misrepresentation seem to be limited only by the ingenuity of the greed that creates them.[37] A manufacturer may give a product a name that the manufacturer knows consumers will confuse with the brand-name of a higher-quality competing product; the manufacturer may write "wool" or "silk" on material made wholly or partly of cotton; the manufacturer may mark a fictitious "regular price" on an article that is always sold at a much lower "sale" price; a business may advertise an unusually low price for an object which the business actually intends to sell at a much higher price once the consumer is lured into the store; a store may advertise an object at an unusually low price, intending to "bait and switch" the unwary buyer over to a more expensive product; a producer may solicit paid "testimonials" from professionals who have never really used the product. We shall return to some of these issues below when we discuss advertising.

The Duty Not to Coerce

People often act irrationally when under the influence of fear or emotional stress. When a seller takes advantage of a buyer's fear or emotional stress to extract consent to an agreement that the buyer would not make if the buyer were thinking rationally, the seller is using duress or undue influence to coerce. An unscrupulous funeral director, for example, may skillfully induce guilt-ridden and grief-stricken survivors to invest in funeral services they cannot afford. Since entry into a contract requires *freely* given consent, the seller has a duty to refrain from exploiting emotional states that may induce the buyer to act irrationally against his or her own best interests. For similar reasons, the seller also has the duty not to take advantage of gullibility, immaturity, ignorance, or any other factors that reduce or eliminate the buyer's ability to make free rational choices.

Problems with the Contractual Theory

The main objections to the contract theory focus on the unreality of the assumptions on which the theory is based. First, critics argue, the theory unrealistically assumes that manufacturers make direct agreements with consumers. Nothing could be farther from the truth. Normally, a series of wholesalers and retailers stand between the manufacturer and the ultimate consumer. The manufacturer sells the product to the wholesaler, who sells it to the retailer, who finally sells it to the consumer. The manufacturer never enters into any direct contract with the consumer. How then can one say that manufacturers have contractual duties to the consumer?

[37] See, for example, the many cases cited in George J. Alexander, *Honesty and Competition* (Syracuse, NY: Syracuse University Press, 1967).

Advocates of the contract view of manufacturers' duties have tried to respond to this criticism by arguing that manufacturers enter into "indirect" agreements with consumers. Manufacturers promote their products through their own advertising campaigns. These advertisements supply the promises that lead people to purchase products from retailers who merely function as "conduits" for the manufacturer's product. Consequently, through these advertisements, the manufacturer forges an indirect contractual relationship not only with the immediate retailers who purchase the manufacturer's product but also with the ultimate consumers of the product. The most famous application of this doctrine of broadened indirect contractual relationships is to be found in a 1960 court opinion, *Henningsen* v. *Bloomfield Motors*.[38] Mrs. Henningsen was driving a new Plymouth when it suddenly gave off a loud cracking noise. The steering wheel spun out of her hands, the car lurched to the right and crashed into a brick wall. Mrs. Henningsen sued the manufacturer, Chrysler Corporation. The court opinion read:

> Under modern conditions the ordinary layman, on responding to the importuning of colorful advertising, has neither the opportunity nor the capacity to inspect or to determine the fitness of an automobile for use; he must rely on the manufacturer who has control of its construction, and to some degree on the dealer who, to the limited extent called for by the manufacturer's instructions, inspects and services it before delivery. In such a marketing milieu his remedies and those of persons who properly claim through him should not depend "upon the intricacies of the law of sales. The obligation of the manufacturer should not be based alone on privity of contract [that is, on a direct contractual relationship]. It should rest, as was once said, upon 'the demands of social justice'." *Mazetti* v. *Armous & Co.* (*1913*). "If privity of contract is required," then, under the circumstances of modern merchandising, "privity of contract exists in the consciousness and understanding of all right-thinking persons . . ." Accordingly, we hold that under modern marketing conditions, when a manufacturer puts a new automobile in the stream of trade and promotes its purchase by the public, an implied warranty that it is reasonably suitable for use as such accompanies it into the hands of the ultimate purchaser. Absence of agency between the manufacturer and the dealer who makes the ultimate sale is immaterial.

Thus, Chrysler Corporation was found liable for Mrs. Henningsen's injuries on the grounds that its advertising had created a contractual relationship with Mrs. Henningsen and on the grounds that this contract created an "implied warranty" about the car which Chrysler had a duty to fulfill.

A second objection to the contract theory focuses on the fact that a contract is a two-edged sword. If a consumer can freely agree to buy a product *with* certain qualities, the consumer can also freely agree to buy a product *without* those qualities. That is, freedom of contract allows a manufacturer to be released from his or her contractual obligations by explicitly *disclaiming* that the product is reliable, serviceable, safe, etc. Many manufacturers fix such disclaimers on their products. The Uniform Commercial Code, in fact, stipulates in Section 2-316:

a. Unless the circumstances indicate otherwise, all implied warranties are excluded by expressions like "as is," "with all faults," or other language that in common under-

[38] *Henningsen* v. *Bloomfield Motors, Inc.*, 32 New Jersey 358, 161 Atlantic 2d 69 (1960).

standing calls the buyer's attention to the exclusion of warranties and makes plain that there is no warranty, and

b. When the buyer before entering into the contract has examined the goods or the sample or model as fully as he desired, or has refused to examine the goods, there is no implied warranty with regard to defects that on examination ought in the circumstances to have been revealed to him.

The contract view, then, implies that if the consumer has ample opportunity to examine the product and the disclaimers and voluntarily consents to buy it anyway, he or she assumes the responsibility for the defects disclaimed by the manufacturer, as well as for any defects the customer may carelessly have overlooked. Disclaimers can effectively nullify all contractual duties of the manufacturer.

A third objection to the contract theory criticizes the assumption that buyer and seller meet each other as equals in the sales agreement. The contractual theory assumes that buyers and sellers are equally skilled at evaluating the quality of a product and that buyers are able to adequately protect their interests against the seller. This is the assumption built into the requirement that contracts must be freely and knowingly entered into: Both parties must know what they are doing and neither must be coerced into doing it. This equality between buyer and seller that the contractual theory assumes, derives from the laissez-faire ideology that accompanied the historical development of contract theory.[39] Classical laissez-faire ideology held that the economy's markets are competitive and that in competitive markets the consumer's bargaining power is equal to that of the seller. Competition forces the seller to offer the consumer as good or better terms than the consumer could get from other competing sellers, so the consumer has the power to threaten to take his or her business to other sellers. Because of this equality between buyer and seller, it was fair that each be allowed to try to out-bargain the other and unfair to place restrictions on either. In practice, this laissez-faire ideology gave birth to the doctrine of "caveat emptor": let the buyer take care of himself.

In fact, sellers and buyers do not exhibit the equality these doctrines assume. A consumer who must purchase hundreds of different kinds of commodities cannot hope to be as knowledgeable as a manufacturer who specializes in producing a single product. Consumers have neither the expertise nor the time to acquire and process the information on which they must base their purchase decisions. Consumers, as a consequence, must usually rely on the judgment of the seller in making their purchase decisions, and are particularly vulnerable to being harmed by the seller. Equality, far from being the rule, as the contract theory assumes, is usually the exception.

6.3 THE DUE CARE THEORY

The "due care" theory of the manufacturer's duties to consumers is based on the idea that consumers and sellers do not meet as equals and that the consumer's interests are particularly vulnerable to being harmed by the manufacturer who

[39] See Friedrich Kessler and Malcolm Pitman Sharp, *Contracts* (Boston: Little, Brown and Company, 1953), p. 1–9.

has a knowledge and an expertise that the consumer does not have. Because manufacturers are in a more advantaged position, they have a duty to take special "care" to ensure that consumers' interests are not harmed by the products that they offer them. The doctrine of "caveat emptor" is here replaced with a weak version of the doctrine of "caveat vendor": let the seller take care. A New York court decision neatly described the advantaged position of the manufacturer and the consequent vulnerability of the consumer:

> Today as never before the product in the hands of the consumer is often a most sophisticated and even mysterious article. Not only does it usually emerge as a sealed unit with an alluring exterior rather than as a visible assembly of component parts, but its functional validity and usefulness often depend on the application of electronic, chemical, or hydraulic principles far beyond the ken of the average consumer. Advances in the technologies of materials, of processes, of operational means have put it almost entirely out of the reach of the consumer to comprehend why or how the article operates, and thus even farther out of his reach to detect when there may be a defect or a danger present in its design or manufacture. In today's world it is often only the manufacturer who can fairly be said to know and to understand when an article is suitably designed and safely made for its intended purpose. Once floated on the market, many articles in a very real practical sense defy detection of defect, except possibly in the hands of an expert after laborious, and perhaps even destructive, disassembly. By way of direct illustration, how many automobile purchasers or users have any idea how a power steering mechanism operates or is intended to operate, with its "circulating work and piston assembly and its cross shaft splined to the Pitman arm"? We are accordingly persuaded that from the standpoint of justice as regards the operating aspect of today's products, responsibility should be laid on the manufacturer, subject to the limitations we set forth.[40]

The "due care" view holds, then, that because consumers must depend upon the greater expertise of the manufacturer, the manufactures not only has a duty to deliver a product that lives up to the express and implied claims about it, but in addition the manufacturer has a duty to exercise due care to prevent others from being injured by the product, *even if the manufacturer explicitly disclaims such responsibility and the buyer agrees to the disclaimer*. The manufacturer violates this duty and is "negligent" when there is a failure to exercise the care that a reasonable person could have foreseen would be necessary to prevent others from being harmed by use of the product. Due care must enter into the design of the product, into the choice of reliable materials for constructing the product, into the manufacturing processes involved in putting the product together, into the quality control used to test and monitor production, and into the warnings, labels, and instructions attached to the product. In each of these areas, according to the due care view, the manufacturer, in virtue of a greater expertise and knowledge, has a positive duty to take whatever steps are necessary to ensure that when the product leaves the plant it is as safe as possible, and the customer has a right to such assurance. Failure to take such steps is a breach of the moral duty to exercise due care and a violation of the injured person's right to expect such care, a right that rests on the consumer's need to rely on the manufacturer's

[40] *Codling* v. *Paglia*, 32 New York 2d 330, 298 Northeastern 2d 622, 345 New York Supplement 2d 461 (1973).

expertise. Edgar Schein sketched out the basic elements of the "due care" theory several years ago when he wrote:

> . . . a professional is someone who knows better what is good for his client than the client himself does. . . . If we accept this definition of professionalism . . . we may speculate that it is the *vulnerability of the client* that has necessitated the development of moral and ethical codes surrounding the relationship. The client must be protected from exploitation in a situation in which he is unable to protect himself because he lacks the relevant knowledge to do so . . . If [a manufacturer] is . . . a professional, who is his client? With respect to whom is he exercising his expert knowledge and skills? Who needs protection against the possible misuse of these skills? . . . Many economists argue persuasively . . . that the consumer has not been in a position to know what he was buying and hence was, in fact, in a relatively vulnerable position . . . Clearly, then, one whole area of values deals with the relationship between the [manufacturer] and consumers.[41]

The due care view, of course, rests on the principle that individuals have a moral duty not to harm or injure others by their acts and that others have a moral right to expect such care from individuals. This principle has been justified from a variety of different positions. Rule-utilitarians have defended it on the grounds that if the rule is accepted, everyone's welfare will be advanced.[42] It has been argued for on the basis of Kant's theory, since it seems to follow from the categorical imperative that people should be treated as ends and not merely as means, that is, that they have a *positive* right to be helped when they cannot help themselves.[43] And Rawls has argued that individuals in the "original position" would agree to the principle because it would provide the basis for a secure social environment.[44] The judgment that individual producers have a duty not to harm or injure, therefore, is solidly based on several ethical principles.

The Duty to Exercise Due Care

According to the due care theory, manufacturers exercise sufficient care when they take adequate steps to prevent whatever injurious effects they can foresee that the use of their product may have on consumers after having conducted inquiries into the way the product will be used and after having attempted to anticipate any possible misuses of the product. A manufacturer, then, is *not* morally negligent when others are harmed by a product and the harm was not one that the manufacturer could possibly have foreseen or prevented. Nor is a manufacturer morally negligent after having taken all reasonable steps to protect the consumer and to ensure that the consumer is informed of any irremovable risks that might still attend the use of the product. A car manufacturer, for example, cannot be said to be negligent from a moral point of view when people carelessly misuse the cars the manufacturer

[41] Edgar H. Schein, "The Problem of Moral Education for the Business Manager," *Industrial Management Review*, 8 (1966): 3–11.

[42] See W. D. Ross, *The Right and the Good* (Oxford: The Clarendon Press, 1930), ch. 2.

[43] Donagan, *Theory of Morality*, p. 83.

[44] Rawls, *Theory of Justice*, pp. 114–17; 333–42.

produces. A car manufacturer would be morally negligent only if the manufacturer had allowed unreasonable dangers to remain in the design of the car that consumers cannot be expected to know about or that they cannot guard against by taking their own precautionary measures.

What specific responsibilities does the duty to exercise due care impose on the producer? In general, the producer's responsibilities would extend to three areas:[45]

Design The manufacturer should ascertain whether the design of an article conceals any dangers, whether it incorporates all feasible safety devices, and whether it uses materials that are adequate for the purposes the product is intended to serve. The manufacturer is responsible for being thoroughly acquainted with the design of the item, and to conduct research and tests extensive enough to uncover any risks that may be involved in employing the article under various conditions of use. This requires researching consumers and analyzing their behavior, testing the product under different conditions of consumer use, and selecting materials strong enough to stand up to all probable usages. The effects of aging and of wear should also be analyzed and taken into account in designing an article. Engineering staff should acquaint themselves with hazards that might result from prolonged use and wear, and should warn the consumer of any potential dangers. There is a duty to take the latest technological advances into account in designing a product, especially where advances can provide ways of designing a product that is less liable to harm or injure its users.

Production The production manager should control the manufacturing processes to eliminate any defective items, to identify any weaknesses that become apparent during production, and to ensure that short-cuts, substitution of weaker materials, or other economizing measures are not taken during manufacture that would compromise the safety of the final product. To ensure this, there should be adequate quality controls over materials that are to be used in the manufacture of the product and over the various stages of manufacture.

Information The manufacturer should fix labels, notices, or instructions on the product that will warn the user of all dangers involved in using or misusing the item and that will enable the user to adequately guard himself or herself against harm or injury. These instructions should be clear and simple, and warnings of any hazards involved in using or misusing the product should also be clear, simple, and prominent. In the case of drugs, manufacturers have a duty to warn physicians of any risks or of any dangerous side-effects that research or prolonged use have revealed. It is a breach of the duty not to harm or injure if the manufacturer attempts to conceal or down-play the dangers related to drug usage.

[45] Discussions of the requirements of "due care" may be found in a variety of texts, all of which, however, approach the issues from the point of view of legal liability: Irwin Gray, *Product Liability: A Management Response* (New York: AMACOM, 1975), ch. 6; Eugene R. Carrubba, *Assuring Product Integrity* (Lexington, MA: Lexington Books, 1975); Frank Nixon, *Managing to Achieve Quality and Reliability* (New York: McGraw-Hill Book Co., 1971).

In determining the safeguards that should be built into a product, the manufacturer must also take into consideration the *capacities* of the persons who will use the product. If a manufacturer anticipates that a product will be used by persons who are immature, mentally deficient, or too inexperienced to be aware of the dangers attendant on the use of the product, then the manufacturer owes them a greater degree of care than if the anticipated users were of ordinary intelligence and prudence. Children, for example, cannot be expected to realize the dangers involved in using electrical equipment. Consequently, if a manufacturer anticipates that an electrical item will probably be used by children, steps must be taken to ensure that a person with a child's understanding will not be injured by the product.

If the possible harmful effects of using a product are serious, or if they cannot be adequately understood without expert opinion, then sale of the product should be carefully controlled. A firm should not oppose regulation of the sale of a product when regulation is the only effective means of ensuring that the users of the product are fully aware of the risks its use involves.

Problems with "Due Care"

The basic difficulty raised by the "due care" theory is that there is no clear method for determining when one has exercised enough "due care." That is, there is no hard and fast rule for determining how far a firm must go to ensure the safety of its product. Some authors have proposed the general utilitarian rule that the greater the probability of harm and the larger the population that might be harmed, the more the firm is obligated to do. But this fails to resolve some important issues. Every product involves at least some small risk of injury. If the manufacturer should try to eliminate even low-level risks, this would require that the manufacturer invest so much in each product that the product would be priced out of the reach of most consumers. Moreover, even *attempting* to balance higher risks against added costs involves measurement problems: How does one quantify risks to health and life?

A second difficulty raised by the "due care" theory is that it assumes that the manufacturer can discover the risks that attend the use of a product before the consumer buys and uses it. In fact, in a technologically innovative society new products whose defects cannot emerge until years or decades have passed will continually be introduced into the market. Only years after thousands of people were using and being exposed to asbestos, for example, did a correlation emerge between the incidence of cancer and exposure to asbestos. Although manufacturers may have greater expertise than consumers, their expertise does not make them omniscient. Who, then, is to bear the costs of injuries sustained from products whose defects neither the manufacturer nor the consumer could have uncovered beforehand?

Thirdly, the due care view appears to some to be paternalistic. For it assumes that the *manufacturer* should be the one who makes the important decisions for the consumer, at least with respect to the levels of risks that are proper for consumers to bear. But one may wonder whether such decisions should not be left up to the free choice of consumers who can decide for themselves whether or not they want to pay for additional risk reduction.

6.4 THE SOCIAL COSTS VIEW OF THE MANUFACTURER'S DUTIES

A third theory on the duties of the manufacturer would extend the manufacturer's duties beyond those imposed by contractual relationships and beyond those imposed by the duty to exercise due care in preventing injury or harm. This third theory holds that a manufacturer should pay the costs of *any* injuries sustained through any defects in the product, *even when the manufacturer exercised all due care in the design and manufacture of the product and has taken all reasonable precautions to warn users of every foreseen danger*. According to this third theory a manufacturer has a duty to assume the risks of even those injuries that arise out of defects in the product that no one could reasonably have foreseen or eliminated. The theory is a very strong version of the doctrine of "caveat vendor": let the seller take care.

This third theory, which has formed the basis of the legal doctrine of "strict liability," is founded on utilitarian arguments.[46] The utilitarian arguments for this third theory hold that the "external" costs of injuries resulting from unavoidable defects in the design of an artifact constitute part of the costs society must pay for producing and using an artifact. By having the manufacturer bear the external costs that result from these injuries as well as the ordinary internal costs of design and manufacture, all costs will be internalized and added on as part of the price of the product. Internalizing all costs in this way, according to proponents of this theory, will lead to a more efficient use of society's resources. First, since the price will reflect *all* the costs of producing and using the artifact, market forces will ensure that the product is not overproduced, and that resources are not wasted on it. (Whereas if some costs were not included in the price, then manufacturers would tend to produce more than is needed.) Second, since manufacturers have to pay the costs of injuries, they will be motivated to exercise greater care and to thereby reduce the number of accidents. Manufacturers will therefore strive to cut down the social costs of injuries, and this means a more efficient care for our human resources. In order to produce the maximum benefits possible from our limited resources, therefore, the social costs of injuries from defective products should be internalized by passing them on to the manufacturer, even when the manufacturer has done all that could be done to eliminate such defects. And third, internalizing the costs of injury in this way enables the manufacturer to distribute losses among all the users of a product instead of allowing losses to fall on individuals who may not be able to sustain the loss by themselves.

Underlying this third theory on the duties of the manufacturer are the standard utilitarian assumptions about the values of efficiency. The theory assumes that an efficient use of resources is so important for society that social costs should be allocated in whatever way will lead to a more efficient use and care of our resources. On this basis, the theory argues that a manufacturer should bear the social costs for injuries caused by defects in a product, even when no negligence was involved and no contractual relationship existed between the manufacturer and the user.

[46] See, for example, Michael D. Smith, "The Morality of Strict Liability In Tort," *Business and Professional Ethics*, 3, no. 1 (December 1979): 3–5; for a review of the rich legal literature on this topic, see Richard A. Posner, "Strict Liability: A Comment," *The Journal of Legal Studies*, 2, no. 1 (January 1973): 205–21.

Problems with the Social Costs View

The major criticism of the social costs view of the manufacturer's duties is that it is unfair.[47] It is unfair, the critics charge, because it violates the basic canons of compensatory justice. Compensatory justice implies that a person should be forced to compensate an injured party only if the person could foresee and could have prevented the injury. By forcing manufacturers to pay for injuries that they could neither foresee nor prevent, the social costs theory (and the legal theory of 'strict liability' that flows from it) treats manufacturers unfairly. Moreover, insofar as the social costs theory encourages passing the costs of injuries on to all consumers (in the form of higher prices), consumers are also being treated unfairly.

A second criticism of the social costs theory attacks the assumption that passing the costs of all injuries on to manufacturers will reduce the number of accidents.[48] On the contrary, critics claim, by relieving consumers of the responsibility of paying for their own injuries, the social costs theory will encourage carelessness in consumers. And an increase in consumer carelessness will lead to an increase in consumer injuries.

A third argument against the social costs theory focuses on the financial burdens the theory imposes on manufacturers and insurance carriers. Critics claim that a growing number of consumers successfully sue manufacturers for compensation for any injuries sustained while using a product, even when the manufacturer took all due care to ensure that the product was safe.[49] Not only have the number of "strict liability" suits increased, critics claim, but the amounts awarded to injured consumers have also escalated. Moreover, they continue, the rising costs of the many liability suits that the theory of "strict liability" has created have precipitated a crisis in the insurance industry because insurance companies end up paying the liability suits brought against manufacturers. These high costs have imposed heavy losses on insurance companies and have forced many insurance companies to raise their rates to levels that are so high that many manufacturers can no longer afford insurance. Thus, critics claim, the social costs or "strict liability" theory wreaks havoc with the insurance industry; it forces the costs of insurance to climb to unreasonable heights; and it forces many valuable firms out of business because they can no longer afford liability insurance nor can they afford to pay for the many and expensive liability suits they must now face.

Defenders of the social costs view, however, have replied that in reality the costs of consumer liability suits are not large. Studies have shown, they say, that the number of liability suits filed in state courts increased only 9 percent between 1978 and 1984 (when population grew by 6 percent).[50] Less than 1 percent of product-related injuries result in suits and successful suits average payments

[47] George P. Fletcher, "Fairness and Utility in Tort Theory," *Harvard Law Review*, 85, no. 3 (January 1972): 537–73.

[48] Posner, *Economic Analysis of Law*, pp. 139–42.

[49] See "Unsafe Products: The Great Debate Over Blame and Punishment," *Business Week*, 30 April 1984; Stuart Taylor, "Product Liability: the New Morass," *New York Times*, 10 March 1985; "The Product Liability Debate," *Newsweek*, 10 September 1984.

[50] "Sorting Out the Liability Debate," *Newsweek*, 12 May 1986.

of only a few thousand dollars.[51] Defenders of the social cost theory also point out that insurance companies and the insurance industry as a whole have remained profitable (with overall profits of $1.7 billion in 1985) and claim that higher insurance costs are due to factors other than an increase in the amount of liability claims.[52]

The arguments for and against the social costs theory deserve much more discussion than we can give them here. The theory is essentially an attempt to come to grips with the problem of allocating the costs of injuries between two morally innocent parties: The manufacturer who could not foresee or prevent a product-related injury, and the consumer who could not guard himself or herself against the injury because the hazard was unknown. This allocation problem will arise in any society that, like ours, has come to rely upon a technology whose effects do not become evident until years after the technology is introduced. Unfortunately, it is also a problem that may have no "fair" solution.

6.5 ADVERTISING ETHICS

The advertising industry is a massive business. Over $75 billion is spent each year on advertising.[53] Sixteen billion dollars is spent on television advertising alone; another $20 billion is spent on newspaper advertisements.[54] There are over six thousand advertising agencies doing business in the United States, many of which employ several thousand people.

Who pays for these advertising expenditures? In the end, advertising costs must be covered by the prices consumers pay for the goods they buy: The consumer pays. What does the consumer get for his or her advertising dollar? According to most consumers, they get very little. Surveys have shown that 66 percent of consumers feel that advertising does not reduce prices; 65 percent believe it makes people buy things they should not buy; 54 percent feel advertisements insult the intelligence, and 63 percent feel advertisements do not present the truth.[55] On the other hand, defenders of the advertising industry see things differently. Advertising, they claim, "is, before all else, communication."[56] Its basic function is to provide consumers with information about the products available to them, a beneficial service.[57]

[51] Ernest F. Hollings, "No Need for Federal Product-Liability Law," *Christian Science Monitor*, 20 September 1984; see also Harvey Rosenfield, "The Plan to Wrong Consumer Rights," *San Jose Mercury News*, 3 October 1984.

[52] Irvin Molotsky, "Drive to Limit Product Liability Awards Grows as Consumer Groups Object," *New York Times*, 6 March 1986.

[53] U.S. Bureau of the Census, *Statistical Abstract of the United States, 1985*, 105th ed. (Washington, DC: U.S. Government Printing Office, 1984), p. 548.

[54] *Ibid.*, p. 549.

[55] Raymond A. Bauer and Stephen A. Greyser, *Advertising in America: The Consumer View* (Cambridge: Harvard University Press, 1968), p. 394.

[56] Walter Weir, *Truth in Advertising and Other Heresies* (New York: McGraw-Hill Book Company, 1963), p. 154.

[57] See also, J. Robert Moskin, ed., *The Case for Advertising* (New York: American Association of Advertising Agencies, 1973), *passim.*

Is advertising then a waste or a benefit? Does it harm consumers or help them?

A Definition

Commercial advertising is sometimes defined as a form of "information" and an advertiser as "one who gives information." The implication is that the defining function of advertising is to provide information to consumers. This definition of advertising, however, fails to distinguish advertisements from, say, articles in publications like *Consumer Reports,* which compare, test, and objectively evaluate the durability, safety, defects, and usefulness of various products. A 1981 study found that more than half of all television ads contained no consumer information whatsoever about the advertised product, and that only half of all magazine ads contained more than one informational cue.[58] Consider how much information is conveyed by the following advertisements:

> "When the sun goes down and the moon comes up, it's a whole different animal . . . There is a special feel in an Oldsmobile."
>
> "Be a Part of It" (Canadian Club)
>
> "If You Smoke, Please Try Carlton."
>
> "Coke Adds Life"
>
> "Tradition With a Dash of the Unexpected" (Aramis Cologne)

Advertisements often do not include much objective information for the simple reason that their primary function is not that of providing unbiased information. The primary function of commercial advertisements, rather, is to sell a product to prospective buyers, and whatever information they happen to carry is subsidiary to this basic function and usually determined by it.

A more helpful way of characterizing commercial advertising is in terms of the buyer-seller relationship: Commercial advertising can be defined as a certain kind of communication between a seller and potential buyers. It is distinguished from other forms of communication by two features. First, it is publicly addressed to a mass audience as distinct from a private message to a specific individual. Because of this public feature, advertising necessarily has widespread social effects.

Second, advertising is intended to *induce* several members of its audience to buy the seller's products. An advertisement can succeed in this intent in two main ways: (1) by creating a desire for the seller's product in consumers and (2) by creating a belief in consumers that the product is a means of satisfying some desire the buyer already has.

Discussion of the ethical aspects of advertising can be organized around

[58] See "Ads Infinitum," *Dollars & Sense,* May/June 1984. For an ethical analysis of the information content of advertising see Alan Goldman, "Ethical Issues in Advertising," pp. 242–49 in *New Introductory Essays in Business Ethics,* Tom Regan, ed. (New York: Random House, Inc., 1984), pp. 235–70; The view that advertising is justified by the "indirect" information it provides is advanced in Phillip Nelson, "Advertising and Ethics," in *Ethics, Free Enterprise, and Public Policy,* Richard T. DeGeorge and Joseph A. Pichler, eds., New York: (Oxford University Press 1978), pp. 187–98.

the various features identified in the definition above: its social effects, its creation of consumer desires, and its effects on consumer beliefs.

We will begin by discussing the *social effects* of advertising.

Social Effects of Advertising

Critics of advertising claim that it has several adverse effects on society: It degrades people's tastes, it wastes valuable resources, and it creates monopoly power. We will examine these criticisms one by one.

Psychological Effects of Advertising A familiar criticism of advertising is that it debases the tastes of the public by presenting irritating and aesthetically unpleasant displays.[59] To be effective advertisements must often be intrusive, strident, and repetitive. So that they will be understood by the most simple-minded person, advertisements are often boring, insipid, and insult the intelligence of viewers. In illustrating the use of toothpaste, mouthwashes, deodorants, and undergarments, for example, advertisements sometimes employ images that many people find vulgar, offensive, disgusting, and tasteless. Yet, although these sorts of criticisms may be quite accurate, they do not seem to raise important ethical issues. It is certainly unfortunate that advertisements do not measure up to our *aesthetic* norms, but this does not imply that they also violate our *ethical* norms.

More to the point is the criticism that advertising debases the tastes of consumers by gradually and subtly inculcating materialistic values and ideas about how happiness is achieved.[60] Since advertising necessarily emphasizes the consumption of material goods, people are led to forget the importance of their other, more basic, needs and of other more realistic ways of achieving self-fulfillment. As a result, personal efforts are diverted from "nonmaterialistic" aims and objectives that are more likely to increase the happiness of people, and are instead channeled into expanded material consumption. Consumer advocate Mary Gardiner Jones writes:

> The conscious appeal in the television commercial is essentially materialistic. Central to the message of the TV commercial is the premise that it is the acquisition of *things* that will gratify our basic and inner needs and aspirations. It is the message of the commercial that all of the major problems confronting an individual can be instantly eliminated by . . . the use of a product . . . A second inescapable premise of these ads is that we are all externally motivated, concerned to do and be like our neighbors or to emulate popular successful individuals . . . Personal success in the TV ad is externally contrived, not the product of years of study and training . . . In addition, . . . the TV commercial presents a very special and limited view of American society. Here, according to the TV commercial . . . is what the young

[59] See Stephen A. Greyser, "Irritation in Advertising," *Journal of Advertising Research*, 13, no. 3 (February 1973): 7–20.

[60] See Michael Schudson, *Advertising, the Uneasy Persuasion* (New York: Basic Books, Inc., Publishers, 1984), p. 210; David M. Potter, *People of Plenty* (Chicago: The University of Chicago Press, 1954), p. 188; International Commission for the Study of Communication Problems, *Many Voices, One World* (London: Kogan Page, 1980), p. 110.

> and successful are wearing and how they furnish their homes . . . [But] the TV world [is] typically that of the white suburban middle-income, middle-class family.[61]

The difficulty with this criticism, however, is that it is uncertain whether advertising actually has the large psychological effects the criticism attributes to it.[62] A person's beliefs and attitudes are notoriously difficult to change without there being in the first place a willingness to accept the message being offered. Thus, the success of advertising may depend more on its appeal to the values consumers already possess than on its ability to instill new values. If this is so, then advertising does not so much create society's values as reflect them.

Advertising and Waste A second major criticism brought against advertising is that it is wasteful.[63] Economists sometimes distinguish between "production costs" and "selling costs." Production costs are the costs of the resources consumed in producing or improving a product. Selling costs are the additional costs of resources that do not go into changing the product but are invested instead in persuading people to buy the product. The costs of resources consumed by advertising, critics claim, are essentially "selling costs": They are not used to improve the product but to merely persuade people to buy it. The resources consumed by advertisements do not add anything to the utility of the product. Such resources, critics conclude, are "wasted" because they are expended without adding to consumer utility in any way.

One reply made to this argument is that advertising does in fact produce something: It produces and transmits information on the availability and the nature of products.[64] But as many have pointed out, even in these respects, the information content of advertisements is minimal and could be transmitted by substantially less expensive means.[65]

Another more persuasive reply to the argument is that advertising serves to produce a beneficial rise in demand for *all* products. This rising general demand in turn makes mass production possible. The end result is a gradually expanding economy in which products are manufactured with ever greater efficiency and ever more cheaply. Advertising, then, adds to consumer utility by serving as an

[61] Mary Gardiner Jones, "The Cultural and Social Impact of Advertising on American Society," in *Consumerism,* 2nd ed., David Aaker and George S. Day, eds. (New York: The Free Press, 1974), p. 431.

[62] Stephen A. Greyser, "Advertising: Attacks and Counters," *Harvard Business Review,* 50(10 March 1972): 22–28.

[63] For an overview of the economic literature on this issue see Mark S. Albion and Paul W. Farris, *The Advertising Controversy, Evidence on the Economic Effects of Advertising* (Boston, MA: Auburn House Publishing Company, 1981), pp. 69–86, 153–70; for an informal discussion of the issue see Jules Backman, "Is Advertising Wasteful?" *Journal of Marketing* (January 1968); 2–8.

[64] Phillip Nelson, "The Economic Value of Advertising," in Yale Brozen, *Advertising and Society* (New York: New York University Press, 1974), pp. 43–66.

[65] Richard Caves, *American Industry: Structure, Conduct, Performance* (Englewood Cliffs, NJ: Prentice-Hall, Inc., 1972), p. 101.

incentive to greater consumption and thereby indirectly motivating a greater productivity and efficiency and a lower price structure.[66]

There is, however, substantial uncertainty surrounding the question whether advertising is responsible for a rise in the total consumption of goods.[67] Studies have shown that advertising frequently fails to stimulate consumption of a product, and consumption in many industries has increased in spite of minimal advertising expenditures. Advertising thus appears to be effective for individual companies not because it *expands* consumption, but only because it *shifts* consumption away from one product to another. If this is true, then economists are correct when they claim that beyond the level needed to impart information, advertising becomes a waste of resources because it does nothing more than shift demand from one firm to another.[68]

Moreover, even if advertising were an effective spur to consumption, many authors have argued, this is not necessarily a blessing. E. F. Schumacher, Herman E. Daly, and other economists have claimed that the most pressing social need at present is finding ways of *decreasing* consumption.[69] Increasing consumption has led to a rapid industrial expansion that has polluted much of the natural environment and has rapidly depleted our nonrenewable resources. Unless we limit consumption, we will soon outrun the finite natural resources our planet possesses with disastrous consequences for us all. If this is so, then the claim that advertising induces ever higher levels of consumption is not in its favor.

Advertising and Market Power Since the early 1950s, Nicholas Kaldor and others have claimed that the massive advertising campaigns of modern manufacturers enable them to achieve and maintain a monopoly (or oligopoly) power over their markets.[70] And monopolies, as we have seen, lead to higher consumer prices. Kaldor's argument was simple. Large manufacturers have the financial resources to mount massive and expensive advertising campaigns to introduce their products. These campaigns create in consumers a "loyalty" to the brand-name of the manufacturer, giving the manufacturer control of a major portion of the market. Small firms are then unable to break into the market because they cannot finance the expensive advertising campaigns that would be required to get consumers to switch their brand loyalties. As a result, a few large oligopoly firms emerge in control of consumer markets from which small firms are effectively barred. Advertising, then, is supposed to reduce competition, and to raise barriers to entry into markets.

[66] David M. Blank, "Some Comments on the Role of Advertising in the American Economy—A Plea for Reevaluation," in *Reflections on Progress in Marketing*, L. George Smith, ed. (Chicago: American Marketing Association, 1964), p. 151.

[67] See the discussion in Thomas M. Garrett, *An Introduction to Some Ethical Problems of Modern American Advertising* (Rome: The Gregorian University Press, 1961), pp. 125–30.

[68] *Ibid.*, p. 177.

[69] See E. F. Schumacher, *Small Is Beautiful* (London: Blond and Briggs, Ltd., 1973); and Herman E. Daly, ed., *Toward a Steady-State Economy* (San Francisco: W. H. Freeman, 1979), 'Introduction.'

[70] Nicholas H. Kaldor, "The Economic Aspects of Advertising," *The Review of Economic Studies*, 18 (1950–51): 1–27; see also William S. Comanor and Thomas Wilson, *Advertising and Market Power* (Cambridge: Harvard University Press, 1975). A readable review of the economic literature on this issue can be found in Albion and Farris, *The Advertising Controversy*, pp. 45–68.

But is there a connection between advertising and market power? If advertising does raise costs for consumers by encouraging monopoly markets, then there should be a statistical connection between the amount of advertising revenues spent by an industry and the degree of market concentration in that industry. The more concentrated and less competitive industries should exhibit high levels of advertising, while less concentrated and more competitive industries should exhibit correspondingly lower levels. Unfortunately, the statistical studies aimed at uncovering a connection between advertising intensity and market concentration have been inconclusive.[71] Some concentrated industries (soaps, cigarettes, breakfast cereals) expend large amounts on advertising, but others (drugs, cosmetics) do not. Moreover, in at least some oligopoly industries (the auto industry, for example) smaller firms spend more per unit on advertising than the large major firms. Whether advertising harms consumers by diminishing competition is an interesting but unsettled question.

The criticisms of advertising based on its social effects are inconclusive. They are inconclusive for the simple reason that it is unknown whether advertising has the capacity to produce the effects that the criticisms assume it has. To establish the case for or against advertising on the basis of its effects on society will require a great deal more research on the exact nature of the psychological and economic effects advertising has.

Advertising and the Creation of Consumer Desires

During the late 1950s John K. Galbraith and others began to argue that advertising is manipulative: It is the creation of desires in consumers for the sole purpose of absorbing industrial output.[72] Galbraith distinguished two kinds of desires: those that have a "physical" basis, such as desires for food and shelter, and those that are "psychological in origin," such as the individual's desires for goods that "give him a sense of personal achievement, accord him a feeling of equality with his neighbors, direct his mind from thought, serve sexual aspiration, promise social acceptability, enhance his subjective feeling of health, contribute by conventional canons to personal beauty, or are otherwise psychologically rewarding."[73] The physically based desires originate in the buyer and are relatively immune to being changed by persuasion. The psychic desires, however, are capable of being managed, controlled, and expanded by advertising. Since the demand created by physical needs is finite, producers soon produce enough to meet these needs. If production is to expand, therefore, producers must create new demand by manipulating the pliable psychic desires through advertising. Advertising is therefore used to create psychic desires for the sole purpose of "ensuring that people buy what is produced"—that is, to absorb the output of an expanding industrial system.

[71] See L.G. Telser, "Some Aspects of the Economics of Advertising," *Journal of Business* (April 1968), pp. 166–73; for a survey of studies on this issue, see James M. Ferguson, *Advertising and Competition: Theory Measurement and Fact* (Cambridge, MA: Ballinger Publishing Company, 1974), ch. 5.

[72] See John Kenneth Galbraith, *The Affluent Society* (Boston: Houghton Mifflin Company, 1958).

[73] John Kenneth Galbraith, *The New Industrial State* (New York: New American Library, 1967), p. 211.

The effect of this management of demand through advertising is to shift the focus of decision in the purchase of goods from the consumer where it is beyond control, to the firm where it is subject to control.[74] Production, then, is not molded to serve human desires; rather human desires are molded to serve the needs of production.

If this view of Galbraith's is correct, then advertising violates the individual's right to choose for himself or herself: Advertising manipulates the consumer. The consumer is used merely as a means for advancing the ends and purposes of producers, and this diminishes the consumer's capacity to freely choose for himself or herself.[75]

It is not clear that Galbraith's argument is correct. As we have already seen, the psychological effects of advertising are still unclear. Consequently, it is unclear whether psychic desires can be manipulated by advertising in the wholesale way that Galbraith's argument assumes.[76]

Moreover, as F. A. von Hayek has pointed out, the "creation" of psychic wants did not originate with modern advertising.[77] New wants have always been "created" by the invention of novel and attractive products (such as, the first bow-and-arrow, the first painting, the first perfume), and such a creation of wants seems harmless enough.

However, although it is unclear whether advertising as a whole has the massive manipulative effects that Galbraith attributes to it, it is clear that some particular advertisements are at least *intended* to manipulate. They are intended, that is, to arouse in the consumer a psychological desire for the product without the consumer's knowledge and without the consumer being able to rationally weigh whether the product is in his or her own best interests. Advertisements that intentionally rely on "subliminal suggestion," or that attempt to make consumers associate unreal sexual or social fulfillment with a product, fall into this class, as do advertisements that are aimed at children.

Suppa Corporation in Fallbrook, California, for example, briefly tested candy advertisements printed on paper on which the word "buy" was written so it would register subconsciously but could not be consciously perceived unless one specifically sought it out. Subsequent tests showed that the ads created more of a desire to buy candy than those printed on paper on which the word "no" appeared in a similar subliminal manner.[78] Manipulative ads aimed at children are exemplified by a criticism The National Advertising Division of the Council of Better Business Bureaus recently leveled at a Mattel, Inc., television commercial aimed at children which mixed animation sequences with group shots of dolls. Children who are still learning to distinguish between fantasy and reality, the Council felt, would

[74] *Ibid.*, p. 215.

[75] See the discussion of manipulation in advertising in Tom L. Beauchamp, "Manipulative Advertising," *Business & Professional Ethics Journal*, 3, nos. 3 & 4 (Spring/Summer 1984); 1–22; see also in the same volume the critical response of R. M. Hare, "Commentary," pp. 23–28.

[76] See George Katova, *The Mass Consumption Society* (New York: McGraw-Hill Book Company, 1964), pp. 54–61.

[77] F. A. von Hayek, "The *Non Sequitur* of the 'Dependence Effect,'" *Southern Economic Journal* (April 1961).

[78] Vance Packard, "Subliminal Messages: They Work; Are They Ethical?" *San Francisco Examiner*, 11 August, 1985; see also W. B. Key, *Media Sexploitation* (Englewood Cliffs, NJ, Prentice Hall, 1976).

not be given "an accurate depiction of the products" pictured in the advertisements.[79] The Council also criticized a Walt Disney Music Co. advertisement of a limited-time offer which conveyed a "sense of urgency" that children might find "overwhelming." Critics have also claimed that television shows of animated characters who resemble toy dolls and figures that are advertised on the same show are in effect prolonged advertisements for these toys. The effect of such "half-hour advertisements," they allege, is to manipulate the vulnerable child by feeding him commercials under the guise of entertainment.[80] Moreover, such "advertisement-programs" often contain high levels of violence since their cartoon superhero characters—like "He-Man," "Rambo," "She-Ra," "GI Joe," and "Transformers"—are themselves violent. Advertising which promotes toys modeled on violent characters or which promotes military toys, indirectly promotes aggression and violent behavior in children who are highly suggestible and easily manipulated, critics claim, and it is therefore unethical.[81] Advertisements of this sort are manipulative, insofar as they circumvent conscious reasoning and seek to influence the consumer to do what the advertiser wants and not what is in the consumer's interests.[82] They violate, that is, the consumer's right to be treated as a free and equal rational being.

Advertising and Its Effects on Consumer Beliefs

The most common criticism of advertising concerns its effect on the consumer's beliefs. Since advertising is a form of communication, it can be as truthful or as deceptive as any other form of communication. Most criticisms of advertising focus on the deceptive aspects of modern advertising.

Deceptive advertising can take several forms. An advertisement can misrepresent the nature of the product by using deceptive mock-ups, by using untrue paid testimonials, by inserting the word "guarantee" where nothing is guaranteed, by quoting misleading prices, by failing to disclose defects in a product, by misleadingly disparaging a competitor's goods, or by simulating well-known brand-names. Some fraudulent forms of advertising involve more complex schemes. Bait advertisements, for example, announce the sale of goods that later prove not to be available or to be defective. Once the consumer is lured into the store, he or she is pressured to purchase another more expensive item.

A long ethical tradition has consistently condemned deception in advertising on the grounds that it violates consumers' rights to choose for themselves (a Kantian argument) and on the grounds that it generates a public distrust of advertising that diminishes the utility of this form and even of other forms of communication

[79] "Ads Aimed at Kids Get Tough NAD Review," *Advertising Age,* 17 June, 1985.

[80] Cynthia Kooi, "War Toy Invasion Grows Despite Boycott," *Advertising Age,* 3 March, 1986.

[81] Howard LaFranchi, "Boom in War Toys Linked to TV," *Christian Science Monitor,* 7 January 1986. LaFranchi notes that the average child watches 800 ads for war toys and 250 war-toy television segments in a year, or the equivalent of 22 days in the classroom. See also Glenn Collins, "Debate on Toys and TV Violence," *New York Times,* 12 December 1985.

[82] See the discussion of manipulation in advertising in Tom L. Beauchamp, "Manipulative Advertising," *Business & Professional Ethics Journal,* 3, nos. 3 & 4 (Spring/Summer 1984); 1–22; and in the same volume the critical response of R. M. Hare, "Commentary," pp. 23–28; see also Alan Goldman, "Ethical Issues in Advertising," pp. 253–60, and Robert L. Arrington, "Advertising and Behavior Control," pp. 3–12, in *Journal of Business Ethics,* 1, no. 1 (February 1982).

(the utilitarian argument).[83] The central problem, then, is not that of trying to understand why deceptive advertising is wrong as much as of trying to understand how it becomes deceptive and therefore unethical.

All communication involves three terms: (1) the author(s) who originates the communication, (2) the medium that carries the communication, and (3) the audience who receives the communication. Since advertising is a form of communication, it involves these three terms and the various ethical problems raised by the fact that it is a form of communication can be organized around these three elements:

The Authors Deception involves three necessary conditions in the author of a communication: (1) The author must intend to have the audience believe something false, (2) the author must know it is false, and (3) the author must knowingly do something that will lead the audience to believe the falsehood. This means that the deliberate intent to have an audience believe something false by merely implying it is as wrong as an express lie. It also means, however, that the advertiser cannot be held morally responsible for misinterpretations of an advertisement when these are the unintended and unforeseen results of unreasonable carelessness on the part of the audience. The "author" of an advertisement includes, of course, not only the heads of an advertising agency, but also the persons who create advertising copy and those who "endorse" a product. By offering their positive cooperation in the making of an advertisement, they become morally responsible for its effects.

The Medium Part of the responsibility for truth in advertising rests on the media that carry advertisements. As active participants in the transmission of a message, they also lend their positive cooperation to the success of the advertisement and so they, too, become morally responsible for its effects. They should, therefore, take steps to ensure that the contents of their advertisements are true and not misleading. In the drug industry, retail agents who serve as company sales agents to doctors and hospitals are in effect advertising "media" and are morally responsible for not misleading doctors with respect to the safety and possible hazards of the drugs they promote.

The Audience The meaning attributed to a message depends in part on the capacities of the person who receives the message. A clever and knowledgeable audience, for example, may be capable of correctly interpreting an advertisement that may be misleading to a less knowledgeable or less educated group. Consequently, the advertiser should take into account the interpretive capacities of the audience when he or she determines the content of an advertisement. Most buyers can be expected to be reasonably intelligent and to possess a healthy skepticism concerning the exaggerated claims advertisers make for their products. Advertisements that will reach the ignorant, the credulous, the immature, and the unthinking, however, should be designed to avoid misleading even those potential buyers

[83] A critical discussion of several definitions of deception in advertising is found in Thomas L. Carson, Richard E. Wokutch, and James E. Cox, "An Ethical Analysis of Deception in Advertising." *Journal of Business Ethics,* 4 (1985); 93–104.

whose judgment is limited. When matters of health or safety, or the possibility of significant injury to buyers is involved, special care should be exercised to ensure that advertisements do not mislead users into ignoring possible dangers.

The third category of issues ("The Audience") raises what is perhaps the most troubling problem in advertising ethics: To what extent do consumers possess the capacity to filter out the "puffery" and bias most advertising messages carry? When an advertisement for a Norelco electric shaver proclaims "You can't get any closer," do consumers automatically discount the vague, nonspecific, and false implication that Norelco was tested against every possible method of shaving and was found to leave facial hair shorter than any other method? Unfortunately, we have very little knowledge of the extent to which consumers are able to filter out the exaggerations advertisements contain.

The moral issues raised by advertising, then, are complex and involve several still unsolved problems. The following summarizes, however, the main factors that should be taken into consideration in determining the ethical nature of a given advertisement:

Social Effects

1. *What does the advertiser intend the effect of the advertisement to be?*
2. *What are the actual effects of the advertisement on individuals and on society as a whole?*

Effects on Desire

1. *Does the advertisement inform or does it also seek to persuade?*
2. *If it is persuasive, does it attempt to create an irrational and possibly injurious desire?*

Effects on Belief

1. *Is the content of the advertisement truthful?*
2. *Does the advertisement have a tendency to mislead those to whom it is directed?*

QUESTIONS FOR REVIEW AND DISCUSSION

1. Define the following concepts: the contractual theory (of a seller's duties), the duty to comply, implied claim, reliability, service life, maintainability, product safety, reasonable risk, duty of disclosure, duty not to misrepresent, duty not to coerce, manufacturer's implied warranty, disclaimer, caveat emptor, due care theory (of a seller's duties), caveat vendor, professional, manufacturer's duty to exercise due care, social costs theory (of a seller's duties), advertisement, production costs, selling costs, to expand consumption, to shift consumption, Kaldor's theory of advertising and market power, brand loyalty, Galbraith's theory of the creation of consumer desires, bait advertisements, deception.

2. Discuss the arguments for and against the three main theories of a producer's duties to the consumer. In your judgment, which theory is most adequate? Are there any marketing areas where one theory is more appropriate than the others?
3. Who should decide (a) how much information should be provided by manufacturers, (b) how good products should be, (c) how truthful advertisements should be? The government? Manufacturers? Consumer groups? The free market? Explain your views.
4. "Advertising should be banned because it diminishes a consumer's freedom of choice." Discuss this claim. Review the materials available in your library and decide whether you agree that "criticisms of advertising based on its social effects are inconclusive."
5. Carefully examine two or more advertisements taken from current newspapers or magazines and assess the extent to which they meet what you would consider adequate ethical standards for advertising. Be prepared to defend your standards.
6. A manufacturer of electric coffee pots recalled the pots (through newspaper announcements) when he found that the handles would sometimes fall off without warning and the boiling contents would spill. Only 10 percent of the pots were returned. Does the manufacturer have any additional duties to those who did not return the pots? Explain your answer.

CASES FOR DISCUSSION

Drugs and Hair Dyes

In January 1978, the Food and Drug Administration (FDA) announced it was considering a regulation that would require hair dyes containing the chemical 4-MMPD (4-Methoxy-M-phenylenediamine sulfate) to carry the following label:

> Warning: Contains an ingredient that can penetrate your skin and has been determined to cause cancer in laboratory animals.

The warning promised to have a significant effect on the sales of the major manufacturers of permanent hair dyes, including Clairol, Cosmair, Revlon, Alberto-Culver, Breck, Helene Curtis, and Tussy. The permanent hair dye sales of these companies had topped $300 million in 1977.

4-MMPD had been suspected of being carcinogenic since March 1975, when Dr. Bruce Ames announced that hair-dye ingredients caused mutations in bacterial genes.[1] Since chemicals that produce bacterial mutations are often also found to cause cancer, bacterial mutations are generally regarded as indications of a potentially carcinogenic substance.

The National Cancer Institute (NCI) subsequently tested 4-MMPD and found that it did indeed cause cancer in laboratory animals. Concurrently, the FDA sponsored studies that showed that about 3 percent of the 4-MMPD in dyes readily penetrates the scalp and enters the bloodstream; only 50 percent of the chemical is subsequently excreted.

In spite of these findings, however, the FDA was unable to do more than propose a warning label, since the 1938 Food, Drug, and Cosmetic Act, which

[1] "Are Hair Dyes Safe?," *Consumer Reports*, 44, no. 8 (August 1979): 456–60.

regulates cosmetics, prohibits the FDA from banning the sale of hair dyes no matter how hazardous their contents. This prohibition was written into the law when a powerful cosmetic lobby convinced Congress in 1938 that hair dyes should be exempt from any law controlling cosmetics.[2] Moreover, the cosmetic industry contested the validity of the NCI tests on the grounds that the large doses of 4-MMPD administered to animals in the tests were "the equivalent of a woman drinking more than 25 bottles of hair dye a day, every day of her life." FDA officials countered that because of test expenses, researchers must expose a few animals to large doses in order to determine the risk of exposing many humans to small doses. After a prolonged legal battle with the cosmetic industry, the FDA succeeded in imposing the proposed warning label.

When it was clear that the FDA would succeed in imposing the warning label, the major hair dye manufacturers implemented essentially similar strategies to avoid the label: They reformulated their hair dyes so that the new dyes contained no 4-MMPD. However, the companies refused to recall the old hair dyes that they had already distributed to retailers and that would continue to be sold over counters for several years. They would affix no warnings to these dyes.

The response of Revlon differed somewhat from that of other manufacturers. Revlon removed the offending 4-MMPD from its dyes and replaced it with a 4-EMPD (4-ethoxy-M-phenylenediamine sulfate), a substance with a chemical structure almost identical to 4-MMPD, but one that did not yet require a warning label.

Several chemical experts later claimed that Revlon's 4-EMPD had a potential for causing cancer similar to that of 4-MMPD.[3] The FDA subsequently tested 4-EMPD and found that it produced bacterial mutations similar to those that 4-MMPD had produced several years before. When questioned about the safety of 4-EMPD, Revlon at first contended that the NCI had tested 4-EMPD and had found it was not hazardous. NCI, however, denied that it had ever tested 4-EMPD. Revlon then corrected itself and admitted that its own biologists had performed bacterial tests on 4-EMPD and, like the FDA, they had found that the substance caused mutations in bacterial genes.[4]

Until animal tests on 4-EMPD are completed, the FDA cannot move to require a warning label against the Revlon substance. Such tests take three to four years to complete, and processing a warning proposal takes another one or two years.

1. In your judgment, was the Food and Drug Administration right in ordering the warning label in January 1978, on the basis of the kinds of tests that it and the NCI had carried out? Defend your answer.
2. In your judgment, was it enough, from an ethical point of view, for the cosmetic companies to fix the warning on their labels or did their duties extend beyond this? Relate your answer to the three theories on the seller's duties discussed in the text and to the legitimacy of imposing risk.
3. In your judgment, should the FDA also have imposed some restrictions on the adver-

[2] Darla Miller, "Well, Does She or Doesn't She—Know If Her Hair Dye Is Safe," *San Jose Mercury*, 5 December 1979, pp. 1C, 3C.

[3] *Ibid.*

[4] "Are Hair Dyes Safe," p. 458.

tisements through which the cosmetic companies promoted their dyes? Explain your answer.

4. Comment on the ethical propriety of the strategies by which the cosmetic companies responded to the FDA announcement of January 1978 and to the requirements of a warning label.
5. Should government have the power to regulate business in the manner described in the case? Should the FDA have more or less control over cosmetic companies? Comment on the business-government relationships illustrated by the case.

Marketing Infant Formula

Dear Friend, In asking for your help in the boycott of Nestlé products, I speak for myself and for the Infant Formula Action Coalition (INFACT). Nestlé, the largest food processer in the world, is actively encouraging mothers in the developing countries in Africa, Asia, and South America to give up breast feeding and turn to powdered milk formula instead. But in such countries water is contaminated, sterilization procedures are unknown, illiteracy makes proper preparation impossible, and poor people try to stretch the powdered milk supply by overdiluting their baby's formula. The tragic results are widespread malnutrition and severe infant diarrhea that often ends in death. Despite worldwide protest, Nestlé continues to put profits first and refuses to halt this traffic with death. So we are trying, by boycott, to compel Nestlé to do what they won't do out of decency. INFACT and I ask you to do two things: Boycott *all* Nestlé products, and send a generous contribution to help us spread the word.

Most sincerely,
Benjamin Spock, M.D.[1]

Dr. Spock's letter supporting the boycott of Nestlé's products was one of several tactics used to get producers of infant formula to change their marketing practices in developing nations. In addition to Nestlé, four other companies have come under fire for their marketing of infant formula in Third World countries: Bristol-Myers, Abbott Laboratories, American Home Products, and Borden's.

Infant formula was developed in the 1920s to provide a medically acceptable alternative to breast milk for mothers who were not able to breast-feed their babies.[2] By the 1960s, 75 percent of all American babies were being fed infant formula, and two kinds of companies were producing and marketing the formulas: drug companies and food companies. The three main American drug companies producing infant formula (Bristol-Myers, Abbott Laboratories, and American Home Products) tended to emphasize dietary research in the development of their formulas and tended to market their formulas through medical channels: physicians, nurses, hospitals, clinics, professional health journals, and medical detail staff. The two

[1] Undated letter printed and distributed by the Newman Center, 1701 University Ave., S. E., Minneapolis, MN 55414.

[2] The information in this and the following paragraph is drawn from James E. Post, "The International Infant Formula Industry," pp. 215–41, in *Marketing and Promotion of Infant Formula in the Developing Nations, 1978*: *Hearing Before the Subcommittee on Health and Scientific Research of the Committee on Human Resources*. U.S. Congress, Senate, 95th Congress. Hereinafter this publication is cited as "*Hearings*."

main food companies (Nestlé—a Swiss company—and Borden's), on the other hand, entered the infant formula business as a way of diversifying the canned milk products they were already producing and they tended to market their product through conventional consumer-oriented mass advertising.

During the 1960s birth rates in the United States and Europe began to level off, and infant formula producers turned to marketing their products in Third World countries where birth rates were still high and where a trend toward urbanization was making large populations accessible to modern mass-marketing techniques. Bristol-Myers pushed hard to extend its marketing into the Caribbean, Central America, and the Philippines; Abbott Laboratories moved into Africa and Southeast Asia; American Home Products expanded into Southeast Asia, Latin America, and Africa; Borden's went into Latin America, the Caribbean, and Southeast Asia; and Nestlé attempted to build up a significant presence in every national market. By the late 1970s Abbott Laboratories' infant formula sales in developing nations totaled about $20 million annually; American Home Products had sales of about $50 million worth of infant formula in developing nations; and Nestlé held about a 50 percent share of the entire infant formula world market estimated to total $1.5 billion in 1978. Borden's succeeded in developing only a narrow share of the infant formula market.

Many medical personnel in Third World countries were happy to see the appearance of the infant formulas. Prior to the introduction of the formulas, infants were regularly weaned from breast-feeding with rice water, sweetened cow's milk, and other supplemental foods, so the formulas provided a preferable method of weaning. Undernourished or sickly mothers, too, had not had a readily available alternative to supplement their breast milk until the formulas appeared. In addition, understaffed hospitals welcomed the appearance of the "mothercraft nurses" whom the formula manufacturers provided and who instructed new mothers on all aspects of hygenic child care and feeding. The nurses, dressed in white uniforms, provided the mothers with free samples (as hospitals do in the United States), and were often paid on a commission basis to promote the formulas. While the drug companies (Bristol-Myers, Abbott Laboratories, and American Home Products) promoted their formulas primarily through these medical avenues, Nestlé and the other food companies tended to rely primarily on intensive mass-media advertising, including sound trucks, newspapers, television, radio, popular magazines, and billboards.

As infant formula manufacturers expanded their marketing into the developing countries in the early 1970s, health officials began to voice a concern that the incidence of malnutrition and diarrhea were rising among Third World babies due to an increasing reliance on infant formulas and a concomitant decline of breast-feeding. In a series of studies, Dr. Derrick B. Jelliffe and other nutrition experts claimed that the trend toward infant formulas was dangerous, and that breast milk was the only ideal food for growing infants because it contains both the nutrients essential to a child's health and the antibodies that protect the child against disease.[3] If a mother is unable to nurse her child, they argued, then commercial formulas would provide a safe substitute only if they could be used under

[3] D. B. Jelliffe, *Child Nutrition in Developing Countries* (Washington, DC: U.S. Government Printing Office, 1966); D. B. Jelliffe, "World Trends in Infant Feeding," *American Journal of Clinical Nutrition*, 29 (1976): 1227.

sanitary conditions and according to the instructions provided with the formulas. In underdeveloped countries, they claimed, these conditions were not available: Hygiene was lacking, sterilization procedures were not employed, and mothers lacked the education to read written instructions. These and other difficulties involved in the use of infant formula by third-world mothers were summarized in 1973 by Dr. Roy E. Brown:

> [As] with other so-called convenience foods, the general public must pay the commercial companies for that convenience. In a newly urbanized [third-world] family, the financial pressures may be extreme, and it is not uncommon for a well-meaning mother to be forced to cut her food costs by over-diluting or "stretching" the infant's formula . . . Added to this are several other related problems in formula preparation. The uneducated mother may easily misread or misunderstand the directions and incorrectly reconstitute the formula. In many new urban centers, the contaminated water supply will contaminate the formula. There is an associated problem with the cleansing of feeding bottles and nipples, and with refrigeration of the prepared formulas . . . The end result is not only poor nutrition but also recurrent bouts of diarrhea that will cause further dietary restriction, modification, and dilution and that will increase the likelihood of malnutrition and possible death.[4]

Dr. Jelliffe estimated that infant deaths in the Third World directly or indirectly attributable to the use of infant formula might be as high as ten million per year. Consequently steps should be taken to encourage breast-feeding among mothers in developing countries and to discourage the use of infant formula preparations.

Critics of the infant formula companies alleged that it was the aggressive marketing practices that the companies were using in the Third World that were encouraging mothers to use infant formula even when it endangered the life and health of their infants. Two kinds of practices drew special criticism: intensive consumer advertising that implied that the use of infant formula was nutritionally or socially superior to breast-feeding, and the use of medical personnel to endorse or promote the infant formulas directly to new mothers. Doug Clement, for example, an organizer of the Infant Formula Coalition that sponsored the Nestlé boycott, argued:

> Mass-media advertising is one way that these formula producers create a market for infant formula in the developing countries. Huge advertisements appear on the sides of panel trucks in Nigeria or stationwagons in Thailand. In Barbados, advertisements for Bristol-Myers' "Enfamil" were on the back covers of the 1975 and 1976 telephone books . . . In the maternity ward of Philippine hospitals there are full-color calendars and posters depicting bright, healthy babies next to large cans of Nestlé's "Lactogen" and "Pelargon" formulas. And in Uruguay newspaper ads display a new Nestlé formula: "Eledon" . . . [Radio] has become an extensive advertising medium for formula marketers in the third-world. In Kenya, for example, infant formula ads made up almost 13 percent of all Swahili radio advertising in 1973; nine-tenths of this advertising was for Nestlé's Lactogen. In Malaysia, where the poor and rural tend to listen to the radio while the relatively rich and urban watch television, Nestlé ran three and a half times as many formula ads on radio as on TV in 1976. "Mother-

[4] Roy E. Brown, "Breast Feeding in Modern Times," *American Journal of Clinical Nutrition*, 26 (May 1973): 485–86.

craft nurses,'' hired by the companies to talk to new mothers about infant care and feeding . . . bring cans of their company's formula when they visit mothers on the maternity wards or in their homes, and often leave [free] samples behind. In their crisp white uniforms, the nurses are seen as medical authorities, and their explicit endorsement of bottle-feeding is a powerful reinforcement of the media message. Such advertising persuades third-world women that formula is the modern, healthy, and Western way to feed babies. Bottle-feeding becomes a status symbol; breast-feeding, a vulgar tradition. [Statement of Doug Clement][5]

All infant formula promotions in the Third World, these critics argued, should unequivocally emphasize the superiority of breast-feeding over bottle-feeding. None should encourage bottle-feeding.

In February 1978, a researcher for the Interfaith Center for Corporate Responsibility (a critic of the infant formula companies) analyzed the labels on several cans of infant formula available in stores in Guatemala. According to the researchers, the Spanish labels read as follows when translated into English:[6]

SIMILAC—American Home Products (no mention of breast-feeding):

There is no food equivalent that more closely resembles the milk of healthy well-fed mothers.
SIMILAC With Iron
Similar to Mother's Milk

WYETH S-26—American Home Products (no mention of breast-feeding):

Nourishes the baby like the mother's breast.
S-6
A superior food for the infant offers the baby all the formula he wants, just as if you were giving him the breast.

NAN—Nestlé:

Maternal lactation is the most adequate for the baby but in case of its total or partial absence, or if for other reasons it is necessary to replace or complement it, you can use NAN with total confidence, a powdered food quantitatively and qualitatively similar to mother's milk, for use right from the infant's birth.

ENFAMIL—BRISTOL MYERS:

Breast milk is best for your infant and is the preferred feeding whenever possible. ENFAMIL is a sound nutritious substitute or supplement for breast milk to be used when breast-feeding is unsuccessful, inappropriate, or stopped early.

[5] Doug Clement, ''Infant Formula Malnutrition: Threat to the Third-World,'' *The Christian Century*, 1 March 1978, p. 209.

[6] *Hearings*, pp. 720–21.

During the early 1970s, Borden's was advertising "KLIM," its principal powdered milk product, in the Caribbean and other developing areas. Magazine and newspaper advertisements showed a picture of a smiling plump baby drinking from a bottle; below the picture of the baby was a slightly smaller picture of a can of Klim and the text: "Give him Klim and watch him grow! Klim is full of goodness to build strong bodies, bones, and teeth. Give your baby the best full cream powdered milk—give him Klim. KLIM IS GOOD FOR YOUR BABY AND YOUR GROWING CHILDREN TOO." The ad contained no mention of breast-feeding nor did it mention that Klim was not an infant formula but was simply a form of powdered milk. In Singapore radio ads often repeated the slogan: "Help your baby grow healthy and happy. Give him [Nestlé's] Lactogen with Honey." Newspaper advertisements carried the same slogan in large type beneath a picture of a plump smiling baby surrounded by a well-dressed family and a picture of a can of Lactogen infant formula; beneath the slogan in much smaller type was the text: "Mother's milk is always best for your baby but when breast-feeding is no longer possible, or when your breast-fed baby is growing so fast that he needs extra feeds, give him Lactogen with Honey and help him grow healthy and happy."

The infant formula companies also promoted their products through the use of "baby booklets" which were distributed to new mothers free of charge. Nestlé, for example, distributed booklets entitled *A Life Begins* and *Your Baby and You* that urged the mother to use "an occasional bottle-feed" when she could not breast-feed her baby "entirely" by herself. The pamphlets also drew attention to various reasons for discontinuing breast-feeding and for substituting formula.

Critics of the infant formula industry employed several strategies as they attempted to pressure the companies into changing their marketing practices. In England, the War On Want, a charity organization, published *The Baby Killer*, an exposé of the infant formula issue and a severe criticism of Nestlé. When a German translation appeared within a year retitled *Nestlé Kills Babies*, Nestlé sued the publishers for defamation and libel. Although Nestlé won the suit in 1976, the lawsuit drew substantial media coverage and focused attention on Nestlé's marketing practices. The following year, in the United States several consumer advocacy groups joined together to form INFACT (Infant Formula Action), a coalition that launched a national boycott of all Nestlé products.

Through 1975, 1976, and 1977, members of the Interfaith Center for Corporate Responsibility (an agency that tries to promote social responsibility in corporations) who held stock in Bristol-Myers, Borden's, Abbott, and American Home Products joined together to sponsor shareholders' resolutions requesting that these companies release information on their infant formula promotion policies. Although these resolutions were all voted down, the companies nonetheless eventually agreed to release the information requested. Subsequently, the Interfaith Center submitted resolutions to American Home Products and Abbott Laboratories asking that these companies cease advertising infant formula to Third World consumers, discontinue using medical personnel and free samples, and include clear instructions and warnings on all infant formula products. Although these resolutions were voted down, they generated substantial publicity for the Interfaith Center and the infant formula issue.

The companies producing infant formula responded to the criticisms in several ways. One response was to argue that withdrawing infant formulas from the Third World would create even greater problems. Abbott Laboratories, for example, argued that the availability of infant formula was a health necessity in Third World countries, and the critical problem was that of developing safe methods of making it available.

> Few would debate that breast-milk alternatives have been necessary . . . [in cases] related to maternal disease, infant deformities, serious illness, prematurity, and inadequacy of breast-milk. In these cases, a formula may be necessary to complement or replace breast-milk if the child is to progress normally. . . . [Another] problem is that women of low socioeconomic status in developing countries are often malnourished . . . they produce an at-risk newborn of low birth weight in up to 50 percent of the cases . . . If fed solely at the breast, low birth weight infants begin to exhibit signs of growth retardation, reduced activity and other symptoms of serious malnutrition at about three months . . . The infant's poor state of malnutrition is associated with higher susceptibility to infection and disease. . . . Over time we believe it will become increasingly clear that a high-quality infant formula, closely patterned after breast-milk and fed with breast-milk may be *nutritionally* preferable for many infants, if the intergenerational cycle of malnourished mothers, malnourished infant is to be broken. . . . So that this point of view is not misinterpreted, we reaffirm that every mother who can, should breast-feed. Even if the breast-milk eventually becomes inadequate, the mother should breast-feed so that the baby receives colostrum and as much benefit as possible from her natural milk . . . [However] in the case of significantly malnourished mothers with low birth weight infants, the advice that nothing but breast-feeding should be offered to a malnourished child for four to six months may prove to be too conservative. Without nutritional intervention and breast-fed only, the infant may be safer but stunted, inactive, and perhaps mentally affected, and the infant's future outcome bleak. A well-nourished infant is less susceptible to infection, so the dangers of early nutritional supplementation need to be weighed against the benefit of resistance to disease.[7]

During the early 1970s, Abbott Laboratories, American Home Products, and Nestlé participated in conferences on infant nutrition that were sponsored by the World Health Organization, UNICEF, and the Protein Advisory Calories Group of the United Nations. Neither Borden's or Bristol-Myers took an active part in these conferences. In November 1975, several infant formula manufacturers formed the International Council of Infant Food Industries (ICIFI) and adopted a code of marketing ethics. Steven Bauer, president of ICIFI, described the code as a "minimum standard" that "addresses itself to matters of ethics and professional standards but not to commercial matters [advertising or marketing policy], which remain the duties and obligations of individual member companies."[8] The ICIFI Code recognized the principle "that breast-milk is the preferred form of nutrition for infants not needing special diets" and that "breast-milk substitutes are intended to supplement breast-milk and [are] for use when mothers cannot, or elect not to, breast-feed for medical or other reasons." The code stated in part:

[7] *Ibid.*, pp. 263–68.

[8] "Marketing Infant Foods," letter of E. Steven Bauer in *The Lancer*, 2 July 1977.

1. The members of ICIFI accept responsibility for the diffusion of information that supports sound infant feeding practices. . . .
2. Product information for the public will always recognize that breast-milk is the feeding of choice with the recommendation to seek professional advice when a supplement or alternative may be required.
3. Product labeling will affirm breast-feeding as the first choice for the nutrition of infants.
4. Product claims will reflect scientific integrity without implication that any product is superior to breast-milk.
5. Explicitly worded instructions and demonstrations for product use will be provided . . .
6. In cooperation with health authorities, professional communications and educational materials will be provided to caution against misuse . . .
7. Members' personnel will observe professional ethics . . . in medical/nursing centers, maternities, and physician's offices and all contacts.
8. Members will employ nurses, nutritionists, and midwives whenever possible to perform mothercraft services . . .
9. Individual contacts by mothercraft personnel and issuance of complimentary supplies of breast-milk substitutes will be in consultation with medical or nursing personnel . . .
10. Mothercraft personnel will support doctors . . . and will not discourage mothers from . . . breast-feeding.
11. Nurses' uniforms will be worn only by persons who are professionally entitled to their use . . .
12. Compensation of mothercraft personnel will be on a basis of quality and level of services performed and without relationship to sales.
13. Adherence to this code will be obligatory on all members of ICIFI . . .[9]

Both Nestlé and American Home Products adopted the code. Abbott Laboratories, however, criticized the marketing code as too weak and subsequently withdrew from the ICIFI:

> Although supportive of the concept, [we] decided not to join the International Council of Infant Food Industries (ICIFI) because we felt that the use of mass-media campaigns for infant formula were inappropriate in third-world settings, and the ICIFI code did not specifically exclude these practices. We subsequently published a printed code outlining our marketing policies. [Statement of Abbott Laboratories spokesperson][10]

Unlike the ICIFI code, the Abbott Laboratories' own marketing code prohibited advertising directly to consumers. The Abbott Laboratories' code stated in part:

1. We believe that unsupervised, direct promotion of infant feeding products to mothers can unjustly impel them to make decisions concerning the care and nutrition of their babies for which they may lack adequate medical or nutritional knowledge.

[9] *Hearings*, pp. 887–88.

[10] *Ibid.*, p. 270.

Therefore, we do not advertise our products through general circulation magazines, directories, newspapers, radio, television, billboards, and other public mass media.

2. We do not encourage use of our products where private purchase would impose a financial hardship on the family, or where inadequate facilities for preparation constitute a hazard to infant health.
3. If any contact with mothers is made . . . it must be with the explicit agreement of a health care professional. Samples are supplied only to professional health care personnel at their request.
4. Company representatives . . . are thoroughly taught the preference and value of breast-feeding . . . Deception and other unethical practices are expressly forbidden. Specifically, any inference that our employees are members of a hospital, clinic, or maternity center staff is contrary to company policy. Even in the case of female employees who are qualified nurses, nurses uniforms are not to be worn. Nurses are reimbursed through adequate salary, not sales commission.
5. Our product label and printed instruction, in addition to stressing the importance of breast-feeding, will emphasize the need for accurate, proper proportions in preparing the formula. Pictographs as well as the written word will be included in appropriate language.
6. We will direct additional company resources to: (a) encourage breast-feeding, (b) promote good overall nutritional practices, (c) improve infant and child care, (d) improve sanitation.
7. Unless proscribed by law, we will terminate any distributor who does not follow the code. The company has devised internal procedures and policy to maintain ongoing surveillance of our marketing practices.[11]

The surveillance system used by Abbott Laboratories consisted of asking all field managers to state in writing twice a year whether they were following the code, and of discussing the code with managers in different countries. Bristol-Myers and other drug companies in the infant formula industry also adopted codes similar to Abbott's.

These codes have not entirely satisfied critics. The ICIFI code, in particular, has been heavily criticized. The United Nations' Protein Advisory Group in a letter dated January 23, 1976, claimed that the ICIFI marketing code (1) implied that only "healthy" mothers should breast-feed their infants, (2) provided no way of ensuring that sales staffs in developing countries would communicate the superiority of breast milk, (3) allowed marketing of formula among illiterate mothers who could not read the instructions for preparing the formula, (4) allowed company sales staff to "be visible in medical wards and maternity institutions," (5) failed to regulate promotional material, and (6) was subject to "several weaknesses, inadequacy, and vagueness."[12] In addition, INFACT critics claimed, the ICIFI code provided no surveillance or enforcement methods, it permitted mass advertising aimed at consumers to continue, it allowed nurses to promote the formula to mothers, and it allowed free samples for mothers of newborns. The code, they claimed, in effect "legitimized" these promotional practices. Doubts about the Abbott Laboratories code and others like it focused primarily on the

[11] *Ibid.*, pp. 206–7.

[12] Investor Responsibility Research Center, "Infant Nutrition, Breast Feeding, and Formula Promotion Practices," Analysis R, 6 April 1977, pp. R-13–R-14.

effectiveness of the company's enforcement efforts, on the propriety of continuing to place their "nurses" in health and maternity institutions, and on doubts whether Abbott could control distribution of its products in the many Third World countries where even pharmaceutical drugs are legally sold over-the-counter without prescription.

1. Describe the marketing strategies of the companies involved in the case (distinguish the marketing methods used by the drug companies from those used by the food companies). Describe the strategies used by the critics of the infant formula companies. Explain the concerns of the critics of the formula companies.
2. Assess the promotional practices of the companies in terms of the moral standards that you think are appropriate for the sort of environment in which the companies are operating. Relate your assessment to the three theories of the manufacturer's duties discussed in the chapter. Are any of these three theories particularly appropriate or inappropriate for the Third World context within which the infant formula companies operate? Evaluate the advertisements used by the companies. Do companies have a duty to ensure that consumers do not misuse their products? Do the duties of the manufacturer end at the point of sale?
3. Compare and contrast the codes adopted by the ICIFI and by Abbott Laboratories. Assess the codes in terms of utilitarian criteria, in terms of their recognition of moral rights, and in terms of their adherence to standards of justice. What explanation can you give for the fact that the food companies tend to adopt the ICIFI code whereas the drug companies tend to adhere to a code like Abbott's?
4. In your judgment, are the infant formula companies morally responsible for the misuse of their products and for whatever infant malnutrition results from the use of infant formula in Third World countries? Are Third World governments responsible? Are Third World mothers responsible? Is the medical profession in the Third World responsible?
5. Identify the probable costs and benefits that would result if the companies were to withdraw their products totally from Third World markets. In your judgment, would the benefits of such a withdrawal outweigh its costs? Suggest some practical alternatives to total withdrawal.
6. "By selling our formulas in the Third World we give the Third World mother a choice she did not have before; it is paternalistic to think we have a right to decide what is best for her. The Third World mother should be as free to decide whether to use the formula as her First World counterpart is." Comment.

Toy Wars*

Early in 1986, Tom Daner, president of the advertising company of Daner Associates, was contacted by Mike Teal, the sales manager of Crako Industries. Crako Industries is a family-owned company that manufactures children's toys and had long been a favorite and important client of Daner Associates. The sales manager of Crako Industries explained that the company had just developed a

* Copyright, © 1986, by Manuel Velasquez. Although the events described in this case are real, all names of the individuals and the companies involved are fictitious; in addition, several details have been altered to disguise the identity of participants.

new toy helicopter. The toy was modeled on the military helicopters that had been used in Vietnam and that had appeared in the "Rambo" movies. Mike Teal explained that the toy was developed in response to the craze for military toys that had been sweeping the nation in the wake of the Rambo movies. The family-owned toy company had initially resisted moving into military toys since members of the family objected to the violence associated with such toys. But as segments of the toy market were increasingly taken over by military toys, the family came to feel that entry into the military toy market was crucial for their business. Consequently, they approved development of a line of military toys, hoping that they were not entering the market too late. Mike Teal now wanted Daner Associates to develop a television advertising campaign for the toy.

The toy helicopter Crako designers had developed was about one and one-half feet long, battery-operated, and made of plastic and steel. Mounted to the sides were detachable replicas of machine guns and a detachable stretcher modeled on the stretchers used to lift wounded soldiers from a battlefield. Mike Teal of Crako explained that they were trying to develop a toy that had to be perceived as "more macho" than the top-selling "G.I. Joe" line of toys. If the company were to compete successfully in today's toy market, according to the sales manager, it would have to adopt an advertising approach that was even "meaner and tougher" than what other companies were doing. Consequently, he continued, the advertising clips developed by Daner Associates would have to be "mean and macho." Television advertisements for the toy, he suggested, might show the helicopter swooping over buildings and blowing them up. The more violence and mayhem the ads suggested, the better. Crako Industries was relying heavily on sales from the new toy and some Crako managers felt that the company's future might depend on the success of this toy.

Tom Daner was unwilling to have his company develop television advertisements that would increase what he already felt was too much violence in television aimed at children. In particular he recalled a television ad for a tricycle with a replica machine gun mounted on the handle-bars. The commercial showed the tricycle being pedaled through the woods by a small boy as he chased several other boys fleeing before him over a dirt path. At one point the camera closed in over the shoulder of the boy, focused through the gunsight, and showed the gunsight apparently trying to aim at the backs of the boys as they fled before the tricycle's machine gun. Ads of that sort had disturbed Tom Daner and had led him to think that advertisers should find other ways of promoting these toys. He suggested, therefore, that instead of promoting the Crako helicopter through violence, it should be presented in some other manner. When Teal asked what he had in mind, Tom was forced to reply that he didn't know. But at any rate, Tom pointed out, the three television networks would not accept a violent commercial aimed at children. All three networks adhered to an advertising code that prohibited violent, intense, or unrealistic advertisements aimed at children.

This seemed no real obstacle to Teal, however. Although the networks might turn down children's ads when they were too violent, local television stations were not as squeamish. Local television stations around the country regularly accepted ads aimed at children that the networks had rejected as too violent. The local stations inserted the ads as spots on their non-network programming, thereby circumventing the Advertising Codes of the three national networks. Daner Associates would simply have to place the ads they developed for the Crako helicopter through local television stations around the country. Mike Teal was firm: If Daner Associates would not develop a "mean and tough" ad campaign, the toy company would move their account to an advertiser who would. Reluctantly, Tom Daner agreed to develop the advertising campaign. Crako Industries accounted for $1 million of Daner's total revenues.

Like Crako Industries, Daner Associates was also a family-owned business. Started by his father almost fifty years ago, the advertising firm that Tom Daner now ran had grown dramatically under his leadership. In 1975 the business had grossed $3 million; ten years later it had revenues of $25 million and provided a full line of advertising services. The company was divided into three departments (creative, media, and account executive), each of which had about twelve employees. Tom Daner credited much of the company's success to the many new people he had hired, especially a group with M.B.A.s who had developed new marketing strategies based on more thorough market and consumer analyses. Most decisions, however, were made by a five-person executive committee consisting of Tom Daner, the senior accountant, and the three department heads. As owner-president Tom's views tended to color most decisions, producing what one member of the committee called a "benevolent dictatorship." Tom himself was an enthusiastic, congenial, intelligent and well-read person. During college he had considered becoming a missionary priest but had changed his mind and was now married and the father of three daughters. His personal heros included Thomas Merton, Albert Schweitzer, and Tom Doley.

When Tom Daner presented the Crako deal to his executive committee he found that they did not share his misgivings. The other committee members felt that Daner Associates should give Crako exactly the kind of ad Crako wanted: one with a heavy content of violence. Moreover, the writers and artists in the creative department were enthused with the prospect of letting their imaginations loose on the project, several feeling that they could easily produce an attention-grabbing ad by "out-violencing" current televison programming. The creative department, in fact, quickly produced a copy-script that called for videos showing the helicopter "flying out of the sky with machine-guns blazing" at a jungle village below. This kind of ad, they felt, was exactly what they were being asked to produce by their client.

But after viewing the copy, Tom Daner refused to use it. They should produce an ad, he insisted, that would meet their client's needs but that would also meet the guidelines of the national networks. The ad should not glorify violence and war but should somehow support cooperation and family values. Disappointed and somewhat frustrated, the creative department went back to work. A few days later, they presented a second proposal: an ad that would show the toy helicopter flying through the family room of a home as a little boy plays with it; then the scene shifts to show the boy on a rock rising from the floor of the family room; the helicopter swoops down and picks up the boy as though rescuing him from the rock where he had been stranded. Although the creative department was mildly pleased with their attempt, they felt it was too "tame." Tom liked it, however, and a version of the ad was filmed.

A few weeks later Tom Daner met with Mike Teal and his team and showed them the film. The viewing was not a success. Teal turned down the ad. Referring to the network regulations which other toy advertisements were breaking as frequently as motorists broke the 55-mile-per- hour speed law, he said "That commercial is going only 55 miles an hour when I want one that goes 75." If the next version was not "tougher and meaner," Crako Industries would be forced to look elsewhere.

Disappointed, Tom Daner returned to the people in his creative department and told them to go ahead with designing the kind of ad they had originally wanted: "I don't have any idea what else to do." In a short time the creative department had an ad proposal on his desk that called for scenes showing the helicopter blowing up villages. Shortly afterwards a small set was constructed depicting a jungle village sitting next to a bridge stretching over a river. The ad was filmed using the jungle set as a background.

When Tom saw the result he was not happy. He decided to meet with his creative department and air his feelings. "The issue here," he said, "is basically the issue of violence. Do we really want to present toys as instruments for beating up people? This ad is going to promote aggression and violence. It will glorify dominance and do it with kids who are terrifically impressionable. Do we really want to do this?" The members of the creative department, however, responded that they were merely giving their client what the client wanted. That client, moreover, was an important account. The client wanted an aggressive "macho" ad, and that was what they were providing. The ad might violate the regulations of the television networks, but there were ways to get around the networks. Moreover, they said, every other advertising firm in the business was breaking the limits against violence set by the networks. Tom made one last try: Why not market the toy as an adventure and fantasy toy? Film the ad again, he suggested, using the same jungle backdrop. But instead of showing the helicopter shooting at a burning village, show it flying in to rescue people from the burning village. Create an ad that shows excitement, adventure, and fantasy, but no aggression. "I was trying," he said later, "to figure out a new way of approaching this kind of advertising. We have to follow the market or we can go out of business trying to moralize to the market. But why not try a new approach? Why not promote toys as instruments that expand the child's imagination in a way that is positive and that promotes cooperative values instead of violence and aggression?"

A new film version of the ad was made, now showing the helicopter flying over the jungle set. Quick shots and hightened background music give the impression of excitement and danger. The helicopter flies dramatically through the jungle and over a river and bridge to rescue a boy from a flaming village. As lights flash and shoot haphazardly through the scene the helicopter rises and escapes into the sky. The final ad was clearly exciting and intense. And it promoted the saving of a life instead of violence against life.

It was clear when the final version was shot, however, that it would not clear the network censors. Network guidelines require that sets in children's ads must depict things that are within the reach of most children so that they do not create unrealistic expectations. Clearly the elaborate jungle set (which cost $25,000 to construct) was not within the reach of most children and consequently most children would not be able to recreate the scene of the ad by buying the toy. Moreover, network regulations stipulate that in children's ads scenes must be filmed with normal lighting that does not create undue intensity. Again clearly the helicopter ad which created excitement by using quick changes of light and fast cuts did not fall within these guidelines.

After reviewing the film Tom Daner reflected on some last-minute instructions Crako's sales manager had given him when he had been shown the first version of the ad: The television ad should show things being blown up by the guns of the little helicopter and perhaps even some blood on the fuselage of the toy; the ad had to be violent. Now Tom had to make a decision. Should he risk the account by submitting only the rescue mission ad? Or should he let Teal also see the ad that showed the helicopter shooting up the village, knowing that he would probably prefer that version if he saw it? And was the rescue mission ad really that much different from the ad that showed the shooting of the village? Did it matter that the rescue mission ad still violated some of the network regulations? What if he offered Teal only the rescue mission ad and Teal accepted the "rescue approach" but demanded he make it more violent; should he give in? And should Tom risk launching an ad campaign that was based on this new untested approach? What if the ad failed to sell the Crako toy? Was it right to experiment with a client's product, especially a product that was so important to the future of the client's business? Tom was unsure what he should do. He wanted to show Teal only the rescue mission commercial but he felt he first had to resolve these questons in his own mind.

1. From a moral point of view, what, in your judgment, should Tom Daner's final decision be? Justify your answer. What should Tom do if he is asked to make the final ad more violent than the rescue ad he had filmed?
2. Answer the questions Tom Daner asked himself: Was the rescue mission ad really that much different from the ad that showed the shooting of the village? Did it matter that the rescue mission ad still violated some of the network regulations? Was it right to experiment with a client's product, especially a product that was so important to the future of the client's business?

Part Four

BUSINESS AND ITS INTERNAL CONSTITUENCIES

Employee Issues

The process of producing goods forces businesses not only to engage in external exchanges but also to coordinate the activities of the various internal constituencies who must be brought together and organized into the processes of production. Employees must be hired and organized; stockholders and creditors must be solicited; managerial talent must be tapped. Inevitably conflicts arise within and between these internal constituencies as they interact with each other and as they seek to distribute benefits among themselves. The next two chapters explore some of the ethical issues raised by these internal conflicts. Chapter Seven discusses the issue of job discrimination. Chapter Eight discusses the issue of conflicts between the individual and the organization.

7

THE ETHICS OF JOB DISCRIMINATION

INTRODUCTION

In 1989, the Supreme Court, in a decision written by Sandra Day O'Connor, the only female justice to ever sit on the Court, invalidated an affirmative action program of the city of Richmond, Virginia, that required that 30 percent of its construction contracts be awarded to minority businesses so that the effects of past racial discrimination in the construction industry might be remedied. The next day the editor of the *Syracuse Herald-Journal* in Syracuse, New York, sharply criticized the Supreme Court's ruling:

> Assuming that what the Supreme Court ultimately seeks is justice, not merely legal correctness, Monday's ruling against ''set-asides'' for minority contractors is a bad one. For justice is not some intellectual exercise for a jurist in chambers. It is not something for legal scholars to ponder at their ease in the years to come. It is not small talk at the Bar Association cocktail party. Justice—or the absence of it—is what happens to people's lives. And the effect of this ruling— intended or not— will be to deny economic justice to people. . . . [B]itter experience has shown that . . . [u]nless special arrangements are made beforehand—such as with set-asides—minorities often are effectively shut out. Not that those awarding government contracts are necessarily motivated by racism—although that surely happens. But the people in charge tend to favor their friends, the people they know, the people they've done business with before. Cracking that tight little circle can be impossible—or next to impossible—for a minority entrepreneur trying to get a business off the

> ground. There's nothing wrong with free enterprise and a level playing field. . . . But there are capable, worthy people who before affirmative action had no hope of even getting into the game. The upshot of the Supreme Court ruling will be to put many of them back on the sidelines. This is not justice.[1]

The same day, but several thousand miles away, in Nebraska, the editor of the *Omaha World-Herald* congratulated the six members of the Supreme Court who had voted in favor of the ruling:

> A six-member majority on the U.S. Supreme Court dealt sensibly with a lawsuit in which a good cause—helping minority groups enter the work force—was carried to extremes. The decision in a Virginia case should supply some of the balance that was missing from some earlier decisions dealing with affirmative action and racial quotas. Racial discrimination in the workplace is illegal, as it ought to be. . . . [But] some people, even though they hate racial discrimination, have been troubled by the inherent inconsistencies in the use of what amounts to reverse discrimination to correct the "effects of past discrimination." Preferences give special treatment to an individual without regard to whether he has been the victim of past discrimination. Other individuals are penalized, by being passed over, without regard to whether they have discriminated illegally against anyone. To demand preferential treatment, in effect, is to imply that minorities can't compete and succeed on their merits.[2]

The debates over discrimination and its remedies have been prolonged and acrimonious and have continued to this day. Since the 1960s, public concern has swirled around the plight of racial minorities, the inequality of women, and the "harm" that white males have suffered as a result of the preference shown to women and minorities. These continuing debates over racial and sexual equality have been focused largely on business. This is inevitable: Racial and sexual discrimination have had a long history in business, and it is in this area that discriminatory practices have the most substantial and long-lasting consequences.

Perhaps more than any other contemporary social issue, public discussions of discrimination have clearly approached the subject in ethical terms: The words "justice," "equality," "racism," "rights," and "discrimination" inevitably find their way into the debate. This chapter analyzes the various sides of this ethical issue. The chapter begins by examining the nature and extent of discrimination. It then turns to discussing the ethical aspects of discriminatory behavior in employment and ends with a discussion of affirmative action programs.

7.1 JOB DISCRIMINATION: ITS NATURE

Although many more women and minorities are entering formerly male-dominated jobs, they still face problems that they would characterize as forms of discrimination.

> I am twenty-three-years old, I have a B.A. in Spanish literature . . . During my interview for this job my interviewer kept looking at my legs and talking about

[1] *Syracuse Herald-Journal*, 25 January 1989.

[2] *Omaha World-Herald* (Omaha, Nebraska), 25 January 1989.

> how interesting he thought the job would be for me because I would be around men doing interesting work . . . "We usually don't hire married girls," he said. "We like to have young, pretty and available girls around the office." "You know," he added, "it cheers things up a lot.". . . I was hired and took the job because I was desperate. I was told I was awfully pretty and would most certainly be an asset to the office. . . . When I was hired I was told that two people constitute a team that would work on a specific project. . . . the "team" turned out to be a male, making around $15,000, and a female, making $6,000. Most "girls" have the same degrees as the men, or higher ones, but are still in the lower positions. The reason for this, I was told, was that most foreigners (whom the office deals with) don't "respect" women and would feel slighted if they had to deal with "one." (Wasn't that the reason given for not hiring blacks in offices and shops?—blacks would turn away customers!) . . . In my office all the men go out to eat together and all the women go out to eat together . . . the three blacks in the mailroom eat inside. They are not permitted to go out to eat. [Anonymous][3]

And managers face difficult dilemmas in trying to recruit new personnel without engaging in discrimination. In the fall of 1983, for example, Frank Forsberg, company recruiter for Lockheed Corporation, needed to hire several chemists quickly for a job in Saudi Arabia. Since the Saudi government had given Lockheed very few days to submit a proposal for a contract on a job requiring the use of analytical chemists, the company had little time to lose dealing with candidates who later might turn out to be unacceptable. Frank Forsberg, however, decided he first had to take the time to talk with his boss, K. Bentley, director of Lockheed's science and application branch in Houston, concerning a stipulation that Saudis had placed on the personnel sent to Saudi Arabia to do the job. Conferring with Bentley, Forsberg quickly laid the issue on the table: "The customer has stated that no Jewish applicants or women would be acceptable." Saudi culture prohibits dealings between men and women in business and the Saudis considered themselves involved in a religious and political war with Israel. Thus, they had notified prospective suppliers that it would be impossible for women or Jews to operate effectively in their country and that a company's proposal would be disqualified if it included personnel from either group. Bentley was disturbed by Forsberg's suggestion that their recruitment procedures should include explicit references to the exclusion of Jews and women. According to Forsberg: "When I showed it to Bentley he said, 'Do we really have to say this?' and I said, 'If we're going to get this job proposal out on time, we've got to.' " Reluctantly, Bentley agreed that job notices could be posted stating that women and Jewish applicants were not acceptable to the customer requesting the contract. A few days later Forsberg telephoned a Ph.D. candidate named Philip Lurie who had applied for the job, had the right credentials, and seemed one of the best qualified. On the telephone Forsberg asked "You are obviously not a woman, but are you Jewish?" When Lurie replied, "Yes, I am Jewish," Forsberg thought, "That kind of changes everything."[4] It was unclear to him whether he was involved in an illicitly discriminatory activity.

[3] Anonymous, "We Usually Don't Hire Married Girls," quoted in *The Capitalist System* by Richard C. Edwards, Michael Reich, Thomas E. Weisskopf, 2nd ed. (Englewood Cliffs, NJ: Prentice Hall, 1978), pp. 13–15.

[4] This case is based entirely on the information contained in "U.S. Firms Accused of Discriminating to Do Business Abroad," *San Jose Mercury News*, 27 November 1983, p. 1F.

The root meaning of the term "discriminate" is "to distinguish one object from another," a morally neutral and not necessarily wrongful activity. But in modern usage the term is not morally neutral: It is usually intended to refer to the wrongful act of distinguishing illicitly among people not on the basis of individual merit but on the basis of prejudice or some other invidious or morally reprehensible attitude.[5] This morally charged notion of "invidious" discrimination, as it applies to employment, is what is at issue in this chapter.[6] In this sense to discriminate in employment is to make an adverse decision (or set of decisions) against employees (or prospective employees) who belong to a certain class because of morally unjustified prejudice toward members of that class. Discrimination in employment thus must involve three basic elements. First, it is a decision against one or more employees (or prospective employees) that is *not based on individual merit* such as the ability to perform a given job, seniority, or other morally legitimate qualifications. Second, the decision derives solely or in part from racial or sexual prejudice, from false stereotypes, or from some other kind of *morally unjustified attitude* against members of the class to which the employee belongs. Third, the decision (or set of decisions) has a *harmful or negative impact* upon the interests of the employees, perhaps costing them jobs, promotions, or better pay.

Employment discrimination in the United States historically has been directed at a surprisingly large number of groups. These have included religious groups (such as Jews and Catholics), ethnic groups (such as Italians, Poles, and Irish), racial groups (such as blacks, orientals, and Hispanics), and sexual groups (such as women and homosexuals). We have an embarrassingly rich history of discrimination.

Forms of Discrimination: Intentional and Institutional Aspects

A helpful framework for analyzing different forms of discrimination can be constructed by distinguishing the extent to which a discriminatory act is intentional and isolated (or noninstitutionalized) and the extent to which it is unintentional and institutionalized.[7] First, a discriminatory act may be part of the *isolated* (non-

[5] This morally charged meaning is now perhaps the dominant meaning given to the term "discrimination," and is found in any relatively recent dictionary; see, for example, *Webster's New Collegiate Dictionary* (Springfield, MA: G. & C. Merriam Company, 1974), p. 326, where a main meaning attributed to the term "discriminate" is "to make a difference in treatment or favor on a basis other than individual merit," and where a meaning attributed to "discrimination" is "prejudiced or prejudicial outlook, action, or treatment."

[6] For a somewhat lengthy discussion of the meaning of discrimination, see Barry R. Gross, *Discrimination in Reverse* (New York: New York University Press, 1978), p. 6–28. Although modern dictionaries all attest to the morally charged meaning of "discrimination." Gross tries to provide an argument to the effect that the term should retain its morally neutral meaning so that it can be used to apply to "discrimination against white males" that is not based on racial prejudice. In the text, however, I rely more on the morally laden notion of "invidious discrimination" that has been used by the Supreme Court and that is developed, for example, in Ronald Dworkin, "Why Bakke Has No Case," *New York Review of Books*, 10 November 1977, p. 15.

[7] Joe R. Feagin and Clairece Booker Feagin, *Discrimination American Style*, 2nd ed. (Malabar, FL: Robert E. Krieger Publishing Company, 1986), pp. 23–33.

institutionalized) behavior of a single individual who *intentionally* and knowingly discriminates out of personal prejudice. In the anonymous statement quoted above, for example, the attitudes that the male interviewer is described as having may not be characteristic of other company interviewers: His behavior toward female job seekers may be an intentional but isolated instance of sexism in hiring. Second, a discriminatory act may be part of the routine behavior of an *institutionalized* group, which *intentionally* and knowingly discriminates out of the personal prejudices of its members. The Ku Klux Klan, for example, is an organization that intentionally institutionalizes discriminatory behavior. Third, an act of discrimination may be part of the *isolated* (noninstitutionalized) behavior of a single individual who *unintentionally* and unknowingly discriminates against someone because he or she unthinkingly adopts the traditional practices and stereotypes of his or her society. If the interviewer quoted in the anonymous statement above, for example, acted unintentionally, then he would fall into this third category. Fourth, a discriminatory act may be part of the systematic routine of a corporate organization or group that *unintentionally* incorporates into its formal *institutionalized* procedures practices that discriminate against women or minorities. The anonymous statement above, for example, describes an office in which the best-paying jobs are routinely assigned to men and the worst-paying jobs are routinely assigned to women, on the stereotypical assumption that customers will not do business with women. There may be no deliberate intent to discriminate, but the effect is the same: a racially or sexually based pattern of preference toward white males.

Historically, there has been a shift in emphasis from the discussion of discrimination as an intentional and individual matter, to its discussion as a systematic and not necessarily intentional feature of institutionalized corporate behavior. During the early 1960s, employment discrimination was seen primarily as an intentional, calculated act performed by one individual upon another. Title VII of the Civil Rights Act of 1964, for example, seems to have had this notion of discrimination in mind when it stated:

> It shall be an unlawful employment practice for an employer (1) to fail or refuse to hire or to discharge any individual, or otherwise discriminate against any individual with respect to his compensation, terms, conditions, or privileges of employment because of such individual's race, color, religion, sex, or national origin; or (2) to limit, segregate, or classify his employees or applicants for employment in any way that would deprive or tend to deprive any individual of employment opportunities or otherwise adversely affect his status as an employee because of such individual's race, color, sex, or national origin.[8]

But in the late 1960s, the concept of discrimination was enlarged to include more than the traditionally recognized intentional forms of individual discrimination. By the early 1970s, the term "discrimination" was being used regularly to include disparities of minority representation within the ranks of a firm, regardless of whether or not the disparity had been intentionally created. An organization was engaged in discrimination if minority group representation within its ranks was

[8] U.S. Congress, Senate, Subcommittee on Labor of the Committee on Labor and Public Welfare, *Compilation of Selected Labor Laws Pertaining to Labor Relations, Part II*, 93rd Congress, 2nd Session, 6 September 1974, p. 610

not proportionate to the group's local availability. The discrimination would be remedied when the proportions of minorities within the organization were made to match their proportions in the available workforce by the use of "affirmative action" programs. A Department of Labor guidebook for employers issued in February 1970, for example, stated:

> An acceptable affirmative action program must include an analysis of areas within which the contractor is deficient in the utilization of minority groups and women, and further, goals and timetables to which the contractor's good faith efforts must be directed to correct the deficiencies and thus to increase materially the utilization of minorities and women at all levels and in all segments of his work force where deficiencies exist. . . . "Underutilization" is defined as having fewer minorities or women in a particular job classification than would reasonably be expected by their availability.[9]

Many people have criticized the view that an institution is "discriminatory" if a minority group is underrepresented within its ranks. Discrimination is the act of individuals, these critics argue, and it is individual women and minorities whom it mistreats; consequently, we should not say discrimination exists until we know that a specific individual was discriminated against in a specific instance. The problem with this criticism is that it is generally impossible to know whether a specific individual was discriminated against. People compete with each other for jobs and promotions and whether a person wins a specific job or promotion depends to a large extent on chance factors such as who his competitors happened to be, what abilities his competitors happened to have, how interviewers happened to see him, and how he happened to perform at the crucial moments. Consequently, when a minority individual loses in this competitive process, there is generally no way of knowing whether that individual's loss was the result of chance factors or of systematic discrimination. The only way of knowing whether the process itself is systematically discriminating is by looking at what happens to minorities as a *group*: If minorities as a *group* regularly lose out in a competitive process in which their abilities as a *group* match those of non-minorities, then we may conclude that the process is discriminatory.[10]

Nevertheless, during the 1980s, government policy under the Reagan administration tended to favor the view that the focus of society should not be on discrimination in its institutionalized forms. Starting in about 1981, the federal government began to actively oppose affirmative action programs based on statistical analyses of systematic discrimination. The administration held that only individuals who could prove that they had been the victims of discrimination aimed specifically and intentionally at them should be eligible for preferential treatment in hiring or promotions. Although the Reagan administration was largely unsuccessful in its efforts to dismantle affirmative action programs, it did succeed in naming a majority of Supreme Court justices who rendered decisions that tended to undermine some

[9] U.S. Equal Employment Opportunity Commission, *Affirmative Action and Equal Employment: A Guidebook for Employers*, II (Washington, DC: Government Printing Office, 1974): D-28.

[10] The necessity of basing analyses of discrimination on statistical grounds and the uselessness of attempting an individual case-by-case procedure are discussed by Lester Thurow in "A Theory of Groups and Economic Redistribution," *Philosophy and Public Affairs*, 9, no. 1 (Fall 1979): 25–41.

legal supports of affirmative action programs (these are discussed below). These trends were reversed or at least slowed once again in the 1990s, when Bush became president and pledged to "knock down the barriers left by past discrimination." Moreover, Congress stepped in to propose legislation that would support affirmative action programs and that would reverse the Supreme Court rulings that had undermined them. Thus, our society has wavered and continues to waver on the question of whether discrimination should be seen only as an intentional and isolated act, or also as an unintentional and institutionalized pattern revealed by statistics, and whether we should bend our efforts to combating primarily the former or the latter.

For purposes of analysis it is important to keep separate the ethical issues raised by policies that aim at preventing individuals from discriminating intentionally against other individuals, from those raised by "affirmative action" policies which aim at achieving a proportional representation of minorities within our business institutions. We will discuss each of these issues separately below. First, however, we must examine the extent to which our business institutions today are discriminatory. It is a commonly held belief that although business used to be discriminatory, this is no longer the case due to the great strides minorities and women have made during the last few years. If this belief is correct, then there is not much point in discussing the issue of discrimination. But is it correct?

7.2 DISCRIMINATION: ITS EXTENT

How do we estimate whether an institution is practicing discrimination against a certain group? By looking at statistical indicators of how the members of that group are distributed within the institution. A *prima facie* indication of discrimination exists when a disproportionate number of the members of a certain group hold the less desirable positions within the institution in spite of their preferences and abilities.[11] Three kinds of comparisons can provide evidence for such a distribution: (1) comparisons of the *average* benefits the institution bestows on the discriminated group with the average benefits the institution bestows on other groups; (2) comparisons of the proportion of the discriminated group found in the *lowest* levels of the institution with the proportions of other groups found at those levels; (3) comparisons of the proportions of that group that hold the *more advantageous* positions with the proportions of other groups that hold those same positions. If we look at American society in terms of these three kinds of comparisons, it becomes clear that some form of racial and sexual discrimination is present in American society as a whole. For some segments of the minority population (such as young college-educated black males), however, discrimination is not as intense as it once was.

[11] Walter B. Connolly, Jr., *A Practical Guide to Equal Employment Opportunity*, 2 vols. (New York: Law Journal Press, 1975), 1:231-242; for a discussion of the relevance of statistics see Tom Beauchamp, "The Justification of Reverse Discrimination," in W. T. Blackstone and R. Heslep, *Social Justice and Preferential Treatment* (Athens, GA: The University of Georgia Press, 1977), pp. 84–110.

Average Income Comparisons

Income comparisons provide the most obvious indicators of discrimination. If we compare the average incomes of nonwhite American families, for example, with the average incomes of white American families, it turns out that white family incomes are substantially above those of nonwhites, as Table 7.1 indicates.

Table 7.1 also shows that, contrary to a commonly held belief, the income gap between whites and minorities has been *increasing* rather than decreasing. Since 1973, even during periods when the real incomes of whites have gone up, real minority incomes have not kept up. In 1970 the average income for a black family was 65 percent of a white family's average income; by 1989 the black family's income had dropped to only 60 percent of the white family's income.

Income comparisons also provide evidence of large discrepancies based on sex. A comparison of average incomes for men and women shows that women receive only a portion of what men receive. As Table 7.2 shows, the earnings gap between men and women has narrowed. But women in 1989 earned only about 70 cents for every dollar that men earned, which is, nevertheless, an improvement over the 65 cents on the dollar that they used to make in 1970. However, the latest improvements in the ratio of female and male incomes came about partly as a result of *declines* in the average earnings of men. Between 1988 and 1989, while female real earnings increased by 1.8 percent, male real earnings decreased by 1.8 percent. Thus, the disproportionate impact that poor economic

TABLE 7.1 Average Family Incomes for White and Minority Families (in 1989 dollars)

YEAR	WHITE	BLACK	PERCENTAGE OF WHITE	HISPANIC	PERCENTAGE OF WHITE
1989	$43,403	$26,415	60.8	29,197	67.2
1988	42,254	26,536	62.8	28,197	66.7
1987	42,056	25,948	61.7	28,217	67.0
1986	41,201	25,771	62.5	27,650	67.1
1985	39,614	24,614	62.1	26,681	67.3
1984	38,694	23,604	61.0	26,934	69.6
1983	37,433	22,904	61.2	25,425	67.9
1982	36,754	22,177	60.3	25,362	69.0
1981	36,742	22,776	61.9	26,423	71.9
1980	37,530	23,786	63.4	26,508	70.6
1979	39,680	24,780	62.4	28,648	72.2
1978	39,672	25,502	64.3	27,875	70.2
1977	38,872	24,477	62.9	27,200	69.9
1976	38,192	24,573	64.3	26,282	68.8
1975	37,133	23,973	64.5	25,574	68.8
1974	38,362	24,264	63.2	27,298	71.1
1973	39,554	24,596	62.1	27,716	70.0

Source: U.S. Bureau of the Census, Current Population Reports, Series P-60, No. 168, Table 2.

TABLE 7.2 Median Weekly Earnings and Average Annual Income by Sex (in 1989 dollars)

YEAR	WEEKLY EARNINGS OF WORKING PERSONS: WOMEN	WEEKLY EARNINGS OF WORKING PERSONS: MEN	WEEKLY EARNINGS OF WORKING WOMEN AS A PERCENTAGE OF MEN'S
1988	$ 315	$ 449	70.1%
1987	303	433	69.9
1986	290	419	68.2
1985	277	406	68.2
1984	265	391	67.7
1983	252	378	66.6
1982	238	364	65.3
1981	219	339	64.6
1980	201	312	64.4
1979	182	291	62.5

YEAR	AVERAGE ANNUAL INCOME OF ALL PERSONS: WOMEN	AVERAGE ANNUAL INCOME OF ALL PERSONS: MEN	ANNUAL INCOME OF ALL WOMEN AS A PERCENTAGE OF MEN'S
1989	$13,226	$25,746	51%
1988	12,904	25,213	51
1987	12,594	24,885	50
1986	12,152	24,689	49
1985	11,724	23,800	49
1984	11,438	23,198	49
1983	11,079	22,636	49
1982	10,530	22,334	47
1981	10,149	22,529	45
1980	10,191	23,084	44
1979	10,292	24,443	42
1975	10,402	24,037	43
1970	10,029	24,087	42

Source: U.S. Dept. of Labor Statistics, *Handbook of Labor Statistics*, Bulletin 2340, Table 41, and U.S. Bureau of the Census, Current Population Reports, Series P-60, No. 168, Table 13.

conditions has had on male earnings is partly responsible for recent improvements in the ratio of female-to-male earnings.

The disparities in earnings between men and women begin as soon as men and women leave school. In 1976, ten years after "affirmative action" was instituted, the average *starting* salary offered to women college graduates majoring in marketing was $9,768, while male graduates were offered average starting salaries of $10,236; women graduates majoring in humanities were offered $8,916, while men were offered $9,792; women social science graduates were offered $9,240,

TABLE 7.3 Median Incomes for Men and Women by Education, 1989

EDUCATION	WOMEN'S MEDIAN INCOME	MEN'S MEDIAN INCOME
Elementary		
8 years or less	$12,188	$17,555
High School		
1 to 3 years	13,923	21,065
4 years	17,528	26,609
College		
1 to 3 years	21,631	31,308
4 years	26,709	41,892
5 years or more	32,050	46,842

Source: U.S. Bureau of the Census, Current Population Reports, Series P-60, No. 168, Table 12.

while men were offered $10,392.[12] A census bureau study of men and women aged 21 to 22 found that white women's starting salaries in 1980 were 83 percent of white men's, an actual *decline* from 1970 when white women earned 86 percent of what white men earned.[13] Yet the same study found that between 1970 and 1980 white women had substantially *increased* their job qualifications relative to men: Although the same proportion (27 percent) of men had four or more years of college in 1980 as in 1970, women with four or more years of college entering the labor force increased from 19 percent in 1970 to 27 percent in 1980. Overall, as Table 7.3 shows, in 1989 women with four years of college earned substantially less than men with four years of college; in fact, a male high school graduate commands almost as much as a woman with four years in higher education. Table 7.4 shows that women who recently graduated from high school and college still have substantially lower earnings than their male peers. Not surprisingly, the income distribution between men and women in the United States is sharply skewed in favor of men. Table 7.5 shows that women's incomes consistently fall into the lowest brackets, while men's incomes cluster around the most lucrative ones.

Although young black college male graduates (between the ages of 22 and 27) earn about the same as young white male graduates of the same age, there is little improvement in the relative earnings of older blacks.[14] Moreover, devastatingly high unemployment rates among young blacks (33 percent among blacks aged 16 to 19 in 1988; 20 percent among those aged 20 to 24) have more than

[12] U.S. Dept. of Labor, *The Earnings Gap Between Women and Men* (Washington, DC: U.S. Government Printing Office, 1979), p. 6.

[13] Robert Pear, "Women's Pay Lags Further Behind Men's," *New York Times*, 16 January 1984, p. 1; see also, "Gender Gap/Dollar Gap," *Los Angeles Times*, 25 January 1984.

[14] Daniel S. Hamermesh & Albert Rees, *The Economics of Work and Pay, 3rd Ed.* (New York: Harper & Row Publishers, Inc., 1984), p. 319.

TABLE 7.4 Average Earnings of Men and Women Recently Out of School, 1989 (full- time workers)

EDUCATION	AVERAGE EARNINGS OF 18-TO-24-YEAR-OLDS		AVERAGE EARNINGS OF 25-TO-29-YEAR-OLDS	
	MEN	WOMEN	MEN	WOMEN
Elementary				
8 years or less	$10,653	(NA[a])	$13,617	(NA)
High School				
1 to 3 years	12,297	10,301	17,268	13,001
4 years	14,732	12,189	21,143	15,247
College				
1 to 3 years	15,692	13,591	23,041	17,693
4 years	22,255	17,584	29,233	21,800
5 years or more	(NA)	(NA)	32,092	24,489

Source: U.S. Bureau of the Census, Current Population Reports, Series P-60, No. 162, Table 36.

[a] NA = Not Applicable.

TABLE 7.5 Distribution of Income Among Women and Men, 1989

TOTAL MONEY INCOME	PERCENTAGE OF WOMEN WITH THAT INCOME	PERCENTAGE OF MEN WITH THAT INCOME
$1 to $2,499	16.6	6.9
$2,500 to $4,999	13.4	5.9
$5,000 to $9,999	21.4	13.1
$10,000 to $14,999	14.7	12.8
$15,000 to $24,999	19.0	21.6
$25,000 to $49,999	13.0	29.2
$50,000 to $74,999	1.4	6.7
$75,000 and over	0.5	3.8

Source: U.S. Bureau of the Census, Current Population Reports, Series P-60, No. 168, Table 13.

obliterated the advances made by the small percentage (11 percent in 1988) of young blacks who graduate from college.

The earnings disparities between men, women, and minorities cut across all occupations, as the summary in Table 7.6 shows.

Lowest Income Group Comparisons

The lowest income group in the United States consists of those people whose annual income falls below the poverty level. In 1989 the poverty level was set at $12,675 for a family of four, at $9,885 for a family of three, and $8,076 for a family of two (by comparison, the average tuition, room, and board fees for one

TABLE 7.6 Median Incomes of Men and Women by Occupation, 1989

OCCUPATION	MEDIAN EARNINGS	
	WOMEN	MEN
Executive, administrators, and managerial	$24,589	$40,103
Professional specialty	27,933	39,449
Technical and related support	21,768	31,371
Sales	16,057	29,676
Administrative support, including clerical	17,517	25,138
Precision production, craft, and repair	17,457	26,499
Machine operators, assemblers, and inspectors	14,463	22,343
Transportation and material moving	16,288	23,612
Handlers, equipment cleaners, laborers	14,095	18,046
Service workers	11,669	18,903
Farming, forestry, and fishing	11,305	13,885

Source: U.S. Department of the Census Current Population Reports, Series P-60, No. 168, Table 12.

person to attend a private college for one year in 1988 totaled $13,330).[15] As Table 7.7 shows, poverty has tended to increase in America since 1979. The greatest increase, however, has been among Hispanic minorities. As the table indicates, the poverty rate among minorities has consistently been two to three times higher than among whites every year for the past decade. This is not surprising, since minorities have lower average incomes.

In view of the lower average incomes of women, it also comes as no surprise that families headed by single women fall below the poverty level much more often than families headed by single men. As Table 7.8 indicates, families headed by women are almost three times more likely to be impoverished than families headed by men.

The bottom income groups in the United States, then, are statistically correlated with race and sex. In comparison to whites and to male-headed families, larger proportions of minorities and of female-headed families are poor.

Desirable Occupation Comparisons

The evidence of racial and sexual discrimination provided by the quantitative measures cited above can be filled out qualitatively by examining the occupational distribution of racial and sexual minorities. As the figures in Table 7.9 suggest, larger percentages of white males move into the higher paying occupations, while minorities and women are channeled into those that are less desirable. Consequently, although more minorities have moved into middle-management positions, they have not yet been allowed into senior management and top executive positions.[16]

[15] U.S. Bureau of the Census, *Statistical Abstract of the United States, 1990*, p. 160.

[16] Robert S. Greenberger, "Many Black Managers Hope to Enter Ranks of Top Management," *Wall Street Journal*, 15 June 1981, p. 21.

TABLE 7.7 Whites and Minorities Below Poverty Levels

YEAR	PERCENTAGE OF WHITES BELOW POVERTY LEVEL	PERCENTAGE OF BLACKS BELOW POVERTY LEVEL	PERCENTAGE OF HISPANICS BELOW POVERTY LEVEL
1989	10.0	30.7	26.2
1988	10.1	31.3	26.7
1987	10.4	32.4	28.0
1986	11.0	31.1	27.3
1985	11.4	31.3	29.0
1984	11.5	33.8	28.4
1983	12.1	35.7	28.0
1982	12.0	35.6	29.9
1981	11.1	34.2	26.5
1980	10.2	32.5	25.7
1979	9.0	31.0	21.8
1978	8.7	30.6	21.6
1977	8.9	31.3	22.4
1976	9.1	31.1	24.7
1975	9.7	31.3	26.9
1974	8.6	30.3	23.0
1973	8.4	31.4	21.9

Source: U.S. Bureau of the Census, Current Population Reports, Series P-60, No. 168, Table 19.

TABLE 7.8 Poverty in Families Headed by Females and Males

YEAR	PERCENTAGE OF FAMILIES HEADED BY FEMALES THAT ARE BELOW POVERTY LEVEL	PERCENTAGE OF FAMILIES HEADED BY MALES THAT ARE BELOW POVERTY LEVEL
1989	32.2	12.1
1988	33.4	11.8
1987	34.2	12.0
1986	34.6	11.4
1985	34.0	12.9
1984	34.5	13.1
1983	36.0	13.2
1982	36.3	14.4
1981	34.6	10.3
1980	32.7	11.0
1979	30.4	10.2
1978	31.4	9.2
1977	31.7	11.1
1976	33.0	10.8
1975	32.5	8.0
1974	32.1	8.9
1973	32.2	10.7

Source: U.S. Bureau of the Census, Current Population Reports, Series P-60, No. 168, Table 21.

TABLE 7.9 Annual Earnings of Occupations and Percent of Males, Females, and Minorities in Occupations, 1988

	MEDIAN ANNUAL EARNINGS (1988)	PERCENTAGE OF TOTAL			
		MALE	FEMALE	BLACK	HISPANIC
Executive, administrative and managerial					
Managers, real estate	$22,048	55.28%	44.8%	6.2%	6.6%
Managers, marketing	36,504	68.0%	32.0%	3.6%	2.6%
Professional specialty					
Teachers, except college	25,324	27.1%	72.9%	8.8%	3.9%
Lawyers and judges	47,268	80.5%	19.5%	2.3%	1.9%
Technical sales, and administrative support					
Administrative support	16,536	19.9%	80.1%	11.3%	6.5%
Technicians	23,296	52.1%	47.9%	9.4%	4.3%
Service occupations					
Private household	7,280	3.7%	96.3%	22.5%	16.7%
Protective services	21,684	85.6%	14.4%	16.7%	6.3%
Precision production, craft, and repair					
Mechanics and repairers	22,828	96.7%	3.3%	7.1%	7.6%
Extractive occupations	26,156	97.9%	2.1%	5.4%	7.5%
Operators, and laborers					
Machine operators	15,704	59.2%	40.8%	14.8%	13.3%
Transportation	20,228	91.0%	9.0%	14.9%	7.1%
Farming, forestry, fishing					
Agricultural	11,596	81.8%	18.2%	10.0%	21.3%
Managers, Farm	14,456	85.0%	15.0%	1.1%	1.6%

Source: U.S. Department of Labor *Handbook of Labor Statistics*, August 1989, pp. 194–8, and U.S. Bureau of the Census, *Statistical Abstract of the United States, 1990*, pp. 389–91.

Just as the most desirable occupations are held by whites, while the less desirable are held by blacks, so also the most well-paying occupations tend to be reserved for men, and the remainder for women. Table 7.10 illustrates the disparities. Studies indicate that despite two decades of women entering the workforce in record numbers, women managers still are not being promoted from middle-management positions into senior or top-management posts, which continue to be dominated by males.[17]

These statistics are not explainable in terms of the lower educational levels of minorities and women. In 1989, if both worked full time, a male high school

[17] Karen Blumenthal, "Room at the Top," *Wall Street Journal*, 24 March 1986; Marilyn Loden, "Disillusion at the Corporate Top," *New York Times*, 9 February 1986; Carol Kleiman, "Women Still Bound Tightly by Job Stereotype," *San Jose Mercury*, 9 February 1986; Warren Boeker, Rebecca Blair, M. Frances Van Loo, and Karlene Roberts, "Are the Expectations of Women Managers Being Met?" *California Management Review*, Spring 1985.

TABLE 7.10 Median Weekly Earnings and Percentage of Men and Women in Different Occupations, 1988

OCCUPATION	EARNINGS	PERCENTAGE IN OCCUPATION	
		MEN	WOMEN
Child care workers	119	1	99
Secretaries	312	2	98
Kindergarten teachers	321	3	97
Teacher's aides	224	4	96
Typists	299	5	95
Bookkeepers	308	9	91
Elementary school teachers	481	15	85
Cashiers	192	20	80
Waiter/Waitresses	189	23	77
Computer operators	342	34	66
Social workers	423	36	64
Accountants	501	48	52
Secondary school teachers	521	51	49
School administrators	671	56	44
Management analysis	672	63	37
Computer programmers	588	68	32
Marketing managers	702	69	31
Lawyers	914	74	26
Blue collar supervisors	589	92	8
Electrical engineers	741	93	7
Aerospace engineers	805	95	5
Airplane pilots	811	98	2

Source: U.S. Dept.of Labor, *Handbook of Labor Statistics*, Bulletin 2340, Table 43.

graduate earned $26,609, about equal to the $26,709 that a female needed a college diploma to earn. That same year, the income of families headed by blacks aged 25 to 44 who had one to three years of college ($22,537), was close to that of families headed by whites aged 25 to 44 but who had only one to three years of high school ($21,266).[18] And as we noted above, women who recently graduated from high school and college still get substantially lower starting salaries and afterwards continue to earn less than their male peers.

Nor can the large disparities between white males and women or minorities be accounted for by the preferences of the latter. It is sometimes suggested that women choose to work in those jobs that have relatively low pay and low prestige. It is suggested sometimes, for example, that women believe that only certain jobs (such as secretary or kindergarten teacher) are "appropriate" for women; that many women choose courses of study that suit them only for such jobs; that many women choose those jobs because they plan to raise children and these jobs are relatively easy to leave and reenter; that many women choose these jobs

[18] U.S. Bureau of the Census, Current Population Reports, Series P-60, No. 168, *Money Income and Poverty Status in the United States: 1989* (Washington, DC: U.S. Government Printing Office, 1990), pp. 25, 42–3.

because they have limited demands and allow them time to raise children; that many women defer to the demands of their husbands' careers and choose to forgo developing their own careers. Although choice undoubtedly plays some role in pay differentials, however, researchers who have studied the differences in earnings between men and women have all concluded that wage differentials cannot be accounted for simply on the basis of such factors. One study found that, at most, only half of the earnings gap might be accounted for by women's choices.[19] The majority of studies, however, have demonstrated that only a much more negligible portion of the gap can be accounted for on the basis of male and female differences in education, work experience, work continuity, self-imposed work restrictions, and absenteeism.[20] These studies show that such differences can at most account for about one third of the wage gap between white men and white women, and only about one quarter of the wage gap between white men and black women. The repeated and extensive nature of these studies utterly discredit the idea that women earn less than men because women choose to sacrifice their careers for the sake of their family responsibilities. A report of the National Academy of Sciences concluded that "about 35–40 percent of the disparity in average earnings is due to sex segregation because women are essentially steered into lower-paying 'women's jobs.' "[21] Some studies have shown that perhaps only one tenth of the wage differences between men and women can be accounted for by differences in their "personalities and tastes."[22] Similar studies have shown that at least half of the earnings differences between white and minority workers cannot be accounted for by differences of work history, of on-the-job training, of absenteeism, nor of self-imposed restrictions on work hours and location.[23]

To make matters worse, several unexpected trends that emerged in the early nineties and that will be with us until the end of the century promise to increase the difficulties facing women and minorities. A major study of economic and population trends during the nineties concluded that the 1990s would be characterized by the following.

First, most new workers entering the labor force during the 1990s will not be white males, but women and minorities. Although a generation ago white

[19] Jacob Mincer and Solomon W. Polachek, "Family Investments in Human Capital: Earnings of Women," *Journal of Political Economy*, 82 (March/April, 1982, Part II): pp. s76–s108.

[20] See Mary Corcoran, Greg J. Duncan, and Martha S. Hill, "The Economic Fortunes of Women and Children," in *Black Women in America*, Micheline R. Malson, Elisabeth Mudimbe-Boyi, Jean F. O'Barr, and Mary Wyer, eds. (Chicago: The University of Chicago Press, 1988), pp. 97–113; Mary Corcoran, "A Longitudinal Approach to White Women's Wages," *Journal of Human Resources*, vol. 18, no. 4 (Fall 1983), pp. 497–520; and Paula England, "The Failure of Human Capital Theory to Explain Occupational Sex Segregation," *Journal of Human Resources*, 17, no. 3 (Summer 1982): 358–70.

[21] "Study Blames Barriers, Not Choices, For Sex Segregation," *San Jose Mercury News*, 20 December 1985, p. 21E.

[22] Randall K. Filer, "Sexual Differences in Earnings: The Role of Individual Personalities and Tastes," *The Journal of Human Resources*, 18, no. 1 (Winter 1983).

[23] Mary Corcoran and Greg J. Duncan, "Work History, Labor Force Attachment, and Earnings Differences Between the Races and Sexes," *The Journal of Human Resources*, 19, no. 1 (Winter 1979): 3–20; see also Gerald Jaynes and Robin Williams, eds., *A Common Destiny: Blacks and American Society*, (Washington, DC: National Academy Press, 1989), pp. 319–23.

males held the largest share of the job market, between 1985 and the year 2000 white males will comprise only 15 percent of all new workers entering the labor force. Their place will be taken by women and minorities. Three fifths of all new entrants coming into business between 1985 and 2000 will be women, a trend created by sheer economic necessity as well as cultural redefinitions of the role of women. By the year 2000, about 47 percent of the workforce will be women, and 61 percent of all American women will be employed. Native minorities and immigrants will make up 42 percent of all new workers during this decade.[24]

Second, this large influx of women and minorities will encounter major difficulties if current trends do not change. First, as we saw, a sizable proportion of women are still concentrated in traditionally female jobs that pay less than traditionally male jobs. Second, at the present time women encounter barriers (a so-called "glass ceiling" through which they may look but not pass) when attempting to advance into top-paying top management positions. A 1987 survey found that of 800 newly promoted corporation chairmen, presidents, and vice presidents, over 97 percent were men; in fact, the study found that the percentage of women being promoted to the vice presidential level was declining. Less than 2 percent of all officers of Fortune 500 companies are women. Third, married women who want children, unlike married men who want children, currently encounter major difficulties in their career advancement. A 1984 survey found that 52 percent of the few married women who were promoted to vice president remained childless, while only 7 percent of the married men had no children. A 1983 survey found that during the ten years following their graduation, 54 percent of those women who had made significant advances up the corporate ladder had done so by remaining childless. Another study found that women with professional careers are six times more likely than their husbands to have to be the one who stays home with a sick child; even women at the level of corporate vice president report that they must carry a greater share of such burdens than their husbands.[25]

The large numbers of minorities entering the workforce will also encounter significant disadvantages if current trends do not change. As these large waves of minorities hit the labor market, they will find that most of the new good jobs awaiting them require extremely high levels of skill and education that they do not have. Of all the new jobs that will be created between now and the year 2000, more than half will require some education beyond high school and almost a third will require a college degree. Among the fastest-growing fields will be professions with extremely high education requirements, such as technicians, engineers, social scientists, lawyers, mathematicians, scientists, and health professionals; while those fields that will actually see declines in numbers consist of jobs that require relatively low levels of education and skills, such as machine tenders and operators, blue collar supervisors, assemblers, hand workers, miners, and farmers. Even those new jobs that require relatively less skills will have tough requirements: Secretaries, clerks, and cashiers will need the ability to read and

[24] The data in this paragraph are drawn from William B. Johnston and Arnold E. Packer, *Workforce 2000: Work and Workers for the Twenty-first Century* (Indianapolis, IN: Hudson Institute, 1987).

[25] All of the studies in this paragraph are cited in Clint Bolick and Susan Nestleroth, *Opportunity 2000* (Indianapolis, IN: Hudson Institute, 1988), pp. 21–22.

write clearly, to understand directions, and to use computers; assembly-line workers are already being required to learn statistical process control methods employing basic algebra and statistics. The new jobs waiting for minorities will thus demand more education and higher levels of language, math, and reasoning skills.

Unfortunately, although a significant proportion of whites are educationally disadvantaged, minorities are currently the least advantaged in terms of skill levels and education. Studies have shown that only about three fifths of whites, two fifths of Hispanics, and one quarter of blacks could find information in a news article or almanac; only 25 percent of whites, 7 percent of Hispanics, and 3 percent of blacks could interpret a bus schedule; and only 44 percent of whites, 20 percent of Hispanics, and 8 percent of blacks could figure out the change they were due from buying two items.[26] Minorities are also much more disadvantaged in terms of education. In 1988, when 80 percent of all whites between the ages of 18 and 21 had received their high school diplomas, only 70 percent of blacks the same age had graduated, and only 54 percent of Hispanics had. The situation for male minorities in this age group was even worse: Only 65 percent of black male youths and only 48 percent of Hispanic male youths graduated from high school.[27] In that same year, while 42 percent of whites ages 18 to 21 were in college, only 27 percent of blacks and 21 percent of Hispanics were. Thus, although future new jobs will require steeply increasing levels of skills and education, minorities are falling behind in their educational attainment.

In recent years, moreover, an especially troublesome obstacle that working women face has been brought to light: sexual harassment. In 1987, for example, 42 percent of all women working for the federal government reported that they had experienced some form of uninvited and unwanted sexual attention, ranging from sexual remarks to attempted rape or assault. Victims of such verbal or physical forms of sexual harassment were most likely to be single or divorced, between the ages of 20 and 44, have some college education, and work in a predominantly male environment or for a male supervisor.[28] An earlier study of sexual harassment in business found that 10 percent of 7,000 people surveyed reported that they had heard of or observed a situation in their organizations as extreme as: "Mr. X has asked me to have sex with him. I refused, but now I learn that he's given me a poor evaluation. . . ."[29] A 1987 federal court vividly described the injuries that sexual harassment can inflict upon a person:

> Cheryl Mathis's relationship with Mr. Sanders began on terms she described as good, but it later became clear that Sanders sought some kind of personal relationship with her. Whenever Mathis was in his office he wanted the door to outside offices closed, and he began discussing very personal matters with her, such as the lack of a sexual relationship with his wife. He then began bombarding her with unwelcome invitations for drinks, lunch, dinner, breakfast, and asking himself to her house. Mathis made it clear that she was not interested in a personal relationship with her

[26] *Ibid.*, p. 67.

[27] See U.S. Bureau of the Census, *Statistical Abstract of the United States, 1990* (Washington, DC: U.S. Government Printing Office, 1990), pp. 150–51.

[28] Reported in Terry Halbert and Elaine Inguilli, eds., *Law and Ethics in the Business Environment* (St. Paul, MN: West Publishing Co., 1990), p. 298.

[29] Eliza G. C. Collins and Timothy B. Blodgett, "Sexual Harassment . . . Some See It . . . Some Won't," *Harvard Business Review*, vol. 59, no. 2, March/April 1981.

> married boss. . . . Sanders also commented on Mathis's appearance, making lewd references to parts of her body. As Mathis rejected Sanders's advances, he would become belligerent. By the spring of 1983 Mathis began to suffer from severe bouts of trembling and crying which became progressively worse and eventually caused her to be hospitalized on two separate occasions, once for a week in June, 1983, and again in July for a few days. During this entire summer Mathis remained out on sick leave, not returning to work until September, 1983. . . . As soon as she returned to work, Sanders's harassment resumed . . . and once again she was forced to seek medical help and did not work. . . . The harassment not only tormented . . . Mathis, it created hostility between her and other members of the department who apparently resented the plaintiff's familiarity with Sanders.[30]

In 1988 about 5,000 cases of sexual harassment were filed with the federal government's Equal Employment Opportunity Commission, and thousands of other complaints were lodged with state civil rights commissions.

It is clear, then, that unless a number of current trends change, women and minorities, who will comprise the bulk of new workers between now and the end of the century, will find themselves in highly disadvantaged positions as they enter the workforce.

The various statistical comparisons that we have examined, together with the extensive research showing that these differences are not due in any simple way to differences in preferences or abilities, indicate that American business institutions incorporate some degree of systematic discrimination, much of it, perhaps, an unconscious relic of the past. Whether we compare average incomes, proportional representation in the highest economic positions, or proportional representation in the lowest economic positions, it turns out that women and minorities are not equal to white males, and the last twenty years have seen but small narrowings of the racial and sexual gaps. Moreover, a number of ominous trends indicate that unless we embark on some major changes, the situation for many minorities and women will worsen.

Of course, finding that our economic institutions as a whole still embody a great deal of discrimination does not show that any particular business is discriminatory. To find out whether a particular firm is discriminatory, we would have to make the same sorts of comparisons among the various employment levels of the firm that we made above among the various economic and occupational levels of American society as a whole. To facilitate such comparisons within firms, employers today are required to report to the government the numbers of minorities and women their firm employs in each of nine categories: officials and managers, professionals, technicians, sales workers, office and clerical workers, skilled craftworkers, semiskilled operatives, unskilled laborers, and service workers.

7.3 DISCRIMINATION: UTILITY, RIGHTS, AND JUSTICE

Given the statistics on the comparative incomes and low-status positions of minorities and women in the United States, the question we must ask ourselves is this:

[30] *Charlotte Lynn Rawlins Yates and Cheryl Jenkins Mathis* v. *Avco Corporation*, 814 F. 2d 630 (1987), U.S. Court of Appeals, Sixth Circuit.

Are these inequalities wrong, and if so, how should they be changed? To be sure, these inequalities directly contradict the fundamental principles on which the United States was founded: "We hold these truths to be self-evident: that all men are created equal and endowed by their creator with certain inalienable rights."[31] But historically we have often tolerated large discrepancies between these ideals and reality. The ancestors of most black Americans living today, for example, were brought to this country as slaves, treated like cattle, and lived out their lives in bondage, in spite of our ideals of "equality." As the personal property of a white owner, blacks prior to the Civil War were not recognized as people, and consequently had no legal powers, no claims on their bodies or their labors, and were regarded by the Supreme Court in one of its opinions, as "beings of an inferior order . . . and so far inferior that they had no rights that the white man was bound to respect."[32] Women were treated comparably. Through much of the nineteenth century, women could not hold office, could not vote, could not serve on juries nor bring suit in their own names; a married woman lost control over her property (which was acquired by her husband), she was considered incapable of making binding contracts, and, in a major opinion, she was declared by the Supreme Court to have "no legal existence, separate from her husband, who was regarded as her head and representative in the social state."[33] Why are these forms of inequality wrong? Why is it wrong to discriminate?

The arguments mustered against discrimination generally fall into three groups: (1) utilitarian arguments, which claim that discrimination leads to an inefficient use of human resources; (2) rights arguments, which claim that discrimination violates basic human rights; and (3) justice arguments, which claim that discrimination results in an unjust distribution of society's benefits and burdens.

Utility

The standard utilitarian argument against racial and sexual discrimination is based on the idea that a society's productivity will be optimized to the extent that jobs are awarded on the basis of competency (or "merit").[34] Different jobs, the argument goes, require different skills and personality traits if they are to be carried out in as productive a manner as possible. Furthermore, different people have different skills and personality traits. Consequently, in order to ensure that jobs are maximally productive, they must be assigned to those individuals whose skills and personality traits qualify them as the most competent for the job. Insofar as jobs are assigned to individuals on the basis of other criteria unrelated to competency, productivity must necessarily decline. Discriminating among job applicants on the basis of race, sex, religion, or other characteristics unrelated to job perfor-

[31] Thomas Jefferson, *Declaration of Independence*.

[32] *Dred Scott* v. *Sanford*, 60 U.S. (19 How) (1857) at 407 and 421. See Don E. Fehrenbacher, *The Dred Scott Case* (New York: Oxford University Press, 1978).

[33] *Bradwell* v. *Illinois*, 83 U.S. (16 Wall) (1873). See Leo Kanowitz, *Women and the Law* (Albuquerque, NM: University of New Mexico Press, 1969), p. 36

[34] Norman Daniels, "Merit and Meritocracy," *Philosophy and Public Affairs*, 7, no. 3 (Spring 1978): 208–9.

mance is necessarily inefficient and therefore contrary to utilitarian principles.[35]

Utilitarian arguments of this sort, however, have encountered two kinds of objections. First, if the argument is correct, then jobs should be assigned on the basis of job-related qualifications *only so long as such assignments will advance the public welfare*. If, in a certain situation, the public welfare would be advanced to a greater degree by assigning jobs on the basis of some factor not related to job performance, then the utilitarian would have to hold that in those situations jobs should *not* be assigned on the basis of job-related qualifications, but on the basis of that other factor. If, for example, society's welfare would be promoted more by assigning certain jobs on the basis of *need* (or sex or race) instead of on the basis of job qualifications, then the utilitarian would have to concede that *need* (or sex or race) and not job qualifications is the proper basis for assigning those jobs.[36]

Second, the utilitarian argument must also answer the charge of opponents who hold that society as a whole may benefit from some forms of sexual discrimination. Opponents might claim, for example, that society will function most efficiently if one sex is socialized into acquiring the personality traits required for raising a family (nonaggressive, cooperative, caring, submissive, etc.) and the other sex is socialized into acquiring the personality traits required for earning a living (aggressive, competitive, assertive, independent).[37] Or one might hold that one sex ends up with the traits suited for raising a family as a result of its inborn biological nature, while the other sex ends up with the traits suited for earning a living as a result of its own biology.[38] In either case, whether sexual differences are acquired or natural, one might argue that jobs that call for one set of sexually based traits rather than another, should be assigned on the basis of sex because placing people in jobs that suit their personality traits promotes society's welfare.[39]

The utilitarian argument against discrimination has been attacked on several fronts. None of these attacks, however, seem to have defeated its proponents. Utilitarians have countered that using factors other than job-related qualifications in fact never provides greater benefits than the use of job-related qualifications.[40]

[35] For economic analyses of the costs and benefits associated with discrimination, see Gary S. Becker, *The Economics of Discrimination*, 2nd ed. (Chicago: The University of Chicago Press, 1971); Janice Fanning Madden, *The Economics of Sex Discrimination* (Lexington, MA: D. C. Heath and Company, 1973). For a critical review of this literature see Annette M. LaMond, "Economic Theories of Employment Discrimination," in *Women, Minorities, and Employment Discrimination*, Phyllis A. Wallace and Annette M. LaMond, eds. (Lexington, MA: D. C. Heath and Company, 1977), pp. 1–11.

[36] *Ibid.*, p. 214.

[37] See the discussion of this view in Sharon Bishop Hill, "Self-Determination and Autonomy," in *Today's Moral Problems*, 2nd ed., Richard Wasserstrom, ed. (New York: Macmillan, Inc., 1979), pp. 118–33.

[38] See Steven Goldberg, *The Inevitability of Patriarchy* (New York: William Morrow & Co., Inc., 1973); and J. R. Lucas, "Because You Are a Woman," *Philosophy*, 48: 166–71.

[39] On this issue see Janet S. Chafetz, *Masculine, Feminine, or Human?: An Overview of the Sociology of Sex Roles* (Itasca, IL: Peacock, 1974); and Joyce Trebilcot, "Sex Roles: The Argument from Nature," *Ethics*, 85, no. 3 (April 1975): 249–55.

[40] See, for example, Thomas Nagel, "Equal Treatment and Compensatory Discrimination," *Philosophy and Public Affairs*, 2 (1973): 360; and Ronald Dworkin, *Taking Rights Seriously* (Cambridge: Harvard University Press, 1977), pp. 232–37.

Moreover, they claim, studies have demonstrated that there are few, or no, morally significant differences between the sexes.[41]

Rights

Nonutilitarian arguments agaist racial and sexual discrimination may take the approach that discrimination is wrong because it violates a person's basic moral rights.[42] Kantian theory, for example, holds that human beings should be treated as "ends" and never used merely as "means." At a minimum, this principle means that each individual has a moral right to be treated as a free person equal to any other person and that all individuals have a correlative moral duty to treat each individual as a free and equal person. Discriminatory practices violate the principle in two ways. First, discrimination is based on the belief that one group is inferior to other groups: that blacks, for example, are less competent or less worthy of respect than whites or perhaps that women are less competent or worthy of respect than men.[43] Racial and sexual discrimination, for instance, may be based on stereotypes that see minorities as "lazy" or "shiftless" and see women as "emotional" and "weak." Such degrading stereotypes undermine the self-esteem of those groups against whom the stereotypes are directed and thereby violate their right to be treated as equals. Secondly, discrimination places the members of groups which are discriminated against in lower social and economic positions: Women and minorities have fewer job opportunities and they are given lower salaries. Again, the right to be treated as a free and equal person is violated.[44]

A group of Kantian arguments, related to those above, holds that discrimination is wrong because the person who discriminates would not want to see his or her behavior universalized.[45] In particular, the person would not want to be discriminated against on the basis of characteristics that have nothing whatever to do with the person's own ability to perform a given job. Since the person who discriminates would not want to see his or her own behavior universalized, it is, according to Kant's first categorical imperative, morally wrong for that person to discriminate against others.

Justice

A second group of nonutilitarian arguments against discrimination views it as a violation of the principles of justice. John Rawls, for example, argues that among the principles of justice that the enlightened parties to the "original position" would choose for themselves is the principle of equal opportunity: "Social and

[41] Susan Haack, "On the Moral Relevance of Sex," *Philosophy*, 49: 90-95: Jon J. Durkin, "The Potential of Women," in *Women in Management*, Bette Ann Stead, ed. (Englewood Cliffs, NJ: Prentice Hall, 1978), pp. 42–46.

[42] Richard Wasserstrom, "Rights, Human Rights, and Racial Discrimination," *The Journal of Philosophy*, 61 (29 October 1964): 628–41.

[43] Richard Wasserstrom, "Racism, Sexism, and Preferential Treatment: An Approach to the Topics," *UCLA Law Review*, 24 (1977): 581–622.

[44] This is, for example, the underlying view in John C. Livingston, *Fair Game*? (San Francisco: W. H. Freeman and Company, 1979), pp. 74–76.

[45] Richard M. Hare, *Freedom and Reason* (New York: Oxford University Press, 1963), pp. 217–19.

economic inequalities are to be arranged so that they are attached to offices and positions open to all under conditions of fair equality of opportunity."[46] Discrimination violates this principle by arbitrarily closing off to minorities the more desirable offices and positions in an institution, thereby not giving them an opportunity equal to that of others. Arbitrarily giving some individuals less of an opportunity to compete for jobs than others is unjust, according to Rawls.

Another approach to the morality of discrimination that also views it as a form of injustice is based on the formal "principle of equality": Individuals who are equal in all respects relevant to the kind of treatment in question should be treated equally, even if they are dissimilar in other nonrelevant respects." To many people, as we indicated in Chapter Two, this principle is the defining feature of justice.[47] Discrimination in employment is wrong because it violates the basic principle of justice by differentiating between people on the basis of characteristics (race or sex) that are not relevant to the tasks they must perform. A major problem faced by this kind of argument against discrimination, however, is that of defining precisely what counts as a "relevant respect" for treating people differently and explaining why race and sex are not relevant, while something like intelligence or war service may be counted as relevant.

Discriminatory Practices

Regardless of the problems inherent in some of the arguments against discrimination, it is clear that there are strong reasons for holding that discrimination is wrong. It is consequently understandable that the law has gradually been changed to conform to these moral requirements and that there has been a growing recognition of the various ways in which discrimination in employment occurs. Among the practices now widely recognized as discriminatory are the following:[48]

Recruitment Practices Firms that rely solely on the word-of-mouth referrals of present employees to recruit new workers tend to recruit only from those racial and sexual groups that are already represented in their labor force. When a firm's labor force is composed only of white males, this recruitment policy will tend to discriminate against minorities and women. Also, when desirable job positions are advertised only in media (or by job referral agencies) that are not used by minorities or women (such as, in English newspapers not read by Spanish-speaking minorities), or are classified as "for men only," recruitment will also tend to be discriminatory.

Screening Practices Job qualifications are discriminatory when they are not relevant to the job to be performed, as, for example, requiring a high school diploma or a credential for an essentially manual task in places where minorities statistically have had high secondary-school drop-out rates. Aptitude or intelligence tests used to screen applicants become discriminatory when they serve to disqualify members from minority cultures who are unfamiliar with the language, concepts,

[46] John Rawls, *A Theory of Justice* (Cambridge: Harvard University Press, Belknap Press, 1971), pp. 83–90.

[47] Charles Perelman, *The Idea of Justice and the Problem of Argument* (London: Routledge and Kegan Paul, 1963).

[48] Feagin and Feagin, *Discrimination American Style*, pp. 43–77.

and social situations used in the tests but who are in fact fully qualified for the job. Job interviews are discriminatory if the interviewer routinely disqualifies women and minorities by relying on sexual or racial stereotypes. These stereotypes may include assumptions about the sort of occupations "proper" for women, the sort of work and time burdens that may fittingly be "imposed" on women, the ability of a woman or a minority person to maintain "commitment" to a job, the propriety of putting women in "male" environments, the assumed effects women or minorities would have on employee morale or on customers, and the extent to which women or minorities are assumed to have personality and aptitude traits that make them unsuitable for a job. Such generalizations about women or minorities are not only discriminatory, they are also false.

Promotion Practices Promotion, job progression, and transfer practices are discriminatory when employers place white males on job tracks separate from those open to women and minorities. Seniority systems will be discriminatory if past discrimination has eliminated minorities and women from the higher, more senior positions on the advancement ladder. To rectify the situation, individuals who have specifically suffered from discrimination in seniority systems should be given their rightful place in the seniority system and provided with whatever training is necessary for them. When promotions rely on the subjective recommendations of immediate supervisors, promotion policy will be discriminatory to the extent that supervisors rely on racial or sexual stereotypes.

Conditions of Employment Wages and salaries are discriminatory to the extent that equal wages and salaries are not given to people who are doing essentially the same work. If past discrimination or present cultural traditions result in some job classifications being disproportionately filled with women or minorities (such as, secretarial, clerical, or part-time positions), steps should be taken to make their compensation and benefits comparable to those of other classifications.

Discharge Firing an employee on the basis of his or her race or sex is a clear form of discrimination. Less blatantly discriminatory are layoff policies that rely on a seniority system in which women and minorities have the lowest seniority because of past discrimination.

Sexual Harassment

Women, as was earlier noted, are victims of a particularly troublesome kind of discrimination that is both overt and coercive: They are subjected to sexual harassment. While males are also subjected to some instances of sexual harassment, it is women who are by far the most frequent victims. But for all its acknowledged frequency, sexual harassment still remains difficult to define clearly and difficult also to police and prevent. In 1978 the Equal Employment Opportunity Commission published a set of "guidelines" defining sexual harassment and setting out what, in its view, was prohibited by the law. In their current form the guidelines state:

> Unwelcome sexual advances, requests for sexual favors and other verbal or physical contact of a sexual nature constitute sexual harassment when (1) submission to such conduct is made either explicitly or implicitly a term or condition of an individual's

> employment, (2) submission to or rejection of such conduct by an individual is used as the basis for employment decisions affecting such individual, or (3) such conduct has the purpose or effect of unreasonably interfering with an individual's work performance or creating an intimidating, hostile or offensive working environment.[49]

The guidelines state, further, that sexual harassment is prohibited and that an employer is responsible for all sexual harassment engaged in by employees, "regardless of whether the employer knew or should have known" the harassment was occurring and regardless of whether it was "forbidden by the employer."

In several major respects, the guidelines are clearly morally justified. They are intended to outlaw those situations in which an employee is coerced into giving in to another employee's sexual demands by the threat of losing some significant job benefit, such as a promotion, a raise, or even the job. This kind of degrading coercion exerted on employees who are vulnerable and defenseless, inflicts great psychological harms on the employee, violates the employee's most basic rights to freedom and dignity, and is an outrageously unjust misuse of the unequal power that an employer can exercise over the employee. It is thus a crude violation of the moral standards of utilitarianism, rights, and justice.

However, several aspects of these guidelines merit further discussion. First, the guidelines prohibit more than particular acts of harassment. In addition to prohibiting harassing *acts*, they also prohibit conduct that "creates" an "intimidating, hostile or offensive working environment." That means that an employer is guilty of sexual harassment when the employer allows an *environment* that is hostile or offensive to women, even in the absence of any particular incidents of sexual harassment. But this raises some difficult questions. If the mechanics in a garage are accustomed to placing pin-ups in their place of work and are accustomed to recounting off-color jokes and using off-color language, are they guilty of creating an environment that is "hostile and offensive" to a female coworker? In a well-known case, for example, a federal court described the following real situation:

> For seven years the [female] plaintiff worked at Osceola as the sole woman in a salaried management position. In common work areas [she] and other female employees were exposed daily to displays of nude or partially clad women belonging to a number of male employees at Osceola. One poster, which remained on the wall for eight years, showed a prone woman who had a gold ball on her breasts with a man standing over her, golf club in hand, yelling "Fore!" And one desk plaque declared "Even male chauvinist pigs need love. . . ." In addition, Computer Division Supervisor Dough Henry regularly spewed anti-female obscenity. Henry routinely referred to women as "whores," "cunt," "pussy," and "tits. . . ." Of plaintiff, Henry specifically remarked, "All that bitch needs is a good lay" and called her "fat ass."[50]

[49] Equal Employment Opportunity Commission, *Title 29 Code of Federal Regulations*, Section 1604.11, Sexual Harassment.

[50] *Rabidue* v. *Osceola Refining Company*, 805 F. 2d 611 (1986), U.S. Court of Appeals, Sixth Circuit, Circuit Judge Keith, Dissenting in Part, quoted in Terry Halbert and Elaine Inguilli, eds., *Law and Ethics in the Business Environment* (St. Paul, MN: West Publishing Co., 1990), p. 301.

Should this kind of situation count as the kind of "intimidating, hostile or offensive working environment" that the guidelines prohibit as sexual harassment? The answer to this legal question is unclear, and different courts have taken different positions on the question. But a different question and one that is more relevant to our inquiry is this: Is it morally wrong to create or to allow this kind of environment? The answer to this question seems in general to be yes, since such an environment is degrading, it is usually imposed by more powerful male parties upon more vulnerable female employees, and it imposes heavy costs upon women since such environments tend to belittle them and make it more difficult for them to compete with males as equals. Nevertheless, some critics object that these kinds of environments were not created to intentionally degrade women, that they are part of the "social mores of [male] American workers," that it is hopeless to try to change them, and that they do not unjustly harm women since women have the power to take care of themselves.[51] A *Forbes* magazine article, for example, recently asked rhetorically, "Can women really think they have the right to a pristine work environment free of rude behavior?"[52] Such sentiments are indicative of the uncertainties surrounding this issue.

A second important point to note is that the guidelines indicate that "verbal or physical contact of a sexual nature" constitutes sexual harassment when it has the "effect of unreasonably interfering with an individual's work performance." Many critics have argued that this means that what counts as sexual harassment depends on the purely subjective judgments of the victim. According to the guidelines verbal contacts—presumably conversations—of a sexual nature count as prohibited sexual harassment when they "unreasonably" interfere with work performance. But sexual conversations that are "unreasonable" interferences to one person, critics claim, may be well within reasonable limits to another person since people's tolerance—even enjoyment—of sexual conversations differs. What one person believes is innocent innuendo or flirting or an enjoyable sexual joke, may be taken by another as an offensive and debilitating "come-on." The critics claim that a person who in all innocence makes a comment that is taken wrongly by another person, may find himself the target of a sexual harassment complaint. However, supporters of the guidelines reply that our law courts are well experienced with defining what is "reasonable" in the more or less objective terms of what an average competent adult would feel to be reasonable, so this concept should present no major difficulties. Critics, however, have countered that this still leaves open the question of whether the guidelines should prohibit sexual conversations that the average *woman* would find unreasonable or that the average *man* would find unreasonable—two standards, they claim, that would have drastically different implications.

A more fundamental objection to the prohibition of "verbal conduct" that creates an "intimidating, hostile or offensive working environment" is that these kinds of prohibitions in effect violate people's right to free speech. This objection is frequently made on university campuses where prohibitions of speech that creates a hostile or offensive environment for women or minorities are not unusual, and

[51] This was, for example, the position of the majority opinion in *Rabidue* vs. *Osceola Refining Company*.

[52] Gretchen Morgenson, "Watch That Leer, Stifle That Joke," *Forbes*, 15 May 1989, p. 72.

where such prohibitions are generally characterized as requiring "politically correct speech." Students and faculty alike have objected that free speech must be preserved on university campuses because truth is found only through the free discussion and examination of all opinions, no matter how offensive, and truth is the objective of the university. Similar claims cannot usually be made about a business corporation, of course, since its objective is not the attainment of truth through the free discussion and examination of all opinions. Nevertheless, it can be argued that employees and employers have a right to free speech and that prohibitions of speech that creates an environment that some feel to be offensive are wrong even in corporate contexts, because such prohibitions violate this basic right. The reader will have to decide whether such arguments have much merit.

A third important feature of the guidelines to note is that an employer is guilty of sexual harassment even if the employer did not know and could not have been expected to know that it was going on, and even if the employer had explicitly forbidden it. This violates the common moral norm that a person cannot be held morally responsible for something of which they had no knowledge and which they had tried to prevent. Many people have suggested that the guidelines are deficient on this point. However, supporters reply that the guidelines are morally justified from a utilitarian point of view for two reasons. First, over the long run, they provide a strong incentive for employers to take steps that will guarantee that the harm of sexual harassment is eradicated from their companies, even in those areas of the company of which they usually have little knowledge. Moreover, the harms inflicted by sexual harassment are so devastating, that any costs imposed by such steps will be balanced by the benefits. Second, the guidelines in effect ensure that the harms inflicted by sexual harassment are always transferred to the shoulders of the employer, thereby making such harms part of the costs of doing business that the employer will want to minimize in order to remain competitive with other businesses. Thus, the guidelines in effect internalize the costs of sexual harassment so that competitive market mechanisms can deal with them efficiently. The guidelines are also just, supporters claim, because the employer is usually better able to absorb the costs of sexual harassment, than the innocent injured employee who would otherwise have to suffer the losses of harassment alone.

Beyond Race and Sex: Other Groups

Are there other groups that deserve protection from discrimination? The Age Discrimination in Employment Act of 1967 prohibited discriminating against older workers merely because of their age, until they reached age sixty-five. This act was modified in 1978 to prohibit age discrimination until workers reach age seventy.[53] On October 17, 1986, new legislation was enacted prohibiting forced retirement at any specific age. Older workers are thus in theory protected against discrimination by federal laws. Nevertheless, because of widespread stereotypes about the abilities and capacities of older workers, subtle discrimination against the aged continues to pervade America.[54]

[53] Barbara Lindemann Schlei and Paul Grossman, *Employment Discrimination Law, 1979 Supplement* (Washington, DC: The Bureau of National Affairs, Inc., 1979), p. 109–20.

[54] John Lawrie, "Subtle Discrimination Pervades Corporate America," *Personnel Journal*, January 1990, pp. 53–55.

While older workers at least have some legal protections against discrimination, such protections are nonexistent for workers with unusual sexual preferences. A court held, for example, that Liberty Mutual Insurance Company was not acting illegally when it refused to hire a male merely on the grounds that he was "effeminate," and a court also cleared Budget Marketing, Inc., of acting illegally when that company fired a male who began to dress as a female prior to a sex-change operation.[55]

Many companies have fired or canceled the health benefits of those workers who are found to have the virus for acquired immune deficiency syndrome (AIDS).[56] As of 1990, over 300,000 individuals had been diagnosed as carrying the virus, although only a portion of them had yet suffered symptoms or debilitation that affected their ability to perform well on the job. Several court decisions have held that AIDS qualifies as a "handicap" under federal law (the Vocational Rehabilitation Act of 1973), and federal law prohibits federal contractors, subcontractors, or employers who participate in federally funded programs from firing such handicapped persons, so long as they can perform their jobs if some "reasonable" accommodation is made. However, businesses that are not covered by this federal law (i.e., businesses that do not participate in a federally funded program or who do not hold federal contracts of at least $2,500 or who are not subcontractors to such employers) are not prevented by this law from firing AIDS-infected employees at will.[57] Some states and some cities have enacted laws to prevent discrimination against AIDS victims, but most employers are free to discriminate against them as they choose.

Many companies also have policies against hiring overweight persons, a class of people that most state laws do not protect. Philadelphia Electric Company, for example, refused to hire Joyce English simply because she weighed 300 pounds.[58] Should any of these groups—gays, transexuals, AIDS victims, obese persons—be protected against job discrimination? Some have argued that they should be protected on the same grounds that women and ethnic minorities are currently protected.[59] But at the present time these groups remain as vulnerable as women, minorities and older workers once were.

[55] See *Smith* v. *Liberty Mutual Insurance Company*, 395 F. Supp., 1098 (1975), and *Sommers* v. *Budget Marketing Inc.*, 667 F. 2d 748 (1982).

[56] Terence Roth, "Many Firms Fire AIDS Victims, Citing Health Risk to Co-Workers," *Wall Street Journal*, 12 August 1985; Dorothy Townsend, "AIDS Patient Sues Kodak Over Firing, Claims Bias," *Los Angeles Times*, 2 April 1986; Jim Dickey, "Firing Over AIDS Test Claimed," *San Jose Mercury News*, 11 October 1985, p. 1B.

[57] Joseph G. Ormsby, Geralyn McClure Franklin, Robert K. Robinson, and Alicia B. Gresham, "AIDS in the Workplace: Implications for Human Resource Managers," *SAM Advanced Management Journal*, Sprint 1990, pp. 23–27.

[58] Robert N. Webner, "Budding Movement Is Seeking to Stop Fat Discrimination," *Wall Street Journal*, 8 October 1979, p. 33.

[59] See Richard D. Mohr, "Gay Rights," in *Philosophical Issues in Human Rights*, Patricia H. Werhane, A. R. Gini, and David Ozar, eds. (New York: Random House, Inc., 1986), pp. 337–41; David Margolick, "Court Blocks Job Denials for Obesity," *New York Times*, 8 May 1985, p. 18; Cris Oppenheimer, "A Hostile Marketplace Shuts Out Older Workers," *San Jose Mercury News*, 9 December 1985.

7.4 AFFIRMATIVE ACTION

All of the equal opportunity policies discussed above are ways of making employment decisions blind with respect to sex and race. These policies are all negative: They aim to prevent any further discrimination. They therefore ignore the fact that as a result of past discrimination women and minorities do not now have the same skills as their white male counterparts and that because of past discrimination women and minorities are now underrepresented in the more prestigious and desirable job positions. The policies discussed so far do not call for any positive steps to eliminate these effects of past discrimination.

In order to rectify the effects of past discrimination, many employers have instituted affirmative action programs designed to achieve a more representative distribution of minorities and women within the firm by giving preference to women and minorities. Affirmative action programs, in fact, are now legally required of all firms that hold a government contract. What does an affirmative action program involve? The heart of an affirmative action program is a detailed study (a "utilization analysis") of all the major job classifications in the firm.[60] The purpose of the study is to determine whether there are fewer minorities or women in a particular job classification than could be reasonably expected by their availability in the area from which the firm recruits. The utilization analysis will compare the percentage of women and minorities in each job classification with the percentage of those minority and female workers available in the area from which the firm recruits who have the requisite skills or who are capable of acquiring the requisite skills with training the firm could reasonably supply. If the utilization analysis shows that women or minorities are underutilized in certain job classifications, the firm must then establish recruiting goals and timetables for correcting these deficiencies. Although the goals and timetables must not be rigid and inflexible quotas, they must nonetheless be specific, measurable, and designed in good faith to correct the deficiencies uncovered by the utilization analysis within a reasonable length of time. The firm appoints an officer to coordinate and administer the affirmative action program, and undertakes special efforts and programs to increase the recruitment of women and minorities so as to meet the goals and timetables it has established for itself.

Supreme Court decisions have not been clear about the legality of affirmative action programs. A large number of federal court decisions have agreed that the use of affirmative action programs to redress imbalances that are the result of previous discriminatory hiring practices is legitimate. Moreover, in 1979 the U.S. Supreme Court ruled that companies legally can use affirmative action programs to remedy a "manifest racial imbalance" whether or not the imbalance resulted from past discriminatory job practices.[61] In June 1984, however, the Court ruled that companies may not set aside the *seniority* of white workers during layoffs in favor of women and minority workers hired under affirmative action plans so long as the seniority system was adopted without a discriminatory motive. Thus,

[60] On the requirements of affirmative action programs, see Connolly, Jr., *A Practical Guide to Equal Employment Opportunity*, 1:359–73.

[61] *United Steelworkers of America* v. *Weber*, 99 S. Ct. 2721 (1979).

although affirmative action programs that give preferences to women or minorities as a group were not declared illegal, their effects could disappear during hard times since the "last hired, first fired" rule of seniority would hit strongest at women and minorities recently hired through the programs.[62] The 1984 Supreme Court decision also included a nonbinding "advisory" statement that "If individual members of a . . . class demonstrate that they have been actual victims of the discriminatory practice, they may be awarded competitive seniority and given their rightful place on the seniority roster. However . . . mere membership in the disadvantaged class is insufficient to warrant a seniority award; each individual must prove that the discriminatory practice had an impact on him."[63] To many this seemed to imply that affirmative action programs that awarded jobs on the basis of membership in a disadvantaged class were not completely legal; others, however, interpreted the "advisory" more narrowly to mean merely that awarding *seniority* could not be based on mere membership in a disadvantaged class.[64] This latter interpretation seemed to be supported by another Supreme Court ruling on May 19, 1986, which held that although layoffs based on race were unconstitutional, racial hiring goals were a legally allowable means for remedying past discrimination. The 1986 Supreme Court majority opinion stated that layoffs based on race "impose the entire burden of achieving racial equality on particular (white) individuals, often resulting in serious disruption of their lives. . . On the other hand, racial preferences in hiring merely deny a future employment opportunity, not the loss of an existing job, and may be used to cure the effects of past discrimination."[65]

In 1989 the Supreme Court issued five decisions that further complicated the legal standing of affirmative action programs. In January of that year, in *City of Richmond* v. *J. A. Croson Co.*, the Court ruled that affirmative action plans of a public governmental body that sets aside a certain percentage of its public monies for minority contractors is unconstitutional. Such set-aside programs could be used by public bodies only as "a last resort" in an "extreme case" and only if there was hard and specific proof of previous racial bias by that governmental body. On June 5, in *Wards Cove Packaging Co.* v. *Antonio*, the Court ruled that even when statistics showed that there are dramatic racial imbalances in an employer's jobs, the imbalances are legally permissible if the employer provides a "business explanation" for the imbalances, and the burden is on minorities to prove to the court that the explanation is not adequate. The court also ruled that the burden is on minorities to identify and prove that specific employment practices of the employer caused specific racial imbalances. A few days later, on June 12, in *Martin* v. *Wilks*, the Supreme Court ruled that even when affirmative action programs had been approved by courts of law several years ago, white employees

[62] Rogene A. Buchholz, *Business Environment and Public Policy* (Englewood Cliffs, NJ: Prentice Hall, 1982), pp. 287–88.

[63] Quoted in "High Court Dumps Quotas in Labor Case," *Washington Times*, 13 June 1984, p. 1.

[64] "A Right Turn on Race?," *Newsweek*, 25 June 1984, pp. 29–31; Stuart Taylor, "Reagan Attack on Quotas in Jobs Goes to High Court," *New York Times*, 6 August 1985, p. 17.

[65] Aaron Epstein, "Layoffs Can't Favor Minority Workers," *San Jose Mercury News*, 20 May 1986, p. 1a.

could sue to challenge the program by claiming unfair treatment *at any later point in time*, so long as they had not been involved in the litigation that had resulted in the court-approved program. The same day, in *Lorrance* v. *AT&T Technologies*, the Supreme Court ruled, however, that women and minorities could not sue to challenge a seniority system as discriminatory if they waited until years later when they were personally affected by its discriminatory impact. Unlike challenges to affirmative action programs, which white males were free to file at any future time without limit, challenges to discriminatory seniority systems had to be filed by women and minorities the moment the system was put into place, even though they might not have been around when it was put into place and so could not have been affected by the system until years later. On June 15, in *Patterson* v. *McLean Credit Union*, the Court ruled that an 1866 civil rights law that gives minorities "the same right . . . to make and enforce contracts . . . as is enjoyed by white citizens," and which had been used by minorities to sue private employers for compensatory and punitive damages when they were victims of racial harassment while on the job, could no longer be used by minority victims of on-the-job racial harassment. Instead, the Court ruled, minorities had to use Title VII of the 1964 Civil Rights Act which does not allow for compensatory and punitive damages, which has restrictive time limits, and which only allows for recovery of back pay if the victim is fired.

Thus, the Supreme Court has vacillated on the constitutionality of affirmative action programs. Depending on the period in question, the issue at stake, and the current makeup of the Court, it has tended both to support and to undermine affirmative action programs. Like the public itself, which remains deeply divided on the issue, the Supreme Court has had trouble making up its mind whether to support or attack these programs.[66]

Affirmative action programs have been attacked mainly on the grounds that, in attempting to correct the effects of past discrimination, these programs themselves have become racially or sexually discriminatory.[67] By showing preference to minorities or women, the programs institute a form of "reverse discrimination" against white males.[68] A forty-five-year-old electrical worker at a Westinghouse plant, for example, is quoted as saying:

> What does bother me is the colored getting the preference *because* they're black. This I am against. I say, I don't care what his color is. If he has the ability to do the job, he should get the job—not *because* of his color. They shouldn't hire 20 percent just because they're black. This is discrimination in reverse as far as I'm concerned. . . . If they want it, they can earn it like I did. I am not saying deprive them of something—not at all.[69]

[66] See, for example, "The New Politics of Race," and "A Crisis of Shattered Dreams," in *Newsweek*, 6 May 1991, pp. 22–26, 28–31.

[67] See, for example, Barry R. Gross, *Discrimination in Reverse*: *Is Turnabout Fair Play*?; for a contrasting view see also Alan H. Goldman, *Justice and Reverse Discrimination* (Princeton: Princeton University Press, 1979).

[68] See, for example the articles collected in Barry R. Gross, ed., *Reverse Discrimination* (Buffalo: Prometheus Books, 1977).

[69] Theodore V. Purcell and Gerald F. Cavanagh, *Blacks in the Industrial World* (New York: The Free Press, 1972), p. 164.

Affirmative action programs are said to discriminate against white males by using a nonrelevant characteristic—race or sex—to make employment decisions, and this violates justice by violating the principles of equality and of equal opportunity.

The arguments used to justify affirmative action programs in the face of these objections tend to fall into two main groups.[70] One group of arguments interprets the preferential treatment accorded to women and minorities as a form of *compensation* for past injuries they have suffered. A second set of arguments interprets preferential treatment as an *instrument* for achieving certain social goals. Whereas compensation arguments for affirmative action are backward looking insofar as they focus on the wrongness of *past* acts, the instrumentalist arguments are forward looking insofar as they focus on the goodness of a future state (and the wrongness of what happened in the past is irrelevant).[71] We will begin by examining the compensation arguments and then turn to the instrumentalist arguments.

Affirmative Action as Compensation

Arguments that defend affirmative action as a form of compensation are based on the concept of compensatory justice.[72] Compensatory justice, as we noted in Chapter Two, implies that people have an obligation to compensate those whom they have intentionally and unjustly wronged. Affirmative action programs are then interpreted as a form of reparation by which white male majorities now compensate women and minorities for unjustly injuring them by discriminating against them in the past. One version of this argument holds, for example, that blacks were wronged in the past by American whites and that consequently blacks should now receive compensation from whites.[73] Programs of preferential treatment provide that compensation.

The difficulty with arguments that defend affirmative action on the basis of the principle of compensation is that the principle of compensation requires that compensation should come only from those specific individuals who intentionally inflicted a wrong, and it requires them to compensate only those specific individuals whom they wronged. For example, if five red-haired persons wrongfully injure five black-haired persons, then compensatory justice obligates only the five red-

[70] See Bernard Boxill, *Blacks and Social Justice* (Totowa, NJ: Rowman & Allanheld, 1984), pp. 147–72; see also the essays collected in Marshall Cohen, Thomas Nagel, and Thomas Scanlon, eds., *Equality and Preferential Treatment* (Princeton: Princeton University Press, 1977); and William T. Blackstone and Robert D. Heslep, eds., *Social Justice & Preferential Treatment* (Athens, GA: The University of Georgia Press, 1977).

[71] George Sher, "Reverse Discrimination, the Future, and the Past," in *Ethics*, 90 (October 1979): 81–87, and George Shere, "Preferential Hiring," in *Just Business,* Tom Regan, ed. (New York: Random House, Inc., 1984), pp. 32–59. An excellent discussion of affirmative action programs is Robert K. Fullinwider, *The Reverse Discrimination Controversy* (Totowa, NJ: Rowman and Littlefield, 1980).

[72] Paul W. Taylor, "Reverse Discrimination and Compensatory Justice," *Analysis*, 33 (1973): 177–82; see also, Anne C. Minas, "How Reverse Discrimination Compensates Women," *Ethics*, 88, no. 1 (October 1977): 74–79.

[73] Bernard Boxhill, "The Morality of Reparations," *Social Theory and Practice 2*, no. 1 (1972): 113–22.

haired persons to give to only the five black-haired persons whatever the black-haired persons would have had if the five red-heads had not injured them. Compensatory justice, however, does not require that compensation should come from *all* the members of a group that contains some wrongdoers, nor does it require that compensation should go to *all* the members of a group that contains some injured parties. In the example above, although justice requires that the five red-haired persons must compensate the five black-haired persons, it does *not* require that all red-haired persons should compensate all black-haired persons. By analogy, only the specific individuals who discriminated against minorities or women in the past should now be forced to make reparation of some sort, and they should make reparation only to those specific individuals against whom they discriminated.[74] Since affirmative action programs usually benefit all the members of a racial or sexual group, regardless of whether they specifically were discriminated against in the past, and since these programs hinder every white male regardless of whether he himself specifically discriminated against someone in the past, it follows that such preferential programs cannot be justified on the basis of compensatory justice.[75] In short, affirmative action programs are unfair because the beneficiaries of affirmative action are not the same individuals who were injured by past discrimination, and the people who must pay for their injuries are usually not the ones who inflicted those injuries.[76]

Various authors have tried to counter this objection to the "affirmative action as compensation" argument by claiming that actually *every* black person (or every woman) living today has been injured by discrimination and that *every* white person (or every male) has benefited from those injuries. Judith Jarvis Thomson, for example writes:

> But it is absurd to suppose that the young blacks and women now of an age to apply for jobs have not been wronged . . . Even young blacks and women have lived through downgrading for being black or female . . . And even those who were not themselves downgraded for being black or female have suffered the consequences of the downgrading of other blacks and women: lack of self-confidence and lack of self-respect.[77]

And Martin Redish writes:

[74] Alan H. Goldman, "Limits to the Justification of Reverse Discrimination," *Social Theory and Practice*, vol. 3, no. 3.

[75] See Karst and Horowitz, "Affirmative Action and Equal Protection," *Virginia Law Review*, 60 (1974).

[76] There are innumerable discussions of this objection to the compensation justification; see, for example, the series: Michael Bayles, "Reparations to Wronged Groups," *Analysis*, 33, no. 6 (1973); L. J. Cowan, "Inverse Discrimination," *Analysis*, 33, no. 10 (1972); Roger Shiner, "Individuals, Groups, and Inverse Discrimination," *Analysis*, 33 (June 1973); Paul Taylor, "Reverse Discrimination and Compensatory Justice," *Analysis*, 33 (June 1973); James Nickel, "Should Reparations Be to Individuals or Groups?," *Analysis*, 34, no. 9: 154–160; Alan H. Goldman, "Reparations to Individuals or Groups?," *Analysis*, 35, no. 5: 168–70.

[77] Judith Jarvis Thomson, "Preferential Hiring," *Philosophy and Public Affairs*, 2, no. 4 (Summer 1973): 381; for a similar claim with respect to blacks, see Graham Hughes, "Reparation for Blacks?," *New York University Law Review*, 43 (1968): 1072–73.

> It might also be argued that, whether or not the [white males] of this country have themselves participated in acts of discrimination, they have been the beneficiaries—conscious or unconscious—of a fundamentally racist society. They thus may be held independently "liable" to suppressed minorities for a form of unjust enrichment.[78]

It is unclear whether these arguments succeed in justifying affirmative action programs that benefit groups (all blacks and all women) instead of specific injured individuals and that penalize groups (white males) instead of specific wrongdoers.[79] Has every minority and woman really been injured as Thomson claims, and are all white males really beneficiaries of discrimination as Redish implies? And even if a white male happens (through no fault of his own) to benefit from someone else's injury, does this make him "liable" for that injury?

Affirmative Action as an Instrument for Achieving Social Goals

A second set of justifications advanced in support of affirmative action programs is based on the idea that these programs are morally legitimate instruments for achieving morally legitimate ends. Utilitarians, for example, have claimed that affirmative action programs are justified because they promote the public welfare.[80] They have argued that past discrimination has produced a high degree of correlation between race and poverty.[81] As racial minorities were systematically excluded from better-paying, and more prestigious, jobs, their members have become impoverished. The kinds of statistics cited earlier in this chapter provide evidence of this inequality. Impoverishment in turn has led to unmet needs, lack of self-respect, resentment, social discontent, and crime. The public welfare, therefore, will be promoted if the position of these impoverished persons is improved by giving them special educational and employment opportunities. If opponents object that such affirmative action programs are unjust because they distribute benefits on the basis of an irrelevant criterion such as race, the utilitarian can answer that *need*, not race, is the criterion by which affirmative action programs distribute benefits. Race provides an inexpensive *indicator* of need because past discrimination has created a high correlation between race and need. Need, of

[78] Martin H. Redish, "Preferential Law School Admissions and the Equal Protection Clause: An Analysis of the Competing Arguments," *University of California at Los Angeles Review* (1974), p. 389; see also, Bernard R. Boxill, "The Morality of Preferential Hiring," *Philosophy and Public Affairs*, 7, no. 3 (Spring 1978): 246–68.

[79] Robert Simon, "Preferential Hiring: A Reply to Judith Jarvis Thomson," *Philosophy and Public Affairs*, 3, no. 3 (Spring 1974): 312–20; Gertrude Ezorsky, "It's Mine," *Philosophy and Public Affairs*, 3, no. 3 (Spring 1974): 321–30; Robert K. Fullinwider, "Preferential Hiring and Compensation," *Social Theory and Practice*, 3, no. 3 (Spring 1975): 307–20.

[80] For examples of utilitarian arguments, see Thomas Nagel, "Equal Treatment and Compensatory Discrimination," *Philosophy and Public Affairs*, 2, no. 4 (Summer 1973): 348–63; James W. Nickel, "Preferential Policies in Hiring and Admissions, A Jurisprudential Approach," *Columbia Law Review*, 75: 534–58; Ronald Dworkin, "The De Funis Case: The Right to Go to Law School," *New York Review of Books*, 23, no. 1 (5 February 1976): 29–33.

[81] Owen M. Fiss, "Groups and the Equal Protection Clause," *Philosophy and Public Affairs*, 5, no. 2 (Winter 1976): 150–51.

course, is a just criterion of distribution.[82] And appealing to the reduction of need is consistent with utilitarian principles since reducing need will increase total utility.

The major difficulties encountered by these utilitarian justifications of affirmative action have concerned, first, the question whether the social costs of affirmative action programs (such as, the frustrations felt by white males) outweigh their obvious benefits.[83] The utilitarian defender of affirmative action, of course, will reply that the benefits far outweigh the costs. Second, and more important, opponents of these utilitarian justifications of affirmative action have questioned the assumption that race is an appropriate indicator of need. It may be inconvenient and expensive to identify the needy directly, critics argue, but the costs might be small compared to the gains that would result from having a more accurate way of identifying the needy.[84] Utilitarians answer this criticism by arguing that *all* minorities (and women) have been impoverished and psychologically harmed by past discrimination. Consequently, race (and sex) provide accurate indicators of need.

Although utilitarian arguments in favor of affirmative action programs are quite convincing, the most elaborate and persuasive array of arguments advanced in support of affirmative action have proceeded in two steps: First, they have argued that the *end* envisioned by affirmative action programs is equal justice, and second, they argue that affirmative action programs are morally legitimate *means* for achieving this end.

The end that affirmative action programs are supposed to achieve is phrased in various ways: (1) In our present society, it is argued, jobs are not distributed justly because they are not distributed according to the relevant criteria of ability, effort, contribution, or need.[85] Statistics show that jobs are in fact still distributed according to race and sex. One end of affirmative action is to bring about a distribution of society's benefits and burdens that is consistent with the principles of distributive justice, and that eliminates the important position race and sex currently have in the assignment of jobs.[86] (2) In our present society, women and minorities do not have the equal opportunities that white males have and that justice demands. Statistics prove this. This lack of equal opportunity is due to subtle racist and sexist attitudes that bias the judgments of those (usually white males) who evaluate job applicants and that are so deeply entrenched that they are virtually ineradicable by good faith measures in any reasonable period of time.[87] A second end of affirmative action programs is to neutralize such conscious and unconscious bias in order to ensure equal opportunity to women and minorities.

[82] James W. Nickel, "Classification of Race in Compensatory Programs," *Ethics*, 84, no. 2 (1974): 146–50.

[83] Virginia Black, "The Erosion of Legal Principles in the Creation of Legal Policies," *Ethics*, vol. 84, no. 3 (1974); William T. Blackstone, "Reverse Discrimination and Compensatory Justice," in *Social Justice and Preferential Treatment*, Blackstone and Heslep, eds. (Athens, GA: University of Georgia Press, 1977).

[84] Robert K. Fullinwider, "On Preferential Hiring," in *Feminism and Philosophy*, Mary Vetterling-Braggin, Frederick A. Elliston, and Jane English, eds. (Totowa, NJ: Littlefield, Adams and Company, 1978), pp. 210–24.

[85] See Nickel, "Preferential Policies."

[86] Nagel, "Equal Treatment and Compensatory Discrimination."

[87] Lawrence Crocker, "Preferential Treatment," in *Feminism and Philosophy*, Vetterling-Braggin et al., eds., pp. 190–204.

(3) The lack of equal opportunity under which women and minorities currently labor has also been attributed to the privations they suffered as children. Economic privation hindered minorities from acquiring the skills, experience, training, and education they needed to compete equally with white males.[88] Furthermore, since women and minorities have not been represented in society's prestigious positions, young men and women have had no role models to motivate them to compete for such positions as young white males have. Few black youths, for example, are motivated to enter the legal profession:

> Negro youth in the north, as well as the south, have been denied an inspiring image of the Negro lawyer, at least until recent years. On the contrary, they have been made sharply aware of the lack of respect and dignity accorded the Negro lawyer . . . Negro youth also know in what lack of regard the Negro, if employed in law enforcement at all, is held. . . . Such knowledge does little to inspire Negroes to do anything but avoid involvement with the law whatever its form.[89]

A third end of affirmative action programs is to neutralize these competitive disadvantages with which women and minorities are currently burdened when they compete with white males, and thereby bring women and minorities to the same starting point in their competitive race with others. The aim is to ensure an equal ability to compete with white males.[90]

The basic *end* that affirmative action programs seek is a more just society, a society in which an individual's opportunities are not limited by his or her race or sex. This goal is morally legitimate insofar as it is morally legitimate to strive for a society with greater equality of opportunity. The *means* by which affirmative action programs attempt to achieve a just society is giving qualified minorities and females preference over qualified white males in hiring and promotion and instituting special training programs for minorities and females that will qualify them for better jobs. By these means, it is hoped, the more just society outlined above will eventually be born. Without some form of affirmative action, it is argued, this end could not be achieved.[91] But is preferential treatment a morally legitimate *means* for attaining this end? Three reasons have been advanced to show that it is not.

First, it is often claimed that affirmative action programs "discriminate" against white males.[92] Supporters of affirmative action programs, however, have pointed out that there are crucial differences between the treatment accorded to whites by preferential treatment programs and immoral discriminatory behavior.[93] To discriminate, as we indicated earlier, is to make an adverse decision against

[88] George Sher, "Justifying Reverse Discrimination in Employment," *Philosophy and Public Affairs*, 4, no. 2 (Winter 1975): 159–70.

[89] Carl and Callahan, "Negroes and the Law," *Journal of Legal Education*, 17 (1965): 254.

[90] Kaplan, "Equal Justice in an Unequal World," *N.W.U. Law Review*, 61 (1966): 365.

[91] Theodore V. Purcell and Gerald F. Cavanagh, *Blacks in the Industrial World* (New York: The Free Press, 1972), pp. 30–44. See also, the articles on alternative feminist futures collected in Carol Gould, ed., *Beyond Domination* (Totowa, NJ: Rowman and Allenheld, 1983).

[92] Carl Cohen, "Race and the Constitution," *The Nation*, 8 February 1975; Lisa H. Newton, "Reverse Discrimination as Unjustified," *Ethics*, 83 (1973): 308–12.

[93] Ronald Dworkin, "Why Bakke Has No Case."

the member of a group because members of that group are considered inferior or less worthy of respect. Preferential treatment programs, however, are not based on invidious contempt for white males. On the contrary, they are based on the judgment that white males are currently in an advantaged position and that others should have an equal opportunity to achieve the same advantages. Moreover, racist or sexist discrimination is aimed at destroying equal opportunity. Preferential treatment programs are aimed at restoring equal opportunity where it is absent. Thus, preferential treatment programs cannot accurately be described as "discriminatory" in the same immoral sense that racist or sexist behavior is discriminatory.

Second, it is sometimes claimed that preferential treatment violates the principle of equality itself ("Individuals who are equal in all respects relevant to the kind of treatment in question should be treated equally") by allowing a nonrelevant characteristic (race and sex) to determine employment decisions.[94] But defenders of affirmative action programs have replied that sexual and racial differences are now relevant to making employment decisions. These differences are relevant because when society distributes a scarce resource (such as jobs) it may legitimately choose to allocate it to those groups that will best advance its legitimate ends. Since, in our present society, allocating scarce jobs to women and minorities will best achieve equality of opportunity, race and sex are now relevant characteristics to use for this purpose. Moreover, as we have seen, the reason that we hold that jobs should be allocated on the basis of job-related qualifications is that such an allocation will achieve a socially desirable (utilitarian) end: maximum productivity. When this end (productivity) conflicts with another socially desirable end (a just society), then it is legitimate to pursue the second end even if doing so means that the first end will not be as fully achieved.

Third, some critics have objected that affirmative action programs actually harm women and minorities because such programs imply that women and minorities are so inferior to white males that they need special help to compete. This attribution of inferiority, critics claim, is debilitating to minorities and women and ultimately inflicts harms that are so great that they far outweigh the benefits provided by such programs. In a widely read and much-acclaimed book, for example, the black author Shelby Steele criticized affirmative action programs in business and education:

> [I]n theory, affirmative action certainly has all the moral symmetry that fairness requires—the injustice of historical and even contemporary white advantage is offset with black advantage; preference replaces prejudice, inclusion answers exclusion. It is reformist and corrective, even repentent and redemptive. . . . But after twenty years of implementation, I think affirmative action has shown itself to be more bad than good and that blacks . . . now stand to lose more from it than they gain. . . . I think that one of the most troubling effects of racial preferences for blacks is a kind of demoralization, or put another way, an enlargement of self-doubt. Under affirmative action the quality that earns us preferential treatment is an implied inferiority. However this inferiority is explained—and it is easily enough explained by the myriad deprivations that grew out of our oppression—it is still inferiority. . . . Even when the black sees no implication of inferiority in racial preferences, he

[94] *Ibid.*

> knows that whites do, so that—consciously or unconsciously—the result is virtually the same. The effect of preferential treatment—the lowering of normal standards to increase black representation—puts blacks at war with an expanded realm of debilitating doubt, so that the doubt itself becomes an unrecognized preoccupation that undermines their ability to perform, especially in integrated situations.[95]

Steele's eloquently expressed view is one that many other minorities have come to hold.[96]

This third objection to affirmative action programs has been met in several ways. First, while many minorities concede that affirmative action carries some costs for minorities themselves, they also hold that the benefits of such programs still outweigh the costs. A black worker, for example, who won several jobs through affirmative action, is reported as saying, "I had to deal with the grief it brought, but it was well worth it."[97] Second, proponents of affirmative action programs also argue that these programs are based *not* on an assumption of minority or female inferiority but on a recognition of the fact that white males, consciously or unconsciously, will bias their decisions in favor of other white males. The only remedy for this, they argue, is some kind of affirmative action program that will force white males to counter this bias by requiring them to accept that proportion of minority applicants that research shows are qualified and willing to work. As studies repeatedly show, even when women and minorities are more qualified, white males are still granted higher salaries and positions by their white male counterparts. Moreover, they claim, the unjustified attributions of inferiority that many minorities experience are the result of lingering racism on the part of coworkers and employees, and such racism is precisely what affirmative action programs are meant to eradicate. A third response that supporters of affirmative action make is that although a portion of minorities may be made to feel inferior by current affirmative action programs, nevertheless many more minorities were made to feel much more devastatingly inferior by the overt and covert racism that affirmative action is gradually eroding. The overt and covert racism that pervaded the workplace prior to the implementation of affirmative action programs systematically disadvantaged, shamed, and undermined the self-esteem of all minorities to a much higher degree than is currently the case. Finally, proponents argue that it is simply false that showing preference toward a group makes members of that group feel inferior: For centuries white males have been the beneficiaries of racial and sexual discrimination without apparent loss of their self-esteem. If minority beneficiaries of affirmative action programs are made to feel inferior, it is due to lingering racism, not to the preference extended to them and their fellows.

Strong arguments can be made in support of affirmative action programs, then, and strong objections can be lodged against them. Because there are such powerful arguments on both sides of the issue, the debate over the legitimacy of affirmative action programs continues to rage without resolution. The review of

[95] Shelby Steele, *The Content of Our Character: A New Vision of Race in America* (New York: St. Martin's Press, 1990), pp. 112, 113, 117–118.

[96] Sonia L. Nazario, "Many Minorities Feel Torn by Experience of Affirmative Action," *Wall Street Journal*, 27 June 1989, pp. A1, A7.

[97] *Ibid.*

the arguments above, however, seems to suggest that affirmative action programs are at least a morally permissible means for achieving just ends, even if they may not show that they are a morally required means for achieving those ends.

Implementing Affirmative Action and Managing Diversity

Opponents of affirmative action programs have argued that other criteria besides race and sex have to be weighed when making job decisions in an affirmative action program. First, if sex and race are the only criteria used, this will result in the hiring of unqualified personnel and a consequent decline in productivity.[98] Second, many jobs have significant impacts on the lives of others. Consequently, if a job has significant impact on, say, the safety of others (such as the job of flight controller or surgeon), then criteria other than race or sex should have a prominent place and should override affirmative action.[99] And, third, opponents have argued that affirmative action programs, if continued, will turn us into a more racially and sexually conscious nation.[100] Consequently, the programs should cease as soon as the defects they are meant to remedy are corrected.

The following guidelines have been suggested as a way of folding these sorts of considerations into an affirmative action program when minorities are underrepresented in a firm:[101]

1. Both minorities and nonminorities should be hired or promoted only if they reach certain *minimum levels* of competency or are capable of reaching such levels in a reasonable time.
2. If the qualifications of the minority candidate are only *slightly less* (or equal to or higher) than those of the nonminority, then the minority should be given preference.
3. If both the minority and the nonminority candidates are adequately qualified for a position but the nonminority candidate is *much more* qualified, then:
   a. if performance in the job directly affects the lives and safety of people (such as a surgeon or an airline pilot), or if performance on the job has a substantial and critical effect on the entire firm's efficiency (such as, head comptroller), then the more qualified nonminority should be given preference; but
   b. if the position (like most positions in a firm) does not directly involve safety factors and does not have a substantial and highly critical effect on a firm's efficiency, then the minority person should be given preference.
4. Preference should be extended to minority candidates only so long as their representation throughout the various levels of the firm is not proportional to their availability.

The success or failure of an affirmative action program also depends in part on the accommodations a company makes to the special needs of a racially and sexually diverse workforce. Both women and minorities encounter special work-

[98] Sidney Hook, "Discrimination Against the Qualified?" *New York Times*, 1971.

[99] See Nickel, "Preferential Policies," p. 546.

[100] For example, Gross, *Discrimination in Reverse*, p. 108; for a reply to Gross see Boxill, "The Morality of Preferential Hiring."

[101] Theodore V. Purcell, "A Practical Way to Use Ethics in Management Decisions," Paper for the Drew-Allied Chemical Workshop, June 26–27, 1980; and Nickel, "Preferential Policies."

place problems, and companies need to devise innovative means for addressing these needs. The major problems faced by women relate to the fact that a large number of married couples have children, and it is women who physically bear children and who in our culture carry most of the burden of raising and caring for them. Some people have suggested that companies respond by creating two career tracks for women: one track for women who indicate that they plan to have and actively participate in raising their own children while pursuing their careers, and the other track for women who either plan not to have children or plan to have others (husbands or child care providers) raise their children while they devote themselves to pursuing their careers by putting in extra hours, making sacrifices in their personal lives, traveling, transferring, and relocating to advance their careers, and taking every opportunity for professional development.[102] This approach, however, has been criticized as unjust because it may force women, unlike men, to choose between their careers and their families, and it may result in a lower-status cohort of "mommies" who are discriminated against in favor of a high-status cohort of "career females." Others have suggested that so long as our culture continues to put child care tasks primarily on women, companies should help women by providing more generous family leave policies (IBM provides up to eight weeks of paid maternity leave, up to an additional year of unpaid leave for a new parent with the option of part-time work during that year and a guarantee of their jobs when they return, and pays up to $1,750 of adoption expenses); by providing more flexible work schedules (allowing parents to schedule their arrival and departure times to fit the needs of their children's schedules, or to work four ten-hour days in a week instead of five eight-hour days, allowing mothers of school-age children to work full time during the school year and either rely on temporary replacements during vacations or allow mothers to only work part time); by providing "sick leave" for parents whose children are sick (or for nonparents who have special needs); allowing special job-arrangements for parents (letting new parents spend several years working part time while their children are growing up and guaranteeing their jobs when they return, or letting two parents share the same job); and by providing child care support (setting up a child care facility at or near the workplace, reimbursing employees for child care expenses, setting up a child care referral service, providing special day care personnel who can care for employees' sick children or providing an on-site clinic that can care for sick children while parents work).[103]

The special needs of minorities differ from those of women. Minorities are much more economically and educationally disadvantaged than nonminorities, with fewer work skills, fewer years of formal education, poor-quality educations, and poor or nonexistent English language skills. To meet their needs, companies have to begin providing on-the-job education in work skills, basic reading, writing, and computational skills, and English language skills. Newark New Jersey's Prudential Insurance, for example, provides computer-assisted training in reading and math for entry-level applicants. Northeast Utilities in Hartford, Connecticut, pro-

[102] Felice N. Schwartz, "Management Women and the New Facts of Life," *Harvard Business Review* (January–February, 1989), pp. 65–76.

[103] Bolick and Nestleroth, *Opportunity 2000*, pp. 28–50.

vides five weeks of training in vocational skills and English language skills for its Hispanic recruits, while Amtek Systems in Arlington, Virginia, provides similar programs for Asians. Minorities also often have cultural values and beliefs that can give rise to misunderstandings, conflicts, and poor work performance. To deal with this issue, companies have to train their managers to manage a culturally diverse workforce by educating them on those minority cultures represented in their workforce, and helping managers learn to become more aware of, to listen to, communicate with, and understand people from diverse backgrounds.[104]

The controversy over the moral propriety of affirmative action programs has not yet died. The Supreme Court has ruled that such programs do not violate the Civil Rights Act of 1964. It does not follow that these programs do not violate any moral principles. If the arguments examined above are correct, however, then affirmative action programs are at least consistent with moral principles. But the arguments themselves continue to be the subject of intense debate.

Comparable Pay for Jobs of Comparable Worth

During the last few years several groups have advanced a proposal to deal with sexual discrimination that is much more radical and far reaching than affirmative action programs. Affirmative action programs attempt to increase the proportions of women in positions where they are under-represented but they leave untouched the wages and salaries that attach to the positions women already tend to hold. That is, affirmative action programs do not address the problem posed by the fact that jobs that women historically have filled tend to pay low wages and salaries, and merely ensure that more women are hired into those jobs with higher wages and salaries. In contrast to this, the new so-called "comparable worth" programs that many groups have advocated to deal with sexually biased earnings attempt to alter the low wages and salaries that market mechanisms tend to assign to jobs held by women. Unlike affirmative action programs, a comparable worth program does not attempt to place more women into those positions that have higher salaries; instead, a comparable worth program attempts to place higher salaries on those positions that most women already hold.

Comparable worth programs proceed by measuring the value of each job to an organization (in terms of skill requirements, educational requirements, tasks involved, level of responsibility, and any other features of the job that the employer thinks deserve compensation) and ensuring that jobs of equal value are paid the same salary regardless of whether external labor markets pay the same rates for those jobs.[105] For example, studies have shown that legal secretaries and instrument repair technicians hold jobs that have the same relative value for a firm in terms of problem-solving, know-how, and accountability.[106] Nevertheless legal secretar-

[104] *Ibid.*, pp. 65–94; see also, Beverly Geber, "Managing Diversity," *Training*, pp. 23–30.

[105] See Donald J. Trieman and Heidi I. Harmann, eds., *Women, Work, and Wages: Equal Pay for Jobs of Equal Value* (Washington, DC: National Academy Press, 1981) and *Comparable Worth: A Symposium on the Issues and Alternatives* (Washington, DC: Equal Employment Advisory Council, 1981).

[106] Darla Miller, "On the Way to Equitable Pay," *San Jose Mercury News*, 15 July 1981, pp. 1C, 3C.

ies, who are virtually all female, command $9,432 less on the job market than instrument repair technicians, who are predominantly male. A comparable worth program in a firm would adjust the salaries of these two occupations so that they are paid approximately the same.

Thus, in a comparable worth program each job is assigned a certain number of points for difficulty, for skill requirements, for experience, for accountability, for work hazards, for knowledge requirements, for responsibility, for working conditions, and for any other factors that are deemed worthy of compensation. Jobs are then assumed to deserve equal pay if they score equal points, and higher (or lower) pay if they have higher (or lower) scores. Job market considerations are used to determine the actual salary to be paid for jobs with a given number of points, but when jobs have the same scores, they are paid the same salaries. For example, since the job market pays instrument repair technicians $9,432 more than legal secretaries (although these jobs have approximately equal values), a comparable pay program might raise the salaries of the secretaries by $9,432, or perhaps lower the salaries of technicians by the same amount, or it might raise the salaries of secretaries by half that amount and lower that of technicians by the same amount. Job market considerations thus play a small role in setting comparable worth salaries, but they do not determine the salary of one job relative to another.

The fundamental argument in favor of comparable worth programs is one based on justice: Justice requires that equals should be treated as equals.[107] Proponents of comparable worth programs argue that at present jobs filled by women are paid less by job markets than jobs filled by men even when the jobs are in effect equal insofar as they involve equal responsibilities and require equal abilities. Once jobs are objectively evaluated, they claim, it is clear that many women's jobs are equivalent to men's jobs and, in justice, should be paid the same even if discriminatory job markets place them on different wage scales. That certain jobs involve equal responsibilities and abilities, is evident, proponents claim, from an examination of the jobs themselves.

The main arguments against comparable worth programs focus on the appropriateness of markets as determinants of salaries.[108] Opponents of comparable worth argue that there is no "objective" way of evaluating whether one job is "equivalent" to another than by appealing to labor markets which register the combined evaluations of hundreds of buyers and sellers.[109] Only the market forces of supply and demand can determine the "true" worth of a job and only market forces can achieve an approximate capitalist justice by ensuring that each laborer receives a price for her labor that exactly equals the value both she and the buyer

[107] For these and other arguments see "Paying Women What They're Worth," *Report from the Center for Philosophy & Public Policy, University of Maryland*, 3, no. 2 (Spring 1983): 1–5.

[108] See *Pay Equity: Equal Pay for Work of Comparable Value*, Joint Hearings before the Subcommittees on Human Resources, Civil Service, and Compensation and Employee Benefits of the Committee on Post Office and Civil Service, House of Representatives, September 16, 21, 30, and December 2, 1982 (Washington, DC: U.S. Government Printing Office, 1983); Caroline E. Mayer, "The Comparable Pay Debate," *The Washington Post National Weekly Edition*, 6 August 1984; Nina Totenberg, "Why Women Earn Less," *Parade Magazine*, 10 June 1984.

[109] Joanne Jacobs, "Only the Market Can Establish Comparable Worth," *San Jose Mercury News*, 12 October 1984, p. 7B.

places on it. Assigning salaries by assigning "points" to a job is much more arbitrary and less objective than doing so by relying on market forces. Moreover, opponents argue, if the job market pays those who enter a certain occupation a low salary, this is because there is a large supply of workers who want that occupation relative to the demand for that occupation. So-called "women's jobs" have low salaries because there are too many women bidding for those jobs and they thereby drive those salaries down. The solution is not to distort markets by assigning higher "comparable worth" salaries for jobs that are already overcrowded. It is much better to allow the low salaries to stand so they can channel women into other areas of the economy where demand is lower as indicated by the existence of higher salaries. Finally, opponents say, the higher-paying "male jobs" are as open to women as to men. If women choose to enter the lower-paying jobs instead of the higher-paying ones, this is because they derive some utility from (i.e., get some benefits from) the lower-paying jobs that they do not get from the higher-paying ones: Perhaps the lower-paying jobs are "cleaner," or more personally rewarding, or less arduous. Thus women do receive some compensation from the jobs they continue to select even though this might not be in the form of a salary.

Defenders of comparable worth programs answer these criticisms by replying that job markets are not "objective." Women's jobs are paid less, proponents claim, because current job markets are discriminatory: They arbitrarily assign lower salaries to "women's" jobs precisely because they are filled by women. As proof that job markets assign lower salaries to some jobs precisely because they are filled with women, proponents of comparable worth programs point to figures such as those in Table 7.10 which show that there is a consistent relationship between the percentage of women in an occupation and that occupation's salary: The more an occupation is dominated by women, the less it pays. A pattern this consistent indicates that the low wages of women's jobs are not a matter of chance overcrowding of women into this or that occupation. Instead, it is an indication that women are consistently perceived by those in the labor markets as being less capable, skilled, or committed than men. Because of these subjective and discriminatory biases, buyers in job markets systematically underprice the talents of women. As a result job markets undervalue the jobs women take. Consequently, job markets are not adequate indicators of appropriate wage scales for women's jobs.

As with affirmative action, comparable worth continues to be a highly controversial issue.

Conclusions

Earlier sections examined several future trends that will affect the future status of women and minorities in the workforce between now and the year 2000. Of particular significance is the fact that over the next decade, only a tiny portion of new workers will be white males. Most new workers will be women and minorities, and unless major changes are made to accommodate their needs and special characteristics, they will not be incorporated smoothly into the workplace.

We have reviewed a number of programs that provide special assistance to women and minorities on moral grounds. However, it should be clear, in view of the future demographic trends, that enlightened self-interest should also prompt business to give women and minorities a special hand. For the costs of not assisting the coming influx of women and minorities with their special needs, will not be borne entirely by women and minorities themselves. Unfortunately, if businesses do not accommodate themselves to these new workers, American businesses will not be able to find the workers they need and they will suffer recurrent and crippling shortages over the next decade. For the pool of traditional white male workers simply will be so small, that businesses will not be able to rely on them to fill all their requirements for skilled and managerial positions.

Many businesses, aware of these ominous trends, have undertaken programs to prepare themselves now to respond to the special needs of women and minorities. To respond to women's needs, for example, many companies have instituted day care services and flexible working hours that allow women with children to care for their children's needs. Other companies have instituted aggressive affirmative action programs aimed at integrating large groups of minorities into their firms where they are provided with education, job training, skills, counseling, and other assistance designed to enable them to assimilate into the workforce. The belief of such companies is that if they act now to recruit women and minorities, they will be familiar with their special needs and will have a large cadre of women and minorities capable of bringing other women and minorities along. James R. Houghton, chairman of Corning Glass Works, is quoted as saying: "Valuing and managing a diverse work force is more than ethically and morally correct. It's also a business necessity. Work force demographics for the next decade make it absolutely clear that companies which fail to do an excellent job of recruiting, retaining, developing and promoting women and minorities simply will be unable to meet their staffing needs."[110]

QUESTIONS FOR REVIEW AND DISCUSSION

1. Define the following concepts: job discrimination, institutionalized/isolated discrimination, intentional/nonintentional discrimination, statistical indicators of discrimination, utilitarian argument against discrimination, Kantian arguments against discrimination, formal principle of "equality," discriminatory practices, affirmative action program, utilization analysis, "reverse discrimination," compensation argument for preferential treatment, instrumental argument for preferential treatment, utilitarian argument for preferential treatment, the end goals of affirmative action programs, invidious contempt, comparable pay.
2. In your judgment, was the historical shift in emphasis from intentional/isolated discrimination to nonintentional/institutionalized discrimination good or bad? Justify your judgment.
3. Research your library for statistics published during the last year that tend to support or refute the statistical picture of racism and sexism developed in Section 7.2 of the text. In view of your research and the materials in the text, do you agree or disagree with the statement "the position of women and minorities relative to white males has changed considerably." Explain your position fully.

[110] Quoted in Investor Responsibility Research Center, "Equal Employment Opportunity, 1990 Analysis E" (Washington, DC: Investor Responsibility Research Center, Inc., 1990.), p. e–4.

4. Compare and contrast the three main kinds of arguments against racial and sexual job discrimination. Which of these seem to you to be the strongest? The weakest? Can you think of different kinds of arguments not discussed in the text? Are there important differences between racial discrimination and sexual discrimination?
5. Compare and contrast the main arguments used to support affirmative action programs. Do you agree or disagree with these arguments? If you disagree with an argument, state clearly which part of the argument you think is wrong and explain why it is wrong. (It is not enough to say, "I just don't think it is right.")
6. "If employers only want to hire [the best qualified] young white males, then they have a right to do so without interference, since these are their businesses." Comment on this statement.

CASES FOR DISCUSSION

Brian Weber[1]

The Kaiser Aluminum plant in Gramercy, Louisiana, opened in 1958. From the beginning, the Kaiser Gramercy plant had relatively few black workers. By 1965, although 39 percent of the local work force was black, Kaiser had hired only 4.7 percent blacks. In 1970, a federal review of Kaiser employment practices at the Gramercy plant found that of 50 professional employees, none were black; of 132 supervisors, only 1 was black; and of 246 skilled craftworkers, none were black. A 1973 federal review found that although Kaiser had allowed several whites with no prior craft experience to transfer into the skilled craft positions, blacks were not transferred unless they possessed at least five years of prior craft experience. Since blacks were largely excluded from the crafts unions, they were rarely able to acquire such experience. As a result, only 2 percent of the skilled craftworkers at Gramercy were black. A third federal review in 1975 found that 2.2 percent of Kaiser Gramercy's 290 craftworkers were black; that of 72 professional employees, only 7 percent were black; and that of 11 draftsmen, none were black. Moreover, although the local labor market in 1975 was still 39 percent black, the Kaiser Gramercy plant's overall work force was only 13.3 percent black. Only the lowest-paying category of jobs—unskilled laborers—included a large proportion (35.5 percent) of blacks, a proportion that was brought about by implementing a 1968 policy of hiring one black unskilled worker for every white unskilled worker.

By 1974, Kaiser was being pressured by federal agencies to increase the number of blacks in its better-paying skilled crafts positions. Moreover, the United States Steelworkers Union was simultaneously pressing Kaiser to institute a program for training its own workers in the crafts, instead of hiring all its crafts workers from outside the company. As a response to both of these pressures, Kaiser agreed in 1974 to set up a training program that was intended to qualify its *own* workers (both white and black) for crafts positions, and that was also intended to eliminate

[1] See Rick Harris and Jack Hartog, "The Catch-22 Case," *Civil Rights Digest*, 11, no. 2 (Winter 1979): 2–11.

the manifest racial imbalance in its crafts positions. According to the agreement with the union, Kaiser workers would be trained for crafts positions, in order of seniority, at Kaiser's own expense ($15,000–20,000 per year per trainee). One half of the slots in the crafts training program would be reserved for blacks until the percentage of black skilled craftworkers in the Gramercy plant approximated the percentage of blacks in the local labor force. Openings in the program would be filled by alternating between the most senior qualified white employee and the most senior qualified black employee.

During the first year of the program, thirteen workers were selected for the training program: seven blacks and six whites. Brian Weber, a young white worker who had applied to the program, was not among those selected. Brian, a talkative, likeable southerner and father of three, had been working as a blue-collar lab analyst in the Gramercy plant. His position was rated as "semiskilled." He wanted very much to enter one of the skilled jobs. Upon investigation Weber found that he had several months more seniority than two of the black workers who had been admitted into the training program. Forty-three other white workers who were also rejected had even more seniority than he did. Junior black employees were thus receiving training in preference to more senior white employees. Weber later found that none of the black workers who had been admitted to the program had themselves been the subject of any prior employment discrimination by Kaiser.[2]

1. In your judgment, was the Kaiser plant practicing discrimination? If you believe it was discriminating, explain what kind of discrimination was involved and identify the evidence for your judgment; if you believe it was not discriminatory, prepare responses to the strongest objections to your own view. Was Kaiser management morally responsible for the situation in its plant? Why?
2. In your judgment, did the management of Kaiser act rightly when it implemented its preferential treatment program? Explain your judgment in terms of the ethical principles that you think are involved. Does the fact that none of the black workers had themselves been subject to any prior employment discrimination by Kaiser absolve Kaiser from any ethical duty to rectify the racial imbalance in its workforce? What policies would you have recommended for Kaiser?
3. Was Brian Weber treated fairly or unfairly? Explain your judgment on the basis of the moral principles that you think are involved. What is the value of seniority relative to equality of opportunity? As a manager, how would you have dealt with Brian and others who felt as he did? Should seniority serve as a basis for deciding who gets trained for a job? What kinds of qualifications do you believe should be taken into account?

Comparable Pay in San Jose

On Sunday, July 5, 1981, the city employees of San Jose, California, went on strike. The strike was unusual: For the first time in U.S. labor history workers

[2] Weber subsequently sued Kaiser and the case was eventually heard by the U.S. Supreme Court. The Court ruled that Kaiser's affirmative action program was not in violation of the Civil Rights Act of 1964.

were striking over the issue of equal pay for "comparable" work. Striking city employees agreed that men and women always received equal pay when they held the same job. But, they said, jobs that women traditionally filled paid less than those that men traditionally filled. These "disparities," city workers held, were discriminatory and had to end. The strike was unusual for a second reason: It was illegal. Civil Service regulations stipulate that city workers do not have the right to strike.

The strike arose out of a study commissioned by the San Jose city council in 1979, that was designed to find whether women were paid less than men for nonmanagement city jobs. The city council, which had been pressured to do the study by the city workers' union—the American Federation of State, County and Municipal Employees (AFSCME)—asked Hay Associates, a San Francisco consulting firm, to prepare the study.

Hay Associates began their study by sending questionnaires to all city employees. The questionnaire asked each one to describe the tasks, problems, requirements, responsibilities, and working conditions involved in his or her job. The Hay consultants then had the city's personnel department review these questionnaires and conduct on-the-job interviews with about 20 percent of the employees. On the basis of these questionnaires and interviews, the personnel department wrote new job descriptions for each city job indicating its duties, requirements, responsibilities, and working conditions.

Hay Associates then convened a committee of ten city employees and asked them to rate the new job descriptions of 225 nonmanagement city government jobs, using Hay's widely respected rating system and guided by Hay consultants. The committee was comprised of workers familiar with many job classifications and included four union members and one management representative. The committee met with the Hay consultants two or three times a week for five months to review the new job descriptions and assign points to each job in each of four categories: knowhow, problem-solving, accountability, and working conditions. The discussions of the committee were often heated since a final judgment could not be made until seven of the ten members reached agreement. Using tables provided by Hay Associates the committee members had to assign points to each job in each of the four categories.

The assignment of points used complicated criteria that took into account every aspect of the four categories. The Hay criteria, for example, took into account both the scope and depth of knowledge required by each job including knowledge of practical procedures, techniques, and skills gained through formal training and education or experience. Education was broken down into primary, elementary vocational, advanced vocational, and basic technical-specialized. These subcategories were further broken down into more detailed criteria. Other categories measured human relations requirements for each job. Using these guides, the committee gave each job a numerical rating that constituted the "value" of the job and was intended to be a measure of the utility of the job relative to the needs of the organization and to other jobs in the organization.

Once the committee had assigned numerical ratings to each job, those jobs with comparable values were grouped together into the same "Job Grade"; fifteen job grade levels were assigned. Table 7.11 indicates the numerical rating assigned

TABLE 7.11 Numerical Ratings Assigned by Hay Study to Selected City Jobs in Selected Job Grades with Salary and Predominant Sex Comparisons

JOB AND SALARY	PREDOMINANT SEX	KNOW-HOW	PROBLEM-SOLVING	ACCOUNTABILITY	WORKING CONDITIONS	TOTAL POINTS
Job Grade 15						
Senior Chemist $29,094	Male & Female	264	115	115	7	501
Senior Librarian $23,348	Female	264	100	132	0	496
Job Grade 12:						
Planner II $25,636	Male	200	76	76	0	352
Librarian II $21,268	Female	200	57	87	0	344
Job Grade 8:						
Executive Secretary $19,994	Female	132	38	43	0	213
Electrician $26,338	Male	132	38	38	16	224
Library Assistant $18,226	Female	152	33	38	0	223
Job Grade 6:						
Painter $24,518	Male	115	22	22	14	173
Secretary $17,784	Female	115	29	33	0	177
Senior Telephone Operator $15,210	Female	115	25	38	0	178
Senior Water System Technician $21,710	Male	115	22	25	10	172
Job Grade 1:						
Custodian $15,210	Male	66	8	12	12	98
Data Entry Operator I $13,052	Female	76	10	12	0	98

Source: Hay Associates Study, 1980, American Federation of State, County and Municipal Employees, Local 101. Quoted in *San Jose Mercury*, 15 July 1981.

TABLE 7.12 Comparable Male and Female City Jobs with Salary Comparisons

JOB FILLED PREDOMINANTLY BY MALES	ANNUAL SALARY	COMPARABLE JOB FILLED PREDOMINANTLY BY FEMALES	ANNUAL SALARY	SALARY DIFFERENCE
Custodian	$15,210	Library Page	$11,154	$4,056
Park Ranger	18,304	Senior Typist	15,600	2,704
Equipment Operator	18,304	Police Records Clerk	15,600	2,704
Gardener	19,292	Secretary	17,784	1,508
Planner II	25,636	Librarian II	21,268	4,368
Civil Engineer	21,528	Neighborhood Recreation Supervisor	18,460	3,068
Metal Worker	24,180	Executive Secretary	19,994	4,186
Plumber	26,260	Programmer Analyst	21,396	4,862
Electrician	28,964	Buyer	22,256	8,708

Source: Hay Associates Study, 1980, American Federation of State, County and Municipal Employees, Local 101. Quoted in *San Jose Mercury*, 8 July 1981.

to several jobs along with an indication of the salary and whether the job is predominantly filled by males or females.

As the examples in Table 7.12 indicate, city jobs dominated by women were paid less than jobs dominated by men even when, as the numerical ratings assigned by the Hay committee suggested, those jobs involved equal or "comparable" requirements. Table 7.12 lists examples of several city jobs that the Hay committee judged to be comparable to each other but which were not paid comparable salaries. The examples in Table 7.12 also suggest that jobs filled predominantly by women were being paid less than jobs filled predominantly by men.

In order to develop a method of comparing salaries, the Hay consultant group used a complicated statistical formula to compute the average or "trend" salaries of jobs with the same numerical ranking. The Hay formula took into account the relative value of each job to the city organiza tion based on comparisons with other jobs and salaries of comparable numerical ranking. These averages were pictured as a "trend line" on a graph on which average salaries were placed on one axis and numerical rankings were placed on the other axis. The "trend line" thus was supposed to indicate what a job would be paid if salary were based solely on the value of the job as computed by the Hay study. The Hay study found that the salaries of most jobs dominated by women fell 2 to 10 percent below this trend line (i.e., below the computed average salary of jobs with the same numerical value), while jobs dominated by men were 8 to 15 percent above the trend line (above the computed average salary of jobs with the same numerical value).

TABLE 7.13

JOB FILLED PREDOMINANTLY BY WOMEN	1980–81 ACTUAL SALARY	1980–81 "TREND-LINE" SALARY
Senior Librarian	$23,438	$29,858
Acquisition Librarian	24,847	28,031
Librarian II	21,350	27,170
Executive Secretary	20,071	24,600
Secretary	17,852	19,653
Typist Clerk II	14,355	16,913

Sources: Hay Associates Study, 1980, and American Federation of State, County and Municipal Employees, Local 101. Quoted in *San Jose Mercury,* 15 July 1981.

Nine months and $100,000 later the committee finished its work and Hay Associates submitted a report of its results. A few months later, on July 5, 1981, the city workers went on strike demanding that the salaries of all jobs filled predominantly by women should be raised to the levels of the Hay study trend line. As Table 7.13 shows this would require a large increase in the salaries of a number of jobs filled predominantly by women.

Several city council members strongly objected to the demand of the city workers. San Jose city salaries, they pointed out, were on a par with the average salaries paid in that area of California. The salary schedule for almost every significant job category, in fact, equaled or exceeded the average marketplace salary other private and public employers in the area paid their workers for holding the same job. A survey of fifteen other cities and counties, for example, revealed that the average 1979 salary for the job of ''Typist Clerk II'' was $14,472; San Jose city workers that year earned $14,340 for the same job. In some nearby areas (Alameda County) the job of Typist Clerk II had paid as little as $12,588. The job of ''Data Entry Operator'' was paid an average of $15,096 by other area employers in 1979; San Jose city paid $15,036. In Oakland, a few miles away, the same job was paid $13,692 that year. A ''Clerk Typist'' in 1979 was paid $12,996 by the city of San Jose, while private employers throughout the county paid the same job an average of $12,000. An ''Account Clerk II'' with three years experience was paid $13,596 by the city that year, while private employers in the area paid $12,600 for the same job.

Some city council members argued that job salaries always should be based on the going rate in the local labor market. Salaries should not be based on the subjective estimates of what a committee thinks the job is ''worth'':

> The monetary worth of a job in our economic system is what an employer must pay to attract and keep a qualified work force. The comparable worth concept would replace this market value definition of job worth with an artificial determination of worth made by committee on the basis of subjective ratings of various aspects of

> each job. This approach, although well-intentioned, flies in the face of the very basis of our free enterprise system. (Statement of Claude Fletcher, San Jose City Council member)[1]

Other local leaders, including much of the local business community, agreed with the dissident council members:

> As a taxpayer, you'd expect the city administration to run an efficient operation and not to pay wages that are substantially above the going rate in the workplace. In a free enterprise system you can't say you're going to turn your back on the laws of supply and demand and maintain a cost-effective organization. (Statement of Joe Henson, vice president of management services for IBM)[2]

The American Federation of State, County and Municipal Employees, the city workers' union, did not agree with these free enterprise sentiments. The marketplace had built-in biases against women, they held, and it had to be changed by relying on more equitable methods that based salaries on the true value of a job as measured by its contribution to the organization:

> We're talking about fundamentally altering the marketplace because the marketplace is inherently discriminatory. . . There is no free market. The system of wages was set up by a grand conspiracy, so to speak, that has held down the wages of women to minimize labor costs. . . . When we've had shortages of nurses there's been no concerted effort to raise their wages. And the suppression of wages here in Silicon Valley exceeds the suppression of wages in San Jose. Look at the hundreds of ads in the San Jose Mercury News for clerical positions. Why don't they raise the wages to fill those jobs? Because private industry believes you can get more for less—except for mangement. (Statement of William Callahan, business agent for AFSCME.[3]

The union held that the reason why the marketplace undervalued women's jobs was because of the widespread continuation of past trends that had to be changed now and that could only be changed through union bargaining. In a pamphlet union leaders wrote:

> Discriminatory wage patterns continue because jobs are currently not paid according to their relative value to the organization and jobs of equal value are not assigned similar wages. . . . The employer may argue that wages must be comparable to those being paid by other area employers whether they are discriminatory or not. But there will be no pay equity unless the general level of pay for women's jobs is raised in accordance with the findings of the job comparability study. (Statement in "Pay Equity: A Union Issue for the 1980's" by AFSCME.[4]

Neither the San Jose city council nor other city officials were unanimously set against the union's views on comparable pay for comparable work. A few days after the strike began, Janet Gray Hayes, the major of San Jose, said that she felt that comparable work was "an issue whose time has come."[5] That same

[1] Philip J. Trounstine, "Sex Bias Called Inherent," *San Jose Mercury*, 9 July 1981, p. 1B.

[2] *Ibid.*

[3] *Ibid.*

[4] *Ibid.*

[5] *Ibid.*

day Francis Fox, San Jose's city manager, said that in spite of strong opposition from angry business and government leaders from around the nation, he was in favor of comparable pay and was "willing to take the heat because it's the right thing to do."[6] A majority of the council members also favored some form of comparable pay adjustment.

Disagreements between the city and the union, however, centered on how large that adjustment should be. The city council offered the union a package that would increase wages by 12 percent over two years and that in addition earmarked $1.45 million for the purpose of moving city pay rates part of the way toward the Hay Associates "trend line." The city worker's union, however, had demanded that all jobs be moved all the way to the trend line over a four-year time period. The council had rejected that demand as too costly.

By Tuesday July 8, 1981, striking city workers had shut down virtually all city construction projects and closed thirteen of the city's sixteen libraries. The union claimed that 1,000 of its members were on strike although city officials claimed the number was closer to 500. The hardest hit city services included libraries, city garages, city clerks, the auditors' office, and the finance office. Tuesday night 700 striking city workers met at the union's headquarters to consider the council's offer. The city workers resoundingly rejected the offer by voice vote both because they felt that the wage increase was too small and because they felt the comparable pay adjustment did not go far enough.

Earlier on the afternoon of July 8, the city council had instructed City Manager Francis Fox to send a letter to all striking workers warning them that the work stoppage was "an illegal strike" according to civil service ordinances which stated that "Failure to report for duty . . . within 48 hours . . . may be deemed to constitute resignation from the Service and the position may be declared vacant." Fox's letter warned that "If you return to work on or before Monday, July 13, or your first scheduled work shift after Monday, your job will be waiting. If you fail to return, you will be considered as having resigned."[7] In effect the letter promised to fire workers who had not returned to their jobs by Monday July 13.

City Manager Fox and the union negotiator Frank Le Sueur met together over the next few days to consider a compromise. By the weekend they had reached a tentative agreement, subject to the approval of the city council, that would provide $3.2 million over four years to bring all jobs up to the Hay trend line. On Sunday July 12 the city council met to consider the tentative settlement worked out by Fox and Le Sueur. The council unanimously voted to reject it. When their vote was announced outside their chambers, a bitter crowd of union members and union officials broke open the closed doors of the chambers and charged into the meeting room loudly denouncing the council's vote as "unbelievable arrogance and carelessness." Angered, Francis Fox promised that he would push forward with his plan to fire all striking workers on Monday.

After the disturbance, council members turned back to work and developed

[6] *Ibid.*

[7] Ed Pope, "Striking S.J. Workers Turn Down City Offers," *San Jose Mercury*, 8 July 1981, p. 1.

two broad counter proposals. The first proposal, called "Plan A," promised general wage increases of 8.5 percent each year for the next two years but provided nothing for comparable pay adjustments; instead, under Plan A, the council would promise to put the issue of comparable pay before city voters on the following November ballot. The second proposal, called "Plan B," would offer general wage increases of 7.5 percent in 1981–82 and 8 percent in 1982–83 for the 2000 workers represented by the union; in addition Plan B would set aside $1.4 million for comparable pay adjustments for female-dominated jobs. Discussion of the proposals during the meeting was heated. Plan A was unanimously approved early in the discussions. But Plan B was strongly opposed by some. Both Francis Fox and Mayor Hayes had earlier vowed not to go above a 6 percent wage increase, although both were strongly in favor of some comparable pay adjustments. Other council members were unequivocally opposed to any comparable pay adjustment. Eventually, however, Plan B also received the required six votes.

On Monday morning at 11 a.m., both general proposals were presented to the union at a secret meeting at a hotel near the airport. By now the union had lost confidence in their negotiator, Frank Le Sueur. He had been replaced by two other city workers. The new union negotiators agreed to present and recommend Plan B to the city workers. They also agreed that no pay adjustments would total more than 15 percent for any job grade. Under the plan female jobs would increase at a faster rate than male-dominated jobs: female-dominated jobs would receive the general 7.5 percent wage increase plus an additional percentage increase designed to bring them closer to the Hay trend line, while male-dominated jobs would receive only the general 7.5 percent wage increase. Librarians (a female-dominated job), for example, would receive a 7.5 percent wage increase plus another 7.5 percent comparable pay adjustment increase; Typist clerks (the largest female-dominated category) would receive a 3.5 percent comparable pay adjustment in addition to the 7.5 percent general wage increase.

On Monday night the city council met once again to make a final decision on Plan B. Several city council members still objected to the plan and insisted that the city manager should follow through with his promise to fire striking workers. The majority of the council, however, was in favor of the plan and voted to adopt it as their official offer by a vote of 8–3.

The next day union members met and voted 295–27 to accept the city council's offer of Plan B.

1. In your judgment, did the fact that San Jose city jobs filled mostly by men paid more than those filled mostly by women, constitute a form of unjust discrimination? What kind of discrimination was invoked?
2. In your judgment, would an individual city employee have been morally justified in deciding to join the strike? Why or why not? Were members of the city council justified in their argument that the salary scales were morally legitimate because they equaled or exceeded average regional salaries?
3. In your judgment, was the Hay Associates' method of establishing the comparability of jobs adequate or inadequate? Explain your answer. Is there an adequate moral

justification for setting salaries by the Hay Associates' method in "a free enterprise system"?

4. Would the city council have been morally justified to fire the striking city workers? Why or why not?
5. Evaluate the final plan accepted by both the union and the city council. In your judgment, is there a moral requirement for all or some private businesses to adopt such a plan? Explain your answer. What, in your judgment, is the morally best way of dealing with the kinds of salary "discrepancies" described in the case?

8

THE INDIVIDUAL IN THE ORGANIZATION

INTRODUCTION

What are organizations like? Here are some descriptions of life inside organizations by three people positioned at different organizational levels:

Spot-welder at a Ford Assembly Plant:

> I start the automobile, the first welds. . . . the welding gun's got a square handle, with a button on the top for high voltage and a button on the bottom for low. . . . We do about thirty-two jobs per car, per unit. Forty-eight units an hour, eight hours a day. Thirty-two times forty-eight times eight. Figure it out. That's how many times I push that button. . . . It don't stop. It just goes and goes and goes. . . . I don't like the pressure, the intimidation. How would you like to go up to someone and say, "I would like to go to the bathroom?" If the foreman doesn't like you, he'll make you hold it, just ignore you. . . . Oh, yeah, the foreman's got somebody knuckling down on him, putting the screws to him. But a foreman is still free to go the bathroom, go get a cup of coffee. He doesn't face the penalties. . . . When a man becomes a foreman, he has to forget about even being human, as far as feelings are concerned. You see a guy there bleeding to death. So what, buddy? That line's gotta keep goin'.[1]

[1] Studs Terkel, *Working: People Talk About What They Do All Day and How They Feel About What They Do* (New York: Pantheon Books, Inc., 1979), pp. 159, 160, 161.

Plant Manager at Ford Assembly Plant:

I'm usually here at seven o'clock. . . . Then I go out on the floor, tour the plant. . . . I'll change my tour so they can't tell every day I'm going to be in the same place at the same time. The worst thing I could do is set a pattern where they'll always know where I'll be. I'm always stopping to talk to foremen or hourly fellas. . . . I may see a water leak, I say to the foreman, "Did you call maintenance?" Not do it myself, let him go do it. By the time I get back in the office, I have three or four calls, "Can you help me on this?" This is how you keep in contact. . . . The operating committee meets usually every other day: my assistant plant managers; an operations manager, he has two production managers; a controller; an engineering manager; a quality control manager; and a materials manager. That's the eight key figures in the plant. . . . You can't run a business sitting in the office 'cause you get divorced too much from the people. The people are the key to the whole thing. If you aren't in touch with the people they think he's too far aloof, he's distant. It doesn't work.[2]

Ex-President of Conglomerate:

I don't know of any situation in the corporate world where an executive is completely free and sure of his job from moment to moment. . . . The danger starts as soon as you become a district manager. You have men working for you and you have a boss above. You're caught in a squeeze. The squeeze progresses from station to station. I'll tell you what a squeeze is. You have the guys working for you that are shooting for your job. The guy you're working for is scared stiff you're gonna shove him out of his job. . . . There's always the insecurity. You bungle a job. You're fearful of losing a big customer. You're fearful so many things will appear on your record, stand against you. You're always fearful of the big mistake. You've got to be careful when you go to corporation parties. Your wife, your children have to behave properly. You've got to fit in the mold. You've got to be on guard. When I was president of this big corporation . . . [the] corporation specified who you could socialize with, and on what level. . . . The executive is a lonely animal in the jungle who doesn't have a friend.[3]

Not everyone experiences organizations as these three people do. Nonetheless, these three descriptions of organizational life touch on many of the most problematic characteristics of business organizations: the alienation experienced by assembly line workers; the feelings of oppression created by the exercise of authority; the responsibilities heaped on the shoulders of managers; the power tactics employed by managers anxious to advance their career ambitions; the pressures felt by subordinates and superiors as they both try to get their jobs done. Other problems could be added to the list: health problems created by unsafe working conditions, conflicts of interest created by an employee's allegiance to other causes, the absence of due process for nonunionized employees; invasion of privacy by a management's legitimate concern to know its own workers. The list could go on.

[2] *Ibid.*, pp. 178, 179.

[3] *Ibid.*, pp. 405, 406.

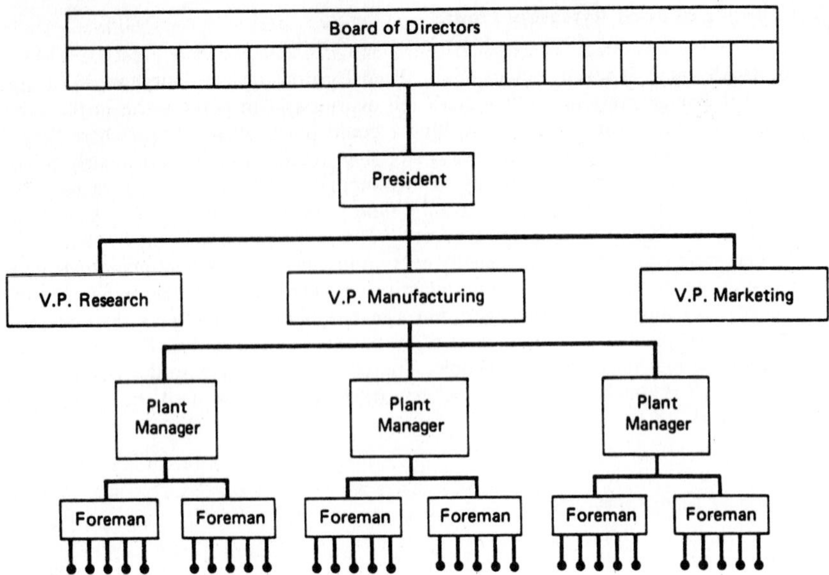

FIGURE 8-1

This chapter explores these and other problems raised by life within business organizations. The chapter is divided into two main parts. The first part begins by describing the traditional model of the organization: the organization as a "rational" structure. The following sections then discuss, first, the employee's duties to the firm as defined by this traditional model, and second, the employer's duties to the employee, again as defined by this model. The second main part of the chapter turns to describing a more recent view of the organization: the organization as a "political" structure. The last sections discuss the two main ethical issues raised by this more recent "political" analysis of the firm: employee rights and organizational politics.

8.1 THE RATIONAL ORGANIZATION

The more traditional "rational" model of a business organization defines the organization as a structure of formal (explicitly defined and openly employed) relationships designed to achieve some technical or economic goal with maximum efficiency.[4] E. H. Schein provides a compact definition of an organization from this perspective:

> An organization is the rational coordination of the activities of a number of people for the achievement of some common explicit purpose or goal, through division of labor and function and through a hierarchy of authority and responsibility.[5]

[4] See James D. Thompson, *Organizations in Action* (New York: McGraw-Hill Book Company, 1967), pp. 4–6; see also, John Ladd, "Morality and the Ideal of Rationality in Formal Organizations," *Monist*, 54 (1970).

[5] E. H. Schein, *Organizational Psychology* (Englewood Cliffs, NJ: Prentice Hall, 1965), p. 8.

If the organization is looked at in this way, then the most fundamental realities of the organization are the formal hierarchies of authority identified in the "organizational chart" that represents the various official positions and lines of authority in the organization. Figure 8.1 provides a simplified example.

At the bottom of the organization is the "operating layer": those employees and their immediate supervisors who directly produce the goods and services that constitute the essential outputs of the organization. The work of the Ford spot-welder quoted at the beginning of this chapter was located at this level. Above the operating layer of laborers are ascending levels of "middle managers" who direct the units below them and who are in turn directed by those above them in ascending formal lines of authority. The plant manager quoted above worked within these middle levels of the organization. At the apex of the pyramid is "top management": the board of directors, the chief executive officer, and his or her staff. The ex-president quoted earlier inhabited these upper levels of the organization.

The rational model of an organization supposes that most information is collected from the operating layers of the organization, rises through the various formal management levels, each of which aggregates the information, until it reaches top management levels. On the basis of this information the top managers make general policy decisions and issue general commands, which are then passed downward through the formal hierarchy where they are amplified at each managerial level until they reach the operating layer as detailed work instructions. These decisions of the top managers are assumed to be designed to achieve some known and common economic goal such as efficiency, productivity, profits, maximum return on investment, etc. The goal is defined by those at the top of the hierarchy of authority who are assumed to have a legitimate right to make this decision.

What is the glue that holds together the organization's many layers of employees and managers and that fixes these people onto the organization's goals and formal hierarchy? Contracts. The model conceives of the employee as an agent who freely and knowingly agreed to accept the organization's formal authority and to pursue its goals in exchange for support in the form of a wage and fair working conditions. These contractual agreements cement each employee into the organization by formally defining each employee's duties and scope of authority. By virtue of this contractual agreement, the employee has a moral responsibility to obey the employer in the course of pursuing the organization's goals, and the organization in turn has a moral responsibility to provide the employee with the economic supports it has promised. For, as we have already discussed at some length, when two persons knowingly and freely agree to exchange goods or services with each other, each party to the agreement acquires a moral obligation to fulfill the terms of the contract. Utilitarian theory provides additional support for the view that the employee has an obligation to loyally pursue the goals of the firm: Businesses could not function efficiently and productively if their employees were not single-mindedly devoted to pursuing their firm's goals. If each employee were free to use the resources of the firm to pursue his or her *own* ends, chaos would ensue and everyone's utility would decline.

The basic ethical responsibilities that emerge from these "rational" aspects of the organization focus on two reciprocal moral obligations: (1) the obligation of the *employee* to obey organizational superiors, to pursue the organization's goals, and to avoid any activities that might threaten that goal, and (2) the obligation of the *employer* to provide the employee with a fair wage and fair working conditions. These duties in turn are presumed to be defined through the organization's formal lines of authority and through the contracts that specify the employee's duties and working conditions. We will examine these two reciprocal duties in turn.

8.2 THE EMPLOYEE'S OBLIGATIONS TO THE FIRM

In the rational view of the firm, the employee's main moral duty is to work toward the goals of the firm and to avoid any activities which might harm those goals. To be unethical, basically, is to deviate from these goals in order to serve one's own interests in ways that, if illegal, are counted as a form of "white collar crime."[6]

As administrator of the company's finances, for example, the financial manager is entrusted with its funds and has the responsibility of managing those funds in a way that will minimize risk while ensuring a suitable rate of return for the company's shareholders. Financial managers have this contractual duty to the firm and its investors because they have contracted to provide the firm with their best judgment and to exercise their authority only in the pursuit of the goals of the firm and not for their own personal benefit. Financial managers fail in their contractual duty to the firm when they misappropriate funds, when they waste or squander funds, when they are negligent or fraudulent in the preparation of financial statements, when they issue false or misleading reports, and so on.

These traditional views of the employee's duties to the firm have, of course, made their way into the "law of agency," that is, the law that specifies the legal duties of "agents" (employees) toward their "principals."[7] The "restatement" of the law of agency, for example, states in section 385 that "an agent is subject to a duty to his principal to act solely for the benefit of the principal in all matters connected with his agency"; and section 394 prohibits the agent from acting "for persons whose interests conflict with those of the principal in matters in which the agent is employed."[8] In short, the employee must pursue the goals of the firm and must do nothing that conflicts with those goals while he or she is working for the firm.

There are several ways in which the employee might fail to live up to the

[6] The classic analysis of white collar crime is Edwin H. Sutherland, *White Collar Crime* (New York: Holt, Rinehart and Winston, Inc., 1949); see also U.S. Chamber of Commerce, "White Collar Crime: The Problem and Its Import," in Sir Leon Radzinowicz and Marvin E. Wolfgang, *Crime and Justice*, vol. I, *The Criminal in Society*, 2nd ed. (New York: Basic Books, Inc., 1977), pp. 314–55; and Donald R. Cressey, *Other People's Money* (Glencoe, IL: The Free Press, 1953). The most recent and most extensive analysis of white collar crime is Marshall B. Clinard, Peter C. Veager, Jeanne Brissette, David Petrashek, and Elizabeth Harries, *Illegal Corporate Behavior* (Washington, DC: U.S. Government Printing Office, 1979).

[7] See Philip I. Blumberg, "Corporate Responsibility and the Employee's Duty of Loyalty and Obedience: A Preliminary Inquiry," in *The Corporate Dilemma*, Dow Votaw and S. Prakash Sethi, eds. (Englewood Cliffs, NJ: Prentice Hall, 1973), pp. 82–113.

[8] Quoted in *ibid.*, pp. 87 and 88.

duty to pursue the goals of the firm: The employee might act on a "conflict of interest," the employee might steal from the firm, or the employee might use his or her position as leverage to force illicit benefits out of others through extortion or commercial bribery. We will turn now to examine the ethical issues raised by these tactics.

Conflicts of Interest

Conflicts of interest in business arise when an employee or an officer of a company is engaged in carrying out a task on behalf of the company and the employee has a private interest in the outcome of the task (a) that is possibly antagonistic to the best interests of the company, and (b) that is substantial enough that it does or reasonably might affect the independent judgment the company expects the employee to exercise on its behalf.[9] Or, more simply, conflicts of interest arise when the self-interest of employees in positions of trust leads them to discharge their offices in ways that may not be in the best interests of the firm. An official of a corporation, for example, is involved in a conflict of interest if he holds stock in one of the companies submitting bids for a construction contract. His interest in seeing the value of the stock improve may tempt him to give the contract to the building company in which he holds stock, even though it did not offer the best terms to the corporation for which he works.

Conflicts of interest need not be financial. For example, if my daughter-in-law is a saleswoman for a firm that manufactures the type of tools that my company purchases, I have an interest in seeing her succeed and may be motivated to give her my company's business even though other firms may offer better terms.

Conflicts of interest can also arise when officers or employees of one company hold another job or consulting position in an outside firm with which their own company deals or competes. An employee of one bank, for example, could be involved in a conflict of interest if the employee took a job serving a competing bank, or if the employee took a job serving an insurance company that leased the employee's own bank's equipment or facilities: At the very least the employee's loyalties would be divided between serving the interests of each competing firm. Similarly, a conflict of interest would be created if an accountant working for an insurance company also provides "independent" auditing services for some of the firms the insurance company insures: The accountant might be tempted to pass on to the insurance company some of the private information gathered when auditing the books of those other firms.

Conflicts of interest may be actual or potential.[10] An *actual* conflict of interest occurs when a person actually discharges his or her duties in a way that is prejudicial to the firm and does it out of self-interest. A *potential* conflict of interest occurs when a person is merely motivated or tempted by self-interest to act in a way that is prejudicial to the firm. In the first case cited above, for example, the

[9] Conflicts of interest are discussed in M. Davis, "Conflict of Interest," *Business and Professional Ethics Journal,* 1, no. 4 (Summer 1982): 17–29; see also Twentieth Century Fund, ed., *Abuse on Wall Street: Conflicts of Interest in the Securities Markets* (Westport, CT: Quorum Books, 1980).

[10] Thomas M. Garrett and Richard J. Klonoski, *Business Ethics,* 2nd ed. (Englewood Cliffs, NJ: Prentice Hall, 1986), p. 55.

official of the corporation is involved in a merely *potential* conflict of interest, so long as his judgment is not biased by his stockholdings and he gives the contract to the construction company which offers his employer the best terms. The conflict of interest becomes *actual* if his judgment is biased toward the construction company in which he holds stock, and he acts on this bias.

If we accept the view (outlined in Chapter Two) that agreements impose moral duties, then *actual* conflicts of interest are unethical because they are contrary to the implied contract that a worker freely accepts when taking a job with a firm. The administrative personnel of a firm are hired to use their unbiased judgment to advance the goals of the firm. By accepting the position within the firm, the employee contracts to administer the assets of the firm in accordance with these goals and in return takes the salary connected with fulfilling this administrative task. To break this contractual relation violates the rights and duties created by the contract.

Potential conflicts of interest may or may not be ethical depending on the probability that the employee's judgment will be affected by the conflicting interest or will appear to be affected. Obviously, there are no general rules for determining whether or not an employee's private and conflicting interests are significant enough to affect his or her judgment: Much depends on the employee's personal psychology and intentions, on the employee's position in the firm and the nature of the employee's job, on how much he or she stands to gain from the transactions involved, and on the impact the employee's actions will have on others inside and outside the firm. To avoid problems many companies (a) specify the amount of stock that the company will allow employees to hold in supplier firms, (b) specify the relationships with competitors, buyers, or suppliers that the company prohibits employees from having, and (c) require key officers to disclose all their outside financial investments.

Conflicts of interest can be created by a variety of different kinds of situations and activities. Two kinds of situations and activities demand further attention: bribes and gifts.

Commercial Bribes and Extortion A *commercial bribe* is a consideration given or offered to an employee by a person outside the firm with the understanding that when the employee transacts business for his or her own firm, the employee will deal favorably with that person or with that person's firm. The consideration may consist of money, tangible goods, the "kickback" of part of an official payment, preferential treatment, or any other kind of benefit. A purchasing agent, for example, is accepting a bribe when he or she accepts money from a supplier who gives it to the agent in order to receive favored treatment in the agent's purchasing decisions. On the other hand, an employee is engaged in commercial *extortion* if the employee demands a consideration from persons outside the firm as a condition for dealing favorably with those persons when the employee transacts business for his or her firm. Purchasing agents, for example, who will buy only from those salespeople who give them certain goods or services are involved in extortion. Extortion and the acceptance of bribes obviously create a conflict of interest that violates the moral duty that the employee's work contract establishes—that is, the duty to use one's unbiased judgment in the pursuit of the employer's legitimately established goals.

Gifts Accepting gifts may or may not be ethical. The purchasing agent, for example, who accepts gifts from the salesperson with whom he or she deals without asking for the gifts and without making such gifts a condition of doing business with them, may be doing nothing unethical. If the agent does not give favored treatment to those from whom he or she accepts gifts and is not prejudiced against those who fail to give a "gift," no *actual* conflict of interest is created. A *potential* conflict of interest, however, may exist and the act may encourage a practice that in some instances becomes an actual conflict of interest or that may be subtly affecting the independence of a person's judgment. Vincent Barry suggests that the following factors should be considered when evaluating the morality of accepting a gift:[11]

1. What is the value of the gift? That is, is it substantial enough to influence one's decisions?
2. What is the purpose of the gift? That is, is the gift intended or accepted as a bribe?
3. What are the circumstances under which the gift was given? That is, was the gift given openly? Was it given to celebrate a special event (Christmas, a birthday, a store opening)?
4. What is the position of the recipient of the gift? That is, is the recipient in a position to influence his own firm's dealings with the giver of the gift?
5. What is the accepted business practice in the area? That is, is the gift part of an open and well-known industry practice?
6. What is the company's policy? That is, does the company forbid acceptance of such gifts?
7. What is the law? That is, is the gift forbidden by a law, such as a law prohibiting gifts in sports recruiting?

Employee Theft

The employee of a firm has a contractual agreement to accept only certain specified benefits in exchange for his labor and to use the resources and goods of the firm in pursuit only of the legitimate aims of the firm. For the employee to appropriate additional benefits for herself or to convert company resources to the employee's own use are forms of theft since to do either is to take or use property that belongs to another (the employer) without the consent of its rightful owner.

Employee theft is often petty: involving the theft of small tools, office supplies, or clothing. At the managerial level, petty theft sometimes occurs through the manipulation or padding of expense accounts, although the amounts involved are sometimes substantial. Other forms of managerial theft, sometimes referred to as "white collar crime," are embezzlement, larceny, fraud in the handling of trusts or receiverships, and forgery. The ethics of these forms of theft, however, are relatively clear. Not always as clear are some particularly modern kinds of theft: thefts involving various forms of information.

Computer Theft What are the ethics of using a computer to gain entry into a company's data bank? Of copying a company's computer programs? Of

[11] Vincent Barry, *Moral Issues in Business* (Belmont, CA: Wadsworth Publishing Company, Inc., 1986), pp. 237–38.

using or copying a company's computerized data? Of using a company computer during one's own time? Unless authorized explicitly or through a company's formal or informal policies, all such activities are unethical forms of theft since they all involve taking or using property that belongs to someone else without the consent of its rightful owners. Of course, the information contained in a data bank and the programs provided by a company are not *tangible* property, and the employee who examines, uses, or copies such information or programs might leave the original information or programs unchanged (the company might never even realize what the employee did). Nevertheless, unauthorized examination, use, or copying of computer information or programs constitutes theft. It is theft because information gathered in a computer bank by a company and computer programs developed or purchased by a company, are the property of that company.

Such theft is best understood by considering the nature of property: Property consists of a bundle of rights that attach to some identifiable asset. The most important of these rights are the right to exclusive use of the asset, the right to decide whether and how others may use the asset, the right to sell, trade, or give away the asset, the right to any income generated by the asset, and the right to modify or change the asset.[12] (These rights, of course, are limited by the rights of others, such as the right not to be harmed.) All of these rights can and do attach to those computers, computer data, and computer programs that a company used its own resources to develop or which the company purchased with its own resources. Such information or programs consequently are the property of the company and only the company has the right to its use or benefits. To usurp any of the rights that attach to property, including the rights pertaining to use, is a form of property theft and is therefore unethical.

Trade Secrets "Proprietary information" or "trade secrets" consist of nonpublic information (1) that concerns a company's own activities, technologies, future plans, policies, or records, and which, if known by competitors, would materially affect the company's ability to compete commercially against those competitors; (2) that is owned by the company (although it might not be patented or copyrighted) because it was developed by the company for its private use from resources it owns or it was purchased for its private use from others with its own funds; and (3) that the company indicates through explicit directives, through security measures, or through contractual agreements with employees that it does not want anyone outside the company to have that information. For example, if a company, using its own engineering and laboratory resources, develops a secret process to manufacture computer "floppy disks" that can carry more computer data than any other company's disks, and it takes explicit measures to ensure that process is not known to anyone else, detailed information about that process is a "trade secret." Similarly, lists of suppliers or customers, research results, formulas, computer programs, computer data, marketing and production plans, and any other information that is developed by a company for its own private use from its own resources, can all constitute "trade secrets." Since employees, especially those involved in company research and development, often have access

[12] See Lawrence C. Becker, *Property Rights* (London: Routledge & Kegan Paul, 1977), p. 19.

to trade secrets which the company must entrust to them if it is to carry on its business, they often have the opportunity to use such secrets for their own advantage by dealing with competitors. Such use of trade secrets by employees is unethical because it is using the property of another agent for a purpose not sanctioned by that other agent, and because the employee has an implied (or even, in some cases, an explicit) contract not to use company resources for purposes not sanctioned by the company.[13] An engineering employee, for example, who is hired to oversee the development of a secret manufacturing process that gives her company a competitive edge over others, acts wrongly if she decides to leave that company to work for a competitor who promises her a higher salary in exchange for setting up the same process she developed while being paid to do so by her former employer.

However, skills that an employee acquires by working for a company do not count as trade secrets since trade secrets consist of information and not skills. The skills that an employee develops are considered part of his or her own person and are not the property of an employer like proprietary information is. Unfortunately, it is not always easy to distinguish skills from trade secrets. The situation, for example, might resemble that of Donald Wohlgemuth, a general manager dissatisfied with his salary and his working conditions, who oversaw a B.F. Goodrich secret technology for making spacesuits for the government.[14] Wohlgemuth subsequently negotiated a job with International Latex, a Goodrich competitor, at a much higher salary. At Latex, however, he was to manage a division that involved, among other things, the manufacture of spacesuits for the government. Goodrich managers objected to his working for a competitor where he might use the information and skills Goodrich had paid to develop. When they questioned the ethics of his decision, Wohlgemuth heatedly replied that "loyalty and ethics have their price and International Latex has paid the price." The Ohio Court of Appeals, ruled that Goodrich could not keep Wohlgemuth from selling his skills to another competitor, but it imposed on Wohlgemuth an injunction restraining him from disclosing to Latex any of the trade secrets of B.F. Goodrich. The court did not explain, however, how Wohlgemuth, Goodrich, or Latex were to distinguish between the information and the skills Wohlgemuth had acquired while working for Goodrich.

Some companies have tried to avoid the problem of trade secrets by having employees sign contracts agreeing not to work for competitors for one or two years after leaving the company, but courts have generally rejected the validity of such contracts. Other companies have dealt with these problems by agreeing to provide departing employees with continuing remuneration or future retirement benefits in exchange for their not revealing proprietary information.

The ethical issue of misusing proprietary information has become much more prominent in the last decade as new "information technologies" (such as the computer) have increasingly turned information into a valuable asset to which employees have regular access. As information technologies continue to develop this issue will continue to grow in importance.

[13] For more extended discussion of the ethics of trade secrets see DeGeorge, *Business Ethics*, pp. 292–98.

[14] This case is recounted in Michael S. Baram, "Trade Secrets: What Price Loyalty?" *Harvard Business Review* (November/December 1968).

Before leaving the subject of proprietary information, it is worth recalling that a company's property rights over proprietary information are not unlimited. In particular, they are limited by the rights of other agents, such as the rights of employees to know the health risks associated with their jobs. A company's right to keep information secret is not absolute but must be balanced against the legitimate rights of others.

Insider Trading

As a start, we can define insider trading as the act of buying and selling a company's stock on the basis of "inside" information about the company. "Inside" or "insider" information about a company is confidential or proprietary information about a company that is not available to the general public outside the company, but which would have a material or significant impact on the price of the company's stock. The president of a defense company, for example, may learn that her company is about to receive a multibillion-dollar contract from the government before any member of the outside public is aware of this. She may then purchase a large block of the stock of her company, knowing that its value will rise when the news of the contract becomes public and other buyers and sellers of stock bid up its price. Her purchase of stock is insider trading. The president may also tip off her father, who also hurries out to buy some stock before the general public learns about the contract. His purchase is also insider trading.

Insider trading is illegal, and during the latter half of the 1980s a large number of stockbrokers, bankers, and managers were prosecuted for insider trading. Insider trading is also considered unethical, not merely because it is illegal, but because, it is claimed, the person who trades on insider information in effect "steals" this information and thereby gains an unjust or unfair advantage over the member of the general public.[15] However, several people have argued that insider trading is actually socially beneficial and, on utilitarian grounds, should not be prohibited but encouraged.[16]

First, it is sometimes argued, the insider and his friends bring their inside information to the stock market and, by trading on it, they bid up the price of the stock (or bid it down) so that its stock market price rises (or falls) to reflect the true underlying value of the stock. Experts on the stock market tell us that the stock market functions most efficiently when the market price of each company's stock equals the true underlying value of the stock as determined by the information available. When insiders trade stocks on their inside information, and bid up (or down) the value of stocks, they in effect bring their information to the market, and by their purchases "signal" to others the information they have about what those stocks are really worth. So insider traders perform the valuable service of making their inside information available to the stock market, thereby ensuring

[15] See, for example, Patricia H. Werhane, "The Ethics of Insider Trading," *Journal of Business Ethics*, vol. 8, no. 11 (November 1989), pp. 841–45.

[16] See Bill Shaw, "Should Insider Trading Be Outside the Law?" *Business and Society Review*, Summer 1988, pp. 34–37; the main defender of insider trading along the lines sketched below is Henry G. Manne, *Insider Trading and the Stock Market* (New York: The Free Press, 1966) and "In Defense of Insider Trading," *Harvard Business Review*, 113 (November/December, 1966), pp. 113–122. A recent defense of insider trading who also provides a complete bibliography of Manne's work is Robert W. McGee, "Insider Trading: An Economic and Philosophical Analysis," *The Mid-Atlantic Journal of Business*, vol. 25, no. 1 (November 1988), pp. 35–48.

that the market value of stocks more accurately reflects their true underlying value and securing a more efficient market.

Second, it is argued, insider trading does not harm anyone. Critics of insider trading sometimes claim that the insider who has special "inside" information somehow harms those people who unwittingly sell their stocks to him, not realizing that he knows their stocks are worth more than he is paying them for the stock. But those who defend the ethics of insider trading point out that when people sell their stocks, it is because they need or want the money at that moment. And whether they sell to the insider or some other party, they will get whatever the current market price of their stock is. Later, of course, when the insider's information becomes available to everyone, they will regret selling, because the value of the stock they sold will rise. But at the moment they wanted to sell their stock, they would not have gotten more for their stock from others than what the insider gave them. Moreover, the defenders of insider trading argue, when insiders begin buying up stock on the basis of their inside information, the price of the stock gradually begins to rise. This means that people who need to sell their stocks during that period of rising prices will get more for their stock than they would have received if the insider had not stepped in to raise the price. So not only does the insider not harm those who sell stocks to him right from the beginning, he also benefits those who sell stocks to him or to others later.

Third, the defenders of insider trading argue, it is untrue that the insider trader has an unfair advantage over others who do not have access to his inside information. The fact is that many of the people who buy and sell stocks on the stock market have more or better information than others. Experts, for example, tell us that they can analyze and research coming economic trends, future industry events, probable new discoveries, and other occurrences, and that they can use their analyses to generate information about the value of certain stocks that is not generally available to the public. There is clearly nothing wrong or unfair about this. More generally, there is nothing basically unethical or unfair about having an information advantage over others in the stock market.

Those who claim that insider trading is unethical, however, point out that the defenders of insider trading conveniently ignore several important facts about insider trading. First, the information that the insider trader uses, is information that does not belong to him. The executives, managers, employees, and others who work inside a company and who are aware of inside events that will affect the price of the company's stock do not themselves own the company. The resources they work with, including the information that the company makes available to them, are resources that belong collectively to the shareholders. And employees have an ethical (or "fiduciary") duty to refrain from using company information to benefit themselves or their friends. Just as all employees have an ethical duty to use company resources only for the benefit of the shareholder-owners, so also do they have an ethical duty to use company information only for the benefit of shareholder-owners. So an insider who takes confidential inside company information and uses it to enrich himself is in effect a thief stealing what is not his. Like any common thief who violates the moral rights of those from whom he steals, the insider trader is violating the moral rights of all shareholders, especially those shareholders who unwittingly sell him their stock.

Second, argue those who hold that insider trading is unethical, the information advantage of the insider really is unfair or unjust. Because the information of the insider is information that he stole, it is quite unlike the information advantage of stock experts or analysts. The information advantage of the insider is unfair because it is unjustly stolen from others—the company's owners—who made the investments that ultimately produced the information he stole. The insider's advantage ultimately comes from stealing the fruits of someone else's labor or resources. This is quite unlike the information advantage of the analyst who owns the information he uses because it was produced through his own labors or purchases.

Third, argue those who claim that insider trading is unethical, it is untrue that no one is harmed by insider trading. Both empirical and theoretical studies have shown that insider trading has two effects on the stock market that are harmful to everyone in the market and to society in general. First, insider trading tends to reduce the size of the market, and this harms everyone. Everyone knows that the insider has an advantage over others, so the more inside trading that people suspect is going on in the market, the more they will tend to leave the market and the smaller it will get. And the reduced size of the market will have a number of harmful effects, including (1) a decline in the liquidity of stocks because it is harder to find buyers and sellers for stock; (2) an increase in the variability of stock prices because small variations will make relatively larger differences in the smaller market; (3) a decline in the market's ability to spread risk because there are fewer parties among whom to spread risks; (4) a decline in market efficiency due to the reduced number of buyers and sellers, (5) a decline in the utility gains available to traders because of the decline in available trades.[17]

The second effect of insider trading is that it increases the costs of buying and selling stocks in the market (i.e., the transaction costs), and this is also harmful. Stocks in the New York stock market are always bought and sold through an intermediary called a "specialist" who charges a small fee for purchasing the stocks of those who want to sell and for holding the stocks for those who want to buy them later. But when a specialist senses that insiders are coming to him, he will realize that the stocks insiders are selling to him and, which he will have to hold for others, might later turn out to be worth far less (otherwise, why would the insiders with their inside information have gotten rid of them?). So to cover himself from potential future losses, he will start to raise the fee he charges for his services as an intermediary (by increasing the bid-ask spread). The more insiders there are, the more the specialist must raise his fees, and the more costly it becomes to make stock exchanges. Although in the extreme case, the costs may rise so high that the market in stocks breaks down completely, in the less extreme case the rising costs will merely make the stock market just that much more inefficient. In either case, insider trading has a harmful effect on the market.[18]

There are, then, good reasons supporting the view that insider trading is

[17] See H. Mendelson, "Random Competitive Exchange: Price Distributions and Gains from Trade," *Journal of Economic Theory* (December, 1985), pp. 254–80.

[18] See L. R. Glosten and P. R. Milgrom, "Bid, Ask, and Transaction Prices in a Specialist Market with Heterogeneously Informed Traders," *Journal of Financial Economics* (March 1985), pp. 71–100; T. Copeland and D. Galai, "Information Effects on the Bid-Ask Spread," *Journal of Finance* (December 1983), pp. 1457–69; G. J. Bentson and R. Hagerman, "Determinants of Bid-Ask Spreads in the Over-the-Counter Market," *Journal of Financial Economics* (January–February 1974), pp. 353–64; P. Venkatesh and R. Chiang, "Information Asymmetry and the Dealer's Bid-Ask Spread: A Case Study of Earnings and Dividend Announcements," *Journal of Finance* (December 1986), pp. 1089–1102.

unethical on the grounds that it violates people's rights, that it is based on an unjust informational advantage, and that it harms society's overall utility. In short, insider trading violates our standards of rights, of justice, and of utility. But the issue continues to be greatly debated and is still not completely settled.

The law on insider trading, however, is fairly settled, although its exact scope is unclear. The Securities and Exchange Commission has prosecuted a large number of insider trading cases, and court decisions in these cases have tended to establish that insider trading is illegal and that it consists of trading in a security while in possession of nonpublic information that can have a material effect on the price of the security, and that was acquired, or was known to have been acquired, in violation of a person's duty to keep the information confidential.[19] As this definition indicates, it is not just company employees who can be guilty of insider trading, but anyone who knowingly buys or sells stock using information that they know was acquired by a person who had a duty to keep that information confidential. Anyone is guilty, that is, who trades on stock knowingly using stolen private information that can affect the stock's price.

8.3 THE FIRM'S DUTIES TO THE EMPLOYEE

The basic moral obligation that the employer has toward employees, according to the rational view of the firm, is to provide them with the compensation they have freely and knowingly agreed to receive in exchange for their services. There are two main issues related to this obligation: the fairness of wages and the fairness of employee working conditions.[20] Both wages and working conditions are aspects of the compensation employees receive from their services, and both are related to the question of whether or not the employee contracted to take a job *freely* and *knowingly*. If an employee was "forced" to accept a job with inadequate wages or inadequate working conditions, then the work contract would be unfair.

Wages

From the employee's point of view, wages are the principal (perhaps the only) means for satisfying the basic economic needs of the worker and the worker's family. From the employer's point of view, wages are a cost of production that must be kept down lest the product be priced out of the market. Every employer, therefore, faces the dilemma of setting fair wages: How can a fair balance be struck between the employer's interests in minimizing costs and the workers' interest in providing a decent living for themselves and their families?

There is, unfortunately, no simple formula for determining a "fair wage." The fairness of wages depends in part on the public supports that society provides the worker (social security, Medicare, unemployment compensation, public education, welfare, etc.), on the freedom of labor markets, on the contribution of the worker, on the needs of the worker, and on the competitive position of the firm.

[19] Gary L. Tidwell and Abdul Aziz, "Insider Trading: How Well Do You Understand the Current Status of the Law?" *California Management Review*, vol. 30, no. 4 (Summer 1988), pp. 115–123.

[20] The following analysis of wages and working conditions draws from Garrett, *Business Ethics*, pp. 53–62.

Although there is no way of determining fair salaries with mathematical exactitude, we can at least identify a number of factors that should be taken into account in determining wages and salaries.[21]

1. The going wage in the industry and the area Although labor markets in an industry or an area may be manipulated or distorted (by job shortages, for example), they generally provide at least rough indicators of fair wages if they are competitive and if we assume competitive markets are just. In addition, the cost of living in the area must be taken into account if employees are to be provided with an income adequate to their families' needs.

2. The firm's capabilities In general, the higher the firm's profits, the more it can and should pay its workers, while the smaller its profits, the less it can afford. Taking advantage of cheap labor in captive markets when a company is perfectly capable of paying higher wages is exploitation.

3. The nature of the job Jobs that involve greater health risks, that offer less security, that require more training or experience, that impose heavier physical or emotional burdens, or that take greater effort should carry higher levels of compensation.

4. Minimum wage laws The minimum wages required by law set a floor for wages. In most circumstances, wages that fall beneath this floor are unfair.

5. Relation to other salaries If the salary structure within an organization is to be fair, workers who do roughly similar work should receive roughly similar salaries.

6. The fairness of wage negotiations Salaries and wages that result from "unfree" negotiations in which one side uses fraud, power, ignorance, deceit, or passion to get its way will rarely be fair. When the management of a company, for example, uses the threat of relocation to force wage concessions out of a wholly dependent community, or when a union "blackmails" a failing company with a strike that is certain to send the firm into bankruptcy, the resulting wages have little likelihood of being fair.

Working Conditions: Health and Safety

Each year more than 5,900 workers are killed and over 5,700,000 are seriously injured as a result of job accidents.[22] Ten percent of the job force suffers a job-related injury or illness each year, for a loss of over 31 million work days annually. Delayed occupational diseases resulting from exposure to chemical and physical hazards kill off additional numbers. Annual costs of work-related deaths and injuries are estimated to be $8 billion.[23]

Workplace hazards include not only the more obvious categories of mechanical injury, electrocution, and burns, but also extreme heat and cold, noisy machin-

[21] See Garrett, *Business Ethics*, pp. 38–40, and Barry, *Moral Issues in Business*, pp. 174–75.

[22] Keith Davis and William C. Frederick, *Business and Society: Management, Public Policy, Ethics* (New York: McGraw-Hill Book Company, 1984), p. 266.

[23] Rollin H. Simonds, "OSHA Compliance: Safety Is Good Business," *Personnel*, July–August 1973.

ery, rock dust, textile fiber dust, chemical fumes, mercury, lead, beryllium, arsenic, corrosives, poisons, skin irritants, and radiation.[24] A government description of occupational injuries is dismaying:

> Three and a half million American workers exposed to asbestos face a dual threat: Not only are they subject to the lung-scarring pneumoconiosis of their trade, *asbestosis*, but they are endangered by *lung cancer* associated with inhalation of asbestos fibers. Recent studies of insulation workers in two states showed 1 in 5 deaths were from lung cancer, seven times the expected rate; half of those with twenty years or more in the trade had x-ray evidence of asbestosis; 1 in 10 deaths were caused by *mesothelioma*, a rare malignancy of the lung or pleura which strikes only 1 in 10,000 in the general working population. Of 6,000 men who have been uranium miners, an estimated 600 to 1,100 will die during the next twenty years as a result of *radiation exposure*, principally from lung cancer. Fifty percent of the machines in industry generate *noise* levels potentially harmful to hearing. Hundreds of thousands of workers each year suffer skin diseases from contact with materials used in their work. The *dermatoses* are the most common of all occupational illnesses. Even the old, well-known industrial poisons, such as mercury, arsenic, and lead, still cause trouble.[25]

In 1970 Congress passed the Occupational Safety and Health Act and created the Occupational Safety and Health Administration (OSHA) "to assure as far as possible every working man and woman in the nation safe and healthful working conditions."[26] Unfortunately, from the beginning OSHA found itself embroiled in controversy. But in spite of the severe criticism it has received,[27] an inadequate number of field inspectors (800), and often inefficient forms of regulation, the existence of OSHA has led many firms to institute their own safety programs. A 1975 poll revealed that 36 percent of the firms surveyed had implemented safety programs as a result of OSHA, while 72 percent said that the existence of OSHA had influenced them in their safety efforts.[28]

Although more attention is now being paid to worker safety, occupational accident rates have not necessarily been declining. Between 1961 and 1970, the number of injuries per million working hours in manufacturing industries rose by almost 30 percent: from 11.8 injuries per million, to 15.2 per million.[29] By 1973, the rate had moved up to 15.3 per million, and by the late 1970s, the incidence of disabling injuries continued to be 20 percent higher than in 1958.[30]

Risk is, of course, an unavoidable part of many occupations. A race-car

[24] William W. Lowrance, *Of Acceptable Risk* (Los Altos, CA: William Kaufmann, Inc., 1976), p. 147.

[25] U.S. Department of Health, Education and Welfare, "Occupational Disease . . . The Silent Enemy," quoted in *ibid.*, p. 147.

[26] *Occupational Safety and Health Act of 1970,* Public Law, 91–596.

[27] See, for example, Robert D. Moran, "Our Job Safety Law Should Say What It Means," *Nation's Business,* April 1974, p. 23.

[28] Peter J. Sheridan, "1970–1976: America in Transition—Which Way Will the Pendulum Swing?," *Occupational Hazards* (September 1975), p. 97.

[29] Davis and Frederick, *Business and Society,* p. 266.

[30] Barry, *Moral Issues in Business* p. 178; see also "Workplace Injuries Increase," *San Francisco Chronicle,* 14 November 1985.

driver, a circus performer, a rodeo cowboy, all accept certain hazards as part of their jobs. And so long as they (1) are fully compensated for assuming these risks and (2) freely and knowingly choose to accept the risk in exchange for the added compensation, then we may assume that their employer has acted ethically.[31]

The basic problem, however, is that in many hazardous occupations, these conditions do not obtain:

1. Wages will fail to provide a level of compensation proportional to the risks of a job when labor markets in an industry are not competitive, or when markets do not register risks because the risks are not yet known. In some rural mining areas, for example, a single mining company may have a monopoly on jobs. And the health risks involved in mining a certain mineral (such as uranium) may not be known until many years afterwards. In such cases, wages will not fully compensate for risks.
2. Workers might accept risks unknowingly because they do not have adequate access to information concerning those risks. Collecting information on the risks of handling certain chemicals, for example, takes up a great deal of time, effort, and money. Workers acting individually may find it too costly, therefore, to collect the information needed to assess the risks of the jobs they accept.
3. Workers might accept known risks out of desperation because they lack the mobility to enter other less risky industries or because they lack information on the alternatives available to them. Low-income coal miners, for example, may know the hazards inherent in coal mining, but since they lack the resources needed to travel elsewhere, they may be forced to either take a job in a coal mine or starve.

When any of the three conditions above obtain, then the contract between employer and employee is no longer fair; the employer has a duty, in such cases, to take steps to ensure that the worker is not being unfairly manipulated into accepting a risk unknowingly, unwillingly, or without due compensation. In particular:

1. Employers should offer wages that reflect the risk-premium prevalent in other similar but competitive labor markets.
2. To insure their workers against unknown hazards the employer should provide them with suitable health insurance programs.
3. Employers should (singly or together with other firms) collect information on the health hazards that accompany a given job and make all such information available to workers.

Working Conditions: Job Satisfaction

The rational parts of the organization put a high value on efficiency: All jobs, all tasks, are to be designed so as to achieve the organization's goals as efficiently as possible. And since efficiency is achieved through specialization, the rational aspects of organizations tend to incorporate highly specialized jobs.[32]

[31] See Russell F. Settle and Burton A. Weisbrod, "Occupational Safety and Health and the Public Interest," in *Public Interest Law*, Burton Weisbrod, Joel F. Handler, and Neil K. Komesar, eds. (Berkeley: University of California Press, 1978), pp. 285–312.

[32] Thompson, *Organizations in Action*, pp. 51–82.

Jobs can be specialized along two dimensions.[33] Jobs can be specialized *horizontally* by restricting the range of different tasks contained in the job and increasing the repetition of this narrow range of tasks. The spot-welder quoted in the introduction to this chapter, for example, does nothing but apply welds to car bodies, "thirty-two jobs per car, forty-eight (cars) an hour, eight hours a day." Jobs can also be specialized *vertically* by restricting the range of control and decision making over the activity that the job involves. Whereas the job of the spot-welder is highly specialized vertically, the job of the plant manager is much less vertically specialized.

Job specialization is most obvious at the operating levels of organizations. Assembly-line work usually consists of closely supervised, repetitive, and simple tasks. Low-level clerical jobs also tend to be fragmented, repetitive, dull, and closely monitored as this example shows:

> I worked for a while at the Fair Plan Insurance Company, where hundreds of women sat typing up and breaking down sextuplicate insurance forms. My job was in endorsements: *First, third, and fourth copies staple together/place the pink sheet in back of the yellow/If the endorsement shows a new mortgagee/stamp the fifth copy "certificate needed . . ."* Other sections, like coding, checks, filing, and endorsement typing, did similar subdivided parts of the paperwork. The women in the other sections sat at steel desks like mine, each working separately on a stack of forms or cards. Every section had a supervisor who counted and checked the work. She recorded the number of pieces we completed, and the number of errors we made, on our individual production sheets. These production sheets were the basis for our periodic merit raises. Aside from counting and checking, the supervisor also tried to curtail talking and eating at desks.[34]

The debilitating effects that job specialization can have on workers were first noted over two hundred years ago by Adam Smith when he wrote:

> In the progress of the division of labor, the employment of the far greater part of those who live by labor, that is, of the great body of the people, comes to be confined to a few very simple operations, frequently to one or two. But the understandings of the greater part of men are necessarily formed by their ordinary employments. The man whose whole life is spent in performing a few simple operations has no occasion to exert his understanding. . . . He naturally loses, therefore, the habit of such exertion and generally becomes as stupid and ignorant as it is possible for a human creature to become. . . . It corrupts even the activity of his body, and renders him incapable of exerting his strength with vigor and perseverance, in any other employment than that to which he has been bred.[35]

More recent research on the mental health of assembly-line workers has tended to corroborate Smith's early suspicions. In a study of auto workers, for example, A. W. Kornhauser found that about 40 percent suffered some sort of mental health problem and that only 18 percent could be considered to have "good mental

[33] Henry Mintzberg, *The Structuring of Organizations* (Englewood Cliffs, NJ: Prentice Hall, 1979), pp. 69–72.

[34] Barbara Garson, *All the Livelong Day: The Meaning and Demeaning of Routine Work* (Garden City, NY: Doubleday & Co., Inc., 1975) p. 157. Reprinted by permission of Doubleday & Co.

[35] Adam Smith, *The Wealth of Nations* (New York: Modern Library, 1937), p. 734.

health."[36] A later study found that many American workers suffered from ulcers, lack of self-esteem, anxiety, and other psychological and psychosomatic diseases.[37] In a survey of fifteen years of research on job satisfaction, Stanislav Kasl found that, among other factors, low job satisfaction was related to "lack of control over work; inability to use skills and abilities; highly fractionated, repetitive tasks involving few diverse operations; no participation in decision-making," and that poor mental health was related to similar factors.[38]

Not all workers are equally affected by job specialization. Older workers and workers in large urban areas seem to show more tolerance for routine monotonous jobs, apparently because older workers scale down their expectations over the years, while urban workers reject the Puritan work ethic and so prefer not to become involved in their work.[39] Nonetheless, only 24 percent of all blue-collar workers would choose the same type of work if they could start all over again, an indication that a substantial portion of workers do not find their jobs intrinsically satisfying.[40]

The injuries that highly specialized work has upon the well-being of workers poses an important problem of justice for employees. The most narrowly specialized forms of work are those that require the least skills (since one of the functions of specialization is to dispense of the need for training). And unskilled labor, of course, commands the lowest levels of compensation. As a consequence, the psychological costs of dull, meaningless, and repetitive work tend to be borne by the group of workers that is paid least: unskilled laborers.

Not only may the injuries of specialization be inequitable, they are often also related to a lack of freedom. Unskilled workers often have no real freedom of choice: They must either accept work that is meaningless and debilitating or else not work at all. The freedom that is essential to a fair work contract is therefore often absent.

Excessive job specialization is undesirable for other reasons than that it places unjust burdens on workers. There is also considerable evidence that it does not contribute to efficiency. Research findings during the 1970s and early 1980s have demonstrated that there is a linkage between worker productivity and programs that improve the quality of work life for workers by giving workers greater involvement in and control over a variety of work tasks.[41]

How should these problems of job dissatisfaction and mental injury be dealt with? A few years ago, Hackman, Oldham, Jansen, and Purdy argued that there are three determinants of job satisfaction:

[36] A. W. Kornhauser, *Mental Health of the Industrial Worker: A Detroit Study* (Huntington, NY: R. E. Krieger, 1965).

[37] H. Sheppard and N. Herrick, *Where Have All the Robots Gone?* (New York: The Free Press, 1972).

[38] Stanislav Kasl, "Work and Mental Health," in *A Matter of Dignity,* W. J. Heisler and John W. Houck, eds. (Notre Dame, IN: University of Notre Dame Press, 1977).

[39] See J. L. Pierce and R. B. Dunham, "Task Design: A Literature Review," *Academy of Management Review,* October 1976, pp. 83–97.

[40] *Work in America: Report of a Special Task Force to the Secretary of Health, Education, and Welfare* (Washington, DC: Congressional Quarterly, Inc., 1973), p. 15.

[41] See the review of the research on this issue in John Simmons and William Mares, *Working Together* (New York: Alfred A. Knopf, Inc., 1983).

> *Experienced Meaningfulness.* The individual must perceive his work as worth-while or important by some system of values he accepts.
>
> *Experienced Responsibility.* He must believe that he personally is accountable for the outcome of his efforts.
>
> *Knowledge of Results.* He must be able to determine, on some regular basis, whether or not the outcomes of his work are satisfactory.[42]

To influence these three determinants, the authors claim, jobs must be expanded along five dimensions:

1. *Skill Variety* the degree to which a job requires the worker to perform activities that challenge his skills and abilities.
2. *Task Identity* the degree to which the job requires a completion of a whole and identifiable piece of work—doing a job from beginning to end with a visible outcome.
3. *Task Significance* the degree to which the job has a substantial and perceivable impact on lives of other people, whether in the immediate organization or the world at large.
4. *Autonomy* the degree to which the job gives the worker freedom, independence, and discretion in scheduling work and determining how he will carry it out.
5. *Feedback* the degree to which a worker, in carrying out the work activities required by the job, gets information about the effectiveness of his efforts.[43]

In short, the solution to job dissatisfaction is perceivable enlargement of the narrowly specialized jobs that give rise to dissatisfaction: broadening the job "horizontally" by giving the employee a wider variety of tasks, and deepening the job "vertically" by allowing the employee more perceivable control over these tasks. Jobs can be horizontally enlarged, for example, by replacing single workers performing single repetitive tasks with teams of three or four who are jointly responsible for the complete assembly of a certain number of machines.[44] And such team jobs can be vertically enlarged by delegating to the team the responsibility of determining their own work assignments, work breaks, and inspection procedures.[45]

8.4 THE POLITICAL ORGANIZATION

To anyone who has ever worked within a large organization, the goal-directed and efficient structure that the rational model of the organization attributes to business firms will seem a bit incomplete if not altogether unreal. Although much of the behavior within organizations accords with the orderly picture drawn by the rational model, a great deal of organizational behavior is neither goal directed

[42] Richard Hackman, Grey Oldham, Robert Jansen, and Kenneth Purdy, "A New Strategy for Job Enrichment," *California Management Review*, 17, no. 4 (Summer 1975): 58.

[43] *Ibid.*, p. 59.

[44] Lars E. Björk, "An Experiment in Work Satisfaction," *Scientific American* (March 1975), pp. 17–23.

[45] For a study of how one company set up such programs see Michael Maccoby, "Helping Labor and Management Set Up a Quality-Of-Worklife Program," *Monthly Labor Review* (March 1984).

nor efficient nor even rational. Employees within organizations often find themselves embroiled in intrigues, in on-going battles for organization resources, in feuding between cliques, in arbitrary treatment by superiors, in scrambles for career advancement, in controversies over what the organization's "real" goals are or should be, and in disagreements over strategies for pursuing goals. Such behaviors do not seem to fit within the orderly pattern of the rational pursuit of organizational goals.[46] To understand these behaviors and the ethical issues they raise we must turn to a second model of the firm, one that focuses less on its rational aspects and more on its political features: The "political model of the organization."[47]

The political analysis of the organization that we shall now sketch is a more recently developed view of organizations than the rational analysis. Unlike the rational model, the political model of the organization does not look merely at the formal lines of authority and communication within an organization nor does it presume that all organizational behavior is rationally designed to achieve an objective and given economic goal such as profitability or productivity. Instead the political model of the organization sees the organization as a system of competing power coalitions and of formal and informal lines of influence and communication that radiate from these coalitions.[48] In place of the neat hierarchy of the rational model, the political model postulates a messier and more complex network of clustered power relationships and crisscrossing communication channels (see Figure 8.2).

In the political model of the organization, individuals are seen as grouping together to form coalitions that then compete with each other for resources, benefits, and influence. Consequently, the "goals" of the organization are those established by the historically most powerful or dominant coalition.[49] Goals are not given by "rightful" authority, but are bargained for among more or less powerful coalitions. The fundamental organizational reality, according to this model, is not formal authority or contractual relationships, but *power:* the ability of the individual (or group of individuals) to modify the conduct of others in a desired way without

[46] For a compact contrast of rational and political behaviors, see Robert Miles, *Macro Organizational Behavior* (Santa Monica, CA: Good Year Publishing, 1980), pp. 156–61. A fuller and more historical discussion of the "rational" and "political" approaches to organization is Henry Mintzberg, *Power In and Around Organizations* (Englewood Cliffs, NJ: Prentice Hall, 1983), pp. 8–21.

[47] For more recent analyses of the firm based on the "political" model, see Mintzberg, *Power In and Around Organizations;* Samuel B. Bacharach and Edward J. Lawler, *Power and Politics in Organizations* (San Francisco: Jossey-Bass, Inc., Publishers, 1980), James G. March, "The Business Firm as a Political Coalition," *Journal of Politics,* 24 (1962): 662–68; Tom Burns, "Micropolitics: Mechanisms of Institutional Change," *Administrative Science Quarterly,* VI (1962–62): 255–81; Michael L. Tushman "A Political Approach to Organizations: A Review and Rationale," *Academy of Management Review* (April 1977), pp. 206–16; Jeffrey Pfeffer, "The Micropolitics of Organizations," in *Environments and Organizations,* Marshall W. Meyer, et al., eds. (San Francisco: Jossey-Bass, Inc., Publishers, 1978), pp. 29–50.

[48] See R. M. Cyert and J. G. March, *A Behavioral Theory of the Firm* (Englewood Cliffs, NJ: Prentice Hall, 1963); H. Kaufman, "Organization Theory and Political Theory," *The American Political Science Review,* 58, no. 1 (1964): 5–14.

[49] Walter R. Nord, "Dreams of Humanization and the Realities of Power," *Academy of Management Review* (July 1978), pp. 674–79.

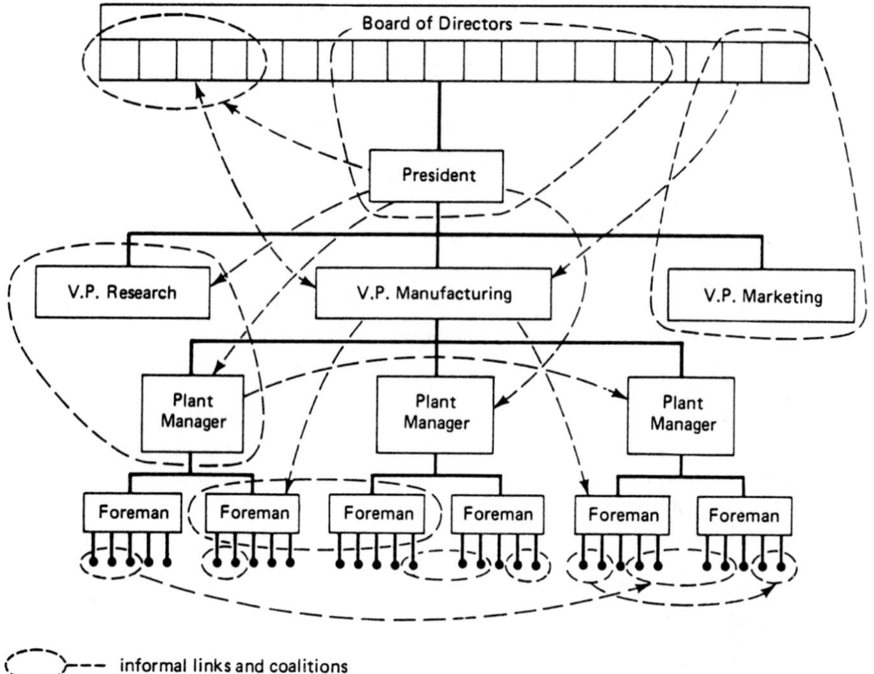

FIGURE 8-2

having one's own conduct modified in undesired ways.[50] An example of an organizational coalition and the nonformal power it can exert even over formal authorities is provided by this account of life in a government agency:

> We had this boss come in from Internal Revenue [to run this OEO department]. He wanted to be very, very strict. He used to have meetings every Friday—about people comin' in late, people leavin' early, people abusin' lunch time. . . . Every Friday, everyone would sit there and listen to this man. And we'd all go out and do the same thing again. Next Friday he'd have another meeting and he would tell us the same thing. (Laughs.) We'd all go out and do the same thing again. (Laughs.) He would try to talk to one and see what they'd say about the other. But we'd been working all together for quite awhile. You know how the game is played. Tomorrow you might need a favor. So nobody would say anything. If he'd want to find out what time someone came in, who's gonna tell 'em? He'd want to find out where someone was, we'd always say, "They're at the Xerox." Just anywhere. He couldn't get through.[51]

[50] On the primacy of power in organizations, see Abraham Zaleznik, "Power and Politics in Organizational Life," *Harvard Business Review* (May–June 1970), pp. 47–60. The definition of "power" in the text is derived from Virginia E. Schein, "Individual Power and Political Behaviors in Organizations: An Inadequately Explored Reality," *Academy of Management Review* (January 1977), pp. 64–72. Definitions of power are, of course, controversial.

[51] Terkel, *Working*, p. 349; Many more examples of political behaviors can be found in Samuel A. Culbert and John J. McDonough, *The Invisible War* (New York: John Wiley & Sons, Inc., 1980).

As this example shows, behavior within an organization may *not* be aimed at rational organizational goals such as efficiency or productivity, and both power and information may travel completely outside (even contrary to) formal lines of authority and communication. Nonetheless, formal managerial authority and formal communication networks provide rich sources of power. The spot-welder quoted earlier was referring to the power of formal authority when he said, "I don't like the pressure. . . . If the foreman doesn't like you, he'll make you hold it. . . . Oh, yeah, the foreman's got somebody knuckling down on him, putting the screws to him." And the ex-president of the conglomerate whom we also quoted earlier was in part referring to the power of formal authority when he said, "You have men working for you and you have a boss above. You're caught in a squeeze. The squeeze progresses from station to station." The formal authority and sanctions put in the hands of superiors, then, are a basic source of the power they wield over subordinates.

If we focus on power as the basic organizational reality, then the main ethical problems we will see when we look at an organization are problems connected with the acquisition and exercise of power. The central ethical issues will focus not on the contractual obligations of employers and employees (as the rational model would focus them), but on the moral constraints to which the use of power within organizations must be subjected. The ethics of organizational behavior as seen from the perspective of the political model, then, will focus on this question: What are the moral limits, if any, to the exercise of power within organizations? In the sections that follow we will discuss two aspects of this question: (1) What, if any, are the moral limits to the power managers acquire and exercise over their subordinates? (2) What, if any, are the moral limits to the power employees acquire and exercise on each other?

8.5 EMPLOYEE RIGHTS

Observers of corporations have repeatedly pointed out that the power of modern corporate management is much like that of a government.[52] Governments are defined in terms of four features: (1) a centralized decision-making body of officials who (2) have the power and recognized authority to enforce their decisions upon subordinates ("citizens"); these officials (3) make decisions that determine the public distribution of social resources, benefits, and burdens among their subordinates and (4) they have a monopoly on the power to which their subordinates are subject. These same four features, observers have argued, also characterize the managerial hierarchies that run large corporations: (1) Like a city, state, or federal government, the top managers of a corporation constitute a centralized decision-making body; (2) these managers wield power and legally recognized authority over their employees, a power that is based on their ability to fire, demote, or promote employees and an authority that is based on the law of agency that stands ready to recognize and enforce managerial decisions; (3) the decisions of managers

[52] For example: Richard Eells, *The Government of Corporations* (New York: The Free Press of Glencoe, 1962); and Arthur Selwyn Miller, *The Modern Corporate State* (Westport, CT: Greenwood Press, 1976).

determine the distribution of income, status, and freedom among the corporation's constituencies; and (4) through the law of agency and contract, through their access to government agencies, and through the economic leverage they possess, managers of large corporations effectively share in the monopoly on power that political governments possess.[53]

These analogies between governments and managements, several observers have held, show that the power managers have over their employees is fully comparable to the power government officials have over their citizens. Consequently, if there are moral limits to the power government officials may legitimately exercise over citizens, then there are similar moral limits that should constrain the power of managers.[54] In particular, these authors argue, just as the power of government should respect the civil rights of citizens, so the power of managers must respect the moral rights of employees. What are these employee rights? The moral rights of employees would be similar to the civil rights of citizens: the right to privacy, the right to consent, the right to freedom of speech, and so on.[55]

The major objection to this view of employee rights is that there are a number of important differences between the power of corporate managers and the power of government officials and these differences undercut the argument that the power of managers should be limited by employee rights comparable to the civil rights that limit the power of government. First, the power of government officials (in theory at least) is based on *consent,* whereas the power of corporate managers is (in theory again) based on *ownership:* Government officials rule because they have been elected or because they have been appointed by someone who has been elected; corporate managers "rule" (if that is the right word) because they own the firm for which workers freely choose to work, or because they have been appointed by the owners of the firm. Consequently, since the power of government rests on the consent of the governed, that power can legitimately be limited when the governed choose to limit it. On the other hand, since the power of managers rests on ownership of the firm, they themselves have the right to impose whatever conditions they choose to impose on employees who freely and knowingly contracted to work on their firm's premises.[56] Second, the power of corporate managers, unlike that of most government officials, is effectively limited by unions: Most blue-collar workers and some white-collar workers belong to a union that provides them with a degree of countervailing power that limits the power of management. Accordingly, moral rights need not be invoked to protect the interests of employees.[57] Third, whereas a citizen can escape the power

[53] See Earl Latham, "The Body Politic of the Corporation," in *The Corporation in Modern Society,* Edward S. Mason, ed. (Cambridge: Harvard University Press, 1960).

[54] See, for example, David W. Ewing, *Freedom Inside the Organization* (New York: McGraw-Hill Book Company, 1977), pp. 3–24; Garrett, *Business Ethics,* pp. 27–30.

[55] David W. Ewing, "Civil Liberties in the Corporation," *New York State Bar Journal,* (April 1978), pp. 188–229.

[56] This ownership and contract argument is the basis of traditional legal views on the employee's duty to obey and be loyal to his employer. See Blumberg, "Corporate Responsibility," pp. 82–113.

[57] Donald L. Martin, "Is an Employee Bill of Rights Needed?" in *The Attack on Corporate America,* M. Bruce Johnson, ed. (New York: McGraw-Hill Book Company, 1978).

of a particular government only at great cost (by changing citizenship), an employee can escape the owner of a particular management with considerable ease (by changing jobs). Because of the relatively high costs of changing citizenship, citizens need civil rights which can insulate them from the inescapable power of government. They do not need similar employee rights to protect them from the power of a corporation whose influence is easily escaped.[58]

Advocates of employee rights have responded to these three objections in a number of ways: First, they claim, corporate assets are no longer controlled by private owners; they are now held by a dispersed and almost powerless group of stockholders. This kind of dispersed ownership implies that managers no longer function as agents of the firm's owners, and, consequently, that their power no longer rests on property rights.[59] Second, although some workers are unionized, many are not and these nonunionized workers have moral rights which managers do not always respect.[60] Third, changing jobs is sometimes as difficult and as traumatic as changing citizenship, especially for the employee who has acquired specialized skills that can be used only within a specific organization.[61]

There is, then, a continuing controversy over the adequacy of the *general* argument that, since managements are like governments, the same civil rights that protect citizens must also protect employees. Whether this general argument is accepted or not, however, a number of independent arguments have been advanced to show that employees have certain *particular* rights that managers should respect. We will look at these arguments next.[62]

The Right to Privacy

Speaking broadly, the right to privacy is the right to be left alone. We will not discuss this broad characterization of the right to privacy, however, but will concentrate on privacy as the right of a person not to have others spy on his or her private life. In this more narrow sense, the right to privacy can be defined as the right of persons to determine the type and extent of disclosure of information about themselves.[63]

The employee's right to privacy has become particularly vulnerable with

[58] *Ibid.*

[59] The classic exposition of this view is Adolf Berle and Gardner Means, *The Modern Corporation and Private Property,* 1932; a more recent exposition of similar themes is Adolf Berle, *Power without Property* (New York: Harcourt Brace Jovanovich, Inc., 1959); see also John Kenneth Galbraith, "On the Economic Image of Corporate Enterprise," in *Corporate Power in America,* Ralph Nader and Mark J. Green, eds. (Middlesex, England: Penguin Books, 1977); and John J. Flynn, "Corporate Democracy: Nice Work if You Can Get It," in *ibid.*

[60] Jack Stierber, "Protection Against Unfair Dismissal," in *Individual Rights in the Corporation,* Alan F. Westin and Stephen Salisbury, eds. (New York: Pantheon Books, Inc., 1980).

[61] David W. Ewing, *Freedom Inside the Organization* (New York: McGraw-Hill Book Company, 1977), pp. 36–41.

[62] Several of these arguments are summarized in Patricia H. Werhane, *Persons, Rights, and Corporations* (Englewood Cliffs, NJ: Prentice Hall, 1985), pp. 108–22.

[63] See Charles Fried, *An Anatomy of Values: Problems of Personal and Social Choice* (Cambridge: Harvard University Press, 1970), p. 141.

the development of recent technologies.[64] Employees who use phones and computers can be legally monitored by their employer, who may wish to check how fast they are working, whether they are engaged in personal or business-related activities, or simply what they are doing. Polygraph, or "lie detector" machines, although generally prohibited by federal law in most industries, are still allowed during internal investigations of suspected employee theft or economic loss and in a number of "exempt" industries. Computerized methods of obtaining, storing, retrieving, collating, and communicating information have made it possible for employers to collect and keep personal information about their employees, such as company medical records, credit histories, criminal and arrest histories, FBI information, and employment histories. Genetic testing, although not yet widely used by many companies, already allows employers to test an employee for about fifty genetic traits that indicate that the employee will be more likely than others to develop certain diseases (such as cystic fibrosis or sickle-cell anemia) or be affected by certain workplace toxins or occupational hazards. It is expected that in the future, genetic tests of workers and job candidates will enable employers to screen out a wide range of workers whose genes indicate that they are likely to add to the company's medical insurance costs or add to the costs of installing workplace protections. Urine tests allow companies to screen out employees who take drugs, drink alcohol, or smoke tobacco at home. Written psychological tests, personality inventory tests, and "honesty" tests make it possible for an employer to uncover a wide range of personal characteristics and tendencies that most persons would rather keep private, such as their level of honesty or their sexual orientation.

Not only have these innovations made a person's privacy more vulnerable, but they have come at a time when managers are particularly anxious to learn more about their employees. Advances in industrial psychology have demonstrated relationships between an employee's private home life or personality traits, and on-the-job performance and productivity.

There are two basic types of privacy: psychological privacy and physical privacy.[65] *Psychological* privacy is privacy with respect to a person's inner life. This includes the person's thoughts and plans, personal beliefs and values, feelings, and wants. These inner aspects of a person are so intimately connected with the person that to invade them is almost an invasion of the very person. *Physical* privacy is privacy with respect to a person's physical activities. Since people's inner lives are revealed by their physical activities and expressions, physical privacy is important in part because it is a means for protecting psychological privacy. But many of our physical activities are considered "private" apart from their connection to our inner life. A person normally feels degraded, for example, if

[64] See John Hoerr, "Privacy in the Workplace," *Business Week,* 28 March 1988, pp. 61–65, 68; Susan Dentzer, "Can You Pass the Job Test?" *Newsweek,* 5 May 1986; Sandra N. Hurd, "Genetic Testing: Your Genes and Your Job," *Employee Responsibilities and Rights Journal,* vol. 3, no. 4 (1990), pp. 239–52; U.S. Congress, Office of Technology Assessment, *Genetic Monitoring and Screening in the Workplace,* OTA-BA-455 (Washington, DC: U.S. Government Printing Office, October 1990); Arthur R. Miller, *The Assault on Privacy: Computers, Data Banks and Dossiers* (Ann Arbor: University of Michigan Press, 1971.

[65] See Garrett, *Business Ethics,* pp. 47–49, who distinguishes these two types of privacy (as well as a third kind, "social" privacy).

forced to disrobe publicly or to perform biological or sexual functions in public. Physical privacy, therefore, is also valued for its own sake.

The purpose of rights, as analyzed in Chapter Two, is to enable the individual to pursue his or her significant interests and to protect these interests from the intrusions of other individuals. To say that persons have a moral right to something is to say at least that they have a vital interest in that "something." Why is privacy considered important enough to surround it with the protection of a right?[66] To begin with, privacy has several *protective* functions. First, privacy ensures that others do not acquire information about us that, if revealed, would expose us to shame, ridicule, embarrassment, blackmail, or other harm. Second, privacy also prevents others from interfering in our plans simply because they do not hold the same values we hold. Our private plans may involve activities that, although harming no one, might be viewed with distaste by other people. Privacy protects us against their intrusions and thereby allows us the freedom to behave in unconventional ways. Third, privacy protects those whom we love from being injured by having their beliefs about us shaken. There may be things about ourselves that, if revealed, might hurt those whom we love. Privacy ensures that such matters are not made public. Fourth, privacy also protects individuals from being led to incriminate themselves. By protecting their privacy, people are protected against involuntarily harming their own reputations.

Privacy is also important because it has several *enabling* functions. First, privacy enables a person to develop ties of friendship, love, and trust. Without intimacy these relationships could not flourish. Intimacy, however, requires both sharing information about oneself that is not shared with everyone and engaging in special activities with others that are not publicly performed. Without privacy, therefore, intimacy would be impossible and relationships of friendship, love, and trust could not exist. Second, privacy enables certain professional relationships to exist. Insofar as the relationships between doctor and patient, lawyer and client, psychiatrist and patient all require trust and confidentiality, they could not exist without privacy. Third, privacy also enables a person to sustain distinct social roles. The executive of a corporation, for example, may want, as a private citizen, to support a cause that is unpopular with his or her firm. Privacy enables the executive to do so without fear of reprisal. Fourth, privacy enables people to determine who they are by giving them control of the way they present themselves to society in general and of the way that society in general looks upon them. At the same time, privacy enables people to present themselves in a special way to those whom they select. In both cases, this self-determination is secured by the right of the individual to determine the nature and extent of disclosure of information about oneself.

It is clear, then, that our interest in privacy is important enough to recognize it as a right. However, this right must be balanced against other individuals' rights and needs. Employers in particular sometimes have a legitimate right to inquire into the activities of employees or prospective employees. The employer

[66] The analyses in this paragraph and the following are drawn from Fried, *Anatomy of Values*, pp. 137–52; Richard A. Wasserstrom, "Privacy" in *Today's Moral Problems*, 2nd ed., Richard A. Wasserstrom, ed. (New York: Macmillan, Inc., 1979); Jeffrey H. Reiman, "Privacy, Intimacy and Personhood," *Philosophy and Public Affairs*, 6, no. 1 (1976): 26–44; and James Rachels, "Why Privacy Is Important," *Philosophy and Public Affairs*, 4, no. 4 (1975): 295–333.

is justified in wanting to know, for example, what a job candidate's past work experience has been and whether the candidate has performed satisfactorily on previous jobs. An employer may also be justified in wanting to identify the culprits when the firm finds itself the subject of pilferage or employee theft, and of subjecting employees to on-the-job surveillance in order to discover the source of thefts. How are these rights to be balanced against the right to privacy? Three elements must be considered when collecting information that may threaten the employee's right to privacy: relevance, consent, and method.[67]

Relevance The employer must limit inquiry into the employee's affairs to those areas that are directly relevant to the issue at hand. Although employers have a right to know the person they are employing and to know how the employee is performing, employers are not justified in inquiring into any areas of the employee's life that do not affect the employee's work performance in a direct and serious manner. To investigate an employee's political beliefs or the employee's social life, for example, is an invasion of privacy. Moreover, if a firm acquires information about an employee's personal life in the course of a legitimate investigation, it has an obligation to destroy the information, especially when such data would embarrass or otherwise injure the employee if it were leaked. The dividing lines between justified and unjustified investigation are fairly clear with respect to lower level employees: There is clearly little justification for investigating the marital problems, political activities, or emotional characteristics of clerical workers, sales workers, or factory laborers. The dividing line between what is and what is not relevant, however, becomes less clear as one moves higher in the firm's management hierarchy. Managers are called on to represent their company before others and the company's reputation can be significantly damaged by a manager's private activities or emotional instability. A vice president's drinking problem or membership in a disreputable association, for example, will affect the vice president's ability to adequately represent the firm. The firm in such cases may be justified in inquiring into an officer's personal life or psychological characteristics.

Consent Employees must be given the opportunity to give or withhold their consent before the private aspects of their lives are investigated. The firm is justified in inquiring into the employee's life only if the employee has a clear understanding that the inquiry is being made and clearly consents to this as part of the job or can freely choose to refuse the job. The same principle holds when an employer undertakes some type of surveillance of employees for the purpose, say, of uncovering or preventing pilferage. Employees should be informed of such surveillance so they can ensure they will not inadvertently reveal their personal lives while under surveillance.

Methods The employer must distinguish between methods of investigation that are both ordinary and reasonable, and methods that are neither. Ordinary

[67] The remarks that follow are based in part on Garrett, *Business Ethics*, pp. 49–53; for a more stringent view which concludes that polygraphs, for example, should not be used at all by employers, see George G. Brenkert, "Privacy, Polygraphs, and Work," *Business and Professional Ethics Journal*, 1, no. 1 (Fall 1981): 19–35.

methods include the supervisory activities that are normally used to oversee employees' work. Extraordinary methods include devices like hidden microphones, secret cameras, wiretaps, lie detector tests, personality inventory tests, and spies. Extraordinary methods are unreasonable and unjustified unless the circumstances themselves are extraordinary. Extraordinary methods of investigation might be justified if a firm is suffering heavy losses from employee theft that ordinary supervision has failed to stop. Extraordinary devices, however, are not justified merely because the employer hopes to be able to pick up some interesting tidbits about employee loyalties. In general, the use of extraordinary devices is justified only when the following conditions have been met: (1) The firm has a problem that can be solved in no other manner than by employing such extraordinary means; (2) the problem is serious and the firm has well-founded grounds for thinking that the use of extraordinary means will identify the culprits or put an end to the problem; (3) the use of the extraordinary devices is not prolonged beyond the time needed to identify the wrongdoers or after it becomes clear that the devices will not work; (4) all information that is uncovered but that is not directly relevant to the purposes for which the investigation was conducted is disregarded and destroyed; (5) the failure rate of any extraordinary devices employed (such as lie detectors, drug tests, or psychological tests) is taken into account and all information derived from devices with a known failure rate is verified through independent methods that are not subject to the same failure rates.

Freedom of Conscience

In the course of performing a job, an employee may discover that a corporation is doing something that he or she believes is injurious to society. Indeed, individuals inside a corporation are usually the first to learn that the corporation is marketing unsafe products, polluting the environment, suppressing health information, or violating the law.

Employees with a sense of moral responsibility who find that their company is injuring society in some way will normally feel an obligation to get the company to stop its harmful activities and consequently will often bring the matter to the attention of their superiors. Unfortunately, if the internal management of the company refuses to do anything about the matter, the employee today has few other legal options available. If, after being rebuffed by the company, the employee has the temerity to take the matter to a government agency outside the firm, or worse, to disclose the company's activities to a public medium, the company has the legal right to punish the employee by firing him or her. Furthermore, if the matter is serious enough, the company can reinforce this punishment by putting the matter on the employee's record and, in extreme cases, seeing to it that the employee is black-balled by other companies in the industry.[68]

Several authors have argued that this is in effect a violation of an individual's right to freedom of conscience.[69] It is a violation of the right to freedom of con-

[68] For examples see Alan F. Westin, *Whistle Blowing, Loyalty and Dissent in the Corporation* (New York: McGraw-Hill Book Company, 1981), and Frederick Elliston, John Keenan, Paula Lockhart, Jane van Schaick, *Whistleblowing, Managing Dissent in the Workplace* (New York: Praeger Publishers, Inc., 1985).

[69] For example, Ewing, *Freedom Inside the Organization*, pp. 115–27.

science because the individual is forced to cooperate with an activity that violates the individual's personal moral beliefs. What is the basis of this right? The right to freedom of conscience derives from the interest that individuals have in being able to adhere to their religious or moral convictions.[70] Individuals who have religious or moral convictions commonly see them as absolutely binding and can transgress them only at great psychological cost. The right to freedom of conscience protects this interest by requiring that individuals may not be forced to cooperate in activities that they conscientiously believe are wrong.

These arguments, however, have not yet had a substantial effect on the law, which still by and large reinforces the employee's duty of maintaining loyalty and confidentiality toward the employer's business.[71] In the absence of legal protections of the employee's right to freedom of conscience, some authors have supported the practice of "whistleblowing."[72]

Whistleblowing

Whistleblowing is an attempt by a member or former member of an organization to disclose wrongdoing in or by the organization. In 1981, for example, Mr. Mackowiak, was hired as a welding inspector by University Nuclear Systems, Inc. (UNSI), a firm responsible for installing the heating, ventilating, and air conditioning system at a nuclear power plant owned by the Washington Public Power Supply system. Mackowiak was supposed to inspect the work of UNSI employees and make sure it conformed to federal quality and safety standards, a task that was mandated by federal regulations requiring builders of nuclear power plants to give their inspectors the authority and organizational freedom they needed to fulfill their role as independent observers of the construction process. However, Mackowiak claimed, some UNSI employees would not give him access to areas in which work was not up to federal specifications. Mackowiak brought the problem to his superiors. When he was unable to get them to respond to his concerns, Mackowiak "blew the whistle" on the company. He met with officials of the Nuclear Regulatory Commission at his home and disclosed to them his concerns about the safety and quality control of the work of UNSI. The NRC took his allegations seriously, acted on them, and conducted a full investigation of UNSI that rectified the problems. The company, however, found out that Mackowiak had talked to federal agents and in early 1982 he was fired because, the company said, he had a "mistrustful attitude toward management" although his "inspection qualifications/expertise is excellent and he is a good inspector."[73]

Whistleblowing can be internal or external. If the wrongdoing is reported only to those higher in the organization, as Mackowiak initially did, it is internal

[70] See John Rawls, *A Theory of Justice* (Cambridge: Harvard University Press, 1971), pp. 205–11.

[71] See Blumberg, "Corporate Responsibility."

[72] E.g., Ralph Nader, Peter J. Petkas, and Kate Blackwell, *Whistle Blowing* (New York: Grossman Publishers, 1972); and Charles Peters and Taylor Branch, *Blowing the Whistle: Dissent in the Public Interest* (New York: Praeger Publishers, Inc., 1972); for a recent comprehensive study of whistleblowing see Frederick Elliston, John Keenan, Paula Lockhart, and Jane van Schaick, *Whistleblowing Research, Methodological and Moral Issues* (New York: Praeger Publishers, Inc., 1985).

[73] *Mackowiak* v. *University Nuclear Ssytems, Inc.*, 753 F. 2d 1159 (9th Cir. 1984).

whistleblowing. When the wrongdoing is reported to external individuals or bodies such as government agencies, newspapers, or public interest groups, the whistleblowing is said to be external.

As Mackowiak's experience shows, blowing the whistle is often a brave act of conscience that can carry heavy personal costs. A recent study of whistleblowers found that the average whistleblower is a 47-year-old family man who has been a conscientious employee for seven years and who has strong belief in universal moral principles.[74] The same study reported that 100 percent of the whistleblowers surveyed who worked for private businesses were fired by their employers, 20 percent could still not find work at the time of the survey, 25 percent had suffered increased financial burdens on their family, 17 percent lost their homes, 54 percent had been harassed by their peers at work, 15 percent viewed their subsequent divorce as a result of their whistleblowing, 80 percent suffered physical deterioration, 86 percent reported emotional stress including feelings of depression, powerlessness, isolation, and anxiety, and 10 percent reported having attempted suicide. Nevertheless, most of the whistleblowers surveyed had few regrets and would do it again. Typical of the comments they made to the survey team were the following: "This has turned out to be the most frightening thing I have ever done. But it has also been the most satisfying. I think I did the right thing, and I have caused some changes to be made in the plant," "Do what is right. Lost income can be replaced. Lost self-esteem is more difficult to retrieve," "Finding honesty within myself was more powerful than I expected."

It is sometimes argued that external whistleblowing is always wrong on the grounds that employees have a contractual duty to be loyal to their employer and to keep all aspects of the business confidential. When an employee accepts a job, the argument goes, the employee implicitly agrees to keep all aspects of the business confidential and to singlemindedly pursue the best interests of the employer. The whistleblower violates this agreement and thereby violates the rights of his or her employer.

Although part of what this argument asserts is true, the conclusion is false. It is true that an employee enters an agreement to act on behalf of his or her employer in all matters pertaining to the business and that the employee also implicitly agrees to keep trade secrets and other proprietary information secret. However, this agreement is not unqualified, and it does not impose on the employee unlimited obligations toward his or her employer. As we saw in an earlier discussion, agreements and contracts are void if they require a person to do something immoral. Consequently, if an employee has a moral obligation to prevent other people from being harmed and the only way to prevent the harm is by blowing the whistle on one's employer, an employment agreement cannot require the employee to remain silent. In such a situation, the employment agreement would be void because it would require the employee to immorally fail to do what he is morally obligated to do. External whistleblowing is justified, then, if it is necessary to prevent a wrong that one has a moral right or a moral duty to prevent, or if it will yield a benefit that one has a moral right or duty to provide.

It is also false, as it is sometimes argued, that external whistleblowing is always morally justified on the grounds that all persons, including employees,

[74] C. H. Farnsworth, "Survey of Whistleblowers Finds Retaliation but Few Regrets," *New York Times*, 21 February 1988.

have a right to freedom of speech. When employees disclose what is going on in a firm to external parties, the argument holds, they are merely exercising their right to freedom of speech and their act is therefore morally justified. However, this argument ignores the fact that the right to freedom of speech, like all other rights, is limited by the rights of other persons. In particular, an employee's right to freedom of speech is limited by the rights of the employer and other parties. Because of the employment contract, the employer has a right to have employees keep proprietary matters secret, and the right to have the employee pursue the employer's best interests, provided the employee is not thereby forced to do anything immoral. Moreover, other parties—such as stockholders or fellow employees—who can be injured by external whistleblowing also have a right to not be subjected to such injuries needlessly or without a proportionately serious reason. External whistleblowing, then, can be justified only if other means—such as internal whistleblowing—of preventing a wrong have been tried but have failed, and only if the harm that is to be prevented is much more serious than the harm that will result to other parties.

External whistleblowing, then, is morally justified if

1. There is clear, substantiated, and reasonably comprehensive evidence that the organization is engaged in some activity that is seriously wronging or will seriously wrong other parties.
2. Reasonably serious attempts to prevent the wrong through internal whistleblowing have been tried and have failed.
3. It is reasonably certain that external whistleblowing will prevent the wrong.
4. The wrong is serious enough to justify the injuries that external whistleblowing will probably inflict on oneself, one's family, and other parties.

But to say that external whistleblowing is justified is not the same as saying that it is obligatory. Although it may be morally permissible for a person to blow the whistle on a company, this does not mean that the person also has a moral duty or moral obligation to do so.[75] Under what conditions is it not only permissible but obligatory for a person to engage in external whistleblowing? Whistleblowing is merely a means to an end—the end of correcting or preventing a wrong—so a person has an obligation to take this means only to the extent that he or she has an obligation to achieve the end. Clearly, then, a person has a moral obligation to engage in whistleblowing only when he or she has a moral obligation to prevent the wrong that whistleblowing will prevent. When, then, does a person have an obligation to prevent a wrong? Assuming that conditions 1 through 4 above are met, so that whistleblowing is at least permissible, a person also has an obligation to blow the whistle when (1) that specific person has a moral duty to prevent the wrong, either because it is part of the person's specific professional responsibilities (e.g., as an accountant, environmental officer, professional engineer, lawyer, etc.) or because no one else can or will prevent the wrong in which the company is involved and (2) the wrong involves serious

[75] Richard T. DeGeorge, *Business Ethics* 3rd ed. (New York: Macmillan Publishing Company, 1990) p. 211; see also Richard DeGeorge, "Whistleblowing: Permitted, Prohibited, Required," In *Conflicting Loyalties in the Workplace,* F. A. Elliston, ed. (Notre Dame, IN: University of Notre Dame Press, 1985). My discussion draws heavily on DeGeorge.

harm to society's overall welfare, or a serious injustice against a person or group, or a serious violation of the basic moral rights of one or more people. For example, when a company is involved in activities that can result in substantial health injuries to many people who have a right to be protected from such injuries, and no one else in the company is willing to bring these activities to a halt, then I have an obligation to do everything I can to prevent the wrong, even if this means resorting to whistleblowing.

It must be recognized, however, that the occurrence of justified external whistleblowing generally indicates a failure in an organization's internal communication system. External whistleblowing is a symptom of a structural problem: the absence of company mechanisms that enable concerned employees to effectively voice their concerns through internal whistleblowing. Most companies have no clear policies or procedures that allow employees to voice their moral concerns outside the standard chain of command. When employees encounter waste, fraud, abuse, or managerial inepitude, they have no way of taking their concerns to those within the organization who can do something about the issue. Moreover, even when companies have "open door" policies that say that employees can take concerns to those higher in the organization, fear of reprisal will often prevent them from going over the head of their immediate supervisor. As a result, frustrated and morally conscientious employees either leave the organization or take to external whistleblowing.[76]

To overcome these problems, many companies have implemented programs that provide channels and procedures that facilitate internal whistleblowing. FMC corporation, for example, has an "ethics hotline"—a toll-free telephone number—that any employee can call to report suspected legal or ethical violations to an "ethics officer" whose full-time responsibility is responding to any calls that come in.[77] If the employee wishes to remain anonymous, he or she is assigned a number that can be used for identification in any future communications. The ethics officer is empowered to conduct a full investigation of the allegations and is empowered to take the results of the investigation to higher management, including, if necessary, the audit committee of the board of directors. To ensure that employees are not penalized for using the hotline, it is a company policy that any supervisor who retaliates against an employee who reports a violation is subject to punishment. And to ensure that employees are aware of the hotline and encouraged to use it, FMC regularly reminds employees of the hotline in the company paper and in other company documents, and calls it to the attention of new employees in their initial orientation training sessions.

The Right to Participate and Participatory Management

A democratic political tradition has long held that government should be subject to the consent of the governed because individuals have a right to liberty

[76] See Rowe and Baker, "Are You Hearing Enough Employee Concerns?" *Harvard Business Review*, May–June 1984.

[77] For a description of these and other effective corporate ethics programs, see Manuel G. Velasquez, "Corporate Ethics: Losing It, Having It, Getting It," pp. 228–44 in Peter Madsen and Jay M. Shafritz, eds., *Essentials of Business Ethics* (New York: Meridian Books, 1990).

and this right implies that they have a right to participate in the political decisions which affect them. Within a democracy, therefore, decision-making usually has two characteristics: (1) Decisions that affect the group are made by a majority of its members, (2) decisions are made after full, free, and open discussion.[78] Either all the members of the group participate in these decision-making processes or they do so through elected representatives.

A number of authors have proposed that these ideals of democracy should be embodied in business organizations.[79] Some have argued that enabling the individual employee within the organization to participate in the decision-making processes of the organization is an "ethical imperative."[80] As a first step toward such democracy, some have suggested that, although decisions affecting workers should not be made *by* workers, they should, nonetheless, be made only after full, free, and open discussion *with* workers. This would mean open communication between workers and their supervisors, and the establishment of an environment that encourages consultation with workers. Employees would be allowed to freely express criticism, to receive accurate information about decisions that will affect them, to make suggestions, and to protest decisions.

A second further step toward "organizational democracy" would give individual employees not only the right to consultation but also the right to make decisions about their own immediate work activities. These decisions might include matters such as working hours, rest periods, the organization of work tasks, and the scope of responsibility of workers and supervisors.

A third step toward extending the ideals of democracy into the workplace would allow workers to participate in the major policy decisions that affect the general operations of the firm. European firms, for example, particularly in West Germany, have adopted the concept of "codetermination."[81] Starting in 1951, German law required that each firm in the basic industries (coal, iron, and steel) should be administered by an eleven-member board of directors composed of five directors elected by stockholders, five directors elected by employees, and one director elected by the other ten. Further extension of the law to firms with more than twenty workers required such firms to have twelve-member boards composed of eight directors elected by stockholders and four directors elected by employees. These "Work Councils" decide issues such as plant shut-down or relocation, mergers with other firms, substantial product diversification, or the introduction of fundamentally new labor methods.

Full organizational democracy has not been particularly popular in the United States. Part of the reason, perhaps, is that employees have not shown a great deal of interest in participating in the firm's broader policy decisions. A more

[78] Robert G. Olson, *Ethics* (New York: Random House, Inc., 1978), pp. 83–84.

[79] Martin Carnoy and Derek Shearer, *Economic Democracy, the Challenge of the 1980s* (White Plains, NY: M. E. Sharpe, Inc., 1980); Warren G. Bennis and Philip E. Slater, *The Temporary Society* (New York: Harper & Row, Publishers, Inc., 1968); Vincent P. Mainelli, "Democracy in the Workplace," *America,* (15 January 1977), pp. 28–30; see also the essays in *Self-Management: New Dimensions to Democracy,* Ichak Adizes and Elizabeth Mann Borgese, eds. (Santa Barbara, CA: Clio Books, 1975).

[80] Marshall Sashkin, "Participative Management Is an Ethical Imperative," *Organizational Dynamics,* 12, no. 4 (1984), pp. 4–22.

[81] Frederick D. Sturdivant, *Business and Society,* 3rd. ed. (Homewood, IL: Richard D. Irwin, Inc., 1985), pp. 326–27.

important reason, however, is that American ideology distinguishes sharply between the power exercised in political organizations and the power exercised within economic organizations: Whereas power in political organizations should be democratic, power in economic organizations should be left in the private hands of managers and owners.[82] Whether this ideological distinction is valid is something the reader must decide. Many authors continue to argue that, given the large and dominant role that business organizations are now playing in our daily lives, democracy will soon touch only the peripheral areas of our lives if it continues to be restricted to political organizations.[83]

Some management theories, moreover, have urged managers to adopt a leadership style characterized as "participative leadership," on the utilitarian grounds that such a leadership style will increase worker satisfaction and favorably affect the organization's performance and productivity. Such theories are heavily dependent on assumptions about human nature and human motivation. One of the earliest such theories, for example, that of Douglas McGregor, described two "theories" or sets of assumptions managers can make about employees.[84] In one theory, Theory X, managers assume that employees are naturally indolent and self-centered, prefer to be led, are resistent to change, and need to be rewarded, punished, and controlled in order to get them to achieve organizational objectives. Managers who subscribe to Theory X tend to be more authoritarian, directive, controlling, and less consultative. In the other theory, Theory Y, managers assume that employees want, and can develop the capacity, to accept responsibility, have an inherent readiness to support organizational goals, and can determine for themselves the best means for achieving these goals and willingly direct their efforts toward those means. Theory Y, McGregor held, is a more accurate description of the modern workforce, and managing according to Theory Y means that the manager would delegate decisions, enlarge job responsibilities, use a participative and consultative style of management, and allow employees to evaluate themselves on the basis of their achievement of objectives they had set for themselves as means toward broader company objectives. Theory Y leadership, McGregor held, will create a more effective and ultimately more productive organization.

A later theory, that of Raymond Miles, largely agreed with McGregor's but went a step beyond his by distinguishing not two but three "models" or sets of assumptions managers can make about employees.[85] The "traditional" model assumes that most employees dislike work, most neither want nor are capable of being creative or self-directed, and most care more about how much they earn than what they do. Under these assumptions the manager must provide all direction, must closely supervise and control employees, and must establish all work routines and procedures. The second and more enlightened "human relations" model assumes that most employees want to belong and be recognized, that they want to

[82] See Robert A. Dahl, *After the Revolution? Authority in a Good Society* (New Haven: Yale University Press, 1970), pp. 117–18.

[83] C. Pateman, "A Contribution to the Political Theory of Organizational Democracy," *Administration and Society*, 7 (1975): 5–26.

[84] Douglas McGregor, *The Human Side of Enterprise* (New York: McGraw-Hill, 1960).

[85] Raymond E. Miles, *Theories of Management: Implications for Organizational Behavior and Development* (New York: McGraw-Hill, 1975), p. 35.

feel useful and important, and that meeting these needs is more important to them than what they earn. The human relations manager tries to keep employees informed, listens to them, allows them some self-direction and self-control, and tries to make each feel useful and important. The third and most enlightened model is the "human resources" model, which assumes that most employees do not find work inherently distasteful, that people want to contribute to meaningful goals that they helped establish, and that most employees can be creative and responsible and can exercise more self-direction and self-control than they presently have. The human resources manager tries to create an environment in which everyone can contribute to the limits of their ability, encourages full employee participation on important matters, continually expands employee self-direction and self-control, and tries to make use of "untapped" human resources. Miles held that worker satisfaction and organizational effectiveness and productivity would all be increased by the use of human resources management.

Yet another theory, developed by Rensis Likert, went one more step beyond Miles's theory to posit not three but four "systems of organization": system 1, the "exploitive authoritative"; system 2, the "benevolent authoritative"; system 3, the "consultative"; and system 4, the "participative."[86] As their titles suggest, these systems of leadership range from the absence of trust in system 1 to complete mutual trust between manager and employee in system 4; from lack of employee freedom to discuss problems to complete freedom; from no use of employee ideas to constant use; from no employee involvement in decisions to full involvement; from absolute management control of work to employee self-control; from no teamwork to a substantial amount of cooperative teamwork; from all influence and decisions coming from the top, to influence and decisions flowing upward, downward, and laterally. Likert argues that system 4, which incorporates the highest levels of employee participation and self-direction, is likely to yield the highest levels of organizational effectiveness and productivity.

If participative management styles like those advocated in different ways by McGregor, Miles, and Likert do make organizations more effective and productive, then on utilitarian grounds, managers would have a moral obligation to seek to implement these styles. However, the research that has been conducted on whether participative management is more effective and productive has not come to firm conclusions. In some cases, participative management has been spectacularly successful, enabling entire plants to be turned from unproductive "disasters" into highly efficient dynamos.[87] But in other cases participative management has not had substantial positive effects on performance or productivity.[88] Moreover, critics of the participative approach to management have argued both that people are different and do not all want or can participate in management decision-making, and that organizations and organizational tasks are different and are not all suited to participatory management. If this is correct, then the utilitarian argument in

[86] Rensis Likert, "From Production- and Employee-Centerdness to Systems 1–4," *Journal of Management*, 5 (1979), pp. 147–156.

[87] See, for example, William F. Dowling, "At General Motors: System 4 Builds Performance and Profits," *Organizational Dynamics*, vol. 3, no. 3 (1975), pp. 26–30.

[88] For a review of the literature, see Edwin A. Locke, David M. Schweiger, and Gary P. Latham, "Participation in Decision Making: When Should It Be used?" *Organizational Dynamics*, vol. 14, no. 3 (1986), pp. 58–72.

favor of participative management can at most show that managers have an obligation to use participative management with the right people and in the right organizational contexts.

The Right to Due Process versus Employment-at-Will

When a General Motors internal investigation uncovered what it considered sufficient evidence of a secret employee scheme to defraud the company, without consulting the employees the team felt were involved, GM quickly doled out what one journalist called "an almost ruthless brand of corporate justice" in his description of the subsequent firings at GM's Tarrytown, New York offices:

> Only a few days remained until Christmas, and the General Motors employees working in the modern Chevrolet Division office here were looking forward to the long paid holiday—totally unprepared for the ordeal most of them were about to face. Suddenly, without warning, about 25 salaried employees were summoned, one by one. They each were funneled through a three-room "assembly line" where solemn-faced GM officials from Detroit fired them, stripped them of their company cars and other benefits, and gave them cab fare home. One worker, with more than 20 years of service, recalls watching in disbelief as a GM functionary with a map and a ruler measured off the distance to his home and handed him $15. Within a few hours it was over. GM had all but wiped out the staff of the zone sales and service office that supervises the Chevrolet dealers in the New York City area.[89]

Until recently, American labor law has given a prominent position to the principle of "employment-at-will," the doctrine that unless employees are protected by an explicit contract (such as union employees), employers "may dismiss their employees at will . . . for good cause, for no cause, or even for causes morally wrong, without being thereby guilty of legal wrong."[90] The doctrine of employment-at-will is based on the assumption that, as owner of a business, the employer has a right to decide freely who will work for the business, so long as the employee freely accepts and freely can reject that work. As owner of the property constituting the business, therefore, the employer has the right to hire, fire, and promote employees of the business on whatever grounds the employer chooses. In this view the employee has no right to object to or contest the employer's decisions because as a nonowner the employee has no right to determine how the business will be run, and because as a free agent the employee freely agreed to accept the authority of the employer and always remains free to work elsewhere.

The doctrine of employment-at-will has come under considerable attack.[91] First, employees often are not free to accept or reject employment without suffering considerable harm, since often they have no other job available. Moreover, even when they are able to find alternative employment, workers pay the heavy costs

[89] Greg Conderacci, "Motorgate: How a Floating Corpse Led to a Fraud Inquiry and Ousters by GM," *Wall Street Journal*, 24 April 1982, pp. 1, 16.

[90] Quoted in Lawrence E. Blades, "Employment at Will versus Individual Freedom," *Columbia Law Review*, 67 (1967): 1405.

[91] See, for example, Patricia H. Werhane, *Persons, Rights, and Corporations* (Englewood Cliffs, NJ: Prentice Hall, 1985), pp. 81–93; Richard DeGeorge, *Business Ethics*, pp. 204–7.

involved in engaging in a job search and of going unpaid while they are doing so. Consequently, one of the fundamental assumptions on which employment-at-will is based—that employees "freely" accept employment and are "free" to find employment elsewhere—is erroneous. Second, employees generally make a conscientious effort to contribute to the firm but do so with the understanding that the firm will treat them fairly and conscientiously in return. Workers surely would not freely choose to work for a firm if they believed the firm would treat them unfairly. There is, therefore, a tacit agreement that the firm makes to treat workers fairly, and workers therefore have a quasi-contractual right to such treatment. Third, workers have a right to be treated with respect as free and equal persons. Part of this right is the right to nonarbitrary treatment and the right not to be forced to suffer harm unfairly or on the basis of false accusations. Since firings and reductions in pay or status obviously harm employees—particularly when they have no other job alternatives—these violate the employee's right when they are arbitrary or based on false or exaggerated accusations. For these reasons, a recent trend away from the doctrine of employment-at-will has developed and has been replaced gradually by the view that employees have a right to "due process."[92]

For many people, the most critical right of employees is the right to due process. For our purposes, "due process" refers to the fairness of the process by which decision-makers impose sanctions on their subordinates. An ideal system of due process would be one in which individuals were given clear antecedent notice of the rules they were to follow, which gave a fair and impartial hearing to those who are believed to have violated the rules, which administered all rules consistently and without favoritism or discrimination, which was designed to ascertain the truth as objectively as possible, and which did not hold people responsible for matters over which they had no control.

It is obvious why the right to due process is seen by many people as the most critical right of employees: If this right is not respected, employees stand little chance of seeing their other rights respected. Due process ensures that individuals are not treated arbitrarily, capriciously, or maliciously by their superiors in the administration of the firm's rules, and sets a moral limit on the exercise of the superior's power.[93] If the right to due process were not operative in the firm, then even if the rules of the firm protect the employee's other rights, these protections might be enforced sporadically and arbitrarily.

The most important area in which due process must play a role is in the hearing of grievances. By carefully spelling out a fair procedure for hearing and processing employee grievances, a firm can ensure that due process becomes an institutionalized reality. Here is an example of one company's fairly simple set of procedures for ensuring due process in grievances:

> All problems should be taken up initially with the employee's immediate supervisor. Most of the problems will be settled at this point to the satisfaction of the employee. There may be times, however, when the nature of the problem is such that the

[92] Robert Ellis Smith, *Workrights* (New York: E. P. Dutton, 1983), pp. 209–15.

[93] See T. M. Scanlon, "Due Process," in *Due Process*, J. Roland Pennock and John W. Chapman, eds. (New York: New York University Press, 1977), pp. 93–125.

> supervisor may not be able to give an immediate answer. In those instances where the immediate supervisor is unable to solve the problem within two working days following the date of presentation by the employee, the employee may review the problem with his departmental manager or superintendent. In situations where, after having discussed his problem with his immediate supervisor and departmental manager or superintendent, an employee still has questions, he may take the problem to the personnel manager for disposition.[94]

Trotta and Gudenberg identify the following features as the essential components of an effective grievance procedure:

1. Three to five steps of appeal, depending upon the size of the organization. Three steps usually will suffice.
2. A written account of the grievance when it goes past the first level. This facilitates communication and defines the issues.
3. Alternate routes of appeal so that the employee can bypass his supervisor if he desires. The personnel department may be the most logical alternate route.
4. A time limit for each step of the appeal so that the employee has some idea of when to expect an answer.
5. Permission for the employee to have one or two co-workers accompany him at each interview or hearing. This helps overcome fear of reprisal.[95]

Employee Rights and Plant Closings

During the last two decades American manufacturing plants have been losing ground to foreign competitors. In 1960, for example, American car companies had 95 percent of the domestic automobile market; by 1984 their share had shrunk to 75 percent, foreign competitors having taken the rest.[96] Similarly, while 95 percent of our domestic steel came from American companies in 1960, by 1984 U.S. companies provided only 75 percent of our steel. The pattern is similar in other parts of the world. In 1960 the U.S. share of the world market in manufactured goods was 25 percent; by 1984 it had shrunk to 16 percent.

A number of factors have contributed to the loss of the United States' manufacturing competitiveness. First, blue-collar wages tend to be much lower in other countries: Whereas American steelworkers earn $23 an hour including benefits, Korean workers earn $2 an hour. Second, some foreign competitors (Japanese steelmakers, for example) have invested in more efficient equipment, have cultivated more productive employer-employee relations, have more cooperative employee work rules, and have instituted other programs that have raised worker productivity relative to the United States. Third, governments of some foreign manufacturing industries (the government of the French steel industry, for example) have provided planning, financial subsidies, protective tariffs, favorable tax rates,

[94] Quoted in Maurice S. Trotta and Harry R. Gudenberg, "Resolving Personnel Problems in Nonunion Plants," in Westin and Salisbury, *Individual Rights*, p. 306.

[95] *Ibid.*, pp. 307–8.

[96] William E. Diehl, *Plant Closings* (New York: Division for Mission in North America, Lutheran Church in America, 1985), p. 2. Much of the discussion below draws on this excellent work, which may be acquired by writing to its publisher at 231 Madison Avenue, New York, NY 10016.

and other "industrial policies" designed to nurture and support their industrial base, whereas the United States government has done little in this direction.

As American manufacturing plants have become less competitive, many have been shut down, throwing their employees out of work. Between 1969 and 1976 alone about 30 percent of all large U.S. manufacturing plants (those with more than 100 workers) closed down.[97] Each year during this period approximately 3.2 million workers lost their jobs. Although the national average unemployment rate in 1985 hovered around 7.3 percent (over 8 million people), cities and towns formerly dependent on manufacturing facilities that had shut down continued to face double-digit unemployment.

The loss of competitiveness is not the only reason plants shut down, of course. Plants also close because their products become obsolete (facilities manufacturing kerosene lamps, for example); their manufacturing technology becomes obsolete (a mill using water power, for example); demand shifts away from a certain product design before the plant has time to retool (in 1973, for example, the energy crisis within months shifted demand away from large American cars to the smaller cars being manufactured abroad); the plant is taken over in a merger and the new managers decide to consolidate operations in a few large facilities (a small profitable steel operation, for example, may be closed down after a merger and its operations shifted to another plant that is more efficient and has an even higher profit margin); or managers make the wrong decisions or put short-term profits ahead of long-term investment (a team of managers, for example, might put off buying new equipment in order to show higher earnings on their quarterly report).

Whatever the cause, whether foreign competition, changes in domestic demand, or mismanagement, plant closings impose high costs on workers and their communities. Workers' life savings are exhausted. Many lose their homes to foreclosure; are forced to accept menial jobs with drastically lower salaries and status; lose their pension rights, and suffer acute mental distress resulting in feelings of worthlessness and self-doubt, psychosomatic illnesses, alcoholism, family quarrels, child and spouse abuse, divorce, and suicide.[98] Communities are harmed because closed plants mean declining tax revenues, the loss of business from unemployed workers, and increased revenues that must be spent to provide social services for the unemployed.[99] In some cases, entire towns have been reduced to ghost towns when the plant on which most of the local labor force depended left.

Plant closings are not always avoidable in a market economy such as ours. However, although shutdowns are sometimes necessary, the moral rights of workers involved should continue to be respected, even when a business is forced to close.[100] Among the rights that must be respected are the workers' right to be treated only as they freely and knowingly consent to be treated, a right that requires they be

[97] Edward S. Herman, *Corporate Control and Corporate Power* (New York: Cambridge University Press, 1981), pp. 85–113.

[98] Barry Bluestone and Bennett Harrison, *The Deindustrialization of America* (New York: Basic Books, Inc., Publishers, 1982), pp. 140–90.

[99] Don Stillman, "The Devastating Impact of Plant Relocations," in *The Big Business Reader*, Mark Green, ed. (New York: The Pilgrim Press, 1983), pp. 137–48.

[100] For a discussion of the ethical issues involved in plant closings see Judith Lichtenberg, "Workers, Owners, and Factory Closings," *Philosophy and Public Policy* (January 1985).

informed about impending shutdowns that will affect them. Other countries, such as Sweden, Germany, and Great Britain all require extended advance notice of impending plant closures. As the laws of these same countries also recognize, workers have a right, too, to participate (through their unions, for example) in closure decisions perhaps even by being given the opportunity to purchase the plant and operate it themselves. Moreover, utilitarian principles imply that the harm caused by layoffs should be minimized, and this in turn means that the costs of plant closings should be absorbed by those parties who have the greater resources and who would therefore be harmed the least by having to pay the costs. Consequently, since the corporate owner of a plant scheduled for shutdown often has greater resources than the workers, it should bear much of the costs of retraining, transfer, relocation, and so forth, by developing and paying for programs to deal with these. Many companies have successfully implemented such programs. Finally, considerations of justice imply that workers and communities that have made substantial contributions to a plant during its operating life should be repaid by company assurances that it will not unjustly abandon worker pension plans, worker health plans, worker retirement plans, and community reliance on tax revenues.

These ethical considerations are nicely embodied in the suggestions that William Diehl, a former senior vice president in the steel industry, makes concerning eight steps that companies can take to minimize the harmful effects of plant closings.[101]

1. *Advance Notice* If the company can notify workers of a closing date twelve to eighteen months in advance, they would have time to prepare for it. . . . One day's notice of closing is totally unjust and unacceptable.
2. *Severance Pay* A commonly suggested formula is for each worker to receive severance pay equal to one week's earnings for every year of service . . .
3. *Health Benefits* Worker's health benefits should be covered by the company for at least one additional year after the employee is dismissed.
4. *Early Retirement* Workers who are within three years of normal retirement should be retired on full pension, with years of service computed as if they had worked until age sixty-five.
5. *Transfer* In the case of a multiplant corporation, all workers at the facility should have the opportunity to transfer to an equally paying job at another plant, with full moving expenses covered by the employer.
6. *Job Retraining* Company-sponsored training programs should be established to train and place workers in other jobs in the local community. These programs should also include family counseling for all employees.
7. *Employee Purchase* Workers and the local community should be given the opportunity to purchase the plant and operate it under an employee Stock Ownership Plan (ESOP) . . . [if] viable. . . .
8. *Phasing Out of Local Taxes* Companies should phase out their local taxes over a five year period. This may involve a voluntary contribution to the local taxing authority if the plant and equipment are disposed of in a way that will severely reduce property taxes.

[101] Diehl, *Plant Closings*, pp. 14–16.

Unions and the Right to Organize

Just as owners have the right to freely associate with each other to establish and run a business for the achievement of their morally legitimate ends, so also workers have the right to freely associate with each other to establish and run unions for the achievement of their morally legitimate common ends. The same rights of free association that justify the formation and existence of corporations also underlie the worker organizations we call "unions."[102]

The worker's right to organize into a union also derives from the right of the worker to be treated as a free and equal person. Corporate employers, especially during periods of high unemployment or in regions where only one or a very few firms are located, can exert an unequal pressure on an employee by forcing the employee to accept their conditions or go without an adequate job. Unions have traditionally been justified as a legitimate "countervailing" means for balancing the power of the large corporation so that the worker in solidarity with other workers can achieve an equal negotiating power against the corporation.[103] Unions thus achieve an equality between worker and employer that the isolated worker could not secure, and they thereby secure the worker's right to be treated as a free and equal person in job negotiations with powerful employers.

Not only do workers have a right to form unions, but their unions also have a right to strike.[104] The right of unions to call a strike derives from the right of each worker to quit his or her job at will so long as doing so violates no prior agreements or the rights of others. Union strikes are therefore morally justified so long as the strike does not violate a prior legitimately negotiated agreement not to strike (which the company might have negotiated with the union) and so long as the strike does not violate the legitimate moral rights of others (such as citizens whose right to protection and security might be violated by strikes of public workers such as firefighters or police).

In spite of the well-accepted view that unions and union strikes are legitimate, there has been a good deal of dissatisfaction toward them. While unions represented 35 percent of the workforce in 1947, they represented only 22 percent by the early 1980s.[105] From an earlier record of winning 75 percent of all union elections, unions must now be satisfied with winning only about 45 percent of worker votes.[106] Analysts predict that by the year 2000 unions will represent only 13 percent of the labor force.

There are a variety of factors responsible for this decline in union membership, including an increase in white-collar and female workers, a shift from manufacturing to service industries, and a decline in public confidence in unions. But one of the major causes is rising opposition to unions on the part of managers and a disturbing increase in the use of illegal tactics to defeat union organizing

[102] Richard DeGeorge, *Business Ethics,* p. 192.

[103] J. K. Galbraith, *American Capitalism: The Concept of Countervailing Power* (Boston: Houghton Mifflin, 1952).

[104] Douglas Fraser, "Strikes: Friend or Foe of American Business and the Economy?" *Los Angeles Times,* 3 November 1985.

[105] Ron Chernow, "Grey Flannel Goons: The Latest in Union Busting," in *The Big Business Reader,* Mark Green, ed. (New York: The Pilgrim Press, 1983), pp. 47–59.

[106] "Beyond Unions," *Business Week,* 8 July 1985.

campaigns.[107] This is unfortunate and shortsighted since the decline in the effectiveness of unions has been accompanied by a consequent increase in the appeal to legislatures and the courts to establish rigid legal protections against the abuses that unions were originally established to secure. As the effectiveness of workers' rights to unionize and strike continues to shrink, we can count on a proliferation of laws to secure the rights that worker organizations can no longer accomplish.

8.6 ORGANIZATIONAL POLITICS

The discussion so far has focused primarily on formal power relationships within organizations: that is, the ethical issues raised by the power that the formal structure of the organization allows managers to exercise over their subordinates. These power relations are sanctioned and overt: They are spelled out in the firm's "organizational chart," inscribed in the contracts and job descriptions that define the employee's duties to the firm, recognized by the law (of agency), openly employed by superiors, and largely accepted as legitimate by subordinates.

The ethical constraints on the use of this formal power that we reviewed above have also been approached from a largely formal perspective. The rights to privacy, to due process, to freedom of conscience, and to consent can all be formalized within the organization (by formulating and enforcing rules, codes, and procedures) just as the power relationships they constrain are formalized.

But as we have already seen, organizations also contain informal pockets and channels of power: sources of power that do not appear on organizational charts and uses of power that are covert and perhaps not recognized as legitimate. We must turn now to look at this underbelly of the organization: organizational politics.

Political Tactics in Organizations

There is no settled definition of "organizational politics." For our purposes, however, we can adopt the following definition: "Organizational politics" are the processes in which individuals or groups within an organization use nonformally sanctioned power tactics to advance their own aims; such tactics we shall call "political tactics."[108]

A word of caution is necessary, lest the reader interpret "their own aims" to mean "aims in conflict with the best interests of the organization." Although the aims of a coalition in a firm may conflict with the best interests of the firm (a problem we will examine), such conflict is neither inevitable nor even, perhaps, frequent. Two factors tend to suppress such conflicts: (1) The careers of individuals often depend on the health of their organizations and (2) long-time association with an organization tends to generate bonds of loyalty to the organization. Often, therefore, what one person *perceives* as a conflict between a certain group's aims and the best interests of the organization is in fact a conflict between the beliefs

[107] *Ibid.*

[108] This definition is from Bronston T. Mayes and Robert W. Allen, "Toward A Definition of Organizational Politics," *Academy of Management Review* (October 1977), pp. 672–78; for a popular overview of the issues raised by organizational politics, see "Playing Office Politics," *Newsweek*, 16 September 1985, pp. 54–59.

of that person and the beliefs of the group concerning what the "best interests" of the organization are: The group may genuinely believe that X is in the best interests of *both* the organization and itself, while the person may genuinely believe instead that Y, which conflicts with X, is what is in the best interests of the organization.

Because organizational politics aim at advancing the interests of one individual or group (such as, acquiring promotions, salary or budget increases, status, or even more power) by exerting nonformally sanctioned power over other individuals or groups, political individuals tend to be *covert* about their underlying intents or methods.[109] Virginia E. Schein, for example, gives this illustration of a department head intent on strengthening her position in an organization:

> The head of a research unit requests permission to review another research group's proposal in case she can add information to improve the project. Her covert intent is to maintain her current power, which will be endangered if the other research group carries out the project. Using her informational power base, her covert means are to introduce irrelevant information and pose further questions. If she sufficiently confuses the issues, she can discredit the research group and prevent the project from being carried out. She covers these covert intents and means with the overt ones of improving the project and reviewing its content.[110]

The fact that political tactics are usually covert means that they can easily become deceptive or manipulative. This is evident if we examine more examples of organizational political tactics. In a recent study of managerial personnel, respondents were asked to describe the political tactics they had experienced most frequently in the organizations in which they had worked.[111] The following kinds of tactics were reported.

Blaming or attacking others Minimizing one's association with an outcome that is failing or has failed by blaming one's rivals for the failure or "denigrating their accomplishments as unimportant, poorly timed, self-serving, or lucky."

Controlling information Withholding information detrimental to one's aims or distorting information "to create an impression by selective disclosure, innuendo," or overwhelming the subject with "objective" data (graphs, formulas, tables, summations) designed to create an impression of rationality or logic and to obscure important details harmful to one's interests.

Developing a base of support for one's ideas Getting others to understand and support one's ideas before a meeting is called.

Image building Creating the appearance of being thoughtful, honest, sensitive, on the inside of important activities, well-liked, confident.

Ingratiation Praising superiors and developing good rapport.

Associating with the influential

[109] Miles, *Macro Organizational Behavior*, pp. 161–64.

[110] Schein, "Individual Power and Political Behaviors," p. 67.

[111] Robert W. Allen, Dan L. Madison, Lyman W. Porter, and Patricia A. Renwick, Bronston T. Mayes, "Organizational Politics," *California Management Review*, 22, no. 1 (Fall 1979): 77–83.

Forming power coalitions and developing strong allies

Creating obligations Making others feel obligated to oneself by performing services or favors for them.

Some researchers have argued that the basic source of power is the creation of dependency: A acquires power over B by making B dependent upon A for something. Some authors identify the following political tactics by which such dependencies can be created:[112]

Getting control over scarce resources desired by others Controlling employees, buildings, access to influential persons, equipment, useful information.

Establishing favorable relationships Getting others to feel obligated to oneself; making others think one is a friend; building a reputation as an expert; encouraging others to believe that one has power and that they are dependent on that power.

Anyone who has ever worked within organizations can undoubtedly think of many examples of the use of political tactics in organizational life. Here is a former executive's description of the use of some "ploys" he encountered during his corporate career:

> [This is] a ploy for many minor executives to gain some information: I heard that the district manager of California is being transferred to Seattle. He knows there's been talk going on about changing district managers. By using this ploy—"I know something"—he's making it clear to the person he's talking to that he's been in on it all along. So it's all right to tell him. Gossip is another way of building up importance within a person who starts the rumor. He's in, he's part of the inner circle . . . When a top executive is let go. . . . suddenly everybody in the organization walks away and shuns him because they don't want to be associated with him. In corporations, if you back the wrong guy, you're in his corner and he's fired, you're guilty by association. . . . A guy in a key position, everybody wants to talk to him. All his subordinates are trying to get an audience with him to build up their own positions.[113]

The Ethics of Political Tactics

Obviously, political behavior in an organization can easily become abusive: Political tactics can be used to advance private interests at the expense of organizational and group interests; they can be manipulative and deceptive; and they can seriously injure those who themselves have little or no political power or expertise. On the other hand, political tactics can also be put at the service of organizational and social goals, they may sometimes be necessary to protect the powerless, and they are sometimes the only defense a person has against the manipulative and deceptive tactics of others. The dilemma for the individual in an organization is

[112] These are culled from the pages of John P. Kotter, *Power in Management* (New York: American Management Association, 1979), a book which argues that "skillfully executed power-oriented behavior" is the mark of the "successful manager."

[113] Terkel, *Working*, pp. 407, 409, 410.

knowing where the line lies that separates morally legitimate and necessary political tactics from those that are unethical.

Very few authors have examined this dilemma.[114] This is unfortunate because, although few organizations are totally pervaded by political behavior, it is also the case that no organization is free of it: We are all political animals even if our political campaigns are largely confined to the office. We shall here only be able to make a start at analyzing the many complex ethical issues raised by the political maneuvering that inevitably goes on within organizations. The issues can best be approached by addressing three questions that can focus our attention on the morally relevant features of using political tactics. (1) The *utilitarian* question: Are the goals one intends to achieve by the use of the tactics socially beneficial or socially harmful? (2) The *rights* question: Do the political tactics used as means to these goals treat others in a manner consistent with their moral rights? (3) The *justice* question: Will the political tactics lead to an equitable distribution of benefits and burdens?[115]

The utility of goals Utilitarian principles require that managers pursue those goals that will produce the greatest social benefits and the least social harm. If we assume that business organizations generally perform a socially beneficial function and that activities that harm the organization will probably diminish these social benefits, then utilitarianism implies that the individual manager should avoid harming the organization and that the manager should work to ensure that the organization carries out its beneficial social functions as efficiently as possible. The basic function of most businesses, for example, is to produce goods and services for consumers. Insofar as a business organization is serving this function in a socially beneficial and nonharmful way, the employee should avoid harming the business and should strive to ensure that the business carries on its productive function with a minimum of waste. Two kinds of political tactics directly contradict this norm and are therefore typically judged unethical: political tactics that involve the pursuit of personal goals at the expense of the organization's productive goals, and political tactics that knowingly involve inefficiency and waste. Suppose, for example, that the head of a research unit secretly withholds critical information from other research units in the same company so that his own unit will look better than the others. As a result, his career ambitions are advanced and his unit gets a larger budget allocation the following year. Was his tactic of withholding information to gain an edge on others morally legitimate? No: The tactic was clearly inconsistent with the efficient pursuit of the company's productive functions.

Of course, businesses do not always have socially beneficial and nonharmful goals. Pollution, planned obsolescence, price-fixing, and the manufacture of hazardous products are some obvious organizational goals that utilitarianism would condemn. To the extent that a business pursues such goals, the employee has a duty

[114] See John R. S. Wilson, "In One Another's Power," *Ethics*, 88, no. 4 (July 1978): 299–315; L. Blum, "Deceiving, Hurting, and Using," in *Philosophy and Personal Relations*, A. Montefiore, ed. (London: Routledge and Kegan Paul, 1973).

[115] Gerald F. Cavanagh, Dennis J. Moberg, and Manuel Velasquez, "The Ethics of Organizational Politics," *Academy of Management Review* (July 1980); Manuel Velasquez, Dennis J. Moberg, and Gerald F. Cavanagh, "Organizational Statesmanship and Dirty Politics: Ethical Guidelines for the Organizational Politician," *Organizational Dynamics* (Autumn 1983): 65–80.

not to cooperate (unless, perhaps, the employee is threatened with personal losses of such magnitude that he or she is in effect coerced to comply). Utilitarian principles imply that to voluntarily pursue goals that are socially harmful or to voluntarily cooperate in such a pursuit is immoral, regardless of what kinds of political tactics one uses.

Unfortunately, organizational goals are not always clear because there may be no consensus over what the organization's goals actually are. This is especially the case, for example, when a company is in the process of undergoing a change in management or a change in organization and more or less widespread bargaining erupts over what the new goals should be. When organizational goals are in the process of being redefined in this way, the various coalitions and individuals within the organization will usually attempt to use political tactics to install the goals that each wants, either through a unilateral exercise of power (a new management, for example, may try to get rid of all the old staff and to hire its own "team") or through political compromise (the new management may try to persuade the old staff to accept new goals). In such fluid situations the individual has no choice but to examine the goals being proposed by the various coalitions, and to make a conscientious attempt to determine which goals are in the long run the most socially beneficial. Whereas the use of political tactics to install illegitimate organizational goals would be unethical, political tactics may be used to ensure the installation of morally legitimate goals *provided that the tactics meet the two criteria here following.*

The consistency of political means with moral rights Some political tactics are obviously deceptive, as when a person creates the impression that he or she has an expertise that the person does not in fact have. Other tactics are manipulative. It is manipulative, for example, to feign love in order to extract favors from a person. Deception and manipulation are both attempts to get a person to do (or believe) something that that person would not do (or believe) if he or she knew what was going on. These sorts of political tactics are unethical to the extent that they fail to respect a person's right to be treated not merely as a means but also as an end; that is, they fail to respect a person's right to be treated only as he or she has freely and knowingly consented to be treated. Such moral disrespect is exhibited in many of those political tactics that take advantage of our emotional dependencies and vulnerabilities, both of which provide others with the cheapest and most reliable levers for acquiring power over us. A skilled administrator, for example, can become adept at pretending friendship and concern, and adept at getting others to look upon him or her with affection, respect, loyalty, indebtedness, trust, gratitude, and so on. The administrator can then exploit these feelings to get subordinates to do things for him or her that they ordinarily would not do, especially if they knew the deception involved and knew the covert motives on which the administrator acted. A skillful administrator might also learn to take advantage of particular individuals' personal vulnerabilities such as vanity, generosity, sense of responsibility, susceptibility to flattery, gullibility, naiveté or any of the other traits that can lead a person to unwittingly put himself or herself at the mercy of others. By covertly taking advantage of these vulnerabilities, the manager can get employees to serve the manager's aims, even though they would not do so if they knew the covert motives on which the manager acted.

But are deceptive and manipulative political tactics always wrong? What if

I am forced to work in an organization in which others insist on using deceptive and manipulative tactics against me? Must I remain defenseless? Not necessarily. If the members of an organization know that certain kinds of covert political tactics are in common use within an organization, and if, nonetheless, they freely choose to remain within the organization and become skillful in using and defending themselves against these tactics, then one can presume that these organizational members have tacitly consented to having those kinds of covert political tactics used against themselves. They have freely agreed to play an organizational game, as it were, in which everyone knows that fooling the other players and maneuvering them out of winning positions is all part of the game. Dealing with them on the basis of this tacit consent would not violate their right to be treated as they have freely and knowingly chosen to be treated.

However, the use of deceptive or manipulative political tactics is clearly unethical when: (1) they are used against persons who do not know, or do not expect, that these kinds of tactics will be used against themselves or (2) they are used against persons who are not free to leave the organization in which these tactics are being used or (3) they are used against persons who are not skilled at defending themselves against these tactics. Using a deceptive or manipulative tactic in any of these instances violates the moral respect due to persons, especially if the tactic injures a person by maneuvering the person into unknowingly acting against his or her own best interests.

The equity of the consequences Political tactics can create injustices by distorting the equality of treatment that justice demands. An individual who controls an organization's budget or information system, for example, may covertly administer that system unjustly by showing favoritism to those persons or groups who can advance the individual's career. Such political tactics blatantly violate the basic principle of distributive justice discussed earlier: Individuals who are similar in all relevant respects should be treated similarly, and individuals who are dissimilar in relevant respects should be treated dissimilarly in proportion to their dissimilarity.

Political tactics can also create injustices among those employees who have few or no political skills. Those without political skills are easily maneuvered into accepting a smaller share of the organization's benefits than their abilities or needs may merit in comparison to others. Benefits are then no longer distributed to these people on the basis of their relevant characteristics: An injustice is committed against them.

Not only can political tactics leave others better or worse off than they deserve, but politics can also be used to gain unjust advantages for oneself. An engineer who is competing with another engineer for promotion to department head, for example, may cultivate and flatter her superiors, while simultaneously using innuendo to discredit her rival. As a result she may get the promotion, even though the other engineer was more qualified. Using political tactics in this way to acquire advantages on the basis of nonrelevant characteristics is also unjust.

In addition to these immediate inequities, the prolonged prevalence of political tactics within an organization can generate long-term and debilitating organizational effects. Several researchers have found that the use of power in organizations tends to routinize the dehumanized treatment of less powerful individuals. David Kipnis, for example, found that individuals who exercise power find themselves increasingly tempted to (a) increase their attempts to influence the behavior of the less powerful, (b) devalue the worth of the performance of the less powerful, (c) attribute the cause of the less powerful's efforts to power controlled by themselves rather than to the less powerful's motivations to do well, (d) view the less powerful as objects of manipulation, and (e) express a preference for the maintenance of psychological distance from the less powerful.[116] Power, in short, corrupts.

Chris Argyris and others have maintained, on the other hand, that those who are controlled by the powerful, "tend to feel frustration, conflict, and feelings of failure," that they "adapt" by leaving the organization, by trying to climb the organization's ladder, by retreating to aggression, daydreaming, regression, or simple apathy; and that the organization itself becomes characterized by competition, rivalry, and hostility.[117] In deciding whether to use political tactics, the individual should seriously consider, therefore, the long-range consequences that the exercise of power implied by these tactics can have on oneself and on others.

QUESTIONS FOR REVIEW AND DISCUSSION

1. Define the following concepts: the rational model of the organization, employee's obligations to the firm, law of agency, conflict of interest, actual/potential conflicts of interest, commercial bribe, commercial extortion, morality of accepting gifts, insider information, theft, fair wage, OSHA, unfairly imposed employee risk, horizontal/vertical job specialization, job satisfaction, the political model of the organization, power, government-management analogy, right to privacy, physical/psychological privacy, relevance, consent, extraordinary methods, right to freedom of conscience, whistleblowing, right to participate, right to due process, organizational politics, political tactics.
2. Relate the theory of the employee's obligations to the firm in this chapter to the discussion on contractual rights and duties in Chapter Two. Relate the six criteria for just wages in this chapter to the various standards of justice developed in Chapter Two. Relate the problems of job satisfaction described in this chapter to the discussion of alienation in Chapter Three. Relate the discussions of employee rights in this chapter to the theory of moral rights developed in Chapter Two.
3. Compare and contrast the rational model of the organization with the political model of the organization. Would you agree with the following statement: "The rational model of the organization implies that the corporation is based on consent, while the political model implies that the corporation is based on force"? Which of the two models do you think provides the more adequate view of the university? Of the company you work for? Explain your answers.
4. In view of the contractual agreement that every employee makes to be loyal to the employer, do you think whistleblowing is ever morally justified? Explain your answer.
5. Do you agree or disagree with the claim that corporate managements are so similar to governments that employees should be recognized as having the same "civil rights" as citizens have?

[116] David Kipnis, "Does Power Corrupt?," *Journal of Personality and Social Psychology*, 24, no. 1 (1972): 33.

[117] Chris Argyris, *Personality and Organization* (New York: Harper & Brothers, 1957), pp. 232–37.

CASES FOR DISCUSSION

DBCP

For over a year, rumors had been circulating among the workers of the Occidental Chemical Plant in Lathrop, California, that the men working in their Agricultural Chemical Division were unable to have children. In June of 1977, the union asked some of their men to volunteer for semen analysis. Seven people volunteered. All had abnormally low sperm counts. Follow-up studies on five of the men on July 22 showed that they were functionally sterile. All had been involved in the production of Dibromochloropropane (DBCP).[1] News of the sterility among the workers in the Occidental plant sent shock waves through the industry. The two major producers of DBCP, Dow Chemical and Shell Chemical, were especially concerned about their workers. Subsequent tests on 432 DBCP workers in California, Colorado, and Arkansas revealed that one third had been rendered infertile by DBCP.[2]

DBCP is a widely used pesticide. In 1951 Dow discovered that DBCP was a highly effective soil fumigant capable of eliminating small worms that attack the root systems of corn, soybeans, grapes, citrus, peaches, figs, walnuts, pineapples, and other crops. After carrying out initial toxicology tests from 1952 to 1954, Dow concluded that, although DBCP produced slight skin irritations and was highly toxic when taken orally or when its vapors were inhaled, it could be used safely when handled carefully in well-ventilated areas. By 1957 Dow was manufacturing and selling DBCP. The labels included the following warnings:

> Warning. Harmful liquid and vapor; causes skin irritation and blisters on prolonged contact; avoid breathing vapor; avoid contact with eyes, skin, and clothing; do not take internally; and use only with adequate ventilation.[3]

Shell started its production of DBCP in 1955 after commissioning several research studies by the University of California to determine the toxicologic properties of DBCP. These tests also showed DBCP was toxic when taken orally or inhaled but revealed "no indications of testicular effect."[4]

In 1958 Shell received a "confidential report" from a University of California researcher, Dr. Charles Hine, describing the results that inhaling DBCP had on rats. The rats were exposed to DBCP fumes in concentrations of 5, 10, 20, and 40 ppm (parts per million) five days a week for ten weeks. No rats survived 40 ppm. Subsequent autopsy showed damage to the liver, lung, kidney, brain, adrenals, and testes of the rats. "Testes decreased in size at 5 ppm, but the difference was not significant until 10 ppm."[5] Since Shell had partially funded the study, the information was considered the confidential property of Shell.

[1] U.S. Congress, Senate, *Worker Safety in Pesticide Production: Hearings before the Subcommittee on Agricultural Research and General Legislation of the Committee on Agriculture, Nutrition, and Forestry,* 95th Congress, 1st session, 13 and 14 December 1977, pp. 3–5.

[2] Ronald B. Taylor, "Pesticides," *San Jose Mercury,* 1 July 1979, p. 1F.

[3] *Worker Safety in Pesticide Production,* p. 120.

[4] *Ibid.,* p. 126.

[5] *Ibid.,* p. 126.

In 1961 the results of the Shell study were combined with the results of a similar study of the effects of DBCP on rats, guinea pigs, rabbits, and monkeys that Dr. T. Torkelson had carried out for Dow. The combined study was published in 1961 in the *Journal of Toxicology and Applied Pharmacology*. The joint study concluded in part:

> The most striking observation at autopsy [of the animal] was severe atrophy and degeneration of the testes of all species. In the rats this was characterized by degenerative changes in the seminiferous tubules, an increase in sertoli's cells, a reduction in the numbers of sperm cells, development of abnormal forms of sperm cells . . . Until further experience is obtained, close observation of the health of the people exposed to this compound should be maintained.[6]

The Torkelson-Hine study recommended that occupational exposure to DBCP be controlled to less than 1 ppm in air.

Dow and Shell submitted the results of the Torkelson study to the federal government in 1961 to obtain registration of DBCP in accordance with a new law that had been passed in 1959. After submitting the study to the federal government, Dow asked that the information be treated as a confidential trade secret and that it not be revealed to competing companies seeking to register their products.[7] Although the study had already been published in a public journal, Dow now held that, since Dow had paid for the study, the information was proprietary and that competing companies should pay for their own registration studies.

> One of the primary reasons for our efforts to protect our health and safety data as trade secret is the major competitive harm that would result from its release. We cannot afford to continue to spend millions of dollars each year on pesticides research if our data are to be made publicly available. Such release would permit our competitors, both here and abroad, to enter the market in competition with us for a fraction of the cost and with very little of the risk. . . . therefore, in order to protect our own business interests and proprietary rights, as well as the viability of the free enterprise system, we are compelled to seek judicial relief for the protection of our valuable scientific data . . . [T]he cost of registration of pesticides has become so immense that some protection of our competitive position is essential if the pesticide industry in this country is to continue its investment in the research necessary to develop safer and more effective pesticides. [Statement of Dow representative][8]

In spite of the recommendation in the Torkelson study that workers exposed to DBCP be kept under "close observation," and in spite of the evidence of testicular damage caused by DBCP, neither Dow Chemical nor Shell Chemical carried out sperm tests on those workers involved in the production of DBCP between 1955 and 1977.

> In 1961, we weren't in the habit of thinking in terms of sperm and getting these kinds of tests. In fact, even today this is a difficult problem. It is a difficult problem because of social difficulties that people may have, because of church attitudes. In no way have we been able to get a 100 percent response for sperm. [Statement of Dow representative][9]

[6] *Ibid.*, pp. 24, 25.
[7] *Ibid.*, p. 28.
[8] *Ibid.*, p. 28.
[9] *Ibid.*, p. 24.

But why weren't the workers made aware of the results of the studies and informed that sperm tests were available to them? Couldn't workers then decide for themselves (as they did after the revelations of sterility among Occidental workers) whether to take the sperm tests or to refrain because of "church," "social," or other reasons? When asked these questions, a Dow spokesman replied as follows:

> I can only surmise that in the early 1960s and late 1950s, chlorinated and brominated compounds were known to have caused a big impact on kidney and liver. This is what the doctors were monitoring for . . . But the feeling was, when . . . you look at liver, you look at spleen, and you look at heart, these, too, are organs of concern. . . . If one was to look at the medical information and go back to the historical observations of people you will find that most of the studies were done on kidney, on liver, on passage of urine, on feces, on many of these kinds of observational studies. Blood sampling and sperm tests were just not part of a routine physical examination. [Statement of Dow representative][10]

The position of Shell Chemical was similar:

> [Until] the recent past, industrial physicians did not consider the testes as a primary target organ, concern was for such organs as the liver, kidney, and lungs . . . Significantly, neither the 1958 nor the 1961 reports recommended explicitly doing fertility testing or measuring sperm density. They did indicate an apparent less dense sperm concentration in those animals which showed significant, discernible testicular degeneration . . . The logical conclusion was that the decreased sperm counts were secondary to the atrophy [reduction in size] of the testes. And so, the conclusion at that time by practitioners in occupational health was that if the DBCP concentration was kept within the limits recommended and that if the testicular integrity was maintained, there was no reason, given the state-of-the-art at that time, to do sperm testing on workers. [Statement of Shell Chemical representative][11]

The National Cancer Institute undertook studies of the possible carcinogenic effect of DBCP on rats in 1972. A large number of the rats developed stomach tumors after DBCP was orally administered. This result was published in summary abstract form in 1975 and in final form in 1977. In 1979 Hazelton Laboratories completed a study of the effects on rats of inhaling DBCP at the low-dose levels encountered in plants manufacturing DBCP. After reading a preliminary draft of the study, a scientist is reported as saying "those rats had tumors all the way up to their brains. We're going to have an outbreak of similar problems in workers, I'm pretty sure."[12]

After being informed of the sterility found among DBCP workers in the Occidental plant, Dow and Shell suspended production of DBCP in August 1977. Officials of the two companies held that the cost of protecting workers against DBCP was greater than the slim profits that could be made from its sales.[13] First Dow (on August 25, 1977) and then Shell (August 26) announced a recall of all DBCP.

[10] *Ibid.*, pp. 24, 25, 26.

[11] *Ibid.*, p. 32.

[12] Taylor, "Pesticides."

[13] *Ibid.*

Although the federal EPA had banned all uses of DBCP shortly after the sterile workers were discovered in 1977, pressures from agricultural interests led EPA assistant director, Steven D. Jellinek, to lift the ban partially on September 19, 1978. DBCP remained illegal for use on most vegetables, but it could be manufactured and used on gardens (home gardens, golf courses, public parks), pineapples, tree fruit, grapes, and ornamental flowers so long as EPA label restrictions were followed and so long as manufacturers allowed workplace concentrations of no more than one-part-per-billion. Dow and Shell declined to resume production of DBCP, but Amvac Chemical Corporation of Los Angeles was soon producing some 2,500 gallons per day.[14]

The Environmental Protection Agency pointed out that if the pesticide were completely banned, farmers would suffer a $400 million loss from crop damages in the first three years of the ban.[15] A citrus grower in California reported that, since 1977 when he stopped using DBCP in his 25-acre lemon grove in California, "production has gone from 1,400 boxes to 800 boxes, to less than 300 boxes."

Since Amvac found its American markets largely closed off after the ban, it decided to begin marketing DBCP more aggressively in foreign countries whose environmental laws were not as stringent as those of the United States. The decision of Dow, Shell, and later Occidental, to discontinue production of the suspected carcinogenic pesticide provided a window of opportunity for Amvac in overseas countries. In its 1979 annual report, Amvac made the following statement:

> Management believes that because of the extensive publicity and notoriety that has arisen over the sterility of workers and the suspected mutagenic and carcinogenic nature of DBCP, the principal manufacturers and distributors of the product (Dow, Occidental, and Shell chemical) have, temporarily at least, decided to remove themselves from the domestic marketplace and possibly from the world marketplace . . . Notwithstanding all the publicity and notoriety surrounding DBCP it was [our] opinion that a vacuum existed in the marketplace that [we] could temporarily occupy. [We] further believed that with the addition of DBCP, sales might be sufficient to reach a profitable level.

Critics charged that Amvac was now shipping the pesticide to less developed nations whose farm workers, often illiterate, were even less knowledgeable of its dangers than American ones had been. In third world countries, they claimed, workers would apply the pesticide with their bare hands using no protective gear, unable to read warnings which were written in English anyway, and utterly unaware of the pesticide's sterilizing effects and its potentially carcinogenic nature. A former Amvac executive was quoted as replying, however, that "Quite Frankly, without DBCP, Amvac would go bankrupt."[16] Moreover, defendants of the company argued, these pesticides were especially important for agrarian third world nations that desperately needed to raise their agricultural yields both to promote their development and to feed their populations. If their governments felt that the benefits of increased yields balanced the risks of their using DBCP, then this was a judgment and decision that was rightfully theirs to make.

[14] *Ibid.*, p. 2F.

[15] *Ibid.*, p. 1F.

[16] David Weir and Mark Schapiro, *Circle of Poison* (San Francisco, CA: Institute for Food and Development Policy, 1981), p. 22.

1. In your judgment, did Dow and Shell before 1977 do all they should have done for workers involved in the manufacture of DBCP? Explain your answer in terms of the ethical principles that you believe are involved.
2. In your judgment, did Dow and Shell do all they should have done for workers who might use their products? Explain.
3. In your judgment, were Dow and Shell morally responsible for the sterility of the DBCP workers?
4. Do you agree with Dow's arguments for classifying health studies as "trade secrets"?
5. In view of the potential crop losses predicted by the EPA, do you think it would be morally permissible to manufacture DBCP so long as potential employees were informed of the risks involved?
6. In your judgment, was Amvac ethically justified in its decision to continue to produce DBCP and to market it in less developed Third World nations?

Bendix Politics

On September 24, 1980, William Agee, chairman of Bendix Corporation was scheduled to address a special meeting of 600 company staff members at Bendix headquarters in Southfield, Michigan. There was plenty to talk about since under Agee's leadership the company was undergoing a major change in direction and a controversial major internal reorganization. Not only were employees concerned that theirs might be one of the dozens of jobs that would be cut from the new organization, there was also some residual uneasiness over Agee's firing of William Panny, the former president, and the simultaneous resignation of Jerome Jacobson, the former executive vice-president for strategic planning. At the meeting Agee planned to announce his choice for Jacobson's replacement: Mary Cunningham, a young (twenty-nine-year-old) Harvard Business School Graduate who had been with Bendix for fifteen months. There was a problem, however.

As he usually did when preparing a meeting, Agee solicited reports from his senior executives concerning what they felt were the most significant issues on the minds of Bendix employees. One of the items that appeared was a concern over the nature of the relationship between Agee and Cunningham and the rising rumors over what was termed "this whole female thing." Since Mary Cunningham's arrival at Bendix she had been working closely with Bill Agee, and he had quickly promoted her from his executive assistant to vice president for corporate and public affairs. Both handsome people, the two necessarily worked and traveled together and gossip started when first Cunningham and then Agee separated from their spouses. As one Bendix staff member put it:

> There were rumors for a long time, and they just grew and grew. The two of them were seen together at the GOP convention [in July 1980]. The TV camera panned in on them, with Agee on one side of Gerald Ford and Mary on [Agee's] other [side], and people thought it was really stupid of them to be seen like that. But they acted like they didn't care. And with her being his top business aide, they traveled all over the country together. That got tongues to wagging. It was almost inevitable.[1]

[1] *The Detroit News,* 5 October 1980, p. 4C.

Agee decided to deal with the rumors. At the September 24th meeting with 600 employees present, he announced Mary Cunningham's promotion to vice president for strategic planning, and then made the following statement:

> I know it has been buzzing around that Mary Cunningham's rise in this company is very unusual and that it has something to do with a personal relationship we have. Sure it's unusual. Her rise in this company is unusual because she's a very unusual and very talented individual. It is true that we are very close friends and she's a very close friend of my family. But that has nothing to do with the way that I and others in this company evaluate performance. Her rapid promotions are totally justified.[2]

If the announcement was intended to lay "the female issue" to rest, it failed. Prior to the meeting, William Agee had received a telephone call from a newspaper reporter who indicated that some Bendix people who were unhappy with Agee had gotten in touch with him. They were planning to "leak" Agee's statement to the press. It might be better, the reporter had suggested, if Agee allowed him to be present at the meeting. Agee had acquiesced. The day after the meeting the reporter printed the story, rumors and all, on the front page of a Detroit newspaper. By evening, the story had hit the news wires, and over the next few days it became national news.

The event focused national attention on Bendix at the very time the organization was undergoing substantial changes. Some of the changes dated back to 1976 when William Agee took over the chairmanship of Bendix after W. Michael Blumenthal left the job to become secretary of the treasury under President Jimmy Carter. William Agee introduced a new, more open style of management into Bendix. The year after he took over as chairman he installed a special telephone line through which employees could contact him directly with complaints. He got rid of the large meeting table in the center of the headquarters' meeting room and replaced it with large comfortable chairs. He discarded the policy of reserving the best company parking space for himself, saying that it was deserved by the person who arrived first at work each day.

The most important changes, however, grew out of a need to reevaluate the company's major operations. Ranked as the 88th-largest industrial company in the United States, Bendix sales had been steadily growing. In 1979 sales were \$3.8 billion, up from \$2.6 billion in 1975, and profits were \$162.6 million, up from 1975 profits of \$79.8 million. Bendix had large operations, however, in the automotive industry and in the forest products industry, and neither of these industries was doing well. DBA, its largest foreign automotive subsidiary, in fact, had a long history of deficits. And its forest products plants had been unable to develop more efficient technologies. As a consequence, Bendix earnings from these operations had started to slide and only its income from other investments had kept Bendix's overall income high. One obvious solution was to dispose of its holdings in these industries and to buy into other more profitable businesses.

When William Agee took over the helm of Bendix, he hired William P. Panny as president (formerly a vice president of Rockwell International) to assist him in these changes. It was widely thought that eventually Panny would succeed

[2] See *Newsweek,* 6 October 1980, p. 79; and *Wall Street Journal,* 26 September 1980, p. 33.

Agee. Together, the two of them sold off a large part of the ailing DBA automotive subsidiary, reduced its workforce, and closed some of its plants. By 1980, a much reduced DBA would once again be operating in the black. Moreover, by 1979 Agee had begun work on selling off the Bendix forest products business. In September of 1980, he announced the completion of negotiations to sell off the forest products operations for $435 million. Other divestitures and further diversifications were in the offing.

During these major change-overs, disagreements had begun to emerge between Agee and Panny. In 1978, William Agee felt that Bendix should purchase ASARCO, a mining company which had lost $30 million in 1977. Agee believed that ASARCO would be worth much more in the future than the then depressed price of its stock indicated. But Panny argued against the purchase as unreasonable and held that at most Bendix should purchase 20 percent of the company. Panny carried the day with the Bendix management team and only 20 percent of ASARCO was purchased. The next year ASARCO's profits climbed to $259 million and the price of its stock doubled.

More important, however, was a disagreement over whether Bendix should abandon the automotive business altogether. Agee's publicly stated view was that the automobile industry was "in the winter of its life."[3] Panny, however, disagreed. Bendix had been in the automotive industry for decades and the company had acquired great familiarity and experience with its workings. It would be unwise, Panny felt, to turn from a well-known business to others in which the company had little experience and with which its employees were not familiar.

In June of 1979 Agee hired Mary Cunningham to serve as his executive assistant. Mary Cunningham was described as an "unusually brilliant," "uncommonly ambitious," "politically astute," "beautiful," "sophisticated," "poised" woman with "high ideals." Almost immediately after arriving from the Harvard Business School, she was assigned to put her extensive financial analytical skills to work on some major Bendix investment projects. One of her largest projects was an analysis of the possible acquisition of the Warner and Swasey Company, a machine-tool business. The investment looked good. Bendix already had a machine-tool business that, together with the acquisition of Warner and Swasey, would make Bendix the second largest U.S. machine-tool builder. Relying on the analysis, Agee purchased Warner and Swasey in April 1980 for $300 million. The buy paid off: Warner and Swasey was holding $65 million in liquid assets and $40 million in stock, which, when disposed of, made their real purchase price $195 million.

In June of 1980, Bill Agee promoted Mary Cunningham, then only twenty-nine, to vice president for corporate and public affairs. (The move was not unusual for Agee; in 1979 he had promoted Bernard B. Winograd, who was then twenty-eight, to corporate treasurer.) By now the two were working closely together. A company staff person described her with the words: "She's his key advisor; she counsels him on the most important things in the company."[4] But some insiders sensed trouble. Later, a Bendix executive commented, "She is very smart and

[3] Peter W. Bernstein, "Upheaval at Bendix," *Fortune,* 3 November 1980, p. 52.

[4] *Wall Street Journal,* 26 September 1980, p. 33.

she knows how corporations work—that's how she's done so well—but when it came to her relationship with Bill Agee, she didn't act smart, she didn't use her political sense."[5]

Several Bendix managers now began to complain that Cunningham had too much access to Agee and that he was becoming increasingly inaccessible to others. Said one official:

> People don't like the way she conducts herself. She's not as careful as she should be. She's always invoking the chairman's authority for everything she does. Mary has so clearly identified herself with him that people don't feel they can question her or contradict her.[6]

The feelings of the managers were further ruffled when Agee had Cunningham carry out an in-depth analysis of Bendix's automotive business in June 1980. Mary Cunningham angered several managers when she inspected the floors of the automotive plants without first telling the plant managers that she was going to do so. Bendix managers (including Mr. Panny) afterwards harshly criticized the three-volume analysis that Mary Cunningham and her seven-person staff (derisively referred to as "Snow White and the Seven Dwarfs") had produced. The Cunningham report, according to the managers, was unenlightening and did not contain anything they did not already know.[7]

Agee's reorganization of the company had now started to move into its internal affairs. In early 1980 Agee announced that the company would be internally reorganized. Up to this time Bendix had been highly centralized: Most company divisons were run out of corporate headquarters in Southfield near Detroit. Agee intended to make the divisions much more autonomous. Panny, however, strongly opposed the reorganization, arguing that the company was not ready to be decentralized and that the employees did not want it.

In September 1980, Agee fired Panny. According to *Fortune Magazine* it was rumored in Detroit that several Bendix executives had earlier gone to Panny to "complain" about Cunningham's relationship to Agee.[8] Panny, according to the *Fortune* rumor, was "planning" to bring the matter to the Bendix board of directors, but Agee fired him before he had the chance. A few hours later, Jerome Jacobson, a Bendix executive, resigned from his position as vice president for strategic planning.

Matters then became more heated. According to author Gail Sheehy, who interviewed both Cunningham and Agee, "anonymous letters" now began to be sent to Bendix board members, making "malicious references" to the conduct of the pair.[9] The letters, according to Sheehy, urged board members, to "investigate their relationship" at once.

Agee acted quickly. First he arranged meetings with Bendix's top managers

[5] *San Jose Mercury,* 10 October 1980, p. 20A.

[6] S. Freedberg, G. Storch, and C. Teegartin, "Two At the Top," *The Detroit News,* 5 October 1980, p. 5C.

[7] Bernstein, "Upheaval at Bendix," p. 52.

[8] *Ibid.,* p. 53.

[9] Gail Sheehy, "Cunningham Encounters the Mildew of Envy," *Detroit Free Press,* 13 October 1980, p. 4B.

and with the board's executive committee. To each group he said the same thing: The rumors going around were utterly false; he and Cunningham had "no romantic involvement."[10] Then he moved to promote Mary Cunningham to the vacated position of vice president for strategic planning. At the fateful company meeting of September 24, he announced her promotion, and simultaneously attempted to lay "the female issue" to rest. The next day, however, the story was reported in the nation's newspapers along with the rumors suggesting that Mary Cunningham's rapid promotions were due to her "romantic involvement" with Bill Agee.

The day the news broke in the papers, Mary Cunningham decided she had to move quickly if she was to out maneuver "them." (She did not know who had sent the anonymous letters.) Her first instinct was to resign, since this would prevent the board from firing her first and would ensure that Bill Agee would not be compromised by her continuing presence in the company. But by the next day she had instead decided to request a temporary leave of absence from the company. This tactic would leave her with a palatable option should the board want her to leave, but at the same time it would pressure the board to take the option of retaining her. Since the board had publicly approved her promotion only a few days earlier, it would probably not be willing to reverse itself publicly so soon afterwards. Consequently, on September 28, she submitted to the board a letter requesting an "immediate but temporary" leave which "should not be construed in any sense as tantamount to resignation." The letter continued by explaining that a resignation would set "a dangerous precedent" because it would enable "female executives to be forced out of a company through malicious gossip" and would also "tend to confirm the most base and erroneous assumptions suggested by the media."[11]

The next afternoon a committee comprised of a few members of the Bendix board of directors met and decided to announce in the name of the board that they had "complete confidence" in Mary Cunningham and that "it would be unjust for a corporation to respond to speculation in the media by accepting her request."[12] After the meeting, one of the board members gave her a bit of advice: She should be careful because she was being used by others to get at Bill Agee and if the thing went on for much longer Agee's position would be in danger.[13]

The drama was not yet over. Mary Cunningham was still unsure whether it might not be better for her to resign. When the full board met a few days later and the members discussed the issue among themselves, a large number felt that she should not continue on at Bendix. Too many difficulties would confront her if she continued in her present role, they felt. This was made known to Cunningham. Subsequently, on October 9, she issued another statement:

> I have submitted my resignation, effective today, as an officer of the Bendix Corporation . . . I am convinced that the unusual convergence of events beyond my control has substantially impaired my ability to carry out my responsibilities as a corporate

[10] Bernstein, "Upheaval at Bendix," p. 54.

[11] *San Jose Mercury,* 1 October 1980, p. 12A.

[12] *Ibid.*

[13] Gail Sheehy, "Cunningham's Idealism Gets Lost in Corporate Jungle," *Detroit Free Press,* 14 October 1980, p. 3B.

officer of Bendix . . . I am grateful for the many supportive communications from the business community and others concerned with the right to be judged on merit alone.[14]

1. List all the political tactics that you think were used by the various parties involved in the case. Explain why you classify these as "political tactics."
2. In your judgment, were any of these political tactics morally legitimate? Were any morally illegitimate? Explain your answer in terms of the relevant moral principles involved.
3. Was William Panny treated fairly? Was Mary Cunningham treated fairly? Explain your answer fully.
4. Is it possible to eliminate from an organization the kinds of political tactics that you think were being used in Bendix? If you do not think it is possible, explain why; if you think it is possible, describe the methods by which such tactics can be eliminated.

The Coors Tests

On April 5, 1977, the members of Brewery Workers Local No. 366 walked off the job at the Adolf Coors Brewery Plant in Golden, Colorado.[1] The wildcat strike was motivated in part by Coors's use of lie detector tests in a preemployment examination required of prospective employees. Said an officer of the union: "When you get through being grilled on that lie detector, you feel dirty."[2]

To support their case the union collected several notarized affidavits in which striking employees alleged that the company had asked them improper questions during the lie detector test. Two of the notarized affidavits read in part as follows:[3]

> In April of 1973, I, John A. K __________, had to submit to a polygraph test for employment at the Adolph Coors Company in Golden, Colorado. Of the many personal questions asked, the two listed below were particularly aggravating.
>
> 1. Are you a homosexual?
> 2. Do you know of any reason that you could be blackmailed?

> I, Oliver A. D. __________, was hired by the Adolph Coors Company on October 23, 1972. Below are listed some of the questions I was asked on the lie detector while going through my screening for a job.
>
> Do you get along with your wife?
> What is your sex preference?
> Are you a communist?
> Do you have money in the bank?
> Have you ever stolen anything and was [sic] not caught at it?

[14] *Detroit Free Press*, 10 October 1980, p. 15A.

[1] "Bitter Beercott," *Time*, 26 December 1977, p. 15.

[2] *Ibid.*

[3] Copies of these affidavits were obtained from Brewery Bottling, Can and Allied Industrial Union-Local No. 366; 4510 Indiana Street, Golden, CO.

> I feel that these questions were degrading and an invasion of my privacy. I also feel these questions are unnecessary for the Coors Company to ask of anyone seeking a job with them.

Coors executives responded to these allegations by saying that they did not know these alleged questions were being asked of their prospective employees. The polygraph questionnaires, they said, were administered by an outside agency which Coors had hired before 1975.[4]

However, Coors was unwilling to give up using polygraph tests altogether. In 1960, a member of the Coors family had been kidnapped and killed. In August 1977, a bomb was planted in a Coors recycling plant. Chairman William Coors and his brother, Joseph Coors, both said they wanted to ensure that they did not hire someone who might again endanger their families or their employees. In addition, the Coors brothers felt that the polygraph tests would reveal some information that the company should have:

> [The tests reveal] whether the applicant may be hiding some health problem . . . [and ensure that] the applicant does not want the job for some subversive reason such as sabotaging our operation. [Statement of William Coors]

Coors therefore continued to use the polygraph test but formulated a standard questionnaire that the polygraph agency was to use in the preemployment examination. The new questionnaire consisted of seven question areas. Before a job applicant even made an appointment with the polygraph agency, the applicant was given a copy of the questions and was asked to review the questions carefully. If he had any hesitations about answering the questions on a lie detector, he was invited to discuss his problems with the employment staff. The seven questions were as follows:

1. Did you tell the complete truth on the employment application?
2. Have you ever used any form of illegal drug or narcotic on the job?
3. Has the use of alcohol frequently impaired your ability to perform on the job?
4. Are you concealing any information about subversive, revolutionary, or communistic activity?
5. Are you applying for a job with this company so you can do it or any of its employees harm?
6. Are you presently wanted by the authorities for a felony?
7. Have you ever stolen any kind of merchandise, material, or money from an employer?[5]

Coors assured each applicant that these were the only questions that he or she had to answer. The polygraph agency was to adhere to the questionnaire.

Although the wildcat strike ran out of steam and was abandoned, new problems forced Coors managers to reconsider its use of polygraphs. In 1985 and again in 1986 Congress began to consider bills preventing employers from requiring workers and job applicants to take polygraphs. The House passed a bill in March

[4] "Bitter Beercott."

[5] A copy of the questionnaire was also obtained from Brewery Bottling, Can, and Allied Industrial Union-Local No. 366.

1986 preventing the use of polygraphs except in unusual circumstances, but these efforts came to nothing when a similar bill did not make it through the Senate. Eighteen states, however, already prohibited or limited the use of polygraphs in business. Fearing that the tests would be outlawed, Coors managers decided to change their applicant tests. In August 1986 the company announced that it would no longer require polygraph tests of its job applicants. In place of the polygraph it would now require applicants to submit to a drug test, to a twelve-page psychological test called the Stanton Survey, which inquired into the applicant's attitude toward theft and dishonesty, and to a background check by Equifax Services, a national audit and loss-control company.[6]

Coor's decision to use a drug test came on the heels of a report of the President's Commission on Organized Crime issued on March 3, 1986, that highlighted the use of illegal drugs in the United States and that recommended that government and private businesses begin programs of testing their employees and job applicants for the use of drugs. On September 15 President Reagan signed an executive order requiring those federal employees who held "sensitive" posts to be tested for the use of illegal drugs. It was estimated that between 5 and 13 percent of American workers abused illegal drugs (marijuana was estimated to account for 95 percent of this abuse). In June 1984, a report of the Research Triangle Institute had estimated that the abuse of illegal drugs cost the U.S. $60 billion in 1983 alone; lost worker productivity accounted for $33 billion of these costs.[7] Employers felt that the use of drugs by employees affected their job performance, their judgment, and their skills, and that it therefore lowered productivity and increased accidents.

The drug test used by Coors would be conducted at a private medical laboratory at a cost of $20 per test. Critics of the test were concerned because of the high error rate that the commonly used drug tests had exhibited. In 1985 the Center for Disease Control had found that of thirteen testing laboratories examined, only one correctly identified traces of cocaine at least 80 percent of the time, that tests for five other drugs were wrong more than half of the time, and that tests for certain drugs were wrong 100 percent of the time.[8] A Northwestern University study found that the most commonly used drug test, the EMIT urinalysis test developed by Syva, was wrong 25 percent of the times that it indicated drugs were present in a urine sample.[9] Over-the-counter drugs such as "Contac" and "Sudafed" showed up as amphetamines; cough medicine containing dextromethorphan would show up as morphine; poppy seeds on pastries showed up as morphine; and the prescription drug Amoxicillin showed up as cocaine.

Critics were also concerned that the commonly used drug tests were invasions of privacy. The drug tests, they pointed out, did not show whether an employee was under the influence of drugs at the time of testing since drugs such as marijuana showed up in urine samples as long as one month after the drug was used. Nor

[6] "Three New Tests to Replace Coor's Traditional Polygraph," *Oakland Tribune*, 30 August 1986.

[7] "Battling Drugs on the Job," *Time*, 27 January 1986, p. 43.

[8] *New York Times*, 16 September 1986.

[9] See Patricia A. Hunter, "Your Urine or Your Job," *Loyola of Los Angeles Law Review*, 19 (June 1986): 1451–93; Mark Rust, "Drug Testing," *ABA Journal*, 1 November 1986, pp. 51–54.

did the tests show whether the employee's performance was in any way affected by drugs. Employers, critics argued, do not have a right to inquire into what the employee does during his or her private time; employers have a right to place requirements on employees only during their working hours and only such requirements as are directly related to job performance.[10]

1. Would Coors have been justified in using a polygraph and in asking the questions alleged in the notarized affidavits? Explain your answer fully in terms of the ethical principles involved.
2. Was Coors justified in using a polygraph to gather responses to any or all of the seven questions in its revised questionnaire? Explain your answer fully.
3. Could Coors have protected its interests by using any other methods? Explain your answer fully.
4. In your judgment, was Coors justified in using the three kinds of tests that it implemented in 1986? Are drug tests justified for job *applicants?* Is random drug testing or mass drug testing of a company's *employees* justified? Explain your answers fully.

H. J. Heinz Company Incentives

Top managers throughout H. J. Heinz Corporation still liked the management incentive plan (MIP) that H. J. Heinz had decided on during the late 1960s. With reported sales of $2.2 billion and net income of $99.1 million in 1978, H. J. Heinz was by then one of the largest multinationals in the world, owning and operating over 30 companies that manufactured and marketed food products in over 150 countries, and maintaining an enviably consistent, almost predictable rise in annual earnings throughout the decade. The corporate officers and small staff at H. J. Heinz Corporate World Headquarters in Pittsburgh monitored the performance of their almost completely autonomous operating companies through conventional budgets and financial reports and did not inquire into the operating details of its companies unless they deviated from the earnings and goals set for them each year. The top management at each Heinz company reported to world headquarters directly but had total responsibility for their own company's operations and for all employees at their companies, all of whom reported only to them and not to corporate headquarters in Pittsburgh.[1]

The MIP affected 225 Heinz managers including officers and senior managers at corporate headquarters and the top managers at each Heinz company. The MIP awarded "points" to these managers, and year-end incentive compensation depended on points earned, sometimes totaling 40 percent of net compensation. Points were awarded to the top managers of each of the operating companies according to whether their companies reached the profit goals set by corporate staff at world headquarters. Two goals were set for the managers of each company each year: a "fair" goal of exceeding the previous year's after-tax profits by perhaps 15 percent, and an "outstanding" goal above even that. No points were awarded if the fair goal was not achieved, a certain number of points were awarded

[10] *Ibid.*

[1] The information in this and the following paragraph is drawn from Richard J. Post and Kenneth E. Goodpaster, "H. J. Heinz Company: The Administration of Policy," in Kenneth E. Goodpaster, *Ethics in Management* (Boston: Harvard Business School, 1984), pp. 77–86.

if it was achieved, and an additional larger number of points were awarded for achieving the outstanding goal. Career advancement was also linked to consistent achievement of the goals through the years. The MIP was given a great deal of the credit for Heinz's consistent earnings growth.

In April 1979, attorneys for Campbell Soup Company, a competitor then suing H. J. Heinz for allegedly monopolizing the ketchup market, notified Heinz's general legal counsel that while investigating Heinz's financial relationships with an advertising agency, they had uncovered an unusual practice.[2] One of the Heinz subsidiary companies, Heinz USA, had asked the ad agency to fix its invoices so that services the ad agency actually rendered to Heinz USA in 1975, were billed and paid for by Heinz USA in 1974 and described on the invoices as being rendered in 1974. Instead of listing the items as assets consisting of prepaid 1975 expenses, Heinz USA had charged them off as a 1974 expense and deducted them from its 1974 income reports. As a result, the income Heinz USA had reported was understated for 1974, and 1975 income was overstated by an equal amount. On hearing of this, H. J. Heinz corporate officials at Pittsburgh, including James Cunningham, corporate president and CEO, decided to launch an audit of all Heinz companies.

The audit, completed in 1980, discovered that since 1971 top managers at several of the Heinz companies had been routinely transfering expenses for goods and services from the year in which they were delivered, to an earlier year in their income reports. Moreover, auditors discovered, the managers' reports also routinely had been transfering sales income from the year in which goods were actually sold to an earlier or a later year. By means of such transfers, which totaled about $8.5 million and which violated both explicit Heinz corporate policy and generally accepted accounting principles, the managers ensured that their profit goals would be met each year, and that any profits in excess of those goals in effect would be transfered to following years as a hedge against a possible future decline in revenues.[3] As a Heinz employee explained to the auditors:[4]

> If this year's goal is, say, $20 million net profit after tax (NPAT), it can be anticipated that next year's goal will be, say, 15 percent higher, or $23 million NPAT. This year seems to be a good one and it is anticipated that earnings will be $24 million NPAT. But if that figure is reported to world headquarters, it is likely that next year's goal will be about 15 percent higher than the $24 million NPAT, or approximately $27 million NPAT. Of course, there is no assurance that there will not be some unforeseen disaster next year. Thus, if it is possible to mislead world headquarters as to the true state of the earnings of the [subsidiary] and report only the $20 million NPAT, which is the current fiscal year's goal, and have the additional $4 million NPAT carried forward into next year, the [subsidiary] will have a good start toward achieving its expected $23 million NPAT goal next year and will not have to reach $27 million NPAT.

[2] Thomas Petzinger, "Heinz to Probe Prepayments to Suppliers By Using Outside Lawyers, Accountants," *Wall Street Journal,* 30 April 1979, p. 5; Thomas Petzinger, "Results in Probe of Heinz Income Juggling Expected to Be Announced by Early April," *Wall Street Journal,* 18 March 1980.

[3] Thomas Petzinger, "Heinz Discloses Profit-Switching at Units Was Much Broader Than First Realized," *Wall Street Journal,* 13 September 1979.

[4] "Report of the Audit Committee to the Board of Directors: Income Transferal and Other Practices," H. J. Heinz Company, form 8-K, May 7, 1980, quoted in Post and Goodpaster, *op. cit.,* p. 80.

TABLE 8.1 Change in Sales, Net Income and Earnings per Share H. J. Heinz Company.

In thousands except for per share amounts	1971	1972	1973	1974	1975	1976	1977	1978
Sales as previously reported	$876,451	$1,020,958	$1,116,551	$1,349,091	$1,564,930	$1,749,691	$1,868,820	$2,150,027
Net increase (decrease) resulting from restatement to correct improper treatment of sales	—	—	14,821	(1,777)	(4,747)	4,725	8,480	9,409
Sales as restated	$876,451	$1,020,958	$1,131,372	$1,347,314	$1,560,183	$1,754,416	$1,877,300	$2,159,436
Net income as previously reported	$ 37,668	$ 42,287	$ 21,552	$ 64,320	$ 66,567	$ 73,960	$ 83,816	$ 99,171
Net increase (decrease) in income before income taxes resulting from restatement:								
Correct improper treatment of sales, net of related costs	—	—	1,968	309	(1,527)	1,815	1,294	2,872
Correct improper recognition of income/expense	1,290	512	1,813	5,615	(1,861)	(684)	3,822	(1,417)
	1,290	512	3,781	5,924	(3,388)	1,131	5,116	1,455
Income tax effect	(671)	(263)	(1,566)	(2,698)	1,254	(604)	(2,203)	(680)
Net adjustments	619	249	2,215	3,226	(2,134)	527	2,913	775
Net income as restated	$ 38,287	42,536	$ 23,767	$ 67,546	$ 64,433	$ 74,487	$ 86,729	$ 99,946

Source: H. J. Heinz Company, "1979 Annual Report," p. 50.

Unaware of what was being done by its subsidiary companies, Heinz corporate headquarters had used the falsified financial reports of its subsidiaries as the basis for the corporate income statements it issued each year to investors and to the government's Securities and Exchange Commission. As a result of the audit, H. J. Heinz was forced to provide the financial community with revised financial statements for each year since 1971 as part of its 1979 annual report (see Table 8.1).

The audit also discovered a number of other unusual practices in the corporation's foreign subsidiaries.[5] One Heinz company, Star-Kist, a producer of canned fish products, operated in a country whose laws prohibited the payment of interest to nonresidents, thereby in effect making it illegal for Star-Kist to provide interest-bearing loans to local businesses. Owners of local fishing fleets who regularly needed loans to operate their fleet turned to local competitors of Star-Kist, who agreed to provide the loans if the fleets would work for them instead of for Star-Kist. To get around the prohibition on interest, Star-Kist provided "free" loans to fishing fleets and billed them for "supplies" that were never provided. Payments for these "supplies" were equivalent to the interest the loans would have carried. Another Heinz subsidiary made a number of "questionable" payments to lower level government employees in a foreign country where such payments were said to be common. In each case, the payments were intended to ensure that the government employees would resolve a pending dispute in favor of the Heinz subsidiary. There was no evidence that officials at H. J. Heinz corporate headquarters knew of these or any of the other practices uncovered by the audit.

QUESTIONS

1. Identify the corporate policies and systems that made these incidents possible. In view of these policies, were the managers involved morally responsible for what they did? What changes would you have recommended?
2. What consequences did the issuing of inaccurate corporate financial statements have on parties outside H. J. Heinz? What social costs, violations of rights, and injustices do you believe were associated or could have been associated with the issuing of inaccurate financial statements?
3. In your judgment, were the "questionable" payments and practices engaged in by subsidiaries operating in foreign countries unethical? Explain.

[5] See "Report of the Audit Committee," summarized in Post and Goodpaster, *op. cit.*, pp. 81–82.

INDEX